P9-DFE-045

Mastering Public Speaking

EDITION 8

GEORGE L. GRICE
Radford University, *Professor Emeritus*

JOHN F. SKINNER
San Antonio College

PEARSON

Boston • Columbus • Indianapolis • New York • San Francisco • Upper Saddle River
Amsterdam • Cape Town • Dubai • London • Madrid • Milan • Munich • Paris • Montreal • Toronto
Delhi • Mexico City • São Paulo • Sydney • Hong Kong • Seoul • Singapore • Taipei • Tokyo

Editor-in-Chief, Communication: Karon Bowers
Director of Development: Eileen Calabro
Senior Development Editor: Carol Alper
Editorial Assistant: Megan Sweeney
Marketing Manager: Blair Zoe Tuckman
Associate Development Editor: Angela Mallowes
Senior Digital Editor: Paul DeLuca
Digital Editor: Lisa Dotson
Associate Managing Editor: Bayani Mendoza de Leon

Production/Project Manager: Raegan Keida Heerema
Project Coordination, Text Design, and Electronic
    Page Makeup: Cenveo Publisher Services/Nesbitt
    Graphics, Inc.
Cover Design Manager: Nancy Danahy
Senior Cover Designer: Nancy Sacks
Senior Manufacturing Buyer: Mary Ann Gloriande
Printer/Binder: R. R. Donnelley Willard
Cover Printer: Lehigh-Phoenix Color/Hagerstown

Credits and acknowledgments borrowed from other sources and reproduced, with permission, in this textbook appear on the appropriate page within text or on page 415.

Library of Congress Cataloging-in-Publication Data
Grice, George L.
    Mastering public speaking / George L. Grice, John F. Skinner. — 8th ed.
        p. cm.
    Includes bibliographical references and index.
    ISBN 978-0-205-02939-6
    1. Public speaking.   I. Skinner, John F. II. Title.
    PN4129.15.G75 2012
    808.5'1—dc23

                                    2011043500

Copyright © 2013, 2010, 2007, 2004 by Pearson Education, Inc.

All rights reserved. Manufactured in the United States of America. This publication is protected by Copyright, and permission should be obtained from the publisher prior to any prohibited reproduction, storage in a retrieval system, or transmission in any form or by any means, electronic, mechanical, photocopying, recording, or likewise. To obtain permission(s) to use material from this work, please submit a written request to Pearson Education, Inc., Permissions Department, One Lake Street, Upper Saddle River, New Jersey 07458, or you may fax your request to 201-236-3290.

10 9 8 7 6 5 4 3 2 1—RRD—14 13 12 11

www.pearsonhighered.com

ISBN 10: 0-205-02939-6
ISBN 13: 978-0-205-02939-6

To Wrenn, Evelyn, Carol, and Leanne

To Suzanne, Drew, and Devin;
Beverley, G.W., Rick, Randy,
and the memory of my grandmother,
Gertrude Viola Wallace

and

To the memory of Robert C. Jeffrey,
our teacher and friend

Brief Contents

Contents

1   An Introduction to Public Speaking   1

4   Listening   57

7 Researching Your Topic   107

8 Supporting Your Speech   127

9   Organizing the Body of Your Speech   147

14   Using Presentational Aids   241

17 The Structure of Persuasion   301

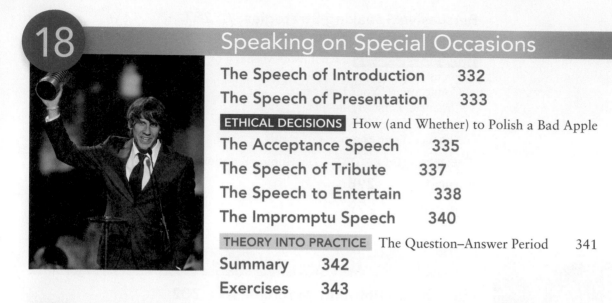

Preface to the Student

The word began as the spoken word. Long before anyone devised a way to record messages in writing, people told one another stories and taught each other lessons. Societies flourished and fell, battles were waged and won—all on the basis of the spoken word. Ancient storytellers preserved their cultures' traditions and history by translating them orally to eager audiences. Crowds might wander away from unprepared, unskilled speakers, but the most competent, skilled storytellers received widespread attention and praise.

After the development of script and print, people continued to associate marks on the page with the human voice. Even today, linked as we are by Twitter, IMs, and Facebook updates, a speaker standing at the front of a hushed room makes a special claim on our attention and our imagination. As you develop and deliver speeches in class—and in future years as you deliver reports, sell products, present and accept awards, or campaign for candidates—you continue an ancient oral tradition. This book is about the contract that always exists between a speaker and an audience, and about the choices you make in your roles as speaker and listener.

We developed this book with two principles in mind. First, public speaking, like ancient storytelling, requires a level of competence that develops from skills handed down from patient teacher to interested student. Yet this is more than a skills course. The master speaker is principled as well as skilled. We want to instruct you in how to make wise choices as you select topics and then research, organize, practice, and deliver your speeches. Just as important, we want to spur you at each point in the speech-making process to think about why you make the choices you do.

Our second guiding principle has been most economically stated by British journalist and author Gilbert K. Chesterton: "There are no uninteresting subjects; there are only uninterested people." This book is for those who believe, as we do, that the lessons we have to teach one another can enrich the lives of every listener. This course will give you the chance to investigate subjects that appeal to you. We challenge you to develop speech topics creatively, and then to listen to one another's speeches expecting to learn.

Public speaking is an important part of communication, and communication is not only part of your education but is also the way you gain and apply your learning. A liberating and lifelong education occurs only through communication, with ourselves and those around us. We wish each of you the kind of education Steve C. Beering, former president of Purdue University, described so eloquently:

> Education is dreaming, and thinking, and asking questions. It is reading, writing, speaking, and listening. Education is exploring the unknown, discovering new ideas, communicating with the world about us. Education is finding yourself, recognizing human needs, and communicating that recognition to others. Education is learning to solve problems. It is acquiring useful knowledge and skills in order to improve the quality of life. Education is an understanding of the meaning of the past, and an inkling of the potential of the future. Education represents self-discipline, assumption of responsibility and the maintenance of flexibility, and most of all, an open mind. Education is unfinishable. It is an attitude and a way of life. It makes every day a new beginning.[1]

Preface to the Instructor

In 1993, we published the first edition of *Mastering Public Speaking* to show students both the hows and the whys of public speaking. Ours was the first major public speaking textbook to devote an entire chapter to speaker and listener ethics and another to managing speaker nervousness. We also introduced students to the "4 S's," a practical mnemonic device for organizing each major idea in a speech.

The text's instructional approach mirrored our view of the public speaking instructor as a "guide on the side" rather than a "sage on the stage." Our goal is to empower students to take responsibility for their own learning by challenging them to make the decisions required of public speakers. By incorporating into our text many credible examples, both actual and hypothetical, we hoped to inspire and encourage students to achieve the full potential of public speech.

To support our goals, we also wanted to help instructors shape the public speaking classroom into a community of caring, careful thinkers. We sought to improve the quality of feedback in the classroom by analyzing the elements of sound critiques and providing a helpful model for discussing speeches.

We live in a changed world in the early twenty-first century. New media have altered our expectations of what a public speech can accomplish, and new research tools have sent us scrambling to ensure that we know as much about these emerging technologies as do most of our students, but in our view, the fundamentals of public speaking remain the same. Sensitive audience analysis, adequate research, clear organization, and forceful delivery remain the key ingredients for effective speeches. Therefore, our basic instructional approach in this text remains constant: We seek to engage students in the principles, practice, and ethics of public speaking— both as speakers and as listeners.

Changes in the Eighth Edition

Although our basic approach remains the same, we have made changes and improvements to strengthen it. Instructors who have taught from previous editions suggested some of these changes. We made others to help students navigate through the technological advances that have broadened the menu of research and presentational aid options for public speakers.

Major pedagogical changes to this edition include the following:

- This edition provides a more focused discussion of content.
- Learning objectives in each chapter (and in new Appendix A) orient students preparing to read and focus on content mastery.
- Greater use of bulleted and numbered lists highlights concepts and strategies.
- Clearer organization of chapter summaries beneath headings enhances student review of material.

After studying this chapter, you should be able to

1 Define ethics.

2 Understand how ethical principles should guide your actions.

3 Incorporate six ethical responsibilities into your speaking.

4 Incorporate four ethical responsibilities into your listening.

5 Understand and apply fair use guidelines.

6 Understand types of plagiarism.

7 Apply five guidelines to avoid plagiarism.

8 Appreciate, understand, and use civility as a speaker and listener.

SUMMARY

The Importance of Listening

- The personal costs of poor listening include lost opportunities, embarrassment, financial losses, and lost time.

Listening vs. Hearing

- *Listening* differs from *hearing* in four ways: (1) Listening is intermittent, while hearing is continuous; (2) listening is a learned behavior, while hearing is natural for most people; (3) listening is active; hearing is passive; and (4) listening implies doing something with the message received.

the listener's body. *Psychological distractions* include worry, distraction, or preconceived attitudes toward the speaker or the message. *Factual distractions* are caused by our tendency to listen for small supporting details, even when we miss the speaker's main point. *Semantic distractions* are confusion over the meanings of words.

Improving Listening

- Both speakers and listeners can contribute to effective listening.
- Listeners should develop a genuine desire to listen; focus on the speaker's message; listen

---

Throughout this edition, we've replaced and updated many student and professional examples, using actual classroom and contest speakers for most of these. In addition, we have incorporated changes specific to chapter content. The most significant changes are as follows:

- Chapter 1, "An Introduction to Public Speaking," more clearly illustrates how students use critical thinking skills as they research, construct, and deliver their speeches.
- Chapter 2, "The Ethics of Public Speaking," introduces the concept of civility in public speaking. Students are encouraged to foster a civil classroom of respectful, attentive learners. The chapter also contains a new extended example of appropriate and inappropriate source citation.
- Chapter 4 is now titled "Listening" and focuses entirely on listening, a skill students should be developing from the beginning of the semester. The section on critiquing speeches has been expanded and moved to new Appendix A: "Giving and Receiving Criticism." Focusing solely on offering and receiving constructive feedback, this appendix can be assigned at the instructor's discretion—after students have learned guidelines for the content, organization, and delivery of speeches.
- Chapter 5, "Analyzing Your Audience," discusses diversity, and additional examples throughout the book include relevant topics, speech excerpts, and photos.
- Chapter 7, "Researching Your Topic," provides updated coverage of electronic research sources, databases, and academic search engines. The new

"Theory Into Practice" feature—"Evaluating Internet Resources"—more clearly integrates information, previously in Chapter 8, to the topic of research. This chapter also includes a clear statement cautioning students on the use of *Wikipedia* as a source for their speeches. Finally, updated samples are offered for APA and MLA references.

- Chapter 14, "Using Presentational Aids," updates the types and methods of incorporating presentational aids. A new section on PowerPoint contains suggestions for designing and displaying visual aids to enhance a presentation. A "Theory Into Practice" feature presents a more focused outline for "Designing Visual Aids."

- Appendix A, "Giving and Receiving Criticism," continues our strong emphasis on speech criticism but moves it to a stand-alone topic for instructors who want to highlight and assign it at the appropriate time of the semester or quarter.

- Appendix B, "Sample Speeches," includes two new student speeches that complement the speeches retained from the previous edition, providing excellent and contemporary examples from which students can learn. The new student speech on flash mobs in Appendix B is available online in video format on the accompanying MySpeechLab website.

Special Features

An integral part of the learning materials in this book are the many special features. We've included these to help students understand and learn public speaking concepts. We have retained the following popular instructional features:

- **Theory Into Practice** boxes, many of which have been newly revised and edited, reinforce the text's instructional approach and help students to understand and apply communication concepts and strategies to enhance their public speaking competence.

THEORY INTO PRACTICE

TIP   Gaining Perspective

In this chapter, we present eleven strategies for building your speaking confidence. You incorporate these suggestions as you prepare and deliver your speeches. However, what should you do *after* your speech? You've heard the expression, "Experience is the best teacher." Well, there's some truth in that folk wisdom; you can use your public speaking experiences to build your confidence.

After each speech, assess your performance by asking and answering important questions. Your instructor will give you feedback for some of these questions; others you will need to answer for yourself because you alone know the true answers.

- How did you react when you walked to the front

- How did your audience respond to your speech? What did their nonverbal communication convey as you delivered your speech? What feedback did you receive from your classmates and instructor following the speech?

Remember, don't be too critical as you evaluate your performance. You will do some things well, and this should build your confidence. Focus on other aspects of your speech that you can improve.

Suppose that you encounter a serious problem: You lose your place, your mind goes blank, and you bury your head in your notes and race to the end of your speech. Use this as a learning experience. Ask yourself *why* you forgot: Did you try to memorize your speech

KEY POINTS

To Prepare for the Interview

1. Determine whom you want to interview.
2. Decide the format for the interview.
3. Schedule the interview.
4. Research the person to be interviewed.
5. Prepare a list of questions.

- **Key Points** boxes appear throughout the book to reinforce instruction and aid student review. They summarize important material and offer helpful guidelines throughout the public speaking process.

- **Ethical Decisions** boxes deepen students' understanding of the difficult choices speakers and listeners can face. These boxes present mini cases and ask students to choose between controversial courses of action. Thought-provoking questions follow each scenario, providing springboards for engaging classroom debates.

ETHICAL DECISIONS

Ghosting 101

Listening to a speaker, we usually expect to hear the authentic thoughts of that individual. That seems to be a basic principle of the speaker-audience contract. Yet politicians often do not write the speeches they deliver. Instead they rely on speechwriters, sometimes called "ghostwriters." Journalist Ari Posner laments this tradition, observing, "If college or high school students relied on ghosts the way most public figures do, they'd be expelled on charges of plagiarism."[13] Is the practice of ghostwriting in politics ethical? What are the benefits and drawbacks of politicians' relying on speechwriters? Is it ever ethical for these leaders to deliver speeches they did not write? If so, what principles of audience analysis should guide the use of these speeches?

- **Speaking with Confidence** boxes feature the voices of real students from public speaking classes throughout the country explaining how this text helped them build their confidence in public speaking.

SPEAKING WITH CONFIDENCE

Before presenting my speech on how to start a new small business, I began gathering and evaluating the supporting materials I would use to support my key ideas. Like most speakers, I searched online for information. I was careful to be selective and to avoid web pages that were based on personal opinion and bias. I supplemented the examples and statistics I found with my own expert testimony as a successful, self-employed businessman. I cited my sources to establish my credibility and let my listeners assess the quality of my data and documentation. Knowing that I had selected and tested my supporting materials allowed me to minimize my use of qualifiers such as "I think," "this might," and "maybe." I was confident with what I said, and the audience could be confident with what they heard.

Jovan Coker
Radford University

EXPLORING ONLINE

Occasion-Generated Topics

www.scopesys.com/anyday
www.brainyhistory.com

With just a few mouse clicks, you can search for occasion-generated speech topics at the AnyDay-In-History and Brainy History websites. These pages let you discover events that occurred on any day and month you select. They also list names of people who were born or who died on that date, along with holidays and religious observances.

- **Exploring Online** features, sidebars that capture the creativity and commitment necessary to master public speaking, appear several times in every chapter and direct students to a wealth of Internet information that we consider especially interesting or useful.

- **Sample speeches** appear in selected chapters and in Appendix B as models for students to learn from or critique.

◖ Annotated Sample Speech

James Chang delivered the following persuasive speech and placed first at the 2003 Interstate Oratorical Association National Speech Contest. As you read his speech, notice how he used Monroe's motivated sequence to frame his problem–solution discussion of contributing to sustainable charity programs.

Sustainable Giving[15]

James Chang, Cypress College

Attention
In his introduction (paragraphs 1 and 2), James focuses his audience's *attention* on the pervasive problem of poverty. He appeals to his listeners' self-interest (values) by suggesting that they are, unintentionally, part of the problem.

1 Beatrice Biira, a 9-year-old girl in Uganda, lives in abject poverty. Living in a shanty home where the rain seeps through the roof every night, neither she nor any of her siblings has ever stepped foot in a school. Her story, sadly, is not unique. The World Bank in 2001 concluded that nearly three billion people live on less than two dollars a day. We hear this and we want to help, so we write checks to groups who claim that they will make a difference by donating food, clothing, and other short-term essentials, and we feel like we have helped make a difference in Beatrice's life, and, indeed, we probably have.

2 But what happens after the food runs out? Despite our best intentions, by donating to charities that offer short-term aid, we inadvertently perpetuate the cycle of poverty. Thus, I am advocating today that potential donors to charities should give to organizations that provide solutions that are sustainable in nature

---

- **Practice Critique** activities, included in the end-of-chapter exercises, give students an opportunity to learn how to provide helpful and thoughtful evaluations of others' speeches. These activities correlate with student speeches that appear in Appendix B and in selected chapters.

◖ EXERCISES

1. **Practice Critique.** You have just been appointed judge for a public speaking contest. Your task is to present the award for "best introduction" from among the four student speeches in Appendix B. Read these speeches and evaluate their introductions using the guidelines presented in this chapter. Select the introduction you think is best and explain the reasons for your selection.

2. Evaluate the chapter openings you have read thus far in this book. Which are most and least successful at getting your attention? What made them effective or ineffective?

3. Select a magazine and examine the various ways journalists begin their stories. Which of the seven attention-getting devices discussed in this chapter do they employ? Are there other attention-getting techniques you can identify?

4. Examine the attention-getting step of Jennell

5. Suppose the specific purpose of a speech is to persuade an audience to contribute money for needed playground equipment for a local elementary school. Write a statement establishing the importance and relevance of the topic for each of the following audiences:

   a. Parents of children who attend the school

   b. Senior citizens on limited, fixed incomes whose children and grandchildren no longer attend the school

   c. Traditional-age college students

6. Locate the preview statements in the introductions of the student speeches in Appendix B.

7. Rewrite the closure statement of Jennell Chu's speech in Appendix B using two strategies other than the one Chu uses. Discuss the strengths and weaknesses of each closure statement. Which closure strategy do you prefer? Why?

8. Prepare three conclusions for the same body

Resources in Print and Online

NAME OF SUPPLEMENT	AVAILABLE	INSTRUCTOR OR STUDENT SUPPLEMENT	DESCRIPTION
Instructor's Classroom Kit, Volumes I and II (Vol. 1 ISBN: 0205856942 Vol. 2 ISBN: 0205856950)	In print Online	Instructor Supplement	Pearson's unparalleled Classroom Kit includes every instruction aid a public speaking professor needs to manage the classroom. Organized by chapter, each volume contains materials from the Instructor's Manual and Test Bank, as well as slides from the PowerPoint™ Presentation Package that accompanies this text. The fully updated Instructor's Manual offers a chapter-by-chapter guide to teaching Public Speaking, including chapter overviews, chapter summaries, learning objectives, lecture outlines, discussion questions, activities, and handouts. The Test Bank contains multiple choice, true/false, completion, short answer, and essay questions. Each question has a correct answer and is referenced by page, skill, and topic. Electronic copies of all of the resources are available on Pearson's Instructor's Resource Center at www.pearsonhighered.com/irc (access code required).
MyTest (ISBN: 0205857361)	Online	Instructor Supplement	This flexible, online test-generating software includes all questions found in the Test Bank sections of the Classroom Kits, allowing instructors to create their own exams. Instructors can also edit any of the existing test questions and add new questions. Other special features of this program include random generation of test questions, creation of alternate versions of the same test, scrambling of question sequence, and test preview before printing. Available at www.pearsonmytest.com (access code required).
PowerPoint™ Presentation Package (ISBN: 0205857353)	Online	Instructor Supplement	This text-specific package consists of a collection of lecture outlines and graphic images keyed to every chapter of the text. Available for download on Pearson's Instructor Resource Center at www .pearsonhighered.com/irc (access code required).
Pearson's ClassPrep	Online	Instructor Supplement	Pearson's ClassPrep collects the very best class presentation resources—art and figures from our texts, videos, lecture activities, audio clips, classroom activities, and much more—in one convenient online destination. You may search through ClassPrep's extensive database of tools by content topic (arranged by standard topics within the public speaking curriculum) or by content type (video, audio, activities, etc.). You will find ClassPrep in the Instructor's section of MySpeechLab (access code required).
A Guide for New Public Speaking Teachers, Fifth Edition (ISBN: 0205828108)	In print Online	Instructor Supplement	Prepared by Jennifer L. Fairchild, Eastern Kentucky University, this guide helps new teachers prepare for and teach the introductory public speaking course effectively. It covers such topics as preparing for the term, planning and structuring your course, evaluating speeches, using the textbook, integrating technology into the classroom, and much more (available for download at www.pearsonhighered.com/irc; access code required).
Pearson's Contemporary Classic Speeches DVD (ISBN: 0205405525)	DVD	Instructor Supplement	This exciting supplement includes over 120 minutes of video footage in an easy-to-use DVD format. Each speech is accompanied by a biographical and historical summary that helps students understand the context and motivation behind each speech. Speakers featured include Martin Luther King, Jr., John F. Kennedy, Barbara Jordan, the Dalai Lama, and Christopher Reeve. Please contact your Pearson representative for details; some restrictions apply.

NAME OF SUPPLEMENT	AVAILABLE	INSTRUCTOR OR STUDENT SUPPLEMENT	DESCRIPTION
Pearson's Public Speaking Video Library	VHS/DVD	Instructor Supplement	This collection contains a range of types of speeches delivered on a multitude of topics, allowing you to choose the speeches suited to your students. Please contact your Pearson representative for details and a complete list of videos and their contents to choose which would be most useful in your class. Samples from most of our public speaking videos are available on www.mycoursetoolbox.com. Some restrictions apply.
Public Speaking in the Multicultural Environment, Second Edition (ISBN: 0205265111)	In print	Student Supplement	Prepared by Devorah A. Lieberman, Portland State University, this booklet helps students learn to analyze cultural diversity within their audiences and adapt their presentations accordingly (available for purchase).
The Speech Outline (ISBN: 032108702X)	In print	Student Supplement	Prepared by Reeze L. Hanson and Sharon Condon of Haskell Indian Nations University, this workbook includes activities, exercises, and answers to help students develop and master the critical skill of outlining (available for purchase).
Speech Preparation Workbook (ISBN: 013559569X)	In print	Student Supplement	Prepared by Jennifer Dreyer and Gregory H. Patton of San Diego State University, this workbook takes students through the stages of speech creation—from audience analysis to writing the speech—and includes guidelines, tips, and easy-to-fill-in pages (available for purchase).
Study Card for Public Speaking (ISBN: 0205441262)	In print	Student Supplement	Colorful, affordable, and packed with useful information, the Pearson Study Cards make studying easier, more efficient, and more enjoyable. Course information is distilled down to the basics, helping students quickly master the fundamentals, review a subject for understanding, or prepare for an exam. Because they are laminated for durability, they can be kept for years to come and pulled out whenever students need a quick review (available for purchase).
Pearson Public Speaking Study Site	Online	Student Supplement	This open access student Web resource features practice tests, learning objectives, and Web links organized around the major topics typically covered in the Introduction to Public Speaking course. The content of this site has even been correlated to the table of contents of your book (available at www.pearsonpublicspeaking.com).
VideoLab CD-ROM (ISBN: 0205561616)	CD-ROM	Student Supplement	This interactive study tool for students can be used independently or in class. It provides digital video of student speeches that can be viewed in conjunction with corresponding outlines, manuscripts, notecards, and instructor critiques. Following each speech are a series of drills to help students analyze content and delivery (available for purchase).
MySpeechLab	Online	Instructor & Student Supplement	MySpeechLab is a state-of-the-art, interactive, and instructive solution for public speaking courses. Designed to be used as a supplement to a traditional lecture course or to completely administer an online course, MySpeechLab combines a Pearson eText, MySearchLab™, Pearson's MediaShare, multimedia, video clips, activities, research support, tests, and quizzes to completely engage students. MySpeechLab can be packaged with your text and is available for purchase at www.myspeechlab.com (access code required). See next page for more details.

MySpeechLab®

The moment you know.

Educators know it. Students know it. It's that inspired moment when something that was difficult to understand suddenly makes perfect sense. Our MyLab products have been designed and refined with a single purpose in mind—to help educators create that moment of understanding with their students.

The new MySpeechLab delivers **proven results** in helping individual students succeed. It provides **engaging experiences** that personalize, stimulate, and measure learning for each student. And, it comes from a **trusted partner** with educational expertise and a deep commitment to helping students, instructors, and departments achieve their goals.

MySpeechLab can be used by itself or linked to any learning management system. To learn more about how the new MySpeechLab combines proven learning applications with powerful assessment, read on!

MySpeechLab delivers **proven results** in helping individual students succeed.

- Pearson MyLabs are currently in use by millions of students each year across a variety of disciplines.
- MySpeechLab works—but don't take our word for it. Visit our MyLab/Mastering site (www.pearsonhighered.com/mylabmastering) to read white papers, case studies, and testimonials from instructors and students that consistently demonstrate the success of our MyLabs.

MySpeechLab provides **engaging experiences** that personalize, stimulate, and measure learning for each student. MySpeechLab is available for Public Speaking courses.

- **The Pearson eText:** Identical in content and design to the printed text, the Pearson eText lets students access their textbook anytime, anywhere, and any way they want—including downloading to an iPad. Students can take notes and highlight, just like a traditional book.

- **Assessments:** Pre- and Post-Tests for each chapter enable students and instructors to track progress and get immediate feedback. Results from the Pre- and Post-Tests generate a personalized study plan that helps students master course content. Chapter Exams allow instructors to easily assign exams online. Results feed into the MyLab grade book.

- **MediaShare:** A cutting-edge video upload tool that allows students and instructors to upload speeches or group projects for viewing, commenting, and grading (whether face to face or online). Grades can be imported into most learning management systems. Structured much like a social networking site, MediaShare can help promote a sense of community among students.

- **Videos and Video Quizzes:** Interactive videos provide students with the opportunity to watch and evaluate multimedia pertaining to chapter content. Many videos are annotated with critical thinking questions or include short, assignable quizzes that report to the instructor's grade book.

- **ClassPrep** collects the very best class presentation resources in one convenient online destination, so instructors can keep students engaged throughout every class.

- **MyOutline:** This valuable tool provides step-by-step guidance and structure for writing an effective outline, along with a detailed help section to assist students in understanding the elements of an outline and how all the pieces fit together. Students can download and email completed outlines to instructors, save for future editing or print—even print as notecards. Instructors can choose from our templates or create their own structure for use.

- **Topic Selector:** This interactive tool helps students get started generating ideas and then narrowing down topics. Our Topic Selector is question based, rather than drill-down or simply a list of ideas, in order to help students really learn the process of selecting their topic. Once they have determined their topic, students are directed to credible online sources for guidance with the research process.

- **MySearchLab:** Pearson's MySearchLab™ is the easiest way for students to start a research assignment or paper. Complete with extensive help on the research process and four databases of credible and reliable source material, MySearchLab™ helps students quickly and efficiently make the most of their research time.

- **Audio Chapter Summaries:** Every chapter includes an audio chapter summary, formatted as an MP3, perfect for students reviewing material before a test or instructors reviewing material before class.

MySpeechLab comes from a **trusted partner** with educational expertise and a deep commitment to helping students, instructors, and departments achieve their goals.

- Pearson supports instructors with workshops, training, and assistance from Pearson Faculty Advisors—so you get the help you need to make MySpeechLab work for your course.
- Pearson gathers feedback from instructors and students during the development of content and the feature enhancement of each release to ensure that our products meet your needs.

No matter what course management system you use—or if you do not use one at all, but still wish to easily capture your students' grade and track their performance—Pearson has a MySpeechLab option to suit your needs. A MySpeechLab access code is no additional cost when packaged with print versions of selected Pearson Communication texts. To get started, contact your local Pearson Publisher's Representative at www.pearsonhighered.com/replocator.

◖ Acknowledgments

We are, first and foremost, grateful to the many university, college, and community college educators whose enthusiasm contributed to the success of previous editions of this textbook. This eighth edition of *Mastering Public Speaking* is the product of more than just two authors. Although we have tried to speak with one voice for the sake of our readers, the truth is that many voices resonate throughout this text: the voices of our teachers, our colleagues, our editors, and our students. What we know, what we value, and what we write are shaped in part by their influence and insight. Wherever possible, we have tried to acknowledge their contributions. For all their influence on this text we are thankful.

We thank the entire editorial and production staffs at Pearson for their contributions to this eighth edition. We are indebted to Karon Bowers for her faith in this project and her wise counsel. We are especially grateful to Carol Alper, senior development editor, for her thoughtful suggestions, her masterful multitasking, and her patience. Thanks to Blair Tuckman, marketing manager; Megan Sweeney, editorial assistant; Raegan Heerema, project manager; Mary Sanger, project manager for Nesbitt Graphics; Joan Flaherty, copyeditor; and Annette Linder, Lee Scher, and Carolyn Arcabascio, photo researchers. Thank you all for making writing as fun as it can be.

Many students, authors, and publishers graciously allowed us to quote material in this book. Especially helpful were the comments from students and their instructors. A number of students responded to our call for feedback about classroom experiences or topics in *Mastering Public Speaking* that increased their confidence. We thank them all, particularly the students selected for the "Speaking with Confidence" features in this edition. We are especially grateful to Dolly Conner and Daniel Mansson for introducing us to several of these students.

We have benefited immensely from the encouragement and advice of our colleagues at Radford University and San Antonio College, particularly Dolly Conner, Sandy French, Kristin Froemling, David Mrizek, Jolinda Ramsey, Suzanne Skinner, and Karin Wilking. Leonard Ziegler, Debra Coates, and Lora Gordon, many thanks for your help with student photographs. Chris Skinner, thanks for your help in videotaping and transferring videos to DVD.

In addition, *Mastering Public Speaking* has been shaped and refined by the close readings and thoughtful suggestions of a number of reviewers. We would like to thank the following reviewers for their comments on this edition:

Barbara Ruth Burke, *University of Minnesota, Morris*
Rebecca J. Franko, *California State Polytechnic University*
Nancy Legge, *Idaho State University*

Stacey M. Macchi, *Western Illinois University*
David C. McLaughlin, *Montana State University*
Deborah Stieneker, *Arapahoe Community College*
Kimberly Warren-Cox, *Jackson State Community College*

We would also like to acknowledge reviewers of previous editions:

Linda Anthon, *Valencia Community College*
Barbara L. Baker, *Central Missouri State University*
Elizabeth Bell, *University of South Florida*
Jim Benjamin, *University of Toledo*

Kathy Berggren, *Cornell University*
Tim Borchers, *Moorhead State University*
Sue E. Brilhart, *Southwest Missouri State University*

Gwendolyn Brown, *Professor Emerita, Radford University*
Carl R. Burgchardt, *Colorado State University*
Sharon Cline, *University of North Dakota*
Dolly Conner, *Radford University*
Pamela Cooper, *Northwestern University*
Michael Cronin, *Professor Emeritus, Radford University*
Sherry Dewald, *Red Rock Community College*
Thomas E. Diamond, *Montana State University*
Terrence Doyle, *Northern Virginia Community College*
Rebecca J. Franko, *California State Polytechnic University, Pomona*
John Fritch, *Southwest Missouri State University*
Robert W. Glenn, *University of Tennessee*
Deborah Anne Gross, *Gwynedd Mercy College*
Trudy L. Hanson, *West Texas A&M University*
Dayle C. Hardy-Short, *Northern Arizona University*
Deborah Hatton, *Sam Houston State University*
Kimberly Batty Herbert, *Clovis Community College*
Susan Kilgard, *Ann Arundel Community College*
Leslie A. Klipper, *Miramar College*

Mary Kaye Krum, *formerly of Florence-Darlington Technical College*
Linda Kurz, *University of Missouri, Kansas City*
Bruce Loebs, *Idaho State University*
Sean McDevitt, *Lakeland College*
Patricia Palm McGillen, *Mankato State University*
David B. McLennan, *Peace College*
Dante E. Morelli, *Suffolk County Community College*
Eileen Oswald, *Valencia Community College*
Rosemarie Rossetti, *Ohio State University*
Jim Roux, *Horry-Georgetown Technical College*
Edward H. Sewell, *Virginia Polytechnic Institute and State University*
Frances Swinny, *Professor Emerita, Trinity University*
Jason J. Teven, *California State University, Fullerton*
Cory Tomasson, *Illinois Valley Community College*
Beth M. Waggenspack, *Virginia Polytechnic Institute and State University*
Doris Werkman, *Portland State University*
Dianna R. Wynn, *Midland College*

We also appreciate the many talented individuals who prepared the array of supplemental materials listed in the "Resources in Print and Online" section in this preface. Their contributions to the effective teaching and learning of public speaking are immeasurable.

Finally, we are indebted to all our public speaking students who have crafted their messages, walked to the front of their classrooms, and informed, persuaded, entertained, and challenged us. Without their ideas and experiences, writing and revising this book would have been impossible, just as without tomorrow's students it would be unnecessary.

An Invitation

We welcome your feedback about the eighth edition of *Mastering Public Speaking*. Please contact us by email at the following addresses:

ggrice@radford.edu
jskinner@alamo.edu

We look forward to hearing from you.

—George L. Grice and John F. Skinner

An Introduction to Public Speaking

1

- **Why Study Public Speaking?**
  Personal Benefits
  Professional Benefits
  Public Benefits

- **Definitions of Communication**

- **Levels of Communication**
  Intrapersonal Communication
  Interpersonal Communication
  Group Communication
  Public Communication
  Mass Communication

- **Elements of Communication**
  Speaker
  Message
  Listener
  Feedback
  Channel
  Environment
  Noise

- **The Public Speaker as Critical Thinker**
  Theory Into Practice: Thinking about Speaking

After studying this chapter, you should be able to

1. Identify the benefits of studying public speaking.

2. Define communication.

3. Explain the triangle of meaning.

4. Describe the levels of communication.

5. List and define the seven elements of communication.

6. Discuss how these components function in the communication elements model.

7. Explain how the eight critical thinking skills can help you develop and evaluate speeches.

> The only reason to give a speech is to change the world.
>
> —Nick Morgan

Why Study Public Speaking?

Today, beyond the relative security of the college or university classroom, thousands of speakers will stand in front of audiences and deliver speeches. And during those same 24 hours, people will make millions of business presentations. These speakers will express their ideas, champion their causes, and promote their products or services. Those who succeed will make sales, enlist support, and educate and entertain their listeners. Many will also enhance their reputations as effective speakers. To achieve these goals, each will use the skills, principles, and arts that are the subject of this textbook.

Consider, too, that somewhere on a college campus right now is the student who will one day deliver an inaugural address after being sworn in as president; the student(s) who will appear on national television to accept the Heisman Trophy, a Tony Award for Best Performance—Leading Actress in a Play, or the Academy Award for Best Director; the student who will present breakthrough medical research findings to a national conference of doctors and medical technicians, or whose words will usher passage of important legislation.

We began this chapter with a quotation by educator and author Nick Morgan. He credits that statement to an old friend, a speechwriter, who "meant it as a challenge. It was his way of saying that, if you're going to take all the trouble to prepare and deliver a speech, make it worthwhile. Change the world. Otherwise, why bother?"[1] Today, Morgan gives this advice at workshops for leaders of corporations, colleges, and government. Though changing the world may seem unrealistic and intimidating at this stage of your life, you do have the opportunity to help shape the values, beliefs, and behaviors of those around you and in this class. As Henry Ward Beecher stated, "The humblest individual exerts some influence, either for good or evil, upon others." Ethical and effective communicators can make a permanent, positive difference in the lives of others.

You may be taking this course as an elective because you want to improve your public speaking skills in the relative security of a classroom. Or you may be in the class because it is a requirement for graduation. If that's the case, you may rightfully be asking, "Why should I take a course in public speaking?" The answer is that studying and practicing public speaking benefits you personally, professionally, and publicly.

Personal Benefits

This course can benefit you personally in three ways.

- Acquire academic skills. According to a Carnegie Foundation report,

  To succeed in college, undergraduates should be able to write and speak with clarity, and to read and listen with comprehension. Language and thought are inextricably connected, and as undergraduates develop their linguistic skills, they hone the quality of their thinking and become intellectually and socially empowered.[2]

Look at some of the chapter titles in this textbook. They include words such as *analyzing*, *researching*, *organizing*, *wording*, and *delivering*. These are skills you will use in constructing and delivering your speeches. They are also *transferable* skills, meaning they can help you throughout your academic studies and in your chosen career.

- Gain knowledge. According to one study, we remember only 10 percent of what we read, 20 percent of what we hear, 30 percent of what we see, and 70 percent of what we speak.[3] Speaking is an active process. You discover ideas, shape them into a message, and deliver that message using your voice and body. The act of speaking is a crucial test of your thinking skills. In this course, you will learn a lot about the topics on which you choose to speak. By learning how to construct an effective speech, you will also learn to be a better listener.
- Build self-confidence. We devote Chapter 3 to discussing the fear of public speaking. In this course, you can learn how to turn this apprehension into confidence. You will do so by reading this textbook, by listening to your instructor, and, most important, by doing. The confidence and poise you gain as you begin to master public speaking will help you when you give an oral report in your British literature class or when you urge your school board to retain the music education program.

Great speaking requires practice, but your efforts will reward you with transferable skills, increased knowledge, and greater confidence.

Professional Benefits

Studying communication, specifically public speaking, is also important to helping you achieve two professional goals.

- Advance in your career. Numerous studies document a strong relationship between communication competence and career success. In a 2011 report, the National Association of Colleges and Employers listed the characteristics that employers consider most important in hiring an employee. Verbal communication skills were at the top of the list.[4]
- Secure employment. In another survey, one thousand randomly selected human resource managers were asked to determine the "factors most important in helping graduating college students obtain employment." Oral communication skills ranked first; written communication, second; and listening, third.[5] The researchers concluded:

  It appears that the skills most valued in the contemporary job-entry market are communication skills. The skills of listening, oral communication (both interpersonal and public), written communication, and the trait of enthusiasm are indicated to be the most important. Again, it would appear to follow that university officials wishing to be of the greatest help to their graduates in finding employment would make sure that basic competencies in oral and written communication are developed. Courses in listening, interpersonal, and public communication would form the basis of meeting the oral communication competencies.[6]

Oral communication clearly plays a critical role in your professional life. This course will instruct you in two of those vital skills: public speaking and listening.

Public Benefits

> Speech is civilization itself. The word, even the most contradictory word, preserves contact—it is silence which isolates.
>
> —Thomas Mann

Finally, public speaking can help you play your role as a member of society. Public speaking is an important part of creating and sustaining a society of informed, active citizens. A democratic society is shaped in part by the public eloquence of its leaders:

A noted talk show host who encourages parents "to jump-start a child's imagination" through the power of reading

Two former presidents who tap a nation's generosity to aid earthquake victims in Haiti

But a democratic society is also shaped by the quiet eloquence of everyday citizens:

The police officer who informs residents of a crime-plagued area how to set up a Neighborhood Watch program

The social worker who addresses the city council and secures funding for a safe house for abused and runaway children

Actress Angelina Jolie uses her access to the media to urge more people to get involved. A goodwill ambassador for the United Nations, she urges the international community to address global poverty and refugee issues.

In each of these instances, the speaker used the power of the spoken word to address a need and solicit an appropriate audience response. Active civic participation requires citizens to "speak out" about injustices and inequities. And though we increasingly use social media like Facebook and Twitter to alert and quickly mobilize groups of people, activism will always involve one or more individuals stirring groups of people through public speech.

While we recognize effective speaking when we meet someone who always says just the right thing or who says things in funny and colorful ways, few of us have been trained to speak well. That's a shame in light of the personal, professional, and public benefits public speaking can offer. To appreciate the power of communication, you must understand just what it is. That requires a look at some definitions of communication and at some of its essential components.

Definitions of Communication

The word *communicate* comes from the Latin verb *communicare*, meaning "to share." The concept of sharing is important in understanding communication and is implicit in our definition of the term. Simply stated, when you communicate, you share, or make common, your knowledge and ideas with someone else.

Some scholars view communication primarily as a *process*. For example, Thomas Scheidel provides a process perspective when he defines communication as "the transmission and reception of symbolic cues."[7] Other scholars see communication as an outcome or a *product* and define it simply as "shared meaning." We believe both of these perspectives are valid: communication is both a *process* and a *product*. **Communication**, then, is *the sharing of meaning by sending and receiving symbolic cues*.

Figure 1.1 represents Charles Ogden and I. A. Richards's triangle of meaning,[8] an illustration of the three elements necessary for communication: interpreter, symbol, and referent. The word *interpreter* refers to both the sender and the receiver of a message. The **interpreter** is simply the person who is communicating, with words or other symbols.

The second element of this model, the **symbol**, is anything to which people attach or assign a meaning. Symbols can be pictures, drawings, or objects. Even colors can function as symbols; political pundits reduce us to living in blue or red states. Police officers' uniforms and squad cars are symbols of their authority. The most familiar symbols, however, are words. Many words refer to particular objects, places, and people: *chair*; *Long Beach, California*; and *Eudora Welty*, for example. Some words refer to concepts, such as *freedom of expression*, *existentialism*, and *fair play*.

The third and final element of the triangle of meaning is the **referent**, the object or idea for which the symbol stands. Both the sender and the receiver of a message have a referent for the symbols used. This referent depends on each individual's knowledge and experience. People cannot exchange referents in the way they can exchange objects. For example, someone can hand you a paper clip, and that paper clip is the same in your hand as it is in your friend's hand. Your friends, however, cannot transfer their ideas or information to you. All they can do is to code their ideas into symbols and

communication
The process of sharing meaning by sending and receiving symbolic cues.

interpreter
Any person using symbols to send or receive messages.

symbol
Anything to which people attach meaning.

referent
The object or idea each interpreter attaches to a symbol.

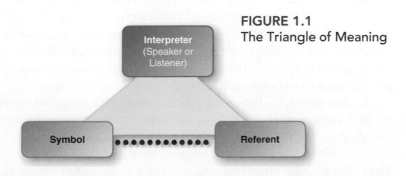

FIGURE 1.1
The Triangle of Meaning

hope that the ideas you decode will be similar to the ones they intended. In short, as senders, we select a symbol based on our referent. That symbol, in turn, triggers the receiver's referent.

Countless jokes and situation comedy plots revolve around interpreters who attach different referents to the same symbol. The *New Yorker* cartoon above illustrates one such outcome. However, miscommunication can sometimes be serious and divisive. Consider the experience of Muslim American Zayed M. Yasin, the Harvard student whose graduation speech was one of three the selection committee chose in the spring of 2002. A furor began when the campus newspaper, the *Harvard Crimson*, published the titles of the three student commencement speeches. Yasin's speech, to be delivered less than nine months after September 11, 2001, was titled "Of Faith and Citizenship: My American Jihad." His aim, he said, was to rescue the word *jihad* from extremists who had co-opted it to justify terrorism. He defined the term as a spiritual quest, "the determination to do right and justice even against your personal interests."[9] Among the definitions of the Arabic word are "striving," "effort," and "struggle," but many of those who protested the selection of Yasin's speech equated the term *jihad* with a "holy war." After the protests began on his campus, Yasin met with members of the selection committee, retitled his speech "Of Faith and Citizenship" for the printed program, and delivered the text of the speech without changing a word.[10]

As this example demonstrates, communication is clearest only when all its interpreters attach similar referents to the message being communicated. You can, no doubt, think of experiences you have had when people misinterpreted what you said because they attached different referents to your words. The most important thing to remember about the triangle of meaning and the process of communication is this: *Words and other symbols have no inherent meaning. People create meaning; words do not.* A word takes on the meaning that each interpreter attaches to it.

What does the triangle of meaning have to do with public speaking? As you will discover throughout this book, this model applies to public speaking just as it does to all other forms of communication. If speakers and listeners always used specific symbols, interpreted them objectively, and attached similar referents to them, few communication problems would arise from the content of the message. As a result, your work in a public speaking class could be limited to improving your organization and polishing your style of delivery. Yet many of our communication problems can be traced directly to difficulties in the relationships between interpreters, the symbols they use, and the referents behind those symbols.

As a public speaker, you must try to ensure that the message your audience hears matches as closely as possible the message you intended. You do that by paying particular attention to your content, organization, and delivery, all major subjects of this book. To understand the complexity of public speaking, you need to realize how it relates to other levels of communication.

◑ Levels of Communication

Communication can occur on five levels: intrapersonal, interpersonal, group, public, and mass communication. Each level is distinguished by the number of people involved, the formality of the situation, and the opportunities for feedback. Public communication is the subject of this book. Yet public speaking incorporates elements of the other four levels. A brief look at each will help you better understand public speaking.

Intrapersonal Communication

Intrapersonal communication is communication with yourself, and it serves many functions. For example, if you woke up this morning and panicked because you overslept and were late for a class, you were communicating intrapersonally. If in the middle of a public speech you tell yourself, "This is really going well," or "I can't believe I just said that," you are also communicating intrapersonally.

As these examples demonstrate, much intrapersonal communication is geared toward a specific, conscious purpose: evaluating how we are doing or did in a particular situation, solving a problem, relieving stress, or planning for the near or distant future. Though we all have probably uttered something aloud to ourselves at times of stress, joy, puzzlement, or discouragement, intrapersonal communication is typically silent. We sit quietly as we reflect on a speaker explaining the difference between ambient and progressive jazz. We are attentive as we hear another speaker

intrapersonal communication
Cognition or thought; communicating with oneself.

explain the preparations for a first skydive. Both as public speakers and as audience members for others' speeches, we communicate intrapersonally a great deal. Keep in mind that intrapersonal communication is a continuous process of self-feedback and that it involves only one person.

Interpersonal Communication

interpersonal communication
Communication between individuals in pairs; also called *dyadic communication*.

As soon as our communication involves ourselves and one other person, it moves to a second level: **interpersonal communication**. This is sometimes called *dyadic communication*; *dyad* is Latin for "pair." Face-to-face conversations between friends, colleagues, acquaintances, or strangers are a common form of interpersonal communication. Even instant messaging between two friends is interpersonal.

Whenever two communicators are face to face or speaking on the telephone, the opportunity for verbal interaction exists. If someone had secretly recorded your last conversation with your best friend and transcribed it for you to read, you might be surprised by the number of incomplete sentences each of you spoke. Ideas that do not appear to make much sense in writing are likely quite clear in conversation. Your best friend often knows how you are going to finish a sentence and either finishes it for you or nods agreement and switches to another idea.

Group Communication

group communication
Three or more people interacting and hoping to influence one another to pursue a common goal.

The next level, **group communication**, generally takes place with three or more people interacting and influencing one another to pursue a common goal. Although researchers place varying limits on the size of a group, everyone recognizes that a sense of cohesion or group identity is essential to any definition of this level of communication.

Seven students who get together and spend half the night quizzing one another for an upcoming exam are obviously engaged in group communication. Presenting a speech in class is not group communication. However, if your presentation generates questions and discussion, your public speaking class might qualify as an example of group communication.

The important thing to remember about group communication is that the people involved must have a sense of group identity. A group of fourteen people, for example, is not just seven dyads, or pairs, of people. They must all believe and accept that they belong together for some reason, whether they face a common problem, share similar interests, or simply work in the same division of a company.

Informational presentations to small groups often encourage questions and comments from audience members, thus increasing speaker-listener interaction.

As long as members are relatively free to contribute to the discussion, what occurs is clearly group communication. However, once someone stands up and begins to present a report or make a speech, the communication shifts to the fourth level—public communication.

Public Communication

Public communication, the subject of this course, occurs when one person speaks face to face with an audience. That audience may be small or large. As the size of the audience grows, the flow of communication becomes increasingly one directional, from speaker to audience. When the audience is large, individual members have less opportunity for verbal interaction with the speaker.

For example, your public speaking class is probably small enough that you feel free to ask your instructor questions during class. In a lecture class of several hundred students, however, you might feel more pressure to keep silent, even if you had a legitimate question. If you were part of an audience of several thousand people, not only might you feel pressure to keep quiet during a speech, but even if you did ask a question the speaker probably could not hear it.

Public communication, therefore, is a more one-directional flow of information. It is also more formal than the other types of communication we have discussed so far. Whether the audience is 20 or 20,000, public communication always involves one person communicating to an audience that is physically present.

public communication
One person communicating face to face with an audience.

Mass Communication

What happens if we sit in front of our television sets or computer monitors and see video clips from that small class or large public assembly? Such a situation represents the fifth and final level of communication—**mass communication**. Once an audience becomes so large that it cannot be gathered in one place, some type of print or electronic medium—newspaper, magazine, radio, television, or computer, among others—must be placed between speaker or writer and the intended audience. The physical isolation of speaker and audience severely limits the possibilities for spontaneous interaction between them. In fact, an important characteristic of mass communication is that audience feedback is *always* delayed. If an article inspires or angers you, you may write a letter to the editor or post a response. You have taken the opportunity to send feedback, but it is delayed.

A second characteristic of mass communication is that the method of message transmission can become very important. Advertisements reach different sizes and types of audiences via radio, television, billboards, magazines, newspapers, and websites. Advertising agencies, political consultants, and the people who use them know very well that the *way* a message is sent can be as important as that message's *content*, something public speakers should also remember.

mass communication
One person or group communicating to a large audience through some print or electronic medium.

KEY POINTS

Levels of Communication

1. Intrapersonal
2. Interpersonal
3. Group
4. Public
5. Mass communication

You will master public speaking skills more quickly and easily if you remain aware of the connections between public communication and the four other levels of communication. In this class, you may use interpersonal and group communication to determine speech topics and how you approach them. You may interview an expert on a topic you are considering for a speech. Through informal conversations with classmates, you will form a clearer picture of your audience by discovering their interests, attitudes, and values. You may offer others feedback on their speeches and receive their comments on yours. If you have the opportunity to tape your speeches, you will gain experience with one of the media of mass communication. Certainly, you will consult print and electronic resources as you research your speech. And as you deliver your public speeches, you will give yourself intrapersonal feedback about the job you are doing and the positive responses we hope you'll be receiving.

Elements of Communication

Now let's look at the elements of communication to see how they apply, specifically, to the complex activity of public speaking. Remember, the better you understand how communication works in general, the better you will be able to make it work for you in specific speaking situations. Just as important, knowing these elements will let us see where some common communication problems arise.

Today, the most widely accepted model of communication has seven components, as illustrated in Figure 1.2, the communication elements model. Although we can identify the individual elements of the communication process, we cannot assess them in isolation. Contemporary scholars emphasize the transactional, interactive nature of communication. Each element simultaneously influences, and is influenced by, the others.

Speaker

speaker
The sender, encoder, or source of the message.

Human communication starts with a person, the **speaker**. We could also call this person the sender, the source, or the encoder. **Encoding** is the process of putting ideas into symbols. We encode so much and so well that we are aware of the process only when we find ourselves "at a loss for words" while either speaking or writing.

encoding
The process of selecting symbols to carry a message.

Message

message
Ideas communicated verbally and nonverbally.

Linked to the speaker is the **message**, the ideas actually communicated. Speech communication scholar Karlyn Kohrs Campbell captures the connection between messages and people when she writes:

> Ideas do not walk by themselves; they must be carried—expressed and voiced—by someone. As a result, we do not encounter ideas neutrally, objectively, or apart from a context; we meet them as someone's ideas.[11]

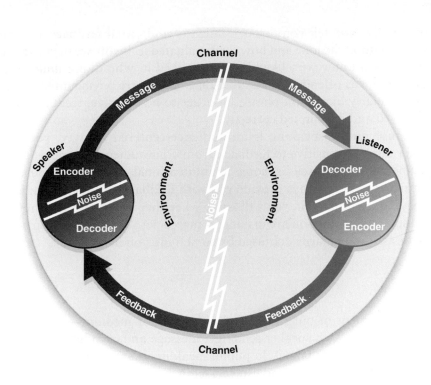

FIGURE 1.2
The Communication Elements Model
A speaker encodes a message and sends it through a channel to a listener, who decodes it. The listener provides feedback and sends it through a channel to a speaker. This interaction takes place in an environment with varying levels of internal and external noise.

The ideas of the message originate with the speaker, who determines the form that the message will initially take. However, others who may participate in the communication process further shape that message.

Listener

The message is sent to a **listener**—the decoder or receiver. This person shapes the message by **decoding** it—that is, attaching meanings to the words, gestures, and voice inflections received. Is every listener's decoded message identical to the one the speaker encoded? Remember our earlier discussion of the triangle of meaning; communication involves more than a single message. The truth is, there are as many messages as there are communicators involved. As long as these messages are similar, communication is usually effective.

Nor does the message stop as it is received. Instead, it is transformed—added to or diminished—as it is joined by other messages that originate with each listener. It is a mistake to assume that a person in the communication process is either a sender or a receiver of messages. We perform both roles simultaneously.

Feedback

The interactions between listeners and senders provide the fourth element in our model of communication—**feedback**. Feedback includes all messages, verbal and nonverbal, sent by listeners to speakers. If you tell a joke,

EXPLORING ONLINE

Comparing Communication Models

http://web.sfc.keio.ac.jp/~masanao/Mosaic_data/com_model.html

Visit this site, maintained by Keio University in Japan, to view and compare a variety of communication models. The site includes linear, interactional, and transactional models. For explanations of each model, you must consult the sources cited.

listener
The receiver, or decoder, of the message.

decoding
The process of attaching meanings to symbols received.

feedback
Verbal and nonverbal responses between communicators about the clarity or acceptability of messages.

your listeners will tell you through laughter and visual feedback whether they understood the joke and how they evaluated it. If you are paying attention, you will know who liked it, who disliked it, who didn't understand it, and who was offended by it. Note that "if you are paying attention" is the particularly important phrase. In order to be effective, feedback must be received and interpreted correctly.

Because public speaking is an audience-centered activity, you as a speaker must be sensitive to feedback from your audience. Some feedback is deliberate and conscious; some is unintentional and unconscious. But your audience will always provide you with feedback of some kind. If you are paying attention to it, you will know when they appreciate your humor, understand the point you are making, disagree with the position you advocate, or are momentarily confused by something you have said.

Channel

channel
The way a message is sent.

The fifth element of our model is the **channel**, or medium—the way the message is sent. Each speaker sending a message and each listener providing feedback uses a channel. In public speaking, the medium is vibrations in the air between speaker and listener, set in motion by the speaker's voice. Vocal elements such as rate, volume, quality, and pitch also carry part of the message. Visual elements—another channel for the message—include eye contact, facial expression, gestures, movement, and presentational aids. As a public speaker, you must learn to use and control all these channels.

Environment

environment
The occasion, social context, and physical setting for communication.

The sixth element of the communication model is the **environment**. Three factors shape an environment: (1) the occasion during which the communication occurs, (2) the larger social context in which the communication takes place, and (3) the physical setting where the communication occurs. The *occasion* refers to the reasons why people have assembled. Circumstances may be serious or festive, planned or spontaneous. Occasions for communication may be as relaxed and informal as a party with friends, as rule-bound as a college debate, or as formal and traditional as a commencement address.

The larger *social context* involves a variety of people and opinions that can vary by culture and affect the appropriateness of the messages that you communicate. For instance, if the members of your audience are from a collectivist culture (such as Latin America or Asia), they may be persuaded by cooperation more than by competition, which may play better in an individualistic culture such as the United States. However, although cultural tendencies do exist, a speaker would be advised to avoid stereotyping the audience; there will always be individual differences in any collected audience.

The physical setting for your classroom speeches is probably apparent to you. You know the size of the room and the number of people in the audience. You know whether the seating arrangement is fixed or flexible. You know whether the room has a lectern or Internet access. You know, or may

Effective public speakers adapt their speaking styles to the physical settings and the occasions for their speeches.

soon discover, potential problems with the setting: the table at the front of the room is wobbly, the air seems stuffy about halfway through each class meeting, one of the fluorescent lights flickers. Each of these distracting elements is a form of noise—the final element for which any accurate model of communication must account.

Noise

Noise is anything that distracts from effective communication, and some form of noise is always present. Three forms of noise exist, distinguished by their sources. First, much noise is **physical**—that is, it occurs in the physical communication environment: the sounds of traffic, the loud *whoosh* of an air conditioner or a heater, the voices of people talking and laughing as they pass by a classroom. However, some physical noise may not involve a sound at all. If your classroom is so cold that you shiver or so hot that you fan yourself, then its temperature is a form of noise. If the room's lighting is poor, then that form of noise will certainly affect the communication occurring there. Anything in the immediate environment that interferes with communication is physical noise.

A second type of noise is **physiological**; a bad cold that affects your hearing and speech, a headache, and an empty growling stomach are examples. Each of these bodily conditions can shift your focus from communicating with others to thinking about how uncomfortable you feel, a form of intrapersonal communication.

The third and final type of noise is **psychological**. This type of noise refers to mental rather than bodily distractions. Anxiety, worry, daydreaming, anticipation, and even joy over some recent event can distract you from the message at hand.

Each form of noise—physical, physiological, and psychological—can occur independently or in combination. Some form of noise is always present, so as a speaker you must try to minimize its effects in public

noise
Anything that distracts from effective communication.

physical noise
Distractions originating in the physical environment.

physiological noise
Distractions originating in the bodies of communicators.

psychological noise
Distractions originating in the thoughts of communicators.

KEY POINTS

Elements of Communication

1. Speaker
2. Message
3. Listener
4. Feedback
5. Channel
6. Environment
7. Noise

communication. For example, by varying your rate, volume, and pitch, or through lively physical delivery, you can combat noise and rivet the audience's attention to your message.

As you can see, public speaking is more complicated than just saying the right words. Communication is dynamic and transactional. Speaker, message, listener, feedback, channel, environment, and noise all interact to influence each other. Unlike that paper clip—the same in every hand that holds it—the message that emerges in communication will never be identical to what any one speaker intended.

Part of mastering public speaking begins with basic skills: organizing a presentation with an identifiable introduction, body, and conclusion; providing previews, summaries, and transitions; deciding whether the oral message needs the support of visual aids; and using appropriate grammar, pronunciation, and articulation.[12] However, to design, develop, and deliver a speech that is appropriate to you, your audience, and the communication context requires some higher-order thinking. Public speaking involves choices, and to choose appropriately, you must sharpen your thinking skills.

◖ The Public Speaker as Critical Thinker

We began this chapter by discussing benefits you gain from studying and practicing public speaking. One of those benefits is that public speaking uses and develops your critical thinking ability. **Critical thinking** is "reasonable reflective thinking that is focused on deciding what to believe or do."[13] If you have ever questioned the answers you were offered, viewed yourself as part of a larger group, looked for patterns you thought no one else had noticed, or followed a hunch to solve a problem in your own way, you have already begun to cultivate your critical thinking ability.[14] You probably also recognize its importance to your personal and professional life. The authors of a national assessment of educational progress underscored the importance of developing critical thinking skills as follows:

> In a world overloaded with information, both a business and a personal advantage will go to those individuals who can sort the wheat from the chaff, the important from the trivial. . . . Quality of life is directly tied to our ability to think clearly amid the noise of modern life, to sift through all that competes for our attention until we find what we value, what will make our lives worth living.[15]

Drawing from the works of Stuart Rankin and Carolyn Hughes, Robert Marzano and his colleagues have identified eight categories of critical thinking skills (see Table 1.1). As a public speaker, you will exercise all of these skills, sometimes in a different order or in combination, as you develop and deliver your speech.

To see how one student used these eight critical thinking skills to develop, deliver, and evaluate her speech, read this chapter's "Theory Into Practice" feature.

critical thinking
The logical, reflective examination of information and ideas to determine what to believe or do.

TABLE 1.1   Eight Categories of Critical Thinking Skills

THIS SKILL . . .	ENABLES THE PUBLIC SPEAKER TO . . .
Focusing	Define problems, set goals, and select pieces of information
Information gathering	Formulate questions and collect data
Remembering	Store information in long-term memory and retrieve it
Organizing	Arrange information so that it can be understood and presented more effectively
Analyzing	Clarify existing information by examining parts and relationships
Generating	Use prior knowledge to infer and elaborate new information and ideas
Integrating	Combine, summarize, and restructure information
Evaluating	Establish criteria and assess the quality of ideas

Source: Adapted from Robert J. Marzano, Ronald S. Brandt, Carolyn Sue Hughes, Beau Fly Jones, Barbara Z. Presseisen, Stuart C. Rankin, and Charles Suhor, *Dimensions of Thinking: A Framework for Curriculum and Instruction,* Alexandria, VA: Association for Supervision and Curriculum Development (1988), 66, 70–112. Reprinted by permission. The Association for Supervision and Curriculum Development is a world-wide community of educators advocating sound policies and sharing best practices to achieve the success of each learner. To learn more, visit ASCD at www.ascd.org.

THEORY INTO PRACTICE

TIP   Thinking about Speaking

Effective public speakers care about their topics and their audiences. As they research, construct, and deliver their speeches, they use the critical thinking skills discussed in this chapter. Consider how one student employed each of these skills in developing her speech.

- **Generating** Wanda's first assignment in her public speaking class was to prepare and deliver a speech about someone she admired. She immediately began generating a list of names: her mother, who held down two jobs to help raise five children; a high school teacher who inspired Wanda to go to college; Coretta Scott King, First Lady of the Civil Rights Movement; and Thurgood Marshall, the first African American to serve on the U.S. Supreme Court.

- **Focusing** Wanda recalled how Marshall's commitment to justice for all was one of the reasons she decided to become a prelaw major. So she decided to focus her speech on Marshall.
- **Information gathering and remembering** She devised a research plan and began to gather her supporting materials. Remembering the moving tributes following Marshall's death, Wanda located some of these articles and also found several books about him.
- **Analyzing and focusing** She analyzed her audience, the occasion, and the information she had collected and began to focus her speech further. Wanda decided that a biography of Marshall's life was far too encompassing for a 3- to 5-minute speech. She also chose not to discuss his more controversial decisions on abortion and capital punishment.

(Continued)

- **Organizing, focusing, and integrating** Wanda organized her key ideas and integrated her supporting materials around two central images: closed doors and open doors. First, she would describe some of the doors closed to African Americans during much of Marshall's life: equal education, housing, public transportation, and voting. She would recount that Marshall, the great-grandson of a slave, was denied admission to the University of Maryland Law School. Second, she would tell how Marshall fought to open these doors by expanding access to housing, public transportation, and voting. And she would, of course, note that it was Marshall who successfully argued the case of *Brown v. Board of Education of Topeka* (1954), which declared

racial segregation in public schools unconstitutional. She would conclude her story by observing that it was Marshall who litigated the admission of the first African American to graduate from the University of Maryland Law School.
- **Evaluating** Wanda evaluated each of these examples as she prepared her speech to ensure that her ideas were well supported.
- **Remembering** As she constructed her speaking notes, Wanda used only a brief outline to help her remember her ideas.
- **Evaluating** After delivering her speech, she evaluated her speaking strengths and weaknesses to improve her skills for her next speech.

SUMMARY

Why Study Public Speaking?

- Public speaking teaches skills that can help you succeed academically, learn actively, and develop confidence. These are the personal benefits of public speaking.
- Public speaking helps you get the job you want and advance in it. These are the professional benefits of public speaking.
- Public speaking helps you take an active role in society and get things done. These are the public benefits of public speaking.

Definitions of Communication

- Communication is the process of sharing meaning by sending and receiving symbolic cues.
- Communication involves individuals (interpreters) attaching referents (meanings) to a variety of symbols (words, gestures, and voice qualities).

Levels of Communication

- The five levels of communication are intrapersonal, interpersonal, group, public, and mass communication.

Elements of Communication

- Communication involves seven key elements: speaker, message, listener, feedback, channel, environment, and noise.

The Public Speaker as Critical Thinker

- Developing and delivering a public speech exercises eight critical thinking skills: focusing, information gathering, remembering, organizing, analyzing, generating, integrating, and evaluating.

EXERCISES

1. If your class includes international students, ask them to describe the roles speaking plays in their native cultures. Are students encouraged to speak in class? Or are such behaviors discouraged? Are speaking skills considered more important for one gender than for the other? What general differences do international students notice in the speaking skills of U.S. students compared with those of their own cultures?

2. Jot down a few of your most embarrassing experiences. Review your list, noting incidents that resulted from a breakdown in communication because you and someone else did not share similar referents. Can you think of other examples of miscommunication based on individuals having different referents for the same message?

3. List examples of words that trigger referents that are different because of the users' ages, genders, religious experiences, educational backgrounds, political affiliations, and economic status. Discuss how a speaker could enhance shared meaning in each of these examples.

4. Using the communication elements model (Figure 1.2) as a guide, analyze a lecture given by an instructor in one of your classes. Focus specifically on the listeners and feedback. Was the instructor attentive to the students' verbal and nonverbal behaviors? If not, what could the instructor have done to make the communication event more of a two-way experience? If yes, give examples to illustrate the instructor's attentiveness to student feedback.

5. Find a magazine or journal article, in print or online, that discusses speech communication in business and professional environments. Write a one-page summary and attach it to a copy of the article.

6. Analyze the physical noise in your classroom. As a listener, how does this affect your reception of your instructor's message? As a speaker, how might you minimize the effect of this noise? If you were redesigning the classroom, what changes would you make to minimize this type of noise?

The Ethics of Public Speaking

2

After studying this chapter,
you should be able to

1 Define ethics.

2 Understand how ethical
principles should guide your
actions.

3 Incorporate six ethical
responsibilities into your
speaking.

4 Incorporate four ethical
responsibilities into your
listening.

5 Understand and apply fair use
guidelines.

6 Understand types of
plagiarism.

7 Apply five guidelines to avoid
plagiarism.

8 Appreciate, understand, and
use civility as a speaker and
listener.

Knowledge is not a loose-leaf notebook of facts. Above all, it is a responsibility for the integrity of what we are, primarily of what we are as ethical creatures.

—Jacob Bronowski

Commercial cartographers once produced maps containing small errors, such as nonexistent streets or bodies of water with funny, fictitious names. Known as "copyright traps," these errors were used to establish ownership and to serve as grounds for legal action against anyone copying the maps without permission.[1]

Today, musicians, mapmakers, photographers, artists, and software creators are likely to place electronic watermarks or fingerprints in their original works using the techniques of steganography.[2] The ID tag hidden in an MP3 file and the electronic watermark on a DVD have the same purpose: to protect the value of the original works and the reputations of their creators.

As a classroom public speaker, you may create a product that leaves no permanent record, except possibly in the memories of some of your listeners. Nevertheless, the speeches you deliver will have a unique value, reflecting your originality, exercising your critical thinking, and building your credibility.

In Chapter 1 we observed that ideas cannot be separated from the people who voice them. Everything you do or say affects the credibility your audience assigns you; that credibility in turn affects the believability of your ideas. Your personal credibility is as important as the perceived credibility you have with various audiences. One of your goals as a speaker should be to make choices that develop and maintain that integrity.

Effective, ethical public speakers understand and respect their audiences. They demonstrate this respect by honoring an unwritten contract with their listeners. Terms of this contract require that audience members expect to learn, listen without prejudging you or your ideas, and, ultimately, evaluate your message and give you feedback. As a speaker, you assume responsibility for being well prepared, communicating ideas clearly in order to benefit the audience, and remaining open to feedback that will improve your speaking. In this chapter, we focus on these mutual responsibilities as we examine ethical speaking, ethical listening, and plagiarism.

◖ Definition of Ethics

It is virtually impossible to read a newspaper or listen to a newscast today without encountering the topic of ethics. We hear of politicians selling out to special-interest groups, stockbrokers engaging in insider trading, accountants "cooking the books," and contractors taking shortcuts in construction projects. We read stories of people who agonized over the decision to allow—and in some cases help—a terminally ill loved one to die.

When we talk about **ethics**, we refer to the standards we use to determine right from wrong, or good from bad, in thought and behavior. Our sense of ethics guides the choices we make in all aspects of our professional and private lives. You should not be surprised that your academic studies include a discussion of ethics. You are, after all, educating yourself to function in a world where you will make ethical decisions daily. In Chapter 1 we established the importance of speech communication in our lives. We

ethics
Standards used to discriminate between right and wrong, good and bad, in thought and action.

© 1992 by P. S. Mueller. Reprinted by permission.

will now examine why it is important for you to ensure that you communicate ethically.

Principles of Ethics

In discussing communication ethics, Donald Smith notes that communication is an ethically neutral instrument: "[S]peaking skill per se is neither good nor bad. The skill can be used by good persons or bad persons. It can be put to the service of good purposes [or] bad purposes...."[3] In this course, you will learn fundamental communication skills that will empower you as both a speaker and a listener. How you exercise these skills will involve ethical choices and responsibilities.

Two principles frame our discussion of ethics.

- First, *all parties in the communication process have ethical responsibilities.* Assume, for example, that a classmate lets you know that he plans to argue in a persuasive speech that "hate speech"—such as protests at military funerals—should be constitutionally protected and is good for the country. Another classmate objects to that position and spreads false claims about what the speaker intends to argue. Students who knew the facts of this case might agree that both students acted unethically, or at least intemperately. As this example demonstrates, all parties involved in communication share ethical obligations.
- Second, *ethical speakers and listeners possess attitudes and standards that pervade their character and guide their actions before,*

A speech is a solemn responsibility. The man who makes a bad thirty-minute speech to 200 people wastes only a half hour of his own time. But he wastes 100 hours of the audience's time—more than four days— which should be a hanging offense.

—Jenkin Lloyd Jones

during, and after their speaking and listening. Ethical speakers and listeners do more than just abstain from unethical behaviors. Ethics is as much a frame of mind as it is a pattern of behavior. Ethics is a working philosophy you apply to your daily life and bring to *all* speaking situations.

Consider the actions of the speaker in the following incident:

Lisa presented a persuasive speech on the need for recycling paper, plastic, and aluminum products. To illustrate the many types of recyclables and how overpackaged many grocery products are, she used as an effective visual aid a paper grocery bag filled with empty cans, paper products, and a variety of plastic bottles and containers. After listening to her well-researched, well-delivered speech, with its impassioned final appeal for us to help save the planet by recycling, the class watched in amazement as she put the empty containers back in the bag, walked to the corner of the room, and dropped the bag in the trash can! After a few seconds, someone finally asked, "You mean you're not going to take those home to recycle them?" "Nah," said Lisa. "I'm tired of lugging them around. I've done my job."

You may or may not believe that people have an ethical responsibility to recycle. But regardless of your views on that issue, you likely question the ethics of someone who insists, in effect, "Do as I say, not as I do." Lisa's actions made the entire class question her sincerity. Ethical standards cannot be turned on and off at an individual's convenience.

◑ Ethical Speaking

Maintaining strong ethical attitudes and standards requires sound decision making at every step in the speech-making process. In this section, we present six guidelines to help you with these decisions.

Speak to Benefit Your Listeners

First, *ethical public speakers communicate in order to benefit their listeners as well as themselves.* Speakers and listeners participate in a transactional relationship; both should benefit from their participation. Listeners give speakers their time; in return, speakers should provide information that is interesting or useful.

Informative speakers have an obligation to benefit their audiences. As in the following example, however, students sometimes lose sight of that responsibility.

Assigned to give an informative speech demonstrating a process or procedure, plant lover Evelyn decided to show how to plant a seed in a pot. Her instructor was worried that this subject was something everyone already knew. Evelyn was, after all, speaking to college students who presumably could read the planting instructions on the back of a seed packet. The instructor did not want to discourage Evelyn but wanted the class to benefit from her speech.

Without saying, "You cannot speak on this topic," the instructor shared her concerns with Evelyn. She found out that Evelyn had several other plant-related topics in mind. Evelyn agreed that a more unusual topic would be more interesting to the class and more challenging for her to deliver. On the day she was assigned to speak, Evelyn presented an interesting speech demonstrating how to propagate tropical plants by "air layering" them. Evelyn got a chance to demonstrate her green thumb, and her classmates learned something most had never heard of before.

You may often speak for personal benefit, and this is not necessarily unethical. You may, for instance, urge a group to support your candidacy or to buy your product. It is appropriate to pursue personal goals but not at the expense of your listeners. As one popular book on business ethics states, "There is no right way to do a wrong thing."[4] Speakers whose objective is to persuade should do so openly and with the goal of benefiting both the audience and themselves. A public speaker may try to inform, convince, persuade, direct, or even anger an audience. Ethical speakers, however, do not deceive their listeners. They are up front about their intentions, and those intentions include benefiting the audience.

EXPLORING ONLINE

Ethical Decision Making

www.scu.edu/ethics

Ethical speakers and listeners should consider the values that shape their decision making. The Markkula Center for Applied Ethics at Santa Clara University is devoted to the study of ethics. Access articles, case studies, and other resources relating to business, global, government, media, and technology ethics.

Speak Up about Topics You Consider Important

Second, ethical public speakers make careful decisions about whether or not to speak. If an issue is trivial, silence is sometimes the best option. There are times, though, when people have an ethical obligation to convey information or when they feel strongly about an issue or an injustice. *Ethical communicators speak up about topics they consider important.* Our nation's history has been shaped by the voices of Thomas Jefferson, Frederick Douglass, Susan B. Anthony, Martin Luther King, Jr., Cesar Chavez, and other advocates. You may never have the sweeping historical impact of these famous speakers, but you do have an opportunity to better the communities of which you are a part. You have a chance to share information your classmates can use to help them get more from their college experience or function better in their careers and personal lives. You can educate others about problems you feel need to be confronted. This class provides a training ground to hone your skills as speaker and listener. Use these skills as you move from involvement in class and campus issues to improvement of your community.

Choose Topics That Promote Positive Ethical Values

Third, *ethical speakers choose topics that promote positive ethical values.* Unless you are assigned a topic, selecting a topic is one of the first ethical choices you will make. You give your topic credibility simply by selecting

Wangari Muta Maathai founded the Green Belt Movement to reforest Africa. She was awarded the Nobel Peace Prize for her advocacy of women's rights, democratic reform, and environmental conservation.

it. As an ethical speaker, your choice should reflect what you think is important for your audience.

In the course we teach, many student speeches have expanded our knowledge or moved us to act on significant issues. But consider this list of informative speech topics that students have chosen:

How to get a fake ID

How to "walk" (avoid paying) a restaurant check

How to get a faculty parking permit

How to get out of a speeding ticket

Even though they were informative rather than persuasive speeches, each of these how-to topics implies that its action is acceptable. We suggest that all these speakers disrespected their listeners, failed to consider the values they were promoting, and presented unethical speeches.

<blockquote>
A mind that is stretched to a new idea never returns to its original dimension.

—Oliver Wendell Holmes
</blockquote>

Use Truthful Supporting Material and Valid Reasoning

Fourth, *ethical speakers use truthful supporting materials and valid reasoning*. Listeners have a right to know both speakers' ideas and the material supporting their claims. Ethical speakers are well informed and should test the truthfulness and validity of their ideas. They should not knowingly use false information or faulty reasoning. Yet sometimes students present incomplete or out-of-date material, as in this example:

> Janet presented an informative speech on the detection and treatment of breast cancer. Her discussion of the disease's detection seemed thorough, but when she got to her second point, she said that the only treatments were radical mastectomy, partial mastectomy, radiation therapy, and chemotherapy. She failed to mention lumpectomy, a popular surgical measure often combined with radiation or chemotherapy. Her bibliography revealed that her research stopped with sources published in the early 1980s, explaining the gap in her speech content.

Janet was uninformed and ended up being embarrassed. But what if Janet had known of the lumpectomy procedure and had simply not wanted to do further research to find out about it? Then we would question her ethics.

In this case, some listeners did not notice the factual errors and the lapses in content while others did. Not getting caught in a factual or logical error does not free the speaker of the ethical responsibility to present complete, factual information. If you speak on a current topic, use the most recent information you can find and try to be as well informed as possible.

EXPLORING ONLINE

Checking Fairness in News Reporting

www.uiowa.edu/~commstud/resources/media/mediawatch.html

Sponsored by the University of Iowa's Department of Communication Studies, this website posts links to dozens of media watch organizations representing diverse political and journalistic perspectives.

Consider the Consequences of Your Words and Actions

Fifth, *ethical speakers concern themselves with the consequences of their speaking*. Mary Cunningham observed, "Words are sacred things. They are also like hand grenades: Handled casually, they tend to go off."[5] Ethical speakers respect the power of language and the process of communication.

It is difficult to track, let alone to predict, the impact of any one message. Your audience interprets your statements and may communicate them to others. Individuals may form opinions and behave differently because of what you say or fail to say. Incorrect information and misinterpretations may have unintended and potentially harmful consequences. If you provide an audience with inaccurate information, you may contaminate the quality of their subsequent decisions. If you persuade someone to act in a particular way, you are partly responsible for the impact of the person's new action.

Strive to Improve Your Public Speaking

Finally, *ethical speakers strive to improve their public speaking.* Speakers who use the guidelines we have presented accept their obligation to communicate responsibly. Their ideas have value, are logically supported, and do not deceive their listeners. We would argue, however, that this is not enough.

Ethical speakers are concerned not only with *what* they say but also with *how* they say it. As a result, they work actively to become more effective communicators. This course provides you with an opportunity to begin mastering public speaking. You will learn how to select, support, evaluate, organize, and deliver your ideas. Your professional and public life beyond the classroom will extend your opportunities to speak publicly. Speakers have "the opportunity to learn to speak well, and to be eloquent [advocates of] truth and justice." If they fail to develop these abilities, they have not fulfilled their "ethical obligation in a free society."[6]

> **KEY POINTS**
>
> **Responsibilities of an Ethical Speaker**
>
> 1. Speak to benefit your listeners.
> 2. Speak up about topics you consider important.
> 3. Choose topics that promote positive ethical values.
> 4. Use truthful supporting material and valid reasoning.
> 5. Consider the consequences of your words and actions.
> 6. Strive to improve your public speaking.

Ethical Listening

The guidelines for ethical speaking we've just discussed probably make perfect sense to you. If some seem intimidating, if you feel that the future of free expression in a democratic society rests squarely on your shoulders, remember that no individual bears such a responsibility alone. Members of your audience are obligated to adhere to four basic principles, and you share these ethical responsibilities as you listen to others' speeches.

Seek Exposure to Well-Informed Speakers

First, *ethical listeners seek out speakers who expand their knowledge and understanding, introduce them to new ideas, and challenge their beliefs.* These listeners reject the philosophy, "My mind's made up, so don't confuse me with the facts." A controversial speaker visiting your campus can expand your knowledge or intensify your feelings about a subject, whether you agree or disagree with the speaker's viewpoint. Even in situations in which you are a captive audience, such as this class, ethical listening should be the standard.

Avoid Prejudging Speakers or Their Ideas

Second, *ethical listeners listen openly without prejudging speakers or their ideas*. This may be difficult. Listening without bias may require that we temporarily suspend impressions we have formed based on the speaker's past actions. But the rewards of doing so can be great, as in this example:

> Linda's first speech in class completely confused her classmates. She seemed nervous and unsure of herself and what she was going to say. The point of her speech eluded everyone. Class discussion after the speech focused primarily on Linda's delivery and some of the distracting mannerisms she exhibited and needed to control. When she went to the front of the room to begin her next speech weeks later, no one was really expecting to be impressed. But they were.
>
> Linda's second speech dealt with the problem of homelessness. Her opening sentence told the class that three years before, she had been living on the street. She had their attention from that point on. In addition to citing recent newspaper and magazine articles, Linda had conducted a great deal of original research. She had interviewed the directors of local shelters and a number of the homeless people who took refuge there, and she quoted these individuals. Her speech was well organized and well delivered. It was both educational and inspiring.
>
> When discussing the speech later, classmates kept referring to her first speech and noting the remarkable improvements Linda had made. One person was blunt, but apparently summed up the feelings of a number of listeners that day: "Linda, I wasn't expecting much from you because your first speech was so unclear to me, but today you had a topic that you obviously care about, and you made us understand and care about it, too. I can't get over the difference between those two speeches!"

When listening to your classmates, assume that you may learn something important from each speaker and therefore listen intently. Information and ideas are best shared in an atmosphere of civility and mutual respect.

Evaluate the Speaker's Logic and Credibility

Listening eagerly and openly does not imply a permanent suspension of judgment, however. The third standard is that *ethical listeners evaluate the messages presented to them*. A listener who accepts a premise without evaluating its foundation is like someone who buys a used car without looking under the hood. The warning "let the buyer beware" is good advice not only for consumers of products but also for consumers of messages.

As a listener, you should critically evaluate a speaker's ideas. Is each idea logically constructed? Is each supported with evidence that is relevant, sufficient, and authoritative? In Chapters 8 and 17, you will learn specific strategies to help you answer these questions as you evaluate a speaker's evidence and logic.

Ethical listening involves thinking critically about a speaker's message. How often do you make a conscious effort to evaluate the meaning and logic behind the messages you hear and read each day?

Beware of the Consequences of Not Listening Carefully

Fourth, *ethical listeners concern themselves with the consequences of their listening.* As the following example illustrates, listeners who assimilate only part of a speaker's message because they fail to listen actively are responsible for the distorted message that results.

> Eduardo, a staff writer for the campus newspaper, mentioned in a speech that the online version of the paper was sponsoring a contest for best research suggestions. The student emailing the HTML page with the most useful research links, as judged by the publication staff, would win first prize: a new BlackBerry. Ted listened to his classmate Eduardo, but the only words that stood out were the name of the paper and the prize. At the next class meeting, Ted told Eduardo, "I called the paper yesterday asking how to get my free BlackBerry and they told me I had to develop a web page and enter some kind of contest." Eduardo replied, "I told you about that contest in my speech. Weren't you listening?"

Ted may have been embarrassed, but he didn't suffer greatly as a result of not listening to Eduardo. In other cases, however, the consequences of not listening are more serious. When you fail to listen to someone's directions and are late for an interview, you miss an employment opportunity. In both of these examples, the listener, not the speaker, bears responsibility for the breakdown in communication.

At other times, listener and speaker may share responsibility for unethical behavior. For example, audience members who become victims of scams because they did not listen critically share responsibility for their victimization with the speaker. Voters who tolerate exaggerated, vague, and inconsistent campaign statements from those who ask to represent them are similarly complicit in ethically lax political campaigns and partially responsible for the results of those campaigns.

KEY POINTS

Responsibilities of an Ethical Listener

1. Seek exposure to well-informed speakers.
2. Avoid prejudging speakers or their ideas.
3. Evaluate the logic and credibility of the speaker's ideas.
4. Beware of the consequences of not listening carefully.

In the past, views of communication ethics implied a dotted line across the front of a classroom, with ethics being solely the speaker's responsibility. In contrast, we view ethics as a shared responsibility of the speaker and each listener. An absence of ethical motives among speakers and listeners devalues the currency of communication. Two aspects of ethics, however, do begin as the speaker's responsibility: understanding fair use guidelines and avoiding plagiarism. These two topics deserve special attention.

◖ Fair Use Guidelines

If the person behind the counter in a copy shop has ever made you feel like a criminal for asking to copy a magazine or journal article—never mind a few pages or photographs from a book—you have experienced one of the quirks of copyright law. The copy shop operates to make a profit; you probably don't have any commercial use of the material in mind. As a result, the copy shop employee may direct you to a self-service copy machine, where you assume full responsibility for respecting copyright law.

fair use provision
Section of U.S. copyright law allowing limited noncommercial use of copyrighted materials for teaching, criticism, scholarship, research, or commentary.

Copyright law applies to both print and electronic sources, including audio and video works. The "same copyright protections exist . . . regardless of whether the work is in a database, CD-ROM, bulletin board, or on the Internet."[7] Section 107 of the Copyright Law of the United States, commonly called the **fair use provision**, says that "the fair use of a copyrighted work . . . is not an infringement of copyright."[8]

The law also specifies four factors to consider in determining whether your specific use of copyrighted material is fair. The law is ambiguous and can vary depending on the specific nature of the work you wish to use. We are not lawyers and cannot offer assurances that will apply to every case. However, Georgia Harper, copyright expert and Scholarly Communications Advisor for the University of Texas at Austin Libraries, has translated these four factors into rules of thumb that "describe a 'safe harbor' within the bounds of fair use."[9] If you plan to use any copyrighted material in a speech, ask the following four questions:

- *What is the purpose and character of the use?* If your intended use is personal, educational, or nonprofit, chances are it is fair use. Use of copyrighted material for purposes of research, scholarship, teaching, commentary, and news reporting usually falls under fair use.
- *What is the nature of the work to be used?* Use of published sources that report news and factual information weighs in favor of fair use. Fair use favors published works more than unpublished works, reinforcing the rationale "that authors should be able to decide when to publish their work."[10]
- *How much of the work will you use?* Noncommercial use of a small portion, excerpt, or clip of a copyrighted work likely qualifies as fair use. Commercial uses that exceed strict length limits, however, require permission.

• *What effect would your use have on the market value of the work?* Information from published sources for class speeches and papers are usually considered fair use. Class assignments fall into the category of "one-time use"; speeches are seldom recorded and distributed.[11]

These guidelines seem to suggest that most copyrighted sources for classroom speeches and papers are covered by fair use. However, what if you publish your work beyond the classroom? What if you post your speech on the Internet, and it includes a clip from a popular movie? What if you include images from copyrighted sources on a blog or in an article you submit to a newspaper? What if you conduct a problem-solving workshop for an on-campus or off-campus organization and you draw heavily from suggestions in a copyrighted source? What if you get paid for the workshop? Be careful. You may be leaving that "safe harbor" of fair use.

Answering these questions requires an understanding of copyright law that is beyond the scope of this textbook. Fortunately, there are some excellent websites that offer more information, analysis, and guidelines. We introduce you to four of these sites in the "Exploring Online" feature "Fair Use and Copyright."

We reiterate one final point. The fair use provision does *not* give you the right to use another's work without crediting that person, agency, or organization. Unattributed use—even fair use—of someone else's work leaves you open to charges of plagiarism, an issue that seems to grow more important in these days of cut-and-paste Internet research.

◐ Plagiarism

The word *plagiarize* comes from a Latin word meaning "to kidnap," so in a sense a plagiarist is a kidnapper of ideas and words. A modern definition of **plagiarism** is "literary—or artistic or musical—theft. It is the false assumption of authorship: the wrongful act of taking the product of another person's mind, and presenting it as one's own."[12]

When you write a paper and submit it to a teacher, you are in effect publishing that work. If, in that paper, you copy something from another source and pass it off as your own work, you are plagiarizing. This act is such a serious offense that in most colleges and universities it is grounds for failing the course or dismissal from the school. Yet recent history has shown us numerous examples of politicians, educators, historians, and other public figures caught plagiarizing materials, either consciously or unconsciously. Plagiarism is an offense serious enough to derail a candidate's campaign for office, to force the resignation of a corporate officer, or to end a student's academic career. Students in a public speaking class should certainly understand what is and what is not plagiarism.

Plagiarism applies to more than simply the copying of another's words. You may also plagiarize another's ideas and organization of material. For example, if you presented a speech organized around the five stages of

EXPLORING ONLINE

Fair Use and Copyright
These four websites provide a wealth of information related to copyright, fair use, and public domain.

www.copyright.gov/laws/

http://copyright.lib.utexas.edu/copypol2.html

www.lib.purdue.edu/uco/CopyrightBasics/fair_use.html

http://fairuse.stanford.edu/

• The U.S. Copyright Office website describes current copyright law and the fair use provision.
• Georgia Harper's "Copyright Crash Course" discusses clearly and in detail issues for instructors and students to consider, including liability for copyright infringement and applying the "four-factor use test."
• The Purdue University Copyright Office presents a series of charts and checklists to help you "make a good faith determination" that your use of copyrighted material is fair.
• The Stanford Copyright & Fair Use website links you to an entire chapter, with links, on fair use that includes summaries of fair use court cases.

plagiarism
The unattributed use of another's ideas, words, or pattern of organization.

You must renounce imagination forever if you hope to succeed in plagiarism. Forgery is intention, not invention.

—Horace Walpole

EXPLORING ONLINE

Copyright Violations

www.benedict.com

The Copyright Website contains some interesting recent examples of alleged copyright violations in the visual, audio, and digital arts. Enter the site at this address, and then click on the tabs to see and hear these examples, read about the allegations, and discover how they were resolved.

> Your manuscript is both good and original; but the part that is good is not original, and the part that is original is not good.
>
> —Samuel Johnson

intentional plagiarism
The deliberate, unattributed use of another's ideas, words, or pattern of organization.

unintentional plagiarism
The careless or unconscious unattributed use of another's ideas, words, or pattern of organization.

paraplage
Plagiarism consisting of half original writing and half quotation from an unattributed source.

dying (denial, anger, bargaining, depression, and acceptance) and did not give credit to Elisabeth Kübler-Ross, you would be guilty of plagiarism. On the other hand, if your speech analyzed the political, economic, and social implications of a pending piece of legislation, you would probably not be guilty of plagiarism. Kübler-Ross developed, explained, and published her framework, or model, in her book *On Death and Dying*, whereas the second example relies on a commonly accepted pattern of analyzing public policy initiatives. The line between legitimate appropriation of material and plagiarism is sometimes unclear. As a speaker, you must always be on guard to credit the source of your ideas and their structure.

Plagiarism can be intentional or unintentional. **Intentional plagiarism** occurs when speakers or writers knowingly present another person's words, ideas, or organization as their own. One category of intentional plagiarism, "self-plagiarism," involves recycling your own work. Revisiting earlier research and extending, elaborating, rethinking, or updating it can be very beneficial. But no one hearing you deliver a speech on "major themes in Thomas Pynchon's novel *Gravity's Rainbow*" is going to be tricked. You're recycling work you did for another class, and many schools now have written policies prohibiting self-plagiarism.

Unintentional plagiarism is "the careless paraphrasing and citing of source material such that improper or misleading credit is given."[13] Intentional plagiarism is considered the more serious offense. Widespread use of the Internet for research may be blurring the distinction between deliberate and accidental plagiarism, however. Web pages are ephemeral; page content and design can change from one day to the next. That quality, together with the ease of browsing numerous sites in a short time, lets readers pick up phrases, ideas, or even organizational patterns almost unconsciously. If a researcher has not printed, bookmarked, or jotted down the URLs for key sites, retracing steps and finding those sites again may be difficult. Unintentional plagiarism may be committed due to ignorance or sloppy research methods, but the effect is still the same: one person is taking credit for the work of another.

To avoid plagiarism, always cite your sources. If you show even a portion of a YouTube video, tell your listeners that you found it on YouTube, the date you first accessed it, and mention the search terms you used to find it. If you want to use video or original writing available on a Facebook page, get permission by emailing the page owner and then cite the source. For information from an online reference work, newspaper, journal, magazine, or blog, simply cite the source and report when the information was posted or when you accessed it. Carefully citing your sources will help you avoid plagiarizing.

Unintentional plagiarism sometimes occurs because of a common misconception that by simply changing a few words of another's writing, you have paraphrased the statement and need not cite it. Michael O'Neill refers to this "hybrid of half textual source, half original writing" as a **paraplage**.[14] Note the differences and similarities in the original and adapted passages of the following statement.

Statement by Erik Vance

In the mid-1940s, Norman Borlaug started the Green Revolution on a small farm in southern Mexico. His idea was simple. As the human population skyrocketed, he would grow a new kind of wheat with a thicker stem and bigger seed heads, thus increasing its yield and allowing farmers to grow more wheat—and feed more people—per acre.

The results were staggering. Within two decades, Mexico's wheat harvest had swollen six-fold, thanks to crops descended from Borlaug's original modified wheat. Borlaug then turned his talents toward rice in the Philippines, and high-yield crops spread into almost every major food staple. In all, Borlaug's revolution helped feed millions of people in poor and developing countries who would otherwise have starved—an achievement that earned him the 1970 Nobel Peace Prize.[15]

Speaker's Paraplage of Erik Vance

The Green Revolution started back in the 1940s as the human population skyrocketed. Working on a small farm in Mexico, Norman Borlaug developed a strain of wheat with thick stems and bigger seeds. As a result, farmers could increase their yields and feed more people.

Just two decades later, the Mexican wheat harvest had increased to six times what it was previously. Borlaug turned to genetically modifying rice, helping to feed millions of people. For his efforts, Borlaug earned the Nobel Peace Prize in 1970.

Speaker's Appropriate Citation of Erik Vance

As suspicious as some people are of "genetically modified" foods, the first such foods saved millions of lives. Freelance science writer Erik Vance tells the story of Norman Borlaug's experiments in the July/September 2010 issue of *Conservation Magazine*. Borlaug grew a new kind of wheat with thicker stems and bigger seed heads, and therefore resistant to the effects of wind and water.

Vance calls the results "staggering" and says that "Within two decades, Mexico's wheat harvest had swollen six-fold." After Borlaug turned his attention to rice, he saved millions of people.

Notice that the appropriate citation above tells the listener something about Vance's credentials and explains exactly where his words appeared. With that information, any listener wanting to read the entire article could find it quickly.

The ability to paraphrase effectively tests your critical thinking skills of analyzing, integrating, and generating. To improve your paraphrasing, consider the following guidelines from the Purdue University Online Writing Lab:

1. Reread the original passage until you understand it fully.
2. Set the original aside; write your paraphrase on a notecard or on paper or type it into a computer file.
3. Below your paraphrase, write a few words to remind you later how you might use this material in your speech. Near your paraphrase, write a key word or phrase in all capital letters to indicate its subject.

EXPLORING ONLINE

The Purdue Online Writing Lab

http://owl.english.purdue.edu/

The Purdue Online Writing Lab offers a wealth of information for writers including information on how to reference materials correctly.

THEORY INTO PRACTICE

TIP   How to Avoid Plagiarism

To avoid plagiarizing, let the following five simple rules guide you:

1. *Take clear and consistent notes while researching.* As you review your notes, you should be able to discern which words, ideas, examples, and organizational structures belong to which authors.
2. *Record complete source citations.* Each sheet of notes, each photocopied article, and each printed page of a document you have accessed should indicate its source(s).
3. *Clearly indicate in your speech any words, ideas, examples, or organizational structures that are not your own.* If you cite a source early in your speech and then use another idea from that author later, you must again give that author credit. You do not need to repeat the complete citation, however. Use an abbreviated citation, such as "Vance says that" in our earlier example, if you have provided the full citation earlier in your speech.
4. *Use your own words, language style, and thought structure when paraphrasing.* Remember that both content and structure distinguish another person's statements. When paraphrasing what another person has written or said, you should use not just your own words but also your own language style and thought structure. Otherwise, you are "para-plaging."
5. *When in doubt, cite the source.* If you are unsure whether you really need to acknowledge a source, it's always wise to err on the side of caution.

4. Check your version against the original to make sure that your paraphrase accurately expresses all the essential information in a new form.
5. Use quotation marks to identify any unique terms or phrases you have borrowed exactly from the source.
6. Record the source on your notecard so that you can credit it easily if you incorporate the material in your speech.[16]

We have discussed some of the dangers of hiding the true authorship of words and ideas. There are also at least two benefits of crediting sources. First, speakers who cite their sources increase their credibility, or believability, with the audience. When you quote from a book, an article, or an interview and name the author or speaker of those words, you show the audience that you have researched the topic and that you know what you are talking about. Second, and far more important, acknowledging your sources is the right thing to do. It is honest. Good ideas and memorably worded thoughts are rare enough that the original writer or speaker deserves credit.

◖ Civility in the Classroom

As Keith gave his first graded speech in his public speaking class, he thought, "This is going well." Then from the audience came a ringing sound. He stumbled over a few words as he noticed his classmate Eden reaching into her book bag to retrieve her cell phone. When the entire class heard Eden whisper, "I can't talk now. I'm in my speech class. I'll call you when it's over," the instructor asked Keith to stop until he regained the attention of all his listeners.

Sound familiar? We hope not, but we suspect that you and some of your instructors have had similar experiences. Unfortunately, examples of disrespectful and discourteous communication occur not only in classrooms but also in politics, in workplaces, in meetings, on blogs, and on Internet message boards. The Institute for Civility in Government laments "the lack of civility in our society in general and our public discourse in particular."[17] Communication professors Rod Troester and Cathy Sargent Mester define **civility** as a "set of verbal and nonverbal behaviors reflecting fundamental respect for others and generating harmonious and productive relationships."[18] Sometimes equated with courtesy and etiquette, civility is a more complex pattern of behavior that involves attitudes, such as respect, and behaviors, such as providing classmates feedback on their speeches.

We have argued that your public speaking class is a community of learners. You will be a part of that community for the rest of the semester or quarter, and the population will function best if all members exhibit respect and mutual support. The following guidelines, discussed more fully in subsequent chapters, will contribute to your enjoyment and success in this class as both a speaker and a listener.

civility
Communication behaviors that reflect respect for others and foster harmonious and productive relationships.

Speaking with Civility

- *Have good motives.* Select topics that benefit your listeners and the communities to which they belong.
- *Prepare and assess what you will say.* Support your ideas with quality evidence and examples.
- *Respect your listeners.* Appreciate the diversity of your audience and adapt your messages to all your listeners.
- *Speak with conviction.* Believe in your topic and convey that commitment as you speak.
- *Encourage the other side to be heard.* Value public discussion and debate, and answer questions others may have about your topic.
- *Welcome feedback.* Appreciate and act on suggestions and criticisms to improve your speaking competence.

The hallmark of civil debate is when you can acknowledge that which is good in the position of the person with whom you disagree.

—Sidney Callahan[19]

Listening with Civility

- *Give speakers your full attention.* Observe classroom courtesy. Don't text message, check your email, or walk into class when another student is speaking. And, of course, don't sleep or study for another class when your instructor or classmates are speaking.
- *Expect to learn something.* Don't prejudge speakers or their ideas. Value and learn from people's differences, believing with Malcolm Forbes that "education's purpose is to replace an empty mind with an open one."

- *Evaluate the merits of the speaker's ideas and supporting material.* Take responsibility for how you act on the information a speaker has presented.
- *Provide the speaker constructive feedback.* Contribute to the learning of others.

The civil classroom doesn't just happen; civility is a choice. It requires work on the part of the instructor and each student, but the results surely include more effective and enjoyable learning. Some advocates even assert that civility "reduces the literal and figurative costs of stress and leads to greater productivity, better health, and more happiness."[20]

Civility grows from mutual respect; it connects us with others. The attitudes and behaviors you develop and practice in this class can serve you well into the future. Civility is "the glue that holds us together and allows us as citizens of a representative democracy to dialogue with each other."[21]

SUMMARY

Definition of Ethics

- *Ethics* refers to fundamental questions of right and wrong in thought and behavior.

Principles of Ethics

- All parties in communication—speakers and listeners—have ethical responsibilities.
- Ethical speakers and listeners possess attitudes and standards that pervade their character and guide their actions before, during, and after their speaking and listening.

Ethical Speaking

- Ethical speakers speak to benefit their listeners, not merely to fulfill their own needs; they choose topics and issues they consider important; they choose topics that promote positive ethical values; and they present audiences with ideas backed by logical reasoning and authentic, up-to-date supporting materials. Ethical speakers care about the consequences their words and actions may have for their listeners, and they seek to improve their public speaking.

Ethical Listening

- Ethical listeners welcome challenges to their beliefs, just as they embrace learning; they listen openly, without prejudging the speaker or the speaker's ideas; they evaluate the speaker's ideas before acting on them; and they care about and accept responsibility for the consequences of their listening.

Fair Use Guidelines

- Speakers planning to use copyrighted materials in their speeches need to be aware of the *fair use provision* of copyright law. Factors that determine whether a particular use is fair are the speaker's purpose, the nature of the work used, the proportion of the entire work that a speaker wants to use, and the effect that widespread use such as the speaker intends would have on the market value of the original work.

Plagiarism

- Both speakers and listeners need to be aware of *plagiarism*, the unattributed use of another's ideas, words, or organization. Plagiarism may be either *intentional* or *unintentional*.

- To avoid plagiarizing, speakers should establish a clear and consistent method of note taking; record a complete source citation on each page of notes or each photocopied article; clearly indicate in the speech any words, ideas, or organizational techniques not their own; use their own words, language style, and thought structures when paraphrasing; and, when in doubt, acknowledge the source. Careful source citation increases a speaker's credibility with the audience and is ethically right.

Civility in the Classroom

- Civility in the classroom is a two-way street. Speakers should have good motives, prepare and assess what they will say, respect their listeners, speak with conviction, encourage the other side to be heard, and finally, welcome feedback.
- Listeners, on the other hand, should give speakers their full attention, expect to learn something, evaluate the merits of the speaker's ideas and supporting material, and finally, provide the speaker constructive feedback.

EXERCISES

1. Select two individuals prominent on the international, national, state, or local scene whom you consider ethical speakers. What characteristics do they possess that make them ethical? Select two people you consider unethical. What ethical standards do you think they disregard or abuse?

2. Consider the following scenario. State representative Joan Richards is running for a seat in the state senate. She worked hard as a legislator and was voted the best representative by the Better Government League (BGL). The BGL voted her opponent, incumbent Mike Letner, one of the ten worst senators in the state. Many political analysts think Richards would be the superior senator. Letner has taken a "no new taxes" pledge and has challenged Richards to do the same. Richards personally thinks taxes may have to be raised in order to keep the state solvent. Nevertheless, she knows that unless she promises to oppose any new taxes, she will lose the election. What should Richards do?

3. Answer each of the following questions and be prepared to defend your position.

   a. Should a speech instructor have the right to censor topics students select for their speeches?

   b. Should students have the right to use profanity and obscenity in their speeches in this class?

   c. Should the Ku Klux Klan be allowed to hold a rally on your campus?

   d. Should lawyers defend clients they know are guilty?

4. Find an article on any subject written by an expert. Summarize the article in one or two paragraphs. Use appropriate source citations, paraphrasing, and quotations to avoid plagiarism.

5. In researching your speech on discrimination against women in the workplace, you discover two polls reaching conflicting conclusions. One shows that experts generally agree with your position; the other shows that they disagree. Is it ethical to present your listeners only the poll that supports your position, or should you acknowledge the other? On what basis should you make this decision?

6. Ethical behavior is something we should demand in national, state, and local political campaigns. We should also expect it of candidates and the electorate in campus politics. Using the ethical guidelines discussed in this chapter, develop a code of ethics that you think should govern speech in student government campaigns on your campus. Also, suggest specific guidelines for the voter, the receiver of these messages.

Speaking Confidently

3

- **Recognize That Speaker Nervousness Is Normal**

- **Control Speaker Nervousness**

- **Learn How to Build Speaker Confidence**
  Know How You React to Stress
  Know Your Strengths and
    Weaknesses
  Know Speech Principles
  Know That It Always Looks Worse
    from the Inside
  Know Your Speech
  Believe in Your Topic
  View Speech Making Positively
  Visualize Success
  Project Confidence
  Test Your Message
  Practice Your Delivery
  Theory Into Practice: Gaining
    Perspective

- **Prepare Your First Speech**
  Understand the Assignment
  Develop Your Speech Content
  Organize Your Speech
  Word Your Speech
  Practice Your Speech
  Deliver Your Speech
  Evaluate Your Speech

After studying this chapter, you should be able to

1. Recognize that public speaking nervousness is normal.

2. Understand that a speaker's goal is not to eliminate nervousness but to control and channel it.

3. Apply eleven guidelines for building speaker confidence.

4. Understand that a public speech is a blend of content, organization, and delivery.

5. Use the seven guidelines of the speech-making process to develop your speeches.

6. Evaluate and learn from your speech after delivering it.

> The best speakers know enough to be scared. Stage fright is the sweat of perfection. The only difference between the pros and the novices is that the pros have trained the butterflies to fly in formation.
>
> —Edward R. Murrow

communication apprehension
The fear or anxiety associated with real or anticipated communication with another person or persons.

◼◗ Recognize That Speaker Nervousness Is Normal

Communication apprehension is the "fear or anxiety associated with either real or anticipated communication with another person or persons," and one form, public speaking anxiety, is especially widespread.[1] In fact, the first edition of *The Book of Lists* reported a survey that asked 3,000 Americans, "What are you the most afraid of?" "Speaking before a group" came in first, ahead of heights, insects, financial problems, deep water, sickness, and even death.[2] Psychiatrists John Greist, James Jefferson, and Isaac Marks contend that public speaking anxiety is "probably the most common social phobia."[3] So, if you are nervous about public speaking and experience what we sometimes call "platform panic," you are in good company.

Our experience and research confirm the prevalence of this common fear among college students. When asked to list their communication weaknesses, a clear majority of students rank speaking before a group as their primary fear. James McCroskey has studied the anxieties of public speaking extensively. His Personal Report of Public Speaking Anxiety (available on MySpeechLab.com) assesses the fear college students have about giving public speeches. His data, collected from several thousand students, confirm that public speaking generates greater apprehension than other forms of communication and that this fear spans several levels:

High anxiety 40%

Moderately high anxiety 30%

Moderate anxiety 20%

Moderately low anxiety 5%

Low anxiety 5%

Note that nearly three-fourths of college students fall into the moderately high to high anxiety range! This means that the person who always has the quick response, who can make others laugh, and who always looks "together" may be just as worried as you are about giving a speech. McCroskey and coauthor Virginia Richmond conclude, "What this suggests, then, is that it is 'normal' to experience a fairly high degree of anxiety about public speaking. Most people do. If you are highly anxious about public speaking, then you are 'normal.'"[4]

What is this platform panic and how does it affect us? Chemically and physiologically, we all experience stage fright in the same way. Adrenaline is suddenly pumped into the bloodstream. Respiration increases dramatically, and so do heart rate and perspiration. You may have heard stories of a 135-pound person lifting the front of a car to help rescue someone pinned under it. Such incidents happen because the body is suddenly mobilized to do what must be done.

Yet the body can be similarly mobilized in stressful situations that are not life-threatening. Athletes waiting for the game to begin, actors for the curtain to go up, and speakers for their call to the lectern often feel their bodies marshaling all their resources either to perform to capacity or to get away from the threatening situation. This phenomenon is called, appropriately, the *fight-or-flight syndrome*.

As the time approaches for your first speech, you may experience any of several symptoms to varying degrees. Students tell us that their symptoms include blushing or redness, accelerated heart rate, perspiring, dry mouth, shaking, churning stomach, increased rate of speech, forgetfulness and broken speech, and nervous mannerisms such as playing with jewelry, tapping fingers, and clutching the lectern. Realize that these symptoms are typical of a public speaker. If you experience any of them, you have plenty of company.

◗ Control Speaker Nervousness

Before discussing what your goal should be regarding speaker nervousness, it is important to note what it should not be. Do *not* make it your goal to eliminate nervousness. Such a goal is counterproductive for at least two reasons. First, nervousness is natural; attempting to eliminate it is unrealistic. Most experienced, successful public speakers still get nervous before they speak. In addition, focusing on eliminating your nervousness may make you more nervous.

A second reason why you should not try to eliminate nervousness is that some anxiety can actually benefit a speaker. Nervousness is energy, and it shows that you care about performing well. Use that nervous energy to enliven your delivery and to give your ideas impact. Instead of nervously tapping your fingers on the lectern, for example, you can gesture. Rather than shifting your body weight from foot to foot, incorporate motivated movement into your speech.

Your goal, then, is to control and channel your nervousness. The coping strategies we suggest in the next section and in Chapter 13 will enable you to control the symptoms of nervousness and to channel that energy into dynamic, effective vocal and physical delivery.

Nervous energy is a sign that you care about your speech performance. Try to channel that energy into gestures and body movement that will enhance your message.

◗ Learn How to Build Speaker Confidence

James Belasco, professor and consultant to major corporations, describes how he uses nervousness as a transforming agent:

> Fear is a wonderful stimulant. It quickens the mind, sharpens the senses, heightens performance. I've learned to focus the stimulant on doing better, rather than worrying about doing worse. When fear runs through my system, I ask myself, "What can I do to remove the potential cause of failure?" "What can I do to ensure success?" I've evolved rituals to answer these questions constructively.[5]

The rituals Belasco then describes are quite practical and make a lot of sense. Get up early, practice saying the first part of each main point in the speech while in the shower, and get to the speech setting early to get the feel of the place.[6] Whether or not you develop your own "readiness rituals," the following eleven suggestions offer a systematic way to become a more confident communicator. If you consider and use these suggestions, you will control your nervousness and channel it into a dynamic and effective speaking style.

Know How You React to Stress

EXPLORING ONLINE

Relaxation Techniques
www.webmd.com/balance/
stress-management/features/
blissing-out-10-relaxation-tech-
niques-reduce-stress-spot

WebMD's Stress Manage-
ment Center offers ten relaxation techniques to help you
"bliss out" and reduce stress.

Nervousness affects different people in different ways. Perhaps you feel that your hands or knees shake uncontrollably as you speak in public. The people sitting next to you may not experience those symptoms of nervousness but may have difficulty breathing comfortably and feel that their voices are shaky. Whatever your individual responses to stress, don't wait until you are delivering a public speech to discover them.

Knowing your reactions to stressful situations helps you in two ways. First, it lets you predict and cope with these physical conditions. Your dry mouth or sweaty palms will not surprise you. Second, because you are anticipating these physical conditions, you will be better able to mask them from the audience. How do you do this? Try these techniques.

If you know that your hands shake when you are nervous, don't hold a sheet of paper during the speech; the shaking paper will only amplify the movement of your hands and will telegraph your anxiety to your audience. If your voice is likely to be thin and quivery as you begin speaking, take several deep, slow breaths before you begin talking. If you get tense before speaking, try some muscle relaxation techniques: tense your hands, arms, and shoulders, and then slowly relax them. If you get flustered before speaking, make sure you arrive on time or even a little early—never late. If looking at an audience intimidates you, talk to audience members beforehand, and when you speak, look for friendly faces in the audience.

Know Your Strengths and Weaknesses

Surgeons spend many hours learning to use the equipment they need to perform operations. Each surgeon knows just what each instrument is capable of doing and strives to use it effectively. As a public speaker, your instruments are your voice, body, mind, and personality. Get to know these instruments, and you can use them effectively to create and communicate messages.

To know yourself, you must honestly assess both your strengths and your weaknesses. Use your strengths to communicate your message with force and impact. If you are a lively and enthusiastic person, channel that energy to reinforce your speech physically and enliven your listeners. If you have a talent for creating memorable phrases, use that creativity to help your listeners attend to and remember your ideas. Just as you can tap your strengths in these ways, you can minimize or avoid your weaknesses if you know them. If you are not effective in delivering humor, don't begin your speech with a joke. To do so would risk failure at this critical point in the speech, and that would make you even more nervous.

The more you understand your strengths and weaknesses, the better you will be able to craft your speech to your abilities. The more confident you are that you can accomplish what you set out to do, the less nervous you will be. One note of caution, however: Don't be too critical of yourself and construct a "safe" speech because you have exaggerated your weaknesses. Instead, expand your abilities by incorporating new strategies into your speech making. Only through thoughtful, measured risk taking will you develop as a public speaker.

Know Speech Principles

If you are confident that you have constructed an effective speech, you will be more confident as you step to the lectern. This textbook and your instructor will assist you in learning speech principles. What are the five functions of an effective speech introduction? How should you construct the body of your speech, and how should you develop each key idea? What strategies help you conclude your speech? How can you use your voice and body to communicate your ideas dynamically? What strategies help you word ideas correctly, clearly, and vividly? We address all these questions, and many others, in this book. As you begin to apply what you learn, you will feel more confident about the content, organization, and delivery of your ideas.

Know That It Always Looks Worse from the Inside

Remember that your audience cannot see your internal state. Because you feel nervous, you focus on your anxiety, exaggerate it, and become more nervous. Many times students have lamented their nervousness after concluding

---

ETHICAL DECISIONS

Being Yourself

Sondra is preparing a speech on defensive driving. A drama major, she is comfortable playing all sorts of characters on stage, but the thought of standing in front of an audience and delivering a speech terrifies her. She has visions of herself clutching the lectern, staring blankly at her notes, and mumbling inaudibly. "I'll feel so exposed—I don't think I can get through it just being my ordinary self," Sondra confides to her friends. She asks their help in brainstorming ways to prepare herself before she comes to class on speech day.

One friend reminds Sondra of their beginning yoga class and recommends yoga and meditation to help her relax.

"Perhaps a glass of wine would relax you," suggests her friend Amy.

"Amphetamines would perk you up; you'd zip right through your speech before you even had time to get scared," offers Edward.

"Or you could dress like a car crash dummy and deliver your speech in character," jokes her boyfriend, Steve.

What do you think of these suggestions? In Chapter 2 we noted that ethical speakers enter into and honor an unwritten contract with their listeners. How should the terms of that contract guide Sondra as she wrestles with how to control her nervousness? Could she follow any of her friends' advice and still "be herself" as she speaks? What advice would you offer if you were her friend?

a speech, only to learn that classmates envied them for seeming so calm. The authors of a study of 95 speakers found that "untrained audiences are not very good at detecting the self-perceived anxiety of beginning speakers."[7] Even if you feel extremely nervous, your audience probably won't realize it. Knowing this should make you more secure and lessen your anxiety.

One of our students, Susan, wrote the following in her self-evaluation of her first graded classroom speech: "Too fast, too rushed. I forgot half of it. Yuck! Yuck! Yuck!" Yet here are a few of the comments her classmates wrote:

"Wow! You seemed really relaxed! Your speech was organized, informative, and interesting."

"Definitely the best speech given so far."

"She seemed to know what she was talking about."

Susan obviously experienced her speech in a radically different way than her classmates and instructor. Asked about her listeners' written comments, Susan responded, "Wow! What you said is definitely true. It does look worse from the inside."

If Susan had not received feedback from her audience, she would probably have retained her high level of public speaking fear, perhaps even avoiding future opportunities to share her ideas with others. By offering honest evaluation, her classmates let Susan see her speech from "the other side," lessened her anxieties, and motivated her to continue improving her public speaking skills.

Know Your Speech

Knowing your strengths and weaknesses, speech principles, and your audience gains you little if you do not know your speech. If you don't know what you want to say, you won't say it. If you think you will forget, you probably will. The more confident you are about your message, the less nervous you will be.

SPEAKING WITH CONFIDENCE

I love to talk, so I never thought that speaking in front of a crowd, big or small, could place my nerves on a roller coaster. However, I found myself breathing so hard even before I arrived at my public speaking class. It was such a relief to learn that nervousness is quite common and that others are just as nervous as I am. Some methods I use to boost my public speaking confidence are to prepare (practicing in front of a mirror helps me), to take deep breaths before I get up to speak, and, finally, to just do it! When I stood in front of my classmates and began to speak, I scanned the audience and became familiar with some friendly faces, and this put me more at ease. Also, moving my hands for appropriate gestures helped me relax. With practice, you can keep nervousness from having a negative effect on your speech. All of these techniques have helped me build confidence in my public speaking ability.

Mariely Sanchez-Moronta
Marymount Manhattan College

If you choose a subject you love, whether it be a favorite hobby, job, class, or poet, you will become deeply involved in developing your speech. This involvement, in turn, may reduce your inhibitions about speaking in public.

You certainly don't need to memorize the entire speech. Yet, to be well prepared, you should know the outline of your major points and the order in which you want to present them. If you forget your notes or drop them and cannot get them back into proper order, you should still be able to deliver the speech. Take a minute to number your notecards, and you have one less worry.

Believe in Your Topic

If you are giving an informative speech, you must believe that what you say will benefit your listeners. If you are giving a persuasive speech, be committed to the belief you attempt to initiate in your audience. Convincing your audience that they should listen to your speech is easier if you believe that the topic is important. The more you believe in your topic, the more earnestly you will want to inform or convince your listeners. In short, if you doubt the importance of the topic, you will feel and seem tentative.

View Speech Making Positively

More and more we are discovering and investigating the mind's ability to affect behavior. Doctors have learned, for example, that patients' attitudes about their illnesses significantly affect their speeds of recuperation or their chances for recovery. One method for reducing communication anxiety is called **cognitive restructuring**. This approach recognizes that nervousness is, in part, caused by illogical beliefs. If speakers can restructure their thinking and focus on positive rather than negative self-statements, they reduce their anxiety. Cognitive restructuring involves two steps. First, identify your negative self-statements ("Everyone will laugh at me when I give my speech"). Second, replace the

cognitive restructuring
A strategy for reducing communication anxiety by replacing negative thoughts and statements with positive ones.

negative thoughts with positive ones ("My classmates understand what it's like to be nervous and will support my speaking efforts").

If you view public speaking as a tedious chore, your audience will sense it from your vocal and physical delivery and perhaps even from your choice of speech topic. On the other hand, if you look at public speaking as an opportunity, your positive attitude will help you control your nervousness. The following examples illustrate how you can replace negative thoughts with positive ones.

Replace the negative thought . . .	with a positive thought.
"My audience will probably be bored with my speech."	"I found the topic of how music affects our moods interesting, and my audience will, too."
"When I get up to speak, my mind will probably go blank, and I'll have nothing to say."	"I've rehearsed my speech, and I have a good set of speaking notes. If I momentarily forget a point, I'll just look at my notecards and then continue."

Thinking positively can help turn anxiety into anticipation. Genuine enthusiasm about the chance to speak in public will guide your choice of topic and will reveal itself to the audience through your lively delivery. Seek out opportunities to test and develop your communication skills. Volunteer for oral reports in classes, speak out at organizational meetings, or offer to introduce a guest speaker at your club's banquet. This positive attitude, coupled with practice and experience, will help make you less apprehensive and more confident.

Visualize Success

In football games, place kickers stand on the sidelines before taking the field, usually in deep concentration and away from other players. They visualize the football being snapped and placed. They imagine themselves approaching the ball and kicking it. As they mentally watch the football go through the goalposts, the referee lifts his arms to signal a field goal, and the crowd cheers. Through this ritual, place kickers focus on their task, visualizing how they can accomplish it.

Like athletes, public speakers can also use **visualization** to reduce their nervousness and improve their performance. A study of 430 college speech students revealed lowered speech anxiety among those who visualized themselves delivering an effective presentation.[8] Rodney describes how he used positive visualization to build his confidence:

visualization
A strategy for reducing communication anxiety by picturing yourself delivering a successful speech.

> The week before I gave my speech, I would find quiet spots where I could relax. I would close my eyes and visualize myself giving an effective presentation. I saw myself arriving at my classroom on the day I was to speak. Calmly, I would walk to my seat. I'd sit down, check my speaking notes to see that they were in order, and collect my thoughts. When Dr. Conner called my name, I got up from my seat and walked confidently to the front of the room. I put my notes on the lectern, looked at my classmates, and smiled. I paused, took a breath,

and then began. I visualized myself being relaxed and delivering my speech as I had planned, with clarity and poise. I felt good talking about a topic that was so important to me. I visualized my classmates smiling at my humor and nodding in agreement as I explained my ideas. I concluded with a dramatic story that really drove home my point. I paused, then walked to my seat. My classmates applauded, and one of them even whispered to me, "Great speech, Rod!"

Project Confidence

Daryl Bem's theory of self-perception states that if you perceive yourself acting a particular way, you will assume that you feel that way.[9] Thus, if you want to feel confident, act confident. Begin by identifying characteristics of speakers who seem confident; then incorporate those behaviors into your speaking. For example, instead of walking tentatively to the lectern, approach it confidently. Instead of avoiding eye contact with your listeners, look directly at them. Instead of leaning on the lectern or shifting your weight from foot to foot, stand erect and still. Instead of tapping your fingers on the lectern or jingling change in your pocket, use your hands to gesture emphatically. Displaying confident behaviors such as these will make you *appear* and *feel* more confident.

Test Your Message

Confident speakers must believe that their speech content will interest listeners or satisfy an audience need. If your listeners are bored with your topic, you will sense it, and that will make you more nervous. If the audience is interested in the content of your speech, they will be attentive.

As a speaker, you can test your message by practicing your speech in front of friends. Can they restate your main points after listening to you? Do they find your supporting material believable? Does your delivery detract from or reinforce your message? Answers to these questions will guide your subsequent practice sessions. The more confident you are that your message will achieve the desired effect on your audience, the less nervous you will be.

Practice Your Delivery

The previous coping strategies have implied the importance of practice. Practicing your speech is so important that it deserves its own discussion. The late Jack Valenti, former presidential speechwriter, correctly observed, "The most effective antidote to stage fright and other calamities of speech making is total, slavish, monkish preparation."[10]

Your approach to practice sessions will vary, depending on how your presentation develops. Sometimes you may practice specific sections of your speech that give you difficulty. But you should also practice your speech several times from start to finish without stopping. Too often when students mess up in practice, they stop and begin again. This is not a luxury you have when you address an audience. As you rehearse your speech, practice recovering from mistakes. Knowing that you can make it through your speech despite blunders should make you more confident.

EXPLORING ONLINE

Cognitive Therapy

www.csulb.edu/~tstevens/
Cognitive%20Therapy.htm

Dr. Tom Stevens, professor emeritus of psychology at California State University, Long Beach, presents seven steps to cognitive restructuring, as well as an overview of other therapies.

EXPLORING ONLINE

Reducing Anxiety

www.ljlseminars.com/anxiety.htm

This article, "Overcoming Speaking Anxiety in Meetings and Presentations" by Lenny Laskowski, a Connecticut speech consultant, lists and briefly discusses ten steps for reducing speech anxiety.

KEY POINTS

Guidelines for Building Speaker Confidence

1. Know how you react to stress.
2. Know your strengths and weaknesses.
3. Know speech principles.
4. Know that it always looks worse from the inside.
5. Know your speech.
6. Believe in your topic.
7. View speech making positively.
8. Visualize success.
9. Project confidence.
10. Test your message.
11. Practice your delivery.

You should also occasionally practice your speech in an environment laden with distractions. Students who practice only in the silence of an empty classroom may not be prepared for distractions that arise when they actually deliver their speeches—for example, a student coming into the classroom during the speech, a lawn mower passing by the window, or two students talking in the back of the room. These distractions, especially those stemming from rudeness, should not occur; in reality, though, they sometimes do. Practicing with the television on in the background or in your room with noise in the hallway forces you to concentrate on what you are saying and not on what you are hearing. You develop poise as a speaker only through practice.

The eleven coping strategies we've discussed will help you channel your nervous energy into dynamic, confident delivery. After each speech, reflect on the experience and gauge your success using the suggestions in this chapter's "Theory Into Practice" feature. In addition, the "Speaking with Confidence" boxes throughout this book reveal how other public speaking students developed their self-assurance using some of these principles. For now, however, you can begin training those butterflies to fly in formation as you prepare your first speech in this class.

THEORY INTO PRACTICE

 **Gaining Perspective**

In this chapter, we present eleven strategies for building your speaking confidence. You incorporate these suggestions as you prepare and deliver your speeches. However, what should you do *after* your speech? You've heard the expression, "Experience is the best teacher." Well, there's some truth in that folk wisdom; you can use your public speaking experiences to build your confidence.

After each speech, assess your performance by asking and answering important questions. Your instructor will give you feedback for some of these questions; others you will need to answer for yourself because you alone know the true answers.

- How did you react when you walked to the front of the room, turned, and looked at the audience looking at you?
- Did you remember what you planned to say?
- Did you have trouble finding your place in your notes?
- What techniques did you try in your speech that worked? What didn't work?
- Did you get less or more nervous as the speech progressed?

- How did your audience respond to your speech? What did their nonverbal communication convey as you delivered your speech? What feedback did you receive from your classmates and instructor following the speech?

Remember, don't be too critical as you evaluate your performance. You will do some things well, and this should build your confidence. Focus on other aspects of your speech that you can improve.

Suppose that you encounter a serious problem: You lose your place, your mind goes blank, and you bury your head in your notes and race to the end of your speech. Use this as a learning experience. Ask yourself *why* you forgot: Did you try to memorize your speech instead of speaking from notes? Were your notes disorganized, or did they contain too little or too much information? Did you focus too little on the audience?

Once you face a problem and determine its cause, you will be better able to plan so that it does not occur again. You don't *discover* confidence; you *build* it. Each public speech provides an opportunity to improve and enhance your confidence for your next speech.

Prepare Your First Speech

This class may require you to give your first speech before you have read much of this textbook. What is absolutely necessary to know, then, in order to deliver that first speech successfully? Preparing your first speech will be easier if you keep in mind two principles of public speaking. First, the more effectively you prepare, the better the speech you will deliver and the more confident you will feel. Only then can you recognize what you already do competently and begin to identify skills you want to improve. In addition, your confidence will grow with each speaking experience throughout this course and later in your life.

The second principle is that every public speech is a blend of *content*, *organization*, and *delivery*. Each of these aspects affects the others. For example, choosing a topic you already know well or have researched thoroughly should easily translate into animated, confident delivery. Elements of speech delivery such as pause and movement can emphasize your speech's organization. Moreover, as you will soon learn, any speech on any topic should be well organized. The more you know about the principles of speech content, organization, and delivery, the better your first speech will be. The following seven guidelines will help you toward that goal.

Understand the Assignment

For your first speech assignment, your instructor may prescribe a specific purpose or leave that choice to you. Often your first speech assignment is to introduce yourself or a classmate and is therefore informative rather than persuasive. The speech may be graded or ungraded. Whether your instructor is trying an innovative assignment or using one that has been tested and proven, he or she is your first and final authority for the specific details of the assignment.

A primary, vital requirement for preparing any speech is to know exactly what you are expected to do. The following questions can help you identify your goals for the speech:

- What am I supposed to do in this speech: inform, persuade, or entertain?
- What are my minimum and maximum time limits for the speech?
- Are there special requirements for the delivery of the speech? If so, what are they?

Develop Your Speech Content

As you select a speech topic, you need to decide the number of main ideas you will cover. To determine what those ideas will be, think about what you would want to hear if you were in the audience. If your instructor assigns you a topic, the specific details you include and the order in which you say them will be uniquely your own. If you are asked to choose a topic, you have even greater creative latitude. In either case, keep your audience in mind. The topic you select or the way you approach an assigned topic should be guided by what you think your listeners will find most interesting or useful.

If your assignment is to introduce yourself, begin by jotting down as many aspects of your life as you can. Audit your history, assess your current circumstances, and project your future goals. Among others, topics that apply to your life and the lives of all your listeners include accomplishments, aspirations, career plans, educational backgrounds, heroes, hobbies, personal values, pet peeves, prized possessions, skills, special interests, and unusual life events.

In addition, you may have a particularly interesting work history or may have traveled to unusual places or come from a different country. You could decide to limit your speech to one of the preceding areas or to combine several that you think your listeners will find most interesting.

If the ideas you disclose are truly unusual, your speech will be memorable. But don't be intimidated or worried if your experiences seem fairly tame and ordinary. Some of your listeners will be relieved to find that their backgrounds are similar to yours. Whether ordinary or extraordinary, your background and your classmates' will provide the basis for conversation before class, for classroom discussion, and for audience analysis as you prepare for future speeches.

If your first speech topic is not assigned, brainstorm for topics that interest you and those that you think would benefit or interest your audience. Your speaking occasion, the time of year that you speak, and upcoming or recent holidays can also suggest topic ideas. In addition, consider subjects that you discover as you conduct research. Don't settle for the first topic that comes to mind, however. If you generate many possible topics and spend some time reflecting on them, the subject you finally choose will probably be more satisfying for you and more interesting to your listeners. To make sure that you have a clear grasp of your speech topic, answer questions such as these:

- What is my speech topic, and why have I chosen it?
- Who are the people in my audience?
- What do I want my listeners to know or remember when I'm finished speaking?

The best way to answer that last question is to ask, "What aspects of my topic interest me and are likely to interest my audience?" Select only a few points to discuss. A time limit of 2 to 4 minutes, for example, may seem endless to you right now. It's not; it goes by very quickly. As you develop your speech content, check to be sure that everything you say is relevant to your purpose and to those few main points you want your listeners to remember. Limiting the number of main ideas should give you enough time to develop them with adequate supporting materials—definitions, stories, statistics, comparisons, and contrasts—that are interesting and relevant to your listeners. Once you have done this preliminary work, you are ready to assess your speech content by asking questions such as the following:

- Have I selected a few key points that I can develop in the time allowed?
- Is everything that I say relevant to my topic?

- Do I use a variety of specific supporting materials, such as examples and stories, to develop my key points?
- Will my supporting materials be clear and interesting to my audience?
- Do I acknowledge sources for anything I quote or paraphrase from other speakers or writers?

Once you begin to generate the main ideas of your topic and to choose those that you think the audience will find most interesting, you have begun to organize your content.

Organize Your Speech

Organizing a speech is similar to writing an essay. Every essay must have an introductory paragraph, a body, and a concluding paragraph. A speech has the same three divisions: an introduction, a body, and a conclusion. To determine whether your ideas are clearly organized and easy to follow, you must consider the organization of each of these three parts of your speech.

Organize Your Speech Introduction. Though usually brief, your speech introduction serves five vital functions. First, it focuses the audience's attention on your message. You want to command their attention with your first words. How can you do this? Question your audience, amuse them, arouse their curiosity about your subject, or stimulate their imaginations.

Second, your introduction should clarify your topic or your purpose in speaking. If your listeners are confused about your exact topic, you limit their ability to listen actively. To minimize any chances of this, state your purpose clearly in a well-worded sentence.

A third function of your introduction is to establish the significance of your topic or to explain your interest in it. Fourth, your introduction should help establish your credibility as a speaker on that topic. Reveal any special qualifications you have for speaking on the topic, and use your words, voice, and body to instill confidence in your listeners that you have prepared thoroughly. Finally, your introduction should highlight or preview the aspects of your subject that you will discuss in the body. Well-planned and well-delivered opening remarks will make the audience want to listen and will prepare them for what comes next. To check the integrity of your speech introduction, answer the following questions:

What are the parts of my introduction?
- What is my attention getter?
- What is my statement of purpose?
- What rationale do I provide for speaking about this topic?
- How do I establish my credibility to speak on this topic?
- What are the points I will cover in my speech?

Organize the Body of Your Speech. The body of your speech is its longest, most substantial section. Though it follows your introduction, you should prepare the body of your speech first. Here you introduce your key ideas and support or explain each one. You should develop only two or three main ideas in a first speech, because you can more easily develop them within your time limit. Your audience will also more easily grasp and remember a few well-developed ideas. Restricting your main points to a few is particularly important in a first speech because it may be the shortest presentation you make during the semester or quarter.

Your organizational goal in the body is to structure your main points so clearly that they are both distinct and unmistakable to your listeners. To help you do so, we recommend a four-step sequence—the "4 S's"—for organizing each of your main ideas. First, *signpost* each main idea. Typical signposts are numbers ("first" or "one") and words such as *initially* and *finally*. Second, *state* the idea clearly. Third, *support*, or explain, the idea; this step will take you the most time. Finally, *summarize* the idea before moving to your next one. These four steps will help you highlight and develop each of your main ideas in a logical, orderly way. The following questions and outline form should help you determine whether the body of your speech is well organized:

Have I organized the body of my speech clearly?

  I. What is my first main idea?
   A. What will I say about it?
   B. How will I summarize it?
 II. What is my second main idea?
   A. What will I say about it?
   B. How will I summarize it?
III. What is my third main idea?
   A. What will I say about it?
   B. How will I summarize it?

Organize Your Speech Conclusion. Your speech conclusion is a brief final step with three main functions. The first is the summary, a final review of the main points you have covered. Summarizing may be as simple as listing the key ideas you discussed in the body of the speech. You should not introduce and develop any new ideas in the conclusion. When you summarize, you bring your speech to a logical close.

The conclusion's second function is to activate an audience response by letting your listeners know whether you want them to accept, use, believe, or act on the content of your speech. Whether your speech is informative or persuasive, you want the audience to have been involved with your information and ideas. This is your last opportunity to highlight what you want your listeners to take away from your speech.

Finally, your conclusion should provide your speech with a strong sense of closure. To do this, end on a positive, forceful note. You can use many of the same techniques here that you used to get the audience's attention at the speech's beginning: question the audience, amuse them, stimulate their imaginations, and so forth. Your final remarks should be carefully thought out and extremely well worded. Ask and answer these questions to test your speech conclusion:

What are the parts of my conclusion?

- What is my summary statement?
- What am I asking my audience to remember or do?
- What is my closing statement?

If you answer each of the questions we've posed so far, you should have an interesting, well-developed speech that is easy to follow. Both your content and your organization are in good shape.

Up to this point, you have spent most of your time thinking about the speech and jotting down ideas. Now you have to word those ideas and practice getting them across to your audience through your vocal and physical delivery.

Word Your Speech

Unless your instructor requests that you do so, avoid writing out your first speech word for word. Even though having the text of your speech in front of you may make you feel more secure, students who deliver speeches from manuscripts often suffer two consequences. One is that what they say tends to sound like writing rather than speech. In Chapter 12 we'll examine some of the important differences between oral and written styles.

A second problem is a lack of eye contact. Effective speakers make eye contact with their listeners. If you are reading, you can't do this. Therefore, if you have a choice, speak from just a few notes rather than from a prepared manuscript.

The language of your speech should be correct, clear, and vivid. To illustrate this, assume that you have been assigned a practice speech of self-introduction early in the course. Assume, too, that you have decided to make your travels one of your main points. "I've traveled quite a bit" is a vague, general statement. Without supporting materials, the statement is also superficial. Instead, suppose you said,

> I've traveled quite a bit. I had lived in five states before I was in middle school, for example. When I was seven, my father worked in the booming oil business, and my family even got a chance to live in South America for more than a year. My brother and I went to an American school in the tiny village of Anaco, Venezuela; we were students 99 and 100 in a school that taught grades 1 through 8. Instruction in Spanish started in the first grade, and by the time we returned to the States, I was bilingual. I have vivid memories of picking mangoes and papayas off the trees, swimming outdoors on Christmas day, and having my youngest brother born in Venezuela.

The second statement is a great deal clearer and more vivid than the first. It begins with the general comment, but then amplifies it with details. The language is personal, conversational, and crisp. The following questions should help you test the language of your speech:

- Does my speech sound conversational?
- Do I use language correctly?
- Will the language of my speech be clear to my listeners?
- Will the language of my speech be vivid for my listeners?

Practice Your Speech

Mental rehearsal is no substitute for oral and physical practice. Merely thinking about what you plan to say will never adequately ready you to deliver a prepared speech. As we said toward the beginning of this chapter, speech making is an active process. You gain a heightened knowledge of what you plan to say and increased confidence in your abilities just by practicing your speech out loud. Before you can do that, however, you must create the notes you will use to practice and deliver the speech.

Preparing thoroughly, practicing often, and wanting to communicate with your audience are keys to any successful speech.

Prepare Your Notes. Make certain that your speaking notes are in the form of key words or phrases, rather than complete sentences. Remember, you want your listeners to recall your main *ideas*, not necessarily your exact wording. The goal in preparing your notes should be the same: You should need only a word or phrase to remind you of the order of your ideas. As you elaborate those points, your specific wording can change slightly each time you practice. Make sure that your notes are easy to read. If your speaking notes are on notecards, be certain to number the cards and have them in the correct order before each practice session.

Practice Productively. Most of your practice will probably be done in seclusion. Practice any way that will help you, being sure to stand as you rehearse. Visualize your audience, and gesture to them as you hope to when giving the speech. You may even want to record and listen to your speech or watch it on video if you have access to that equipment. Give yourself the opportunity to stop for intensive practice of rough spots. Just make sure that you also practice the speech from beginning to end without stopping.

As valuable as solitary practice is, you should also try your speech out on at least a few listeners, if possible. Enlist roommates and friends to listen to your speech and help you time it. The presence of listeners should make it easier to practice the way that you approach your speaking position before you speak and the way you leave it after finishing. Your rehearsal audience can tell you if there are parts of your speech that are too complex and hard to grasp. They may also be able to suggest clearer, more colorful, or more powerful ways of wording certain statements. A practice audience can point out strengths of your delivery and help you eliminate distractions. Most important, serious practice in front of others should focus your attention on the important interaction involved in delivering a speech to an audience. The following questions make up a checklist for your speech practice:

- Have I practiced my speech as I intend to deliver it in class?
- Have I made my speaking notes concise and easy to use and read?
- Have I recorded my speech and made changes after listening to or viewing it?

- How many times have others listened to my speech, and what suggestions have they offered for improving it?
- Have I timed my speech? Is the average time within my overall time limit?
- What adjustments can I make in my speech if it is too long or too short?

Deliver Your Speech

Your speech delivery is made up of your language, your voice, and your body. Speaking in public should feel natural to you and seem natural to your audience. You want to be conversational and to talk *with* your listeners, not *at* them. Use a presentational style with which you are comfortable but that also meets the requirements of your audience, your topic, and your speaking occasion.

Effective vocal delivery is energetic, easily heard, and understandable. Your voice should also show that you are thinking about what you are saying as you deliver your speech. With practice, your voice can communicate humor, seriousness, sarcasm, anger, and a range of other possible emotions. Check your vocal delivery by answering the following questions:

- Do I speak with enough volume to be heard easily?
- Do I change the pitch of my voice enough to create a lively vocal delivery?
- Do I vary my rate of speaking to match my audience's comprehension of what I am saying?

The message your listeners see should match the one they hear. Effective physical delivery is direct and immediate; effective speakers demonstrate their involvement in their topics and in their speaking situations by interacting with their audiences. You must make eye contact with all of your audience. Your facial expression should signal that you are thinking moment to moment about what you are saying. Physical delivery is not limited to your face, however. Gestures with your arms and hands and selective movement from place to place can emphasize what you say and mark important transitions in your speech.

If you are concentrating on your message and your audience's nonverbal feedback, your physical delivery will most likely seem natural. To gauge your directness, immediacy, and involvement, answer the following questions about your physical delivery:

- Are my clothing and other elements of my appearance appropriate to my topic, my audience, and the speaking occasion?
- Do I look at members of my audience most of the time I am speaking? Do I look at listeners in all parts of the room?
- Do my gestures add emphasis to appropriate parts of the speech? Do my gestures look and feel natural and spontaneous?
- Do my facial expressions show that I am thinking about what I am saying rather than about how I look or sound?
- If I include place-to-place movement, does it serve a purpose?

Your goal should be delivery that looks and sounds effortless. Yet, ironically, that will require significant practice and attention to the vocal and physical elements of your delivery.

Evaluate Your Speech

Don't forget your speech as soon as you deliver your final words and return to your seat. While the experience is fresh in your memory, evaluate what you said, your organization, and your delivery. What sorts of feedback did you get from your listeners? In short, how did you respond to the challenge of preparing and delivering a speech? To evaluate the kind of speaker you are now and the kind of speaker you can become, answer the following questions:

- What did I do well?
- What areas can I target for improvement in this class?
- What specific efforts do I need to make in order to improve my next speech?

No matter what your level of public speaking experience, you will benefit from recognizing two concerns that you probably share with everyone in class. First, most of your classmates are probably as apprehensive as you are about their first speech. Almost everyone worries about questions such as, "Will I be able to get through my speech? Will I remember what I wanted to say? Will I be able to make my listeners understand what I want to say? Will I sound okay and look as though I know what I'm doing?" Your nervousness is natural, typical, and healthy. In fact, your anxiety is a sign that you have reasonably high expectations of yourself and that you care about doing well.

Second, you should know that public speaking is a teachable skill, much like math, reading, and writing. So, yes, you can *learn* to speak well. We share responsibility for part of that learning with your instructor. You are also responsible for much of your learning through your own effort and initiative. If you skipped the student preface to this book, we urge you to turn back and read it. Written primarily for you, this preface condenses our philosophy about this course and about education in general.

We began this chapter by focusing on speaker nervousness, because we know that it is a real worry for most people. We have suggested some techniques to help manage and channel your platform panic into a lively, enthusiastic speech. We have also sketched in broad strokes the process of developing and delivering an effective speech. If you think about public speaking for a moment, though, you will realize that the worst thing that could happen to you is that you might embarrass yourself. Stop and ask yourself, "Have I ever embarrassed myself before?" Unless you never leave your house, the answer to that question is yes. You may have even embarrassed yourself so badly that you thought, "I'll never be able to face them again" or "I'll never live this down." But you do. The sun rises the next day. None of us is perfect, and it is unreasonable to expect perfection of ourselves or the people around us. So the best advice of all may be, "Keep public speaking in perspective." Your audience is made up of peers. They are pulling for you. Use this friendly atmosphere as a training ground to become a more effective speaker.

SUMMARY

Recognize That Speaker Nervousness Is Normal

- Speaker nervousness is natural.
- Your goal should be not to eliminate but rather to control and channel it.

Learn How to Build Speaker Confidence

- To control nervousness: (1) know how you react to stress, (2) know your strengths and weaknesses, (3) know basic speech principles, (4) know that it always looks worse from the inside, (5) know what you plan to say without memorizing your speech, (6) believe in your topic, (7) have a positive attitude about speech making, (8) visualize yourself speaking successfully, (9) project confidence, (10) test your message prior to delivering it in class, and (11) practice as much as possible in a variety of situations.

Prepare Your First Speech

- Prepare thoroughly for your first speech by (1) understanding the speaking assignment, (2) developing adequate content of a narrow topic, (3) organizing the various sections of the speech, (4) wording your ideas effectively, (5) practicing productively, (6) delivering the speech, and (7) evaluating your performance.
- Realize that your nervousness is normal and that you can learn to be an effective speaker.

EXERCISES

1. Complete McCroskey's Personal Report of Public Speaking Anxiety (found on MySpeechLab.com) and determine your score. Into which group does your score place you, and how do you compare with other college students whose survey results we discussed early in this chapter? Which coping strategies discussed in this chapter seem most promising in building your confidence?

2. Divide a sheet of paper into two columns. In Column A, list nervous symptoms you experience when speaking to a group of people. In Column B, list ways you can control each symptom. For example:

Column A	Column B
Play with ring on my finger, turning it while speaking.	Remove ring before speaking. Keep hands apart by gesturing more often.

3. Interview someone who frequently gives public speeches and ask how he or she handles speaker anxiety. Based on your interview, compile a list of suggestions for controlling nervousness. How does that list compare with the one in this chapter?

4. After you present your first speech in this class, answer the following questions:
   a. What were three strengths of my speech?
   b. What are two areas I should target for improvement?
   c. What are some specific strategies I can use to improve each targeted area?

Listening

4

After studying this chapter,
you should be able to

1 Appreciate the importance of
listening.

2 Distinguish between listening
and hearing.

3 Understand and apply the
six-step process of listening.

4 Recognize obstacles to
effective listening.

5 Incorporate guidelines to
become a better listener.

Listening is a magnetic and
strange thing, a creative
force. The friends who listen
to us are the ones we move
forward toward, and we want
to sit in their radius. When
we are listened to, it creates
us, makes us unfold and
expand.

—Karl A. Menninger,
Love Against Hate[1]

Effective public communication occurs in the charged space between a speaker and an audience, with each party leaning slightly toward the other. Within that space, for the duration of a speech, the contract binding public speakers and their audiences is in effect. We discussed that contract in Chapter 2, where we maintained that, as members of a community of learners in the classroom, each speaker and each listener bears ethical responsibilities. Among the commitments of the ethical speaker are being well prepared, communicating information and ideas clearly in order to benefit the audience, and remaining open to feedback and criticism that will improve future speeches. Among the responsibilities of ethical listeners are listening openly, listening critically, and providing feedback to assist the speaker's thinking on the topic and to help him or her improve as a public speaker. If the mutual respect and civility implicit in this speaker-listener contract exists, then listening is the paper on which participants write their contract.

In this chapter, we focus on the topic of listening. As we look at the process, problems, and potential of listening, we will provide you with the tools you need to improve your listening skills.

The Importance of Listening

You probably remember playing the game of telephone when you were a child. Someone whispered a phrase or sentence to another person, who whispered it to the next one, and so on. The last person to receive the message then said it aloud. Usually, the final message bore little resemblance to what the first person whispered, and the group laughed at the outcome.

Unfortunately, examples of poor listening exist in areas of life where the results are often far from humorous. In fact, researchers estimate that U.S. businesses lose billions of dollars each year simply because of ineffective listening.

Of course, ineffective listening is not confined to commercial settings. You can probably think of several examples of problems, or at least embarrassing situations, caused by your own ineffective listening. For example, you asked a question the teacher had just answered. You didn't realize that a complete sentence outline of your informative speech was due a week before you were scheduled to speak. You arrived at a party dressed in jeans, a T-shirt, and flip-flops only to find everyone else dressed formally.

Each day, you send and receive both oral and written messages. Of the four roles you perform—speaker, listener, writer, and reader—you spend the most time as a listener. College students, for example, spend approximately 53 percent of their communication time listening.[2] Yet, despite listening's monopoly on your time, you probably know less about this activity than about other forms of communication. While you have taken several courses teaching you to read and write, you have probably never taken one in listening. In short, you have received the least training in what you do the most!

It will probably not surprise you, then, to learn that most of us are inefficient listeners. In fact, immediately after listening to your classmates' speeches, chances are high that you will remember, at most, only 50 percent of what you heard, and 2 days later only 25 percent. This doesn't surprise listening expert Robert Montgomery, who says:

> Listening is the most neglected and the least understood of the communication arts. It has become the weakest link in today's communications system. Poor listening is a result of bad habits that develop because we haven't been trained to listen.

But there is good news, as Montgomery adds, "Fortunately, it is a skill that can be learned."[3]

Listening versus Hearing

Does the following situation sound familiar? You are watching *The Daily Show with Jon Stewart*, listening to a CD, or doing economics homework when your mother walks by and tells you to put out the trash. Fifteen minutes later, she walks back to find you still preoccupied with television, music, or homework, and the trash still in the kitchen. Your mother asks, "Didn't you hear me?" Well, of course you did. You *heard* the direction to put out the trash just as you heard Stewart joking with Samantha Bee, Stevie Ray Vaughn playing a riff, the dog barking at a passing car, and the air conditioner clicking on in the hall. You heard all these things, but you might not have been *listening* to any of them.

What is the difference between **listening** and **hearing**? The two activities differ in at least four important ways.

Listening Is Intermittent

Listening is not a continuous activity but occurs only from time to time when we choose to focus and respond to stimuli around us. Hearing, on the other hand, is a continuous function for a person with normal hearing.

Listening Is a Learned Skill

Hearing means simply receiving an aural stimulus. Unless you have a hearing loss, you don't need training to hear. We hear sounds before we are born, and throughout our lives we hear sounds even as we sleep. Listening, however, must be taught and learned.

listening
The intermittent, learned, and active process of giving attention to aural stimuli.

hearing
The continuous, natural, and passive process of receiving aural stimuli.

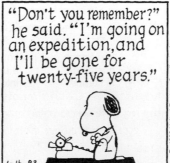

PEANUTS: © United Features Syndicate, Inc. Reprinted by permission.

EXPLORING ONLINE

Listening
www.listen.org

Sponsored by the International Listening Association, this website offers a wealth of quality information about listening. Click on "Listening Resources" to find a host of excellent quotations, articles, and other resources on the topic of listening.

Listening Is Active

The act of hearing is passive; it requires no work. Listening, in contrast, is active. It requires you to concentrate, interpret, and respond—in short, to be involved. You can hear the sound of a fire engine as you sit at your desk working on your psychology paper. You listen to the sound of the fire engine if you concentrate on it, identify it as a fire engine rather than an ambulance, wonder if it is coming in your direction, and then turn back to your work as you hear the sound fade away.

Listening Implies Using the Message Received

Audiences assemble for many reasons. We choose to listen to gain new information; to learn new uses for existing information; to discover arguments for beliefs or actions; to laugh and be entertained; to celebrate a person, place, object, or idea; and to be inspired. There are literally thousands of topics you could listen to—for example, regulating the Internet, the history of blue jeans, crimes of ethnic intimidation, preparing lemongrass chicken, digital photography, and the life of Arthur Ashe. Some of these topics might induce you to listen carefully. Others might not interest you, so you choose not to listen. The perceived usefulness of the topic helps determine how actively you will listen to a speaker. Listening implies a choice; you must choose to participate in the process of listening.

◖ The Process of Listening

In Chapter 1, we introduced the listener as one component of communication. Indeed, the listener is vital to successful communication; without at least one listener, communication cannot occur beyond the intrapersonal level. Remember that any time two people communicate, two messages are involved: the one the sender intends and the one the listener actually receives. These messages will never be identical because people operate from different frames of reference and with different perceptions. To better understand this concept, examine the six steps in the process of listening shown in Figure 4.1.

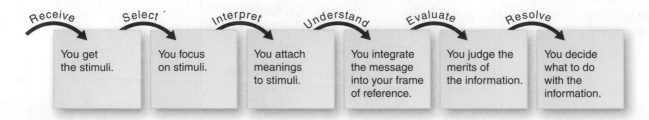

FIGURE 4.1
The Process of Listening

Receive

The first step in listening is to *receive* sounds, the auditory stimuli. In other words, hearing is the first step in effective listening. Some people, such as those with a hearing loss, unintentionally filter or leave out part of the stimulus. Whenever we filter, parts of the messages available to us will be lost.

Select

Individuals *select* different stimuli from those competing for their attention, a phenomenon sometimes called *selective perception*. When the police gather reports from various witnesses to a traffic accident, they often find conflicting information. Each bystander's report will be shaped by where the person was standing or sitting, what the person was focusing on at the moment of impact, how the person was feeling, and a host of other factors. Each witness has a selective perception of the event.

In public speaking situations, the audience reacts in a similar way. One person may focus primarily on what speakers are saying, another on their voices or gestures, still another on what they are wearing or even on the distracting hum of the heating system. If you are intrigued by the speaker's accent, you have selected to focus on that element of speech delivery, and you will probably hear a slightly different speech than the person sitting next to you. You may even be distracted by internal noise, such as worrying about an upcoming exam or trying to resolve a conflict with your roommate. As William James said more than 100 years ago, our view of the world is truly shaped by what we decide to heed.

> Millions of items of the outward order are present to my senses which never properly enter into my experience. Why? Because they have no interest for me. My experience is what I agree to attend to.
>
> —William James[4]

Interpret

Individuals not only choose differently among stimuli competing for their attention, but they also *interpret* those stimuli differently. Interpreting is the process of decoding the message. When you interpret, you attach meanings to the cluster of verbal and nonverbal symbols the speaker provides—words, tone of voice, and facial expression, for example. As we noted in our discussion of the triangle of meaning in Chapter 1, the speaker's knowledge and experience must be similar to the listener's if communication is to be clear and effective.

If you were unable to sense when your friends were serious or joking, you'd have a hard time interpreting and understanding what they told you.

Understand

Once you have decoded, or attached meanings to, a speaker's symbols, you begin fitting the message into your framework of knowledge and beliefs. To *understand* a speaker, you must consider both the content and context of a message. Is the speaker attempting to inform or persuade you? Is the speaker serious or joking? In short, what is the speaker trying to do?

Evaluate

Before acting on the message you have decoded and understood, you *evaluate* it. Evaluating is the process of judging the speaker's reliability and the quality and consistency of her or his information. Is the speaker making eye contact with you? Does he or she speak fluently, without unnecessary pauses or filler words? Do the speaker's gestures and other body language seem relaxed and spontaneous? In short, does the person seem well prepared, confident, and sincere? If the answer to any of these questions is no, you may wonder whether the speaker has ulterior motives. As you evaluate the speaker's message, you decide whether you believe the data presented and whether you agree or disagree with the position the speaker advocates.

Resolve

The final step in listening, resolving, involves deciding what to do with the information we have received. As listeners, we can *resolve* to accept the information, reject it, take action on it, investigate it further, or just try to remember the information so that we can resolve it later.

Obviously, we do not consciously think about each of these six steps every time we listen to someone. As the significance of the message increases for us, we become more involved in the process of listening—a point every speaker should remember.

◖ Obstacles to Effective Listening

Speakers and audience members should recognize some of the reasons why effective listening is so difficult. Learning to listen better is easier if you know what you're up against. For this reason, you need to identify the major obstacles to effective listening. We list and discuss five of them in this section.

Physical Distractions

Have you ever told someone that he or she was being so loud that you couldn't hear yourself think? If so, you were commenting on one obstacle to effective listening: physical distraction. **Physical distractions** are interferences coming to you through any of your senses, and they may take many forms: glare from a sunny window, chill from an air-conditioner vent, or the smell of formaldehyde in your anatomy and physiology lab. You may have trouble focusing on the message of a speech if you concentrate on the speaker's outlandish clothing, on a PE class playing a vigorous game of touch football outside, or on the overpowering smell of aftershave on the person near you.

Physiological Distractions

Physiological distractions have to do with the body. Any illness or unusual physiological condition is a potential distraction to effective listening.

EXPLORING ONLINE

Listening Habits
www.listen.org/Habits

Read and reflect on these lists of irritating and poor listening habits compiled by four noted listening researchers and scholars.

physical distractions
Listening disturbances that originate in the physical environment and are perceived by the listener's senses.

physiological distractions
Listening disturbances that originate in a listener's illness, fatigue, or unusual bodily stress.

A bout of flu, a painful earache, or fatigue after a sleepless night will place limitations on your willingness and ability to listen.

Psychological Distractions

Your attitudes also affect your listening behavior. **Psychological distractions,** such as a negative attitude toward the speaker, the topic, or your reason for attending a speech, can all affect how you listen. If you are antagonistic toward the speaker or the point of view he or she is advocating, you may resist or mentally debate the statements you hear. If you are coerced to be in the audience, you may also be more critical and less open-minded about what is being said. In short, if you are concentrating on thoughts unrelated to what the speaker is saying, you will receive less of the intended message.

psychological distractions
Listening disturbances that originate in the listener's attitudes, preoccupations, or worries.

Factual Distractions

College students are often hampered by **factual distractions,** listening disturbances caused by the flood of facts presented to them in lectures. You may be tempted to treat each fact as a potential test question, but this way of listening can pose problems. For example, have you ever taken copious notes in your World Civilization class only to realize later that, although you have lots of facts, you missed the key ideas? Students and other victims of factual distractions sometimes listen for details but miss the speaker's overall point.

factual distractions
Listening disturbances caused by attempts to recall minute details of what is being communicated.

Semantic Distractions

Semantic distractions are those caused by confusion over the meanings of words. Listeners may be confused by a word that they have never heard before or that is mispronounced. If a student gave a speech about her native country, Eritrea, without showing that word on a visual aid, most listeners would probably begin wondering, "How do I spell that?" "Have I ever seen that word on a map before?" "Is this a new name for an established country?" "Is the speaker pronouncing correctly a word I've always heard mispronounced?" These thoughts divert them from the serious business of listening to a speech filled with new and interesting information.

semantic distractions
Listening disturbances caused by confusion over the meanings of words.

◖ Promoting Better Listening

A major theme of this book is that each party in the communication process has a responsibility to promote effective communication. Promoting better listening should be a goal of both the sender and the receiver of the message. How can you encourage better listening?

As a speaker, you can enhance your audience's retention when you select your ideas carefully, organize them clearly, support them convincingly, word them vividly, and deliver them forcefully.

SPEAKING WITH CONFIDENCE

While preparing my persuasive speech to convince my classmates to use lower viscosity synthetic motor oil, I realized the topic would challenge their listening skills. Although I could do very little to control physical and physiological distractions my audience might experience, I considered ways to address other possible distractions. I tried to overcome psychological distractions by stressing the importance of the topic: they would save money on fuel costs and car repairs. To minimize semantic noise, I defined viscosity as oil thickness and explained how oil flows through motor parts. To reduce factual distractions, I supported my ideas with key facts and expert opinions that I cited in my speech. As I spoke, I could see audience members becoming involved in my topic. I had helped make it easier for them to listen to my speech, and I was rewarded with a stronger feeling of confidence as a speaker with an intrigued—dare I say persuaded—audience.

Jodie Moody
Radford University

As a listener, you must also work hard to understand and remember the speaker's message. The following suggestions will help you become a more effective listener. As you master these suggestions, you will find yourself understanding and remembering more of what you hear.

Desire to Listen

Your attitude will determine, in part, your listening effectiveness. Good listeners begin by assuming that each speech might benefit them. You may not find a speech on how financial institutions determine a person's credit rating of great interest right now. The first time you apply for a loan you may be happy that you paid attention.

Good listeners can learn something from any speech, even if it is poorly prepared and awkwardly delivered. For example, you can determine what the speaker could have done to improve the poorly developed speech. This experience lets you apply speech principles you have learned and improve your own speaking.

You may also have the opportunity to offer helpful suggestions to speakers. Listen carefully so that you can help them improve. If you have a genuine desire to listen to a speaker, you will understand and remember more.

Speakers can promote better listening by demonstrating early in their speeches how the information will benefit their listeners. Let your audience know quickly why it is in their interest to listen carefully to your speech.

Focus on the Message

Your first responsibility as a listener is to pay attention to the speaker's message. Yet a speaker's message competes with other, often quite powerful, stimuli for your attention. Often speakers themselves create distractions. They may play with change or keys in their pockets, dress inappropriately, sway nervously from side to side, use offensive language, or say "um"

EXPLORING ONLINE

Improving Listening Skills

www.salisbury.edu/Counseling/
New/listening_skills.html

The Counseling Center of Salisbury University in Maryland lists bad listening habits of students and then suggests good habits to replace them.

throughout their speeches. These quirks can be very distracting. We have had students, for example, who actually counted the number of "ums" in a speech. After a classmate's speech, they would write in their critiques, "You said 'um' 31 times in your speech." While this may have provided the speaker with some valuable feedback, we suspect these listeners learned little else from the speaker's message. You may not be able to ignore distractions completely as you listen, but you can try to minimize them.

Effective speakers can help listeners focus on the message by eliminating distracting mannerisms and by incorporating nonverbal behaviors that reinforce rather than contradict their ideas. For example, appropriate gestures that describe objects, provide directions, and illustrate dimensions can make a speech easier to remember.

Listen for Main Ideas

You are familiar with the cliché that sometimes you can't see the forest for the trees; well, that saying applies to listening. A person who listens for facts often misses the main point of the message. While it is important to attend to the supporting material of a speech, you should be able to relate it to the major point being developed.

When listening to a speech, pay close attention to the speaker's organization. A speech's structure provides a framework for both speakers and listeners to organize the supporting points and materials. Speakers who clearly enumerate key ideas and repeat them at several points in their speeches give their audience a better opportunity to listen attentively. We discuss organizational techniques in Chapters 9 and 10.

Understand the Speaker's Point of View

As we discussed in Chapter 1, each of us has different referents for the words we hear or speak because we have different life experiences that affect how we view our world.

Speaking in favor of agricultural programs that would preserve the family farm, Cathy tried to involve her audience in her speech by tapping their memories. She asked her classmates to think of the houses they grew up in and the memories created there.

> Think of Thanksgiving and family gatherings. Think of slumber parties and birthday celebrations. Of how you changed your room as you moved from child to teenager to young adult. Think of your feelings as you left home to come to college, and of your feelings when you return to those comfortable confines.

After the speech, several students said they were moved by Cathy's eloquence and passion. She had sparked memories that were important to them. Others in the audience, however, said they were unable to relate to the topic in the way Cathy intended. Several had grown up in more than one house. Some were in military families and had moved often. Still others said they had lived in rented townhomes or apartments. And a few commented

Listening requires something more than remaining mute while looking attentive—namely, it requires the ability to attend imaginatively to another's language. Actually, in listening we speak the other's words.

—Leslie H. Farber

that their childhood memories were not fond ones. Both speakers and listeners need to remember that different experiences shape and limit our understanding of another's message.

When speakers and listeners come from different cultures, the chances for misunderstanding increase. Differences in language, education, and customs challenge listeners to work especially hard at understanding the speaker's message and intent. These differences are often evident in today's multicultural classroom. Some foreign students, for example, come from educational environments that are more structured and formal than the typical American college classroom. They may interpret a speaker's casual dress and use of humor as an indication that the speaker is not serious about the speech. On the other hand, some American students may perceive the more formal presentations of some of their foreign classmates as stiff and indicating a lack of interest in the topic. Understanding each other's frame of reference minimizes this distortion.

Speakers should do two things to clarify their points of view. First, explain early in the speech if you have some particular reason for selecting your topic or some special qualifications to speak on it. If you choose to speak on radio formats because you work at your campus radio station or because you are a media studies major, tell the audience a little about your background. Second, try to relate your subject to your listeners' frames of reference. Rather than using technical jargon or complex explanations that may limit the audience's ability to listen effectively, use examples and language your listeners will understand.

What are some of the listening skills these travelers can use to make the communication experience a positive one for both the speaker and audience?

Provide Feedback

A listener can enhance the communication process by providing feedback to the speaker. Although there is greater opportunity for *verbal* feedback in interpersonal and group environments, it is nevertheless also possible in public speaking contexts. The effective speaker will especially read the audience's *nonverbal* cues to assist in the speech's presentation. If listeners understand and accept the speaker's point and nod in agreement, the speaker can move to the next idea. If listeners appear perplexed, that signal should prompt the speaker to explain the idea more fully before moving to the next point.

Listen with the Body

We listen with more than our ears. In a sense, we listen with our entire bodies. If, as your instructor lectures, you lean back, stretch your legs, cross your arms, and glance at a fellow classmate, you detract from your listening effectiveness. Part of listening is simply being physically ready to listen.

THEORY INTO PRACTICE

TIP   Reinforcing the Message

Most Americans speak at rates between 125 and 190 words per minute. Yet as listeners, we can process 400 to 500 words per minute.[5] This means that, depending on the situation, we can listen at a rate up to four times faster than a person speaks! As a result, we can get bored and move our attention back and forth between what the speaker is saying and some extraneous message, perhaps a personal problem that concerns us. Sometimes, the unrelated thought takes over and psychological noise, which we discussed earlier, drowns out the speaker's message. To be a better listener, you must make better use of this extra time. You can increase your listening accuracy and retention by mentally repeating, paraphrasing, and summarizing what the speaker is saying.

Repeat the Message

You use *repetition* when you state exactly what the speaker has said. Consider, for example, a speaker who argues that a tuition increase is necessary to preserve educational excellence at your college or university. The first reason she offers is this: "A tuition increase will enable us to expand our library." If, after the speaker makes this claim, you mentally repeat her argument, you are using repetition to help you remember her message.

Paraphrase the Message

Using *paraphrase* is a second way to help remember the message. By putting the speaker's ideas into your own words, you become actively involved in message transmission. Suppose the same speaker offers this statement to justify one benefit of a tuition increase:

A tuition increase would generate funds that could be used to enhance our library facilities and resources. In the chancellor's budget proposal, one-third of the tuition increase would go directly to the library. The chancellor estimates that this would enable us to increase our database subscriptions and electronic resources by 10 percent. Also, projected construction would create at least twelve new study rooms.

Obviously, it would be difficult to restate the speaker's explanation word for word. Yet you could paraphrase and summarize her message this way:

A tuition hike would increase our library holdings by 10 percent and expand the number of study rooms by twelve.

Summarize the Message

You use *summary* when you condense what a speaker says. The above paraphrase includes summary, as it leaves out some of the specific information the speaker presented. As a speaker concludes her or his message, you should recollect the key points of the speech. Your summary might be, for example, "A tuition increase will help us expand the library, increase the number of faculty, and renovate some of the older dormitories."

By getting you actively involved in the communication process, repetition, paraphrase, and summary increase your chances of understanding and remembering the message.

You can ready yourself for listening if you sit erect, lean slightly forward, and place both feet flat on the floor. As you listen, look at the speaker. As important as the message you hear is the message you see. Remember, you want to detect any nonverbal messages that intensify or contradict the speaker's verbal message.

Some speakers present views that are highly divisive. Whether or not we agree with them, we should withhold judgment until after listening to what they say.

KEY POINTS

Guidelines to Promote Better Listening

1. Desire to listen.
2. Focus on the message.
3. Listen for main ideas.
4. Understand the speaker's point of view.
5. Provide feedback.
6. Listen with the body.
7. Withhold judgment.
8. Listen critically.

Withhold Judgment

You filter what you hear through your own set of beliefs and values. Many of us have a problem withholding judgment. We hear something and immediately label it as right or wrong, good or bad. The problem is that once we do that, we cease to listen objectively to the rest of the message.

It is difficult to withhold judgment, of course, when you listen to a speech advocating a position you strongly oppose. The following are topics student speakers sometimes discuss: legalization of drugs, capital punishment, abortion, flag burning, euthanasia, gun control, and embryonic stem cell research. We suspect you have some fairly strong opinions on most of these issues. You may even find it difficult to listen to a speech opposing your view without silently debating the speaker. Yet, as you mentally challenge these arguments, you miss much of what the speaker is saying. If you can suspend judgment until after speakers have presented and supported their arguments, you will be a better listener.

Listen Critically

Even though listeners should understand a speaker's point of view and withhold judgment, they should nevertheless test the merits of what they hear. If you accept ideas and information without questioning them, you are in part responsible for the consequences. If the speaker advocating a tuition increase quotes from the chancellor's budget proposal before it has even been submitted, you have every right to be skeptical. "Will the final budget actually earmark one-third of the tuition increase for library use? Will the board of regents accept the chancellor's proposal? Or is this all speculation?" Decisions based on incorrect or incomplete data are seldom prudent and are sometimes disastrous.

Critical listeners examine what they hear by asking several questions: Is the speech factually correct? Are sources clearly identified, and are they unbiased and credible? Does the speaker draw logical conclusions from the data presented? Has the speaker overlooked or omitted important information? Speakers help listeners answer those questions by presenting credible information, identifying their sources, and using valid reasoning.

John Marshall, chief justice of the United States from 1801 to 1835, once stated, "To listen well is as powerful a means of communication and influence as to talk well." If you use these eight suggestions, you will become a better listener.

SUMMARY

The Importance of Listening

- The personal costs of poor listening include lost opportunities, embarrassment, financial losses, and lost time.

Listening vs. Hearing

- *Listening* differs from *hearing* in four ways: (1) Listening is intermittent, while hearing is continuous; (2) listening is a learned behavior, while hearing is natural for most people; (3) listening is active; hearing is passive; and (4) listening implies doing something with the message received.

The Process of Listening

- Listening involves six steps. The listener *receives* sound stimuli, *selects* particular parts of the total stimulus field for attention, *interprets* or decodes the message, *understands* by matching the speaker's message with the listener's frame of reference, *evaluates* the reliability of the speaker and the speaker's message, and *resolves*, or decides, what to do with the information received.

Obstacles to Listening

- *Physical distractions* are listening obstacles that originate in the physical environment. *Physiological distractions* arise from conditions in the listener's body. *Psychological distractions* include worry, distraction, or preconceived attitudes toward the speaker or the message. *Factual distractions* are caused by our tendency to listen for small supporting details, even when we miss the speaker's main point. *Semantic distractions* are confusion over the meanings of words.

Improving Listening

- Both speakers and listeners can contribute to effective listening.
- Listeners should develop a genuine desire to listen; focus on the speaker's message; listen for the speaker's main ideas; understand the speaker's point of view; provide the speaker with feedback; listen with the whole body; withhold judgment about the speaker and the message until after hearing and considering both; and listen critically.
- Listeners can also reinforce a speaker's message by using repetition, paraphrase, and summary.
- Speakers should express a sincere desire to communicate; minimize distracting behaviors and use forceful delivery to underscore their messages; organize their speeches carefully to highlight their key ideas; reveal their credentials and motives for speaking on a particular topic; adapt to feedback from listeners; and present logically supported ideas and cite credible sources.

EXERCISES

1. List what you perceive to be your listening strengths and weaknesses. Beside each weakness, indicate specific strategies that could minimize this problem.

2. Listen to a speech or lecture, paying particular attention to the five types of distractions discussed in this chapter. Give examples of distractions you encountered. What could you or the speaker have done to minimize these interferences? Discuss these options.

3. Suppose you are asked to speak to a group of students at a local high school on the topic "What College Offers You." Half of the audience plans to attend college; the rest does not. All the students have been requested to stay after school on the first sunny day this spring to attend the assembly. What are your listeners' likely psychological distractions with which you must contend? What strategies could you use to minimize them in your speech?

4. Sit in a different seat and next to a different classmate each class for the next 2 weeks. After this time period, analyze whether your location affected your listening attentiveness. If so, how?

Analyzing Your Audience

5

- **Recognize the Value of Audience Diversity**

- **Analyze Your Audience *before* the Speech**
  Analyze Audience Demographics
  Analyze Audience Psychographics
  Analyze Audience Needs
  Analyze Specific Speaking Situations

- **Analyze Your Audience *during* the Speech**
  Theory Into Practice: Using an Audience Questionnaire
  Audience Attention
  Audience Understanding
  Audience Evaluation

- **Analyze Your Audience *after* the Speech**

After studying this chapter, you should be able to

1. Recognize the benefits of diversity.

2. Understand how to become an audience-centered speaker.

3. Recognize that audience analysis occurs before, during, and after a speech.

4. Analyze your audience according to their demographics.

5. Analyze your audience according to their psychographics.

6. Analyze your audience according to their needs.

7. Gather information about your audience by constructing and administering a questionnaire.

8. Use information you have gathered about your audience to develop your speech.

9. Analyze your audience during your speech.

10. Analyze your audience after your speech.

There are some who speak well and write badly. For the place and the audience warm them, and draw from their minds more than they think of without that warmth.

—Blaise Pascal

EXPLORING ONLINE

Speech Texts

www.americanrhetoric.com

To compare the texts of Abraham Lincoln's and Edward Everett's speeches at Gettysburg, visit this award-winning site. American Rhetoric has thousands of speeches available in print, audio, and occasionally video formats. The list of speakers includes some international figures, as well as Americans from all walks of life.

Today we would call it an urban legend—the tale about Abraham Lincoln and how he wrote the Gettysburg Address. As the story goes, Lincoln was such a great thinker and accomplished speaker that he wrote his now-famous speech on some scraps of paper while on the train to Gettysburg, Pennsylvania.[1] Repeated for many years, the story seemed plausible because the speech is only 272 words long. Like other stories that seem too good to be true, however, this one is false. Today, we have a better picture of how Lincoln composed the Gettysburg Address.

Lincoln had anticipated for some time an occasion for an important speech on the same theme. The words of the speech began to take shape in his mind long before he wrote them on paper. Thomas Scheidel points out that in informal remarks 4 months before delivering the Gettysburg Address Lincoln had said,

> How long ago is it?—eighty-odd years since, on the Fourth of July for the first time in the history of the world a nation by its representatives, assembled and declared as a self-evident truth, that "all men are created equal." … Gentlemen, this is a glorious theme, and the occasion for a speech; but I am not prepared to make one worthy of the occasion.[2]

Lincoln was asked to speak at a ceremony dedicating a memorial cemetery for soldiers who had died in the Civil War battle at Gettysburg. He was not the main speaker on this occasion, however; Edward Everett, the most famous orator of his day, had top billing. Everett spoke for 1 hour and 57 minutes to an audience estimated at between 15,000 and 50,000 people seated and standing outdoors.[3] On November 19, 1863, Lincoln rose and, holding two pieces of paper, spoke ten sentences in less than 3 minutes.[4] He began his speech:

> Four score and seven years ago our fathers brought forth on this continent a new nation, conceived in liberty and dedicated to the proposition that all men are created equal.

Lincoln's careful audience analysis helped him decide the topic, length, and scope of his remarks at Gettysburg. Making speeches "worthy of the occasion" requires meticulous audience analysis today, just as it did in Lincoln's time.

◖Recognize the Value of Audience Diversity

In interpersonal communication, you adapt your message to one other person. The quantity and character of your communication depend on your relationship to that other individual. Your task as a public speaker is more challenging, however, for each added person increases the diversity of any audience. Each audience member is unique.

Today's college classroom, like most segments of American life, is increasingly diverse. Your classmates may differ from one another in terms of age, gender, ethnicity, educational background, beliefs, values, and numerous other characteristics. Talking *across* those differences *about* those differences can reveal what you have in common and build your sense of community. Your challenge as a public speaker is to recognize how your listeners differ from one another and to understand, respect, and adapt to this diversity as you develop and deliver your speeches. Evidence shows that it's a challenge worth taking.

Based on his research and his review of other scholars' studies, education professor Jeffrey Milem concludes that students benefit when they interact with peers of different backgrounds:

- They become more engaged in their own learning.
- They improve their critical thinking skills.
- They enhance their interpersonal and social competence.
- They are more satisfied with their college experience.
- They are more likely to engage in community service.
- They demonstrate greater acceptance of people from other cultures.

Milem argues that diverse environments provide students "opportunities to develop the skills and competencies they will need to function effectively as citizens of an increasingly diverse democracy."[6]

If you value your listeners and want to communicate successfully, then you must consider their diversity and view public speaking as an audience-centered activity. You can accomplish this in three ways:

1. *Recognize your own place as part of the audience.* You must admit that you are only one part of the total audience, a fact that should make you want to learn as much as possible about the other parts.
2. *Respect your listeners.* Respect and care for the audience means wanting to enhance their knowledge and understanding by providing interesting or useful information. To do this, you must recognize and appreciate their beliefs, values, and behaviors.
3. *Recognize and act on audience feedback,* whether it's verbal or nonverbal. Speakers who are attuned to their audience will try to discover and cultivate interests their listeners already have, as well as challenge them with new, useful topics.

To discover who your audience members are and what motivates them, you will exercise at least five critical thinking skills. You will engage in *information gathering* as you collect data to develop an increasingly clearer picture of who your listeners are. As you exercise the skill of *remembering*, you'll tap your memories of what your listeners have said and done. You will *focus* on elements of the picture that seem most relevant to topic areas you are considering for your speeches. As you combine, summarize, and restructure pieces of information about your listeners, you will exercise the critical thinking skill of *integrating*. Finally, you will *analyze* the information you have collected by examining individual characteristics of your listeners and the relationships among those characteristics.

Reading America is like scanning a mosaic. If you look only at the big picture, you do not see its parts—the distinct glass tiles, each a different color. If you concentrate only on the tiles, you cannot see the picture.

—Robert Hughes[5]

Ethical public speakers consider the diversity of their audiences and use appropriate channels to communicate with as many of them as possible. Here, an interpreter uses American Sign Language to make the speaker's message accessible to members of the Deaf community.

Audience analysis is a process that shapes and molds the preparation, delivery, and evaluation of any well-planned public speech. In other words, audience analysis occurs *before*, *during*, and *after* the act of speaking. Let's consider more closely how this process works.

◖ Analyze Your Audience *before* the Speech

You will spend more time analyzing your audience before you speak than during or after. Your speech may last only 5 or 10 minutes, for example. Yet, if you care about doing well, your audience analysis before the speech will take considerably more time.

Audience analysis in an online public speaking class poses special challenges. You may or may not have a chance to meet some classmates at a face-to-face orientation session or at other scheduled meetings. Your instructor may invite you to post a message introducing yourself to the class listserv or bulletin board as the class begins. You may be able to administer a questionnaire online to collect student input on a topic area you are considering. Aside from those opportunities, you will have to analyze your classmates based on the messages you read or hear from them.

A traditional face-to-face class provides you the rare opportunity to "live" with your audience for the duration of the course. From the comments they make in and outside class, from the questions they ask other student speakers or your instructor, and from their nonverbal feedback while listening to classroom speeches, you will gradually assemble an increasingly accurate portrait of these people. They will disclose, or you will deduce, information about their beliefs, values, interests, likes, and dislikes. Your audience analysis will be a semester- or quarter-long process, and by the time you deliver your final speech in the class, your audience analysis should be both easier and more accurate than it was at the term's beginning.

Analyze Audience Demographics

demographics
Characteristics of the audience, such as age, gender, ethnicity, education, religion, economic status, and group membership.

audience segmentation
The strategy of dividing an audience into various subgroups based on their demographic and psychographic profiles.

audience targeting
The strategy of directing a speech primarily toward one or more portions of the entire audience.

Your first step as a speaker is to discover and evaluate audience demographics. **Demographics** are characteristics of the audience, such as age, gender, ethnicity, education, religion, economic status, and group membership. Demographic analysis helps you tailor a message to a specific audience by helping you answer the question, "Who is my target audience?"

Part of your audience analysis will involve discovering what you can about the various divisions or subgroups that constitute your listeners. Advertisers and public relations people call this process **audience segmentation**. You might then choose a topic that you believe can relate to all segments of your audience. However, sometimes speakers choose to address only one or more segments of a larger audience, a strategy called **audience targeting**.

For example, if you know that some of your listeners love to travel but are on tight budgets, you could inform them about the option of becoming airline couriers. An informative speech on the dangers of heatstroke and heat exhaustion might be appropriate for athletes in your audience or for those who work outdoors. Of course, you must be sure that your target audience does exist and that it is sufficient in size to justify giving them your primary focus.

You will never know everything about your listeners and will therefore make generalizations from what you do know. One note of caution, however: be careful not to turn these generalizations into stereotypes. This will undermine your speech-making efforts. However, the more you know, the more able you will be to deliver a successful speech.

Seven of the most common characteristics you should analyze about your potential audience are age, gender, ethnicity, education, religion, economic status, and group membership. You will not always be able to learn this much information about your audience. However, keep in mind that the more you know, the better prepared you will be to present a successful speech.

Age. One of the most obvious concerns you have is their age. Your public speaking class may include first-year college students, people returning to college to change careers, and others pursuing interests after retirement. People who are 18 to 20 years old today relate to Watergate and the U.S. boycott of the 1980 Summer Olympics only as important topics of history. While they may be eager to learn more about those topics, it also means they may not understand most casual references to them. Ask a college classroom audience today, "Do you remember where you were on April 20, 1999, when twelve students and one teacher were killed at Columbine High School?" and few if any of your listeners will have a positive answer; most of them were in the first years of elementary school. To make sure your speech on any topic is understandable, you must use supporting materials that are familiar to your listeners, and age is one of the most obvious influences on the audience's frame of reference.

Gender. It is obviously easier to determine the gender of your listeners than their age. However, don't fall into the trap of stereotyping based on gender. What seems to be sensitivity to gender may be disguised sexism: "I'm going to inform you girls about the rules of football," or "This recipe is so easy that even you guys should be able to make it."

Obviously, some speech topics will resonate more with listeners of one gender. An informative speech on the risks of estrogen replacement therapy has more immediate interest for women than men; a speech on prostate cancer, more obvious importance for men than women. But couldn't either of these topics benefit both male and female listeners? You can make virtually every topic relevant to both genders. Rather than using gender to select or eliminate topics, approach any topic so that everyone can get something out of it.

Ethnicity. Ethnicity is the classification of a subgroup of people who have a common cultural heritage with shared customs, characteristics, language, history, and so on. As with gender, avoid ethnic stereotypes. Never assume that because individuals are of the same ethnicity they also share similar experiences and attitudes. Two people of the same ethnicity may have diverse attitudes, interests, and experiences because of differences in their ages, education, income levels, and religion.

Communicating with college students is always somewhat of a challenge. It is not that I have too much difficulty understanding your changing expressions and attitudes. It is that I forget what you never saw.

—Terry Sanford[7]

Effective speakers need to consider the individual life experiences of their audience members to avoid stereotyping and offending some individuals.

> We must make room in our minds for one another.
>
> —Sr. Mary Aquin O'Neill[8]

Education. Your audience's educational level affects what subjects you choose and how you approach them. Students in your class may have attended private schools, had homeschooling, or earned graduate equivalency degrees after interruptions in their high school educations. Others may have lived and studied overseas. Prepared speakers will find out as much as they can about their listeners' levels and types of education.

Remember that education can be informal as well as formal. Listeners who have not completed high school or college are not necessarily uneducated. They may have a wealth of "book" knowledge as well as specialized practical knowledge and training. If you can, find out what your audience knows about a potential speech topic and whether they have experience relevant to it. Then tailor your speech to build upon the knowledge they already have.

Religion. Your audience may include members of various religious groups as well as agnostics and atheists. People from other countries may practice religions you do not know about, or they may practice familiar religions in a different way. Religion will be very important to some listeners and relatively unimportant to others. If your audience's religious views are truly important to a topic you are considering, you need to find out more about their beliefs than the denominational labels they prefer.

Economic Status. Economic status is another key factor affecting audience attitudes and behaviors. Discovering the range of incomes of your classmates' families may be difficult. Certainly, it would be impolite to ask. However, you can probably locate or construct several general profiles of the typical students at your college. Your school's Office of Institutional Research or Office of Student Life may compile and publish student fact books on their websites.

Overall, be realistic, be fair, and be sensitive when choosing topics dealing with economic issues. We remember one student who was offended when a speaker said that students shouldn't go home for spring break but should travel with friends to different parts of the United States to expand their historical and cultural knowledge. The offended student argued that some people simply did not have that option. They needed to work in order to remain in college. On the other hand, we have observed student speakers generate lively audience interest on topics such as summer employment opportunities at national parks and historic sites and how to negotiate the price of a new or used car. Although money may be of greater concern to some people than to others, few people want to spend money needlessly.

Group Membership. We join groups in order to spend time with others who enjoy our hobbies and pastimes, to learn more about subjects that can help us, or to further our political and social goals. Many of these groups are voluntary, such as clubs, honor societies, political parties, environmental groups, and social fraternities or sororities. We may also be required to belong to labor unions and professional associations in order to get or keep jobs or special licenses.

Knowing your listeners' affiliations can be particularly helpful as you prepare persuasive speeches. How you develop your persuasive appeal and select supporting material will reflect assumptions you have made about your audience. If you are speaking to an organization, research the nature of that group as thoroughly as you can.

Analyze Audience Psychographics

Just as you should develop a demographic profile of your audience, you should also generate a psychological profile. **Psychographics** is a term for audience characteristics such as values, beliefs, attitudes, and behaviors. These elements help you understand how your listeners think, feel, and behave. Figure 5.1 illustrates how our behavior is typically shaped by our attitudes, which are based on beliefs, which are validated by values. To better understand the interaction among these elements, we will look at each level of the pyramid, beginning with values and moving upward.

Values. A **value** expresses a judgment of what is desirable and undesirable, right and wrong, or good and evil. Values are usually stated in the

EXPLORING ONLINE

Demographic Profiling

www.census.gov

Want a profile of various demographic characteristics of people in the United States or in your specific geographic area? Need an estimate of the nation's or world's population at this minute? You have access to all this and much more on this site sponsored by the U.S. Census Bureau.

psychographics
Characteristics of the audience, such as values, beliefs, attitudes, and behaviors.

value
Judgment of what is right or wrong, desirable or undesirable, usually expressed as words or phrases.

SPEAKING WITH CONFIDENCE

Audience analysis is important for all public speakers. The more I learned about my classmates, the easier it was to choose a topic that would affect them, to avoid sensitive issues, and to relate to their life experiences. Although I did most of my analysis before my speech, it didn't stop there. I continued to analyze my audience as I spoke. Reading my listeners' expressions and body language helped me determine how my speech was going. For example, if students at the back of the room were having trouble hearing me, I would speak louder. If someone looked confused, I would give an example to clarify my point. If a couple of audience members seemed bored, I might use some humor or walk slightly toward them. And when my classmates smiled approvingly, I was confident that I was getting through to them. Audience analysis during a speech requires quick thinking, but it shows your listeners that you care about them.

Krystal Graves
West Texas A&M University

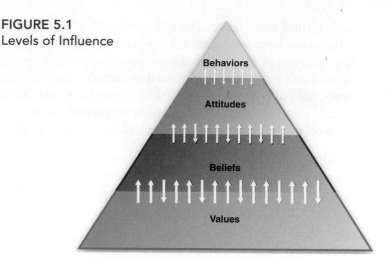

FIGURE 5.1
Levels of Influence

form of a word or phrase. For example, most of us probably share the values of equality, freedom, honesty, fairness, justice, good health, and family. These values compose the principles or standards we use to judge and develop our beliefs, attitudes, and behaviors.

If we value honesty, for example, we are probably offended when we learn that a political leader has lied to us. If we value equality and fairness, we will no doubt oppose employment practices that discriminate on the basis of gender, ethnicity, religion, or age. While our actions may not always be consistent with our values, those standards guide what we believe and how we act. When we act contrary to our values, we may experience conflict or even guilt. That perceived inconsistency or dissonance will often motivate us either to change our behavior to match our beliefs and values or to change our beliefs by rationalizing our behavior.

belief
A statement that people accept as true.

Beliefs. A belief is something we accept as true, and it can usually be stated as a declarative sentence. We probably do not think about many of our beliefs because they are seldom challenged: observing speed limits saves lives, sexual abuse is psychologically harmful to children, illiteracy in the United States undermines economic productivity, and so on.

Other beliefs are more controversial, and we often find ourselves defending them. Each of the following statements is debatable:

- Colleges place too much emphasis on athletics.
- The benefits of surveillance technology in the workplace outweigh its risks.
- Use of the Internet improves the quality of student research.

Those statements you accept as true are part of your beliefs.

attitude
A statement expressing an individual's approval or disapproval, like or dislike.

Attitudes. Attitudes are expressions of approval or disapproval. They are our likes and dislikes. A statement of an attitude makes a judgment about the desirability of an individual, object, idea, or action. Examples include the following: "I support capping enrollment at our college," "I prefer classical music to jazz," "I favor a pass-fail grading system."

Attitudes usually evolve from our values and beliefs. When two values or beliefs collide, the stronger one will generally predominate and determine attitudes. You may value both airline safety and the right to privacy. If a speaker convinces you that a proposed government action will diminish the right to privacy, you may oppose the action. If another speaker demonstrates that the plan is necessary to increase airline passenger safety, you may support the proposal. A single belief in and of itself, is not a reliable predictor of a person's attitude.

Behaviors. A **behavior** is an overt action; it is how we act. Unlike values, beliefs, and attitudes, which are all psychological principles, behaviors are observable. You may feel that giving blood is important (attitude) because an adequate blood supply is necessary to save lives (belief) and because you respect human life (value). Your behavior as you participate in a blood drive and donate blood is a logical and observable extension of your outlook.

behavior
An individual's observable action.

Your knowledge of the foregoing principles will help you analyze your audience and develop its psychological profile. How do you obtain information about your audience's values, beliefs, attitudes, and behaviors? You have two options, both requiring some work.

- The first option is to use your powers of observation and deduction. You can make educated guesses about people's values, beliefs, and attitudes by observing their behaviors. For example, what do your classmates talk about before and after class? What subjects do they choose for classroom speeches? How do they respond to various speeches they hear? How do they dress? What books do they carry with them to class? The answers to these and many other questions help you infer a psychological profile of your audience.
- The second way is to conduct interviews or administer questionnaires. These may be informal or, if you have the time and resources, formal. You could interview classmates informally during conversation before or after class. Questionnaires administered during class may be as simple as asking for a show of hands to answer a question ("How many of you have broadband Internet access?") or as formal as asking classmates to answer a written questionnaire. (We will show you how to construct a questionnaire in the "Theory Into Practice" box on pages 85–86.) Most often you will not have the luxury of using audience interviews and questionnaires for presentations outside the college classroom. Still, if you are addressing a group of strangers, ask your contact person lots of questions about the audience.

EXPLORING ONLINE

Analyzing Psychographics
http://people-press.org
www.gallup.com

What do *you* think? To find out what *others* think, access these sites. The Pew Research Center and the Gallup Organization present the results of opinion polls they've conducted on a variety of political, social, educational, and other topic areas.

Analyze Audience Needs

Once you have considered your audience's demographic and psychographic profiles, you will be in a better position to determine their needs or what motivates them. One particular model, Maslow's hierarchy, will get you thinking about audience needs in an organized way.

Maslow's hierarchy
A model of five basic human needs—physiological, safety, belongingness, esteem, and self-actualization—in an ordered arrangement.

EXPLORING ONLINE

The VALS Survey

www.strategicbusinessinsights.com/vals/ustypes.shtml

Advertisers and other persuaders segment their audiences. The VALS (values and lifestyle) typology, originally developed by the Stanford Research Institute, classifies U.S. consumers according to eight types. To discover how you're classified, access this site, click on the *VALS Survey* link, take the survey, and get an immediate report of your primary and secondary types. How do you think these categories could help you in analyzing your audience?

Maslow's Hierarchy. Sociologist and psychologist Abraham Maslow is best remembered for a model of human needs commonly referred to as **Maslow's hierarchy.**[9] A hierarchy is an arrangement of items according to their importance, power, or dominance. Maslow's thesis was that all human needs can be grouped into five categories, based on the order in which they are ordinarily filled.[10] As a public speaker, you should be aware of the needs dominating any particular audience you address. Maslow's categories, represented in Figure 5.2, are as follows:

1. *Physiological*, or physical, *needs*—basic human requirements for water, food, and sleep. As Maslow and others have observed, hungry people don't play.
2. *Safety needs*—everything that contributes to the "safe, orderly, predictable, lawful, organized world" on which we depend.[11] Having roofs over our heads and reliable transportation are typical safety needs.
3. *Belongingness and love needs*—our relationships with people around us. Giving affection to and receiving affection from other people provides us a sense of community, of fitting in.
4. *Esteem needs*—feelings of individual self-worth and reasonably high self-evaluation that other people confirm and validate as they recognize what we do well. Everyone has certain talents, and we all need a pat on the back from time to time.
5. *Self-actualization needs*—goals we must achieve in order to feel we have reached our potential or fulfilled our destiny. Our cluster of highly individual self-actualization needs can change at different points in our lives.

Note that we all fill our physiological needs in the same way (when it's possible to get those needs met): by taking nutrition and getting rest. The needs at the top of Maslow's model, in contrast, can be both personally distinctive and temporary.

FIGURE 5.2
Maslow's Hierarchy of Needs
From Motivation and Personality, 1st ed., by Abraham H. Maslow, © 1954. Electronically reproduced by permission of Pearson Education, Inc., Upper Saddle River, New Jersey.

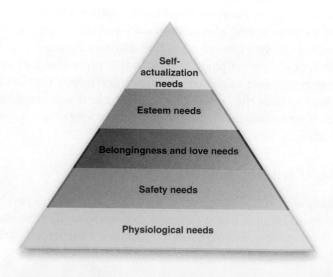

The Importance of Audience Needs. But what does Maslow's hierarchy mean for you in public speaking? Does this model apply to your listeners, and if so, how? We can suggest several ways to make the hierarchy work for you.

First, the people sitting around you in class probably have most of their physiological and safety needs met. This does not mean that you cannot appeal to them on the levels of physiological or safety needs. If you alert listeners to the harms of aggressive driving, dangerous food additives, or potentially deadly drug interactions, for example, you move them to focus on basic issues of survival. In fact, no matter how prosperous and healthy they are, everyone in class would likely be interested in a topic showing them how to save money or demonstrating the health hazards of certain products or practices.

Second, if many of your classmates entered college directly from high school, they are probably interested in being well liked and fitting in. In other words, Maslow's third category, social needs, is extremely important at this point in their lives. If many or most of the people in your class are in their first year of college, their self-esteem may depend partly on whether they succeed or fail in college, and speeches on scholastic success may easily hold their attention.

Finally, although many college students are unsure of the careers they will undertake after graduation, most people have formed, or are forming, self-actualization needs by the time they are in their teens or twenties. Older students may be reassessing and reformulating their self-actualization needs. Those goals are changeable and will adapt as individuals discover new talents, interests, and abilities. For that reason, a college-age audience is likely to be quite receptive to speeches showing how various pursuits can provide personal rewards or self-fulfillment.

It is critical for you to understand, however, that you cannot easily assign all your listeners a specific set of needs. In fact, as Maslow admits, all of us probably have unmet needs at each of the five levels of his hierarchy. We move from one level to another more frequently than we suspect. *Your challenge as a speaker is to identify and emphasize audience needs that are relevant to your topic.*

For example, if you feel secure in your surroundings, you may take your safety needs for granted. However, if you read in your school newspaper reports of several attacks on campus, your concern for your own and others' safety will increase. If you choose to address this issue in a persuasive speech, you will want to stress this need for safety, bringing it to the front of your listeners' awareness. Once the situation is evident to them, you can point out ways to satisfy that need. You might advocate better campus lighting, more security patrols, or personal escort services. Successful speakers identify the unmet needs of their listeners and respond appropriately in an informative, persuasive, or entertaining speech.

Using Maslow's hierarchy can also help the speaker facing an unfamiliar audience. Even though you may initially know little about such an audience, your goal will be to find out as much relevant information as possible about them before the speech. Knowing what motivates them, what they need or want to hear, is an excellent starting point in your audience analysis. It will also help you avoid unfortunate, unnecessary situations such as speaking on the joys of skydiving to a group of people barely able to provide food and clothing for themselves.

Analyze Specific Speaking Situations

Demographic and psychographic analyses give you an arm's-length view of the people who will make up your audience. But who, specifically, is going to be sitting in the audience you will face? Finding this out requires you to analyze your listener's dispositions, the size of your audience, the occasion, the physical environment, and the time of day that your speech will occur.

audience disposition
Listeners' feelings of like, dislike, or neutrality toward a speaker, the speaker's topic, or the occasion for a speech.

Audience Disposition. **Audience disposition** describes how listeners are inclined to react to speakers, their ideas, and the reasons for assembling. After speakers gather information regarding audience beliefs and attitudes, they must assess if their listeners are favorable, unfavorable, or neutral toward the speaker, the topic, and the reasons for assembling.

The higher your speaker credibility, the more likely your audience is to believe you. Thus, if some of your listeners have a neutral or even unfavorable view of you, you will need to work to enhance your image. In Chapter 16 we discuss the importance of speaker credibility, identify its three components, and suggest strategies to enhance your perceived competence, trustworthiness, and dynamism.

A second component of audience disposition is your listeners' attitudes toward your topic. Your audience can be slightly, moderately, or strongly favorable or unfavorable toward your topic, and you should try to determine this level of intensity. A listener who only slightly opposes your position will probably be easier to persuade than one who strongly opposes it.

If you sense that some of your listeners are neutral toward your topic, try to uncover the reasons for their neutrality. Some may be *uninterested*, and you will want to convince these listeners of the topic's importance. Other listeners may be *uninformed*, and your strategy should be to introduce them to the data they need to understand and believe your ideas. Still other listeners may simply be *undecided* about your topic. They may be interested, informed, and aware of the pros and cons of your position. However, they may not have decided which position they support. Your strategy in this instance should be to bolster your arguments and point out weaknesses in the opposition's case. As you can see, evaluating your audience's disposition is a complex activity. The more you know about your listeners, the easier this process becomes.

Frank and Ernest, by Bob Thaves

©1982 Thaves. Reprinted with permission. Newspaper dist. by NEA, Inc.

Listeners can be favorable, unfavorable, or neutral not only to speakers and their topics, but also to the reasons for assembling to hear a speech, the third element of audience disposition. Audiences fall into two categories. A **voluntary audience** has assembled of its own free will. Most adults who attend a worship service or a political rally are there voluntarily. The **captive audience**, in contrast, is required to be present. You may attend a speech by someone visiting your campus because you are required to do so for a particular course. Your reasons for attending a speech or a presentation may significantly affect your disposition as you listen.

We are often tempted to view voluntary audiences as friendly and captive ones as hostile. However, the connection between the audience's reasons for attending and their attitudes is rarely this simple and predictable. Listeners who have assembled freely may well be unfavorable to the speaker or the speaker's cause. Consider the people who attend a political speech or a town hall meeting to protest or to heckle the speaker. Alternatively, a captive audience may actually look forward to a speech. Even members of a captive audience initially unsympathetic to the speaker may find themselves becoming more congenial as a result of the speaker's interesting message or engaging style of delivery.

These three components—the speaker, the speaker's ideas, and the reasons for assembling—combine to form an audience's disposition. Remember that public speaking is an audience-centered activity; keep your listeners' needs and concerns in mind as you construct your message.

Size of the Audience. In speaking before a small group, a speaker may be frequently interrupted with questions. The situation may be so informal that the speaker sits in a chair or on the edge of a table during the presentation. A speaker in such a situation may use jargon and colloquial language, presentational aids, and a conversational style of delivery.

As the audience grows larger, however, the speaker must make adjustments. The language of the speech may become more formal, especially if the speaker knows that the speech will be published or recorded. As the distance between the speaker and the last row of audience members increases, the speaker's volume must increase, gestures and facial expressions must be exaggerated slightly, and presentational aids must be projected in order to be seen. Unless the audience is encouraged to ask questions after the speech, they will likely remain silent. As you can see, the size of your audience affects both the type of speech you deliver and your manner of presentation.

Occasion. The occasion—or the reason for the speaking event—is a critical factor in determining what type of audience you will face. You need to ask yourself (and maybe even some members of the group), "Why is this audience gathering? What special circumstances bring them together?" A class, an annual convention, a banquet, a party, a competition, a reunion, and a regular meeting of an organization are all examples of occasions. These can be formal or informal, serious or fun, planned or spontaneous, closed to the public or open to all.

In addition to a simple description of the occasion, you as a speaker may need to know about the history of the occasion or about the recent

voluntary audience
A group of people who have assembled of their own free will to listen to a speaker.

captive audience
A group of people who are compelled or feel compelled to assemble to listen to a speaker.

history of the group you will address. Say, for example, that the officers of an organization have invited you to speak to their entire membership. If there has been recent conflict between the members and the officers, the majority of your audience may look upon you and your speech skeptically. To understand any occasion, you must know both the purpose and the circumstances of the gathering.

Physical Environment. The physical environment or setting can affect the messages sent by the speaker and received by the audience. For example, the size of the room itself may impede communication. You may be speaking to a large audience through an inadequate or defective public address system. Or, you may compete with a variety of physical noise: the sounds of another meeting next door, a room that is too warm, interruptions from caterers bringing in carts of ice water. Discovering these challenges before you speak will help you prepare your speech and adapt to your audience.

Time. The time at which you deliver your speech is an important part of analyzing the speaking occasion. An address given at 4:00 P.M. on Friday will almost surely find an audience more fatigued and restless than will one given Tuesday at 9:30 A.M. If you are scheduled to speak first in a class that meets at 8:00 A.M., your audience may be half asleep, so you may need to boost your own energy to enliven them.

Your speech's placement in a program may also affect how your audience receives it. If you follow several other speakers, you may need to work harder at getting and keeping your listeners' attention. In short, if your listeners are not at their best, plan on working extra hard to enliven your delivery.

audience profile
A descriptive sketch of listeners' characteristics, values, beliefs, attitudes, and/or actions.

When you use the techniques discussed in this chapter to analyze your audience's demographics, psychographics, and the specific speaking situation, you will be able to construct an **audience profile.** Keep in mind that your understanding of the audience will never be complete. You may have to make educated guesses based on incomplete data. Remember, too, that some information you collect may be irrelevant to your speech topic. Finally, bear in mind that your audience is not a uniform mass but a collection of individuals with varying experiences, values, beliefs, attitudes, behaviors, and personalities.

◗ Analyze Your Audience *during* the Speech

Careful audience analysis before your speech will guide your topic selection, how you focus and develop your subject, and how you plan to deliver your speech. However, even the most thorough, conscientious audience analysis will not guarantee a compelling, effectively delivered speech. Speakers do not perform for audiences; they interact with them. The physical presence of listeners transforms and shapes each public speaking experience. To make that vital connection with your listeners, your audience analysis must continue during the delivery of your speech. Communication scholars suggest that you must be aware of three characteristics of your listeners as you speak.

THEORY INTO PRACTICE

TIP   Using an Audience Questionnaire

If you're unable to learn enough about your listeners through informal means such as observation and discussion, you may have another option. If you need precise, measurable information and have the luxury of ample time and opportunity to collect it, consider administering a questionnaire.

A questionnaire is a set of written questions designed to elicit information about your listeners' knowledge, beliefs, attitudes, or behaviors regarding your specific speech topic.[12] The following guidelines will help you construct and administer a questionnaire and then interpret the results.

Construct a Questionnaire

First, determine what you need to know about your audience. What do they already know about your topic? If you're trying to persuade them, do they agree or disagree with you, or are they undecided? How strongly do they hold these positions?

Second, construct your questions depending on the type and amount of information you seek, how long respondents will have to complete your survey, and how you plan to compile and use the information you gather.

Closed questions, ideal for gathering demographic information, offer respondents a finite set of responses or a scale that asks people to place themselves along a continuum.

- What is your gender?   [ ] Female   [ ] Male
- Are you currently employed?   [ ] Yes   [ ] No
- Smoking is bad for your health.
  [ ] Agree   [ ] Disagree   [ ] Neutral
- The honor code at our school is too strict.
  [ ] Strongly disagree   [ ] Disagree   [ ] Neutral
  [ ] Agree   [ ] Strongly agree

Open questions invite respondents to answer in their own words. Though they take longer to answer, compile, and interpret, open questions often provide unexpected, helpful information or specific examples a speaker may include in a speech.

- What do you think are the qualities of a good supervisor?
- Why did you decide to attend this college?

- What are some activities that contribute to a healthy lifestyle?

Your questions, whether open or closed, should be clear, objective, and focused. Avoid emotional language that may "lead" respondents to a particular response. Pilot test your survey on friends who are similar to your intended audience, timing their completion rate and asking for feedback about your questions' clarity and objectivity. See Figure 5.3 for an example of a clear, objective questionnaire.

Administer a Questionnaire

Because the information you gather will shape your speech, administer any questionnaire at least a week before your speech is due. Your written and oral directions should ensure respondent anonymity. You have an ethical responsibility to consider your listeners' interests, respect their privacy, and not mislead them. Thank respondents for their participation, either orally or on your written questionnaire.

Analyze Questionnaire Responses

First, organize the responses to each question. For closed questions, simply count the number in each response category. Compiling responses to open questions is more subjective and time consuming. Summarizing responses on separate pieces of paper and then tabulating them according to common themes that emerge should speed the process.

Once you have organized the questionnaire responses, you are ready to answer the important question: *So, what does all this information tell me?* Do your listeners agree or disagree with your position on the topic, or are they neutral? Do their beliefs, attitudes, and behaviors vary widely? Do these differences vary according to age, gender, ethnicity, or academic classification? Are there well-worded answers to open questions that you can attribute to the anonymous respondent and use as supporting material? The payoff for all the work you put into constructing, administering, and analyzing the results of your questionnaire is that you have specific information about your audience to help you construct your speech for them.

(Continued)

FIGURE 5.3
Sample Audience
Questionnaire

Please take a few minutes to answer the following questions. The information gathered will be used to assist me in preparing for my persuasive speech. To maintain anonymity, do not include your name. Thank you for your assistance.

1. Please indicate your gender.   [ ] Female   [ ] Male

2. Do you live on or off campus?   [ ] On campus   [ ] Off campus

3. How would you describe your current state of health?
   [ ] Very healthy   [ ] Healthy   [ ] Neutral   [ ] Unhealthy   [ ] Very unhealthy

4. How would you describe your eating habits?
   [ ] Very healthy   [ ] Healthy   [ ] Neutral   [ ] Unhealthy   [ ] Very unhealthy

5. I believe that eating animals is unethical.
   [ ] Strongly disagree   [ ] Disagree   [ ] Neutral   [ ] Agree   [ ] Strongly agree

6. Would you consider changing your eating habits if it would improve your health?   [ ] Yes   [ ] Maybe   [ ] No

7. A vegetarian diet is a healthy diet.   [ ] Agree   [ ] Neutral   [ ] Disagree

8. Are you a vegetarian?   [ ] Yes   [ ] No

9. What do you think are the benefits of a vegetarian diet? (*Please explain your answer.*)

10. What do you think are the drawbacks of a vegetarian diet? (*Please explain your answer.*)

Interpret a Questionnaire

Before he conducted his survey (shown in Figure 5.3), James had planned to persuade his audience to become vegetarians by arguing that eating meat supports and sustains poor treatment of animals. After compiling and analyzing his classmates' responses, James discovered that only two students believed that eating animals is unethical; however, twenty said they would consider changing their eating habits if it would improve their health. James used this information to adapt his speech to his audience. Instead of focusing on the ethical issue of eating meat, he emphasized the health benefits of a vegetarian diet. Because a slight majority had listed the lack of protein as a drawback of a vegetarian diet, James explained how protein-rich foods such as beans and tofu could ensure proper nutrition. Next he outlined some simple steps for selecting tasty vegetarian foods. Because three-fourths of the class lived on campus, he provided several menu selections available in the dining halls and fast-food venues on campus. James's hard work paid off. He delivered a speech that was adapted to his specific audience, and his classmates were impressed that he made the effort to include them in his speech.

Audience Attention

First, you must be aware of the audience's *attention* or interest. Do their eye contact, posture, and other body language indicate that they are concentrating on you and your message? Are there physical distractions in the speech setting that are competing with you for the audience's attention? Do you seem to have the audience's attention throughout some parts of the speech, only to lose it during other parts? If you are concentrating on your message and on your listeners rather than on how you sound and look, you will know the answers to these questions.

If you detect a lapse of audience attention during your speech, how can you recapture it? You could address some of your listeners by name or make a connection between your speech and another one that the audience has already heard. You can also recapture your audience's attention with statements such as "The most important point to remember is. . . ." You may also be able simply to change some aspect of your delivery: speaking more loudly or softly, for example, or moving from the lectern for part of the speech so that you are closer to the audience. Any change in your established pattern of delivery will likely rekindle audience attention and interest. In addition, changing your usual style of delivery may be essential to overcome the distractions of a stuffy room, a noisy heater, or the coughs and other audience noise.

Speakers should assess listeners' responses as they speak and adjust their delivery accordingly.

Audience Understanding

A second characteristic of your audience that you must try to assess is their *understanding* or comprehension of your message. If you have ever produced a false laugh when you didn't really understand a joke, you know how difficult it is to fake comprehension. No matter how hard most of us try to cover up a lack of understanding, something about our voices or our bodies signals to others that we didn't really get it.

Of course, your audience may not try to hide their incomprehension. Members may deliberately tell you with puzzled expressions and other nonverbal cues that they are confused. The worst thing a speaker can do under such circumstances is to continue as if there were no problems. Clarifying something for the audience may be as simple as repeating or rephrasing the problem statement. If a particular word seems to be the source of confusion, defining the word or displaying it may solve the problem.

Audience Evaluation

The third component of audience analysis during the speech is your listeners' *evaluation* of you and your message. Sensitive speakers attuned to their audiences are able to gauge the reactions of those listeners. Do members of the audience seem to agree with what you are saying? Do they approve of the suggestions you are making? Answers to these questions are particularly important when you are seeking to persuade your audience.

ETHICAL DECISIONS

Ghosting 101

Listening to a speaker, we usually expect to hear the authentic thoughts of that individual. That seems to be a basic principle of the speaker-audience contract. Yet politicians often do not write the speeches they deliver. Instead they rely on speechwriters, sometimes called "ghostwriters." Journalist Ari Posner laments this tradition, observing, "If college or high school students relied on ghosts the way most public figures do, they'd be expelled on charges of plagiarism."[13] Is the practice of ghostwriting in politics ethical? What are the benefits and drawbacks of politicians' relying on speechwriters? Is it ever ethical for these leaders to deliver speeches they did not write? If so, what principles of audience analysis should guide the use of these speeches?

Sometimes the answer to such questions will be no. You may be delivering bad news or taking what you know will be an unpopular stand on an issue. Having the audience disagree with the content of your message doesn't necessarily mean that your speech has been a failure. Simply knowing that many listeners agree or disagree with you at the end of a persuasive speech shows that you are an audience-centered speaker.

◖ Analyze Your Audience *after* the Speech

Too often, speakers assume that the speech-making process concludes as you utter your final statement and walk to your seat. However, your influence on audience members can continue for some time. We encourage you to add one additional step: *postspeech analysis*. Part of this step should be self-reflection as you analyze your performance. Did you accomplish what you hoped you would? What do you sense were the strongest aspects of your speech? What were the weakest? How would you rate the content, organization, and delivery of the speech? How can you improve these aspects of your next speech?

Your answers to these questions provide subjective evaluation of your speech efforts. You may be much more critical than your listeners were because only you know how you planned to deliver the speech. For that reason, you should also consider your audience's assessment of your speech content, organization, and delivery.

In this class, that information may come from oral or written critiques from your peers or from comments some of them give you after class. If you give a good speech on an interesting topic, one pleasant reward is having audience members ask questions. The tone and content of those questions will tell you a great deal about how the audience received your message. You will also receive helpful suggestions from your instructor. If you expect to improve as a public speaker, pay attention to the feedback from all your listeners and act on the comments that are particularly relevant.

◖ SUMMARY

Recognize the Value of Audience Diversity

- Your challenge as a speaker is to recognize how your listeners differ from one another and to understand, respect, and adapt to this diversity as you develop and deliver your speeches.

Analyze Your Audience *before* the Speech

- Before the speech, a speaker should consider audience demographics, audience psychographics, and audience needs. Information you gather about these characteristics can help you select a topic and then develop and support it for a particular group of listeners.
- Demographics refer to characteristics of the audience, such as age, gender, ethnicity, education, religion, economic status, and group membership.
- Psychographics is a term for audience psychology and how listeners' thoughts influence their actions. Four key components of audience psychology are values, beliefs, attitudes, and behaviors.

- *Maslow's hierarchy* of needs is a useful tool for analyzing audience motivation by ranking five human needs in terms of their predominance: physiological needs, safety needs, love and belongingness needs, esteem needs, and self-actualization needs.
- Speakers should analyze specific speaking situations by considering the type, disposition, and size of the audience; the occasion and physical environment for the speech; and when the speech is given.
- Gathering information about your audience can be formal or informal. You can observe their behaviors or you can administer a questionnaire and analyze its results.

Analyze Your Audience *during* the Speech

- During a speech, the speaker should pay attention to listeners' attention, comprehension, and evaluation of the speech.

Analyze Your Audience *after* the Speech

- After delivering the speech, a speaker should continue to analyze the audience for signals about their evaluation of the message. Anyone who is serious about improving public speaking must be aware of and act on audience feedback after a speech.

● EXERCISES

1. **Practice Critique.** Select a prepared speech from a published source or electronic database, or use a speech in Appendix B assigned by your instructor. Study the speech to discern how the speaker adapted, or failed to adapt, the message to the audience. Discuss and give examples of how the speaker adapted to the specific audience; for example, what appeals did the speaker use to tap audience values and needs? If you were coaching the speaker, what suggestions would you offer to help her or him better adapt to the audience?

2. Prepare an audience profile of your class using the seven demographic characteristics discussed in this chapter. After you complete your analysis, answer the following questions: Which categories were easiest to determine? Which required more guesswork? Which characteristics do you think will be more important for most speeches given in this class?

3. Based on your analysis of students in this class, predict their opinions on the following questions.

   a. Is a private college education superior to a public one?

   b. What should be the minimum legal age to purchase and consume alcoholic beverages?

   c. Does your college or university place too much emphasis on athletics?

   d. Do social fraternities and sororities do more harm than good?

   After you make your predictions, poll the class to determine their responses to these questions. Were your predictions fairly accurate? Were you surprised at some of the answers? What factors caused you to predict as you did?

4. Select several topics that on first glance appear to be of interest primarily to people of one particular age group, gender, economic status, and so on—for example, the Lamaze method of childbirth, sports and male bonding, and expensive wines. Discuss how speakers could justify these topics as important to a broader audience.

5. Listen to a broadcast debate or discussion on a controversial issue. You can usually find heated discussions on the *PBS NewsHour* and Sunday morning network talk shows. Discuss the differences in positions based on the values supporting each person's arguments.

6. Using the information presented in the "Theory Into Practice" feature in this chapter, construct an audience questionnaire pertaining to the topic of an upcoming speech. Distribute it to your classmates, and then collect, compile, and interpret the results. Write an audience profile based on the results.

Selecting Your Speech Topic

6

- **Generate Ideas**
  Self-Generated Topics
  Audience-Generated Topics
  Occasion-Generated Topics
  Theory Into Practice: Visual
    Brainstorming
  Research-Generated Topics

- **Select Your Topic**

- **Focus Your Topic**

- **Determine Your General Purpose**
  Speeches to Inform
  Speeches to Persuade
  Speeches to Entertain

- **Formulate Your Specific Purpose**

- **Word Your Thesis Statement**

After studying this chapter, you should be able to

1. Understand and apply four approaches to generate speech topics.

2. Use visual brainstorming to focus your topic.

3. Identify your general purpose for speaking.

4. Construct your specific purpose statement.

5. Word your thesis statement.

If I write what you know,
I bore you; if I write what
I know, I bore myself;
therefore, I write what
I don't know.

—Robert Duncan[1]

You can't have good ideas if
you don't have a lot of ideas.

—Linus Pauling

The successful writer begins with a blank sheet of paper or a clear computer screen. The successful director begins with an empty stage. To achieve a finished product—a book or a play—both must go through several complicated steps. Directors must study the literary form, understand its dynamics, research the script, generate ideas, focus and organize those ideas, and then translate them into performance. In so doing, they give the finished product their individual signatures. Writers follow a similar process to complete a project.

As a public speaker, you are both author *and* director, and you seek to fill two voids: a blank sheet of paper and an empty space before an audience. However, before you can exercise your artistry with language, your persistence as a researcher, or any other talents you possess, you must have a topic. Selecting that topic with your audience, your own interests, and your speaking occasion in mind provides your first opportunity to exercise the creativity that will make the speech uniquely yours.

Choosing an excellent speech topic involves several steps, as shown in Figure 6.1. You should (1) generate a list of possible topics, (2) select a topic, (3) focus the topic, (4) determine your general purpose, (5) formulate your specific purpose, and (6) word your thesis statement.

◖ Generate Ideas

brainstorming
Noncritical free association to generate as many ideas as possible in a short time.

The first step in the process of selecting a speech topic is **brainstorming**. This requires you to use the critical thinking skill of *generating*, discussed in Chapter 1. With this technique, you list all the ideas that come to mind without evaluating or censoring any of them. Too often, a speaker spends insufficient time generating a list of potential topics. Yet, as Dr. Pauling suggests, in order to select a good topic, you must generate many topics. As a rule, the larger your list of possible topics, the better the topic you will finally select. Remember, do not evaluate or criticize your list as you brainstorm. What may seem silly to you at first can turn out to be an unusual speech subject with a lot of potential to interest your audience.

Angelita brainstormed topics for her informative speech by listing her interests and activities. She had played the saxophone in her high school band, so she decided to inform her classmates how to play the saxophone. When she shared this idea with her instructor, however, the teacher cautioned her that such a goal was probably unrealistic within the 5- to 7-minute time limits. Hadn't it taken her years to learn how to play the sax? Still interested in this topic area, Angelita consulted encyclopedias and found that this hybrid instrument was popular in military and American jazz bands. She began researching military bands and found the topic fascinating.

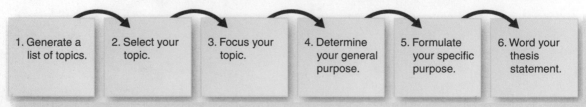

1. Generate a list of topics. 2. Select your topic. 3. Focus your topic. 4. Determine your general purpose. 5. Formulate your specific purpose. 6. Word your thesis statement.

FIGURE 6.1
The Steps in Choosing a Topic for a Speech

She learned that in the early 1600s, when European nations began to create standing armies, those troops needed to march together. Composers wrote marches for this purpose. Military bands played at outdoor celebrations and demonstrations, requiring instruments, such as the saxophone, that were louder than many string instruments. What began as a speech on how to play the saxophone eventually became a very interesting speech on the history of military bands. The topic expanded Angelita's knowledge and also taught her listeners something new.

You can turn brainstorming into productive work toward your speech by asking and answering four questions:

1. What topics interest *you*?
2. What topics interest your *listeners*?
3. What topics develop from the *occasion*?
4. What topics develop from your *research*?

Your answers will help you devise a list of many topics from which you can select the most appropriate.

> There is no such thing as a boring subject. . . . [W]hether it's the plastics industry or the mating habits of a certain insect, you will always find that there are people out there who have devoted their entire lives to the subject. . . . Well, if it can fascinate one person, then you can extract a kind of enthusiasm from that person and transfer it to others out there.
>
> —Ted Koppel

Self-Generated Topics

Self-generated topics come from you—your memory, your notes, your interests, and your experiences. Jot down your hobbies, your favorite courses, books you have read, your pet peeves, names of people who intrigue you, and issues and events that excite you. What are your likes and dislikes? On what topics do you consider yourself knowledgeable? Review your list and beside each item write possible speech topics. If you are irritated by people who are late, you could inform your audience about why people procrastinate or about how to set and meet goals. If you are nearing graduation and have been reading books on how to land your first job, a speech on the dos and don'ts for the employment interview may be fitting.

Self-generated topics may also include subjects you *need* to know. If, for example, you expect to travel soon, you may find yourself riding in taxis, staying in hotels, and dining in restaurants. Are you familiar with tipping etiquette for cabdrivers, baggage carriers, and wait staff? Researching and delivering a speech on tipping will serve your needs and be interesting and informative for your listeners.

Consider the following topics generated by our students, using only their personal interests and knowledge:

self-generated topics
Speech subjects based on the speaker's interests, experiences, and knowledge.

Thinking about your own hobbies and interests is one way to brainstorm for speech topics.

Black history in textbooks	Rappelling
Cyberbullying	Shopping addiction
Deaf culture	Study-abroad programs
Great Barrier Reef	Walker, Alice
Photograph restoration	Wilderness therapy

Use what you know as a starting point in your selection process. Don't worry that you don't know enough about each topic at this stage to construct a speech. What is important is that you have a list of topics that interest you. Because these topics come from *your* knowledge, experience, and interests, your commitment to them is usually strong. Your interest and knowledge will motivate you in preparing your speech. In addition, your enthusiasm for your topic will enliven and enhance your speech delivery.

Self-generated topics can provide you with interesting ideas, but they can also pose some difficulties. One potential pitfall is the use of overly technical language and jargon. If your topic is technical, be especially attentive to the language you choose to convey your meaning. Remember that your speech on any technical topic will lose its intended impact if you fail to define key terms clearly for listeners less knowledgeable about the subject. You will create semantic distractions, one of those major obstacles to listening that we discussed in Chapter 4.

A second potential problem with self-generated topics is a lack of objectivity about the subject. Researching your subject is a process of discovery. When you begin with rigid preconceptions, you may disregard important information that doesn't match your preconceived ideas. To avoid limiting your thinking about a subject, gather some good supporting data before you commit yourself to a specific focus for your topic.

Lack of objectivity about a self-generated topic can take a second form: excessive devotion to the subject. You may choose an interest or a hobby that is a passion of yours. You are enthusiastic about the topic, you already have a wealth of information on it, and doing further research will seem more like a pleasure than a chore. What could possibly go wrong?

"The audience will love this topic," you think. Be careful. Your audience may not share your enthusiasm for aardvarks or restoring Studebaker cars. Your interest in a topic is just one criterion in the selection process. For most speech topics, you must work to generate audience interest. Your audience may not initially share your enthusiasm for aardvarks (or Bob Marley or the history of fireworks or optical illusions), but if you *work* at it, you can *make* them interested.

In addition, be prepared to listen openly to others' speeches. Remember that ethical listeners do not prejudge either a speaker or that speaker's ideas. Granted, some topics seem so narrow or so offbeat that you think, "Who cares?" But a speech might be terrific if the speaker is genuinely interested and has lots of vivid supporting material. Much of the value of education is that it makes you a better (smarter, happier, more well-rounded) person. Some information is intrinsically rewarding and just plain fun to know. Don't dismiss information presented in a speech (or anywhere else) just because it won't make you more money, save you time, or whiten your teeth.

Audience-Generated Topics

audience-generated topics
Speech subjects geared to the interests and needs of a speaker's listeners.

Pursuing **audience-generated topics** is a second way of coming up with speech ideas. What topics interest or seem important to your listeners? If you are asked to speak to a group, it may be because you have expertise in a particular area. In such a case, the topic may be predetermined.

On other occasions, such as in this class, you may not be provided with topics or topic areas. How can you find out what interests your classmates? There are three ways to do this. First, *ask them*. Ask some of your classmates in casual conversation about topics they would like to hear discussed. If possible, you could use a questionnaire to seek topic suggestions from the entire class. When you speak to an organization, ask the person who contacted you about issues of probable interest to the group.

Second, *listen and read*. What do your classmates discuss before and after class? Articles in your campus or local paper or letters to the editor may suggest issues of concern. Finally, *use the audience analysis strategies* detailed in Chapter 5 to generate topics. Consider your listeners' needs. If your class is composed primarily of students just entering college, a speech on the history of your school could be interesting, informative, and appropriate. If your class is composed primarily of seniors, a speech on establishing a good credit history may be timely.

If you are lucky enough to be in a class with a lot of student diversity, you can tap your classmates' lack of knowledge about various topics. Our student Zoljargal surely had this in mind when she chose to inform her listeners about the clothing and cultural festivals of her native Mongolia. Darla, an avid hunter, informed her classmates how to gauge the age of a white-tailed deer. (That speech is in Appendix B.) Blessie, whose parents live in India, informed her classmates how to make a refreshing summertime drink, a mango lassi. Chantal, a doctor and director of the blood bank at an area university hospital, gave her classmates an insider's view of liver transplants. Another student older than her classmates informed them about great blues musician Robert Johnson and his influence on guitarists like Eric Clapton. In each case, these students chose topics by considering both their own knowledge and their peers' lack of knowledge.

You may even find that most of your audience seems to feel one way about a controversial topic while you take the opposite view. You could use this situation to develop and deliver a persuasive speech aimed at winning support for your view of the issue.

The following topics were generated by our students using an audience-centered approach:

Cell phone etiquette	Interviews, dressing for
Cult movie classics	Mnemonic (memory) devices
Ethereal music	Online scholarship searches
Facebook	Road rage
Hazing on college campuses	Test anxiety, how to control
Horror movies, appeal of	TV reality shows, impact of

Occasion-Generated Topics

Occasion-generated topics are a third source of speech subjects. When and where a speech is given may guide you in selecting a topic. A speech on setting goals may benefit your classmates more at the beginning of the term, whereas a speech on stress management may have more impact before exams.

EXPLORING ONLINE

Festivals

www.festivals.com

Speaking near a particularly festive occasion or wondering whether you are? This site is a worldwide guide to festivals. You can search by keyword, location, or subject, or just browse by clicking on art, community, heritage, historical, music, and other topic categories.

EXPLORING ONLINE

Occasion-Generated Topics

www.scopesys.com/anyday

www.brainyhistory.com

With just a few mouse clicks, you can search for occasion-generated speech topics at the AnyDay-In-History and Brainy History websites. These pages let you discover events that occurred on any day and month you select. They also list names of people who were born or who died on that date, along with holidays and religious observances.

occasion-generated topics
Speech subjects derived from particular circumstances, seasons, holidays, or life events.

Rituals and special occasions can provide excellent speech topics. Here guests arrive in traditional dress for a Lapp wedding.

If you are scheduled to speak near a holiday, a speech on the history or importance of that holiday may be appropriate. A speech on a culture different from yours would seem appropriately timed during Diversity Awareness Month, while Banned Books Week may be the ideal occasion for a speech on censorship. To find examples of other holidays, look at your calendar or examine different calendars at a bookstore or online. Specialty calendars or almanacs list unusual but interesting holidays, birth dates of notable and notorious people, or anniversaries of important historical events.

Our students generated the following topics as they focused on different occasions for speeches:

Bat mitzvah (female equivalent of bar mitzvah)

Dia de los Muertos

Dragon Boat Festival in Hong Kong

Festival of the Lanterns

Golden Globe Awards, history of

Hurricanes

Ramadan

Songkran (Water Festival in Thailand)

An occasion-generated topic can often lead you to other interesting topics. Drought conditions in your area may make you consider the subjects of cloud seeding or desalting seawater. Memorial Day may get you thinking about the Wall, the Vietnam Veterans Memorial in Washington, D.C. You may then decide to focus on the competition for the design of the monument; on Maya Lin, whose design won that competition; or on the aesthetics of the wall and the stirring effect it has on visitors.

THEORY INTO PRACTICE

 Visual Brainstorming

Visual brainstorming uses free association around a key word or idea to reveal possible topic areas or clusters of subtopics for speeches. As your thinking suggests additional topics, you will probably be surprised at the web of possible speech topics you have created just from your brainstorming.

Take out a sheet of paper and write your topic in the center. Now, think of how you could divide and narrow that topic. It may help you to think of some generic categories such as "causes," "types," and "solutions" that are appropriate to numerous topics.

As you think of subtopics, draw a line from the center in any direction and write the narrower topic.

Figure 6.2 illustrates the end product of a visual brainstorming exercise on the topic of humor. Certainly you can add to this list, but in just a few minutes our students were able to provide many options for focusing the subject of humor. Some of these, such as the benefits of laughter therapy, are excellent topics that probably would not have occurred to you without this brainstorming exercise.

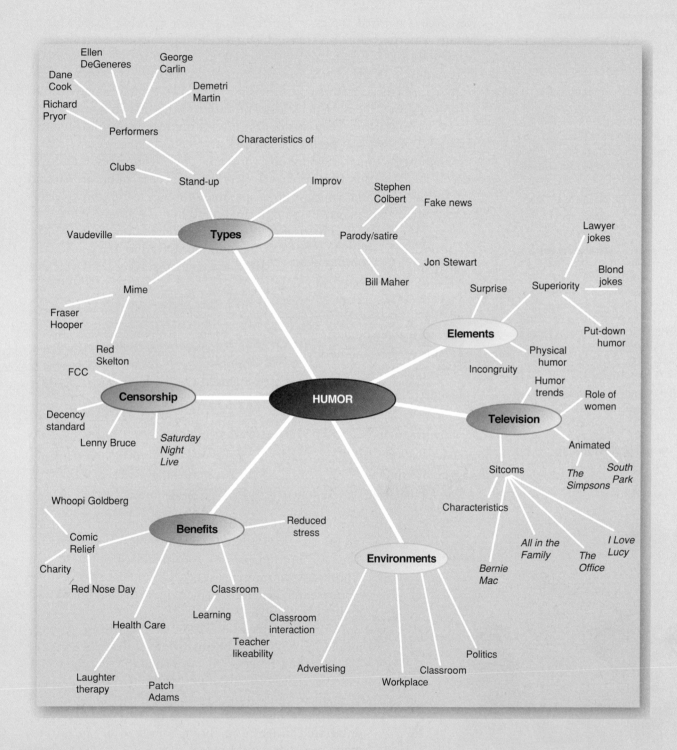

FIGURE 6.2
Visual Brainstorming

Research-Generated Topics

EXPLORING ONLINE

Researching World News

www.onlinenewspapers.com

This site provides access to thousands of newspapers throughout the world. U.S. newspapers are searchable by name and state. Especially helpful is the list of "Top 50 Newspapers for the United States."

research-generated topics
Speech subjects discovered by investigating a variety of sources.

Research-generated topics, a fourth strategy for sparking speech ideas, require you to explore a variety of sources. First, you could consult some of the databases and indexes we list in Chapter 7. Look at the list of subjects and jot down those that interest you. A second research strategy is to browse through magazines or journals in your library, at a local newsstand, or online. Just remember that this exploration is the first step in selecting a speech topic. Don't leap at the first interesting topic you find. A third research strategy is to peruse book titles at a good bookstore or library, noting those that interest you. Bookstores are convenient places to discover speech topics because the books are grouped by general subject area and are arranged to catch your eye. By using these three research tools—databases and indexes, magazines and journals, and books—you may not only discover a speech topic but also locate your first source of information.

Consider the following topics. You might not have thought of these on your own, but all have the potential to be excellent subjects and all came from resources our students found.

Autism spectrum disorder	Nuclear medicine, future of
Breed-specific dog legislation	Obsessive-compulsive disorder
Color's effects on moods	Pet therapy
Cryobiology	Racial profiling
Fingerprints, features of	Sustainable design
Forensic hypnosis	Ties, history of
Identity theft	Tomb sculptures
Marley, Bob	Tuskegee Airmen, the
Nanotechnology	White lung disease
Noh (ancient Japanese) theater	Yoga techniques

visual brainstorming
Informal written outline achieved by free associating around a key word or idea.

It is important that you use all four of these strategies to generate possible speech topics. If you end the topic-generation process too quickly, you limit your options. A substantive list of self-, audience-, occasion-, and research-generated topics gives you maximum flexibility in selecting a subject.

Once you have selected your topic area, use a technique called **visual brainstorming**, described in the "Theory Into Practice" box on pages 96–97, to investigate the range of possibilities within that topic.

You can incorporate research into your discovery and focusing process. For example, if you are really interested in learning about humor in organizations, your research would reveal that there are workshops that teach how to use humor to improve workplace

Visual brainstorming enables speakers to divide topic areas into narrower, more focused speech topics.

morale, enthusiasm, and productivity. There are humor coaches and even a Humor University. Any one or a combination of these subjects could provide the topic for an excellent speech.

Select Your Topic

Once you have generated a list of possible speech topics, you must select the best one. Determining what is best is an individual choice; neither a classmate nor a friend can make that choice. However, asking and answering four questions will help you make a wise decision.

First, *Am I interested in the topic?* The more enthusiastic you are about a topic, the more time and attention you will give to researching, constructing, and practicing your speech. When you enjoy learning, you learn better. As a result, speakers motivated by their topics are almost always more productive than those bored with their topics.

Second, *Is the topic of interest or importance to my audience?* This question helps you avoid choosing a topic that you love but that your audience will never care about. Speech making is easier when your listeners are potentially interested in what you have to say. When your audience is more attentive and receptive, you can relax and make your delivery livelier. Sometimes topics seem to be of little initial interest to an audience but may, nevertheless, be important to their personal or career success. As long as you can demonstrate the importance and relevance of the topic, you will motivate your audience to listen.

A third question you should answer in selecting your speech topic is, *Am I likely to find sufficient authoritative supporting material in the time allotted for researching and developing the speech?* Unless your topic is truly offbeat or brand new, and assuming that you haven't waited until the last minute to start your research, your answer to this question will likely be yes. Even if the topic is so new that it has not yet appeared in articles, chances are good that you'll find information about it on the Internet. In that case, you'll have to judge whether the information you find is authoritative. If your best sources are articles or transcripts that you have to purchase and download, can you afford the expense? If your top sources are items you have to order through interlibrary loan or purchase by mail order, do you have the time? You obviously cannot wait until the week before your speech to order such items. Remember the adage that if something can go wrong, it will. Build some flexibility into your schedule so that you can adapt to any crisis that may arise.

> **KEY POINTS**
>
> **Questions to Guide Topic Selection**
>
> 1. Does this topic interest me?
> 2. Is this topic interesting or important to my listeners?
> 3. Am I likely to find sufficient supporting materials on this topic?
> 4. Do I know enough about this topic to start researching it and to interpret what I discover?

SPEAKING WITH CONFIDENCE

Topic selection can be the most important step of the entire speech. When I brainstormed for topics, I would think about things that really interested me. If you choose something that doesn't excite you, you won't be comfortable speaking about it. Interesting topics, however, make the whole experience more enjoyable. During the past election, I really wanted my classmates to register and vote, so I made this my purpose for speaking. My commitment to this topic motivated me to research and practice my speech. I wanted my audience to share my enthusiasm for voting. Public speaking doesn't have to be boring. You can be creative and have fun with your topic. Knowing that I had something important and interesting for my classmates to hear made me feel more confident delivering my speech.

Bryan McClure
Virginia Tech University

Finally, consider the question, *Do I understand the topic enough to undertake and interpret my research?* A speaker arguing the merits of a tax increase must understand economics in order to assess research data. When you inform the audience about music therapy, you need some understanding of psychological treatment techniques and procedures. A speaker may misinterpret the reasons that violent crime in the United States is higher than in Japan if he or she does not understand Japanese culture. You don't need to know much about your topic as you begin your research, but you must know enough to be able to make sense of the data you discover.

◖ Focus Your Topic

After you select your topic, you must focus it. Even though we have heard students speak on topics that were too narrow, this is rare. More commonly, students tackle topics that are too broad, leaving too little time to develop their ideas. The result is a speech that is more surface than substance.

When you decide on a topic area, use visual brainstorming to determine some of its divisions, or subtopics. The subject of "loneliness," for example, could focus on any of the following topics: the causes of loneliness, the relationship between loneliness and depression, loneliness and the elderly, characteristics of the lonely person, the differences between being alone and being lonely, or strategies for coping with loneliness. You could never discuss all these topics meaningfully in a short speech. Narrowing the scope of your inquiry gives direction to your research and provides sufficient time to support the limited ideas you will present to your audience.

Visual brainstorming is an excellent way of focusing your topic. A second way is through research. The more you read about your subject, the more likely you will discover its many aspects. Some may be too narrow for a complete speech, but others may be suitable for an entire speech or may be combined to form a speech.

For a 5- to 7-minute informative speech assignment, Rob developed three main points in the body of his speech on baseball:

I. The history of baseball
II. How the game is played
III. The uniform and equipment used

As you might guess, Rob found himself rushing through the speech, and he still did not finish it within the time limit. Each of his main points was too broad; he needed to focus his topic further.

Rob could have concentrated on the history of baseball and focused on a specific era that interested him. For example, he could have discussed baseball during the Civil War or focused on the all-black leagues from the 1920s until the integration of baseball during the 1950s. Rob could have spoken about the All-American Girls Professional Baseball League formed during World War II when many professional baseball players were being drafted. Each of these topics would probably have interested and informed Rob's listeners. Notice, too, that each of these narrower

Speaking about a topic you feel strongly about can motivate your desire to speak and energize your delivery.

topics places baseball in a sociological context. Rob's speech on the sport's history could have become a lesson about a particular period of American social history, having appeal even for listeners with no interest in baseball.

● Determine Your General Purpose

Broadly speaking, a speech may have one of three purposes: to inform, to persuade, or to entertain. The general purpose of your speech defines your relationship with the audience. You play the role of mentor when you provide information. You are an advocate when you seek to change beliefs, attitudes, values, or behaviors through a persuasive speech. Your speech to entertain is meant to amuse your audience. As the entertainer, you set a mood to relax your audience using your delivery style, tone, and content.

You may sometimes find it difficult to distinguish these purposes. Because information may affect both what we believe and how we act, the distinction between informative speaking and persuasive speaking is sometimes blurred. A speech meant to entertain is frequently persuasive because it may make a serious point through the use of humor. Despite the overlap between these general purposes, you must be secure about your primary purpose any time you speak in public. A closer look at the objectives and intended outcomes of each general purpose will help you distinguish them.

Speeches to Inform

The objective of a **speech to inform** is to impart knowledge to an audience. You convey this information in an objective and unbiased manner. Your goal is not to alter the listeners' attitudes or behaviors but to facilitate their understanding of your subject and their ability to retain this new information. We discuss the speech to inform in greater detail in Chapter 15. A speech on any of the following topics could be informative:

speech to inform
A speech designed to convey new or useful information in a balanced, objective way.

Art therapy   Middle child syndrome
Billboard liberation   Muralist movement in Mexican art
Hispanic film industry   Poetry slams
History of science-fiction movies   Scottish culture

Speeches to Persuade

speech to persuade
A speech designed to influence listeners' beliefs or actions.

speech to convince
A persuasive speech designed to influence audience beliefs and attitudes rather than behaviors.

speech to actuate
A persuasive speech designed to influence audience behaviors.

A **speech to persuade** seeks to influence either beliefs or actions. The former, sometimes called a **speech to convince**, focuses on audience beliefs and attitudes. A speech designed to persuade audience members to embrace a belief stops short of advocating specific action. Without suggesting a plan of action, a speaker may argue, for example, that polygraph testing is unreliable. Another speaker may try to convince listeners that women have been neglected in medical research without offering a plan to solve the problem.

A speech designed to persuade to action, or a **speech to actuate**, attempts to change not only the listeners' beliefs and attitudes but also their behavior. A speech to actuate could move the audience to boycott a controversial art exhibit, to contribute money to a charity, or to urge their elected officials to increase funding for women's health research. In each case, the speaker's goal would be first to intensify or alter the audience's beliefs and then to show how easy and beneficial taking action could be. We discuss persuasive speeches in Chapters 16 and 17.

Speeches to Entertain

speech to entertain
A speech designed to make a point through the creative, organized use of humorous supporting materials.

A third general purpose of a speech is to entertain. A speech to entertain differs from speaking to entertain. *Speaking to entertain* includes humorous monologues, stand-up comedy routines, and storytelling, for example. When you tell your friends jokes or recount a humorous anecdote, you are trying to entertain them. You are probably not trying to develop a key point in an organized, methodical way.

A **speech to entertain** is more formal than speaking to entertain because it is more highly organized and its development is more detailed. Speeches to entertain are often delivered on occasions when people are in a festive mood, such as after a banquet or as part of an awards ceremony. We discuss the speech to entertain in more detail in Chapter 18, "Speaking on Special Occasions." Remember that all speeches, including those to entertain, should develop a central thought through organized supporting material and ideas. Though the ideas in a speech to entertain will be illustrated and highlighted by humor, a mere collection of jokes does not qualify as a speech. We agree with the communication scholars who contend that a speech to entertain is actually either a speech to inform or a speech to persuade, usually the latter.

◗ Formulate Your Specific Purpose

general purpose
The broad goal of a speech, such as to inform, to persuade, or to entertain.

When you are asked to state the **general purpose** of your speech, you will respond with two words from among the following: *to inform*, *to persuade* (or *to convince* or *to actuate*), or *to entertain*. When asked to state

ETHICAL DECISIONS

Should Instructors Censor?

A colleague of ours had a long and distinguished career teaching communication. After class one day, she returned to her office visibly upset. When questioned by her colleagues, she said one of her students had announced in his speech introduction that his purpose was to teach the class how to make a lethal poison using ingredients people already had in their homes or could easily buy. "Moreover," she said, "to stress the significance of the topic, he assured us that this substance would kill any living animal, certainly even the heaviest human being."

"What did you do?" her colleagues asked. "I sat there thinking of the rash of teenage suicides, even copycat suicides, we've been hearing about lately, and all the other meanness in the world," she replied. "I wrestled with my conscience for about a minute and a half, and then, for the first time since I started teaching, I interrupted a speaker. I told the student I didn't think we needed to hear this information, and asked him to be seated."

Was this teacher's action justified? Did she violate the student's freedom of speech? Placed in that teacher's position, what would you have done?

your specific purpose, however, you must be more descriptive. A **specific purpose** statement has three parts.

First, you begin with the speech's general purpose, stated as an infinitive—for example, "to convince." Second, you name the individuals to whom the speech is addressed, usually phrased simply as "the audience" or "my listeners." Third, you state what you want your speech to accomplish. What should the audience know, believe, or do as a result of your speech? You may want to establish the belief that alcoholism is hereditary. In this case, then, your complete specific purpose statement would be "To convince the audience that alcoholism is hereditary." Other examples of specific purpose statements are:

- To inform the audience on how to communicate constructive criticism
- To inform the audience on celebrity worship syndrome
- To convince the audience that text messaging while driving is a serious problem
- To convince the audience that publically funded professional sports stadiums are a misuse of taxpayers' money
- To move the audience to draft and sign a living will
- To move the audience to spend their spring break building a house for Habitat for Humanity

specific purpose
A statement of the general purpose of the speech, the speaker's intended audience, and the limited goal or outcome.

KEY POINTS

To Develop Your Specific Purpose Statement

1. State your general purpose.
2. Name your intended audience.
3. State the goal of your speech.

Word Your Thesis Statement

A **thesis statement** presents the speech's central idea in one sentence. The thesis statement of a persuasive speech on compulsory national service could be, "Compulsory national service would benefit the nation by promoting the national spirit, the national defense, and the national welfare." This statement is the speech's central idea, a proposition the speaker will support with evidence and argument.

Notice that the process of topic selection has, up to this point, enabled you to focus your subject on something specific and manageable. You are now ready to construct a *working thesis*: a statement that, based on your current research and thinking, summarizes what you will say in your

thesis statement
A one-sentence synopsis of a speaker's message.

speech.[2] Although a thesis statement is designed to keep you focused, it may change as you continue to work on and develop your speech. It gives you a handle on your subject and, as you begin to develop your key ideas, will help you determine whether you can support your thesis statement. In organizing the body of the speech, you may realize that your ideas are not balanced or that two of your main points should be collapsed into one. As you research your speech, you may discover additional ideas that are more important than some you had planned to present. That was the experience of our student who spoke on compulsory national service.

Stuart was developing a persuasive speech advocating a system of compulsory national service (CNS). As he began his research, he planned to focus only on the national security that compulsory military service would provide. His working thesis was, "Compulsory national service would benefit the nation by ensuring its military readiness." Yet his research quickly revealed many other benefits of CNS: domestic conservation and recycling, rural health care, and in-home assistance to the elderly.

By the time he had completed his research, Stuart had broadened the focus of his speech and felt he had developed a much stronger case for instituting a CNS program. When he delivered his speech, he presented three main arguments:

    I. CNS would promote the national spirit.
   II. CNS would promote the national defense.
 III. CNS would promote the national welfare.

Stuart revised his thesis statement to reflect his new organization. In Chapter 10 you will learn how a clearly worded thesis statement will help you construct the preview statement of your speech introduction and the summary step of your conclusion.

The following examples illustrate how you can narrow a topic's focus from a general area to the speech's thesis statement.

Topic Area: Sculpture

Topic: Works by Andy Goldsworthy

General Purpose: To inform

Specific Purpose: To inform the audience about Andy Goldsworthy's sculptures

Thesis Statement: Andy Goldsworthy sculpts wood, ice, and leaves into intricate works in their natural settings.

Topic Area: Police oversight

Topic: Mandatory videotaping of police

General Purpose: To persuade

Specific Purpose: To persuade the audience that all police actions in police stations should be videotaped

Thesis Statement: Videotaping all police actions in police stations will deter police misconduct, discourage false charges of police misconduct, and restore public confidence in police work.

SUMMARY

Generate Ideas

- To choose an appropriate speech topic, brainstorm a list of subjects focused around your interests, the needs and interests of your audience, the occasion for your speech, or the subjects you have researched.

Select Your Topic

- Select your topic after assessing your interest in it; the topic's interest or importance to your audience; your ability to find adequate, quality supporting materials on the topic in the time you have; and your ability to understand what your research reveals about the topic.

Focus Your Topic

- Focus or narrow the topic you've selected by using visual brainstorming and initial research on the subject.

Determine Your General Purpose

- Understand the general purpose of your speech—to inform, to persuade, or to entertain—before moving on to the details of your speech.

Formulate Your Specific Purpose

- Decide what you want your speech to accomplish: what the audience should know, believe, or do as a result of hearing your speech.

Word Your Thesis Statement

- State the central purpose of the speech in one sentence.

EXERCISES

1. Choose a broad subject area and write that topic in the middle of a blank page. Use visual brainstorming to generate a list of specific topics. Continue diagramming as long as it is productive. Review the topics you generated and identify the best ones for a speech in this class.

2. Using the following topic areas, narrow each subject and write a specific purpose statement for an informative speech and a persuasive speech on each topic.
   a. Attractiveness
   b. Class attendance policies
   c. Career planning
   d. Natural disasters
   e. Social media

3. Using what you know (or think you know) about your classmates, generate a list of ten topics you think would interest or be important to them. Share these topics and solicit feedback. How could you generate interest in the topics that were viewed less favorably? What did this activity tell you about how class members perceive each other?

4. Select and read a speech in Appendix B. Determine its general purpose. Word its specific purpose and thesis statement.

Researching Your Topic

7

After studying this chapter, you should be able to

1. Apply the four questions you must ask when developing a research plan.

2. Access and evaluate information you find on the Internet.

3. Use databases and indexes to access information in print, on video, and online.

4. Prepare for and conduct interviews.

5. Determine what information to collect and how to record it.

6. Identify the appropriate time to conclude your research.

7. Compare and contrast APA and MLA styles.

Knowledge is of two kinds.
We know a subject ourselves,
or we know where we can
find information upon it.

—Samuel Johnson

research
The process of gathering evidence and arguments to understand, develop, and explain a speech topic.

If, for example, you are heading toward pharmacy school, studying architecture, or majoring in economics, by the time you graduate you will know about the history of pharmacology or architecture or will understand the interplay of forces that drive an economy. In Samuel Johnson's words, you will "know a subject." Yet your field of study will not stop evolving and developing on the day that you graduate from college. Learning information that becomes a part of who you are makes up only a fragment of your education. An "educated" college graduate in the twenty-first century "will no longer be defined as someone who has absorbed a certain body of factual information, but as one who knows how to find, evaluate, and apply needed information."[1]

Research scholar Patricia Breivik summarizes the snowballing accumulation of information as follows:

> The sum total of humankind's knowledge doubled from 1750–1900. It doubled again from 1900–1950. Again from 1960–1965. It has been estimated that the sum of humankind's knowledge has doubled at least once every 5 years since then.
> . . . It has been further projected that by the year 2020, knowledge will double every 73 days![2]

In light of these circumstances, it is surely smarter to think of being educated as *knowing how to access and analyze* information, rather than *possessing* it.

For public speakers, the challenge is selecting from the wide range of available data the information most appropriate for their speeches. That requires knowing how to research—how to scratch "an intellectual itch."[3]

Research is the gathering of evidence and arguments you will need to understand, develop, and explain your subject. Research is not one step of the speech construction process but should occur throughout that process. You have already seen in Chapter 6 how research can help you select your topic. Once you have chosen a topic, additional research helps you focus and determine your specific purpose. As you begin to construct the body of your speech, you may need to develop some of your ideas further with additional research. Your research continues even as you consult dictionaries, thesauruses, and collections of quotations to help you word your ideas before delivering your speech.

Research is not necessarily a linear process. As a result, you may be exercising and developing a number of critical thinking skills simultaneously. If you have some experience with or knowledge about the topic area, you'll begin by *remembering* and assessing your knowledge. You'll be *information gathering* as you formulate questions you want your research to answer and then collect your data. You will use your *generating* skills to develop new lines of inquiry based on the research you have completed. Throughout the process, you'll be *analyzing* whether and how information from different sources fits together. As you connect items of information, you'll be *integrating* and *organizing*. As you measure the quality and quantity of your research results, you'll be *evaluating*. And because you will often find more information than you can use, your entire research process will have you *focusing* your speech topic more and more narrowly.

The following five-step sequence can help you generate excellent ideas and supporting material regardless of your speech topic.

1. Assess your knowledge of the topic.
2. Develop your research plan.
3. Collect your information.
4. Record your information.
5. Conclude your search.

> If education is what you're left with after you forget everything you've learned, information literacy must be the best skill for . . . growing up in the information age.
>
> —Jenny Sinclair[4]

Assess Your Knowledge

The first question you should ask and answer is, "What do I know that will help me develop my topic?" Your memory has been shaped by what you have read, heard, observed, and experienced. Use that knowledge as a starting point for researching your topic.

For example, a student who worked as a plainclothes security guard for a major department store drew from personal experience in his speech on detecting and apprehending shoplifters. A student who helped her father administer polygraph tests chose as her speech topic the use and misuse of lie detectors. These speakers used their knowledge and experiences as starting points for their research. Both students developed and delivered interesting speeches.

Upon being asked how long he had prepared for one of his speeches, Winston Churchill replied, "For forty years." Communication scholars Robert Jeffrey and Owen Peterson observe, "In a sense, a speaker spends his or her entire life preparing for a speech. Everything we have learned and experienced, as well as the attitudes we have developed, shapes and influences our speech."[5] Your knowledge and experience give you a head start in selecting and developing your topic.

Develop Your Research Plan

Your research plan begins as you answer several questions:

1. What information do I need?
2. Where am I most likely to find it?
3. How can I obtain this information?
4. How will time constraints affect my research options?

The first step in the research process is to assess what you already know about your topic.

Your topic and specific purpose clearly help determine your research plan. If you see a news report about deep brain stimulation to treat Parkinson's disease and you select that topic for a speech, you will obviously need to find and read medical materials. If you decide to speak about the

EXPLORING ONLINE

Online Research Today

www.researchbuzz.org/r/

If you're serious about staying current with Internet research developments, check out ResearchBuzz, produced by Web expert Tara Calishain. At this URL, you can subscribe to a free weekly email newsletter detailing "almost daily updates on search engines, new data managing software, browser technology," and the newest sources of information.

upcoming Oktoberfest celebration or about a new sleep clinic in your area, your best information may not be in print. You will likely spend time talking to people.

Don't assume that all relevant information for a given topic can be found online. Different topics demand different research strategies and a good research plan accounts for these variations. Keep a running list of what you need and where you can obtain it.

You should also prepare a timetable for constructing your speech. If you will be speaking in 2 weeks, you still have time for a lot of online or library research. You may even have time to arrange, conduct, and transcribe interviews. However, 2 weeks is not enough time to order transcripts or recordings and be assured they will arrive by surface mail in time to integrate them into your speech.

◖ Collect Your Information

Once you have developed a research plan, begin collecting the information you need to understand and develop your topic.

The Internet

URL (uniform resource locator)
The standard notation for each Internet website's unique address, often beginning with "http://," "https://," or "www."

search engine
A tool for locating information on the Internet by matching items in a search string with pages that the engine indexes.

If you research primarily online, be aware that **URLs** (**uniform resource locators**)—or website addresses and the routes you use to retrieve information—can change quickly. Thus, we recommend downloading or printing copies of any Web-based information you intend to use in your research. In addition, you may find more information than you can possibly read in the time you have for research. Some 25 percent of college students report finding too much information.[6] How can you determine which information is most useful and which resources are reliable?

While there are a multitude of **search engines** available to conduct online research, such as Yahoo!, Bing, and Ask.com, the most widely used is Google. In 2010, Google held 71.6 percent of the market share for search engines, with Yahoo! a distant second at 14.3 percent. One feature that makes Google such an attractive search engine for students is its Google Scholar search engine, which specifically targets academic resources. This allows students to use a search engine with which they are likely very familiar without connecting to school library databases. Academic opinions regarding Google Scholar appear to be split, however, with one librarian arguing that Google Scholar "is easy to use, saves them [students] time in writing essays, and links to a vast amount of information,"[7] while one university website cautions students, "It is in no way comprehensive, and has limited field searching."[8] We encourage students, therefore, to use Google Scholar as a jumping-off point into a topic, realizing that the most effective next step is to move to academic search engines for full-text and better searching and indexing capabilities. Academic search engines filter the extraneous from the essential and are a key component of serious, targeted searches. Here are three academic search engines and their addresses:

Academic Index	www.academicindex.net
INFOMINE	infomine.ucr.edu
ipl2	www.ipl.org

Information from academic search engines is more focused and of higher quality than what you may find via general search engines such as Google, Bing, Yahoo!, and others.

The **deep Web**, sometimes called the *invisible Web*, contains public, government, corporate, and private information. The "content in the deep web is massive—approximately 500 times greater than that visible to conventional search engines—with much higher quality throughout."[9] Deep Web information often exists in topic-specific databases as multimedia files, graphic files, or in portable document file (PDF) formats.[10] "A full 95 percent of the deep Web is publicly accessible information—not subject to fees or subscriptions."[11] In contrast to static web pages, information in the deep Web is "dynamic"—that is, the pages form only in response to specific research queries.

To explore the deep Web, try either of the following portals:

- CompletePlanet (http://aip.completeplanet.com): "70,000 searchable databases and specialty search engines."
- IncyWincy: The Invisible Web Search Engine (www.incywincy.com): "hundreds of thousands of search engines indexed and searchable."

A popular Internet resource is *Wikipedia*. Once students have selected their speech topics, many turn first to this Web-based, free online encyclopedia with access to more than 3.7 million articles in English and many more in other languages. A recent study revealed that students often begin and end their research at *Wikipedia*.[12] One criticism of *Wikipedia* is that it operates on an "openly editable" model, allowing virtually anyone with an Internet connection to write or edit its entries. This presents problems for students seeking accurate and timely information on their topics. *Wikipedia* acknowledges its limitations as a trusted academic source, stating "Students

EXPLORING ONLINE

Maximizing Your Search

www.alamo.edu/sac/library/faculty/deosdade/searchen.htm

Librarian John Deosdade of the San Antonio College Learning Resource Center has compiled a superb collection called "Search Engines for Quality Web Sites." From this one site you can find and use hundreds of academic and subject-specific search engines that cover everything from Academy Awards to zoos.

deep Web

Huge databases of Internet information posted by public, government, corporate, and private agencies and available only by specific queries.

ETHICAL DECISIONS

The Privacy of Public Information

Jeanine was researching a speech on the problem of child sexual abuse. While she was searching the Internet, she discovered a series of forums devoted to this topic, including a newsgroup and a live chat group. She found thought-provoking and useful discussions in the newsgroup, but the chat discussions were the most intimate and revealing. There, sexual abuse survivors described their memories of actual incidents and talked about how the trauma affected their adult lives.

Jeanine took notes on some of the most remarkable stories and decided to recount one in her speech to add drama. Is this a legitimate way for Jeanine to use her research? Should stories told on the Internet be considered public property, available for anyone to write or speak about? Should Jeanine try to find out whether the speaker would feel comfortable about having the story repeated in a speech? Should she try to verify that the story is true?

THEORY INTO PRACTICE

TIP   Evaluating Internet Resources

When you use the Internet for research, your critical thinking skills may get not just exercise but a full-tilt workout. This is because anything can get posted and quickly communicated to millions of people online. For all the convenience it provides, the Internet forces us to evaluate information. What should you ask about sites that you are considering using to support your speech? Basic questions you may need to ask are listed below.

Purpose

- What seems to be the purpose of this site? To provide information? To promote a position? To sell a product or service?
- What type of site is it? aviation (.aero), commercial (.com, .coop, or .biz), educational (.edu), governmental (.gov), information business (.info), military (.mil), nonprofit organization (.org), personal (.name), or professional (.pro)?
- Is there an institution, agency, or organization identified as sponsoring the site?
- Does the site contain advertising? If so, by whom?
- Who is the author's apparent audience, as reflected by the vocabulary, writing style, and point of view? Students? Professionals? Consumers? Advocates?

Expertise

- Is the author, compiler, or webmaster identified?
- Does the author have verifiable expertise on the subject?
- Are the author's or compiler's credentials provided?
- Do you know the author's occupation?
- Do you know the author's educational background?
- Do you know the author's organizational affiliation?
- Does the author provide contact information, such as an email address, phone number, or mailing address?

- If the site is a compilation, are sources and authors of individual works identified?
- If the site is a research project, does the author explain data, methodology, and interpretation of results? Does the author refer to other works? Provide notes?
- If links to other works are provided, are they evaluated in any way?
- Is the site linked to another site that you already trust or value?
- Are sources or viewpoints missing that you would expect to be present?
- What does this page offer that you could not find elsewhere?

Objectivity

- Does the author's affiliation with an organization, institution, or agency suggest a bias?
- Does the site's sponsorship by an organization or institution suggest an inherent bias?
- Are opposing views represented or acknowledged?
- Are editorial comments or opinions clearly distinguished from facts?

Accuracy

- Can you corroborate the facts using other Internet or library resources (reference works or indexed publications)?
- Is the site inward-focused (providing links only to other parts of the site) or outward-focused (providing links to other websites)?
- Has the author expended the effort to write well, with correct spelling and proper grammar?
- Does the author solicit corrections or updates by email?

Timeliness

- Is the date of publication important to this subject matter?
- Can you tell when the site was created?
- Can you tell when the site was last updated?
- Are links from this site current or broken?[13]

should never use information in *Wikipedia* (or any other online encyclopedia) for formal purposes (such as school essays) until they have verified and evaluated the information based on external sources."[14]

Most *Wikipedia* entries end with notes that identify primary sources of information on the term in question. Be sure to check these sources for any entry you research; in addition carefully check its information against other, better vetted, more academically accepted sources. If you make *Wikipedia* your initial source as you research, make sure that it is not the *only* source you consult.

See the Theory Into Practice feature for recommendations about evaluating information you find on the Internet.

College libraries provide computer terminals to help you research your speech topic. With a few keystrokes you can unlock a wealth of information in and beyond the library.

Library Resources

Though it's certainly not necessary to start your research from your school library these days, that facility contains many resources that you won't find anywhere else. One of the most helpful sources of information is the library staff, particularly reference librarians. A good reference librarian can (1) acquaint you with the library's services and holdings, (2) guide you to particularly helpful sources of information, and (3) instruct you in the use of library equipment. He or she can also guide you to your library's areas of strength, making your research more efficient and your life easier.

database
A huge collection of information arranged for quick retrieval by computer using key words stipulated by a researcher.

Magazines and Journals

Magazine and journal articles are probably the most common source of information for student speeches. With more than 218,000 magazines from which to choose, however, it's helpful to use an index to filter useful from extraneous information.[15] Hundreds of excellent indexes of periodicals exist, and many standard indexes are now available online. These can guide you as you focus your search even more.

The true monster trucks of academic research in periodicals today are full-text **databases**. These databases are powerful because each gives you access to articles in hundreds or even thousands of periodicals and scholarly journals. You can print useful articles or email them to another address. Moreover, if you are a registered college or university student, you have already paid to use these research tools from any computer with Internet access through your school's library website.

Some of the general full-text databases likely available to you are listed in Table 7.1. In addition, specialized indexes exist for almost every academic field. Subject-specific computer databases include *Alternative Health Watch*, *Biography in Context*, *Contemporary Women's Issues*, and so on.

Good libraries are deeply conservative in that they guard and archive the culture's diverse wisdom and beauty, its vast oddities and amusements. But they're also radical bastions of mutual aid. In a "knowledge society" where information carries an ever-steeper price, where the rich get wealthier and the poor have less, libraries are one of the few ways still available for many to educate themselves— ideally, an American right.

—Chris Dodge[16]

TABLE **7.1**   Subscription Databases and Indexes

DATABASE/INDEX	WHAT IT PROVIDES
Academic Search Premier	Full-text database of more than 4,600 academic journals, 3,900 of which are peer-reviewed. See the subject and journal databases designed specifically for colleges and universities.
AccuNet/AP Multimedia Archive	Searchable archive of Associated Press (AP) photos, charts, logos, maps, and other graphics produced for AP, nineteenth century to present. Brief stories accompany most photos 48 hours after publication.
CQ Researcher	Articles on all sides of current, controversial issues. Archive of past articles is searchable by key word, dates, and other criteria.
ERIC	An online digital library with access to more than 1.3 million bibliographic records of journal articles and other education-related materials.
General OneFile	Approximately 80 million articles and records in refereed journals, general interest magazines, newspapers, National Public Radio transcripts, subject-specific collections, and other sources. From this website you can also access InfoTrac Student Edition with access to nearly 9 million articles, updated daily.
LexisNexis Academic	International business, health, law, news, and reference articles, most in full text. Updated continually.
Opposing Viewpoints in Context	Pro–con essays on controversial topics. Includes text of reference works, magazine and newspaper articles, websites, statistics, and images.
Project Muse	Full-text articles from nearly 500 scholarly journals published by scholarly presses in the arts, humanities, social sciences, and mathematics.
Science in Context	Full-text articles from more than 200 magazines, scholarly journals, and links to quality websites. Includes biographies, experiment descriptions, pictures, illustrations, topic overviews, and news of recent scientific discoveries.

Similar print indexes in the reference section of your library may include titles such as *Education Index*, *Hispanic American Periodicals Index*, and *Music Index*. Because these indexes are so specialized, the periodicals and journals they lead you to will likely be written for a specific audience; they may use jargon and technical language familiar only to people in that field. Even if you understand these articles easily, you may have to simplify their language and ideas for a more diverse listening audience.

If you have particular magazines and journals in mind at any stage in your research, you can also check the online versions of these publications. Some magazines provide the full text of current issues along with searchable archives; others give you only sample articles and subscription information. Though browsing individual magazines is not an efficient use of limited research time, searchable online periodicals can be useful.

Newspapers

Newspapers offer abundant information—local, national, or international in scope. Large newspapers such as the *New York Times*, the *Washington Post*, and the *Christian Science Monitor* have been indexed individually in the past. The computer index to the *New York Times*, for example, provides full text of all articles from 1851 to the present.

Today, however, your campus library is more likely to subscribe to powerful databases such as *LexisNexis Academic* that contain full-text newspaper articles in addition to other sources.

Most newspapers now have websites and provide indexes to their own archives. If you have selected a localized topic, you may want to research specific newspapers using a search engine like Google. If you're unsure about newspaper titles, *Newslink* (http://newslink.org) lets you browse lists of U.S. newspapers by state as well as world newspapers by continent or country; click on links to specific papers.

Government Documents

The most prolific publisher in the United States is the federal government. Much of our bureaucracy is devoted to collecting, cataloguing, and disseminating information. Luckily, most of what's available is accessible online: presidential speeches and transcripts of press conferences, pending legislation, contact information for senators and representatives, agency reports, and ordering information for documents not available online in full text. Online, you can take a virtual tour of the White House, listen to audio files of unedited arguments before the Supreme Court, and see digital photographs of historical documents. In short, almost every federal agency has a website.

Your library probably subscribes to several government databases, among them *LexisNexis Government Periodicals Index*, *Federal Register Online*, and *MarciveWeb DOCS*. Searchable by keyword, these databases save you time.

With just a couple of Web addresses, you can access virtually any area of the government. The Library of Congress maintains *THOMAS: Legislative Information on the Internet* at http://thomas.loc.gov. The Government Printing Office maintains a list of links to government information products at www.access.gpo.gov. At those two sites, you can get any information you need from the legislative, executive, or judicial branches of the government.

Books

Books are excellent sources of information. Because they are longer than magazine and newspaper articles, books allow authors to discuss topics in greater depth and often provide an index to key ideas and a list of sources consulted. However, if your speech topic requires the most up-to-date data you can find, information in magazines and newspapers may be more current and accessible than what you find in books. Despite this limitation, books can be an integral part of your research plan. Today the online catalog in most academic libraries permits you to search by subject, title, author, and key word.

EXPLORING ONLINE

Government Documents
http://thomas.loc.gov

This Library of Congress website helps you obtain information from the U.S. Congress. You can download House and Senate committee reports, summaries of bills being considered and notes about their status, copies of laws enacted, and even remarks recorded in the *Congressional Record*. Click on "Help" and access the FAQ (frequently asked questions) feature that provides information that will enhance your research skills as well as instructions on how to conduct a search in *THOMAS*, download a bill or committee report, contact your representative or senators, and cite the documents.

There are times when I think that the ideal library is composed solely of reference books. They are like understanding friends—always ready to meet your mood, always ready to change the subject when you have had enough of this or that.

—J. Donald Adams

Additionally, books you need may be available as ebooks that you can access—"check out"—in your choice of formats after you establish a library account. On the Internet, full-text literary works are also well represented by Literature Online (*LION*, http://lion.chadwyck.com), a searchable subscription database of more than 350,000 British and American works.

Reference Works

Reference works, usually available for use only in the library, include many types of collections to aid you in your research. Many reference works are now online. Whether you are using hard-copy versions in the library, accessing databases through your library's web page, or logging on to the Internet, a few of the reference works you will find most helpful are dictionaries, encyclopedias, almanacs, and books of quotations.

Dictionaries. Dictionaries help you clarify the meanings, spellings, and pronunciations of words. Many good general dictionaries exist, and you undoubtedly use these regularly. A number of more specialized dictionaries covering a wide range of topic areas are also available such as *The Dictionary of Advertising*, *A Dictionary of Slang*, and *A Dictionary of Statistical Terms*.

Thousands of dictionaries exist on the Internet. At YourDictionary.com alone, you can access 2,500 dictionaries, glossaries, and thesauruses in more than 300 languages. Examining some of these dictionaries may generate topics for future speeches and provide information about your current topic.

Encyclopedias. You might have used general encyclopedias, such as *Encyclopedia Americana*, *Encyclopædia Britannica*, and *World Book*, to prepare reports and papers. These multivolume sets of books exist today along with their electronic counterparts, such as *Britannica Online*, the *Video Encyclopedia of the 20th Century*, and the *Encyberpedia*. Some electronic encyclopedias, such as *Encyclopedia.com*, are free. Unless you access others from a library or through a library website, however, you may have to pay for a subscription.

Either in print or as electronic files, encyclopedias organize information on many branches of knowledge. However, you may be less familiar with encyclopedias that focus on specific bodies of knowledge, such as: *Encyclopedia of American Shipwrecks*, *Encyclopedia of Black America*, *Encyclopedia of Jazz*, and *Encyclopedia of Medical History*. Consult your college librarian for advice about subject-specific encyclopedias in the library or online.

Almanacs. Almanacs contain a wide range of specific and statistical information about topics such as education, politics, sports, entertainment, and significant events of a particular year. Almanacs are excellent sources when you need specific facts and background information. What is the exact wording of the Second Amendment of the United States Constitution? In what year was the first *Star Wars* movie released? A good almanac answers these questions and many others. If you selected the history of space flights as your speech topic, an almanac would be a ready reference for the dates, duration, and description of those flights.

General almanacs on library reference shelves include the *World Almanac and Book of Facts*, *Information Please Almanac*, the *New York Times*

Almanac, the *New York Public Library Reference*, and the heavily used *Statistical Abstract of the United States*. Specialized print almanacs cover a wide range of subjects, as illustrated by these examples: *Almanac for Computers*, *Almanac for American Politics*, *Almanac of Higher Education*, and *Almanac of World Crime*.

Today you can find a host of searchable almanacs online. At the online version of the *Information Please Almanac* (www.infoplease.com) you will find more than 50 almanacs grouped into categories ranging from sports to business to science and technology.

Books of Quotations. Captivating quotations, both serious and funny, can enliven the language of your speech. As we noted earlier, they are particularly appropriate in speech introductions and conclusions. Quoting another person also adds authority to your comments and strengthens the development of your ideas. Fortunately, many excellent books of quotations are available in bookstores, libraries, and online. At www.bartleby.com/100, you can access the long-popular *Bartlett's Familiar Quotations*, *The Columbia World of Quotations*, and *Simpson's Contemporary Quotations*. Some other books of quotations include *The American Heritage Dictionary of American Quotations*, *Collins Quotation Finder*, *Famous Last Words*, *Respectfully Quoted: A Dictionary of Quotations from the Library of Congress*, and *The Quotable Woman*. In books or online, collections of quotations are organized alphabetically by author or subject, with handy indexes or search functions.

Television and Radio

You can find ideas for excellent speech topics and materials to support them among the investigative reports on television and radio. Many programs provide transcripts for purchase, with ordering information given at the show's conclusion. Networks now offer transcripts of many of these shows for print or download at their websites. If you require older transcripts, you may have to order them online for a fee. Many National Public Radio programs are archived for downloading as podcasts after their initial broadcast. Some examples of television and radio websites include:

Network	URL
ABC	http://abcnews.go.com
CBS	www.cbsnews.com
CNN	www.cnn.com
CNN/SI	http://sportsillustrated.cnn.com
C-SPAN	www.c-span.org
Fox News	www.foxnews.com
MSNBC	www.msnbc.msn.com
NBC	www.nbc.com/News_&_Sports
NPR	www.npr.org
PBS	www.pbs.org

Your library or DVD rental service may have copies of special televised broadcasts such as the PBS documentary series *Lewis and Clark* or Martin

Scorsese's *Bob Dylan: No Direction Home*. Through informational videos, you can research topics such as military battles, McCarthyism, and space exploration, to name just a few. Commercial videos (as well as websites) can take you on tours of museums such as the Louvre or the Museum of Modern Art and of distant places such as Australia and Italy. Instructional DVDs can teach you how to garden, refinish furniture, and make a sales presentation.

Interviews

Depending on your topic, an interview may be the best source of firsthand information. Today you can interview people by email, instant messaging, Skype; by telephone; or in person. The personal interview can aid you in four ways. First, if published sources are inaccessible, the personal interview may be your only option. The topic you have chosen may be so recent that sufficient information is not yet in print or online. Your topic may also be so localized as to receive little or no coverage by area media.

A second advantage of the personal interview is that it permits you to adapt your topic to your specific audience. Take, for example, the topic of recycling. If you interview the director of your school's physical plant to find out how much trash custodians collect and dispose of each day, you give your speech a personal touch. You could take your speech one step further by figuring out how much your college could contribute to resource conservation. This shows your audience how this topic affects them directly. You will grab their attention.

Third, personal interviews provide opportunities for you to secure expert evaluation of your research and suggestions for further study. The experts you interview may challenge some of your assumptions or data. If this happens, encourage their feedback and don't get defensive. Knowing all the angles can only help you give a more thoughtful speech. Near the end of your interview, ask your interviewee to suggest additional sources that will help you better research and understand your topic.

Open questions, such as those that begin with the phrase, "How do you feel about," can elicit more substantive responses from interviewees than do closed yes or no questions.

Finally, personal interviews can enhance your image as a speaker. Listeners are usually impressed that you went beyond library research in preparing your message for them.

Prepare for the Interview. Once you decide to conduct a personal interview, you must take several steps in preparation. First, determine whom you want to interview. Your interviewee should be someone who is both knowledgeable on the topic and willing to speak with you.

Second, decide on the format for the interview. Will you conduct it face to face, by phone, or online? A face-to-face interview may give you the most information. People tend to open up more when they interact both verbally and nonverbally. In a face-to-face interview, you can listen to what the interviewee says and also observe the nonverbal messages. A phone interview is another possibility when you cannot travel to the expert. A third option, conducting an interview by email or Skype, has both advantages and disadvantages. The email interview is time-consuming because you must prepare a set of questions, send it to the interviewee, and wait for a response. It has the added disadvantage of not allowing for immediate follow-up questions. If something needs clarification, you must email another question. An interview via Skype or by instant messaging eliminates this time lag. However, the email interview often results in more thoughtful and better worded responses than face-to-face, telephone, or Skype interviews.

The third preparation step is to schedule the interview. When requesting an interview, identify yourself and the topic on which you seek information. Let the person know how you intend to use that information, the amount of time needed for the interview, and any recording procedures you plan to use. Some people may object to being quoted or recorded. You are likely to discover that most people you seek to interview are flattered that you selected them as experts and are therefore happy to cooperate.

Fourth, research the interviewee beforehand. Obviously, your selection of this person suggests that you already know something about him or her. In addition, read any articles the interviewee has published on your topic. This enables you to conduct the interview efficiently. You won't ask questions that the person has already answered in print, and your prior reading may prompt some specific questions on points you would like clarified. Also, your research will show that you are prepared. The interviewee will take you and the interview seriously.

Fifth, prepare a list of questions. Always have more questions than you think you will be able to ask, just in case you are mistaken. Mark those that are most important to your research, and ask them first. You may want to have some closed and some open questions, as Joel did when he interviewed a professor of recreation for his speech on how American adults spend their leisure time. *Closed questions* are those that can be answered with a yes, a no, or a short answer. For example, Joel asked, "Do American adults have more time for leisure activities today than they did a generation ago?" and "How many hours per week does the typical adult spend watching TV?" The first question can be answered by a yes or a no, the second with a specific figure.

Open questions invite longer answers and can produce a great deal of information. Joel asked this open question: "How do American adults typically spend their leisure time?" When you ask open questions, sit back and prepare to listen for a while! The less time you have for the interview, the fewer open questions you should ask. Open questions can sometimes result in rambling responses. At times, the interviewee's rambling will trigger questions you would not have thought of otherwise. Joel was surprised to learn that American adults spend approximately 2 hours a week in adult education, a venture he had not included on his initial list of adult leisure activities. When you and the interviewee have plenty of time, and particularly if you are recording the interview, open questions can provide the richest information.

Conduct the Interview. The face-to-face interview is an excellent opportunity to practice your interpersonal communication skills. Specifically, you should follow these guidelines. First, introduce yourself when you arrive, thank the person for giving you time, and restate the purpose of the interview.

Second, conduct the interview in a professional manner. Make sure you arrive appropriately dressed. Be ready and able to set up and handle

KEY POINTS

To Prepare for the Interview

1. Determine whom you want to interview.
2. Decide the format for the interview.
3. Schedule the interview.
4. Research the person to be interviewed.
5. Prepare a list of questions.

If we would have knowledge, we must get a world of new questions.

—Susanne K. Langer

any recording equipment with a minimum of distractions. Try to relax the interviewee—establish a professional atmosphere, pose questions that are clear and direct, listen actively, take notes efficiently, and follow up when necessary. You should control the interview without appearing to be pushy or abrupt.

Third, when you have finished, thank the person again for the interview.

Follow up on the Interview. After the interview, review your notes or listen to your recording. Do this as soon as possible after the interview, when your memory is still fresh. If you are unclear about something that was said, do not use that information in your speech. You should contact your interviewee to clarify the point if you think it will be important to the audience's understanding of the topic.

As a matter of courtesy, you should write to the people you interviewed, thanking them for the time and help they gave you. You may even want to send them a copy of your finished speech if it is in manuscript form.

Calling, Writing, and Emailing for Information

Some years ago, one of our students, Lindahl, wanted to develop an informative speech on the savant syndrome. This was before the film *Rain Man* made many people aware of the special talents and disabilities of savants. Lindahl had seen a *60 Minutes* segment on the syndrome but could not find recent written sources. Her best source, she said, was an article from a 3-year-old issue of *Time*. Others might have abandoned their research and switched topics, but Lindahl followed a hunch that paid off.

The *Time* article quoted several university professors and medical doctors who were engaged in ongoing research on the savant syndrome. Lindahl got their office telephone numbers and called these experts to see if they could recommend new sources she had been unable to locate. The people Lindahl called were flattered by her attention and complimented her perseverance as a researcher. One psychologist mailed her a photocopy of a book chapter she had written on the savant syndrome; a medical doctor mailed Lindahl a packet of journal articles, including the galleys of an article he was about to publish; a psychology professor sent her a tape of savants playing piano concertos they had heard for the first time only moments before. In short, Lindahl received a gold mine of new, expert research as a result of her few long-distance calls. If Lindahl were to conduct such a search today, she might find that email would be a quicker, if less personal, way to contact the experts.

Lindahl was lucky that she began her research more than a month before her speech was due. To take advantage of pamphlets and brochures available through the mail, you will need to plan ahead as well. Thousands of organizations, such as the American Cancer Society and United Way, publish their own informational literature. Political parties and lobbying groups prepare position papers on issues that affect them. Corporations distribute annual reports to their stockholders and will share these on request. You can write to or email any of these organizations. Most post contact information on their websites. You can locate URLs for companies or groups through search indexes available online. Another source that can be helpful is the three-volume *Encyclopedia of Associations*. Each volume lists names, addresses, telephone numbers, email addresses, and URLs for websites, along with descriptions of the organizations. If time permits and research warrants, writing, calling, or emailing these organizations to request information can add relevant primary research to your speech.

Record Your Information

Once you have located information, you must determine what to record and how to record it.

What to Record

When in doubt, record more rather than less. Certainly, it is possible to copy too much information. If you find everything potentially important, your topic probably needs better focus. Without some focus, you risk becoming so bogged down in research that you leave little time for organizing and practicing your speech.

On the other hand, if you are too selective, you may be inefficient. As you research your speech, you may shift your topic focus; hence the supporting material you previously thought was irrelevant becomes important. Discarding unnecessary information is easier than trying to remember a source, retracing your steps, hoping that the information is still on the library shelves or that the Internet source is still live, and then recording that information.

How to Record Information

Traditional advice to researchers is to record each piece of information on a separate notecard, along with the source citation, as you find it. With this strategy, you can organize your speech visually and experiment with different structures. The disadvantage of this method is that it consumes a great deal of library time that might be better devoted to searching for other sources. In addition, much of what you record on notecards may not be used in your speech at all.

SPEAKING WITH CONFIDENCE

Once I choose my speech topic, the fun begins. Sometimes I already know the main points I want to discuss in my speech; sometimes I don't. Either way, what really builds my speech are the interesting and credible supporting materials I find in my research. Of course, it's great to have an informative source like the Internet at my fingertips, but it's also rewarding to use sources that may take a little more time and effort to obtain.

A trip to the library, for example, puts books, newspapers, and journals at my disposal. My favorite source, however, is the interview. Asking an expert specific questions on my topic can yield lots of really helpful information. The person can also direct me to other sources I may not know about. The more I research, the more confident I feel about my speech. So, remember to start researching early and use all the resources available.

Matthew Williams
Radford University

EXPLORING ONLINE

Citing Electronic Sources

www.apastyle.org/apa-style-
help.aspx

www.mla.org

Both the American Psycho-
logical Association and the
Modern Language Asso-
ciation have websites with
examples of documentation
that may be more current
than those in their published
style manuals. The APA site
features its guidelines for
citing information from the
Internet. The only Internet
guidelines for MLA documentation authorized by the MLA
are available at its site.

Another, more common, method is to photocopy material at the library or to print articles you find online. Later, you can review, evaluate, and select from the materials. However, be aware that photocopies or printed articles may lull you into a false sense of accomplishment. What you have copied may turn out to be of little or no use. To avoid this problem, read your material before or very shortly after copying it. Don't wait until the night before your speech to read the information you have been collecting.

Also, remember to note your sources on the copied pages. If the web page URL does not appear as a header or footer on printed pages, be sure to note it. Copy the page or pages containing publication information for each book you use. If you follow these simple directions, photocopying and printing have two additional advantages over using notecards. First, you may not know what you want to use from an article at the time you first find it. If the focus of your speech changes, a different part of the article may become important (indeed, sometimes your research forces you to refocus the speech topic). Second, if you are quoting from or paraphrasing one specific part of an article, you may need to check to make sure that you are not quoting the author out of context. Having a copy of the book chapter, the journal article, or the encyclopedia entry lets you check the context and the accuracy of your quotation.

TABLE **APA Form for Some Common Types of Sources**

Book	Turkle, S. (2011). *Alone together: Why we expect more from tech-nology and less from each other.* New York, NY: Basic Books.
Edited book	Farthing, S. (Ed.). (2010). *Art: From cave painting to street art.* New York, NY: Universe.
Article in weekly magazine	Adee, S. (2011, July 2). Your seventh sense. *New Scientist, 211,* 32–36.
Article in monthly magazine	Warner, J. (2011, May). The humor code. *Wired,* 140–145.
Newspaper article	Stelter, B. (2011, June 21). Upending anonymity, these days the Web unmasks everyone. *New York Times,* pp. A1, A3.
Article in online magazine	Wood, G. (2011, April). Secret fears of the super-rich. *The Atlantic.* Retrieved from http://theatlantic.com/magazine/print/2011/04/secret-fears-of-the-super-rich/8419/
Article in online newspaper	Perlman, D. (2011, July 11). Gray whales—a study in cli-mate change survival. *San Francisco Chronicle.* Retrieved from http://www.sfgate.com/cgi-bin/article.cgi?f=/c/a/2011/07/10/MN0J1K7LKM.DTL
Document avail-able on university website	Osborn, A. (2011, July 7). *Studying abroad in China: A firsthand account.* Retrieved from http://www.american.edu/cas/news/amanda-osborn-boren-award.cfm
Organization website	United States Olympic Committee. (2011, July 11). USOC internships: Frequently asked questions. Retrieved from http://www.teamusa.org/jobs/usoc-internships/frequently-asked-questions
Posting to online forum	Downs, D. A. (2007, December 19). Civility and free speech on campus [Online forum comment]. Retrieved from http//:www.nas.org/nasForum.cfm

If you are gathering information from the Internet, be sure to print the pages you will need or download the information to a disk or flash drive. Remember that what appears on the Internet disappears quickly. If you do not capture it in print or store it in a file when you find it, you may have to forgo using the information in your speech. If you do not know how to create a storage file for Internet material, ask your librarian or computer lab instructor for help.

It is important to record full citations of sources you have consulted in your research in your list of works cited at the end of your speech. Most writer's handbooks recommend a particular form. Two popular forms are presented in the *Publication Manual of the American Psychological Association*, sixth edition (APA) and the *Modern Language Association Handbook for Writers of Research Papers*, seventh edition (MLA). Be sure to check with your instructor, who may prefer one of these or some other bibliographic form.

Copies of the two style manuals we just listed are probably in your library's reference section. Tables 7.2 and 7.3 compare APA and MLA

TABLE 7.3   MLA Form for Some Common Types of Sources

Book	Turkle, Sherry. *Alone Together: Why We Expect More from Technology and Less from Each Other.* New York: Basic Books, 2011. Print.
Edited book	Farthing, Stephen, ed. *Art: From Cave Painting to Street Art.* New York: Universe, 2010. Print.
Article in weekly magazine	Adee, Sally. "Your Seventh Sense." *New Scientist* 2 July 2011: 32–36. Print.
Article in monthly magazine	Warner, Joel. "The Humor Code." *Wired* May 2011: 140–145. Print.
Newspaper article	Stelter, Brian. "Upending Anonymity, These Days the Web Unmasks Everyone." *New York Times* 21 June 2011, late ed.: A1+. Print.
Article in online magazine	Wood, Graeme. "Secret Fears of the Super-Rich." *The Atlantic .com.* Atlantic Monthly Group. April 2011. Web. 10 July 2011.
Article in online newspaper	Perlman, David. "Gray Whales—a Study in Climate Change Survival." *San Francisco Chronicle.* Hearst Communications. 11 July 2011. Web. 12 July 2011.
Document available on university website	Osborn, Amanda. *Studying Abroad in China: A Firsthand Account.* American University. 7 July 2011. Web. 11 July 2011.
Organization website	United States Olympic Committee. "USOC Internships: Frequently Asked Questions." U.S. Olympic Committee, 11 July 2011. Web. 11 July 2011.
Posting to online forum	Downs, Donald A. Online posting. "Civility and Free Speech on Campus." Online posting. *NASOnline Forum.* 19 Dec. 2007. Web. 12 July 2011.

Note: MLA no longer requires URLs for most Web references. However, you should check with your instructor to see if he or she prefers that you include URLs at the end of each reference.

bibliographic styles. Whether you want to cite a segment of National Public Radio's *All Things Considered*, a stop-smoking DVD, or lecture notes you took in an anthropology class, the most recent editions of these reference books are likely to give you a pattern to follow.

◖ Conclude Your Search

As you prepare your speech, you must make choices. Your goal is to support your ideas with the most compelling evidence and arguments you can find. The more you know about your topic, the greater your flexibility in determining its content and, subsequently, its impact. This concept of choice can make your task more complex, but it will also produce a more effective speech.

There is a limit, however, to the time you can spend researching. An important part of effective research is knowing when to stop accumulating materials and when to start using them. In his book *Finding Facts Fast*, Alden Todd provides the following guideline for research projects:

> If the last 10 percent of your planned research time has brought excellent results, you are doubtless on a productive new track and should extend the project. But if the last 25 percent of your scheduled time has brought greatly diminished results, this fact is a signal to wind up your research.[17]

Although Todd's 10/25 formula may not be wholly applicable to your researching a speech for this class, it does highlight an important issue: at some point you must stop researching and start structuring your speech.

In the next chapter, we discuss the purposes and types of supporting material. Understanding these topics will help you evaluate your research and select the best information to support the ideas of your speech.

◗ SUMMARY

Purposes of Research

- Research is the process of gathering information and evidence to understand, develop, and explain your topic. Learning to research is fundamental to mastering public speaking. Knowing your subject thoroughly greatly reduces your speech anxiety.

The Process of Research

- Thorough research of a subject involves five steps. (1) Assess your knowledge of the subject and begin to organize that knowledge.

(2) Develop a research plan for your topic. (3) Collect information from a variety of sources: magazines and journals, newspapers, government documents, books, reference works, electronic media, and interviews. (4) Record the information you consider important and useful. Be sure to record the source of the information—author, title, and publication information—using a current *reference* form. (5) Conclude your search. The quality and quantity of the information you collect will help you focus and organize the subject and will signal when you have exhausted your research efforts.

EXERCISES

1. **Practice Critique.** Suppose that the International Olympic Committee just declared public speaking to be a new event for the Olympic Games. You've been hired as a coach for the U.S. Olympic Public Speaking Team. Suppose, further, that Jennell Chu has entered her speech on flash mobs in the competition. Read the transcript of this speech in Appendix B. Then write Jennell a letter to help her develop a research plan for revising her speech. What information should remain in her speech? What information needs to be updated, clarified, or improved? Where could she search for this information?

2. Select a topic for one of your speeches; then answer the following questions:

    a. What information do I need?

    b. Where am I most likely to find this information?

    c. How can I obtain the information?

    d. How will time constraints affect my research options?

3. Using any magazine or journal index listed in this chapter, construct a bibliography of at least seven sources for an upcoming speech. Locate at least three of these articles.

4. Using a print or an online newspaper index, construct a bibliography of at least five sources for an upcoming speech. Locate at least three of these articles.

5. Which of the reference works discussed in this chapter could you consult to answer the following questions?

    a. What is the derivation of the word *boycott*?

    b. What is the per capita personal income in your state?

    c. Thomas DeCarlo Callaway is the legal name of what contemporary musician?

    d. The first Earth Day was celebrated on what date?

    e. What is the preferred pronunciation of the word *data*? In how many other ways can it be pronounced correctly?

    f. The swallows return to San Juan Capistrano on or around St. Joseph's Day. What is this date?

    g. What is the history of tiramisu?

    h. In what year and what city was the first Super Bowl played? Who won the game?

6. Using books of quotations, such as those listed in this chapter, prepare a list of at least two quotations on each of the following topics:

    a. Making a good first impression

    b. The importance of friendship

    c. The dangers of student apathy

    d. Appreciating diversity

    Bring your list to class and be prepared to discuss how you could use some of the quotations in a speech. Which would contribute to an effective introduction or conclusion? Which could be used to illustrate an idea in the body of a speech?

7. Select an expert to interview for an upcoming speech. Using suggestions in the chapter, arrange, prepare for, and conduct an interview, and follow up on it.

Supporting Your Speech

8

After studying this chapter, you should be able to

1. Identify three purposes of supporting materials.

2. Explain and develop seven types of supporting materials.

3. Apply seven guidelines to evaluate evidence.

4. Distinguish between incomplete and appropriate source citations.

> A fact in itself is nothing. It is valuable only for the idea attached to it, or for the proof which it furnishes.
>
> —Claude Bernard

The speaker began his introduction by describing his first nighttime high-tech treasure hunt. He and his friends had followed the directions provided by their inexpensive global positioning system, ending up beneath a bridge, in front of a large tree. Using the flashlights they were instructed to bring, they quickly found the trail of aluminum strips hanging in the trees and followed it until they were in a deeply wooded area. When the aluminum-foil trail ended, they found the promised container. Inside was a Swatch watch, set to the current time and running, and a small notebook and pencil. The speaker took the watch, left a similar treasure of his own, signed and dated the logbook, and replaced the lid on the container. When he used the term *geocaching* and named the website that had launched his quest, www.geocaching.com, most people in the audience were reaching for pen and paper. This speaker introduced listeners to a novel topic in a particularly vivid way. He successfully used a variety of supporting materials—narration, comparison, examples, and definition— to make his words interesting and memorable.

When you think of argument, you likely think of two people trying to persuade each other. In a real sense, however, all public speaking is argument. We should speak and accept ideas only if they are supported with sufficient evidence and reasoning. Speakers must prove what they assert in both informative and persuasive speeches. Listeners should think critically and evaluate the merits of any statement based on evidence the speaker offers for its support.

Toward the end of Chapter 3, we recommended a formula for structuring each major idea in your speech. This pattern, called the "4 S's," consists of *signposting*, *stating*, *supporting*, and *summarizing* each key idea. In this chapter, we focus on the third of these four S's: *supporting* your major ideas. You will learn more about the purposes of supporting materials, and we will discuss seven types you can use. Finally, we'll suggest ways to evaluate evidence and how to cite it to ensure that you communicate your ideas clearly, memorably, and authoritatively.

◗ Purposes of Supporting Materials

You will use supporting materials in your speech to provide specific points of reference for your audience. Effective supporting materials help you anchor your ideas in the minds of your listeners. They do so by giving your ideas clarity, vividness, and credibility.

Clarity

A sign in an Austrian ski hotel says, "Not to perambulate the corridors in the hours of repose in the boots of ascension."[1] Translation (we assume): "Don't tramp down the halls in ski boots while guests are sleeping." You have no doubt seen other examples of what happens when well-meaning people try to translate something into an unfamiliar language. Yet people can send unclear messages even in their first language. Thus we have an advertisement on a bag of chips: "You may be a winner! Details inside! No purchase necessary."

As a speaker, your first goal is to communicate clearly. *Clarity* refers to the exactness of a message. The clarity of any message you send results partly from your language, as we discuss in Chapter 12. In addition, the supporting material you choose should make your message clear. As you develop a speech, ask yourself, "Does my supporting material really explain, amplify, or illustrate the point I'm trying to make?" If it does not, disregard it and continue your search for relevant material. Clear supporting materials help listeners understand your ideas.

Vividness

Which of the following sentences makes a stronger impression?

> An online practice test program is a helpful teaching tool in the classroom.

or

> An online practice test program is a wise and genial tutor, giving immediate feedback and waiting patiently until the student masters the task at hand.

If you are typical, you chose the second sentence. The first statement seems flat, generic. The second personalizes the technology, gives it human qualities, and creates an image that remains with you for a while.

In this chapter, we use several excerpts from speeches to illustrate various types of supporting materials. Once you finish reading the chapter, you will no doubt remember some of the examples and forget others. Those you remember will be ones you found particularly vivid. *Vivid* supporting materials are striking, graphic, intense, and memorable. A major purpose of supporting materials, then, is to help your audience remember the key points in your speech. You will accomplish this best by using vivid forms of support chosen with your unique audience in mind.

Supporting materials clarify, enliven, and add credibility to your speech. When you prepare your speech, ensure accuracy by recording in complete form any quotations and definitions you plan to use.

Credibility

You gasp as you see the headline "Scientists Discover Microbial Life on Mars." Would it make a difference whether you saw this on the cover of *Scientific American* or the *National Enquirer*? Of course it would. A scientific article reviewed and selected for publication by a panel of experts is significantly more believable than an article from any weekly tabloid. **Credibility** refers to the dependability or believability of a speaker or that speaker's sources.

credibility
The believability or dependability of speakers and their sources.

Many ideas in the speeches you prepare will require simple supporting materials: short definitions, brief examples, or quick comparisons, for example. In other instances, you may present complex or controversial ideas that require several types of supporting materials. Whether your supporting materials are simple or complex, they must be accurate and their sources clearly cited if they are to reinforce your ethos or credibility. A speech with all its ideas and support taken from a single source is too limited. Using several sources to corroborate your ideas and facts can be a valuable and persuasive tool. Your main points will be more credible if you show that these ideas are shared by several experts.

You establish clarity by explaining your idea so that listeners *understand* it. You establish vividness by presenting your idea so that listeners will *remember* it. Finally, you establish credibility by presenting the idea so that listeners *believe* it. If the supporting materials in your speech make the audience understand, remember, and believe what you say, you have done a good job selecting them.

Accomplishing these goals will require you to use four critical thinking skills. *Focus* on and *evaluate* specific pieces of information and measure their quality. *Analyze* the different supporting materials to see how they fit together to clarify your message. Finally, *integrate* as you combine and restructure your information in a way that is both appropriate to your listeners and uniquely your own.

◼● Types of Supporting Materials

To help you achieve clarity, vividness, and credibility in your speaking, consider seven types of supporting materials available to you: example, definition, narration, comparison, contrast, statistics, and testimony. Keep in mind that there is no best type of support for your ideas. Select what is most appropriate to your topic, your audience, and yourself.

Example

example
A sample or illustration of a category of people, places, objects, actions, experiences, or conditions.

An **example** is a specific illustration of a category of people, places, objects, actions, experiences, or conditions. In other words, examples are specimens or representations of a general group. The sound of the word itself gives perhaps the easiest definition to remember: An *example* is a *sample* of something. Measles, mumps, and chicken pox are examples of common childhood illnesses. *Schindler's List* and *Saving Private Ryan* are examples of Steven Spielberg movies. Using examples that are familiar to listeners is an excellent way to make your points clear and memorable. This, of course, requires you to have done some good audience analysis.

Brief Examples. Brief examples are short, specific instances of the general category you are discussing. They may be used individually but are often grouped together. Notice how Jocelyn combined several brief examples early in her speech on the attractions of New York City:

> Your walking tour of midtown Manhattan could take you to places as diverse as St. Patrick's Cathedral, Rockefeller Center, and the Museum of Modern Art. Try not to gawk as you look at some of the most famous architecture in the world—the Chrysler Building, the Empire State Building, and Grand Central Station. Tired of pounding the pavement? Slip into a chair in the Algonquin Hotel's dim lobby, soak up the literary history, ring the bell on your table, and order something to drink. Hungry? You've got the world's table to choose from—everything from four-star restaurants to little holes-in-the-wall serving the best ethnic dishes: Chinese, Vietnamese, Indian, Mexican, Thai.

Extended Examples. Extended examples are lengthier and more elaborate than brief examples. They allow you to create more detailed pictures of a person, place, object, experience, or condition. Later in her speech, Jocelyn developed an extended example of one of her favorite New York City attractions:

> Beginning with my second visit to New York, one of my first stops has usually been the Museum of Modern Art. If you're like me, you'll need to give yourself at least a couple of hours here, because for a small admission price you're going to get a chance to see up close art that you've only seen before as photographs in books. Upstairs on my last visit, I saw works such as Vincent Van Gogh's *Starry Night* and Roy Lichtenstein's huge pop art paintings of comic strip panels. On a wall with a number of other paintings was a canvas so small that I almost missed it. I'm glad I didn't. It was Salvador Dali's famous surrealist work, *The Persistence of Memory*, with its melting clock and watch faces. Then over in a corner is a special room that holds only one painting. As you walk in, you see an expanse of gray carpet and several upholstered benches. One wall is glass, two others are white and bare, but the fourth one holds the three panels of Claude Monet's massive painting, *Water Lilies*.

Notice how vividly this extended example suggests a scene and re-creates an experience. But whether your examples are brief or extended, they can be of two further types: actual and hypothetical.

Actual Examples. An **actual example** is real or true. Each of the examples we've used so far is an actual example. Steven Spielberg did direct the two films listed. The Chrysler Building and the Empire State Building are famous New York landmarks.

Notice how Kyle tells a real story in his speech on the health of 9/11 recovery workers:

> Upon graduating as an NYPD detective, Michael Valentin took an oath to have utmost "loyalty, bravery, and fidelity." So on the morning of 9/11, Valentin could do nothing else than selflessly and heroically put his fears second and head straight to downtown Manhattan. For 2 months he searched for the bodies, but within weeks of working at the site, Valentin began feeling numbness in his hands, coughing up blood, and developed a cancer mass the size of a lemon outside his lung. Now every breath he takes is a choice between a life of pain and no life at all.[2]

actual example
A true instance or illustration.

Later in this chapter, we'll show how Kyle combined this one example with statistics, another type of supporting material, to develop a compelling case for helping 9/11 recovery workers.

hypothetical example
An imaginary or fictitious instance or illustration.

Hypothetical Examples. A **hypothetical example** is imaginary or fictitious. A speaker often signals hypothetical examples with phrases such as, "Suppose that," "Imagine yourself," or "What if." Hypothetical examples clarify and vivify the point you are making, but they do not prove the point.

Notice how the following introduction mentions actual products but places them in a hypothetical situation. The speaker chose this method knowing that not all listeners would have all the products listed. The speaker then generalizes from these examples to support the claim that we live in an electronic world.

> We wake up in the morning to soothing music coming from our AM-FM digital clock radio equipped with a gentle wake-up feature. We stumble downstairs, enticed by the aroma of coffee brewed by a preset coffee maker with 24-hour digital clock timer and automatic shut-off function. We zap on our 37-inch wide-screen HDTV with on-screen display of current time and channel. As we sit in our six-way action recliner, we use our 26-function wireless remote to perform the ritual of the morning channel check. Finding nothing that captures our interest, we decide instead to watch the video of last week's family reunion recorded with our 12X power zoom, fully automatic digital camcorder with self-timer, electronic viewfinder, and "flying erase head for 'rainbow'-free edits." Oh dear! What would our grandparents think? Certainly, we live in an electronic world!

Definition

EXPLORING ONLINE

Online Dictionaries

www.onelook.com

The OneLook Dictionary Search website indexes more than 19 million words in more than one thousand dictionaries. Simply type a word and call up definitions from multiple dictionaries.

A **definition** tells us the meaning of a word, a phrase, or a concept. Definitions are essential if your audience is unfamiliar with the vocabulary you use or if there are multiple definitions of a particular term. You want to clarify terms early in your speech so you don't confuse your listeners and lose their attention.

Definitions can take several forms. Four of the most common are definition by synonym, definition by etymology, definition by example, and definition by operation. Choose the form most appropriate to your audience and to the term you want to clarify.

definition
An explanation of the meaning of a word, phrase, or concept.

definition by synonym
Substitution of a word having similar meaning for the word being defined.

Definition by Synonym. The first type of definition is **definition by synonym**. Synonyms are words that have similar meanings. Consider these pairs of words:

mendacity and *dishonesty*   *pariah* and *outcast*
plethora and *excess*   *anathema* and *curse*
mitigate and *lessen*   *surreptitious* and *secret*

Each word is coupled with one of its synonyms. The first word of each pair may not be a part of your listeners' working vocabularies. As a speaker, you would want to use the second word in each pair; because those words are more familiar, they communicate more clearly. As the joke goes, never use a big word when a diminutive one will do.

Definition by Etymology.

Definition by Etymology. A second type of definition is **definition by etymology**. Etymology is the study of word origins. Describing how a word has developed may clarify its meaning.

You can use this type of definition to highlight the unusual nature of a familiar term. The reference section of your library and a variety of websites have several dictionaries of word origins and histories of word usage. We enjoy browsing in them, and in Chapter 17 we use definition by etymology to explain two fallacies of reasoning. What does an English fox hunt have to do with the red herring fallacy? How did the term *bandwagon fallacy* develop from political parades in the 1800s and early 1900s? Turn to pages 315 and 317 to learn the answers and to see examples of definition by etymology.

definition by etymology
Explanation of the origin of the word being defined.

Definition by Example.

Definition by Example. An example is a specific instance or illustration of a larger group or classification. **Definition by example** uses a specific instance to clarify a general category or concept. In his informative speech on violent crimes, Jacob presented two definitions to help his audience understand the distinction between "assault" and "battery."

definition by example
Providing an instance or illustration of the word being defined.

> Of course, different jurisdictions define crimes in slightly different ways. But, according to the Chicago Police Department website, accessed last Saturday, "In Illinois assault is a threat, while battery is an actual attack." The *New York Public Library Desk Reference* provides a more vivid explanation. Their 2002 calendar draws this distinction: "If you angrily shake your fist at someone, it's legally considered assault. If you follow up your actions by punching the person in the nose, the offense is assault and battery."

Jacob first used definition by synonym and then definition by example to clarify the distinction between these two terms.

You need not confine your definitions by example to language, however. Often audible and visual examples can be the quickest and most vivid ways to define a term or concept.

Audible examples are those you let your audience hear. Speeches on types of music, voice patterns, or speech dialects could define key terms by audible examples. For instance, if you used the word *scat* in a speech on jazz, you could offer a dictionary definition of the term: "jazz singing that uses nonsense syllables."[3] But wouldn't a taped example of Ella Fitzgerald, Al Jarreau, or Bobby McFerrin singing scat be more memorable to your audience? Other terms appropriate for audible definitions include Boston Brahmin dialect, industrial music, straight-ahead jazz, and vocalese.

Visual examples define a term by letting the audience see a form of it. If you're using the term *krumping* in a speech on contemporary dance, you could offer the *Urban Dictionary* definition: a style of dance involving "elaborate face-painting and freestyle dance moves usually performed in competition with other crews."[4] But a more vivid way to define the term would be to show a clip from a Missy Elliott or a Chemical Brothers' video. Speeches on styles of architecture or painting could also benefit from visual definition, as could any of the following terms: *abstract expressionism*, *concrete poetry*, *emoticon [:-o]*, *optical illusion*, and *photorealism*.

Definition by Operation. Sometimes the quickest and liveliest way to define a term is to explain how it is used. **Definition by operation** clarifies a word or phrase by explaining how an object or concept works, what it does, or what it was designed to do. The terms *radar detector*, *MP3 player*, and *laser scalpel* are but a few of the physical objects best defined by explaining their operation.

You can also define concepts, actions, or processes by operation. To define magnetic resonance imaging, you would have to explain how that technology operates. Notice how the following speaker defines an unfamiliar term by explaining its function:

> Humpback whales feed themselves by the technique of "bubble netting." A group of four or five whales will locate a school of krill or other small fish. The whales dive deep, encircling the fish and releasing a curtain of rising bubbles. The bubbles confuse the krill and force them into a tight column. The humpbacks then surface through the middle of the column with their mouths wide open, enjoying the feast.

Definition by operation is often livelier and clearer than many dictionary definitions. It can also be especially useful in the case of new technologies whose dictionary definitions have yet to be written.

Narration

Narration is storytelling, the process of describing an action or a series of occurrences. If you come to school on Monday and tell a friend about something you did during the weekend, you are narrating those events.

Personal Narrative. As a participant in the events, you will probably speak in first person at least part of the time, using the pronouns *I* or *we*. Such a story is called a **personal narrative**. We have suggested that you draw on your own experiences as you select and develop a speech topic, and personal narratives can be rich and interesting supporting materials.

Sultana, a student whose husband is Muslim and who had herself converted to the Muslim religion, used a personal narrative effectively. She told the story of her first experience with the celebration of Ramadan, a period of daylight fasting during the ninth month of the Muslim year:

> My first Ramadan I was a bit nervous. I had just become a Muslim, and I thought, "There is no way I can go from sunup to sunset without food. It's not even logical." I like to eat, as some of you may have noticed. And I thought,

---

definition by operation
Explanation of how the object or concept being defined works, what it does, or what it was designed to do.

narration
The process of describing an action or series of occurrences; storytelling.

personal narrative
A story told from the viewpoint of a participant in the action and using the pronouns *I* or *we*.

"There's no way that I can do this." Also, I was a student at the time, and it was finals. I honestly believe that you can't function if you don't eat. I mean, how can you think and pass a final? But I was determined at least to begin Ramadan; it goes for 30 days. So I set out and the first few days were a bit difficult. You can get hungry; there's no denying that. Your stomach growls out loud in class. But after about 3 days, the body adjusts. You don't really need as much food as most of us consume. You can live a long time on that stored-up fat we have and survive quite well. But the experience provides a lot of self-confidence, because if you can spend 30 days fasting, you can do just about anything.

Her classmates laughed along with Sultana as she poked fun at students' eating habits during the stress of final exams, as well as at her own tendency to be finishing a snack as her speech class started. In addition to creating interest in the topic, Sultana's story reinforced her credibility to speak on the topic of Ramadan. We tend to believe the accounts of people who have experienced events firsthand. That is an important reason for using personal narratives.

Third-Person Narrative. Narratives need not be personal but may relate incidents in the lives of others. When you speak from someone else's point of view and use the pronouns *he*, *she*, or *they*, you are telling a **third-person narrative**.

In the following example, notice how Kimberly used third-person narrative to illustrate the danger of running red lights:

> Michael approached the intersection and noticed it [the light] turn red. He was so late for his appointment that he decided to run right through, hoping no one was coming. There was someone, though, and Michael got broadsided as he ran the light. His car was shoved sideways, narrowly missing a 10-year-old boy riding through the intersection on his bicycle. This scenario may seem like fiction, but in fact, situations like this occur every day, when drivers race to beat the light.[5]

third-person narrative
A story told from the viewpoint of a witness and using the pronouns *he*, *she*, or *they*.

Comparison

Comparison is the process of depicting one item—a person, place, object, or concept—by pointing out its similarities to another, more familiar item. Just as examples can be actual or hypothetical, comparisons can be literal or figurative.

comparison
The process of associating two items by pointing out their similarities.

Literal Comparison. A **literal comparison** associates items that share actual similarities. Roger spoke on the need for a national high-speed rail network. He framed his speech using a comparison with the Interstate Highway System, developed in the 1950s through 1970s. Roger argued that the interstate system significantly promoted economic growth, decreased travel time, and increased travel safety and mobility. The challenge, he noted, was that it required a strong national commitment of vision, patience, and resources. Roger used literal comparison as he presented these same arguments for a high-speed rail system.

literal comparison
Associations between two items that share actual similarities.

figurative comparison
Associations between two items that do not share actual similarities.

Figurative Comparison. When you draw a **figurative comparison**, you associate two items that do not necessarily share actual similarities. The purpose of figurative comparisons is to surprise the listener into seeing or considering one person, place, object, or concept in a new way.

In his persuasive speech, Ben used the following figurative comparison to explain why college students have an elevated risk of contracting bacterial meningitis:

> Everybody comes to school bringing with them their own strain of influenza, like ingredients for a stew. We're all dumped into this crock pot called a campus, put on simmer for 1 or 2 weeks, and it's no wonder it occasionally boils over into something very serious. Have you noticed most campus flu outbreaks occur shortly after summer vacation and around Christmas break? This is because people leave and bring back more than the tinker toys they bargained for. And so the crock pot cycle continues.[6]

Effective figurative comparisons must contain an element of surprise, as well as a spark of recognition. Katherine highlighted the enormous popularity of the social-networking site Facebook when she quoted from the May 2011 issue of *Success*: "If Facebook were a nation, it would be the world's third largest nation, behind only China and India."

contrast
The process of distinguishing two items by pointing out their differences.

literal contrast
Distinctions between two items that share actual differences.

figurative contrast
Distinctions between two items that do not have actual differences.

Contrast

Contrast links two items by showing their differences. A **literal contrast** distinguishes items that do share some similarities. A **figurative contrast**, on the other hand, distinguishes items that share no similarities. In a persuasive speech on the dangers of overexposure to the sun, our student Patricia effectively used the following literal contrast:

> Sunblocks are either chemical or physical. Oils, lotions, and creams that claim a certain SPF factor all contain chemical blocks. On the other hand, zinc oxide, the white or colored clay-looking material you see some people wearing, usually on their noses, is a physical block.

Supporting materials, such as visual aids, can help make complicated concepts clearer and easier for an audience to grasp.

You can use comparison and contrast together in your speech. If you clarify a term by showing how it is similar to something the audience knows, you can often make the term even clearer by showing how it differs from something the audience also knows.

Another student, Paul, used a variety of supporting materials to document problems of exercise anorexia, an addiction to exercise:

> According to *Psychology Today*, June 2005, this disorder can affect 35 percent of those who work out three to five times a week for more than an hour each time. Specific symptoms can be when someone exercises even when ill, or withdraws from others to exercise, or becomes upset if unable to work out. Just like alcoholics, exercise anorexics are literally addicted to their behavior. But unlike alcoholism, exercise anorexia is an even bigger epidemic because people don't recognize that there is a problem.[7]

Paul explained exercise anorexia by comparing and contrasting it with alcoholism. He also demonstrated the dimension of this problem by using statistics, the next type of supporting material we discuss.

Statistics

Statistics are collections of data. Broadly speaking, any number used as supporting material is a statistic. Think of how much trust politicians and the general public put in preference polls gathered before elections. Statistics can predict certain events in our daily lives, such as price increases or decreases on certain goods and services. Used appropriately, statistics can make your ideas clear and vivid, can increase your credibility, and can prove your point.

Used inappropriately, however, statistics may baffle, bore, or even mislead your audience. The following five suggestions should guide you in presenting statistical material.

Do Not Rely Exclusively on Statistics. If statistics are your only form of supporting material, your audience will likely feel bombarded by numbers. Since your listening audience has only one chance to hear and assimilate your statistics, use statistics judiciously and in combination with other forms of support.

Remember Kyle's speech on the health of 9/11 recovery workers? He used a real example, NYPD detective Michael Valentin, to illustrate serious health consequences and to tap listeners' emotions. Kyle then introduced statistics to demonstrate the breadth of this problem:

> But, Valentine is not alone in his illness. A September 5, 2006, *CBS News* article reveals an astonishing 70 percent of the 40,000 recovery workers who responded to the attack on the World Trade Center are suffering lung problems.[8]

Round off Statistics. A statistic of 74.6 percent has less impact and is more difficult for your audience to remember than "nearly three-fourths." No one in your audience will remember the statistic of $1,497,568.42; many, however, may be able to remember "a million and a half dollars." Rounding off statistics for your listeners is neither deceptive nor unethical. Instead, it reflects your concern for helping your audience understand and retain key statistical information.

Use Units of Measure That Are Familiar to Your Audience. In her speech on London tourist attractions, Veronica described the London Eye as being "135 meters high—equivalent to 64 red telephone boxes stacked on top of one another." If she had stopped there, listeners unfamiliar with the metric system or with British phone boxes would have had only a vague idea of the height Veronica was describing. However, she wisely converted meters to feet, adding that the London Eye is 443 feet tall.

Use Presentational Aids to Represent or Clarify Relationships among Statistics. In his first informative speech of the semester, Alec discussed U.S. college study-abroad programs. He accessed a report by

statistics
Data collected in the form of numbers.

EXPLORING ONLINE

Locating Statistics

www.fedstats.gov

Need a statistic to document the extent of a condition or problem? The Federal Interagency Council on Statistical Policy maintains this website, with information and statistics provided by more than 100 U.S. federal agencies. You can search agencies alphabetically or by subject area.

the Institute of International Education listing the percentages of students studying in various host countries: 20.4 percent in the United Kingdom, 9.7 percent in Spain, 9 percent in Italy, 8.3 percent in France, and so forth. Alec decided that his classmates would remember more of this information if he presented it orally and visually. So he constructed a chart that ranked these nations according to the percentage of U.S. students studying there. Listeners were able to see the rankings and focus on the particular countries where they would like to study.

Stress the Impact of Large Numbers. Former U.S. Surgeon General C. Everett Koop used statistics effectively to make his point that tobacco-related diseases cause significant deaths. Notice how he used repetition and helped his audience visualize the enormity of these deaths:

> Let's start with a factual description of the problem. Based on the calculations of the finest statistical minds in the world and the World Health Organization, they have predicted that by 2025, . . . 500 million people worldwide will die of tobacco-related disease. That's a numbing figure. It is too large to take in, so let me put it in other terms for you. That's a Vietnam War every day for 27 years. That's a Bhopal every 2 hours for 27 years. That's a Titanic every 43 minutes for 27 years.
>
> If we were to build for those tobacco victims a memorial such as the Vietnam Wall, it would stretch from here [Washington, D.C.] 1,000 miles across seven states to Kansas City. And, if you want to put it in terms per minute, there's a death [every] 1.7 seconds, or about 250 to 300 people since I began to speak to you this afternoon.[9]

Testimony

Examples, definition, narration, comparison, contrast, and statistics are discrete types of supporting materials. Each is a different strategy for validating the ideas of a speech. Speakers sometimes generate these types of support themselves. Other times, they glean them from their research, citing their sources but justifying the point in their own words. Still other times, speakers find the words and structure of the original source so compelling that they quote directly or paraphrase the source. This latter strategy is known as **testimony**, or quotation.

In his speech "Ribbons: Function or Fashion," Tony discussed how awareness ribbons can inform and connect communities. To give his ideas credibility, he used the testimony of a communication professor and an animal welfare website:

> Dr. Judith Trent, a communication professor at the University of Cincinnati, states in the *Cincinnati Enquirer* of September 18, 2001, that wearing a ribbon "shows you're a part of something that's larger than yourself. It helps to unify and support the cause. It's a public signal about a private thought." By wearing ribbons, people can easily give support and find comfort in people around them. The Purple Ribbon Campaign website, last updated July 15, 2003, states, "Wearing a ribbon allows a person to represent their hopes and drive for a better day to come. It also provides support to others in letting them know that they are not suffering alone."[10]

testimony
Quotations or paraphrases of an authoritative source to clarify or prove a point.

SPEAKING WITH CONFIDENCE

Before presenting my speech on how to start a new small business, I began gathering and evaluating the supporting materials I would use to support my key ideas. Like most speakers, I searched online for information. I was careful to be selective and to avoid web pages that were based on personal opinion and bias. I supplemented the examples and statistics I found with my own expert testimony as a successful, self-employed businessman. I cited my sources to establish my credibility and let my listeners assess the quality of my data and documentation. Knowing that I had selected and tested my supporting materials allowed me to minimize my use of qualifiers such as "I think," "this might," and "maybe." I was confident with what I said, and the audience could be confident with what they heard.

Jovan Coker
Radford University

Tony clearly identified two sources and quoted them directly, trusting their credibility and their words to persuade his listeners. Testimony relies largely on the reputation of the source being quoted or paraphrased.

Expert testimony is not limited to the statements of other people, however. As a speaker, you use *personal testimony* when you support your ideas with your own experiences and observations. Many students select a speech topic because they have some special knowledge or experience with the subject. One student, for example, gave a speech comparing retail prices at large supermarkets to those at convenience stores. He was careful to explain his credentials and establish his expertise in the subject. Not only did he wear his store apron and manager's name tag, but he also said early in his introduction, "As a former receiving control manager, I was in charge of purchasing products for the store, so I have some knowledge of how wholesale prices are translated into the retail prices you and I pay." The speaker enhanced his credibility both verbally and nonverbally. Speakers should choose supporting materials carefully and ethically.

◖ Tests of Evidence

The positions you develop in your speech will be only as strong as the evidence supporting them. Seven guidelines will help you evaluate the validity and strength of your supporting materials. These suggestions will also help you evaluate evidence you hear others present in their speeches.

Is the Evidence Quoted in Context?

Evidence is quoted *in context* if it accurately reflects the source's statement on the topic. Evidence is quoted *out of context* if it distorts the source's position on the topic. For example, suppose Joyce was preparing a speech on hate crimes on campus. She read in the campus paper the following statement by the president of her college:

> We've been fortunate that our campus has been relatively free of bias-motivated crimes. In fact, last year, only two such incidents were reported—the lowest

---

KEY POINTS

Tests of Evidence

1. Is the evidence quoted in context?
2. Is the source of the evidence an expert?
3. Is the source of the evidence unbiased?
4. Is the evidence relevant?
5. Is the evidence specific?
6. Is the evidence sufficient?
7. Is the evidence timely?

EXPLORING ONLINE

Political Information

www.democrats.org

www.rnc.org

The Democratic, Republican, and other political parties maintain websites to promote issues and candidates. These sites offer information and links to party platforms, issues, polls, press releases, and news stories. Although political parties may provide much supporting material for your ideas, remember to evaluate the quality and objectivity of the evidence.

figure in the past 5 years. Yet, no matter how small the number is, any hate crime constitutes a serious problem on this campus. We will not be satisfied until our campus is completely free from all bias-motivated intimidation.

Now, suppose Joyce used the following statement to support her position that hate crimes are prevalent on campus:

> We need to be concerned about a widespread and growing problem on our campus: the prevalence of hate crimes. Just this past week, for example, our president argued that hate crimes constitute, and I quote, "a serious problem on this campus."

The president did say those words, but Joyce failed to mention the president's position that hate crimes on campus are few and decreasing. By omitting this fact, she has distorted the president's message. Joyce has presented the evidence out of context. The evidence you cite in your speech should accurately represent each source's position on the topic.

Is the Source of the Evidence an Expert?

If you delivered a speech advocating the licensing of law clerks to draft wills and conduct other routine legal business, would you rather quote a first-year lawyer or a senior law partner of a major legal corporation? Of course, it would depend on the specific individuals and what they said, but you would probably place more trust in the more experienced person.

An expert is a person qualified to speak on a particular topic. We trust the opinions and observations of others based on their position, education, training, or experience. The chairperson of a committee that has studied the effects of a community-based sentencing program is knowledgeable about that issue. A person completing graduate study on the effects of a local Head Start program on literacy has also developed an area of expertise. As a speaker, select the most qualified sources to support your position.

Our student who compared the pricing policies of large supermarkets and convenience stores was careful to establish his own credibility both verbally and nonverbally. When you fail to present your qualifications or the qualifications of those you quote, you give listeners little reason to believe you.

Is the Source of the Evidence Unbiased?

When Markdown Marty of Marty's Used Cars tells you he has the best deals in town, do you accept that claim without questioning it? Probably not. Marty may be an expert on used cars, but he's understandably biased. When individuals have a vested interest in a product, a service, or an issue, they are often less objective.

You expect representatives of political parties, special-interest groups, business corporations, labor unions, and so forth, to make statements advancing their interests. For example, the supermarket receiving control manager we quoted earlier concluded his speech by stating that it is more economical to shop at large supermarkets than at convenience stores. When you include testimony and quotations in your speeches, try to rely on objective experts who do not have a vested interest in sustaining the positions they voice.

ETHICAL DECISIONS

Biased Sources: To Use or Not to Use

You probably wouldn't be surprised that a Gallup study sponsored by Motorola found that people who use cellular phones are more successful in business than those who don't or that a Gallup poll sponsored by the zinc industry revealed that 62 percent of Americans want to keep the penny. These are just two examples that *Wall Street Journal* writer and editor Cynthia Crossen uses in her book *Tainted Truth: The Manipulation of Fact in America* to illustrate the difficulty of distinguishing between neutral research and commercially sponsored studies.

Assume that you are preparing to give a speech on hormone replacement therapy to counteract the effects of aging. Through an electronic database search, you find a study that shows the substance melatonin prevents cancer, boosts the immune system, and improves the quality of sleep. When you look for the source, you see that the study was sponsored by a pharmaceutical company that produces melatonin. What course of action should you follow? Should you disregard the findings because the study was commercially sponsored, use the findings without mentioning the study's sponsor, mention the findings and acknowledge the study's commercial sponsorship, or treat the findings in some other way?

Is the Evidence Relevant?

Evidence should relate to the speaker's claim. Sounds pretty obvious, doesn't it? However, both speakers and listeners often fail to apply this guideline in evaluating evidence. A speaker who contends that amateur boxing is dangerous but presents only evidence of injuries to professional boxers has clearly violated the relevance criterion. However, many times irrelevant evidence is difficult to detect.

Ryan's speech called for increased funding of medical trauma centers. Throughout his speech, he cited the need for the specialized care provided in these facilities. Yet, when he estimated the demand for this care, he used statistics of emergency room use. Trauma centers are not the same as emergency rooms. Therefore, Ryan's evidence was irrelevant to his argument. As you construct your speech, make certain your evidence relates specifically to your key points.

Is the Evidence Specific?

Which of the following statements is more informative?

The new convention center will increase tourism a lot.
The new convention center will increase tourism by 40 percent.

What does "a lot" mean in the first statement? Twenty percent? Fifty percent? Eighty percent? We don't know. The second statement is more precise. Because it is specific, we are better able to assess the impact of the new convention center. Words such as *lots*, *many*, *numerous*, and *very* are vague. When possible, replace them with specific or precise words or phrases.

Notice how Tasha used specific evidence to document her assertion that there is a need for organ donors.

As of April 22, 2009, at 8 p.m., 101,719 people wait hopefully for an organ, cited by the OPTN, Organ Procurement and Transplantation Network's website. To put this growing number into perspective, The *Saturday Evening Post* of December 1989 reported that at that time, 17,000 names were on the list. That's a 590 percent increase in the past 20 years.[11]

Is the Evidence Sufficient?

In her speech on rap music, Lea played excerpts from two rap songs, one of which she characterized as antiwoman and the other as antipolice. She encouraged her listeners to boycott rap music because "it demeans women and law enforcement officers." Lea did not apply this sixth guideline to her evidence. Two examples do not justify a blanket indictment of rap music.

In considering the guideline of sufficiency, ask yourself, "Is there enough evidence to prove the point?" Three examples of college athletes graduating without acquiring basic writing skills are insufficient to prove that athletes are failing to get a good education. One example may illustrate a claim, but it will rarely prove it. Make certain you have sufficient evidence to support your points.

Is the Evidence Timely?

If you were preparing a travel budget for a trip overseas, which would you find more helpful: an airline ticket pricing schedule you had from last year or one you printed from a travel website this week? Of course you would want to rely on more recent information. The timeliness of information is especially important if you are speaking about constantly changing issues, conditions, or events. What you read today may already be dated by the time you give your speech.

Some speech topics, however, are timeless. If you speak about the gods of Mount Olympus, no one would question your use of Robert Graves's *Greek Gods and Heroes*, published in 1960. As a scholar of mythology, Graves earned a reputation that time is not likely to diminish. Similarly, if you deliver a speech on the ancient Olympic Games, your most authoritative sources may be history textbooks. If, however, your topic concerns current drug-testing procedures in Olympic competition, it would be vital for you to use the most recent sources of the best quality you can find. The date of your evidence must be appropriate to your specific argument.

◖ Citing Your Sources

A bibliography of quality sources you consulted in researching your speech will build your credibility with your instructor. In Chapter 7, we directed you to sources that will help you compile a correct bibliography. However, most of your listeners will not have an opportunity to see it. To acknowledge your sources and to take credit for the research you have done, you will need to provide "oral footnotes" for ideas and supporting materials in your speech that are not your own. Doing so accomplishes two goals. First, clear source citations enhance the credibility of what you say by demonstrating that experts and data support your position. Second, clear source citations help interested listeners find published sources that they might wish to read or study.

How do you "orally footnote" sources as you deliver your speech? Your instructor may require more or less information in oral source citations than we do, so be sure to check. Our rule of thumb is this: give only the information necessary to build the credibility of the source but enough information to help listeners find your source if they wish.

Do you need to include *all* the information that was in your bibliographic entry for the source? No. Only the most active listener would remember the title and page numbers of a journal article or the publisher of a book that you cite, for example. Is there any information not in your bibliography that you *should* mention as you cite a source? Yes. To establish the credibility of any source you name, you need to explain at least briefly that individual's qualifications. You can usually find such information somewhere in the book, magazine, journal, or website you are using. If not, check a biographical database.

If the author is a newspaper or magazine staff writer, however, you do not need to name that individual. If the publication has a corporate author (a group, committee, or organization), just mentioning the name of the group or organization is probably sufficient. The date of publication may be extremely important to building credibility on a current topic. For periodicals published weekly or for online magazines that are frequently updated, specify the date, month, and year that the material was published or that you accessed it.

Orally footnoting Internet sources poses special challenges. Though it is never acceptable just to say, "I found a web page that said . . ." or "I found this on Yahoo!," most listeners will not remember a long URL. If the URL is simple and easily recognizable, mention it: "pbs.org," "cnn.com," or "espn.com," for example. Identifying the sponsor of a website is important. If you cannot identify the group or individual who published and maintains the site, you may need to look for a better source.

Compare the following source citations:

"Who is the fairest one of all, and state your sources!"

Instead of saying:	Say this:
"Studs Terkel says in his book *Will the Circle Be Unbroken?* . . ."	Studs Terkel, Pulitzer Prize–winning oral historian, says in his 2001 book *Will the Circle Be Unbroken?* . . ."
"According to an article I found on the Lexis/Nexis Academic database . . ."	"According to an article in the July 18, 2005, issue of the *Roanoke Times and World News* . . ."
"Leigh T. Hollins says in his article in the journal *Fire Engineering* . . ."	"Leigh T. Hollins, a certified EMT and battalion chief in the Manatee County, Florida, fire department, says in his article in the June 2005 issue of the journal *Fire Engineering* . . ."
"According to the Bureau of Labor Statistics . . ."	"According to figures I found on the U.S. Department of Labor's Bureau of Labor Statistics website on March 3, 2008, . . ."
"I found an article at memory.loc.gov/ ammem/ jrhtml/jr1940.html . . ."	"On March 12 of this year, I found an article entitled 'Breaking the Color Line: 1940–1946.' It's a link from the Recreation and Sports collection of the Library of Congress's website American Memory . . ."

In each case, the oral footnote that takes a few more words, identi-fies the source more clearly and more specifically, and would reinforce the speaker's credibility. The "Theory Into Practice" feature summarizes our advice for citing books, articles, and other types of sources.

THEORY INTO PRACTICE

TIP — Information for Oral Footnotes

If you are citing:	Tell us:
A magazine/journal article	That it is an article, the title of the magazine or journal, the author's name and credentials (if other than a staff writer), and the date of publication
A newspaper article	That it is an article, the name of the newspaper, the author's name and credentials (if other than a staff writer), and the date of the issue you are citing
A website	The title of the web page; the name of the individual, agency, association, group, or company sponsoring the site; and the date of publication, last update, or the date you accessed it
A book	That it is a book, the author's name(s) and credentials, the book's title, and the date of publication
An interview you conducted	That you interviewed the person, the person's name, and his or her position or title
A television or radio program	The title of the show, the channel or network airing it, and the date of broadcast
A videotape or DVD	The title of the tape or disk and the date of publication
A reference work	The title of the work and the date of publication
A government document	The title of the document, the name of the agency or government branch that published it, and the date of publication
A brochure or pamphlet	That it is a brochure; its title; the name of the agency, association, group, or company that published it; and the date of publication (if available)

SUMMARY

Purposes of Supporting Materials

- Supporting materials in a speech achieve three purposes: *clarity*, *vividness*, and *credibility*. Clarity helps the audience understand your ideas. Vividness assists them in remembering your ideas. Credible supporting materials make your ideas believable.

Types of Supporting Materials

- Types of material you can use to support the main ideas of your speech include example,

definition, narration, comparison, contrast, statistics, and testimony.

- *Examples* are samples or illustrations of a category.
- *Definitions* are explanations of an unfamil-iar term or of a word having several possible meanings. We can define terms by synonym, etymology, example, or operation.
- *Narration* is storytelling. Narratives may be personal or third person.
- *Comparisons* associate two or more items to show the similarities between or among

them. Comparisons can be either literal or figurative.

- *Contrasts* function like comparisons except that their purpose is to distinguish or show differences between or among two or more items. Contrasts can be either literal or figurative.
- *Statistics* are data collected in the form of numbers. Used properly, they can bolster a speaker's credibility and lend vivid support to the ideas of the speech.
- You use *testimony* when you cite, quote, or paraphrase authoritative sources. The authorities you cite may employ examples, definitions, narration, comparison, contrast, or statistics. *Personal testimony* comes from your own experience.

Evaluating Evidence

- To ensure that your supporting materials are credible, answer seven questions about each piece of evidence you consider using: Is the evidence quoted in context? Is the source of the evidence an expert? Is the source of the evidence unbiased? Is the evidence relevant to the point you are making? Is the evidence specific? Is the evidence sufficient to prove your point? Is the evidence timely?

Citing Sources

- If you use supporting materials that others have developed, you must cite them in your speech by providing "oral footnotes." You should offer enough information to establish the credibility of the source without overwhelming the listener.

EXERCISES

1. **Practice Critique.** Appendix B includes a transcript of a speech by Chiwoneso Beverley Tinago. After reading this speech, write a critique to Chiwoneso evaluating the evidence she uses to support her ideas. What types of supporting material does she use? Use the tests suggested in this chapter to evaluate her evidence. Give examples of her best supported arguments. Why are they effective? What other types of evidence could she provide to make her arguments more convincing?

2. Rewrite the following sentences to make them more vivid.
   a. The food at the Cozy Café is very good.
   b. I have a lot of homework to do.
   c. The students in my speech class are interesting people.
   d. We have a good time at the beach.

3. Locate a transcript of a speech in *Vital Speeches of the Day* or in some other publication or electronic database. Read it and note in the margins the different types of supporting materials the speaker used. Discuss the materials used most effectively, and account for their effectiveness. Discuss those used least

effectively, and suggest ways the speaker could improve them.

4. Read the following five statements, and indicate those with which you agree or disagree. Discuss the type(s) of supporting materials you would likely use to support your positions.
   a. European soccer is a more popular sport than American football.
   b. The fear of giving a speech can be reduced.
   c. Art is more important than science.
   d. Life in the country is more fun than life in the city.
   e. This state is an excellent place to visit.

5. Discuss a method of definition you could use for each of the following terms:
   a. Deep Web
   b. Aphorism
   c. Contralto
   d. Palpable
   e. Ballistic fingerprinting
   f. Bollywood
   g. Hardscape
   h. Speed dating

Organizing the Body of Your Speech

9

- **Formulate an Organizing Question**
- **Divide the Speech into Key Ideas**
  Topical Division
  Chronological Division
  Spatial Division
  Causal Division
  Pro–Con Division
  Mnemonic Division
  Problem–Solution Division
  Need–Plan Division

- **Develop the Key Ideas**
  Signpost the Idea
  State the Idea
  Support the Idea
  Summarize the Idea
  Theory Into Practice: Applying the "4 S's"

- **Connect the Key Ideas**

After studying this chapter, you should be able to

1. Understand and construct eight patterns for organizing the body of your speech.

2. Identify patterns especially appropriate for informative and persuasive speeches.

3. Select an appropriate organizational pattern for your speech.

4. Apply the "4 S" strategy for developing each key idea.

5. Understand four ways of connecting key ideas.

6. Construct an appropriate transition statement to connect your ideas.

> If you want me to talk for ten minutes, I'll come next week. If you want me to talk for an hour, I'll come tonight.
>
> —Woodrow Wilson

EXPLORING ONLINE

Organization: Why and How

http://grammar.ccc.commnet.edu/grammar/composition/organization.htm

This essay, "Principles of Organization," by Professor John Friedlander of Southwest Tennessee Community College is an excellent explanation of the importance of organization to effective writing, thinking, and speaking. Friedlander also discusses various patterns of organization.

The seventeenth-century mathematician and philosopher Blaise Pascal once wrote to a friend, "I have made this letter longer than usual, because I lack the time to make it short."[1] If you've ever furiously written several pages to answer an essay question only to discover that the answer requires just one brief paragraph, Pascal's comments probably make a great deal of sense to you. It takes time to organize your thoughts to write a coherent letter or give a succinct answer to an essay question. Investing the time to organize simplifies the task in the end. Getting organized will also simplify your speech preparation and make your speech more vivid and memorable for your listeners.

A coherent speech has a beginning, a middle, and an end—what we call the *introduction*, *body*, and *conclusion*. Many speech textbooks and instructors summarize the overall strategy of a speech as follows: "Tell us what you are going to tell us. Tell us. Then, tell us what you told us." Use this organizational perspective in every speech.

In this chapter, we teach you how to organize the body of your speech. In Chapter 10, you will learn how to organize the introduction and the conclusion. Although you deliver it after the introduction, organize the body of your speech first, for in order to "tell us what you are going to tell us," you must first determine what to tell us. In constructing the body of a speech, your best strategy is to formulate an organizing question, divide the speech into key ideas, and then develop each idea.

◖ Formulate an Organizing Question

If your research is productive, you'll gather more information than you can use in your speech. Some of that information will be relevant to your topic; some of it will not. You may also be missing some information that you need to develop your topic fully. Deciding what is relevant, irrelevant, or missing requires your critical thinking skill of *analyzing* as you examine items of information and the relationships among them. You will also be *integrating* as you combine and restructure the pieces of information and *organizing* as you arrange your information so that you can present it effectively, in a way your listeners can understand.

How can you start assessing the information you have, how it fits together, and what you still need? Begin by constructing an organizing question. An **organizing question** is one that, when answered, indicates the ideas and information necessary to develop your topic. The way your question is worded will shape the structure of your speech. For example, if you wanted to speak on the process of selecting a baby's gender, you could ask any of the following organizing questions:

organizing question
A question that, when answered, indicates the ideas and information necessary to develop your topic.

- What issues are involved in gender selection?
- What are the methods of gender selection?
- What are the benefits of gender selection?
- What are the problems with gender selection?

Each of these questions will lead you to a different set of answers—and thus to a different speech. The first two questions are appropriate for an informative speech, the latter two for persuasive speeches.

Suppose you selected the first organizing question: What issues are involved in gender selection? To answer this question, you would probably study the opinions and research of ethicists and medical experts, among others. From the information you collected, you might construct the following thesis statement: "Before deciding on the process of gender selection, parents should consider the ethical, medical, and social issues involved." Constructing, researching, and answering your organizing question helps you focus your speech and determine what information you will need to support it.

What does the National Holocaust Memorial Museum contain? Researching and answering this organizing question will help a speaker focus the speech and determine the information needed to support it.

Write your organizing question on a notecard or a sheet of paper, and keep it in view as you sift through your research. Ask yourself periodically, "What information helps answer this question?" As you continue working, you may change your organizing question; usually it will become more specific, helping you focus your speech further.

You should find that your organizing question suggests a pattern, perhaps several possible patterns, of organization. Consider these examples:

- What does it take to brew a great cup of coffee?
- What does the U.S. National Holocaust Memorial Museum contain?
- Why do some people favor and others oppose the medical use of marijuana for terminally ill patients?

Answering the first question will probably require you to discover and discuss a formula or procedure (chronological organization). The second question calls for a description of the physical areas of the museum (spatial organization). The third question will require you to study and explain the arguments for and against (pro–con organization) the medical use of marijuana.

Divide the Speech into Key Ideas

In the body of the speech, you develop your key ideas according to a specific organizational pattern. Public speakers employ a wide variety of organizational structures. We will discuss eight patterns most commonly used: (1) topical, (2) chronological, (3) spatial, (4) causal, (5) pro–con, (6) mnemonic, (7) problem–solution, and (8) need–plan. The first six patterns are appropriate for either informative or persuasive speeches. Problem–solution and need–plan patterns are appropriate only for persuasive speeches.

As you consider these patterns, keep in mind that no single pattern is best. To be effective, you must select a structure that accomplishes the

KEY POINTS

Patterns for Dividing Your Speech into Key Ideas

1. Topical division
2. Chronological division
3. Spatial division
4. Causal division
5. Pro–con division
6. Mnemonic division
7. Problem–solution division
8. Need–plan division

purpose of your speech. In other words, fit the organization to your topic rather than your topic to the organization.

Topical Division

topical division
Organization of a speech according to aspects, or subtopics, of the subject.

Topical division is the most common organizational pattern for public speeches. This strategy creates subtopics, or categories, that constitute the larger topic. For example, a speech on graffiti is divided topically if it focuses on graffiti as artistic expression, as political expression, and as vandalism. A speech on the American Indian tribal colleges is arranged topically if the speaker's main points include the history of the tribal colleges, examples of the tribal colleges, and success of the tribal colleges.

Coffee-lover Rowena organized her informative speech to cover the following points:

Specific Purpose: To inform the audience on the types and tastes of coffee
Key Ideas: I. Types of coffee
        A. Dark roasts
        B. Blends
        C. Decaffeinated
        D. Specialties
    II. Tastes of coffee
        A. Acidity
        B. Body
        C. Flavor

An example of topical division for a persuasive speech is as follows:

Specific Purpose: To persuade the audience to adopt a pet
Key Ideas: I.   Caring for a pet reduces anxiety and stress.
     II. Caring for a pet increases exercise and physical health.
    III. Caring for a pet decreases loneliness and depression.
    IV. Caring for a pet enhances empathy and self-esteem.

As these examples suggest, topical organization is particularly appropriate as a method of narrowing broad topics, and that may explain its popularity and widespread use.

Chronological Division

chronological division
Organization of a speech according to a time sequence.

The **chronological division** pattern follows a time sequence. This organization is especially appropriate if you are explaining procedures or processes. A simple and familiar example of chronological organization is a recipe. Any well-written recipe is organized in a time sequence: First, make sure that you have these ingredients; second, preheat the oven; and so forth. Topics that begin with phrases such as "the steps to" or "the history of" may be developed chronologically. Examples of such topics include the history of your university, the biography of author Toni Morrison, the stages of intoxication, steps to getting your first job, and how a product is marketed.

The following ideas are developed chronologically:

Specific Purpose: To inform the audience of Elisabeth Kübler-Ross's five stages of dying
Key Ideas: I. Denial
II. Anger
III. Bargaining
IV. Depression
V. Acceptance

Specific Purpose: To inform the audience about the history of garage rock
Key Ideas: I. The 1960s: The "British Invasion" Inspiration
II. The 1980s: The Garage Rock Revival
III. Today: The Neo-Garage Movement

Spatial Division

You use **spatial division** when your main points are organized according to their physical proximity or geography. This pattern is appropriate for a speech discussing the parts of an object or a place. Examples of spatial division are the following:

Specific Purpose: To inform the audience about the halls and palaces of the Forbidden City in Beijing, China
Key Ideas: I. The Halls of Harmony
II. The Palace of Heavenly Purity
III. The Palace of Earthly Tranquility
IV. The Hall of the Cultivation of the Mind

spatial division
Organization of a speech according to the geography or physical structure of the subject.

Speakers often use maps and diagrams to organize their topics spatially and to discuss the parts of places.

Specific Purpose: To inform the audience of the parts of the U.S. National Holocaust Memorial Museum

Key Ideas: I. Four classrooms, two auditoriums, and two galleries for temporary exhibits occupy the lower level.

II. The permanent exhibit occupies four floors of the main building.

III. The library and archives of the U.S. Holocaust Research Institute occupy the top floor.

Causal Division

causal division
Organization of a speech from cause to effect, or from effect to cause.

Choose a **causal division** pattern when you want to trace a condition or action from its causes to its effects, or from effects back to causes. Medical topics in which a speaker discusses the symptoms and causes of a disease can easily be organized using this method of division. Informative speeches on topics such as hurricanes, lightning, earthquakes, and other natural phenomena may also use this pattern. The following speech outline illustrates the causal pattern:

Specific Purpose: To inform the audience about the effects and causes of sports-victory riots

Key Ideas: I. Effects
   A. Death and injuries
   B. Vandalism
   C. Law enforcement costs
II. Causes
   A. The competitive nature of sports
   B. Mob psychology
   C. Unfavorable economic conditions
   D. Inadequate police presence

Because the causal pattern may be used any time a speaker attributes causes for a particular condition, it is suitable for persuasive as well as informative speeches. A speaker could attempt to prove that certain prescription drugs are partly responsible for violent behavior among those who use them; that televising executions would lead to a call for an end to capital punishment; or that new antibiotic-resistant bacteria are promoting the incidence of infections once thought to be under control.

Pro–Con Division

pro–con division
Organization of a speech according to arguments for and against some policy, position, or action.

The **pro–con division** presents arguments for and against a position. Because it is balanced in perspective, this pattern is more appropriate for an informative speech than a persuasive one. After discussing each side of an issue, however, you could choose to defend the stronger position. In this case, your division becomes *pro–con-assessment*, a pattern appropriate for a persuasive speech.

Brian decided to inform his classmates on "snapping." Also known as "cracking," "dissing," and "playing the dozens," this game of insults is part of African-American history and culture. In the book *Snaps*, Brian found examples of this war of words, such as Quincy Jones's snap "Your house is so small, you have to go outside to change your mind."

At first, Brian thought he would use a topical division and discuss (1) the history of snaps, (2) how the game is played, (3) common topics, and (4) sample snaps. As he continued to research his topic, however, he discovered that there is a lively debate as to whether snapping is constructive or destructive. Brian decided to use a pro–con division to tell his listeners about the debate:

Specific Purpose: To inform the audience about the arguments for and against snapping

Key Ideas: I. Snapping should be encouraged.
     A. It is part of African-American history and culture.
     B. It is a nonviolent way of expressing hostility.
     C. It encourages imagination and creative wordplay.
  II. Snapping should be discouraged.
     A. It is demeaning.
     B. It can provoke violence.
     C. It is not an effective way to express anger.

The following outline also demonstrates a pro–con analysis of a controversial issue:

Specific Purpose: To inform the audience of the arguments for and against an increase in the minimum wage

Key Ideas: I. Increasing the minimum wage would be beneficial.
     A. The number of poor people would decrease.
     B. The number of people on welfare would decrease.
     C. The concept of social justice would be affirmed.
  II. Increasing the minimum wage would be harmful.
     A. Unemployment would increase.
     B. Inflation would increase.
     C. Business bankruptcies would increase.

An advantage of the pro–con pattern is that it places an issue in its broader context and provides balance and objectivity. A disadvantage, however, is the time required to do this. You need plenty of time to discuss both sides of an issue in sufficient detail. Therefore, you will probably want to use this strategy only in one of your longer speeches. If you do not devote sufficient time to each idea, a pro–con or pro–con-assessment development may seem simplistic or superficial to your audience.

Mnemonic Division

One of the most creative organizational strategies you can use is **mnemonic division**, organizing a speech according to a special memory device such as alliteration, rhyme, or initial letters that spell a word. If you can recall what the four Cs of diamond grading refer to, you probably memorized that information according to a mnemonic device. The four Cs stand for **c**ut, **c**olor, **c**larity, and **c**arat weight.

EXPLORING ONLINE

Applying Mnemonics
www.mindtools.com/memory.html

To learn more about memory techniques and a variety of mnemonic devices that you could use to organize a speech or to study, visit this site. The links to brief articles give you access to methods of improving your memory.

mnemonic division
Organization of a speech according to a special memory device, such as alliteration, rhyme, or initial letters that spell a word.

Our student Debra applied mnemonic division to one of the main points in her speech on skin cancer. After answering the questions, "Who is at greatest risk for developing skin cancer?" and "What are the three types of skin cancer?" her third point was "What are the warning signs of skin cancer?" To answer that important question, she cited and used the Skin Cancer Foundation's ABCDs of skin cancer: **A**symmetry, **B**order irregularities, **C**olor variations, and **D**iameters larger than typical moles. The brilliance of this mnemonic is that once you hear it explained as clearly as Debra did, you will retain the information for a long time.

If you were giving a speech explaining how to improve listening, you could use the gimmick developed by Robert Montgomery (giving him credit in your speech, of course).[2] Montgomery suggests six guidelines for better listening:

L — Look at the other person.
A — Ask questions.
D — Don't interrupt.
D — Don't change the subject.
E — Express emotions with control.
R — Responsively listen.

No doubt, the word *ladder* would help you remember your major points as you prepared and delivered such a speech. More important, though, the mnemonic would help your listeners retain what you had said.

At times, mnemonic division, sometimes called gimmick division, may seem corny or trivial. If you feel that way about this pattern, you probably should avoid it, as your speech delivery might seem self-conscious. When used well and with confidence, however, the mnemonic helps your audience remember not only what points you have covered but also the order in which you covered them. That is a major accomplishment! In the next section of this chapter, we use a gimmick as we introduce you to our 4 S strategy of developing the ideas of the speech. See if it helps you remember these important points.

Problem–Solution Division

problem–solution division
A rigid organizational pattern that establishes a compelling problem and offers one or more convincing solutions.

The **problem–solution division** is a simple, rigid, organizational approach for a persuasive speech. In this approach, the major divisions of your speech and their order are predetermined: you first establish a compelling problem and then present a convincing solution. Because you advocate a plan of action, this pattern is by nature persuasive.

Speeches that call for a law or some action often use a problem–solution format, as in the following example:

Specific Purpose: To persuade the audience to support reform of our national park system
Key Ideas: I. Our national parks are threatened.
　　　　　　　A. Political influence is a threat.
　　　　　　　B. Environmental pollution is a threat.
　　　　　　　C. Inadequate staffing is a threat.

II. Our national parks can be saved.
  A. The National Park Service should have greater independence.
  B. Environmental laws should be stricter.
  C. Funding should be increased.

A common alternative to the problem–solution division is to divide the speech into a discussion of problems, causes, and solutions. Notice how Matthew uses this approach:

Specific Purpose: To persuade the audience that involuntary psychiatric commitment laws should be reformed

Key Ideas: I. The problems caused by involuntary commitment laws are serious.
  A. Many are potential victims of being wrongfully committed.
    1. The elderly are especially at risk.
    2. The poor are at risk.
    3. All of us are at risk.
  B. Victims face physical and financial dangers.

  II. Two factors perpetuate these problems.
  A. Medicare policies indirectly encourage hospitals to commit patients regardless of their actual health.
  B. Involuntary commitment laws are too vague.

  III. To remedy this problem, we must act on three levels.
  A. The federal government must reform involuntary commitment procedures.
  B. The psychiatric industry must establish greater control over mental hospitals.
  C. We, as individuals, must take action as well.[3]

Need–Plan Division

The **need–plan division** is a variation of the problem–solution division. This fourfold approach (1) establishes a need or deficiency in the present system, (2) presents a proposal to meet the need, (3) demonstrates how the proposal satisfies the need, and (4) suggests a plan for implementing the proposal.

Salespeople often use the need–plan strategy. They demonstrate or create a need, supply the product or service to meet that need, demonstrate or describe how well it will work, and often even arrange an easy payment plan to help guarantee your purchase. This fundamental sales approach is prevalent for one simple reason: it works! You can use this strategy when you want to prompt an audience to action.

Suppose the specific purpose of your speech is to persuade your audience that employers should provide health promotion programs for their employees. Using the need–plan pattern, you could make four arguments. First, employee illness results in absenteeism, lost productivity, and increased health care costs. Second, employers should establish on-site health and fitness centers for their employees. Third, when health promotion programs have been tried, they have reduced absenteeism,

need–plan division
A variation of problem–solution organization that (1) establishes a need or deficiency, (2) offers a proposal to meet the need, (3) shows how the plan satisfies the need, and (4) suggests a plan for implementing the proposal.

SPEAKING WITH CONFIDENCE

Having never spoken in public before, giving a speech to a room full of strangers was quite unnerving. Not to mention that constructing a strong speech can be overwhelming for anyone who lacks the proper tools. By using the 4 S's to properly structure my speeches I was able to create a solid foundation to give me the confidence I needed. I was able to express my thoughts concisely, in a way that benefitted both the audience and me. Even writing and organizing my speech became easier by using this simple but powerful framework. Often times I have found myself referring back to the 4 S's, not only when developing speeches but also when writing papers. The 4 S's makes structuring key points for any topic an effective process.

Melissa Gilbert
San Antonio College

increased productivity, and capped health care costs. As your final step, you could suggest an implementation strategy to include exercise and conditioning programs, alcohol- and drug-awareness education, stress-management workshops, antismoking clinics, and health status testing and evaluation.

Develop the Key Ideas

Assume that your speech is divided into key ideas, that you have selected the most appropriate pattern to organize them, and that you have decided their order in the speech. Now you need to develop each major point. Obviously, the number of major points you can develop in a speech depends on the time you have been given to speak, the topic's complexity, and the audience's level of education and knowledge of the subject. There is no fixed rule, but we recommend that you develop at least two, but not more than five, main points. Many speakers find that a three-point structure works best.

Regardless of the number of points you select, your responsibility is to explain and support each one sufficiently. The organizational strategy we suggest is one we call the "4 S's." Your listeners will better comprehend and remember your speech if you *signpost*, *state*, *support*, and *summarize* each idea.

Signpost the Idea

It's Monday morning and you're sitting in your introductory psychology class. You take notes as Dr. Potter lectures on factors that influence interpersonal attraction. In which scenario will you likely understand and remember more of what she says?

Dynamic speakers combine words and gestures as signposts to guide listeners through their speeches.

1. Dr. Potter presents her material using words and phrases such as "also," "another factor," and "moving on to similarity."

2. Dr. Potter introduces her ideas with statements such as "a third factor of attraction is proximity" and "similarity is a fourth component of attraction."

If you're like most students, you chose the second scenario. In fact, one experiment tested this and found that "students are able to process information more effectively when lecturers use obvious organizational cues." The researcher's advice to teachers is: "Incorporating organizational cues appears to pay substantial dividends. . . ."[4]

That same advice is equally important for public speakers. Because your audience may not consist of note takers, your task is even more challenging. One "obvious organizational cue" you can use is signposting. A **signpost** is a word such as *initially*, *first*, *second*, and *finally*. Just as a highway signpost tells travelers where they are in their journey, so a signpost in a speech tells the audience where they are in the speaker's message. Signposts help listeners follow your organizational pattern and increase the likelihood that they will remember your key ideas.

State the Idea

Each major idea needs to be worded precisely and with impact. In her persuasive speech, Esperanza argued the benefits of a multicultural college experience. Her specific purpose was to persuade the audience that ethnic studies (ES) courses should be required for all students. Her organizing question was:

Why should all students be required to take ES courses?

Using a topical organization, Esperanza presented three reasons to support her proposal. Before we tell you how she actually worded those ideas, let's look at how a less experienced student might have stated them:

1. ES courses promote cultural awareness.
2. I would like to discuss ES courses and what research and expert opinion say about the way they affect conflict that may be ethnic or racial.
3. Third, social skills.

Do these points seem related? Are they easy to remember? No, they're a mess! To avoid clutter, keep the following suggestions in mind when wording your key ideas:

1. *Main headings should clearly state the points you will develop.* The first statement ("ES courses promote cultural awareness") does that; the others do not.
2. *Main headings should usually be worded as complete sentences.* Think of the main heading as a statement that you will prove with your supporting materials. Listeners would probably remember the wording of statement 1 in the previous list. As a result, they would remember the point of the speaker's evidence. That is not true for the other two statements.

KEY POINTS

The "4 S" Strategy of Developing Key Ideas
1. Signpost the idea.
2. State the idea.
3. Support the idea.
4. Summarize the idea.

signpost
Numbers (*one*) or words (*initially, second,* or *finally*) that signal the listener of the speaker's place in the speech.

3. *Main headings should be concise.* You want listeners to remember your key ideas. The first statement is easier to remember than the second. The third statement is the shortest but it isn't a complete sentence. Remembering it doesn't help you understand the point the speaker made.

4. *Main ideas should be parallel to other main ideas.* Parallel wording gives your speech rhythm and repetition, two qualities that help listeners remember your points.

5. *Main ideas should summarize the speech.* When you state your main points, listeners should see how those points answer the organizing question and achieve your specific purpose.

Now let's see how Esperanza worded each of her key ideas:

Specific Purpose: To persuade the audience that ES courses should be required for all students

Key Ideas: I. ES courses promote cultural awareness.
II. ES courses reduce ethnic and racial conflict.
III. ES courses improve social skills.

Each of these main headings clearly states a distinct point that Esperanza will argue. Each statement is a concise, complete sentence. All three sentences are grammatically parallel. Notice, too, that each of the three key ideas directly answers Esperanza's organizing question:

Why should ES courses be required for all students?

An alternative to introducing your key idea as a declarative sentence is to ask a question. For example, the specific purpose of Evan's speech was:

to inform the audience on the civil rights Freedom Rides of 1961.

He organized his supporting materials to answer three questions:

1. What were the goals of the Freedom Riders?
2. What resistance did they confront?
3. What were their successes?

He introduced each of these ideas with a signpost, for example:

The *first* question we must answer to understand this chapter in the Civil Rights Movement is: What were the goals of the Freedom Riders?

He was then ready to answer this question using various types of supporting materials.

You can usually accomplish the first two S's, signposting and stating your idea, in one sentence. For an informative speech assignment requiring the use of visual aids, our student Jennifer decided to speak about Victorian homes—America's "painted ladies." Using spatial organization, she focused her speech on interior details and decoration, taking her listeners on a virtual tour of a Victorian home she called Conglomeration House. Jennifer introduced her first key idea as follows:

The first room we will visit on our tour of a Victorian home is the parlor, the woman's domain.

That sentence clearly signposts and states Jennifer's initial main point.

Support the Idea

This third S is the meat of the "4 S's." Once you have signposted and stated the idea, you must support it. Several categories of supporting materials are at your disposal, limited only by the amount of research you have done and by time limits on your speech. Some of those categories of supporting materials, discussed in detail in Chapter 8, are examples, definitions, comparisons, and statistics.

In her speech on Victorian homes, Jennifer combined specific language with visual aids to depict a different style of each room. For example, as part of her support for the first room, the parlor, she stated the following:

> The parlor in Conglomeration House is done in the Rococo revival style, which is almost exclusively used in interior design. In their book *The Secret Lives of Victorian Homes*, Elan and Susan Zingman-Leith, who restore Victorian houses, give us this wonderful example of this style. [Jennifer showed an enlarged photograph.] Typical of the Rococo theme, the walls are painted white or a pastel color and are broken into panels decorated with wooden molding or even artwork painted directly onto the wall. Around the windows and ceiling are intricately carved wooden details that are influenced by botanical or seashell designs. These are painted to match the color of the walls, but are heavily accented with gilt, or gold-colored paint. Following the pale color scheme, the mantel is made of marble. It is also intricately carved in a botanically inspired design and has cherubs worked into it as well.

Summarize the Idea

A summary at the end of each major division wraps up the discussion and refocuses attention on the key idea. These periodic summaries may be as brief as one sentence. Early in the course, our students sometimes summarize a point by saying, "So I've told you a little about . . ." What you say in these internal summaries within the body needs to be more substantial and more varied than that. An effective summary should reinforce the point you have just developed and also provide a note of closure for that key idea.

If you introduced your idea as a question, your summary should provide the answer. Remember, your point is lost if the audience remembers only your question; they must remember your answer as well.

Jennifer summarized her first key idea with the following statement:

> So the parlor gives us a wonderful example of the Rococo revival architectural style: very feminine, very ornate, and very French.

Such a summary not only clued her audience that she had finished discussing this first room but alerted them that they were about to move to the second room on the tour.

THEORY INTO PRACTICE

TIP   Applying the "4 S's"

Assigned to deliver an informative speech about something that originated or that exists outside of the United States, our student Alex developed the first main point in the body of his speech as follows:

Signpost of key idea
Statement of key idea
Support for key idea

First, I'd like to *describe the Itsukushima Shrine's Grand O-Torii Gate* as I experienced it for the first time. Along the way I'll give you some specific details about the structure. During 1991 and halfway into 1992, I was still in the military and living in Japan. On one of our off weekends, we decided to visit

(narration)

the shrine in Miyajima-guchi, a small town south of the military base where we were stationed. We boarded a train and enjoyed the 30- to 45-minute ride to the small town. From the train station, we walked a short distance to a pier. There we boarded a ferry that took us to Miyajima Island, where the shrine was located. We got off the ferry and walked toward the shrine location, not knowing that it was really close. The tide was in. Suddenly, there

To clarify the look of the Grand O-Torii Gate for his listeners, Alex showed them this view he had seen as he stood on the shore of Miyajima Island at high tide looking out at the Sea of Japan.

We believe that use of the "4 S's" is fundamental to effective organization within the body of any speech. As you begin to master and apply this four-step strategy, it may seem to be a cookie-cutter approach to public speaking. It is exactly that. The "4 S's" are to speech organization what the required movements are to gymnastics—basics that you must learn before you can develop your own style or flair. As you master the "4 S's" and gain confidence in public speaking, clear organization will become almost a reflex reaction performed without conscious effort. As your ability to organize ideas clearly becomes second nature, you will find that the structure of your thinking, writing, and speaking has greatly improved.

appeared this big red Japanese gate in the water about half a football field away from where we were standing near the shore.

    I was already excited from the train ride and the ferry ride. Seeing the Grand O-Torii Gate was kind of like seeing Sleeping Beauty's Castle at Disneyland for the first time. You see it in pictures and movies all the time. But seeing it for real, well, if you've been to Disneyland you know the feeling. This is what the Grand O-Torii Gate looks like when the tide is in. [Alex shows the photograph.] It really looks like it's floating in the water, especially if you have never seen it when the tide is out.

    I promised you some specific details about the structure and I won't let you down. On the 3rd of June 2005, I found a website, www.hiroshima-cdas.or.jp, sponsored by a Japanese Internet service provider. The site mentions that the gate is almost 52½ feet tall and that each pillar is about 44 feet tall and at least 24½ feet around. The gate is constructed entirely of wood from the camphor tree, which is native to the area. Concrete beams and pillars support the O-Torii gate, and it's covered with vermillion, or deep red, lacquer. Because it is out at sea, partially submerged in the water, shipworms and barnacles encrust and slowly deteriorate the wood at the base. I've seen the barnacles but I had no clue of the damage that was going on. Fortunately, plastic resin has been found to be effective in preserving the wood.

    You can now imagine the impression the Grand O-Torii gate made on me even from a distance, but it can be even more awe-inspiring when you get a chance to stand as close to it as I did.

    Japan is, unfortunately, subject to destructive typhoons. That's why governments and organizations have banded together to help preserve this shrine for future generations. So, second, let's examine some of the work required to preserve the gate.

Margin annotations:
- (comparison)
- (visual example)
- (citation, source)
- (statistics)
- (definition)
- Summary of key idea
- (transition to second key idea)

Connect the Key Ideas

A speech is composed of key ideas—the building blocks of your speech—and you have just seen how to develop each according to the "4 S's" approach. For your speech to hang together, you must connect those ideas, just as a mason joins bricks and stones with mortar. A speaker moves from one idea to the next—puts mortar between the units—with the aid of a transition. A **transition** is a statement connecting one thought to another. Without transitions, the ideas of a speech are introduced abruptly. As a result, the speech lacks a smooth flow of ideas and sounds choppy.

transition
A statement that connects parts of the speech and indicates the nature of their connection.

A transition not only connects two ideas but also indicates the nature of their connection. Transitions are usually indicated by *markers*, words or phrases near the beginning of a sentence that indicate how that sentence relates to the previous one.[5] You will use some transitions *within* each of your main points to offer illustrations (*for example*), indicate place or position (*above*, *nearby*), or make concessions (*although*, *of course*).[6] However, the transitions you use *between* the main points of your speech will indicate four basic types of connections: complementary, causal, contrasting, and chronological.

A **complementary transition** adds one idea to another, thus reinforcing the major point of the speech. Typical transitional markers for complementary transitions include *also*, *and*, *in addition*, *just as important*, *likewise*, *next*, and *not only*.

Each of the following transitions uses the complementary approach to reinforce the speaker's thesis:

> It is clear, then, that golf courses have sociological effects on communities where they are located. Just as important, however, are their environmental effects.

> Vocal cues, however, are not the only source of information that may help you determine if someone is lying. You may also look for body cues.

A **causal transition** emphasizes a cause-effect relationship between two ideas. Words and phrases that mark a causal relationship include *as a result*, *because*, *consequently*, and *therefore*.

In his speech, Victor documented problems resulting from excessive noise. As he shifted his focus from cause to effect, he used the following transition:

> We can see, then, that we live, work, and play in a noisy world. An unfortunate result of this clamor and cacophony is illustrated in my second point: excessive noise harms interpersonal interaction.

A **contrasting transition** shows how two ideas differ. These transitions often use markers such as *although*, *but*, *in contrast*, *in spite of*, *nevertheless*, *on the contrary*, and *on the other hand*.

In her tour of Conglomeration House, Jennifer moved her audience from her first to her second main idea with the following clear contrasting transition:

> In sharp contrast to the parlor is the library, the man's retreat in the home. This is the second room we will visit on our tour.

A **chronological transition** shows the time relationships between ideas and uses words or phrases such as *after*, *as soon as*, *at last*, *at the same time*, *before*, *later*, and *while*.

Will informed his classmates on the SQ3R system of studying and remembering written material. He organized his five main points around five key words: *survey*, *question*, *read*, *recite*, and *review*. His transitions emphasized the natural sequence of these stages:

> After surveying, or overviewing, what you are about to read, you are ready for the second stage of the SQ3R system: to question.

complementary transition
Adds one idea to another.

causal transition
Establishes a cause-effect relationship between two ideas.

contrasting transition
Shows how two ideas differ.

chronological transition
Shows how one idea precedes or follows another in time.

A second example of a chronological transition is the following:

> If thorough preparation is the first step in a successful job interview, the second step is to arrive on time.

A good transition serves as a bridge, highlighting the idea you have just presented and preparing your listeners for the one to come. It smoothes the rough edges of the speech and enhances the cohesiveness of your ideas. Note, however, that transitions alone cannot impose order on a speech. The main ideas and their natural links must exist before you can underscore their connections with transitions.[7] Developing and pursuing an organizing question can help ensure that you know your main ideas and their connections in the first place.

Effective transitions require more than just inserting a word or phrase between two ideas. If you find yourself always using a single word such as *now*, *next*, or *okay* to introduce your ideas, you need to work on your transitions. Avoid using weak and pedestrian phrases as transitions, such as "Moving on to my next point" or "The next thing I would like to discuss." Instead, work on composing smooth, functional transition statements as Bonnie did in the following example.

In her persuasive speech, Bonnie advocated voluntary school uniforms for students in kindergarten through high school. She previewed her ideas in her introduction by stating that pilot programs demonstrate that "voluntary uniforms would help create a safer school environment, enhance academic achievement, and promote a positive social climate." In the body of her speech, Bonnie explained and supported each of these points, connecting them by using smooth transitions. Bonnie used the following excellent transition as she moved from her first to her second idea:

> Every student has a right to learn in a safe environment, and school uniforms help eliminate one cause of school violence. But schools should do more than ensure safety; they should promote learning. A second benefit of school uniforms is that they enhance academic achievement.

ETHICAL DECISIONS

Crunch Time

Rosa has delayed working on her speech until the night before it is due. She logs on to the Internet and begins downloading articles relating to her topic: how to avoid harming yourself with prescription drugs. The next morning, she sorts through the material, jotting down examples, statistics, and testimony she finds interesting. However, by the time she needs to leave for class, Rosa's speech is still not well organized, and she admits that her listeners may not be able to follow some of the information she plans to present. Rosa is torn between two courses of action. She does not want to get a failing grade on the speech, and she'd like to get some practice speaking in front of a group, so she is tempted to "wing it" and see what happens. "I can always clear up any confusion by answering questions later," she thinks. "After all, I have done the research." However, because she knows that some people in the audience may get lost and even misinterpret the information she presents, Rosa considers telling her instructor that she is not prepared and suffering the consequences.

What would you do if you were Rosa? Would she be violating any ethical standards if she were to forge ahead and deliver her speech? Do you think that delivering a disorganized speech is an abuse of the power a speaker wields over an audience? Put your thoughts in writing, and be prepared to discuss them with your classmates.

If you follow the guidelines and examples in this chapter, the body of your speech will be well organized. You should now know how to generate an organizing question and use it to select an organizational pattern that is appropriate to your topic, your purpose, and your audience. You should also know how to develop each main idea in the body of your speech according to the "4 S's" and how to connect those main ideas with appropriate transitions. In Chapter 10, you will learn how to extend this excellent organization to the introduction and conclusion of your speech.

SUMMARY

The Importance of Speech Organization

- The chief goal of speech organization is to help your listeners understand and retain information.

The Parts of a Speech

- The three parts of a speech are the *introduction*, *body*, and *conclusion*. You should organize the body first because it is the most substantial part of the speech and its content determines the content of the introduction and the conclusion.

Developing an Organizing Question

- To evaluate the information you have researched and select an appropriate organizational pattern, formulate an *organizing question*. Answering this question will tell you what main ideas and information you need in order to develop your topic. Your answer should also suggest possible ways of organizing the body of your speech.

Patterns of Organization

- There are eight organizational patterns for the body of the speech. Six are appropriate for both informative and persuasive speeches: *topical division*, *chronological division*, *spatial division*, *causal division*, *pro–con division*, and *mnemonic division*.
- Two organizational patterns are appropriate only for persuasive speeches: *problem–solution division* and *need–plan division*.

The "4 S's"

- To organize the presentation of each major idea in the body of your speech, we recommend the memory device we call the "4 S's": *signpost* the idea, *state* the idea, *support* the idea, and *summarize* the idea. Apply these four steps to each major idea in the speech.

Developing Transitions

- Each of the main points you develop needs to be connected to the others by *transitions*. Effective transitions indicate the nature of the relation between the ideas: *complementary*, *causal*, *contrasting*, or *chronological*.

EXERCISES

1. **Practice Critique.** Read the transcript of Julian Fray's speech on steganography in Appendix B. Write a critique of the organization of the body of her speech. Does she focus on a few key ideas? Does she develop each idea using the "4 S" strategy? Are these ideas connected with smooth transitions? What suggestions can you offer to improve Julian's speech in any of these areas? Provide specific examples from her speech to support your comments.

2. Read the student speeches in Appendix B, and formulate organizing questions each speaker might have used.

3. From the list of self-generated topics in Chapter 6, select several that would lend themselves to topical organization. What subtopics could each include?

4. From the list of self-generated topics in Chapter 6, select a topic that would lend itself to spatial division. What are some subtopics a speech on this subject could include?

5. Brainstorm for topics about processes of which you have a working knowledge (how to conduct a library computer search, the best way to study for an exam, etc.). Select one of these topics, and develop three to five key ideas, organizing them according to a time sequence.

6. Select one topic and show how it could be developed using three different organizational patterns. Which do you think would make the best speech? Why?

7. What memory devices or gimmicks have you used recently to help you remember materials in this or another class? For example, you may have used "IRS" to help you remember the elements of the triangle of meaning in Chapter 1.

8. Brainstorm some speech topics that could be developed according to a pro–con division. Select one, and write a specific purpose statement. List the divisions you could use in the body of the speech.

9. Select an organizational pattern you think would be appropriate for speeches with the purposes listed below. Could the specific purpose be achieved using other patterns? Are there some patterns that would clearly be inappropriate?

   a. To inform the audience about relaxation techniques

   b. To inform the audience about the history of Groundhog Day

   c. To inform the audience about the advantages and disadvantages of raising money for charitable causes by telethons

   d. To inform the audience about marriage rituals in various cultures

   e. To persuade the audience that illiteracy is seriously harming national productivity

   f. To persuade the audience that the health benefits from one exercise program are greater than those from another

Introducing and Concluding Your Speech

10

- **Organize the Introduction of the Speech**
  Get the Attention of Your Audience
  State Your Topic
  Establish the Importance of Your Topic
  Establish Your Credibility to Speak on Your Topic
  Preview Your Key Ideas
  Put It All Together

- **Organize the Conclusion of the Speech**
  Summarize Your Key Ideas
  Activate Audience Response
  Provide Closure
  Put It All Together
  Theory Into Practice: Outward Method of Speech Development

After studying this chapter, you should be able to

1 Explain the five functions of a speech introduction.

2 Select an appropriate attention-getting step.

3 Construct and evaluate an effective speech introduction.

4 Explain the three functions of a speech conclusion.

5 Know how to use physical and vocal delivery to signal that you are concluding your speech.

6 Construct and evaluate an effective speech conclusion.

7 Identify the nine steps in a well-organized speech.

8 Apply the outward method of speech development.

I think the end is implicit in the beginning. It must be. If that isn't there in the beginning, you don't know what you're working toward. You should have a sense of a story's shape and form and its destination, all of which is like a flower inside a seed.

—Eudora Welty

EXPLORING ONLINE

Introductions and Conclusions

http://wps.ablongman
.com/ab_public_
speaking_2/24/6223/1593278
.cw/index.html

"Starting a Talk with an Introduction" from this Pearson Allyn & Bacon website offers a list of attention-getting devices for beginning a speech effectively. It also provides links to federal statistics and quotations, organized by themes, that may be useful at the start of a speech.

rhetorical question
A question designed to stimulate thought without demanding an overt response.

direct question
A question that asks for an overt response from listeners.

Although famed Southern writer Eudora Welty refers specifically to beginning and ending a short story or novel, her quotation also applies to public speaking. As a speaker, your first words can make a positive impression on your audience, capture their attention, prepare them to listen more effectively, and enlist their support. These first words are crucial, of course, because they can occur only once in a given speech.

In Chapter 9, you learned how to organize the most substantial part of your speech, the body. In this chapter, we examine how you frame the body of your speech by discussing the objectives of speech introductions and conclusions, as well as specific strategies you can use at these important points.

◖● Organize the Introduction of the Speech

After you work on the body of your speech, you are ready to focus on the introduction and conclusion. An introduction should achieve five objectives: (1) get the attention of your audience, (2) state your topic, (3) establish the importance of your topic, (4) establish your credibility to speak on your topic, and (5) preview the key ideas of your speech. Studying these objectives and the ways to achieve them will enable you to get your speech off to a clear, interesting start.

Get the Attention of Your Audience

Your first objective as a speaker is to secure the audience's attention. The way you get the audience involved in your speech will depend on your personality, your purpose, your topic, your audience, and the occasion. Your options include the following seven possible techniques.

Question Your Audience. A speaker can get an audience involved through the use of questions, either rhetorical or direct. A **rhetorical question** stimulates thought but is not intended to elicit an overt response. For example, consider the following opening questions:

- How did you spend last weekend? Watching television? Going to a movie? Sleeping late?
- What would you do if you saw your best friend copying another student's answers during a test?
- Do you remember what first attracted you to this school?

A speaker who asks any of the above questions does not expect an overt audience response. In fact, it would probably disrupt the rhythm of the presentation if someone answered orally. A question is rhetorical if it is designed to get the audience thinking about the topic.

A **direct question** seeks a public response. Audience members may be asked to respond vocally or physically. For example, the following questions could all be answered by a show of hands:

- How many of you have worked as a volunteer for some charitable group within the last year? The last 6 months?
- Last week the Student Government Association sponsored a blood drive. Raise your hand if you donated blood.

Like the rhetorical question, a **direct question** gets the audience thinking about your topic. However, the direct question has the additional advantage of getting your listeners physically involved in your speech and, consequently, making them more alert. This strategy may be especially appropriate if you are the first or final speaker, or if you give your speech when your listeners are especially tired.

Sometimes a direct question may invite an oral response. In his speech urging classmates to volunteer their efforts at charitable agencies, Lou discovered by a show of hands that only a few people volunteered regularly. He then asked the rest of the class why they did not. Several complained of lack of time. One person said she did not know how to locate groups that need volunteers. Lou continued, incorporating these excuses into his speech and refuting them.

"I didn't answer No. 11, because I thought it was a rhetorical question."

When you ask a direct question and you want oral responses, you need to pause, look at your listeners, and give them sufficient time to respond. If you want a direct question answered by a show of hands, raise your hand as you end the question. In this way, you indicate nonverbally how you want the question answered. If you seek and get oral responses, however, make sure that you neither lose control nor turn your public speech into a group discussion. Practice these techniques as you rehearse in front of friends before making them part of your speech.

There are a few final cautions about using a question to get the audience's attention. First, avoid asking embarrassing questions. "How many of you are on scholastic probation?" "Has anyone in here ever spent a night in jail?" Common sense should tell you that most people would be reluctant to answer direct questions such as these. Second, don't use a question without first considering its usefulness to your speech. Many questions are creative and intriguing. Remember, asking a valid question that listeners answer either openly or to themselves gets them immediately involved and thinking about your speech topic. Just don't rely on a question because you have not developed or found a more creative attention getter.

Arouse Your Audience's Curiosity. A lively way to engage the minds of your listeners is through suspense. Get them wondering what is to come. Jake chose to keep his audience in suspense in his attention-getting step. Notice how he incorporated rhetorical questions in his introduction to heighten his listeners' curiosity:

> **KEY POINTS**
>
> **Functions of a Speech Introduction**
>
> 1. Get the attention of your audience.
> 2. State your topic.
> 3. Establish the importance of your topic.
> 4. Establish your credibility to speak on your topic.
> 5. Preview the key ideas of your speech.

A 76-year-old mother of four slices bread at her kitchen counter. In a moment, her life will be over—cut down by a culprit who has been lying quietly in wait for almost two decades. In a way, she's lucky. This culprit frequently strikes women far younger than she. But nevertheless, in a moment a family will begin to mourn. But who was this stealthy assassin? Some rare and untreatable virus? No. An incredibly patient serial killer? Uh-uh. The truth is this villain is not only far deadlier than both of these, but also the most preventable.[1]

Jake resolved the suspense when he introduced his topic: heart disease in women.

Stimulate Your Audience's Imagination. Another way to engage the minds of your listeners is to stimulate their imaginations. To do this, you must know what referents they share, and this requires some good audience analysis on your part. Notice in the following example how Jennifer began her speech by relating a personal experience that she knew many in her audience would find familiar:

> The year was 1984. Saturday morning had finally arrived, and I was in my Strawberry Shortcake nightgown, complete with Strawberry Shortcake necklace and watch, humming along with the theme to *The Smurfs*. I can still hear it in my head. [She hums part of the show's theme song.] My sister sat beside me with her Optimus Prime Transformer in hand. My younger brother was quietly awaiting *Teenage Mutant Ninja Turtles* to come on. All was right with the world.

In the rest of her speech, Jennifer discussed "retro toys" such as Transformers and Strawberry Shortcake and the reasons for their return to store shelves.

Lori introduced one of her speeches in the following way:

> Imagine yourself on a beach, at night. Through the moonlight you see the palm trees swaying as the warm tropical breeze comes in from the sea. There's an undercurrent of excitement as you all load into the boat. Moonlight shimmers off the waves as you approach your unmarked destination. The boat stops. Backward, with gear intact, you fall into the pitch black water. There are no words to express the sensation of your first night dive. You hear only the sounds of your own breathing. You see only the brilliantly colored marine life that swims in and out of the scope of your flashlight; all else is a black abyss.

In spite of what she says, we would argue that Lori did find some words to express the sensation of night scuba diving. Notice her strong appeals to our senses of sight and hearing. In Chapter 12, we discuss the use of language to create these and other sensory impressions in your audience.

Promise Your Audience Something Beneficial. We listen more carefully to messages that are in our self-interest. If you can promise your audience members something that meets one or more of their needs, you secure their attention very quickly. For example, beginning your speech with the statement "Every person in this room can find a satisfying summer internship related to your major field of study" immediately secures the attention of your listeners—at least those not currently working in their dream jobs. Other effective examples are ones in which a speaker promises

---

EXPLORING ONLINE

Quotations

www.theotherpages.org/quote
.html

The "Quotations Home Page" touts more than 29,000 entries in 30 categories. Use the "by topic" link to get to specific subjects quickly. If you're looking for ideas, or just want to be entertained, browse the many links on this site.

that her information can save audience members hundreds of dollars in income tax next April, or in which a speaker says, "The information I will give you in the next 10 minutes will help you buy an excellent used car with complete confidence." Job satisfaction, savings, and consumer confidence—the promises of these three attention getters—are directly related to the interests of many audience members.

In addition to promising a benefit that meets your listeners' self-interests, you can appeal to their selflessness. Notice how David tapped his audience's altruism with the following attention getter:

> When Tricia Matthews decided to undergo a simple medical procedure, she had no idea what impact it could have on her life. But more than a year later, when she saw 5-year-old Tommy and his younger brother Daniel walk across the stage of *The Oprah Winfrey Show*, she realized that the short amount of time it took her to donate her bone marrow was well worth it. Tricia is not related to the boys who suffered from a rare immune deficiency disorder treated by a transplant of her bone marrow. Tricia and the boys found each other through the National Marrow Donor Program, or NMDP, a national network that strives to bring willing donors and needy patients together. Though the efforts Tricia made were minimal, few Americans make the strides she did. Few of us would deny anyone the gift of life, but sadly, few know how easily we can help.[2]

Amuse Your Audience. The use of humor can be one of a speaker's most effective attention-getting strategies. Getting the audience to laugh with you makes them alert and relaxed. You can use humor to emphasize key ideas in your speech, to show a favorable self-image, or to defuse audience hostility. However, any humor you use should be tasteful and relevant to your topic or the speaking occasion. As a speaker, you must be able to make a smooth and logical transition between your humorous opening and your speech topic. Telling a joke or a funny story and then switching abruptly to a serious topic trivializes the topic and may offend your listeners.

Stacey encouraged her classmates to study a foreign language, introducing her classroom speech with the following attention-getting riddle:

> What do you call someone who is fluent in many languages? A polylingual. What do you call someone who is fluent in two languages? A bilingual. What do you call someone who is fluent in only one language? An American!
>
> This is a joke commonly told among the Japanese. Behind the apparent humor of this joke are some embarrassing truths.

Stacey combined humor and rhetorical questions to get her listeners' attention. She then discussed those "embarrassing truths" and the price we pay for speaking only one language.

Energize Your Audience. Sometimes speakers can command attention simply by their presence. Martin Luther King, Jr., had that ability. Although few people can achieve such dynamism, most speakers can work

EXPLORING ONLINE

Quotations

www.bartleby.com/quotations

If you're searching for a profound or funny quotation to get your listeners' attention, this site offers a searchable database that provides thousands of entries from multiple sources, including the venerable *Bartlett's Familiar Quotations*.

Tasteful and relevant humor can capture your audience's attention and prepare them to listen to the rest of your speech.

to enliven their delivery. A positive attitude, appropriate dress, a confident walk to the platform, direct eye contact, a friendly smile, erect posture, a strong voice, and forceful gestures give an introduction as much impact as any of the preceding strategies. Conversely, the absence of these elements can destroy the effect of even the best-worded opening statement. Remember that an energized delivery is not a stand-alone strategy. It cannot substitute for a well-worded opening statement, but rather it is best used in combination with one of the other attention-getting strategies.

The advantages of an "energized" presence extend far beyond a speech introduction, however. In Chapter 13, we'll give you specific suggestions for achieving dynamic delivery throughout your speech.

Acknowledge and Compliment Your Audience. At some point in your life, you will probably be called on to deliver a formal, public speech to an assembled group. Perhaps you will be the keynote speaker for a convention, or maybe you will accept an award from a civic group. Such an occasion usually requires that you begin by acknowledging the audience and key dignitaries. On July 20, 2011, U.S. Secretary of State Hillary Clinton addressed the Working Women's Forum in Chennai, India. She began by acknowledging its founder and president, Dr. Jaya Arunachalam. Notice how Clinton praised the organization's mission of improving the "economic, social, and cultural status of poor working women" in India.

> I want to thank my friend and your friend, a wonderful woman who is viewed as a leader around the world, Jaya. [Applause] I want you to know that I have admired the work of the Working Women's Forum for many years. [Applause] In 1978, there were only 800 women members. Today, there are more than one million of you. I am honored to be here with you to celebrate your accomplishments in bringing micro-credit to women, in bringing healthcare and other services to women so that they could have a better life for themselves and their children.[3] [Applause]

Secretary Clinton complimented her audience on their accomplishments and used words such as *I*, *my*, *you*, and *your* to demonstrate a shared commitment.

In this class, your classmates make up your audience. You have interacted with them and by now probably know them pretty well. To begin your speech formally by acknowledging and complimenting them would seem stiff and insincere. You should not have to compliment fellow classmates; in fact, if you have prepared well, they should be thanking you for providing excellent information. For your assigned speeches, therefore, choose one of the other attention-getting strategies we have discussed.

State Your Topic

Once you have your audience's attention, state the topic or purpose of your speech directly and succinctly. For an informative speech, your statement of purpose typically takes the form of a simple declarative sentence. "Today,

KEY POINTS

Strategies for Getting Your Audience's Attention

1. Question your audience.
2. Arouse curiosity.
3. Stimulate imagination.
4. Promise something beneficial.
5. Amuse your audience.
6. Energize your audience.
7. Acknowledge and compliment your audience.

SPEAKING WITH CONFIDENCE

If you fail to attain your audience's attention in the introduction, you won't have it in the rest of your speech. My introduction's success in my speech on Virtual Cyber Charter Schools was important not only for the rest of my speech but also because it would become the audience's first impression of me. I asked the audience members to close their eyes and picture a classroom, not one of rows of desks, but one with a computer and headset that existed in virtual space. By starting off with this place I knew well and wanted to share, I felt confident in my ability to deliver an effective introduction.

When I asked my audience to open their eyes, I could see that their imaginations were stimulated. Their genuine interest allowed me to be confident throughout the entire speech, especially in the parts that were complicated, like explaining the nuances between curriculum choices available to cyber students. By asking my audience to close their eyes for the briefest of moments, my own were opened to a whole new facet of myself: self-assurance.

Amanda Gipson
Pennsylvania State University Hazleton

I will show you how you can improve your study skills" clearly informs the audience of your topic.

This second goal of a speech introduction is vitally important, even though the actual statement of purpose will take only a few seconds for you to say. Consider the following beginning section of a speech introduction:

How many of you have had a cholesterol count taken in the last year? Do you know what your numbers are and what they mean? It seems like we have all recently become much more aware of good cholesterol and bad, high-density lipoproteins and low-density ones, the dangers of high-fat diets and how difficult they can be to avoid in these fast-food, nuke-it-till-it's-hot times. People who never really considered exercising are spending a lot of money to join health clubs and work out. They know that a high cholesterol count can mean you are in danger of developing arteriosclerosis and finding yourself a candidate for surgery. Even if you don't have a heart attack, you may be hospitalized for one of several new procedures to clean out arteries clogged with plaque.

Now answer the following question: This speaker's purpose was to

a. discuss the interpretation of cholesterol tests.
b. explain sources of cholesterol in popular foods.
c. encourage exercise as a key to reducing serum cholesterol.
d. explain new nonsurgical procedures for opening clogged arteries.
e. I can't tell what the speaker's purpose was.

Unfortunately, in this case, the correct answer is e. What went wrong? The speaker started off well enough by using two legitimate questions—the first direct, the second rhetorical—as an attention getter. But then things got out of control; for almost a minute of speaking time, the speaker lapsed into a series of generalizations without ever stating the purpose of the speech. This excerpt represents a minute of wasted time! In a 5- to 7-minute speech, that minute represents one-fifth to one-seventh of total speaking time. The speaker has confused the audience with vague statements and has lost their

ETHICAL DECISIONS

Revealing versus Concealing Your Purpose

Yvonne has decided on a specific purpose for her persuasive speech: to convince her classmates that same-sex marriages should be legal. As she analyzes her audience's attitudes, she concludes that many of her classmates disagree with her position, some quite strongly. She is fearful that if she reveals her specific purpose in the introduction, some audience members will stop listening to her speech objectively and will either begin formulating counterarguments or simply tune her out. She decides that, instead, she will delay the announcement of her purpose and present some basic criteria for a good marriage. After securing agreement on these criteria, she will then reveal her purpose for speaking—to an audience that is primed to listen.

Is Yvonne's strategy ethical? Is it acceptable for a speaker to conceal his or her purpose in an introduction in order to keep an audience's attention? If you think this strategy is legitimate, write a few examples of situations in which it would be justifiable. Try to list and explain the ethical guidelines speakers should follow in making decisions about this strategy.

confidence. The real shame is that any of the four purposes just listed could be the goal of a good speech. Prepare properly and you will know your purpose. Then, state that purpose clearly as the second step of your introduction.

Establish the Importance of Your Topic

The third goal in organizing the introduction to your speech should be to convince the listeners that the topic is important to them. You want to motivate them to listen further. In his speech on unsafe water used in dental procedures, Brian selected expert testimony and statistics to show his listeners that they were at risk:

Professor Robert Staat, a microbiologist with the University of Louisville Dental School, reported to *20/20* the results of his research testing water samples from more than sixty dental offices across the country. His investigation revealed that almost 90 percent of water used in dental procedures does not meet federal drinking water standards, and two-thirds of the samples contained saliva from previous patients. After comparing dental water with water collected from public toilets, he discovered that in nearly every case the water from the toilets was cleaner than the water going into our mouths. His conclusion: the water used in most dental procedures is dangerously unsanitary, and we must act to protect ourselves.[4]

Remember the way Jake tapped his listeners' curiosity before introducing his topic of heart disease in women? He then provided statistics and examples to establish the importance of his topic for the women and men in his audience:

"[T]he truth," as stated in the *Pittsburgh Post Gazette* of December 12, 2000, "is that heart disease kills more women every year than all forms of cancer, chronic lung disease, pneumonia, diabetes, accidents, and AIDS combined." Whereas one in twenty-eight women will die of breast cancer, one in five will die of heart disease. And guys, before you take the next nine minutes to decide what you'll eat for lunch, ask yourself one

Speakers can motivate audience members to listen by explaining how the topic affects them.

question, "What would my life be like if the women who make it meaningful are not there?" Clearly, this is an issue that concerns us all.[5]

Establish Your Credibility to Speak on Your Topic

The fourth goal of a speech introduction is to establish your credibility to speak on your topic. Your listeners should understand why you selected your topic and should believe that you are qualified to speak on it. Establishing your credibility begins in the introduction and should continue throughout your speech. Introducing relevant supporting materials and citing their sources are two ways to demonstrate that you have carefully researched and considered your topic.

You can also enhance your credibility by drawing on your experience with your topic. Our student Robert mentioned his work as a veterinarian technician in the introduction to his speech on heartworms in dogs. In the body of his speech, he referred several times to how many cases of infected pets he sees in his work. Our student Humberto mentioned in the introduction of his speech on computer scams that he had once almost been victimized. In the final point of his speech body, he explained how he detected the fake money order he had received as payment for a boat he was selling.

Preview Your Key Ideas

A final objective in organizing your introduction is the **preview**, in which you "tell us what you're going to tell us." The preview, working like a map, shows a final destination and reveals how the speaker intends to get there. As a result, the audience can travel more easily through the body of the speech. A speaker addressing the issue of urban decay could preview her speech by saying, "To better understand the scope of this problem, we must look at four measurable conditions: the unemployment rate, housing starts, the poverty level, and the crime rate." That preview lists the four topics to be covered in the body of the speech and prepares the audience to listen more intelligently.

Preview statements are usually one to three sentences. Rarely do they need to be longer. Each of the following examples is appropriately brief and specific.

preview
A statement that orients the audience by revealing how the speaker has organized the body of a speech.

> Assuming that you have the necessary materials, the three steps to constructing a piece of stained glass are, first, selecting or creating a design; second, cutting the glass; and third, assembling and fixing the individual pieces.

> A person suffering from narcolepsy, then, experiences unexpected attacks of deep sleep. This little-known sleep disorder is better understood if we know its symptoms, its causes, and its treatment.

> Today the *charreada* often draws both participants dressed in their traditional costumes and protestors carrying signs. To understand both sides of this issue, we'll look at those who say that the *charreada* is a valid sport that deserves to be practiced and at those who insist that the *charreada* is cruel and inhumane.

If you have written a thesis statement for your speech, you'll have no trouble constructing a preview statement as clear as any of these examples.

Preview statements, however, are often bland and predictable. Use your creativity to accent the ideas that will follow. For example, Jayme could have used the following preview statement in her speech on e-paper: "To understand the potential impact of e-paper, we must look first at what it is and how it works; next, at its advantages and disadvantages; and finally, at its future." Although this statement previews the key ideas of the speech, it conveys little creativity. Instead, Jayme opted for a longer statement to reinforce the ideas of her speech:

> In order to understand why the impact of e-paper could be of Gutenberg proportions, we must first start with a blank sheet as we explore what e-paper is and how it works; next, fill up the page with its advantages and disadvantages; and finally, widen the margins to discuss future directions of this amazing new technology.[6]

Put It All Together

How does the introduction sound when all five of its functions are working together? Our student Rose showed us that she certainly knows how to develop a complete and effective introduction:

> According to an old Indian saying, every person dies three times. The first time is the moment your life ends. The second is when your body is lowered into the ground. The third is when there is no one around to remember you. I'm going to talk to you today about death, or rather the celebration of death. This is a special celebration that comes from a Mexican tradition called *Día de los Muertos*, or Day of the Dead. Now, it may seem strange and morbid to speak of celebration and death in the same breath, but in the Mexican culture, death is embraced and worshipped just as much as life is. After I give you a little background on *Día de los Muertos*, I'll explain the different ways this holiday is celebrated and show you some of the traditional objects used in the celebration.

Paul began his speech this way:

Paul uses description and visualization to arouse his listeners' curiosity.

> Kristen Walsh was in her mid-twenties when she started working out at her local gym. She progressed from exercising 20 minutes every other morning to working out for 4 hours a day. Her friends admired her discipline. But what Kristen Walsh's friends didn't know was that her exercise regimen had become compulsive.

Paul introduces his topic of exercise anorexia.

Paul presents evidence to establish his topic's importance, build his credibility, and challenge his audience to share his concerns.

> Kristen had fallen victim to what the April 2006 *Journal of Health and Illness* claims is the latest weight loss disorder: exercise anorexia.
>
> According to Dr. Doug Bunnell, director of the National Institute of Exercise Addiction, over 11 million Americans a year are affected by this compulsion to exercise, and cases have nearly doubled over the past decade. Even more tragically, Dr. Bunnell goes on to say that this disease has claimed over two million lives in the last decade. As a result, we must all concern ourselves about exercise anorexia to further prevent people from literally working out to death.

Paul previews the key ideas he will develop in the body of his speech.

> In the next few minutes we will examine the devastating symptoms and effects of exercise anorexia, the causes of this disease, and most important, what we can do to prevent the increase of what many psychologists are calling "the deadly regimen."[7]

If you achieve the five objectives we have outlined for a speech introduction, your audience should be attentive, know the purpose of your speech, be motivated to listen, trust your qualifications to speak on the topic, and know the major ideas you will discuss.

Organize the Conclusion of the Speech

The remaining part of the speech is the conclusion. Although it is often briefer than the introduction, your conclusion is vitally important to achieving your desired response. The conclusion is the last section your listeners hear and see and must be well planned and carefully organized. It will be easier to develop if you work to achieve three goals: summarize your key ideas, activate audience response to your speech, and provide closure.

KEY POINTS

Functions of a Speech Conclusion

1. Summarize your key ideas.
2. Activate audience response.
3. Provide closure.

Summarize Your Key Ideas

In the **summary**, you "tell us what you told us." Of all the steps in the process of organization, this should be the easiest to construct. You have already organized the body of the speech and, from it, constructed a preview statement. The summary parallels your preview. If your speech develops three key ideas, you reiterate them. If your speech is on self-concept enhancement, for example, you may simply say, "A good self-concept, therefore, benefits us in three ways. It enhances our social interaction, our academic achievement, and our career success." A speech on dying might be summarized, "Denial. Anger. Bargaining. Depression. Acceptance. These are the five stages of dying described by Kübler-Ross."

An excellent summary step, however, does more than just repeat your key ideas. It also shows how those ideas support the goal of your speech. Remember Stacey's humorous attention getter to her speech encouraging her classmates to study a foreign language? In the speech, she discussed three harms from the nation's failure to promote bilingualism: "First, we lose economically.... Second, we lose scholastically.... Third, we lose culturally." Notice how Stacey reiterates and reinforces these points in the summary step of her conclusion:

> Clearly, these three points show us that by being monolingual we lose *economically*, *scholastically*, and *culturally*. Becoming proficient in another language and its culture may help us reduce our deficit and increase our competitiveness in world trade by recognizing possible problems in marketing campaigns. We will gain intellectually by increasing our vocabulary and expanding our minds. We will gain culturally by breaking barriers and possibly eliminating misunderstandings that occur as a result of being unfamiliar with another language, its people, and its culture.

The summary step gives the listener one last chance to hear and remember the main points of your presentation. Thus, it reinforces the ideas of the speech and brings it to a logical conclusion.

summary
A statement or statements reviewing the major ideas of a speech.

Activate Audience Response

What do you want your audience to do with the information you have provided or the arguments you have proved? The second function of a speech conclusion is to activate an audience response by letting your listeners know whether you want them to accept, remember, use, believe, or act on the content of your speech. Whether your speech is informative or persuasive, you want your audience to be involved with your information and ideas. The conclusion is your last opportunity to ensure this. If you have provided practical information that can make your listeners smarter, healthier, happier, or wealthier, challenge them to remember and use what they learned. If you have educated them about a problem and proposed a solution to it, remind them of the significance of not acting. If you have spoken on a topic that you find inherently interesting, hoping to generate audience interest by communicating your enthusiasm as well as your information, this is your last opportunity to invigorate or animate your listeners about the subject.

Rather than saying, "I hope you'll find what I've said about the film scores of Philip Glass useful," you might say something like this: "The next time you find your attention drawn to a movie's sound track because you like the music or feel that it could stand on its own, think about the painstaking process of matching sight and sound that an acclaimed composer like Philip Glass has to go through."

In her speech, Kimberly discussed an often overlooked problem: motorists who run red lights. Using vivid examples, expert testimony, and compelling statistics, she documented the problem: More than "200,000 people are injured and more than 800 people die every year in the United States due to motorists running red lights."[8] She called for individual, community, and government action to combat the problem. After reiterating the key ideas in her speech's conclusion, Kimberly sought to activate personal responsibility in her listeners:

> On your way home tonight, when you approach that traffic light, think of the facts we have talked about today. These facts apply to you every time you approach a traffic signal. Don't run red lights! When we take an extra minute or two to stop for the light, we are helping to protect hundreds of innocent people. The lives you save could be your neighbor's, your mother's, or your own.[9]

Providing closure means moving beyond your summary to present a satisfying conclusion to the ideas or issues you have discussed. Referring to your speech introduction, calling for action, and posing a provocative question are all effective strategies for ending a speech.

circular conclusion
A conclusion that repeats or refers to material used in the attention-getting step of the introduction.

Provide Closure

If your summary concludes your speech *logically*, your activation and closure statements end the speech *psychologically*. An effective final statement ties the speech together and provides a strong note of closure. You should not have to tell your listeners that the speech is finished. Your wording, as well as your delivery, should make this clear. Without resorting to saying, "In conclusion," or "To conclude," you should mark the end of your speech by slowing your rate, maintaining direct eye contact with your listeners, and pausing briefly before and after your final sentence.

Sometimes a speaker employs what is called a **circular conclusion**, in which the final statement echoes or refers to the attention-getting step of the introduction. Remember Jennifer, the grown-up Strawberry Shortcake who spoke about retro toys? At the end of her speech, she brought her listeners back to the familiar scene she had created at the start of her introduction:

Toy comebacks seem to run in 20- to 30-year cycles; I wonder how many different Elmos there will be in 20 years. For now, on Saturday morning, the Disney Channel delights us with *The Wiggles*, *Stanley*, and the *Higgleytown Heroes*. The little girl in the Strawberry Shortcake nightgown is my 4-year-old, Maddie. She and her baby sister hold their Care Bear dolls and sing along with the programs. Strawberry Shortcake still brings me joy, only now the joy comes from watching how happy Strawberry and her gang make my little girl.

Your final statement does not have to allude to your attention-getting step. Any of the specific techniques we discussed for gaining audience attention can help bring your speech to a psychologically satisfying conclusion. You can ask a question, even the same one you began with or a variation of it. Or you can answer the question you initially asked. Once you arouse your audience's curiosity in your speech, you must satisfy it in order to provide closure. You could stimulate their imaginations through vivid imagery or promise them that the information you have provided can benefit them. You could conclude with a joke or humorous story relevant to your topic. Through lively delivery, you could energize the audience to act on the information you have provided. In a speech presented on more formal occasions than a classroom assignment, you may end by complimenting and thanking the audience.

Put It All Together

All three functions of the conclusion are important. The summary step reinforces the *ideas* of the speech, while the final two functions reinforce the *impact* of the speech. In the introduction of his speech on breaking the silence about ovarian cancer, Viqar presented a startling statistic: "According to the National Cancer Coalition, every 9 minutes in the United States a woman is diagnosed with ovarian cancer."[10] Notice how Viqar used this statistic to frame his three-step conclusion.

In the last 9 minutes we've explored ovarian cancer and the deadly problems associated with the disease, and analyzed a solution to break the silence.

Viqar restates his key idea.

    In the last 9 minutes, a woman has been diagnosed with ovarian cancer. Women like the mother of Rene Rossi, who in the last 9 months of her life told her daughter, "You must do something about this disease." In the last 9 minutes, you have been given the power to do just that. Do it for the women in our lives—our mothers, our daughters, our loved ones.

Viqar requests audience action.

    Shout out this silent killer.[11]

Viqar provides closure.

A diagram of the individual steps in a well-organized speech would contain the following:

1. Attention-getting step
2. Statement of topic
3. Emphasis on topic's importance
4. Emphasis on speaker's credibility
5. Preview
6. Body of speech
7. Summary
8. Activation of audience's response
9. Closure

This is the correct sequence to follow as you *deliver* a speech. In your *preparation*, however, you should construct the body of your speech first. Some instructors recommend that you develop your introduction next and your conclusion last. Others suggest that you prepare your introduction last. Remember, there is no one correct way of constructing a speech. Select the method that works best for you.

We suggest an alternative strategy (see the "Theory Into Practice" feature). Speakers who begin preparing speeches by starting with the introduction often end up trying to fit the rest of their speech to it. Speakers who develop their introduction, body, and conclusion separately often produce three parts, rather than a unified whole. The outward method of development helps you avoid these pitfalls and enables you to present your ideas clearly, cohesively, and convincingly.

THEORY INTO PRACTICE

TIP   Outward Method of Speech Development

Using the "outward method" of developing a speech, construct the body of your speech first, determining the key ideas and developing them using the "4 S's." Then move outward, working simultaneously on your introduction and conclusion. Word the preview and summary statements that highlight your key ideas. Next, decide how you will state your topic, explain its importance, build your credibility, and activate audience response. Finally, develop the attention getter and the final statement at the same time to increase the unity of your speech.

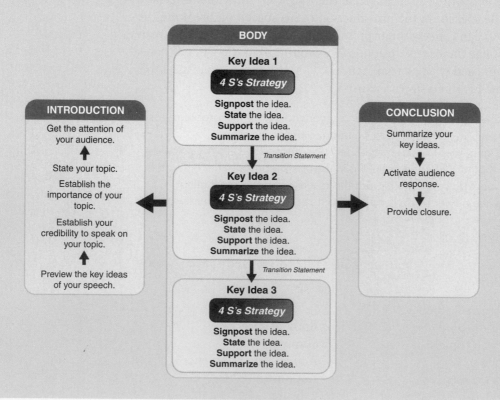

SUMMARY

The Importance of the Introduction and Conclusion

- The introduction and conclusion are brief parts of the speech, but they must be well organized and practiced since they are your first and last chances to create a favorable impression for yourself and your topic.

Functions of an Introduction

- The introduction should achieve five goals: (1) get the attention of your audience; (2) state your topic or purpose; (3) stress the importance or relevance of your topic; (4) establish your credibility to speak on your topic; and (5) preview the key ideas you will develop in the body of the speech.
- To get your audience's attention, you can question your listeners, arouse their curiosity, stimulate their imaginations, promise them something beneficial, amuse them, energize them, or acknowledge and compliment them.

Functions of a Conclusion

- An effective conclusion must do three things: (1) summarize your key ideas or bring your speech to a logical conclusion; (2) secure your listeners' commitment to your information and ideas; and (3) provide closure, or bring the speech to a satisfying psychological conclusion.

The Outward Method of Speech Development

- We recommend that you organize the body of your speech first and then move outward, working simultaneously on your introduction and conclusion.

EXERCISES

1. **Practice Critique.** You have just been appointed judge for a public speaking contest. Your task is to present the award for "best introduction" from among the four student speeches in Appendix B. Read these speeches and evaluate their introductions using the guidelines presented in this chapter. Select the introduction you think is best and explain the reasons for your selection.

2. Evaluate the chapter openings you have read thus far in this book. Which are most and least successful at getting your attention? What made them effective or ineffective?

3. Select a magazine and examine the various ways journalists begin their stories. Which of the seven attention-getting devices discussed in this chapter do they employ? Are there other attention-getting techniques you can identify?

4. Examine the attention-getting step of Jennell Chu's speech in Appendix B. Rewrite the attention getter using two strategies other than the one Chu uses.

5. Suppose the specific purpose of a speech is to persuade an audience to contribute money for needed playground equipment for a local elementary school. Write a statement establishing the importance and relevance of the topic for each of the following audiences:
   a. Parents of children who attend the school
   b. Senior citizens on limited, fixed incomes whose children and grandchildren no longer attend the school
   c. Traditional-age college students

6. Locate the preview statements in the introductions of the student speeches in Appendix B.

7. Rewrite the closure statement of Jennell Chu's speech in Appendix B using two strategies other than the one Chu uses. Discuss the strengths and weaknesses of each closure statement. Which closure strategy do you prefer? Why?

8. Prepare three conclusions for the same body of content. Discuss the advantages and disadvantages of each. Select the one you think is best and explain why.

Outlining Your Speech

11

- **Functions of Outlining**
  Tests Scope of Content
  Tests Logical Relation of Parts
  Tests Relevance of Supporting Ideas
  Checks Balance of Speech
  Serves as Delivery Notes

- **Principles of Outlining**
  Singularity
  Consistency
  Adequacy
  Uniformity
  Parallelism

- **Stages of Outlining**
  The Working Outline
  Theory Into Practice: Visual
    Brainstorming
  The Formal Outline
  The Speaking Outline

After studying this chapter,
you should be able to

1. Understand the five functions
   of outlining.

2. Identify and apply the four
   principles of outlining.

3. Construct key word and
   complete sentence outlines.

4. Understand the three stages of
   outlining.

5. Develop working and formal
   outlines.

6. Prepare your speaking outline.

> Order and simplification are the first steps toward the mastery of a subject.
>
> —Thomas Mann

How long would it take you to memorize and repeat the following 26 letters: *c-p-s-y-n-i-r-t-y-m-v-i-e-m-r-t-o-i-p-o-e-m-o-m-e-m*? A typical learner would need a good deal of practice to remember more than the first four to seven letters.[1] Would it help if the letters were rearranged as follows: *y-m-c-o-i-t-p-s-i-p-t-y-m-m-v-e-n-e-o-i-r-r-m-e-o-m*? Unless you have a photographic memory, such a shuffling of letters is likely no help at all. But what if the letters were scrambled again: *m-y-t-o-p-i-c-i-s-m-e-m-o-r-y-i-m-p-r-o-v-e-m-e-n-t*? Those letters are more recognizable and even more obvious if we eliminated the dashes and used a familiar pattern of grouping and spacing: *my topic is memory improvement*. You could now master the entire sequence of 26 letters in correct order, orally or in writing, without much effort.

Notice that we did not add or delete any letters. We merely reorganized them until they formed a pattern that is easy to recognize and repeat. When you outline, you perform essentially the same task. You organize and reorganize material into a pattern easy to recognize and remember.

In Chapters 9 and 10, we discussed the importance of organization to the delivered speech and suggested some ways of achieving a well-organized presentation. Outlining your speech is the preliminary written work necessary to foster clear organization of your oral message. In this chapter, you will learn why outlines are important to your speech, examine some different types of outlines, and learn how to write an excellent outline.

◖ Functions of Outlining

A well-prepared outline serves five important functions for a speaker:

1. It tests the scope of the speaker's content.
2. It tests the logical relations among parts of the speech.
3. It tests the relevance of supporting ideas.
4. It checks the balance or proportion of the speech.
5. It serves as notes during the delivery of the speech.

Tests Scope of Content

The first purpose of outlining is to test the scope of the speaker's content. Have you narrowed the topic sufficiently to cover your key ideas in some depth? Or are you trying to cover too much material and consequently skimming the surface of the subject, repeating things your audience already knows? Outlining allows you to organize your main ideas and then add, delete, regroup, shuffle, condense, or expand these ideas so you approach your topic in a manageable way. In other words, outlining is a process of setting goals for the speech.

Tests Logical Relation of Parts

Second, outlining allows speakers to test the logical relations among the various parts of the speech. Does one idea in the outline lead to the next in a meaningful way? Do the arguments or subtopics under each of your main points really develop that point? To answer these questions, you must understand the concepts of coordination and subordination. **Coordinate ideas** are those of equal value or importance in the overall pattern of the speech. The following example illustrates the relation between coordinate and subordinate ideas.

If you delivered an informative speech on the functions of service dogs, you might arrange your speech topically and focus on just these two areas:

I. Search functions
II. Protection functions

These two topics are coordinate because they seem to be of equal value. You might have more information on one of them than on the other and thus spend more time in the speech discussing that topic. However, neither is a subtopic of the other. Under that first main topic, you would then list **subordinate ideas**, or subtopics that support it.

I. Search functions
   A. Narcotics detection
   B. Bomb detection
   C. Arson detection
   D. Cadaver location
   E. Disease detection

Notice that points A through E are not only subordinate to the main idea—search functions—but also coordinate with each other since they seem to be equally important. Subordinate points for the second main point could include the following:

II. Protection functions
   A. Seeing-eye dogs
   B. Guard dogs
   C. Attack dogs
   D. Seizure-alert dogs

Your outline is not yet complete, but you can begin to ask yourself the following questions: Are my main points different enough to qualify as separate points? Do my subordinate points really support the main ideas? At this stage, the answers to both of these questions seem to be yes. In this way, the visual form of the outline helps you test the logical connections among parts of your speech. You continue this process to further refine and add to the outline.

Tests Relevance of Supporting Ideas

Third, an outline helps the speaker test the relevance of supporting ideas. To understand how this works, assume that you have written the following portion of an outline for a speech on roller coasters:

coordinate ideas
Ideas that have equal value in a speech.

subordinate ideas
Ideas that support more general or more important points in a speech.

An effective outline can serve as notes to use during the delivery if your speech.

I. Famous roller coasters
   A. Coney Island's "Cyclone"
   B. Montreal's "Le Monstre"
   C. Busch Gardens's "Kumba"
   D. New design technology

Notice that the fourth subpoint, "new design technology," is out of place because it is irrelevant to the main point. How do you solve this problem? One option is to make "new design technology" a separate main point if you can gather adequate supporting material on it; if you can't, eliminate it.

Checks Balance of Speech

A fourth function of outlining is to check the balance or proportion of the speech. Consider the outline on functions of service dogs. If the first main point has five subpoints and the second has four, the speech looks balanced, even though a speaker might spend more time on one of those main points than on the other. Yet if the main point "search functions" had five subpoints and "protection functions" had only two, the outline might not be balanced. This lack of balance could be reflected in the speech.

How can you fix such an imbalance? One option is to focus just on those five search functions by making the subpoints into main points: I. Narcotics detection, II. Bomb detection, III. Arson detection, IV. Cadaver location, V. Disease detection. As you can see, by testing the balance of your speech, an outline can even lead you to alter your specific purpose.

Serves as Delivery Notes

Fifth and finally, a special type of abbreviated outline can serve as notes for the speaker during the speech's delivery. The *speaking outline*, discussed later in this chapter, has only one rule: it must be brief. If you have prepared adequately for your speech, you should need only key words and phrases to remind you of each point you want to discuss. Moreover, having your notes in outline form rather than arranged randomly on notecards or sheets of paper will remind you of the importance of clear organization as you are delivering the speech.

SPEAKING WITH CONFIDENCE

I have come to realize that outlining is an important part of the speech-making process. Having a clear and concise outline builds such self-confidence, not only in my ability to give the speech but in my knowledge of the topic as well. When I sit down to write my outline, all my thoughts seem to flow out onto the page in a step-by-step manner, so that my confidence in the subject builds up. Then, when I am finished with the outline, I feel as if I could give the speech right away because I have so much information down that I could expand on it as little or as much as I needed. Now that I realize how important outlining is, I will always be sure to make one for my speeches because of how much smoother it makes the speech-making process!

Alana Kwast
San Antonio College

Principles of Outlining

Correct outlines take one of two possible forms: the **complete sentence outline** and the **key word or phrase outline**. In a complete sentence outline, each item is a sentence; each item in a key word or phrase outline is a word or group of words. These two forms of outlines should be kept consistent and distinct. Combine them only in the speaker's outline from which you deliver your speech. So far in this chapter, we have used only phrase outlines. More word or phrase outlines and an example of a complete sentence outline follow.

As you construct your outline, you will work more efficiently and produce a clearer outline if you follow a few rules, or principles.

Singularity

First, each number or letter in the outline should represent only one idea. A chief goal of outlining is to achieve a clear visual representation of the connections among parts of the speech. This is possible only if you separate the ideas. For example, suppose a speaker preparing a speech on color blindness has worded a key idea as "causes of and tests for color blindness." The phrase contains two distinct ideas, each requiring separate discussion and development. Instead, the speaker should divide the statement into two coordinate points: "causes of color blindness" and "tests for color blindness."

Consistency

Second, coordinate and subordinate points in the outline should be represented by a consistent system of numbers and letters. Main ideas are typically represented by Roman numerals: I, II, III, and so forth. Label subpoints under the main points with indented capital letters: A, B, C, and so forth. Beneath those, identify your supporting points with indented Arabic numerals: 1, 2, 3, and so on. Identify ideas subordinate to those with indented lowercase letters: a, b, c, and so on. Using this notation system, the labeling and indentation of a typical outline would appear as follows:

I. Main point
   A. Subpoint
      1. Sub-subpoint
      2. Sub-subpoint
      3. Sub-subpoint
   B. Subpoint
      1. Sub-subpoint
      2. Sub-subpoint
         a. Sub-sub-subpoint
         b. Sub-sub-subpoint
II. Main point
   A. Subpoint
   B. Subpoint
      1. Sub-subpoint
      2. Sub-subpoint
   C. Subpoint

---

complete sentence outline
An outline in which all numbers and letters introduce complete sentences.

key word or phrase outline
An outline in which all numbers and letters introduce words or groups of words.

KEY POINTS

Principles of Outlining

1. Each number or letter in the outline should represent only one idea.
2. Coordinate and subordinate points in the outline should be represented by a consistent system of numbers and letters.
3. If any point has subpoints under it, there must be at least two.
4. Each symbol in a sentence outline should introduce a complete sentence. Each symbol in a word or phrase outline should introduce a word or phrase.
5. Coordinate points throughout the outline should have parallel grammatical construction.

Adequacy

A third principle is that if any point has subpoints under it, there must be at least two. A basic law of physics is that you cannot divide something into only one part. If you have an A, you must also have a B. (You may, of course, also have subpoints C, D, and E.) If you have a 1, you must also have at least a 2.

Uniformity

Fourth, each symbol in a sentence outline should introduce a complete sentence. Each symbol in a word or phrase outline should introduce a word or phrase. Keep the form of the outline consistent. Sentences and phrases should be mixed only in your speaking outline.

Parallelism

Finally, coordinate points throughout the outline should have parallel grammatical construction. For example, a key phrase outline of a speech on how to write a résumé begins with a first main point labeled "Things to include." The second point should be "Things to omit," rather than "Leaving out unnecessary information." The first point is worded as a noun phrase; therefore, you should follow it with another noun phrase ("Things to omit") rather than a predicate phrase ("Leaving out unnecessary information"). This does not mean that you must choose noun phrases over verb phrases but rather that all points must match grammatically. In this next example, all coordinate points have parallel grammatical construction.

  I. Including essential information
      A. Address
      B. Career objective
      C. Educational background
      D. Employment history
      E. References
 II. Omitting unnecessary information
      A. Marital status
      B. Religious denomination
      C. Political affiliation

As you can see, coordinate main points I and II are verb phrases, while the coordinate subpoints are all nouns or noun phrases.

◗ Stages of Outlining

If you have difficulty generating or discovering the main points for a speech topic you have chosen, don't worry; you are not alone. Many people are intimidated by the prospect of selecting and organizing ideas, particularly for a first speech. Keep in mind four guidelines to organizing and outlining.

EXPLORING ONLINE

Developing an Outline

http://owl.english.purdue.edu/owl/resource/544/02/

http://owl.english.purdue.edu/owl/resource/673/03/

As it does so well with many topics, the Online Writing Lab at Purdue University presents an excellent rationale for outlining and provides a sample outline. At the second site, OWL provides a list of twenty questions, "thought starters," that suggest ways to explore and develop key ideas.

ETHICAL DECISIONS

Fair and Balanced?

Carter, a member of State U's student government association, helped draft a proposal to reform its bylaws and streamline its operations. He is scheduled to give an informative speech in his public speaking class the week before the student body will vote on the proposal. Carter decides to inform his classmates about the plan's advantages and disadvantages.

As he outlines his speech using a pro–con pattern, Carter identifies three benefits of the change: equal representation of student constituencies, enhanced interaction between students and the SGA, and faster SGA response to campus problems. The only arguments he develops against the proposed change are minor transition problems as the SGA implements the new structure. Carter wants to empower students to make an informed decision and is concerned that his speech may appear self-serving and persuasive.

Should Carter revise his outline to balance both sides of the issue? Is presenting one side more strongly than the other ethical in an informative speech? What outlining principles can help Carter develop his organization and supporting materials? List and explain ethical guidelines that speakers should follow to ensure a fair and balanced discussion of issues.

First, organization is not something that comes to you; rather, it is something that you must seek. Structuring a speech requires you to invest time and thought.

Second, there is no one right way of organizing all speeches on a particular topic. True, some topics logically lend themselves to certain patterns of organization. As you learned in Chapter 9, speeches about processes often almost organize themselves chronologically. Speeches about people may be arranged chronologically or topically. Persuasive speeches on social issues are perhaps most logically organized according to a problem–solution format. Yet different speakers may use different structures. You must determine what works best for you, your topic, and your audience.

Third, the early stages of organizing and outlining a speech are filled with uncertainty. You may find yourself asking, "Do I have enough main points, too many, or too few? Can I find adequate information to support all those main points? Am I overlooking other main points the audience would be interested in hearing me discuss?" Rather than feeling pressured by such questions, look on the early stages of outlining as a period of flexibility. The early, informal versions of your working outline are all provisional—temporary and open to change. Don't be afraid to experiment a little.

Fourth, and finally, identifying the main points in a speech is easier than many people imagine. In the remainder of this chapter, we guide you through the process of outlining, from those first tentative ideas you put on paper to the final outline you use as speaking notes.

The Working Outline

The first step in preparing an outline is to construct a **working outline,** a list of aspects of your chosen topic. Such a list may result from research

> No matter how much fun the detours are, you need a map to keep you on track. Get used to outlining, and your journeys will go a lot smoother.
>
> —Jeff Kirvin[2]

working outline
An informal, initial outline recording a speaker's process of narrowing, focusing, and balancing a topic.

you have already done or some productive brainstorming. Once you have spent significant time researching the subject, you will notice topics that are repeated in different sources on the subject. If, for example, you had selected "super staph"—methicillin-resistant *Staphylococcus aureus* (MRSA)—as the topic for an informative speech and had conducted adequate research, your list of possible aspects of the topic might include its causes, symptoms, diagnosis, treatment, and prevention. Notice that these same topics could be applied to any disease, physical illness, or mental condition.

You can also generate topics by brainstorming and visual brainstorming, techniques we discussed in Chapter 6. Brainstorming can help you generate topics and explore areas of your final topic.[3] Your creative brainstorming might even reveal interesting areas of your topic that have not been adequately treated in the existing research. This discovery provides you an opportunity to conduct original research or experimentation.

As you can see, at this stage, the term *outline* is very loose; the list of key ideas you are developing does not have any numbers or letters attached to it. That's fine, since these notes are for your benefit alone. This working outline is merely a record of the process you go through in thinking about a speech topic.

To illustrate these first steps in preparing an outline, consider the experience of a speaker, Chris, who came up with a speech topic in the following manner:

> As an art major with a brother who's an architect, I'm always interested in stories about important structures. And the designs that usually impress me the most are simple—so clear and straightforward that you end up thinking, "Of course, how else could that building be put together? It's just right."
>
> I first learned about the Gateshead Millennium Bridge when I saw a story about it in *Newsweek*. Later I remembered the story when I read that the bridge had won some design award. That got me interested in researching the structure, and I soon learned that it has won a number of awards and has webcams where you can see live views of the bridge any time you want.
>
> Then I got the chance to travel around England with a group of artists and activists. We eventually went to Newcastle in northeastern England, and I got to see the bridge and walk across it. I thought it was pretty amazing.

At this point, Chris knew that he wanted to talk about this bridge. He also knew from his preliminary research that he would have no trouble finding enough information about it. Just by brainstorming topics that might apply to any bridge, Chris developed the following working outline:

> History of the project
> Design
> Impact

As he researched the bridge further, Chris read several articles about its engineering. He added that topic to his working outline. Then, adding subtopics as he thought of them or encountered them in his research, he developed the visual brainstorming example shown in "Theory Into Practice."

After completing his research on the bridge, Chris realized that the information he had about its engineering was too technical to interest most of his listeners. He also had a great deal of interesting information about the area's history and efforts to revive it economically. However, he could not include all this information within the time limit for his speech. As a result, he decided to focus on just three main points. Chris's working outline was as follows:

I.   Design challenges
II. Specific features of the bridge
III. Impact of the bridge

So was all of that time spent reading the engineering and history articles wasted? "Not at all," Chris says. "Even though I'm not going to have the

THEORY INTO PRACTICE

 **TIP**   Visual Brainstorming

Subject: The Gateshead Millennium Bridge

Visual brainstorming gives form and shape to initial ideas about a topic. This working outline began as Chris jotted down three topics he felt sure about including: history of the project, design, and impact. After some preliminary research, he added engineering and construction as possible subtopics.

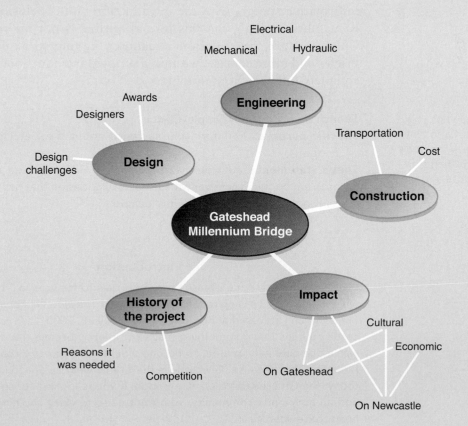

time to discuss the mechanical and electrical engineering or the hydraulics of the bridge, I know those topics better and have more confidence. If someone asks me a technical question about how the bridge operates or why it was built as it was, I feel sure I will either know the answer or remember where to find the answer."

The Formal Outline

formal outline
A complete sentence outline written in sufficient detail that a person other than the speaker could understand it.

Your **formal outline** is a complete sentence outline reflecting the full content and organization of your speech. In its final form, it is the finished product of your research and planning for your speech. A stranger picking up your formal outline should be able to understand how you have organized and supported all your main points. If you keep that goal in mind, you should have no trouble deciding what to include.

If you are required to turn in an outline when you speak, find out if it should be a formal outline or can use key words or phrases. The actual outline should follow the accepted pattern of symbols and indentation that we showed you earlier in this chapter. Some instructors also ask students to label the superstructure of the speech—introduction, body, and conclusion—by inserting those words at the appropriate places in the outline but without any symbols attached to them.

We asked Chris to show you a formal outline of the body of his informative speech, with the introduction and conclusion written out. Remember, though, that his formal outline is not his speaking notes. Unless you are speaking from a manuscript, your speaking notes will be briefer and more concise, without a scripted introduction, conclusion, or complete full-sentence outlining.

Chris's simple title not only gets attention but also hints at his topic. To check the goals of the speech, Chris then states his specific purpose and thesis.

Speech title: Perfect(ly Simple) Design
Specific purpose: To inform the audience about the Gateshead Millennium Bridge
Thesis statement: The Gateshead Millennium Bridge solved a transportation problem on the Tyne River with a spectacular design that has won awards and reinvigorated the area where it is located.

Introduction

I've read and heard the phrase "carrying coals to Newcastle," but I never knew what it meant. According to the third edition of *The New Dictionary of Cultural Literacy,* which I accessed at Bartleby.com on May 28, 2005, "carrying coals to Newcastle" means doing something that's completely useless. Newcastle, England, was a rich coal mining area, so no one would need to carry coals to Newcastle. I mention this because Newcastle is the site of what I want to inform you about today: the Gateshead Millennium Bridge. If you're looking for spectacular design and an active arts community, you don't need to carry anything with you—just head to Newcastle.

As an art major, I'm always interested in stories about important structures. I first learned about the bridge when I saw a story about it in *Newsweek*. Later I read that the bridge had won a design award that's usually given to a building. That got me interested in researching the structure. Then, in the summer of 2003, I got to visit England. We went to Newcastle and I walked across this famous structure. The bridge has a lot to teach us about great design that seems perfectly matched to its function. It's not only great to look at, but surprising to watch in operation.

To appreciate the Gateshead Millennium Bridge more fully, it's useful to know the main challenges its designers faced, specific features of the bridge, and the impact that it's had on the area where it's located.

I. The site of the proposed bridge posed several design challenges.
   A. The industrial towns of Newcastle and Gateshead have faced each other across the River Tyne since Roman times.
      1. The area flourished during the Industrial Revolution.
         a. The territory was rich in coal.
         b. The territory was commercially important because of its port.
      2. Gateshead on the south was in economic shambles by the 1990s.
         a. Industries along the river had closed.
         b. Warehouses and plants were empty.
         c. People moved south in search of work.
      3. Newcastle on the north was better off economically.
      4. Gateshead wanted to encourage some of Newcastle's prosperity to cross the river.
   B. Construction of the bridge could not stop river traffic for an extended time.
   C. The bridge had to allow both foot traffic on it and navigation beneath it.
   D. Once planners chose the design, the bridge developed quickly.
      1. The winning design was announced in 1997.
      2. Construction began in 1999.
      3. The bridge was positioned in November of 2000.
      4. The bridge's opening mechanism was tested for the first time in June of 2001.

II. The Gateshead Millennium Bridge design is so simple that it is revolutionary.
   A. Two parabolic steel arches form the bridge.
      1. The architectural engineering firm of Guilford and Partners and Wilkinson Eyre Architects collaborated on the design of the pedestrian walkway.
      2. The deck contains separate paths for foot and cycle traffic.
         a. The outer bicycle path is almost 1 foot lower than the inner footway.
         b. The bicycle passageway joins two cross-country riverside paths, part of a nationwide network.
      3. The deck was built in thirteen sections.
      4. The supporting arch was built in nine sections.
      5. Eighteen cables connect the supporting arch to the deck.

Note that Chris writes out his entire introduction, gaining audience attention by arousing their curiosity. He builds his credibility by mentioning that he has walked across the bridge, the subject of his speech.

His introduction ends with a clear preview of three main points Chris plans to discuss.

The outline's three main points match Chris's thesis and preview statements. Each item in the outline is a complete sentence. Each level of the outline has at least two headings, and the subordinate points are grammatically parallel.

B. Specific details about the bridge are impressive.
   1. The bridge cost $32 million.
   2. The bridge weighs more than 850 tons.
   3. Its total span is 413 feet.
   4. The supporting arch rises 164 feet above the river level.
   5. The foundation extends down 98 feet to anchor in the riverbed.
   6. Constructed off-site some 6 miles downstream, the completed bridge was carried upstream by the world's second largest floating crane, Hercules II.
   7. The bridge has a striking appearance.
      a. In daylight it looks white with a hint of blue.
      b. At night, changing multicolored lights beneath the pedestrian walkway reflect on the water below.
C. The design of the bridge created the world's first tilting bridge in order to accommodate boat traffic underneath it.
   1. The entire bridge rotates 40 degrees when it opens.
   2. People have nicknamed it the "blinking eye."
   3. The cables connecting the pedestrian path to the supporting arch are horizontal when the bridge is raised.
   4. A series of electric motors and hydraulic rams moves the bridge.
   5. Opening or closing the bridge takes only 4 minutes.
   6. Each opening or closing costs just a little more than $6.50 currently.
   7. Any litter dropped on the bridge rolls into special traps each time it opens.
D. To date, the structure has received more than thirty-seven design awards.
   1. In 2002 the structure won the most prestigious award for British architecture, the RIBA (Royal Institute of British Architects) Stirling Prize.
   2. In 2005 the structure won the International Association for Bridge and Structural Engineering's Outstanding Structure Award.

III. The Gateshead Millennium Bridge has exceeded expectations of its impact on the reinvigoration of the area.
   A. In its first year, 2002, the bridge had over a million visitors, four times the number expected.
      1. The same number visited the nearby Baltic Center.
      2. The new Biscuit Factory is now England's largest commercial art space.
   B. The Sage Gateshead Music Center opened in 2004.
   C. People are now staying in the area in greater numbers.
      1. Forty-six percent of graduates from universities in the area now remain in the area.
      2. The Gateshead-Newcastle area is now one of the top six centers of culture in Great Britain.
      3. The quays are now home to large, new, luxury residential complexes.
      4. The area is now a popular tourist destination and convention hub.

Conclusion

An article in *Tech Directions*, December 2001, reminds us that American architect Louis Sullivan, who created early versions of what we later called skyscrapers, is credited with the saying that "form follows function." In the case of the Gateshead Millennium Bridge, form *is* function. The bridge had to permit river traffic and had to be built offsite so that it didn't stop traffic during its construction. Gateshead Millennium did that. The fact that it was so novel and so great to look at that it attracted a lot of foot traffic was just icing on the cake. It's generated so much traffic, been the subject of so much commentary, and won so many awards that it has helped reinvigorate the towns that it joins.

If you can't get to Newcastle in the near future, you can at least take a virtual stroll across the Gateshead Millennium Bridge. Just do a Google image search to see any of more than 2,000 photos of it. Or go to www.tynebridgewebcam.com to see live pictures that refresh often around the clock from a variety of webcams. If you're lucky, you might get to see the bridge opening or closing. As Chee Pearlman, one of the RIBA Stirling Award jurors, put it: "It's such a stunning move in terms of engineering. And yet so simple. It's a simple motion, and yet it takes your breath away when you watch it happen."

Chris's conclusion begins with a clear summary of his three main points. He then activates audience response by mentioning sources where listeners can see numerous images of the bridge. His final quotation provides a strong sense of closure to the speech.

Bibliography

Booth, Robert. "Stirling Win Is 'Dream Ticket.'" *Building Design* (October 18, 2002): 1.

"Bow of Hope: Wilkinson Eyre's Elegant and Dramatic Contribution to Neglected Gateshead Is a Symbol of Hope and Regeneration." *The Architectural Review* (December 2002): 58–59.

"Bridge on the River Tyne." *The America's Intelligence Wire* (November 4, 2002): n.p.

Cattermole, Howard. "*ISR* Editorial." *Interdisciplinary Science Reviews*, 2004: 113.

Engelbrecht, Gavin. "The Jewel in the Region's Cultural Crown." *European Intelligence Wire* 17 Dec. 2004: n.p.

"Gigantic Floating Crane Places Pedestrian Bridge over River." *Civil Engineering* Feb. 2001: 13.

Johnson, John. "The Gateshead Millennium Bridge." *Physics Review* Apr. 2003: 29–32.

Lewis, Gareth. "Gifford Grabs Glory for Design of Iconic Bridge." *UK Newsquest Regional Press—This Is Hampshire* 19 Apr. 2005: n.p.

McAllister, J. F. O. "From Coal to Culture: This Old Mining Town in the Northeast of England Used to Be a Grimy Industrial Wasteland. Now It's Becoming a Gleaming Cultural Center and—Who Would Have Thought It?—Tourist Destination." *Time International (European Edition)* 30 Aug. 2004: 32.

"Millennium Bridge—Fact Sheet." 5 June 2005. <http://www.gateshead.gov.uk/bridge/facts.htm>.

"News in Brief: Gateshead Wins." *Professional Engineering* 27 Apr. 2005: 4.

Phillips, Tom. "Ornament on Trial." *The Architectural Review* Apr. 2003: 79–87.

Pierce, Alan. "Gateshead Millennium Bridge." *Tech Directions* Dec. 2001: 9.

Pope, Chris. "Raising Eyebrows." *Professional Engineering* 28 Nov. 2001: 23.

"Tyneside's Twin Cities of Culture Are Where the Art Is." *Europe Intelligence Wire* 10 Feb. 2003: n.p.

A formal outline should include a complete bibliography; it's an important resource for interested listeners, including your instructor.

The Speaking Outline

speaking outline
A brief outline for the speaker's use alone and containing source citations and delivery prompts.

Outlining never hurt; how helpful it is depends on what kind of thinker you are.[4]

The **speaking outline,** the one you actually use to deliver your speech, is a pared-down version of your full formal outline. You construct the formal outline for an interested reader having no necessary prior knowledge of your topic. However, you write the speaking outline for yourself. The only rule for the speaking outline is that it be brief.

Why is the speaking outline briefer than the formal outline? Chances are that your instructor will want most or all of your speeches delivered from notes rather than from a written manuscript. Your brief speaking outline, made up of essential words and phrases, serves as your speaking notes. If you spoke from a complete sentence outline, you might be tempted to read the speech, sacrificing eye contact and other vital interaction with your audience. Alternatively, you might try to memorize the formal outline, another dangerous tactic because you then risk forgetting part of the speech. If, instead, you speak using the outline having just key words and phrases to jog your memory, your delivery will seem more natural and conversational, and you will find yourself freer to interact with your audience.

Though the speaking outline leaves out a lot of what the formal outline includes, it also contains some important items not found in the formal outline. For example, you can include directions to yourself about the speech's delivery. A speaker with a tendency to speak too softly could write reminders in the margins, such as "Volume" or "Speak up!" You could also note places where you want to pause, slow down, or use presentational aids. Some speakers find it particularly helpful to make these delivery notes in a color of ink different from the rest of the outline.

Second, most speaking outlines include supporting materials you plan to use. Quotations and definitions should be written in complete sentences, even though the rest of the outline is in words and phrases. When you quote others, you must be exact. For that reason, insert notes about the exact sources you want to cite. Examples, illustrations, and statistics could be noted in only a few words or numbers. Any symbols or abbreviations you are comfortable with are likely appropriate in your speaking outline.

For his speech on the Gateshead Millennium Bridge, Chris condensed his formal outline and added the following notations to create the speaking outline for the actual delivery of the speech:

I. Design challenges
  A. Newcastle & Gateshead face across River Tyne
    1. Area flourished during Industrial Revolution
      a. Coal
      b. Port
    2. Gateshead, on south, in economic shambles by 1990s
      a. Industries closed
      b. Warehouses, plants empty
      c. People went south for work
    3. Newcastle, on north, better off
    4. Gateshead wanted to attract Newcastle's prosperity

B. Construction could not stop river traffic
C. Had to allow foot traffic on it, navigation beneath it
D. Developed quickly
    1. Winning design, 1997
    2. Construction began, 1999
    3. Bridge positioned, November 2000
    4. Bridge's opening mechanism tested, June 2001

PAUSE

(GMB centerpiece . . . why? . . . specific features unique)

II. GMB design: so simple it's revolutionary
  A. 2 parabolic steel arches
    1. Architectural engineers Guilford and Partners, Wilkinson Eyre Architects collaborated on pedestrian walkway design
    2. Deck → separate paths for foot, cycle traffic
      a. Outer bicycle path → almost 1 ft. lower than the inner footway
      b. Bicycle passageway joins 2 cross-country paths, part of national network (*MB Fact Sheet*)
    3. Deck built in 13 sections
    4. Supporting arch built in 9 sections
    5. 18 cables connect 2 arches (*Physics Review*, April 2003)

Artist Tom Phillips in *The Architectural Review*, April 2003: "At the Gateshead Millennium Bridge, exposed technology becomes ornament in itself. . . .

SHOW PHOTO

  B. Specific details of bridge → impressive
    1. $32 million cost
    2. 850+ tons weight
    3. Span → 413 feet
    4. Supporting arch 164 feet
    5. Foundation → 98 feet into riverbed
    6. Constructed off-site, completed bridge carried 6 mi. upstream by Hercules II, world's 2nd largest floating crane (*Civil Engineering*, Feb. 2001)
    7. Striking appearance
      a. Daylight: white, hint blue
      b. Night: changing multicolored lights beneath walkway reflect on water (*MB Fact Sheet*)

Howard Cattermole (strategy manager for Transpower, the New Zealand power grid) said in a 2004 *Interdisciplinary Science Review* editorial: "It has the excitement of a truly great design. An exquisitely slender, slanting, shining white arch supports a sweeping deck with separate pedestrian and cycle lanes." . . . [W]ith seagulls circling and squawking overhead, the feeling is of a pier more than of a bridge."

Delivery prompts are in capital letters so Chris can see them at a glance and not confuse them with content prompts.

Although Chris's speaking outline entries are abbreviated, many are parallel in structure.

Chris's first photo shows the Gateshead Millennium Bridge in its closed position, to allow pedestrian and bicycle traffic between Newcastle and Gateshead across the River Tyne.

Chris's speaking outline contains specific supporting materials such as statistics and quotations, along with information about each source he needs to cite.

    C. World's 1st tilting bridge to allow boat traffic underneath
       1. Entire bridge rotates 40 degrees
       2. "Blinking eye"
       3. Cables horizontal when bridge raised (*Physics Review*, April 2003)
       4. Electric motors, hydraulic rams move bridge

SHOW PHOTO

       5. 4 minutes
       6. Costs $6.50+
       7. Litter → special traps when bridge opens (*Prof. Engineering*, Nov. 28, 2001)

    D. 37 design awards so far
       1. 2002 → most prestigious, RIBA Stirling Prize
       2. 2005 → Int. Assoc. for Bridge & Structural Engineering's Outstanding Structure Award (*Prof. Engineering*, April 27, 2005)

PAUSE

(Worth seeing, but effect on area?)

  III. GMB exceeded expectations
      "Nick Henry, the leader of the Gateshead Council, said: 'It is easy to underestimate the social impact of the project. This is one of the most deprived areas of the UK.'" (Booth article)
         A. 1st year, 2002 → 1+ million visitors, 4 × number expected
            1. Same no. visited Baltic Center
            2. Biscuit Factory now England's largest comm. art space
         B. Sage Gateshead Music Center opened 2004
         C. People now staying in area
            1. 46% of area univ. graduates remain in vicinity
            2. Gateshead-Newcastle now 1 of top 6 centers of culture in GB
            3. Quays home to large, new, luxury residential complexes
            4. Popular tourist destination, convention hub

Chris's second photo shows the bridge opened to allow a tall ship to pass. In this position, the bridge reveals its deck supports, and its suspension cables stand out against the sky. The silvery, undulating structure on the far shore is the Sage Music Center, part of the arts community that has sprung up to revitalize the area.

Someone who knew nothing of the subject and had not seen Chris's formal outline might not be able to make much sense of his speaking outline. That's okay. As long as your notes make sense to you, you're fine. For example, no one would realize that Chris's note in parentheses, "GMB centerpiece . . . why? . . . specific features unique" was his prompt to say, "It was clear that the Gateshead Millennium Bridge was going to be the centerpiece of a special place, but why? We can understand that better if we know some of the specific features that make it unique." If you plan and practice your transitions as carefully as Chris did, you, too, should need only a few words to remind you of what you planned to say in those important sections of your speech.

We believe that keeping your speaking notes in outline form will remind you of the importance of clear organization in the speech you deliver. Ultimately, though, they are *your* notes. As long as they help you without drawing attention to themselves, they are doing their job. If you tend to forget things under pressure, you may need a few more words in notes than some other people do. Resist the temptation to write out too much of the speech, however. If you write it, you'll want to read it. Instead, try the following suggestions:

- Use key words or phrases to remind you of each step in your introduction and conclusion. Then try to deliver those crucial parts of the speech without referring to your notes.
- In the body of the speech, your main ideas must be worded precisely and powerfully. Either write them in complete sentences or use a key word or phrase to remind you of the wording you practiced.
- Don't just read those main ideas when you deliver the speech. Use key words to remind yourself of supporting material and transitions; use numbers to remind you of statistics.
- Include just enough information to be able to cite each of your sources clearly.
- Write out any material you want to quote, using complete sentences. Insert delivery prompts using words, colors, or any other symbols that will jog your memory. We have even had students use a different colored notecard for each main point in the bodies of their speeches. It's an idea we might never have thought of, but it obviously reinforced the organization of the students' speeches. And that's what outlining and preparing speaking notes should do.

SUMMARY

Functions of Outlining

- Outlining serves five main purposes. (1) It allows the speaker to check the scope of the topic. Is the topic too broad? Are you trying to cover too much or too little? (2) It tests the logical relations between main points and subpoints. Are the points related and yet distinctive enough to qualify as separate ideas? (3) It checks the relevance of subpoints. Are supporting ideas all related to the main idea under which they are listed? (4) It gauges the balance of the speech. Does it look as though you will be spending too much time on one of your points and too little on others? Should you eliminate the points that have little support and reorganize those with a great deal of support? (5) It can function as speaking notes, jogging your memory with key words in correct order.

Types of Outlines

- Outlines can take one of two possible forms: the *complete sentence outline* or the *key word or phrase outline*. In the first of these outlines, each item introduced by a number or letter is a complete sentence. The key word or phrase outline avoids complete sentences. The two forms of outlines should generally not be combined.

Principles of Outlining

- Effective outlining is greatly simplified if the speaker remembers these traditional principles: (1) Each symbol—number or letter—should represent only one idea. (2) Coordination and subordination should be represented by a consistent system of letters and numbers properly indented. (3) Any point divided into subpoints must have at least two. (4) Complete sentences and key words should be mixed only in the speaking outline. (5) Coordinate points throughout the outline should have simple, parallel grammatical construction.

Stages of Outlining

- The first phase of outlining is a *working outline*, an informal list of different aspects of the selected speech topic. From there, the speaker should develop a complete sentence outline, or *formal outline*, that is clear and thorough enough to communicate the essence of the speech to any reader. Having checked the scope of the topic and the logical connections, relevance, and balance of the subpoints, the speaker can then select key words and phrases for a *speaking outline*. That outline may also include transitions, quotations, and source citations, as well as personal directions or prompts for the speech's delivery.
- While effective outlining does not guarantee clear organization in the delivered speech, chances are good that any well-organized speech has been carefully outlined at some stage in its development.

EXERCISES

1. **Practice Critique.** Read the transcript of Jennell Chu's speech on flash mobs which appears in Appendix B. As you read, write down an outline of the main ideas that she develops, including the subpoints. Then, using this outline, write brief answers to the following questions and be prepared to discuss them with your classmates: (1) Did Jennell narrow the topic sufficiently to develop her key ideas in some depth? (2) Does one idea in the outline lead to the next in a meaningful way? (3) Do the subtopics under each main idea develop that point? (4) Are the main ideas balanced? In summary, does the outline reveal a well-organized speech? If you were advising Jennell, would you offer any suggestions to help her present her ideas more clearly and support them more effectively?

2. Test your understanding of coordination and subordination by outlining the following statements:
   a. Blind artists draw objects from a single perspective.
   b. Blind artists use lines to represent surfaces.
   c. Blind artists draw distant objects smaller than close ones.
   d. Blind artists use many of the same visual devices as sighted artists.

   Which of the above statements is the key idea? Which statements are subordinate to it? Which statements are coordinate?[5]

3. Select one of the speeches in Appendix B, and prepare a key word or phrase outline of it. Identify three ways the outline reveals whether the speech was well organized, whether the ideas

are balanced, and whether each point directly relates to the specific purpose of the speech.

4. Using the outline you constructed in Exercise 3, reword it as a complete sentence outline. When is it better to develop a key word or phrase outline? When is a complete sentence outline preferred?

5. Listen to a speech in person, on radio or television, on videotape, or online. Outline its main and supporting ideas. Review the outline. Did the speaker try to cover too many points? Are the main points and subpoints relevant, balanced, and logically sequenced? Based on the outline, what suggestions could you give the speaker to improve the speech?

6. Using the entries below, construct an outline of four major points on the topic of "Latin music." The major headings are included in the list:

Mariachi	Ruben Blades
Small folk band	Countries
Cuba	*Merengue*
Styles	Jennifer Lopez
Marc Anthony	*Salsa*
Artists	*Mariachi* band
Puerto Rico	Mexico
Rumba	Enrique Iglesias
Latin big band	Elvis Crespo
Instrumentation	Brazil
Spain	*Mambo*

Wording Your Speech

12

- **Functions of Language**
  Communicate Ideas
  Send Messages about User
  Strengthen Social Bonds
  Serve as Instrument of Play
  Check Language Use

- **Principles of Effective Language Use**
  Use Language Correctly
  Use Language Clearly
  Use Language Vividly
  Use Language Inclusively
  Use Oral Style
  Theory Into Practice: Keys to Effective Oral Style

After studying this chapter, you should be able to

1. Explain the five functions of language.

2. Use language that is clear, correct, and vivid.

3. Use language that is inclusive and respectful.

4. Distinguish between oral and written style.

5. Use oral style when speaking.

Socrates was a famous Greek teacher who went around giving people advice. They killed him. Socrates died from an overdose of wedlock. After his death, his career suffered a dramatic decline.

— From a student paper[2]

Sisters Reunited after 18 Years in Checkout Line at Supermarket

—Newspaper headline[3]

English speakers have access to the richest vocabulary on Earth, largely because we have adopted words so freely from other languages. In fact, three out of five words in English come from a foreign tongue.[1] As a result, the *Oxford English Dictionary* is huge, containing 615,000 words. People who speak English can achieve degrees of subtlety and nuance that are impossible in most languages. So you would think we could manage to be clearer than the speakers and writers in the chapter's opening quotations.

Socrates died of an overdose of hemlock, not wedlock. We doubt that those sisters had to wait in the supermarket checkout line for 18 years, even if there were lots of double-coupon days!

Examples of language abuse, both spoken and written, are all around us. Their effects can be comic or serious. More important for our purposes are examples of words used correctly, clearly, vividly, inclusively, and in an oral style. The way we use words makes us stand out from others. Language empowers us, and we can employ it to serve both ethical and unethical purposes.

In this chapter, you will learn five functions of language. You will also learn five principles of effective language use and suggestions for adhering to them.

◗ Functions of Language

Studying language is important because the more you know about it, the greater influence you will have as you communicate in public. The language we use fulfills at least five functions.[4]

Communicate Ideas

Remember the word *choice*. Every speaker, every writer, every user of language, chooses the words that he or she wants to use. ... Imprecise or weak words detract from the meaning of the message, while the choice of exact words empowers language. Stronger English comes from making stronger choices, and exact wording, when it becomes a habit, can become fun as well as fascinating.

—Jeffrey McQuain[6]

Our language can communicate an infinite number of ideas because we have a structure of separate words. Unlike the sounds most animals make to signal danger, for example, our language allows us to specify the type of threat, the immediacy of the danger, and any number of other characteristics of the situation.[5] However, a speaker's language is effective only if it communicates to listeners. As we mentioned in Chapter 1 in discussing the "triangle of meaning," as long as the speaker and the listener attach similar referents to the words they use, the two can communicate indefinitely.

Send Messages about User

Our vocabulary reveals aspects of our educational background, our age, and even what area or country we call home. In addition, the words we select communicate how we feel about both our listeners and the subject under discussion. Which of these terms suggests the strongest emotion?

　　crisis　　　dilemma　　　problem

Crisis suggests a more powerful feeling than do the other terms. Language can carry considerable emotional impact, and the words you select carry messages—sometimes obvious, sometimes subtle—about your background and the nature and strength of your emotions.

Strengthen Social Bonds

Because it communicates ideas and emotions between people, language also serves a social function. For example, we often use language to identify ourselves as part of a particular group. Think of the slang expressions you use around friends to signal that you are a member of a certain group and in the know. Many of these utterances are fun and harmless, such as the use of *sick* to note something good or desirable.

Other language serves a social function when spoken in unison. A group of kindergarten students reciting the alphabet or counting from 1 to 20 strengthen their group identity and celebrate the group's accomplishment. Repeating a pledge or prayer also reinforces group identity. Or consider the exchange, "Hi, how are you?" and "Fine, how are you doing?" It may be a hollow, automatic social ritual. Nevertheless, such rituals acknowledge the social bond that exists even between strangers.

Serve as Instrument of Play

You have to love the name The Wailin' Jennys, three talented Canadian singer-songwriters (none named Jenny). If you watch TV Land occasionally, you'll probably appreciate the spirit of play in the name of a South Texas band—June with a Cleaver. Our language not only works; it also entertains.

We also use language for the pleasure of its sounds. Many linguists believe we vocalize as children partly because it just feels and sounds good. Luckily, we do not entirely lose that capacity for play as we mature. The jump-rope chant, the forced rhyme of much rap music, and the rapid-fire lyrics of a hit single used in a car commercial are all examples of language used mainly for the sheer fun of its sounds.

Check Language Use

When in doubt, we as speakers will sometimes check with our listeners to see whether they are decoding a message that corresponds to the one we intended: "Do you understand?" "Get it?" As listeners during interpersonal communication, we may even interrupt a speaker to signal our misunderstanding: "Wait a minute. I don't follow you."

These five functions of language should be obvious to you by this point in your public speaking class. The fact that most of your classmates understood the speeches you have given so far testifies to the power of language to carry a speaker's ideas. Yet your listeners have learned more about you than the ideas you communicated. From your language during your speeches and while commenting on others' speeches, they have learned

Nelson Mandela carefully crafts his language to urge his listeners to work toward a day when "we shall, together, rejoice in a common victory over racism."

about your likes and dislikes. They may have even made accurate guesses about aspects of your background. During the semester or quarter, the language you used in your speeches and in class discussion has also established and strengthened the social bonds between you and your classmates. Any time speakers used humor or showed any verbal virtuosity, they invited you to play with language. Whenever you used an interjection such as "Get this" or "This is important" or whenever you questioned a speaker after a speech, you used language to check and measure your understanding.

Although public speaking is generally more formal than casual conversation, the precise level of language you use will depend on what you want your speech to accomplish. At times, we want our language to be "transparent," almost to disappear. In these instances, we focus on getting our meaning across to our listeners quickly and clearly. If you were reporting a fire, a gas leak, or some other emergency to a group of people and advising them to vacate their building, you would try to communicate that information directly, simply, and quickly, without causing panic. You would not waste time mentally editing and practicing the message to make it more clever or more memorable. Because your goal in these circumstances is getting your message across to a listener, you would use language with clear denotations. **Denotation** is the dictionary definition of a word.

denotation
The literal meaning or dictionary definition of a word or phrase.

On other occasions, you speak to get a message across and to convey it in an especially vivid way. At such times, you pay particular attention to the way you encode the message, choosing your words carefully. When your purpose is to signal your feelings about a subject, to strengthen the social bonds between you and your listeners, or to engage them in verbal play, you will likely use language that draws attention to itself and has strong connotations.[7]

SPEAKING WITH CONFIDENCE

Wording my speeches properly was a very high priority for me. I knew that if I did not effectively communicate my ideas, they would fall on deaf ears. I found it extremely important in my persuasive speech on college binge-drinking deaths. Since I was delivering this speech to an audience in a city that ranked in the top 10 for binge drinkers, I had to be sure that the language I used would grab their attention and keep it for the duration of the speech.

I used four techniques that aided in my success in this speech. First, I used language that appealed to the audience's emotions by painting vivid imagery. Second, when delivering quotes and statistics, I tried to use appropriate voice qualities to give them dramatic impact and to stress their logic. Third, I established my credibility by using my personal experiences and education in my field of study for an ethical appeal, while speaking on the audience's level and not using technical jargon. Finally, I imagined that I was speaking to each listener as "a friend." I just conversationally stated the facts and explained how I felt.

By employing these techniques and rehearsing several times, I felt more comfortable and confident in this speech and its delivery than I ever had before.

Suzanne L. Hamilton
San Antonio College

Connotation is the emotional association that a particular word has for an individual listener. The word *fire* may have pleasant connotations for you if you spent some time around a campfire recently. The same word will have negative connotations for someone whose house has burned down.

connotation
The emotional association(s) that a word or phrase may evoke in individual listeners.

Your choice of language depends on the purpose of your speech. Usually, you will use a combination of denotative and connotative language. Whether the wording of your speech is straightforward or evocative, direct or highly embroidered, however, you must use language carefully. The following section offers guidelines for using language that is correct, clear, vivid, inclusive, and in an oral style.

Principles of Effective Language Use

Words are sometimes compared to tools and weapons, and, in a sense, you draw from that arsenal every time you speak. The words you choose help determine your success in informing, persuading, and entertaining your audience. Five principles should guide your use of language and make you a more effective speaker.

KEY POINTS

Principles of Effective Language Use

1. Use language correctly.
2. Use language clearly.
3. Use language vividly.
4. Use language inclusively.
5. Use oral style.

Use Language Correctly

When you use language incorrectly in your speech, you risk sending unintended messages and undermining your credibility. Poorly worded ideas are sometimes evaluated as poor ideas, although this may not be the case. For example, one student, concerned about the increase of sexually transmitted diseases, encouraged her listeners to commit to "long-term monotonous relationships." We hope she meant *monogamous.*

It is important for speakers to rid their speeches of all unnecessary intrusions. Speakers perceived to care about how they state their ideas are also perceived to care about what they say. The following examples illustrate some common language errors we have heard in student speeches:

1. The first criteria for selecting a good wine is to experience its bouquet. (The speaker should use the singular noun *criterion.*)
2. So, you may be thinking, "I could care less about student government elections. They don't affect me." (The speaker should say, "I *couldn't* care less. . . .")
3. Because she failed to wear her seat belt, she was hurt bad: a broken leg, fractured ribs, and a mild concussion. (She was *badly* hurt.)
4. Because they conduct most of their missions at night, a drug trafficker often alludes our understaffed border patrol. (*They* is plural, so the speaker should use *drug traffickers.* Also, the correct word is *elude*, not *allude.*)
5. Less than twenty students attended the lecture given by Dr. Hinojosa last Wednesday. (Use *fewer* for people or items that can be counted. Yes, those "10 Items or Less" supermarket checkout signs are wrong!)

Your language, like your physical and vocal delivery, should be free of all distractions. Errors in subject-verb agreement, misplaced modifiers, and incorrect word choice attract the attention of everyone who recognizes these errors. You won't upset anyone if your language is grammatically correct, but even small errors run the risk of monopolizing some people's attention. In turn, they stop listening carefully to *what* you say because they are paying attention to *how* you say it.

You can speak correctly if you follow a few simple guidelines. First, make a note of grammatical mistakes you hear yourself and other people make in casual conversation. Attentive listening is the first step to improving your use of language. Second, when you are unsure of a word's meaning, consult a dictionary. Third, if you have a question about proper grammar, refer to a handbook for writers. Fourth, when practicing your speech, record it and play it back, listening for mistakes you may not have noticed as you were practicing. Fifth, practice your speech in front of friends and ask them to point out mistakes. These strategies will help you detect and correct errors. Your speaking will improve, and you may save yourself some embarrassment.

Use Language Clearly

The chief virtue that language can have is clearness, and nothing detracts from it so much as the use of unfamiliar words.

—Hippocrates

To achieve clarity, a speaker should use language that is specific and familiar. If you sacrifice either criterion, your language may confuse your listeners.

Use Specific Language. In Chapter 1, we mentioned that many communication problems spring from the fact that there are always two messages involved whenever two people are communicating: the message that the speaker intends and the message that the listener infers or interprets. If you tell your instructor that you missed a deadline because you were "having some problems," you leave yourself open to a wide range of interpretations. Are they health problems, family troubles, or study and work schedule conflicts? These and other interpretations are possible because *problem* is an abstract term.

To clarify your ideas, use the lowest level of abstraction possible. Words are not either abstract or concrete but take on these qualities in relation to other words. Look at the following list of terms:

class
college class
college communication class
Communication Arts & Sciences 100: Effective Speech
CAS 100 at Penn State Hazleton
CAS 100 with Daniel H. Mansson at Penn State Hazleton

The term at the top of this list is more abstract than the phrase at the bottom. As we add those limiting, descriptive words, or *qualifiers*, the referent becomes increasingly specific. The lower the level of abstraction used, the more clearly the listener will understand the speaker.

ETHICAL DECISIONS

Doublespeak or Clearspeak

In his book *The New Doublespeak*, William Lutz writes about the unclear and mis-leading language used in our society. In speeches and public statements, politicians have used phrases such as "revenue enhancement," "receipt proposals," and "wage-based premiums" when they mean *taxes*. Business leaders have referred to "laying off workers" as "work reengineering." Military spokespersons sometimes speak of "neutralizing the opposition" to avoid using the word *killing*.

Lutz argues that the use of such phrases is unethical because the "clearest possible language is essential for democracy to function, for it is only through clear language that we have any hope of defining, debating, and deciding the issues of public policy that confront us." Do you agree with Lutz's position, or do you think it is legitimate for speakers to use this kind of language if it helps achieve their purposes? Can you think of a time when the use of such "doublespeak" would be appropriate? In general, what ethical guidelines should speakers use to govern their choice of language?

Suppose you were giving a speech on how citizens can protect their homes from burglaries and you made the following statement:

> Crime is rampant in our city. Burglary alone has gone way up in the past year or so. So you can see that having the right kind of lock on your door is essential to your safety.

What's wrong with this statement? The language is vague. What does "rampant" mean? How much of an increase is "way up"—15 percent, 50 percent, 400 percent? Is "the past year or so" 1 year, 2 years, or more? What is "the right kind of lock"? As a speaker, you should help your audience by making these ideas more concrete. After some research, you might rephrase your argument like this:

> Last week I spoke with Captain James Winton, head of our City Police Department's Records Division. He told me that crime in our city has increased by 54 percent in the last year, and the number of burglaries has doubled. We can help deter crime by making our homes burglarproof, and one way of doing this is to make sure that all doors have solid locks. I brought one such lock with me: it's a double-keyed deadbolt lock.

Notice the improvement in the second paragraph. The message is clearer, and with that clarity you would gain credibility as a speaker.

Use Familiar Language. Your language may be specific but still not be clear. If listeners are not familiar with your words, communication is impaired.

Speakers sometimes try to impress listeners with their vocabularies. Phrases such as "a plethora of regulations," "this obviates the need for," and "the anathema of censorship" detract from rather than enhance the speaker's message. "We must ever be mindful to eschew verbosity and deprecate tautology" is good advice and fun to say. But if you are trying to communicate with another person, it's probably better to say simply, "Avoid wordiness."

The use of jargon can also undermine clarity. **Jargon** is the special language of a particular activity, business, or group of people. If you inform

EXPLORING ONLINE

Writing Resources Online

http://home.comcast
.net/~garbl/writing/

Garbl's Writing Resources, developed and maintained by Gary B. Larson, provides speech writers with lots of practical information, from basic grammar to style and usage. Especially helpful is the action writing link, which provides information on how to write persuasively. The links to reference sources are also helpful.

jargon
The special language used by people in a particular activity, business, or group.

Writers and poets such as Maya Angelou make the written word come alive through vivid and picturesque language. Successful speakers use these same techniques to make the spoken word evoke vivid images.

your classmates on the development of maglev trains, you will probably also need to tell them that *maglev* is short for "magnetic levitation" and then explain what that means.

If you are certain that the people you are addressing know such terms, jargon presents no problem. In fact, it is usually quite specific and can save a lot of time. Jargon can even increase your credibility by indicating that you are familiar with the subject matter. If you have any doubts about whether your listeners know the jargon, however, either avoid such terms or define each one the first time you use it.

Use Language Vividly

In addition to selecting language that is correct and clear, speakers should choose language that is colorful and picturesque. Vivid language engages the audience and makes the task of listening easier. Read the following critiques of the speeches of the twenty-ninth U.S. president, Warren Harding:

1. Warren Harding was not an effective public speaker. His speeches often were confusing and uninspired. He did not make his points well.
2. "His speeches left the impression of an army of pompous phrases moving over the landscape in search of an idea; sometimes these meandering words would actually capture a straggling thought and bear it triumphantly a prisoner in their midst, until it died of servitude and overwork." William G. McAdoo, Democratic Party leader[8]

Which of these two statements did you enjoy reading more? Which characterization of Harding's speaking did you find more colorful? Which paragraph contains the more vivid images? Which would you like to read again? We're fairly certain that you selected the second statement. Why?

The language of the first critique communicates an idea as simply and economically as possible without calling attention to itself. Its language is transparent. It is also drab and colorless and displays little creativity. The language style is not nearly as lively as the second example. The language of the second statement calls attention to its sounds, textures, and rhythms. Vivid language helps listeners remember both your message and you.

cliché
A once-colorful figure of speech that has lost impact from overuse.

One of the fiercest enemies of vivid language is the **cliché**, a once-colorful expression that has lost most of its impact through overuse. Many clichés involve comparisons. For example, complete the following phrases:

Cute as a _____.

Dead as a _____.

Between a rock and a _____.

Did you have any trouble completing these expressions? Probably not. In fact, *button*, *doornail*, and *hard place* most likely popped into your mind without much thought. Each of these sayings is a cliché, an overworked expression that doesn't require (or stimulate) much thinking. Clichés are bland and hackneyed. Avoid them!

Now that you have seen some of the effects of dull wording, what techniques can you use to make your language more vivid? The answer may be limited only by your imagination. Consider these options: (1) use active language; (2) appeal to your listeners' senses; and (3) use figures and structures of speech. Following these suggestions will give you a good start on making your speeches more colorful and thus more memorable.

Use Active Language. Which of the following statements is more forceful?

> It was decided by the Student Government Association that the election would be delayed for a week.

> The Student Government Association decided to delay the election for a week.

The second one, right? The first sentence uses passive voice, the second active. Active voice is more direct because it identifies the agent producing the action and places it first in the sentence. In addition, active voice is more economical than passive voice; the second sentence is shorter than the first by five words.

Active language, however, involves more than active voice. Active language has energy, vitality, and drive. It is not bogged down by filler phrases such as "you know," "like," "actually," and "stuff like that." Rather than being cliché-ridden, it may convert the commonplace into the unexpected. Language that is lively and active has impact.

In her persuasive speech, Cherie spoke of the injuries, even deaths, children suffer from playing baseball. After detailing ways to make the game safer, she twisted a familiar expression to create a dramatic conclusion: "[C]hildren may be dying to play baseball, but they should never die because of it."[9]

Coining a word or phrase is another way of making your language work for you. During tough economic times the family vacation gives way to the "staycation." A well-turned phrase also actively engages your listeners' minds as they hear the interplay of words and ideas. Indian nationalist leader Mohandas Gandhi, for example, urged his listeners to "live simply so others might simply live."

Appeal to Your Listeners' Senses. Another way you can achieve impact with language is by appealing to your listeners' senses. The obvious and familiar senses are sight, hearing, touch, taste, and smell. To these we can add the sense of motion or movement and the sense of muscular tension. Colorful language can create vivid images that appeal to each of these various senses. Those sharp images, in turn, heighten audience involvement in the speech, inviting listeners to participate with their feelings, thereby increasing their retention of what you have said.

A word is not crystal, transparent and unchanged; it is the skin of a living thought and may vary greatly in color and content according to the circumstances and time in which it is used.

—Oliver Wendell Holmes, Jr.

Assume that you have decided to deliver an informative speech about roller coasters. Such a topic certainly begs for language to create or re-create the various sensations of a coaster ride. But what if you are not confident about your ability to appeal to your audience's various senses in your speech? You can always research this topic and use the words of others, as long as you accurately attribute your quotations. We easily found four magazine articles on roller coasters. Table 12.1 lists and defines the

TABLE 12.1   Types of Sensory Images

THIS SENSORY IMPRESSION:	ACHIEVES THIS EFFECT:	EXAMPLE:
Visual image	Re-creates the sight of something	"The Cyclone differs from other roller coasters in being (a) a work of art and (b) old, . . . decrepit, rusting in its metal parts and peeling in its more numerous wooden parts."
Auditory image	Suggests the sound of something	"Yes it may be anguishing initially . . . terrifying, even, the first time or two the train is hauled upward with groans and and creaks and with you in it. At the top then—where there is a sudden strange quiet but for the fluttering of two tattered flags . . ."
Tactile image	Re-creates the feel of something	"I should mention that a heavy, cushioned restraining bar locks down snugly into your lap and is very reassuring, although, like everything upholstered in the cars, it may be cracked or slashed. . . ."
Thermal image	Creates impressions of heat or cold	"It was an awful moment, with a sickening sense of betrayal and icy-fingered doubt."
Gustatory image	Re-creates the taste of something	Nothing matches the faint metallic taste of fear as you feel the train set free to begin falling from the top of that first hill.
Kinetic image	Creates feelings of motion or movement	"At nearly 65 mph, the train shot into a tunnel and spun 540 degrees around a banked helix. . . ."
Kinesthetic image	Suggests states of muscular tension or relaxation	"My teeth clenched and my knuckles locked bone-white around the lap bar."
Olfactory image	Suggests the smell of something	We are brought to a "quick, pillowy deceleration in the shed, smelling of dirty machine oil. . . ."
Synesthesia	Combines two or more sensory impressions	Riding a coaster is "like driving your car with your head out the window at 70 miles per hour. But to get the full effect, you have to drive it off a cliff."

Sources: Peter Schjeldahl, "Cyclone! Rising to the Fall," *Harper's*, June 1988, 68–70. Examples of visual, auditory, tactile, thermal, and olfactory sensory impressions are from Schjeldahl's article. Other examples are from Richard Conniff, "Coasters Used to Be Scary, Now They're Downright Weird," *Smithsonian*, August 1989, 84–85.

different kinds of sensory images and provides examples from two of these articles. Notice how many of these examples of sensory impressions are not only evocative but also funny and fun to say. However, active language and appeals to the senses are not your only techniques for enlivening your speech language. Public speaking gives you an opportunity to devise some of the figures of speech and to use some special language structures you may have studied in English classes.

Use Figures of Speech. Important ideas are easier to remember if they are memorably worded. Drawing attention to the way you phrase your thoughts can produce memorable effects in your listeners. To enliven your language, you can use various figures and structures of speech. Some of the most common figures of speech are simile, metaphor, and personification. Common structures of speech are alliteration, parallelism, repetition, and antithesis.

Simile and **metaphor** are comparisons of two seemingly dissimilar things. In simile, the comparison is explicitly stated using the words *as* or *like*—for example, "Trying to pin the senator down on the issue is like trying to nail a poached egg to a tree."

In metaphor, the comparison is not explicitly stated but is implied, without using *as* or *like*. Metaphors help us accommodate the new in terms of the familiar. As a nation, we have moved from being "couch potatoes" to "channel surfers." At the same time, television executives and advertisers may conceive of us, remote controls in hand, as a nation of "grazers."

> If we think of ourselves as channel surfers, perhaps we are compensating heavily for sitting in front of the television actually doing nothing. If the industry calls us grazers, perhaps they don't have too high an opinion of us. The metaphors people use give us insights into their conceptual and fantasy worlds. More than that, the metaphors shape how we perceive our "real world," and what we are doing in it.[10]

To produce metaphors is to extend meanings, to improvise, to let your imagination go.[11] Fresh metaphors have the power to surprise us into new ways of seeing things. Theodore Roosevelt created a memorable metaphor when he made the following comparison: "A good political speech is a poster, not an etching."[12]

Personification gives human qualities to objects, ideas, or organizations. "Blind justice," the "angry sea," and "jealousy rearing its ugly head" are all examples of personification. Our student Amanda used personification in her speech on drummers. Notice how the drumbeat takes on human qualities as she introduces her topic:

> It's the catalyst to any gut wrenching rock song, the groove behind any rapper's flow, and the driving force behind any marching band. It's a drum beat. No matter where or when you hear it, a drum beat grabs you by the lapels, screams in your face, and then slams you back into your seat for the ride of your life.

Another student, Phillip, began his speech, "Nearly 8 years ago, a new neighbor moved to East Liverpool, Ohio. But residents of this low-income, minority town didn't greet the newcomer with welcoming signs." This

simile
A comparison of two things using the words *as* or *like*.

metaphor
An implied comparison of two things without the use of *as* or *like*.

personification
A figure of speech that attributes human qualities to a concept or inanimate object.

"Unwanted Neighbor," the title of Phillip's speech, was just "400 yards from an elementary school site." The neighbor? A toxic waste incinerator. Using personification, Phillip made the incinerator an enemy, someone who needed to be turned away.[13]

Use Structures of Speech. In addition to these figures of speech, you can also employ language structures, such as alliteration, parallelism, repetition, and antithesis. **Alliteration** is the repetition of beginning sounds in adjacent or nearby words. A speaker who asks us "to dream, to dare, and to do" uses alliteration. The sounds of words give your speech impact. A student speaking on the topic of child abuse described the victims as "badly bruised and beaten." These words themselves convey a severe problem, and the repetition of the stern, forceful "b" sound vocally accentuates the violence of the act.

Holocaust survivor Elie Wiesel used alliteration in a speech entitled "The Shame of Hunger" when he spoke of "faith in the future," "complacency if not complicity," and "hunger and humiliation."[14]

Speakers use **parallelism** when they express two or more ideas in similar language structure. When they restate words, phrases, or sentences, they use **repetition**. Parallelism and repetition work in concert to emphasize an idea or a call for action. For example, Travis used an alarm clock image to summarize his persuasive speech on the dangers of sleep deprivation. He then used parallelism and repetition in his call to action and closure steps:

> Today, we've sounded the alarm about the harms of sleep deprivation, opened our eyes to the reasons this situation has developed, and finally awakened to the steps we must take to end this nightmare. Before we are all, literally, dead on our feet, let's take the easiest solution step of all. Tonight, turn off your alarm, turn down your covers, and turn in for a good night's sleep.[15]

Antithesis uses parallel construction to contrast ideas. You can probably quote from memory John Kennedy's challenge: "Ask not what your country can do for you, ask what you can do for your country." Dedicating a memorial for soldiers who had died in the Civil War battle at Gettysburg, Abraham Lincoln proclaimed, "The world will little note nor long remember what we say here, but it can never forget what they did here." The fact that we do remember both of these statements attests to the power of antithesis. Notice also that each speaker places what he wants the audience to do or remember at the end of the comparison. Antitheses are usually more powerful if they end positively. Mario Cuomo, an accomplished speaker and former governor of New York, used this strategy when he constructed his keynote address to the 1984 Democratic National Convention. (We think many of you may agree that Cuomo's statement is good advice for today's political leaders.)

> We must get the American public to look past the glitter, beyond the showmanship—to reality, to the hard substance of things. And we will do that not so much with speeches that sound good as with speeches that are good and sound. Not so much with speeches that bring people to their feet as with speeches that bring people to their senses.[16]

alliteration
The repetition of beginning sounds in words that are adjacent, or near one another.

parallelism
The expression of ideas using similar grammatical structures.

repetition
Restating words, phrases, or sentences for emphasis.

antithesis
The use of parallel construction to *contrast* ideas.

Sarah Meinen of Bradley University won the national speech tournament of the Interstate Oratorical Association in 1999 with her speech "The Forgotten Four-Letter Word." She carefully researched and organized her speech on the problem of compassion fatigue, "the inability to care anymore about social issues." She crafted her language carefully, using the figures and structures of speech we have just discussed. Sarah's work paid off. She captured the attention and tapped the concern of her listeners, encouraging them to rekindle a passion for AIDS awareness and activism.

With statistics and expert opinions, Sarah reminded her listeners of the "savage spread" of this "vicious virus" [alliteration]. "AIDS has been too grim, too overwhelming, and it's been around too long" [parallelism and repetition]. She lamented that "despite our exposure to death and destruction, facts and figures, names and Quilt squares, AIDS has slowly faded from our national consciousness . . ." [alliteration and antithesis]. Sarah concluded, "Our well of compassion has run dry . . ." [metaphor].

Sarah urged her listeners to become advocates for change on a national and personal level. "[C]losing our eyes won't make a monster of this magnitude go away" [personification]. "We may be over AIDS, but AIDS is not over . . ." [antithesis]. "We may be immune to the stories and statistics, but none of us is safe from the reality of AIDS" [alliteration and antithesis]. Sarah exhorted her audience to do "whatever you have to do to be shocked, to be scared, to be involved, to be compassionate, and to keep this pandemic from being ignored, dismissed, and forgotten" [parallelism].[17]

Simile, metaphor, personification, alliteration, parallelism, repetition, and antithesis enable speakers to create vivid language and images. Remember, though, that your objective as a speaker is not to impress your listeners with your ability to create vivid language. Vivid language is not an end in itself but rather a means of achieving the larger objectives of the speech. As language expert William Safire notes, "A good speech is not a collection of crisp one-liners, workable metaphors, and effective rhetorical devices; a good speech truly reflects the thoughts and emotions of the speaker. . . ."[18]

Ethical speakers use inclusive language to express their ideas and examples and respect all members of their audience.

Use Language Inclusively

In Chapter 2, we argued that ethics is a working philosophy that we apply to daily life and bring to all speaking situations. Nowhere is this more evident than in the words we select to address and describe others. Ethical communicators neither exclude nor demean others on the basis of their race, ethnicity, gender, sexual orientation, disability, age, or other characteristics. Their language is inclusive, unbiased, and respectful.

EXPLORING ONLINE

Inclusive Language

http://honolulu.hawaii.edu/
intranet/committees/
FacDevCom/guidebk/teachtip/
inclusiv.htm

The Honolulu County Committee on the Status of Women maintains an excellent website on the "Do's and Don'ts of Inclusive Language." This site includes topics such as disabilities, gender-neutral language, sports and home life, names and titles, and pronouns. Also included is a useful and extensive chart of examples of inclusive language.

sexist language
Language that excludes one gender, creates special categories for one gender, or assigns roles based solely on gender.

nonsexist language
Language that treats both genders fairly and avoids stereotyping either one.

At least three principles should guide you as you become a more inclusive communicator.[19] First, *in referring to individuals and groups of people, use the names they wish to be called.* Ethical public speakers are audience-centered. Acceptable terms when referring to race or ethnicity include African American or black; Asian or Asian American; Native American or American Indian; white or Caucasian; and Hispanic, Latino, or Chicano. Refer to individuals' sexual orientations, not their sexual preferences. *Lesbians*, *gay men*, and *bisexual women and men* are acceptable terms. Address females and males who are over age 18 as *women* and *men*, not *girls* and *boys*. Not everyone with these characteristics favors the terms listed, and you should consider those preferences as you address a specific audience. Your goal, though, should be to respect individuals' rights to choose what they wish to be called.

Second, *use the "people first" rule when referring to individuals who have disabilities.* As the name implies, we should place people before their disabilities. Avoid calling someone a disabled person, an epileptic, or an AIDS victim. Instead, refer to *a person with disabilities*, *a person with epilepsy*, or *a person who has AIDS*.

Third, *avoid using language that is gender-biased.* The issue of gender bias is particularly pervasive and problematic. Language is sexist if it "promotes and maintains attitudes that stereotype people according to gender. It [**sexist language**] assumes that the male is the norm—the significant gender. **Nonsexist language** treats all people equally and either does not refer to a person's sex when it is irrelevant or refers to men and women in symmetrical ways when their gender is relevant."[20]

Gender bias occurs when language creates special categories for one gender, with no corresponding parallel category for the other gender. *Man* and *wife*, for example, are not parallel terms. *Man* and *woman* or *husband* and *wife* are parallel. Other examples of nonparallel language are nurse and male nurse, chairman and chairperson, and athletic team names such as *The Tigers* (the men's team) and *The Lady Tigers* (the women's team).

Perhaps the most common display of gender-biased language comes from the inappropriate use of a simple two-letter word: *he*. Sometimes called the "generic he," this word is used to refer to men and women alike, usually with the fallacious justification that there aren't acceptable alternatives without cluttering speech with intrusive phrases such as "he and she" and "him and her." This assumption is false.

Consider the following sentence: "A coach must be concerned with his players' motivation." Sexist, right, since both women and men are coaches? Now, consider how simple it is to remove this gender bias without changing the meaning of the sentence. First, use the plural form: "Coaches must be concerned with their players' motivation." Second, eliminate the pronoun: "A coach must be concerned with player motivation." A third way to avoid gender bias is to include both pronouns: "A coach must be concerned with her or his players' motivation." Although the use of "he and she" may seem wordy and intrusive, speakers sometimes use this double-pronoun construction strategically to remind listeners that both men and women perform the role being discussed.

Speakers exhibit fairness when they express their ideas and examples in language that treats others equally and fairly. The strategies discussed in this section should help you design, develop, and deliver a speech that uses inclusive language and respects your audience. If you'd like to learn more about how to use bias-free language, read the excellent sources we have listed in endnotes 19 and 20.

Speaking inclusively is an ethical obligation for those who value civil discourse. Maggio highlights both the limitations and possibilities of the role language can play in achieving tolerance, acceptance, and change:

> There can certainly be no solution to the problem of discrimination in society on the level of language alone. Replacing *handicap* with *disability* does not mean a person with disabilities will find a job more easily. Using *secretary* inclusively does not change the fact that fewer than 2 percent of U.S. secretaries are men. Replacing *black-and-white* in our vocabularies will not dislodge racism. However, research indicates that language powerfully influences attitudes, behavior, and perceptions. To ignore this factor in social change would be to hobble all other efforts.[21]

Use Oral Style

To speak appropriately, you must recognize that your oral style differs from your written style. Unless your instructor asks you to deliver some speeches from a manuscript, we believe it's better to think of "developing" speeches rather than "writing" them. Avoid writing your speeches for two reasons. First, you will likely try to memorize what you have written, and the fear of forgetting part of the speech will add to your nervousness and could make your delivery stiff and wooden.

Second, and more important, the act of writing itself often affects the tone of the communication. **Tone** is the relationship established by language and grammar between a writer or speaker and that person's readers or listeners. Many of us think of writing as something formal. For that reason, we tend not to write the way that we speak. Novelist and screenwriter Richard Price speaks from his experience about the crucial difference between the written and the spoken word:

> It's amazing how much stuff looks dazzlingly authentic and true and beautiful on the page, but dies in someone's mouth. That's the importance of a read-through for the writer and the director. Because when the actors at a big round table read all the parts of a script, what doesn't work is going to pop up so obviously. And there's no substitute for that. There's no other way you can learn that except to hear it in somebody's mouth.[22]

If you compose parts of a speech on paper, make certain that you read what's on the page out loud to see if it sounds oral rather than written. How can you tell the difference?

EXPLORING ONLINE

Nonsexist Language

http://owl.english.purdue.edu/owl/resource/608/05/

www.ccp.rpi.edu/resources/

These two sites provide useful information on how to avoid stereotypes and make your language nonsexist. The Purdue University Online Writing Lab provides guidelines endorsed by the National Council of Teachers of English for using pronouns and references to various occupations. The Center for Communication Practices at Rensselaer Polytechnic Institute offers Resources for Writers, including information on how to use "gender-fair" language. This article presents specific ways to avoid the sexist use of *he* and *man*.

tone
The relation established by language and grammar between speakers and their listeners.

Our oral style differs from our written style in at least four important ways. First, *in speaking, we tend to use shorter sentences than we write.* Speakers who write out their speeches often find themselves gasping for air when they try to deliver a long sentence in one breath.

Second, *when we communicate orally, we tend to use more contractions, colloquial expressions, and slang.* Our speaking vocabulary is smaller than our writing vocabulary, so we tend to speak a simpler language than we write. Speakers who write out their speeches often draw from their larger written vocabularies. As a result, their presentational style seems formal and often creates a barrier between them and their listeners.

Third, *oral style makes greater use of personal pronouns and references than written style does.* Speakers must acknowledge their listeners' presence. One way of doing this is by including them in the speech. Using the pronouns *I*, *we*, and *you* makes your speech more immediate and enhances your rapport with your listeners. You may even want to mention specific audience members by name: "Last week, John told us how to construct a power résumé. I'm going to tell you what to do once your résumé gets you a job interview." Notice how the name of the student, coupled with several personal pronouns, brings the speaker and audience together and sets up the possibility for lively interaction.

A fourth difference is that *oral style uses more repetition.* Readers can slow down and reread the material in front of them. They control the pace. Listeners don't have that luxury. Speakers must take special care to reinforce their messages, and one way of accomplishing this is by using repetition. Refer to the "Theory Into Practice" feature for help in determining how to incorporate oral style into your speech.

No matter which of the world's nearly 7,000 languages you speak, the words you choose telegraph messages about your background, your involvement with your topic, and your relationship with your listeners.[23] Like the unique voice and body you use to deliver your speeches, your language is an extremely important part of your delivery. If you are conscientious, you must know when to speak simply and directly and when to embellish your language with sensory images, figures of speech, and unusual structural devices. In short, you don't have to be a poet to agree with poet Robert Frost: "All the fun's in how you say a thing."[24]

THEORY INTO PRACTICE

TIP   Keys to Effective Oral Style

Oral style checklist	Instead of this:	Say this:
Use familiar language	Such an action would not be prudent at this juncture.	I don't think we should do that.
Use personal pronouns	People need to stand up and say, "Enough is enough."	We must stand up and say, "Enough is enough."
Use contractions	You will not find him in a library on a weekend if his personal computer is working.	You won't find him in a library on a weekend if his computer's working.
Use short sentences and repetition	According to Nigel Hawkes in his book *Structures: The Way Things Are Built*, an accidental discovery by well diggers in 1974 has led archaeologists in central China to unearth an army of possibly 8,000 terracotta figures of warriors and horses in the tomb of China's first emperor.	According to Nigel Hawkes in his book *Structures: The Way Things Are Built*, well diggers in central China discovered pieces of broken terracotta in 1974. Since then, archaeologists have unearthed what may be a total of 8,000 figures. They are terracotta figures of warriors and horses guarding the tomb of China's first emperor.

SUMMARY

Functions of Language

- Language is a distinctly human instrument. Although other animals produce sounds and noises, human language alone is articulated into words and is capable of expressing an infinite variety of thoughts.
- Language serves five functions: (1) it communicates ideas between speaker and listener; (2) it sends messages, either intentional or unintentional, about the person who uses it; (3) it establishes and strengthens social bonds between groups of people; (4) it is an instrument of play for pleasure, humor, and creativity; and (5) it enables us to monitor and check our use of language.

Principles of Effective Language Use

- Five principles should guide your use of language: (1) use language correctly, (2) use language clearly, (3) use language vividly, (4) use language inclusively, and (5) use oral style.
- Your first obligation as a speaker is to use language *correctly*. To detect and correct language errors: (1) listen to the language you and others use, and focus on how it can be improved; (2) consult a dictionary when you are unsure of a word's meaning; (3) refer to a writer's handbook when you have a question about proper grammar; (4) use a recorder to detect incorrect language use; and (5) practice your speech in front of friends, and ask them to point out your mistakes.

- To use language *clearly*, use specific and familiar language. The more concrete your language, the more closely your referents will match those of your listeners. In addition to being specific, language must also be familiar. Listeners must know the meanings of the words you use.
- To use language *vividly*, use active language, appeal to your listeners' senses, and use figures and structures of speech. Active language avoids *clichés* and filler phrases, using instead active voice, coined words, and well-turned phrases. As a speaker, you can appeal to listeners' senses of sight, sound, feel, temperature, taste, muscular tension, or smell, or a combination of these. Figures and structures of speech include *simile*, *metaphor*, *personification*, *alliteration*, *parallelism*, *repetition*, and *antithesis*.
- To use language *inclusively*, consider audience diversity and avoid stereotypes about people based on characteristics such as race, ethnicity, age, and gender. Nonsexist language treats both females and males symmetrically and fairly, without creating special categories or assigning roles solely according to gender. Speakers who have difficulty selecting inclusive language should consult a dictionary of bias-free terms.
- To achieve an *oral style*, use shorter sentences than you ordinarily write; use contractions, colloquial expressions, and slang when appropriate; use personal pronouns (*I, we, us, they*); and use more repetition than you normally would in writing.

EXERCISES

1. **Practice Critique.** Speech experts consider Martin Luther King, Jr.'s "I Have a Dream" to be one of the most powerful speeches of the twentieth century. Dr. King combined the integrity of his ideas with strong imagery and a masterful delivery to create a memorable speech. Locate a transcript of his speech in a published source or using the Internet links in Appendix B. Write a brief analysis of the language he used to express his ideas and arouse emotions. Note examples of how Dr. King appealed to his listeners' senses and how he used alliteration, parallelism, repetition, antithesis, and metaphor. Comment on Dr. King's use of gender-specific language. If the speech were being delivered today, how might it be rewritten to make the language more inclusive?

2. Generate examples of words and phrases that identify a speaker as being from a particular region of the country. Examples could include the pronoun *y'all*, the use of *pop* for carbonated soft drinks, or the word *grinder* for a submarine sandwich. Do any of these examples also suggest stereotypes about the educational levels of the speakers?

3. Some linguists believe that Shakespeare invented one-tenth of the words he used. According to Richard Saul Wurman in *Information Anxiety*, the Stanford University admissions form asks applicants to invent and explain a new word. Invent, define, and illustrate the use of a new word in a 1- to 2-minute practice speech.

4. Select a one- or two-paragraph passage from a book or magazine. Using the guidelines discussed in this chapter, rewrite the passage for a speech, incorporating elements of oral style.

5. Decide on nonsexist words that could be substituted for each of the following examples:
   a. Manpower
   b. Salesmanship
   c. Mother country
   d. Clothes make the man
   e. Man's best friend
   f. All men are created equal
   g. Brotherly love

6. Listen to your favorite music artist or group. Try to identify at least one example of each of the following language devices in the song lyrics:

   a. Alliteration
   b. Metaphor
   c. Simile
   d. Personification
   e. Visual image
   f. Tactile image
   g. Olfactory image
   h. Gustatory image
   i. Auditory image
   j. Kinesthetic image
   k. Kinetic image

7. Select a speech from a print or online source. Identify examples of as many types of the language devices listed in Exercise 6 as possible.

Delivering Your Speech

13

- **Principles of Nonverbal Communication**

- **Methods of Delivery**
  Speaking Impromptu
  Speaking from Memory
  Speaking from Manuscript
  Speaking Extemporaneously

- **Qualities of Effective Delivery**

- **Elements of Vocal Delivery**
  Rate and Pause
  Volume
  Pitch and Inflection
  Articulation and Pronunciation

- **Elements of Physical Delivery**
  Appearance
  Posture
  Facial Expression
  Theory Into Practice: Dressing for
    Address
  Eye Contact
  Movement
  Gestures

After studying this chapter,
you should be able to

1. Recognize four principles of nonverbal communication.

2. Know the advantages and limitations of the four methods of delivery.

3. Select the delivery method most appropriate to the speaking occasion.

4. Combine different methods of delivery to enhance your delivery.

5. Explain the qualities of effective delivery.

6. List the elements of vocal delivery and incorporate them into your speaking.

7. List the elements of physical delivery and incorporate them into your speaking.

A printed speech is like a dried flower: the substance, indeed, is there, but the color is faded and the perfume gone.

—Paul Lorain

delivery
The way a speaker presents a speech, through voice qualities, bodily actions, and language.

EXPLORING ONLINE

Delivery Advice for Academics

http://pne.people.si.umich.edu/essays.html

Visit this website to see the delivery suggestions one insider gives other academics to improve their "talks." Under "Pedagogical Essays," click "How to Give an Academic Talk" to read a six-page article by Paul N. Edwards of the University of Michigan's School of Information. See his "Usually Better–Usually Worse" chart for a delivery checklist, with explanations that follow.

In Chapter 1, we quoted communication scholar Karlyn Kohrs Campbell: "Ideas do not walk by themselves; they must be carried—expressed and voiced—by someone." Each of us has a unique voice, body, and way of wording ideas. Your manner of presenting a speech—through your voice, body, and language—forms your style of delivery. In other words, *what* you say is your speech content and *how* you say it is your **delivery**. If you and a classmate presented a speech with the same words arranged in the same order (something we don't recommend), your listeners would still receive two different messages. This is because your delivery shapes your image as a speaker and changes your message in subtle ways.

As Paul Lorain's quotation at the beginning of this chapter suggests, your delivery gives color and fragrance to your words. To help you understand how that invigoration occurs, we discuss the qualities and various elements of effective delivery in this chapter. Before we examine the individual elements that constitute physical and vocal delivery, let's first consider some rules that apply to all nonverbal communication and four possible methods of delivering a speech.

Principles of Nonverbal Communication

Your nonverbal behavior communicates a great deal of information concerning your feelings about what you say. In particular, four principles of nonverbal communication provide a framework we will use later to evaluate the specific elements of vocal and physical delivery.

1. *Part of our nonverbal communication is deliberate, and part is unintentional.* You deliberately do certain things to make other people feel comfortable around you or attracted to you. You dress in styles that flatter you or make you comfortable. When speaking or listening to others, you look them in the eyes. You smile when they tell you good news and show concern when they share a problem.

   On the other hand, you may have habits of which you are unaware. You fold your arms, assuming a closed and defensive body position, or jingle your keys when nervous. You tap your fingers on the lectern when anxious or look down at the floor when embarrassed. You can control only those things you know about. Therefore, the first step toward improving your speech delivery is to identify and isolate distracting nonverbal behaviors you exhibit.

2. *Few nonverbal signals have universal meaning.* Standing at a bakery in France, you can't resist the aroma of long, golden loaves of bread hot from the oven. Unable to speak French, you get the clerk's attention, point to the loaves, and hold up two fingers, as in a V for victory. The clerk nods, hands you three loaves, and charges you for all three. Why? The French count from the thumb, whether it is extended or not.

   Just as the meanings of gestures and movements can change from one culture to the next, nonverbal delivery that is appropriate and effective in one speaking situation may be inappropriate and ineffective in another.

3. *When a speaker's verbal and nonverbal channels send conflicting messages, we tend to trust the nonverbal message.* We are reminded of the importance of nonverbal communication when someone breaks a nonverbal rule. One of those rules demands that a person's words and actions match. Suppose Doris walks reluctantly to the front of the classroom, clutches the lectern, stands motionless, frowns, and says, "I'm absolutely delighted to be speaking to you today." Do you believe her? No. Why? Doris's speech began not with her first words, but with the many nonverbal messages that signaled her reluctance to speak. Nonverbal messages should complement and reinforce verbal ones. When they do not, we tend to trust the nonverbal message to help us answer the question, "What's really going on here?" As a result, one final principle of nonverbal communication becomes extremely important.

4. *The message you intend may be overridden by other meanings people attach to your nonverbal communication.* You stare out the window while delivering your speech because you feel too nervous to make eye contact with your listeners. The audience, however, assumes that you are bored and not really interested in speaking to them. Even though it may not be true, your audience's perception that you are disinterested is more important in this situation. Eliminate distracting behaviors that mask your good intentions if you want to present the best speech you can.

This chapter is about the process of presenting your speech vocally and physically. Before we survey the individual elements that make up delivery, it's important to know the possible methods of delivering a speech and the qualities that should mark the method you choose or are assigned.

Methods of Delivery

The four basic ways you can deliver your public speech are (1) impromptu, or without advance preparation; (2) from memory; (3) from a manuscript; or (4) extemporaneously, or from notes.

Speaking Impromptu

We engage in **impromptu speaking** whenever someone calls on us to express an opinion or unexpectedly asks us to "say a few words" to a group. We deal with those special occasions and offer specific guidelines for impromptu speaking in Chapter 18. In these informal situations, other people do not necessarily expect us to be forceful or well organized, and we are probably somewhat comfortable speaking without preparation. The more important the speech, the less appropriate the impromptu method of delivery. Although impromptu speaking is excellent practice, no conscientious person should risk a grade, an important proposal, or professional advancement on an unprepared speech.

EXPLORING ONLINE

Delivering Your Speech

http://wps.ablongman.com/
ab_public_speaking_2

Click on "Deliver" at this Allyn & Bacon site to read information on topics such as modes of delivery, developing dynamism, interacting with your audience, and managing nervousness. By clicking on "Yeas and Nays on Delivery," you can even take a short quiz about your perception of some of your delivery habits. Upon submitting the questionnaire, you get advice based on your answers.

impromptu speaking
Speaking without advance preparation.

Speaking from Memory

speaking from memory
Delivering a speech that is recalled word for word from a written text.

Speaking from memory is similarly appropriate only on rare occasions. We speak from memory when we prepare a written text and then memorize it word for word. At best, a memorized speech allows a smooth, almost effortless-looking delivery because the speaker has neither notes nor a manuscript and can concentrate on interacting with the audience. For most of us, however, memorizing takes a long time. Concentrating on the memory work we've done and our fear of forgetting part of the speech can also make us sound mechanical or programmed. For these reasons, speaking from memory is usually appropriate only for brief speeches, such as those introducing another speaker or presenting or accepting an award.

Speaking from Manuscript

speaking from manuscript
Delivering a speech from a text written word for word and practiced in advance.

Speaking from manuscript, or delivering a speech from a complete text prepared in advance, ensures that the speaker will not be at a loss for words and is essential in some situations. An address that will be quoted or later published in its entirety is typically delivered from a manuscript. Major foreign policy speeches and State of the Union addresses by U.S. presidents are always delivered from manuscript because it is important that the speaker be understood—and *not* misunderstood. Speeches of tribute and commencement addresses are often scripted. Manuscript delivery may be appropriate for any speaking situation calling for precise, well-worded communication.

> If a speech were a style of dress, it would be somewhere between a tuxedo and a flannel shirt. Not stiff. Not sloppy. . . . A speech is more like conversation than formal writing. Its phrasing is loose—but without the extremes of slang, the incomplete thoughts, the interruptions that flavor everyday speech.
>
> —Elinor Donahue[1]

Having every word of your speech scripted may boost your confidence, but it does not ensure effective delivery. You must write the speech in a conversational style. In other words, the manuscript must sound like something you would say in conversation. The text of your speech requires a good deal of time to prepare, edit, revise, and type for final delivery. In addition, if you do not also take time to practice delivering your speech in a fluent, conversational manner and with appropriate emphasis, well-placed pauses, and adequate eye contact, you are preparing to fail as an effective speaker.

Speaking Extemporaneously

speaking extemporaneously
Delivering a speech from notes or from a memorized outline.

The final method of delivery, and by far the most popular, is **speaking extemporaneously,** or from notes. Speaking from notes offers several advantages over other delivery methods. You need not worry about one particular way of wording your ideas because you have not scripted the speech. Neither do you have to worry that you will forget something you have memorized. With your notes in front of you, you are free to interact with the audience in a natural, conversational manner. If something you say confuses the audience, you can repeat it, explain it using other words, or use a better example to clarify it. Your language may not be as forceful or colorful as with a carefully prepared manuscript or a memorized speech, but speaking from notes helps ensure that you will be natural and spontaneous.

Former New York governor Mario Cuomo, skilled in various methods of delivery, reveals that he speaks extemporaneously whenever possible because "it's easier to engage the audience when you have both eyes in direct contact with the people you're addressing, both arms drawing pictures in the air, adding punctuation, fighting off the glaze."[2] The freedom, naturalness, and spontaneity of extemporaneous speaking make this method of delivery particularly attractive.

When speaking either from notes or a manuscript, keep several practical points in mind:

1. *Practice with the notes or manuscript you will actually use in delivering the speech.* If you use sheets of paper, use a weight slightly heavier than bond so that it's easier to handle. Double- or even triple-space a speech manuscript and format text in a font size that's easy for you to see. Both of these strategies will make your words easier to read and help you keep your place. Type sentences on the upper two-thirds of each sheet of paper to help ensure better eye contact. You need to know where things are on the page so that you have to glance down only briefly.

2. *Number your notecards or the pages of your manuscript.* Check their order before you speak.

3. *Determine when you should and should not look at your notes.* Looking at your notes when you quote an authority or present statistics is acceptable. In fact, doing so may even convey to your audience your concern for getting supporting materials exactly right. However, do not look down while previewing, stating, or summarizing your key ideas. If you cannot remember your key points, what hope is there for your audience? Also, avoid looking down when you use personal pronouns such as *I*, *you*, and *we* or when you address audience members by name. A break in your eye contact at these points suddenly distances you from the audience and creates the impression that the speech is coming from a script rather than from you.

4. *Slide your notes or the pages of your manuscript rather than turning them.* To avoid picking them up and turning them over, do not write on the backs of your notes or manuscript. As a rule, if you use a lectern, do not let the audience see your notes after you place them in front of you. The less the audience is aware of your notes, the more direct and personal your communication with them will be.

5. *Devote extra practice time to your conclusion.* The last thing you say can make a deep impression, but not if you rush through it or deliver it while gathering your notes and walking back to your seat. Your goal at this critical point in the speech is the same as your goal for all your delivery: to eliminate distractions and to reinforce your message through your body, voice, and language.

A natural and confident delivery style comes with practice. Record and view yourself on video or rehearse in front of friends to try out gestures and movements that will enhance your effectiveness.

The most satisfactory way of delivering your classroom speeches combines all four of the methods we have discussed. To demonstrate that you are well prepared and to ensure contact with your audience, you may want to memorize your introduction and conclusion. If you deliver the body of your speech extemporaneously, look at your notes occasionally. Just don't look at your notes while you are stating or summarizing each main point. If you quote sources in your speech, you are, in effect, briefly using a manuscript. Finally, as an audience-centered speaker, you should be flexible enough to improvise a bit. You speak impromptu whenever you repeat an idea or think of a clearer or more persuasive example. If you are well prepared, this combination of delivery methods should look natural to your audience and feel comfortable to you.

◖ Qualities of Effective Delivery

As you begin to think about the way you deliver a speech, keep in mind three characteristics of effective delivery. First, *effective delivery helps both listeners and speakers*. Your audience has only one chance to receive your message. Just as clear organization makes your ideas easier to remember, effective delivery can underscore your key points, sell your ideas, or communicate your concern for the topic.

Second, *the best delivery looks and feels natural, comfortable, and spontaneous*. Some occasions and audiences require you to be more formal than others. Speaking to a large audience through a stationary microphone, for example, will naturally restrict your movement. In other situations, you may find yourself moving, gesturing, and using presentational aids extensively. You want to orchestrate all these elements so that your presentation looks and feels relaxed and natural, not strained or awkward. You achieve spontaneous delivery such as this only through practice.

Third, and finally, *delivery is best when the audience is not aware of it*. Your goal should be delivery that reinforces your ideas and is free of distractions. When the audience begins to notice how you twist your ring, to count the number of times you say "um," or to categorize the types of grammatical mistakes you make, your delivery is distracting them from what you are saying. Your delivery has now become a liability rather than an asset.

How can you help ensure effective delivery? Concentrate on your ideas and how the audience is receiving them rather than on how you look or sound. Pay attention to their interest in your speech, their understanding of your message, and their acceptance or rejection of what you are saying. If you notice listeners checking their watches, reading papers, text messaging, whispering to friends, or snoozing, they are probably bored. At this point, you can enliven your delivery with movement and changes in your volume. Such relatively simple changes in your delivery may revive their interest.

But what if you notice looks of confusion on your audience's faces? You want to make certain your listeners understand the point you are making. Slow your rate of delivery, and use descriptive gestures to reinforce your ideas. If you observe frowns or heads shaking from side to side, you've encountered a hostile audience! There are ways to break down the resistance of even an antagonistic group. Look directly at such listeners, establish a conversational tone, incorporate friendly facial expressions, and use your body to demonstrate involvement with your topic.

These helpful tips take practice. Start with the basics. Once you have mastered the essentials of speech delivery, you will be flexible and able to adapt to various audiences. Your delivery will complement your message, not detract from it.

Any prescription for effective delivery will include three basic elements: the *voice*, or vocal delivery; the *body*, or physical delivery; and *language*. In Chapter 12, we discussed how your language contributes to your delivery style. In the remainder of this chapter, we focus on vocal and physical delivery. Let's consider, first, how vocal delivery can enhance your speech.

◑ Elements of Vocal Delivery

Vocal delivery includes rate, pause, volume, pitch, inflection, articulation, and pronunciation.

Rate and Pause

You have probably heard the warning, "Look out for him; he's a fast talker," or words to that effect. Such a statement implies that someone who talks fast may be trying to put something over on us. At the other end of the spectrum, we often grow impatient with people who talk much slower than we do, even labeling them uncertain, dull, or dense. Though these stereotypes may be inaccurate, the impressions people form based on our nonverbal communication can become more important than anything we intend to communicate.

Your **rate**, or speed, of speaking can communicate something, intentionally or unintentionally, about your motives in speaking, your disposition, or your involvement with the topic. Your goal in a speech, therefore, should be to avoid extremely fast or slow delivery. You should instead use a variety of rates to reinforce your purpose in speaking and make you seem conversational.

EXPLORING ONLINE

Assessing Vocal Delivery
www.history.com/video
.do?name=speeches

The History Channel's rich index of speeches and broadcasts that changed the world gives you a chance to appreciate the vocal deliveries of historical and contemporary figures. Just click on a category to browse the clips.

rate
The speed at which a speech is delivered.

ETHICAL DECISIONS

Delivery versus Content

A minister once wrote a delivery prompt in the margin of his speaking notes: "Shout here—argument weak!" Most of us would agree that using delivery to mask weak content is unethical. However, delivery can also demonstrate genuine confidence and enthusiasm for the topic.

As a member of Student Advocates for a Green Environment (SAGE), an organization promoting energy education, conservation, and efficiency across campus, you are selecting a spokesperson to represent SAGE to students, faculty, staff, and administrators. The individual will speak and answer questions in a series of public forums on campus.

Jones and Smith are the two best applicants, and you conclude that each would do a good job. However, you think Jones would be better at constructing the case for SAGE's agenda, but Smith would deliver her ideas with more enthusiasm and confidence. All other factors being equal, which applicant would you select?

What ethical obligations do you have to SAGE? To your audiences? To Jones and Smith? To yourself?

Pauses are a powerful and essential part of any presentation. A pause allows the listener to make a personal connection to the words she just heard. A pause invites the listener to relax into a presentation. A pause makes it possible for the speaker to sense the response of an audience to a presentation. Pauses are those beautiful moments when meaning happens and common ground emerges.

—Achim Nowak[3]

pause
An intentional or unintentional period of silence in a speaker's vocal delivery.

vocalized pause
Sounds or words such as *ah, like, okay, um, so,* and *you know* inserted to fill the silence between a speaker's words or thoughts.

volume
The relative loudness or softness of a speaker's voice.

In Chapter 4, you learned that the typical American speaker talks at a rate between 125 and 190 words per minute. Although we can process information at rates faster than people speak, our comprehension depends on the type of material we are hearing. You should slow down, for example, when presenting detailed, highly complex information, particularly to a group that knows little about your subject. This can work both ways, however. In some situations, speaking slightly faster than the rate of normal conversation may actually increase your persuasiveness by carrying the message that you know exactly what you want to say.

Pauses, or silences, are an important element in your rate of delivery. You pause to allow the audience time to reflect on something you have just said or to heighten suspense about something you are going to say. Pauses also mark important transitions in your speech, helping you and your audience shift gears. World-renowned violinist Isaac Stern was once asked why some violinists were considered gifted and others merely proficient or competent when they all played the correct notes in the proper order. "The important thing is not the notes. It's the intervals between the notes," he responded.

To test the importance of pauses, let's look at a sentence from a speech that President Barack Obama delivered. The president spoke at the memorial service for the victims of the 2011 shooting at a political gathering outside a Tucson, Arizona, supermarket. Try reading this passage without any internal punctuation or pauses:

> But at a time when our discourse has become so sharply polarized—at a time when we are far too eager to lay the blame for all that ails the world at the feet of those who happen to think differently than we do—it's important for us to pause for a moment and make sure that we're talking with each other in a way that heals, not in a way that wounds.

The sentences make sense only if you insert appropriate pauses. Speakers reading from a written text sometimes mark their manuscripts to help them pause appropriately. Now try reading Obama's sentence again, pausing a beat when you see one slash (/) and pausing a bit longer when you encounter two (//).

> But at a time when our discourse has become so sharply polarized // at a time when we are far too eager to lay the blame for all that ails the world / at the feet of those who think differently than we do // it's important for us to pause for a moment / and make sure that we're talking / with each other in a way that heals, // not a way that wounds.[4]

If the pauses marked were meaningful for you, the statement should have gained power. You may even disagree with the placement and length of the pauses we chose. You might say the sentences differently, and that's fine. Public speaking is, after all, a creative and individual process. Remember, though, that to be effective in a speech, pauses must be used intentionally and selectively. If your speech is filled with too many awkwardly placed pauses—or too many **vocalized pauses,** such as "um" and "uh,"—you will seem hesitant or unprepared, and your credibility will erode quickly.

Volume

Your audience must be able to hear you in order to listen to your ideas. **Volume** is simply how loudly or softly you speak. A person who speaks too

Accomplished speakers such as Bill Cosby understand the importance of articulating clearly and adapting their volume to ensure that everyone in the audience can catch every word. If you are using a microphone, continue to speak in a conversational tone, letting it do the work of amplifying your voice.

loudly may be considered boisterous or obnoxious. In contrast, an inaudible speaker may be considered unsure or timid. Adapt your volume to the size of the room. In your classroom, you can probably use a volume just slightly louder than your usual conversational level.

When you speak before a large group, a microphone may be helpful or even essential. If possible, practice beforehand so that the sound of your amplified voice does not startle you. You may even be called on to speak before a large audience without a microphone. This is not as difficult as it sounds. In fact, your voice will carry well if you support your breath from your diaphragm. To test your breathing, place your hand on your abdomen while repeating the sentence "Those old boats don't float" louder and louder. If you are breathing from the diaphragm, you should feel your abdominal muscles tightening. Without that support, you are probably trying to increase your volume from your throat, a mistake that could strain your voice.

At times, you may have to conquer a large space as well as external noise, such as the chattering of people in a hallway, the roar of nearby traffic, or the whoosh of an air-conditioning system. That may require hard work. If you can, use a microphone in such a situation, speak at normal volume, and let the public address system do the work for you. Don't use a microphone unless it is necessary; in a small room, a microphone distances you from the audience.

Pitch and Inflection

Pitch refers to the highness or lowness of vocal tones, similar to the notes on a musical staff. Every speaker has an optimal pitch range, or key. This is the range in which you are most comfortable speaking, and your voice is probably pleasant to hear in this range.

Speakers who are unusually nervous sometimes raise their pitch. Other speakers think that if they lower their pitch, they will seem more authoritative. In truth, speakers who do not use their normal pitch usually sound artificial.

pitch
The highness or lowness of a speaker's voice.

The following practice technique may help you retain or recapture a natural, conversational tone in your delivery. Begin some of your practice sessions seated. Imagine a good friend sitting across from you, and pretend that she asks you what your speech is about. Answer her question by summarizing and paraphrasing your speech: "Mary, I'm going to talk about the advantages of consuming grass-fed rather than grain-fed beef. I've divided my speech into two main arguments. Grass-fed beef has half the saturated fat of grain-fed beef; and grass-fed cattle are treated more humanely than factory-farmed grain-fed beef." Listen closely to the tone of your voice as you speak. You are having a conversation with a friend. You're not tense; you feel comfortable.

Now, keeping this natural, conversational tone in mind, stand up, walk to the front of the room, and begin your speech. Your words will change, but the tone of your speech should be comfortable and conversational, as it was before. In a sense, you are merely having a conversation with a larger audience. We have found this technique helpful for students whose vocal delivery sounds artificial or mechanical. They find their natural pitch ranges and incorporate more meaningful pauses.

A problem more typical than an unusually high- or low-pitched voice is vocal delivery that lacks adequate **inflection**, or changes in pitch. Someone who speaks without changing pitch delivers sentences in a flat, uniform pitch that becomes monotonous. Indeed, the word *monotone* means "one tone," and you may have had instructors whose monotonous droning invited you to doze. Inflection is an essential tool for conveying meaning accurately. You can give a simple four-word sentence four distinct meanings by raising the pitch and volume of one word at a time:

"**She** is my friend." (Not the young woman standing with her.)
"She **is** my friend." (Don't try to tell me she isn't!)
"She is **my** friend." (Not yours.)
"She is my **friend**." (There's nothing more to our relationship than that.)

In public speaking, women can generally make wider use of their pitch ranges than men can without sounding affected or unnatural. For this reason, men often find that they need to vary other vocal and physical elements of delivery—volume, rate, and gestures, for example—to compensate for a limited pitch range.

Articulation and Pronunciation

The final elements of vocal delivery we will discuss are articulation and pronunciation. **Articulation** is the mechanical process of forming the sounds necessary to communicate in a particular language. Most articulation errors are made from habit and take four principal forms: deletion, addition, substitution, and transposition. *Deletion* is leaving out sounds—for example, saying "libary" for "library" or "goverment" for "government." If you have heard someone say "athalete" for "athlete," you've heard an example of an articulation error caused by the *addition* of a sound. Examples of errors caused by the *substitution* of one sound for another are "kin" for "can" and "git" for "get." The final type of articulation error is one of *transposition*, or the reversal

inflection
Patterns of change in a person's pitch while speaking.

EXPLORING ONLINE

Checking Pronunciation
www.m-w.com

Use this Merriam-Webster website to check the pronunciations of unfamiliar words. Enter your query term and click the Search button. To hear the word pronounced correctly, just click the loudspeaker icon near the definition.

articulation
The mechanical process of forming the sounds necessary to communicate in a particular language.

of two sounds that are close together. This error is the vocal equivalent of transposing two letters in a typed word. Saying "lectren" for "lectern" or "hunderd" for "hundred" are examples of transposition errors.

Articulation errors made as a result of habit may be so ingrained that you can no longer identify your mistakes. Your speech instructor, friends, and classmates can help you by pointing out articulation problems. You may need to listen to recordings of your speeches to locate problems and then practice the problem words or sounds to correct your articulation.

Pronunciation, in contrast to articulation, is simply a matter of knowing how the letters of a word sound and where the stress falls when that word is spoken. We all have two vocabularies: a speaking vocabulary and a reading vocabulary.

Most of us make errors in pronunciation primarily when we try to move a word from our reading vocabulary to our speaking vocabulary without consulting the dictionary. In a public speech, the resulting pronunciation error can be a minor distraction or a major disaster, depending on how far off your mispronunciation is and how many times you make the error. If you have any doubt about the pronunciation of a word you plan to use in a speech, look it up in a current dictionary and then practice the correct pronunciation out loud. Apply this rule to every word you select, including those in quotations. If you follow this simple rule, you will avoid embarrassing errors of pronunciation.

Pronunciation of proper nouns—the names of specific people, places, and things—can also pose difficulties. Proper nouns should be pronounced the way that the people who have the name (or who live in the place or who named the thing) pronounce them. For instance, the large city on the Texas Gulf coast is pronounced "HEWstun"; the street in New York City spelled the same way is pronounced "HOWstun." Decide on a reasonable pronunciation, practice it, and deliver it with confidence in your speech. For names of places, consult the *Pronouncing Gazetteer* or the list of geographical names found at the back of many dictionaries.

Once you have mastered these elements of vocal delivery, your speech will be free of articulation errors and mispronounced words. Your voice will be well modulated, with enough inflection to communicate your ideas clearly. You will speak loudly enough that all your listeners can hear you easily. You will adapt your rate to the content of your message, and you will pause to punctuate key ideas and major transitions. In short, your sound will be coming through loud and clear. Now let's consider the picture your listeners will see by examining the aspects of physical delivery.

◑ Elements of Physical Delivery

Physical delivery includes appearance, posture, facial expression, eye contact, movement, and gestures.

Appearance

We all form quick impressions of people we meet based on subtle nonverbal signals. **Appearance**, in particular our grooming and the way we dress,

pronunciation
How the sounds of a word are to be said and which parts are to be stressed.

EXPLORING ONLINE

Pronouncing Proper Names

www.loc.gov/nls/other/sayhow
.html

www.loc.gov/nls/other/ABC
.html

These two excellent sites are products of the National Library Service, a division of the Library of Congress. The first gives you a pronunciation guide to names of public figures. The second is an extensive guide to pronunciations of commercial names.

KEY POINTS

Elements of Vocal Delivery

1. Rate and pause
2. Volume
3. Pitch and inflection
4. Articulation and pronunciation

appearance
A speaker's physical features, including dress and grooming.

is an important nonverbal signal that helps people judge us. Why is appearance so important?

Studies demonstrate that people we consider attractive can persuade us more easily than those we find unattractive. In addition, high-status clothing carries more authority than does low-status clothing. For example, studies show we are more likely to jaywalk behind a person dressed in a dark blue suit, a crisp white shirt, and a dark tie who is carrying an expensive black-leather briefcase than we would behind a person dressed in rags or even in jeans. We will also take orders more easily from that well-dressed person than we would from someone poorly dressed. These studies reinforce the adage that "clothes make the person," a saying any public speaker would do well to remember.

The safest advice on appearance that we can offer the public speaker is to be neat, to be clean, and to avoid extremes in dress and grooming. Use clothes to reinforce your purpose in speaking, not to draw attention. Every moment that the audience spends admiring your suit or wondering why you wore the torn T-shirt is a moment they are distracted from your message. In selecting your clothes, consider the guidelines we discuss in "Theory Into Practice: Dressing for Address."

Clothing also shapes our self-perception. You probably have certain clothes that give you a sense of confidence or make you feel especially assertive or powerful when you wear them. Dressing "up" conveys your seriousness of purpose to your listeners. It also establishes this same positive attitude in your own mind.

Decide what you will wear before the day of your speech and practice at least once in those clothes. One of our students discovered that she was distracted during her presentation because when she moved her arms to gesture, her coat made a rustling sound. She could have eliminated this distraction if she had practiced in that suit coat before the day of her speech. Whatever the problems, it's best to encounter and fix them before the speech. You can then concentrate fully on the speech itself.

Posture

posture
The position or bearing of a speaker's body while delivering a speech.

A public speaker should look comfortable, confident, and prepared to speak. You have the appropriate attire. Your next concern is your **posture**, the position or bearing of your body. The two extremes to avoid are rigidity and sloppiness. Don't hang on to or drape yourself across the lectern, if you are using one. Keep your weight balanced on both legs, and avoid shifting your weight back and forth. Equally distracting is standing on one leg and shuffling or tapping the other foot. You may not realize that you do those things. One student told us that she tied bells to her shoes when she practiced her speeches so that she would "hear what her feet were doing." If you practice in front of friends, ask them to point out delivery distractions. Remember that for your delivery to reinforce your message, it must be free of annoying mannerisms.

Facial Expression

Estimates of the number of possible human facial expressions range from 5,000 to 250,000.[5] Even if the actual number is closer to 5,000, that's

THEORY INTO PRACTICE

TIP Dressing for Address

Consider the Occasion

The speaking occasion dictates, in part, how formally or informally you can dress. A student delivering a valedictory speech would dress differently from one delivering an impromptu campaign speech. A speech in your classroom probably permits you to be more informal than you would be delivering a business presentation to a board of directors or an acceptance speech at an awards ceremony.

Consider Your Audience

Some of your listeners dress more casually than others. In any audience, there is a range of attire. As a rule, dress at or near the top of that range. For speeches outside the classroom, traditional, tasteful, and sub-dued clothing is your wisest choice. You should appear as nicely dressed as the best-dressed people in your audience.

In other words, when in doubt, dress up a little. An audience is more easily insulted if you appear to treat the speaking occasion too casually than if you treat it too formally. Remember, your listeners will make judgments based on your appearance before you even open your mouth.

Consider Your Topic

Though a public speech is not a costumed perfor-mance, your clothing can underscore or undermine the impact you want your speech to have. A hot-pink dress or a lime-green shirt would be entirely appropriate for a speech on Mardi Gras, but not for one on the high cost of funerals. On the other hand, you would look and feel silly wearing a business suit to demonstrate basic poses of Bikram yoga.

Consider Your Image

The clothing you select can shape—or even change—the image you want to create as a speaker. Darker colors convey authority and seriousness; lighter colors establish a friendlier image. A student perceived as the class clown should dress more formally to help dis-pel this image.

still a significant amount of communication potential. Yet, many people giving a speech for the first time put on a blank mask, limiting their **facial expression** to one neutral look. Inexperienced speakers are understandably nervous and may be more concerned with the way they look and sound than they are with the ideas they are trying to communicate.

Your facial expression must match what you are saying. The speaker who smiles and blushes self-consciously through a speech on date rape will simply not be taken seriously and may offend many listeners. If you detail the plight of earthquake victims, make sure your face reflects your concern. If you tell a joke and your listeners can't stop chuckling, break into a smile rather than a frown (unless your frown is part of the joke). In other words, your face should register the thoughts and feelings that motivate your words.

The way to use facial expression appropriately to bolster your message is simple: concentrate as much as possible on the ideas you present and the way your audience receives and responds to them. Try not to be overly con-scious of how you look and sound. This takes practice, but your classroom speeches provide a good forum for such rehearsal. You will learn to interact with the audience, maintain eye contact, and respond with them to your own message. If you do those things, chances are your facial expression will be varied and appropriate and will reinforce your spoken words.

facial expression
The tension and movement of various parts of a speaker's face.

Eye Contact

eye contact
Gaze behavior in which a speaker looks at listeners' eyes.

We've all heard the challenge, "Look me in the eye and say that." We use direct eye contact as one gauge of a person's truthfulness. **Eye contact** can also carry many other messages: confidence, concern, sincerity, interest, and enthusiasm. Lack of eye contact, on the other hand, may signal deceit, disinterest, or insecurity.

Your face is the most important source of nonverbal cues as you deliver your speech, and your eyes carry more information than any other facial feature. As you speak, you will occasionally look at your notes or manuscript. You may even glance away from the audience briefly as you try to put your thoughts into words. Yet you must keep coming back to the eyes of your listeners to check their understanding, interest, and evaluation of your message.

As a public speaker, your goal is to make eye contact with as much of the audience as much of the time as possible. To do this, make sure that you take in your entire audience, from front to back and from left to right. Include all those boundaries in the scope of your eye contact, and look especially at those individuals who seem to be listening carefully and responding positively. Whether you actually make eye contact with each member of the audience is immaterial. You must create that impression. Again, this takes practice.

Movement

movement
A speaker's motion from place to place during speech delivery.

Effective **movement** benefits you, your audience, and your speech. First, place-to-place movement can actually help you relax. Moving to a visual aid, for example, can help you energize and loosen up physically. From the audience's perspective, movement adds visual variety to your speech, and appropriate movement can arouse or rekindle listeners' interest. Most important, though, physical movement serves your speech by guiding the audience's attention. Through movement, you can underscore key ideas, mark major transitions, or intensify an appeal for belief or action.

Remember that your speech starts the moment you enter your audience's presence. Your behavior, including your movement, sends signals about your attitudes toward the audience and your speech topic. When your time to speak arrives, approach your speaking position confidently, knowing that you have something important to say. If you use a lectern, don't automatically box yourself into one position behind it. Even the smallest lectern puts a physical barrier between you and your audience. Moving to the side or the front of it reduces both the physical and the psychological distance between you and your listeners and may be especially helpful when you conclude your speech with a persuasive appeal.

Make certain that your movement is selective and that it serves a purpose. Avoid random pacing. Movement to mark a transition should occur at the beginning or the end of a sentence, not in the middle. Finally, bring the speech to a satisfying psychological conclusion, and pause for a second or two before gathering your materials and moving toward your seat.

SPEAKING WITH CONFIDENCE

Delivery is one of the most important aspects of public speaking, but it can also be intimidating: looking at your audience, wondering if you should move, trying to figure out what to do with your hands. All this requires some planning and work. To improve my delivery, I practiced my entire speech in my room while visualizing my audience. As I spoke, I concentrated on my hand gestures, the amount of eye contact I was making, and the tone and level of my voice. I always timed my speech and made sure I wasn't rushing my delivery, adding pauses where necessary. The more I practiced, the less nervous and more confident I became. My delivery not only made me look more professional, but it also kept my classmates involved in my speech and interested in what I was saying.

Michael Gino
Suffolk County Community College, Selden

Gestures

Gestures—movements of a speaker's hands, arms, and head—seem to be as natural a part of human communication as spoken language. Gestures punctuate and emphasize verbal messages for the benefit of listeners and ease the process of encoding those messages for speakers. Studies show that people asked to communicate without gestures produce labored speech marked by increased hesitations and pauses. Such speakers also demonstrate decreased fluency, inflection, and stress, and they use fewer high-imagery words.[6] Hand gestures, then, seem to help speakers retrieve elusive words from their memories.[7]

> **gestures**
> Movements of a speaker's hands, arms, and head while delivering a speech.

Gestures are important adjuncts to our verbal messages; at times, they even replace words altogether. As a public speaker, you can use gestures to indicate the size of objects, to re-create some bodily motion, to emphasize or underscore key ideas, to point to things such as presentational aids, or to trace the flow of your ideas. If you don't normally gesture in conversation, force yourself to include some gestures as you practice your speech. At first you may feel self-conscious about gesturing. Keep practicing. Gestures that seem natural and spontaneous are well worth whatever time you spend practicing them. They reinforce your ideas and make you seem more confident and dynamic and, like movement, they can help you relax.

Effective speakers understand the importance of vocal and physical interaction with their audience. They talk to their listeners and not to their visual aids.

To be effective, gestures must be coordinated with your words and must appear natural and spontaneous. Any gesture should be large enough for the audience to see it clearly. The speaker who gestures below the waist or whose gestures are barely visible over the top of a lectern may appear timid, unsure, or nervous. Speakers who gesture too much—who talk with their hands—may be perceived as nervous, flighty, or excitable. Therefore, the two extremes to avoid are the absence of gestures (hands clenched on the sides of

KEY POINTS

Elements of Physical
Delivery

1. Appearance
2. Posture
3. Facial expression
4. Eye contact
5. Movement
6. Gestures

the lectern) and excessive gestures (gestures emphasizing everything, so that nothing stands out). Remember, if your audience is waiting for you to gesture or counting your many gestures, they are distracted from your message.

The following two generalizations from research on gestures are particularly helpful for the public speaker. First, people who are confident, relaxed, and have high status tend to expand into the space around them and use gestures that are wider than those of other people. Speakers who wish to emphasize their authority can do so by increasing the width of their gestures. Second, a wide, palms-up gesture creates an openness that is entirely appropriate when a speaker is appealing for a certain belief or urging the audience to some action. A palm-down gesture carries more force and authority and can be used to command an audience into action or to exhort them to a certain belief.

As a speaker, adapt the size of your gestures to the size of your audience. Before a crowd of several thousand, your gestures should be more expansive than when you stand at the front of a small classroom. In a cavernous auditorium, you must adjust your gestures, facial expression, and eye contact so they will be clear to those in the back rows.

These, then, are the tools of vocal and physical delivery, from rate of speaking to hand gestures. Your goal throughout this class and in your future public speaking experience will be to eliminate distracting elements and then work toward delivery that is conversational, forceful, and as formal or informal as your audience and subject require.

One traditional saying is "If it's worth doing, it's worth doing well." That's wise counsel for the public speaker. Delivery is a vital part of your public speech, and effective vocal and physical delivery are assets worth cultivating.

SUMMARY

- Speech *delivery* is composed of a speaker's voice qualities, bodily actions, and language.

Principles of Nonverbal Communication

- Vocal and physical delivery are subject to four principles of nonverbal communication. First, part of our nonverbal communication is intentional, while another part is unconscious and unintentional. Second, few if any nonverbal signals have universal meaning. Third, when a speaker's verbal and nonverbal channels send conflicting messages, we tend to trust the nonverbal message. These three principles contribute to a fourth: the message you intend may be overridden by other messages people attach to your nonverbal communication.

Methods of Delivery

- As a speaker, you can select any of four methods of delivery: *impromptu speaking*, or speaking without advance preparation; *speaking from memory*; *speaking from manuscript*; and *speaking extemporaneously*, or from notes. While each type of delivery is appropriate under certain public speaking circumstances, speeches from a manuscript and particularly from notes have far fewer limitations and more applications than the other two methods of delivery. Those who can speak clearly and emphatically from a few notes after the necessary period of practice have gone a long way toward ensuring success in any public speaking situation.

Elements of Vocal and Physical Delivery

- The nonverbal elements of delivery include everything about your speech that could not be captured and recorded in a manuscript. *Vocal delivery* includes your rate, use of pauses, volume, pitch and inflection, articulation, and pronunciation. Your appearance, posture, facial expression, eye contact, movement, and gestures make up the elements of your *physical delivery*. Your goal with each of these elements should be to eliminate distractions and to work for variety so that you look and sound natural.

- You exercise a good deal of control over most of these physical and vocal elements of delivery. With the confidence that comes from practice, you should be able to adapt your delivery to different speaking situations and audience sizes. Speech delivery should reinforce the clear, forceful communication of your ideas.

EXERCISES

1. **Practice Critique.** Read the transcript of Melissa Janoske's speech on Renaissance fairs that appears in Chapter 15. Focusing on Melissa's use of language, suggest places in the speech where she might incorporate movement and gestures to enhance her delivery. Describe the types of gestures and movements you recommend. Also, using the markings discussed on page 230, note where Melissa could incorporate meaningful pauses to emphasize her ideas.

2. Make a list of famous people you find to be exciting speakers and ones you find boring. Or list instructors who have reputations for being exciting or boring lecturers. How do these individuals' vocal and physical deliveries add to or detract from their ideas? Which of these techniques could you adapt to make your speaking more dynamic?

3. Using the guidelines discussed in the "Rate and Pause" section of this chapter, mark pauses for paragraph 4 of Doris Kearns Goodwin's Speech of Tribute for Timothy Russert in Appendix B. Practice reading this excerpt aloud to convey its meaning with the greatest impact.

4. Select a short passage from a novel, short story, speech, or other prose and copy it. Study the meaning and emotion of the excerpt. After marking the copied text, read the passage aloud, emphasizing key words and phrases and using pauses to enhance the message's impact.

5. Attend a speech and analyze the speaker's vocal and physical delivery. Was the message delivered effectively? What nonverbal elements enhanced and what detracted from the speech? What suggestions could you give the speaker to improve the delivery of the speech?

Using Presentational Aids

14

After studying this chapter, you should be able to

1. Identify the benefits and limitations of using presentational aids.

2. Understand types of presentational aids and their appropriateness.

3. Use various methods and technologies to display your visual and audio aids.

4. Know how to design and display PowerPoint aids.

5. Construct and test presentational aids before you speak.

6. Display and discuss presentational aids as you speak.

A space shuttle exploding in a cloudless azure sky . . .

A Boeing 767 disappearing into the glass and steel frame of a 100-story building . . .

A wall of ocean water racing toward a tropical coastline . . .

Thirty-three Chilean miners rescued after more than 2 months underground . . .

If you form a vivid mental image at the description of any of the events listed at the opening of this chapter, you prove the haunting power of pictures.[1] We have all grown up in a visually oriented society. Even our language reflects the power of the visual message: "A picture is worth a thousand words." "I wouldn't have believed it if I hadn't seen it with my own eyes."

Today, our newspapers, magazines, and computer screens are filled with pictures—black-and-white or color. When the news is bad, we expect to see pictures or video of the airplane wreckage, the flooding, or the aftermath of the earthquake. When the news is good, we expect to see pictures of the winning team or the heroic rescue. We are, indeed, people for whom "seeing is believing." As a speaker, you need not rely only on words to communicate your ideas precisely and powerfully. You can add force and impact to many messages by incorporating a visual dimension.

●The Importance of Using Presentational Aids

A well-designed, appropriate presentational aid can add significantly to the effectiveness of the speech and the speaker. Consider the following four functions as you determine whether to include presentational aids in a particular speech.

Increases Message Clarity

First, presentational aids give your speech greater clarity. They can specify the demographic breakdown of voters in the past election, illustrate the structure of an online course, or explain the process of monitoring and controlling air traffic. You can convey detailed statistical information more clearly in a simplified line graph than by merely reciting the data. Speeches using a spatial organizational pattern often benefit particularly from visual reinforcement.

Reinforces Message Impact

Remember: It is ten times harder to command the ear than to catch the eye.

—Duncan Maxwell Anderson

Second, presentational aids give your speech greater impact. Seeing may encourage believing; certainly, it aids remembering. Duncan Anderson asserts the dramatic power of visual elements to capture an audience's attention. Some people have concluded that adding visual aids to a presentation "has been shown to increase audience retention *at least fivefold*."[2] And a University of Minnesota study found that a presenter using computer-generated transparencies or slides "was perceived to be 43 percent more persuasive than in meetings with unaided presentations."[3]

Each of these studies concludes that a well-constructed presentational aid helps listeners remember more of your speech for a longer period of time. Because they both hear and see the message, listeners are more fully involved in the speech. This greater sensory involvement with the message lessens the opportunity for outside distractions and increases retention.

SPEAKING WITH CONFIDENCE

Visual aids emphasize and stir interest in a speaker's topic. They can add dimension to the spoken word. My persuasive speech was on stem cell research. I knew that this topic was very controversial, and I didn't want my audience to get caught up in their own preconceived opinions. Using a visual aid that included a computer image of Christopher Reeve attached to a respirator in his wheelchair immediately captured the attention of my audience. I proceeded to explain all the possible medical advances and the thousands of individuals who could possibly be cured of their ailments by stem cell research. The visual image accompanied by my words left a lasting impression. Seeing the expressions on the audience's faces when they saw my visual aid helped me to feel more confident in my speaking ability.

Lauren Fishman
Suffolk County Community College, Selden

Increases Speaker Dynamism

Third, presentational aids make you seem more dynamic. Gestures are an important part of your delivery. Most speakers, unfortunately, have difficulty incorporating meaningful gestures into their delivery. Using presentational aids forces you to move, to point, to become physically involved with your speech. Your gestures become motivated and meaningful, and, consequently, you appear more dynamic and forceful.

Enhances Speaker Confidence

A fourth benefit of using presentational aids in your speech is that it can increase your confidence as a public speaker. Clear, attractive presentational aids that you have practiced using can help you relax in three ways. First, knowing that your presentational aids will enhance the clarity and impact of your message should increase your confidence. Second, revealing your presentational aids gives purpose to your movement and gestures, and this will help burn off some of your nervous energy. Finally, if you become nervous when you see the listeners' eyes focused on you, you can use your presentational aids to divert their attention to your speech content. Just remember that the primary purpose of your presentational aids should not be to divert attention from you but to enhance the impact of your message.

Before you plan your presentational aids, ask yourself, "Will such aids make my presentation more effective?" This question is important because any presentational aid, no matter how well designed and planned, involves some distractions for both speaker and audience. It may require setup time, for example. When you uncover the aid for audience view and cover it later, you create a visual break in the speech. In addition, presentational aids remove part of a listener's focus from the speaker. "Quite simply," as one professional speech coach notes, "the moment a visual appears on a screen, the audience will focus on the visual rather than listen to what you, the speaker, are saying.... [T]he visual always wins."[4] So *use presentational aids only if they are necessary to the speech*, and be prepared for possible distractions.

Remember, too, that presentational aids are supplements to, not replacements for, your spoken words. As a speaker, you communicate; your presentational aids simply illustrate.

The requirement for a presentational aid should guide your topic selection, research, and practice of the speech. Don't incorporate a visual aid just to show that you know how to use the technology, to demonstrate your artistic skills, or to add length to a presentation that you fear is too short. Would Martin Luther King, Jr.'s "I Have a Dream" speech really have required a slide show if that technology had been available to him? More important, how different would the effect of that historic speech have been with slides projected on some jumbo screen for his thousands of listeners?

Now that you understand how presentational aids can enhance your speech, some of the problems they may pose, and some of the circumstances in which you should not use them, let's examine the various types of aids you might consider using in a speech.

◖ Types of Presentational Aids

Presentational aids come in many forms, but they can generally be divided into these classifications: objects, pictures, diagrams, graphs, charts, maps, film and video, handouts, and audio aids. You need to determine the type most appropriate to your presentation.

Objects

object
An actual item or three-dimensional model of an item used during the delivery of a speech.

Objects may be either actual size, such as a digital camera, or scaled, such as an architect's model. Other three-dimensional presentational aids are, for instance, a scuba diver's oxygen tank and breathing regulator, a deck of tarot cards, a replica of the Statue of Liberty, or an MP3 player.

Also included under the category of objects are people or animals you employ in delivering a speech. You might enlist a volunteer to help you demonstrate tests for color blindness or, with your instructor's permission, bring in a Jack Russell terrier for a speech on that breed of dog. Objects used effectively give your speech immediacy and carry a great deal of impact.

Pictures

picture
A photograph, painting, drawing, or print used to make a point more vivid or convincing.

Pictures can make a speaker's oral presentation more concrete and vivid. It is difficult to imagine how a speech on the artistic styles of Georgia O'Keeffe or Edward Hopper could be effective without pictures or prints of some of their paintings. A speaker trying to persuade the audience that subliminal messages are common in advertising without showing some examples would be both vague and unconvincing.

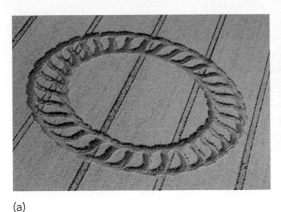

(a)

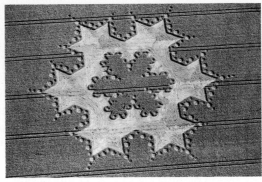

(b)

FIGURE 14.1
Sample Photographs
Photos illustrate visual concepts, here showing (a) relatively simple and (b) more complex crop circles.

Speakers can also use pictures to dramatize a point. Our student Dora delivered an informative speech on crop circles. She used several photographs scanned, enlarged, and printed from a book she had purchased.[5] Some of Dora's photos showed crop circles whose creators were known. Other crop circles had appeared quickly and without a known creator. Dora effectively explored this controversial topic by showing the range of crop circles, from relatively simple (Figure 14.1a) to highly complex (Figure 14.1b). By citing her source and using enlarged photographs that were easy to see, she gave her classmates a clear and vivid glimpse of the phenomenon.

If you are not using your own photographs, you can locate pictures on the Internet in three different ways.[6] First, you can choose a search engine and enter the term you want, followed by the file format extension that you prefer (Eiffel Tower.jpg or roller coaster.gif, for example). Second, all popular search engines have either a toolbar icon or radio button to let you limit your search to pictures, photos, or images. Third, you can use the photograph databases at special websites such as the ones mentioned in the "Exploring Online" feature on this page. Be sure to record information about the source of any photograph so that you can cite it appropriately in your speech and in a written bibliography.

When you use pictures, make sure that you select them with size and clarity in mind. A small snapshot of the Palace of Versailles or a picture from an encyclopedia held up for audience view detracts from, rather than reinforces, the speaker's purpose. Pictures used as visual aids often must be enlarged. You can use a color copier at a copy shop or at your campus multimedia center to enlarge your pictures. If the room where you'll speak has a visual document camera, such as Elmo, you can project small pictures on a screen for easy audience viewing. These document cameras can project transparencies, video, computer slide shows, and computer animation as well as images of three-dimensional objects. Many models feature auto focus and power zoom magnification controlled by wireless remotes.

You can also scan or copy your picture and save it to a disk, a CD, or a flash drive. Then project your visual aid from a computer.

EXPLORING ONLINE

Locating Photographs
www.freefoto.com/index.jsp
www.socialbrite.org/sharing-center/free-photos-directory/

FreeFoto.com offers a collection of more than 130,000 photographs for personal, noncommercial use. Social-brite.org enables you to expand your search with a "Free Photos Directory" with descriptions of and links to dozens of sites.

Diagrams

diagram
A graphic, usually designed on a computer or drawn on poster board, showing the parts of an object or organization or the steps in a process.

Diagrams are graphics showing the parts of an object or organization or the steps in a process. A diagram could show the features of a commercial spacecraft design, the organizational structure of the U.S. judicial system, or the steps in the lost-wax method of casting jewelry. The best diagrams achieve their impact by simplifying and exaggerating key points. For example, no diagram of manageable size could illustrate all the parts of a hybrid, gas-electric car engine. However, a carefully constructed diagram, whether drawn on poster board or projected from the latest high-tech storage device, could isolate and label key parts of that engine design.

Graphs

Graphs can now be easily created using commonly available spreadsheet software and are effective presentational aids taking several forms.

line graph
A diagram used to depict changes among variables over time.

Line Graph. A **line graph** is useful in depicting trends and developments over time. A speaker might convincingly use a line graph to illustrate the rising cost of a college education over the previous 20 years. Some line graphs trace two or more variables—income and expenditures, for example—in contrasting colors.

bar graph
A diagram used to show quantitative comparisons among variables.

Bar Graph. A **bar graph** is useful in comparing quantities or amounts. We can measure the economic health of an institution, a company, or a nation, for example, by learning whether it is "in the red" or "in the black." A bar graph contrasting deficits and profits, showing their relative size, provides a clear, visual indication of economic health, particularly when income is represented in black and deficits in red.

In the following section we show you how Edith used both bar and pie graphs to highlight key statistics.

pie, or circle, graph
A diagram used to show the relative proportions of a whole.

Pie, or Circle, Graph. A third type of graph, the **pie graph** or **circle graph**, is helpful when you want to show relative portions of the various parts of a whole. If you are analyzing the federal budget, for example, a pie graph could illustrate the percentage allocated for defense. Pie graphs can show proportions of 24 hours that people spend in particular activities in a typical day, the causes of cancer deaths, and the composition of your university according to declared majors. When using a pie graph, emphasize the pertinent "slice" of the graph with a contrasting color.

Edith had read and heard conflicting assertions about the amount of renewable energy produced in the United States. She decided to inform her audience of some "facts" about energy consumption so that they could better understand the context of the issue. In her speech she displayed a pie graph (Figure 14.2) that she found on the U.S. Energy Information Administration's website; it showed that renewable energy was a source for 8 percent of energy consumption. She also read statistics that specified how much energy each of the seven types of renewable energy contributed. She reasoned that seven "slices" were too many in a pie graph, so she used a bar graph (Figure 14.3) to show how each source of energy compared to the others.

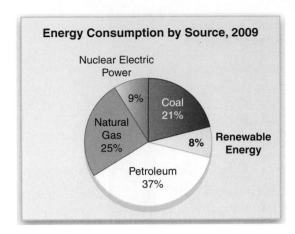

FIGURE 14.2
Sample Pie Graph
Pie graphs compare the percentages of a population, here the sources of energy consumption.

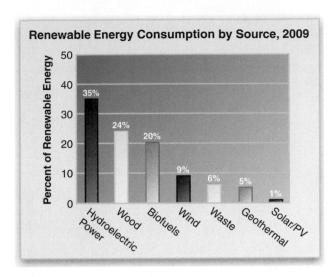

FIGURE 14.3
Sample Bar Graph
Bar graphs compare quantities or amounts, here the sources of renewable energy.

Charts

Like diagrams and graphs, **charts** condense a large amount of information into a small space. Speakers introducing new terms will sometimes list those words on a chart. This strategy is particularly effective if the words can be uncovered one at a time in the order they are discussed. Using charts, you could list the top ten states in per capita lottery ticket sales or rank professional sports according to players' average salaries. A speaker detailing the solution phase of a problem–solution speech could list steps advocated on a chart and introduce them in the order they are discussed.

Joyce chose to inform her audience on how the Internet had facilitated greater global "connectedness." Early in her speech she presented a chart (Figure 14.4) that showed the regional locations of the World's 2,095,006,005 Internet users. Using PowerPoint, she "flew in" her numbered list from bottom to top, creating suspense as to the where her classmates' region ranked on the list.

Maps

Maps lend themselves especially well to speeches discussing or referring to unfamiliar geographic areas. Speakers informing their listeners on the islands of Hawaii, the Battle of Gettysburg, or federal lands currently leased by oil companies would do well to include maps to illustrate their ideas. Although commercial maps are professionally prepared and look good, they may be either too small or too detailed for a speaker's purpose. If you cannot isolate and project a section of the map for a larger audience, prepare a simplified, large-scale map of the territory in question.

chart
A graphic used to condense a large amount of information, to list the steps in a process, or to introduce new terms.

map
A graphic representation of a real or imaginary geographic area.

FIGURE 14.4
Sample Chart
Charts gather information into a convenient format, here the number of Internet users worldwide.

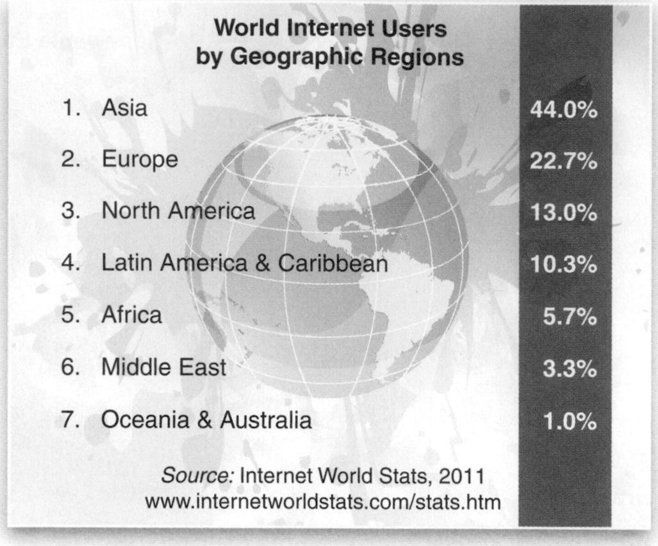

World Internet Users by Geographic Regions

1.	Asia	44.0%
2.	Europe	22.7%
3.	North America	13.0%
4.	Latin America & Caribbean	10.3%
5.	Africa	5.7%
6.	Middle East	3.3%
7.	Oceania & Australia	1.0%

Source: Internet World Stats, 2011
www.internetworldstats.com/stats.htm

Film and Video

film and video
Moving projections used to enhance a speaker's point.

Films and videos are appropriate whenever action will enhance a visual presentation. Though videos carry with them possible distractions, their potential impact is undeniable. Many speeches on social problems are significantly more compelling if the audience not only hears about but also sees graphic evidence of the problem. You can find numerous video clips on the Internet using most search engines. Be sure to note the source of any that you plan to save for multimedia display in your speech so that you can cite them accurately. Moreover, with the widespread popularity of DVDs and updated technology in the classroom, this type of presentational aid is becoming easier and cheaper to use. However, it is important that you, not a presentational aid, organize and present the ideas of your speech. Use only short video clips to illustrate your key ideas.

One popular method for incorporating film clips into speeches is to use Internet-based video caches such as Yahoo!, Hulu, and YouTube. While YouTube and similar sites offer the distinct advantage of not having to buy or rent a DVD, your classroom must have reliable high-speed Internet access in order to smoothly present your clip. It is also somewhat precarious to rely on an Internet-stored video clip that can be removed from the site without notice. One solution to this problem is to use a software program allowing you to download the clips that can then be placed on a thumb drive or other storage device.

Your imagination and your ability to limit yourself to brief clips are your primary obstacles. For example, using YouTube, Google Video, or any of the other video websites, you can show listeners gymnast Alexander Artemev's amazing moves on the pommel horse; vintage concert clips of singer/performer Nina Hagen; world-renowned mime Marcel Marceau's character Bip; or newsreel of the 1940 collapse of the Tacoma Narrows Bridge, known as Galloping Gertie. Video and film can also introduce

EXPLORING ONLINE

Using Audiovisual Aids

www.2myprofessor.com/ Common/guidelines_for_ using_audiovisual.htm

Dr. Mernoush Banton of Florida International University's College of Business Administration maintains this page of practical tips for planning and choosing appropriate presentational aids. Her list of dos and don'ts and her criteria for judging audiovisuals are especially helpful.

ETHICAL DECISIONS

Fair Use or Copyright Infringement

Nicole, a student with a dance background, delivered a speech on the structure and symbolism of *Riverdance* a week before the touring company arrived in town for a series of performances. She illustrated a point in her speech by showing a sequence of less than 2 minutes from a commercial videotape she had rented of a *Riverdance* performance at Radio City Music Hall. That presentational aid certainly made her speech livelier and more vivid for her listeners. Was it, however, a violation of copyright? Using the four guidelines discussed in Chapter 2 (see pages 28–29), determine whether Nicole's use of this material constituted fair use or copyright infringement. Be prepared to defend your answer. Are there other conditions that, had they occurred, would change your answer? If there had been time at the end of class, for example, could Nicole have ethically fulfilled students' requests to see more of the tape?

viewers to aspects of various cultures. One of our students, Henry, delivered an informative speech on the topic of Sufism, an Islamic tradition that is both mystical and multicultural. He informed his listeners how this tradition combines dance and music to express spiritual ecstasy. He played a videotape of the "whirling dervishes" dances of the Mevlevi Order, pointing out the religious significance of the dancers' gestures and movements.

Handouts

A final method of visually presenting material is the **handout**. Copies of any presentational aid—pictures, diagrams, graphs, charts, or maps—may be handed out to individual audience members. Handouts are appropriately used when the information cannot be effectively displayed or projected or when the audience needs to study or refer to the information after the speech.

Gwen, a student presenting her speech "The Power Résumé," used a handout to great benefit. She distributed a sample power résumé and referred to it at key intervals in her speech: "If you look at line 15, you will see . . ." She had numbered the lines of the résumé in the margin so that the audience could find the references without fumbling. Not only could the audience refer to the résumé as Gwen discussed its key features, but many also probably saved it to use later as they prepared their own résumés. In a similar way, if you try to persuade your audience to contribute time and money to local charities, you will more likely achieve your goal if you distribute a handout with the name, address, telephone number, and brief description of each charity.

While working as a student assistant in the Financial Aid Office (FAO), Jake revised and updated a chart of federal financial aid packages available for the 2011–2012 academic school year (see Figure 14.5). Pleased with his efforts, the financial aid staff asked Jake to present his chart to a summer workshop for incoming freshmen and their parents. Because the chart contained many important details, it was too complex for projection; besides, students and their parents might want to refer to it later. So, at the workshop Jake previewed the four categories of aid, distributed his handout, and assisted the financial aid staff as they discussed and answered questions about various aid programs and how to apply for them.

handout
Any graphic visual aid distributed to individual audience members.

FEDERAL STUDENT AID PROGRAMS, 2011			
CATEGORY OF AID	**PROGRAM**	**QUALIFICATIONS**	**PAYBACK REQUIREMENT**
Grants			
	Federal Pell Grant	Need based	none
	Federal Supplemental Educational Opportunity Grant (FSEOG)	Need based	none
	Teacher Education Assistance for College and Higher Education Grant (TEACH)	Must agree to teach	none
	Iraq and Afghanistan Service Grant	Child of deceased service man or woman	none
	Institutional Grants	Merit based	none
Campus-Based Aid			
	Federal Supplemental Educational Opportunity Grants (FSEOG)	Need based	none
	Federal Work-Study (FWS)	Need based	none
	Federal Perkins Loan	Need based	5% interest
Direct Stafford Loans			
	Direct Subsidized Loans	Need based	varies
	Direct Unsubsidized Loans	Not need based	varies
Direct PLUS Loans			
	Direct PLUS Loans for Parents	For parents of qualified students	7.9% interest

Source: Federal Student Aid Office. U.S. Dept. of Education.
https://studentaid.ed.gov/PORTALSWebApp/students/english/campusaid.jsp

FIGURE 14.5
Sample Handout

If you are distributing handouts to listeners who are likely to receive handouts from other speakers on the same day you speak, use colored paper to distinguish your materials. If you are the only speaker and are distributing several handouts, consider putting each one on a different color paper. It's easier to identify which handout you want your listeners to look at if you can say, "On the blue sheet . . . ," for example.

Audio and Other Aids

Audio aids include records, tapes, compact discs, and MP3 files, as well as films and videos. Certain speech topics lend themselves to audio reinforcement of the message. A speech on Janis Joplin, for example, would be more vivid and informative if the audience could see and hear a videotaped clip of one of her performances. Lindahl began her speech on the savant syndrome by playing 30 seconds of a taped piano performance of Chopin's Polonaise no. 6 in A-Flat Major. Her first words were, "The person who was playing that music is considered handicapped, but he heard this piece of music for the first time only minutes before sitting down to play it." The audiotape was a compelling example of one form of the savant syndrome. A speech comparing the jazz styles of Branford and Wynton Marsalis could hardly be effective without letting listeners hear examples from each of those artists.

Audio aids need not be confined to music topics, however. An audience listening to a speech on Winston Churchill could benefit from hearing his quiet eloquence as he addressed Great Britain's House of Commons and declared, "I have nothing to offer but blood, toil, tears, and sweat." And a speaker analyzing the persuasive appeals of radio and television advertisements could play pertinent examples.

You may want to appeal to senses other than sight and hearing. For example, a student of ours gave each audience member an envelope before her speech on aromatherapy. When she discussed the effects of certain scents on behavior, she had students open the envelopes and remove strips of lavender- and vanilla-scented paper, two of the scents she discussed. Think creatively and critically as you consider ways of supporting what you say.

> **audio aid**
> A cassette tape, compact disc, or record used to clarify or prove a point by letting listeners hear an example.

◑ Projection of Presentational Aids

Once you have decided what type of presentation aids will best serve your audience, you must decide how best to display them. **Projection** is especially appropriate when your audience is too large to see the presentational aid easily and clearly. In such a case, you may want to use projections such as PowerPoint slides or transparencies.

A note of caution: As a beginning public speaker, you need to control and be the primary focus of the public speaking event. When you stand at the back of the room and narrate a slide show, you get little experience in speaking before an audience. Presentational aids must always support, not become, your speech.

> **projection**
> A manner of presenting visual aids by casting their images onto a screen or other background.

PowerPoint

PowerPoint is a software program that enables speakers to supplement their presentations with text, graphics, images, audio, and video. Chances are that you have developed PowerPoint slides at some point in your

> **PowerPoint**
> A software program that enables speakers to supplement their presentations with text, graphics, images, audio, and video.

EXPLORING ONLINE

Using PowerPoint

http://office.microsoft.com/
en-us/powerpoint

This site contains numerous links for both novice and experienced users of PowerPoint. Step-by-step instructions will help you design slides and incorporate appropriate color, sound, graphics, and animations.

education. The software's attractions are undeniable. PowerPoint can reassure an inexperienced speaker because in developing your slides you are predetermining your content and organization. Used well, PowerPoint can present a seamless blend of image, text, and spoken word.

Unfortunately, PowerPoint is not always used well. Two communication scholars recently surveyed research and concluded that "students are becoming less and less engaged by professors presenting with PowerPoint."[7] Some corporations have even restricted reliance on the use of PowerPoint in company presentations. Remember that *you* are the presenter—not PowerPoint, Keynote, OpenOffice Impress, or some other software program. Avoid the temptation to blend into the background and narrate a slide show.

Many excellent tutorials can help you learn PowerPoint for the first time or adapt to specific versions of the software. Your college may offer workshops or courses that teach PowerPoint. Additionally, most school libraries have ebooks with tutorials that can walk you through common features of the software. You can access Microsoft's PowerPoint home page using the URL in the "Exploring Online" feature on this page. A Google search for "PowerPoint tutorial" yields hundreds of websites, including some excellent online tutorials for college students.

Among the many display options PowerPoint provides, these are some things to keep in mind:

- Clear the screen when you want listeners to focus just on you. To replace any screen with solid black, just press B on the keyboard. Press the same key again to restore the PowerPoint image. Doing the same with the keyboard letter W replaces the image with a white screen.
- Be familiar with your slides so that you can skip ahead or go back if you need to. Print the Outline View of your slides and keep it handy as a reference. To skip to a slide, just type the number of the slide you want to go to.
- Limit or eliminate moving text. Transitions that have text flying or spiraling in make the audience wait until movement has stopped in order to read. Eliminate animations or sound effects that distract listeners' attention from you and your message.[8]
- While there are exceptions, we think that Guy Kawasaki's 10-20-30 rule establishes solid guidelines for most presentations. Kawasaki, former Apple chief evangelist and current venture capitalist, is well known for touting his 10-20-30 PowerPoint use guidelines. (1) Never use more than 10 slides; (2) Never speak for more than 20 minutes; (3) Never use a font smaller than 30 points. While all three rules may not apply to every speaking class, rule three helps to guard against the problem of too much text on slides. At 30-point font, you are helping ensure that those in the back row will actually see your slides, and you prevent the corresponding problem of reading your speech from a bulleted list crammed into your slides.[9]

You should use PowerPoint ... sparingly. Don't think of it as wallpaper that's always there behind you, but a discrete moment in your talk when you turn to an illustration because it's too difficult to put the idea into mere words.

—Nick Morgan[10]

There are some occasions when using PowerPoint is counterproductive: when you are trying to engage your audience's emotions or imaginations, when you are primarily interested in connecting with your listeners, when you want your listeners to be actively involved in creating the presentation with you, when your preparation time is limited, and when your audience suffers from PowerPoint fatigue.[11]

Document Cameras

Today's high-tech visual presenters such as Elmo offer the advantage of enlarging and projecting visual aids without the work of preparing transparencies. These document cameras can project transparencies, video, computer slide shows, and computer animation as well as images of three-dimensional objects. Many models feature autofocus and power zoom magnification controlled by wireless remotes.

Presentational aids help listeners see as well as hear your message. Well-designed PowerPoint graphics, for example, can enhance the impact of your ideas.

Strategies for Using Presentational Aids

Remember that even the most brilliant presentational aid cannot salvage a poorly planned, poorly delivered speech. Visuals can aid, but they cannot resuscitate, a weak speech. On the other hand, even the most carefully designed and professionally executed visual aid can be spoiled by clumsy handling during a presentation. The effect of public speaking is cumulative, with each element contributing toward one final effect. The following section offers some practical guidelines on how to use presentational aids in your public speech.

Before the Speech

Determine the Information to Be Presented Visually. Sections of a presentation that are complex or detailed may be particularly appropriate for visualization. Be careful, however, not to use too many visual aids. The premium in a speech is on the spoken word. Multimedia presentations can be exciting; they may also be extremely difficult to coordinate. Handling too many objects or charts quickly becomes cumbersome and distracting.

Select the Type of Presentational Aid Best Suited to Your Resources and Speech. The information you need to present, the amount of preparation time you have, your technical expertise at producing the aid, and the cost involved will all influence the visual aid you select. If preparing quality presentational aids to illustrate your speech will take more time, money, or expertise than you have, you are probably better off without them. A presentational aid that calls attention to its poor production is a handicap, no matter how important the information it contains.

EXPLORING ONLINE

Using Presentational Aids

http://cte.uwaterloo.ca/
teaching_resources/tips/
using_visual_aids.html

Sponsored by the University of Waterloo's Centre for Teaching Excellence, this site shares helpful information and charts about using visual aids, including the pros and cons of PowerPoint. You may also link to their discussion of designing visual aids.

KEY POINTS

Strategies for Using
Presentational Aids
before the Speech

1. Determine the information to be presented visually.
2. Select the type of aid best suited to your resources and speech.
3. Ensure easy viewing by all audience members.
4. Make sure that the aid communicates the information clearly.
5. Construct an aid that is professional in appearance.
6. Practice using your aid.
7. Arrange for safe transportation of your aids.
8. Carry backup supplies with you.
9. Properly position the aid.
10. Test your presentational aid.

Ensure Easy Viewing by All Audience Members. A speaker addressing an audience of 500 would not want to use a videotaped presentation displayed on a single television or computer monitor. A bar graph on poster board should be visible to more than just the first four rows of the audience. If possible, practice with your presentational aids in the room where you will speak. Position or project the aid and then sit in the farthest seat possible. (In an auditorium, make it the back row; people will not move forward unless forced to.) If you can read your presentational aid from that distance, it is sufficient in size. If you cannot, either enlarge or eliminate the aid.

Make Sure That the Presentational Aid Communicates the Information Clearly. Simplicity should be your guiding principle in constructing your visual aid. Michael Talman, a graphic design consultant, compares a graphic in a presentation to "going by a highway billboard at 55 miles per hour. Its effectiveness can be judged by how quickly the viewer sees and understands its message."[12] Speakers sometimes construct PowerPoint presentations using all the special effects or posters and slides in Technicolor to make them lively and interesting. However, too many effects or too much color, like too much information, clutters and confuses. Limiting special effects and the range of colors, as well as muting secondary visual elements such as frames, grids, arrows, rules, and boxes, can clarify the primary information you want to convey.[13] Remember that the chief purpose of visual aids is to inform—not to impress—the audience. You may want to use red to indicate a budget deficit, green to indicate growth, or other appropriate colors for a limited number of visual elements. However, as a rule, black or dark blue lettering on a light background is the most visually distinct color combination for text.

Construct a Presentational Aid That Is Professional in Appearance. In the business and professional world, a hand-lettered poster, no matter how neatly done, is inappropriate. Professionals understand the importance of a good impression and are willing to pay graphic designers to help them create polished presentational aids. Today, however, the computer puts a galaxy of inexpensive, professional-looking design options at the fingertips of anyone willing to learn the programs. If you are familiar with a computer graphics program that meets your needs, by all means use it. If you can't use a computer and doubt your freehand skills, another alternative is hiring an art student to draw and letter a presentational aid you have designed.

If you throw together a chart or graph the night before your speech, that is exactly what it will look like. Your hastily prepared work will undermine an image of careful and thorough preparation.

Practice Using Your Presentational Aid. A conscientious speaker will spend hours preparing a speech; presentational aids are a part of that presentation. Just as you rehearse the words of your speech, you should rehearse referring to your aid, uncovering and covering charts, advancing slides, and writing on a whiteboard, flip chart, or a sheet of paper projected by a document camera. In short, if you plan to use presentational aids, learn how *before* your speech; no audience will be impressed by how much you learn during the course of your presentation.

Arrange for Safe Transportation of Your Presentational Aids. Aids worth using are worth transporting safely. The laptop computer you've bought or borrowed needs obvious care. Poster boards should be protected from moisture and bending. Cover your presentational aid with plastic to protect it from that freak rainstorm you encounter just before speech class. If you roll up paper or poster board charts, carry them to different classes, or leave them in a car trunk throughout the day, you cannot expect them to stay flat when you speak.

Carry Backup Supplies with You. An exciting and informative presentation can be ruined when technology fails as you are preparing to speak. Make an inventory of equipment you may need—such as extension cords, bulbs, and batteries—and then take them with you.

Position the Presentational Aid Properly. Get to the place where you will speak *before* the audience arrives. Check out the equipment you will use. If you are using a computer, check to be sure your files are compatible, the projection equipment works, and you can connect to the Internet, if needed. Check the height of the easel if you are using a flip chart or poster boards. If you are projecting text and images, make sure that the equipment works. Position or project your presentational aid in the most desirable location. Make sure that the maximum number of people will see it and that nothing obstructs the audience's view. If you are not to be the first speaker, have your presentational aid and any necessary equipment out of the way but readily located so that you can set up quickly and with little disruption.

Test Your Presentational Aid. Finally, if you are using PowerPoint slides or documents projected by an overhead camera, make sure that they are in focus, in the correct order, and that any remote control you plan to use works. If possible, have any Internet-based videos ready to display to keep the audience from suffering lag time during your speech while you wait for a video to load. If there are people already in the room, you may not want to "give away" your topic by displaying one of your presentational aids. Some speakers prepare a test aid with the word *Test* on it. Although this keeps the audience from seeing part of the speech before you deliver it, it reveals little thought or creativity. A test aid with a creative title for your speech can create interest in your topic without revealing key information. In fact, it could motivate your audience to listen even before you utter your first word.

During the Speech

Not even the most careful preparation of a presentational aid guarantees that it will work for you as you deliver your speech. Keep the following commonsense guidelines in mind as you practice incorporating the aid into your delivery.

THEORY INTO PRACTICE

TIP   Designing Visual Aids

Computer technology has revolutionized the production and display of presentational aids. If you know how, you can use computer programs to design and display professional-looking visual aids. Whether you are preparing PowerPoint slides or other projections, your presentational aids will have a positive impact only if they are clear and readable. Consider the following guidelines before preparing any visuals.[14]

Focus

- *Focus on a few key points.* Resist the temptation to present all your information visually. Select ideas that are the most important or that can best be made through the use of presentational aids.
- *Present ideas one at a time.* Don't let the audience get ahead of you. For example, if you are discussing the first of five solutions for road rage, keep steps 2 through 5 out of audience view. If you are using PowerPoint, build your list through a series of slides. If you display a list of steps using a document camera, cover the steps you have not yet discussed, revealing each when you get to it.

Layout

- *Use a landscape (horizontal) page format rather than a portrait (vertical) format.* Text displayed horizontally is easier to read and gives you a better chance of expressing an idea in a single line.
- *Use left-margin alignment.* It is easier to read than full- or right-margin justification.
- *Use bullets or numbers to highlight your key points.* If you have several key ideas, number them. Listeners can more readily focus on the appropriate part of the visual aid if they see a number when they hear you say, "My third suggestion …"
- *Use no more than six words per line.* Longer sentences are more difficult to read and remember. Learning how to condense and simplify your message also hones your speaking skills.

- *Compose your text in the top half or two-thirds of your slide or document, with no more than six lines per page.* This ensures better viewing for those in the back of the room.

Fonts

- *Use strong, straight fonts.* Arial, Helvetica, and Times New Roman are good choices. Ornate fonts are more difficult to read.
- *Use no more than two fonts per page or screen.* Too many fonts can make your presentational aid more difficult to read.
- *Select a font size large enough to be read easily from the back row.* Minimum font size will vary according to room size and the distance between the projector and the screen. Check font size before your presentation.

Color and Art

- *Use color to enhance your presentational aids.* Research suggests that color can increase the audience's understanding and retention of information. Select colors that highlight the ideas you present. For example, a red line may reinforce a line graph showing a decline in student contributions to charitable organizations. Color can also complement the mood of a speech. A presentational aid for an informative speech on the celebration of Mardi Gras could use bright colors.
- *Limit the number of colors in your presentational aid.* Too many colors make reading a visual aid more difficult. Use no more than six colors per presentational aid and even fewer if the aid contains only text.
- Avoid "chartjunk."[15] Irrelevant graphics and art clutter and detract from your visual aid. An effective presentational aid draws the reader's attention to key points you are making in your speech.

Reveal the Presentational Aid Only When You Are Ready for It. A presentational aid is designed to attract attention and convey information. If it is visible at the beginning of the speech, the audience may focus on it, rather than on what you are saying. Your aid should be seen only when you are ready to discuss the point it illustrates.

If you are using projections, have someone cued to turn the lights off and the projector on at the appropriate time. If your presentational aid is on poster board, cover it with a blank poster board, or turn the blank side to the audience. At the appropriate time, expose the visual aid.

Occasionally, a speaker will stop speaking, uncover a presentational aid, and then continue. This is where rehearsal can really help you. You want to avoid creating unnecessary breaks in the flow of your speech. With practice, you will be able to keep talking as you uncover or project your aid.

Talk to Your Audience—Not to the Presentational Aid. Remember, eye contact is a speaker's most important nonverbal tool. Sustained visual interaction with your audience keeps their attention on you and allows you to monitor their feedback regarding your speech. Turning your back to your listeners undermines your impact. For this reason, use prepared graphics, rather than a dry erase board.

Refer to the Presentational Aid. Speakers sometimes stand at the lectern using their notes or reading their manuscript, relatively far from their aid. This creates two lines of vision and can confuse your audience. It may also give the impression that you must rely on your notes because you do not fully understand what the presentational aid conveys.

Other speakers carry their notes with them as they move to the aid, referring to them as they point out key concepts. This is cumbersome and again reinforces the image of a speaker unsure of what he or she wants to say.

A well-constructed presentational aid should function as a set of notes. The key ideas represented on the aid should trigger the explanation you will provide. You should not need to refer to anything else as you discuss the point your visual aid illustrates. When you practice using your presentational aid, use your aid as your notes.

If you use a computer mouse or a metal or wooden pointer to refer to the aid, have it easily accessible, use it only when pointing to the presentational aid, and set it down immediately after you are finished with it. Too many speakers pick up a pen to refer to their aid and end up playing with it during the rest of the speech.

Finally, point to your presentational aid with the hand closer to it. This keeps your body open and makes communication physically more direct with your audience.

Keep Your Presentational Aid in View until the Audience Understands Your Point. Remember that you are more familiar with your speech than your audience is. Too often, a speaker hurries through an explanation and covers or removes an aid before the audience fully comprehends its significance or the point it makes. Just as you should not reveal your aid too soon, do not cover it up too quickly. You will have invested time and effort

---

KEY POINTS

Strategies for Using Presentational Aids during the Speech

1. Reveal the aid only when you are ready for it.
2. Talk to your audience—not to the aid.
3. Refer to the aid.
4. Keep your aid in view until the audience understands your point.
5. Conceal the aid after you have made your point.
6. Use handouts with caution.

in preparing the aid. Give your audience the time necessary to digest the information it conveys. As you discuss and describe the presentational aid, check your audience response. Many will likely signal their understanding of the presentational aid by nodding their heads or changing their posture.

Conceal the Presentational Aid after You Have Made Your Point. Once you proceed to the next section of your speech, you do not want the audience to continue thinking about the presentational aid. If you are using projections, clear the computer screen or turn off the projector. If the aid is an object or poster board, cover it.

Use Handouts with Caution. Of all the forms of presentational aids, the handout may be the most troublesome. If you distribute handouts before your remarks, the audience is already ahead of you. Passing out information during a presentation can be distracting, especially if you stop talking as you do so. In addition, the rustling of paper can distract the speaker and other audience members. Disseminating material after the presentation eliminates distractions but does not allow the listener to refer to the printed information as you are explaining it. In general, then, use handouts in a public speech only if that is the best way to clarify and give impact to your ideas.

You will encounter some speaking situations, such as a business presentation, that benefit from, and may demand, handout material. Those audiences are often decision-making groups. During an especially technical presentation, they may need to take notes. Afterward, they may need to study the information presented. Handouts provide a record of the presenter's remarks and supplementary information the speaker did not have time to explain.

Presentational aids—objects, graphics, film and video, handouts, and audio aids—can make your speech more effective. By seeing as well as hearing your message, the audience becomes more involved with your speech and more responsive to your appeals.

SUMMARY

Benefits and Types of Presentational Aids

- Presentational aids—objects, pictures, diagrams, graphs, charts, maps, film and video, handouts, and audio aids—can add clarity and impact to a speaker's message, can make a speaker's delivery seem more dynamic, and can increase a speaker's confidence. By seeing as well as hearing your message, the audience becomes more involved with your speech and more responsive to your appeals.

Designing Graphics

- To design graphics that have maximum impact, *focus* on just a few key points and present them one at a time. For graphics that contain text, use horizontal *layout*, with text placed in the top half or two-thirds and with the left margin aligned. Graphics should have no more than six words per line, no more than six lines per page, with bullets or numbers *highlighting* key points. Use strong, straight *fonts*, with no more than two fonts on each graphic. Finally, select *color and art* that amplify the impact of the graphic without cluttering it.

Using Presentational Aids *before* a Speech

- To use these graphics or other presentational aids for maximum impact, take the following steps before the speech: (1) Determine the amount of information to be presented; (2) select the type of aid best suited to your resources and topic; (3) ensure easy viewing by all audience members; (4) ensure that the aid communicates its information clearly; (5) construct an aid that appears carefully or professionally done; (6) practice using the aid; (7) arrange for safe transportation of the aid; (8) carry backup supplies in case of equipment failure; (9) properly position the aid before beginning the speech; and (10) test the aid before using it.

Using Presentational Aids *during* a Speech

- While delivering the speech, remember the following: (1) Reveal the aid only when ready to use it; (2) talk to the audience, not to the aid; (3) refer to the aid; (4) keep the aid in view until the audience understands the point it makes; (5) conceal the aid after making your point with it; and (6) use handouts with caution.

EXERCISES

1. **Practice Critique.** Read the transcript of Melissa Janoske's informative speech, "Renaissance Fairs: The New Vaudeville," in Chapter 15. Although she didn't use presentational aids, several of her classmates commented they wished she had. Write a few suggestions you could offer to Melissa regarding visual aids. What visual content do you think would enhance her speech? What types of aids could she use and how should they be displayed? At what points in her speech should she present them?

2. Select a topic and prepare one PowerPoint slide that illustrates the "Guidelines for Preparing Presentational Aids" discussed in this chapter and one slide that violates one or more of those guidelines. Be sure to include a source line indicating where you got this information. Save the slides to a disk or print them in color. Display your printed slides in class, or project them if multimedia equipment is available, showing the problem slide first. After classmates correctly identify the problems you have illustrated, show the improvements you made on the second slide.

3. Select a graph, diagram, or chart that you find in a magazine, newspaper, or on the Web. Describe how you would adapt it as a presentational aid for a speech.

4. Compile a list of memorable television advertisements. Discuss the visual elements of the ads. What strategies do they use to reinforce the message? Can some of these techniques be adapted to a speech? Are there elements in any of the ads that detract from viewers' remembering the product or brand name? How can a public speaker avoid this pitfall when designing and presenting a presentational aid?

5. Select a statistical table from an almanac, a government report, the *Gallup Poll Monthly, American Demographics,* or some other source. Decide how you could convert the information to a line, bar, or pie graph. Construct the graph on a sheet of paper, poster board, or PowerPoint slide.

6. Sketch a presentational aid you could construct for one of the speeches in Appendix B. Describe how the aid would make the message of the speech clearer and more memorable.

7. Describe at least two different types of presentational aids you could use for a speech having the following specific purposes:

   a. To inform the audience about techniques of handwriting analysis

   b. To inform the audience about "the look" of a Quentin Tarantino film

   c. To inform the audience about the process of photograph restoration

   d. To persuade the audience that federal funding for Parkinson's disease research should be increased

   e. To persuade the audience that [name of building on campus] should be torn down and replaced with another facility

Speaking to Inform

15

- **Characteristics of a Speech to Inform**
- **Informative Speech Topics**
  Speeches about People
  Speeches about Objects
  Speeches about Places
  Speeches about Activities and Events
  Speeches about Processes
  Speeches about Concepts
  Speeches about Conditions
  Speeches about Issues
  Theory Into Practice: Organizing Informative Speeches

- **Guidelines for Speaking to Inform**
  Stress Your Informative Purpose
  Be Objective
  Be Specific
  Be Clear
  Be Accurate
  Limit Your Ideas and Supporting Materials
  Be Relevant
  Use Appropriate Organization
  Use Appropriate Forms of Support
  Use Effective Delivery

- **Annotated Sample Speech: Renaissance Fairs: The New Vaudeville**

After studying this chapter, you should be able to

1. Recognize the three challenges of developing a speech to inform.

2. Understand the characteristics of an informative speech.

3. Distinguish between informative and persuasive speaking.

4. Identify ways of classifying informative speech topics.

5. Use these topic categories to select and organize your speech.

6. Apply ten guidelines for developing an informative speech.

> We are drowning in information and starving for knowledge.
>
> —John Naisbitt

Our thirst for knowledge and stimulation seems insatiable. It has also never been easier to satisfy. It is estimated that in March 2011 there were 245 million Internet users in the United States, an increase of more than 150 percent since 2000.[1] Users logged "onto the Internet to use email, get news, access government information, check out health and medical information, participate in auctions, book travel reservations, research their genealogy, gamble, seek out romantic partners, and engage in countless other activities."[2] Many who want to be connected—"plugged in"—find it amazingly easy to do so.

An informative speech assignment challenges you to take a small step toward building a sense of community within your classroom. Such an assignment also poses at least three challenges:

1. Choosing a topic you find interesting and that your listeners will find interesting or relevant
2. Finding adequate information to make you well informed about the topic
3. Organizing your information in the most fitting manner

These three tasks form the essence of informative speaking, the subject of this chapter.

◖ Characteristics of a Speech to Inform

speech to inform
A speech to impart knowledge, enhance understanding, or facilitate application of information.

We seek knowledge for three reasons: we want to *know*, *understand*, and *use* information. The goals of anyone delivering a **speech to inform**, in turn, are to impart knowledge, enhance understanding, or permit application.

- *To impart knowledge.* Suppose you decided to prepare an informative speech on the general subject of advertising. Your specific purpose could be to inform the audience about advertising in ancient times. Your listeners probably know little about this topic, and you can readily assume that your speech would add to their knowledge.
- *To deepen understanding.* Alternatively, you could inform the audience about how effective advertising succeeds. Using examples your audience already knows, you could deepen their understanding of advertising strategies and principles.
- *To permit application.* A third specific purpose could be to inform your listeners how to prepare effective, low-cost advertisements when they want to promote an event. In this instance, you would help the audience apply basic advertising principles.

When you prepare an informative speech, make sure that you don't slip into giving a persuasive speech. How can you avoid this problem? After all, a persuasive speech also conveys information. In fact, the best persuasive speeches usually include supporting material that is both expository and compelling.

Some topics are easy to classify as informative or persuasive. A speaker urging an audience not to use cell phones while driving is clearly trying to persuade; the speaker is attempting to intensify beliefs and either change or reinforce behavior. On the other hand, a speech charting the most recent options in cell phone technology is a speech to inform. A speech describing different forms of alcohol addiction is informative, whereas a speech advocating the Alcoholics Anonymous program to overcome addiction is persuasive.

Sometimes speakers begin preparing a speech to inform, only to discover that during the speech construction process their objective has become persuasion. In other instances, speakers deliver what they intended to be an informative speech only to find that their listeners received it as a persuasive message. How can this happen? Let's look at the experience of one speaker, Sarah.

> Sarah designed a speech with the specific purpose of informing the audience of the arguments for and against allowing women to serve in military combat. She took care to represent each side's arguments accurately and objectively. After her speech, however, Sarah discovered that some listeners previously undecided on the issue found the pro arguments more persuasive and now supported permitting women to serve in combat roles. But Sarah also learned that others in the audience became more convinced that women should be excluded from such roles. Did Sarah's speech persuade? Apparently for some audience members the answer is yes; they changed their attitudes because of this speech. Yet Sarah's objective was to inform, not to persuade.

In determining the general purpose of your speech, remember that both speakers and listeners are active participants in the communication process. Listeners will interpret what they hear and integrate it into their frames of reference. Your objectivity as a speaker will not stop the listener from hearing with subjectivity. As a speaker, though, you determine *your* motive for speaking. In a speech to inform, it is not to advocate specific beliefs, attitudes, and behaviors on controversial issues. Your objective is to assist your listeners as they come to know, understand, or apply an idea or issue.

Informative Speech Topics

Experts identify several ways of classifying informative speeches. We offer a topical pattern based on the types of topics you can choose for your speech. As you read about these topic categories, keep two guidelines in mind. First, approach each category of topics with the broadest possible perspective. Second, recognize that the categories overlap; the boundaries between them are not distinct. Whether you consider the Great Pyramid of Cheops an object or a place, for example, is much less important than the fact that it's a fascinating informative speech topic. The purpose of our categories is to stimulate—not to limit—your topic selection and development. As you begin brainstorming, consider information you could provide your listeners

KEY POINTS

Topic Categories for Informative Speeches

1. People
2. Objects
3. Places
4. Activities and events
5. Processes
6. Concepts
7. Conditions
8. Issues

We read about, listen to, and watch people who fascinate us. Many of them have unique, interesting stories. Sharing this information with an audience can make an excellent speech.

EXPLORING ONLINE

Online Biographies

www.biography.com

Visit this site for thousands of ideas for speeches about people. You can search alphabetically or by category paragraph-length biographies of more than 25,000 people.

regarding people, objects, places, activities, events, processes, concepts, conditions, and issues.

Speeches about People

People are an obvious and abundant source of topics for an informative speech. A speech about a person gives you the opportunity to expand your knowledge in a field that interests you while sharing those interests with your listeners. If you're an avid photographer, you could discover and communicate something about the life and accomplishments of Ansel Adams, Diane Arbus, Annie Leibovitz, or Alfred Stieglitz. Of course, you don't need to confine your topic to individuals associated with your major or areas of interest. You could interest and inform audiences by discussing the lives and contributions of people such as Bono; Ray Charles; Cesar Chavez; Jimi Hendrix; Jackie Robinson; M. Night Shyamalan; Andy Warhol; Prince William, Duke of Cambridge; or Mark Zuckerberg.

You may choose to discuss a group of people, such as the Four Horsemen of Notre Dame, the Red Hat Society, or the Washermen of Mumbai. You could even compare and contrast two or more individuals to highlight their philosophies and contributions, such as Rachel Carson and Ralph Nader, or Malcolm X and Martin Luther King, Jr.

In considering an informative speech about a person, you must decide what is important and what the audience will remember. Speeches about people organized so that they resemble biographical entries in an encyclopedia amount to lists of dates. Even the most attentive listener will remember few of the details in such a speech.

Speeches about people are often organized chronologically or topically. In her speech about Mark Zuckerberg, cofounder and CEO of the online social network Facebook, Katherine used a chronological pattern to trace his life and accomplishments. She used parallel wording to help her listeners remember her three key points:

   I. Growing Up
  II. Building Up
 III. Leading Up

First, Katherine discussed Zuckerberg's childhood, providing examples of his early predisposition toward technology. Second, she described how he cofounded Facebook during his sophomore year at Harvard University and then dropped out of school to build that enterprise. Finally, Katherine discussed how Zuckerberg's vision for the future of Facebook is reflected in his leadership style, relying not on top-down decision making but on encouraging openness, collaboration, and sharing of information. For example, when you walk into the Facebook headquarters, you see work stations but no individual offices; even Zuckerberg doesn't have a private office.

Speeches about Objects

A second resource of informative topics is objects. Speeches about objects focus on what is concrete rather than on what is abstract. Again, consider objects from the broadest perspective possible so that you can generate a maximum number of topic ideas. Topics for this type of speech could include electric cars, the Great Wall of China, "nanny cams," performance clothing, smart roads, or volcanoes.

Speeches about objects can use any of several organizational patterns. A speech on the Cathedral of Notre Dame could be organized spatially. A speech tracing the development of cyclones and anticyclones evolves chronologically. A speech on the origins, types, and uses of pasta uses a topical division. If the speech focused only on the history of pasta, however, it might best be structured chronologically.

Kevin used a topical organization for his speech on genetically modified (GM) animals, sometimes called *designer animals*:

   I. The process of designing animals
  II. Benefits of GM animals
      A. Medical uses
      B. Commercial uses
 III. Problems of GM animals
      A. Animal health issues
      B. Ethical issues

Speeches about Places

Places are an easily tapped resource for informative speech topics. These speeches introduce listeners to new locales or expand their knowledge of familiar places. Topics may include real places, such as historic sites, emerging nations, national parks, and planets. Topics may also include fictitious places, such as the Land of Oz or the Island of the Lord of the Flies. Speeches about places challenge speakers to select words that create vivid images.

To organize your speech about places, you would typically use one of three organizational patterns: spatial, chronological, or topical. A speech about the Nile, the world's longest river, is organized spatially if it discusses the upper, middle, and lower Nile. A presentation about your college could trace its development chronologically. A speech on Poplar Forest, Thomas Jefferson's getaway home, could use a topical pattern discussing Jefferson's architectural style.

Suppose you selected as your informative speech topic Ellis Island, the site of the chief U.S. immigration center from 1892 to 1954. You could choose any of the following patterns of development:

Pattern: Spatial
Specific Purpose: To inform the audience about Ellis Island's Main Building

EXPLORING ONLINE

Researching Historical Topics

http://memory.loc.gov/ammem/index.html

If you're interested in discussing an informative topic from a historical perspective, check out *American Memory*, historical collections maintained by the Library of Congress. The site contains more than 125 collections, with topics that include the African-American odyssey, early baseball cards (1887–1914), civil war photographs, Hispanic music, occupational folklore, and sound recordings of speeches from World War I.

EXPLORING ONLINE

Touring Museums Online

www.virtualfreesites.com/museums.html

Virtual Tours is an excellent resource for speeches about places. You can read text, view pictures, and, occasionally, listen to audio or see a short movie as you enjoy online guided tours of more than 300 places. From this site, you can access "Virtual Tours of Museums," "Virtual Tours of Exhibits," "Virtual Tours of Special Interest," "Virtual Real-Time Tours," and "Virtual Reality Tours."

Key Ideas: I. The registry room
            II. The baggage room
            III. The oral history studio

Pattern: Chronological

Specific Purpose: To inform the audience of the history of Ellis Island

Key Ideas: I. Years of immigration, 1892–1954
            II. Years of dormancy, 1954–1984
            III. Years of remembrance, 1984–present

Pattern: Topical

Specific Purpose: To inform the audience of the history of Ellis Island

Key Ideas: I. The process of immigration
            II. The place of immigration
            III. The people who immigrated

Notice that each of these outlines is organized according to a distinct pattern. The key ideas in the first outline are organized spatially. Although the specific purposes of the second and third speeches are identical, the former is organized chronologically and the latter topically.

If you choose to speak about a place, avoid making your speech sound like a travelogue. Your speech should identify and develop ideas that contribute to the general education of your listeners.

Speeches about Activities and Events

Activities are things you do by yourself or with others to learn, relax, or accomplish a required task. Among the sources of speech topics are your hobbies, interests, and experiences. Topics that you already know well and are willing to explore more fully often enhance your credibility and energize your delivery.

If you're interested in dancing, a speech on krumping (sometimes called street dancing or clown dancing) could be lively and informative. You could use a topical pattern, informing your audience on these key points:

   I. The origins of krumping
   II. The purposes of krumping
   III. The style of krumping
   IV. The face-painting of krumping

Events are important or interesting occurrences. Examples of topics for this type of speech include the sinking of the *Titanic,* the Woodstock festival, and the rescue of 33 Chilean miners in 2010. For a speech assignment not requiring research, you could speak about an event in your life you consider important, funny, or instructive; for example, "the day I registered for my first semester in college," "the day my first child was born," or "my most embarrassing moment."

Speeches about events typically use a chronological or topical pattern. For example, if your topic is the daring Great Train Robbery that took place in Britain in 1963, you could organize your speech chronologically, describing what happened before, during, and after those famous 15 minutes. Lisa used a topical organization in her speech "World's Longest Yard Sale." She excited her audience with an enthusiastic discussion of this 4-day event. More than 5,000 vendors spanned 450 scenic miles from Kentucky through Tennessee and into Alabama. Lisa divided her topic into two key ideas:

   I. Shopping
     A. Antiques
     B. Collectibles
     C. Furniture
     D. Food
  II. Scenery
     A. Lookout Mountain Parkway
     B. Big South Fork National River
     C. Little River Canyon National Preserve

Speeches about Processes

A process is a series of steps producing an outcome. Your informative speech about a process could explain or demonstrate how something works, functions, or is accomplished. Informative speeches could be on such how-to topics as suiting up and entering a "clean room," making a good first impression, and using an automated external defibrillator. Speeches on global positioning systems, high-pressure processing of juices, nuclear medicine, and cryptography (encoding and decoding messages) are also potentially good informative topics about processes.

Because a process is by definition a time-ordered sequence, speeches about processes commonly use chronological organization. For example, if your specific purpose is to inform your audience of the steps to a successful job interview, you could present these key ideas:

    I. Prepare thoroughly
   II. Arrive promptly
  III. Enter confidently
  IV. Communicate effectively
   V. Follow up immediately

Speeches about processes, however, are not confined to a chronological pattern. The best organization is the one that achieves the purpose of the speech. A student presenting a how-to speech on podcasting would likely choose a chronological pattern if the specific purpose was to explain the steps in the process. Another student might examine the process of podcasting more generally, using a topical pattern to discuss the equipment needed, the most popular file formats, the rapid growth of podcasts, or the effects on traditional broadcasters. Both speeches concern a process, but each uses an organizational pattern suitable for the speaker's specific purpose.

Speeches about Concepts

Speeches about concepts, or ideas, focus on what is abstract rather than on what is concrete. Whereas a speech about an object such as the Statue of Liberty may focus on the history or physical attributes of the statue itself, a speech about an idea may focus on the concept of liberty. Other topics suitable for informative speeches about concepts include ecotourism, objective music, pirate radio, artificial intelligence, endangered languages, and the bystander effect.

Speeches about concepts challenge you to make specific something that is abstract. These speeches typically rely on definitions and examples to support their explanations. Appropriate organizational patterns vary. A speech on Norse mythology could use a topical division and focus on key figures. Speeches about theories, particularly if they are controversial, sometimes use a pro–con division.

Drew, a student of ours, entertained his listeners with a speech on onomastics, or the study of names. Notice how his introduction personalizes his speech and quickly involves his listeners. You can also see from his preview statement that he used a topical organization for this speech about a concept:

> These are some actual names reported by John Train in his books *Remarkable Names of Real People* and *Even More Remarkable Names*. Let me repeat: These are actual names found in bureaus of vital statistics, public health services, newspaper articles, and hospital, church, and school records: E. Pluribus Eubanks, Loch Ness Hontas, Golden Pancake, Halloween Buggage, Odious Champagne, and Memory Leake.
>
> Train says in *Even More Remarkable Names* that "what one might call the free-form nutty name—Oldmouse Waltz, Cashmere Tango Obedience, Eucalyptus Yoho—is the one indigenous American art form."
>
> We're lucky. No one in here has a name as colorful as any of those. But we all have at least two names—a personal and a family name. Today, I'll tell you, first, why personal names developed, and second, the legal status of names. Finally, I have something to tell each of you about the origin of your name.

Speeches about Conditions

Conditions are particular situations: living conditions in a third-world country or social and political climates that give rise to movements such as witchcraft hysteria in Salem, McCarthyism, the women's movement, the civil rights movement, jihad, and national independence movements.

The word *condition* can also refer to a state of fitness or health. Speeches about conditions can focus on a person's health, and, indeed, medical topics are a popular source of student speeches. Informative speeches about crush syndrome, obsessive-compulsive disorder, and progressive supranuclear palsy, for example, can educate listeners about these interesting conditions. A speaker could choose as a specific purpose "to inform the audience about the symptoms, causes, and treatment of preeclampsia." Topical organization is appropriate for many speeches about specific diseases or other health conditions.

This tour guide informs students of the issues, events, and leaders of the civil rights movement.

Jean became interested in the topic of autism. She gathered information from several organizations that conducted research and provided information on this developmental disability. Reviewing the FAQ links on several websites, Jean selected four questions to organize the body of her speech:

 I. What is autism?
 II. What causes autism?
 III. How do you treat autism?
 IV. Is there a cure for autism?

Although the fourth question is closed, requiring only a yes or no answer, Jean used it as an opportunity to discuss types of research being conducted in looking for a cure. At the conclusion of her speech, she gave her audience the URLs for the Autism Society of America and the Center for the Study of Autism websites so they could continue to learn more about this important topic.

States of health also characterize the economy, individual communities, and specific institutions. *Recession*, *depression*, and *full employment* are terms economists use to describe the health of the economy. Speakers inform their listeners about conditions when they describe the state of the arts in their communities, assess the financial situation of most college students, or illustrate how catch limits have affected the whale population, for example.

Speeches about Issues

Speeches about issues deal with controversial ideas and policies. Topics appropriate for informative speeches on issues include the use of polygraphs as a condition for employment, uniform sentencing of criminals, outsourcing jobs, stem cell research, and eliminating sugared soft drinks from school vending machines. Any issue being debated in your school, community, state, or nation can be a fruitful topic for your informative speech.

EXPLORING ONLINE

Discovering Issues

www.aldaily.com

Arts & Letters Daily is an invaluable resource for locating issues in art, criticism, culture, history, literature, music, and philosophy. Updated each weekday and once each weekend, it features current articles, book reviews, essays, and opinions. The site also contains extensive links to newspapers, news and radio services, journals, magazines, Weblogs, music sites, columnists, amusements, and a virtual reference desk.

You may be thinking that controversial issues are better topics for persuasive speeches, but they can also be appropriate for speeches to inform. Just remember that an informative speech on a controversial topic must be researched and developed so that you can present the issue objectively.

Two common organizational patterns for speeches about issues are the topical and pro–con divisions. Speakers predisposed toward one side of an issue sometimes may have difficulty presenting both sides objectively:

> Carl presented a speech on the increasingly popular practice of adopting uniforms for public schools. He presented four good reasons for them: uniforms (1) are more economical for parents, (2) reduce student bickering and fighting over designer clothes, (3) increase student attentiveness in the classroom, and (4) identify various schools and promote school spirit. Carl's only argument against public school uniforms was that they limit students' freedom of expression. His speech seemed out of balance, and most of his classmates thought Carl favored school uniforms. Although the assignment was an informative speech, Carl's pro–con approach was ultimately persuasive. If, like Carl, you feel strongly committed to one side of an issue, save that topic for a persuasive speech.

A second pitfall that sometimes surfaces in the pro–con approach is lack of perspective. Sometimes a speaker will characterize an issue as two-sided when, in reality, it is many-sided. For example, one of our students spoke on the issue of child care. He mentioned the state family leave laws that permit mothers and fathers of newborn infants to take leaves of absence from work while their jobs remain protected. The speaker characterized advocates of such bills as pro-family and opponents as pro-business. He failed to consider that some people oppose such laws because they feel the laws don't go far enough; many state laws exempt small companies with fewer than 50 employees. If you fail to recognize and acknowledge the many facets of an issue in this way, you lose perspective and polarize your topic.

As you begin working on your informative speech, keep in mind this question: "How will the audience benefit from my topic?"

However, what about topics such as the golden age of vaudeville, the origins of superstitions, the history of aviation, the effect of music on livestock production, or the psychological aspects of aging? What about a truly bizarre topic like extreme ironing? Maybe you think that such topics are not relevant to your audience. But part of the process of becoming an educated individual is learning more about the world around you. We are committed to this perspective and believe it is one you should encourage in your listeners.

After you select a topic that meets the criteria discussed in Chapter 6, ask yourself the following three questions: (1) What does the audience already know about my topic? (2) What does the audience need to know to understand the topic? (3) Can I present this information in a way that is easy for the audience to understand and remember in the time allotted? If you are satisfied with your answers to these questions, your next step is to begin developing the most effective strategy for conveying that information. Use the "Theory Into Practice" feature in this chapter to help you select an appropriate organizational pattern.

EXPLORING ONLINE

Choosing and Researching Informative Topics

http://vos.ucsb.edu

Whether you are generating ideas for informative speeches or researching a topic you've already chosen, look at this site if your subject is in the area of the humanities. The Voice of the Shuttle: Web Site for Humanities Research contains numerous links in areas from anthropology to science, technology, and culture. Use the "Search VOS" option to access this site's database of links on your topic.

THEORY INTO PRACTICE

TIP Organizing Informative Speeches

Speeches about	Use	If your purpose is to
People	Topical organization	Explain various aspects of the person's life
	Chronological organization	Survey events in the person's life
Objects	Topical organization	Explain various uses for the object
	Chronological organization	Explain how the object was created or made
	Spatial organization	Describe various parts of the object
Places	Topical organization	Emphasize various aspects of the place
	Chronological organization	Chart the history of or developments in the place
	Spatial organization	Describe the elements or parts of the place
Activities and Events	Topical organization	Explain the significance of the activity or event
	Chronological organization	Explain the sequence of the activity or event
	Causal organization	Explain how one event produced or resulted from another
Processes	Topical organization	Explain aspects of the process
	Chronological organization	Explain how something is done
	Pro–con organization	Explore the arguments for and against the procedure
	Causal organization	Discuss the causes and effects of the process
Concepts	Topical organization	Discuss aspects, definitions, or applications of the concept
Conditions	Topical organization	Explain aspects of the condition
	Chronological organization	Trace the stages or phases of the condition
	Causal organization	Show the causes and effects of the condition
Issues	Topical organization	Discuss aspects of the issue's significance
	Chronological organization	Show how the issue evolved over time
	Pro–con organization	Present opposing viewpoints on the issue

Guidelines for Speaking to Inform

In the remainder of this chapter, we offer ten guidelines you can use as you prepare your informative speech.

Stress Your Informative Purpose

The primary objective of your informative speech is to inform. It is important to be clear about this, especially if your topic is controversial or related to other topics that are controversial. For example, if you are discussing U.S. immigration policy, political correctness, or the role of women in religion, you must realize that some in your audience may already have some very strong feelings about your topic. Stress that your goal is to give additional information, not to change anyone's opinions.

Be Objective

One important criterion for an informative speech is objectivity. If you take a stand, although you may still be informing, you become a persuader. Although both informative and persuasive speakers should support their ideas, informative speakers are committed to presenting a balanced view. Your research should take into account all perspectives. If, as you develop and practice your speech, you find yourself becoming a proponent of a particular viewpoint, you may need to step back and assess whether your orientation has shifted from information to persuasion. If you don't think you can make your speech objective, save the topic for a persuasive speech.

Nothing betrays the image of objectivity that is essential in an informative speech as the inappropriate use of language. For example, in an informative speech on the pros and cons of juvenile curfew laws, one of our students used language that telegraphed his opinion on the issue. Even

SPEAKING WITH CONFIDENCE

Though informative speaking sounds like a simple concept, it is more complicated than it may first appear. It is all too easy to fall into the trap of biased speaking. I selected the hotly debated topic of standardized testing for my informative speech. I then began my research. Throughout the process I would write down notes, only to realize that the information could be interpreted as leaning toward one side of the debate. In order to remain objective, I made an outline to plot the main points that needed to be discussed. I carefully chose ideas that were purely informative, such as "What exactly is standardized testing?" and "When did standardized testing become widely used?" As I constructed my speech, I made sure to use reliable, objective websites that were not gung-ho for either side of the debate. Also, if I had a piece of information that had the slightest inclination of bias, I took it out and saved it for my persuasive speech. Researching an informative speech proved to be more challenging than I anticipated because it's human nature to be biased in any hotly debated issue. But all this work kept me focused. When I delivered my speech, I felt confident that it was strictly informative.

Patty Pak
Virginia Tech University

ETHICAL DECISIONS

Managing Bias in an Informative Speech

Leon serves as historian of his campus fraternity. He considers himself an expert on the subject of Greek life at his school, so he decides to use his observations and experiences as the basis for an informative speech on the pros and cons of joining fraternities and sororities. However, Leon fears that if he reveals that he is a fraternity officer, his listeners will assume that he is not presenting objective information—so he does not mention it.

Is it ethical for Leon to avoid mentioning his fraternity affiliation and position? Is it possible for him to give an unbiased presentation of both sides of the issue? In general, is it ethical for speakers who are strongly committed to an organization, cause, or position to give informative speeches on related topics? If so, what obligations do they have to their audience? What guidelines should these speakers follow to ensure that they will deliver objective information rather than a persuasive speech? Write some suggestions that you can discuss with your classmates.

when explaining the arguments for such laws, he described them as "silly," "costly," and "unenforceable." In an informative speech, your language should be descriptive, not evaluative or judgmental.

Be Specific

Many of us know a little about a lot of subjects. An informative speech gives you the opportunity to fill in the gaps by telling your audience a lot about a little. Narrow your topic. Focus on specific people, objects, places, activities, events, processes, concepts, conditions, and issues. A sports topic could be narrowed to sports commentators, the history of Astroturf, competitive team sports and male bonding, and so on. The more specific you are about your topic, your purpose, and the materials you plan to use in your speech, the more time you will save during your research. Your specific focus will also make your speech easier for the audience to remember.

Be Clear

If you choose your topic carefully and explain it thoroughly, your message should be clear. Don't choose a topic that is too complex, or you risk being too technical for most audiences. You would not be able to give your audience the background knowledge necessary to understand your presentation in the limited time you have. In addition, be careful about using jargon. Impressing the audience with your vocabulary is counterproductive if they cannot understand your message. The purpose of informative speaking is not to impress the audience with complex data but to communicate information clearly.

Ethical decision making requires access to clear and accurate supporting material. Speakers must consider multiple points of view as they research and evaluate their information.

Speeches about processes may use models to describe how something works, functions, or is accomplished.

Be Accurate

Inaccurate information misinforms and has two negative consequences. First, if listeners recognize misstatements, they may begin to question your credibility: "If the speaker's wrong about that, could there be other inaccuracies in the speech?" Accurate statements help you develop a positive image or protect one you have established earlier.

Second, inaccurate information might cause mental or physical harm to listeners. For example, you might give an informative speech on the life-threatening reactions some people have to sulfites, a common ingredient in certain food preservatives. If you didn't mention that these reactions are rare, your audience could leave feeling worried about their health and the damage they may already have suffered. If audience members are unaware of factual errors, they may form invalid beliefs or make unwise decisions.

You must also accurately cite your sources. Some speakers assume that because they do not take a controversial stand in an informative speech, they need not cite sources. While an informative topic may require fewer sources than you would use to establish your side of a debatable point, demonstrating the truth of your ideas and information is essential.

Limit Your Ideas and Supporting Materials

Don't make the mistake of thinking that the more information you put into a speech, the more informative it is. Listeners cannot process all or even most of what you present. If you overload your audience with too much information, they will stop listening. Remember the adage "less is more." Spending more time explaining and developing a few ideas will probably result in greater retention of these ideas by your listeners.

Be Relevant

As you research your topic, you will no doubt discover information that is interesting but not central to your thesis. Because it is so interesting, you may be tempted to include it. Don't. If it is not relevant, leave it out.

Larry delivered an intriguing informative speech on the Jains, a tribe of monks in India whose daily life is shaped by reverence for all living things. As you might guess, the Jains are vegetarians. However, they don't eat vegetables that develop underground because harvesting them may kill insects in the soil. Larry had done a good deal of research on this fascinating topic, including his own travels in India. His firsthand knowledge was both a blessing and a curse. Listening to a speaker who had visited the Jains's monasteries certainly made the topic immediate and compelling. But because he knew so much about the country, Larry included a lot of information about India that was interesting but irrelevant to his main point. His speech became much too long.

To avoid this problem and to keep yourself on track, write out your central thesis and refer to it periodically. When you digress from your topic, you waste valuable preparation time, distort the focus of your speech, and confuse your audience.

Use Appropriate Organization

There is no one best organizational pattern for informative speeches. Choose the pattern that is most appropriate to your topic and specific purpose. However, some patterns are inappropriate for an informative speech. While a pro–con approach is appropriate, a pro–con assessment strategy moves the speech into persuasion. Problem–solution and need–plan patterns are also inherently persuasive. This chapter's "Theory Into Practice" feature offers suggestions for selecting an appropriate organizational pattern. If you have any doubt that your organization is informative rather than persuasive, check with your instructor.

Use Appropriate Forms of Support

Like persuasive speeches, speeches to inform require appropriate supporting materials. These materials should come from sources that are authoritative and free from bias. If you discuss a controversial issue, you must represent each side fairly. For example, if your specific purpose is to inform your audience on the effects of bilingual education, you must research and present information from both its proponents and its critics.

Use Effective Delivery

Some speakers have a misconception that delivery is more important for a persuasive speech than for an informative speech. Regardless of the type of speech, your voice and body should reinforce your interest in and enthusiasm for your topic. Your delivery should also reinforce your objectivity. If you find your gestures, body tension, or voice conveying an emotional urgency, you have likely slipped into persuasion.

After reading this chapter, you should know the principles and characteristics of informative speaking, understand how they contribute to effective speaking, and be able to apply them as you prepare your speeches. Our student Melissa Janoske understood and used these principles when she delivered the following speech to her classmates. As you read her transcript, notice how her supporting materials and organization of the introduction, body, and conclusion contributed to a seamless, organic whole. In the marginal annotations, we have indicated the major strengths of Melissa's speech.

◖ Annotated Sample Speech

Melissa delivered her speech using the extemporaneous speaking style. Following is a transcript of her spoken words.

Renaissance Fairs: The New Vaudeville[3]

Melissa Janoske, Radford University

Melissa's opening comments arouse curiosity about her topic.

1 Imagine you're walking down the street, minding your own business, about to go into a store, when suddenly, someone calls your name. You turn around, and the person advances toward you. Immediately, you find yourself in the middle of a sword fight—right in the middle of the street! As you fight for your life, a crowd gathers, watching and cheering. The fight is treacherous, and your opponent is worthy, but finally, the fight ends when the gleaming edge of your sword pins your opponent onto the cobblestone path below him. Those who have gathered come up and congratulate you.

2 This seemingly outrageous scene is actually fairly commonplace in certain times and places. The year? Well, either 1521 or 2002. The place? Any busy street in Renaissance England, or your local Renaissance festival.

This early source citation builds Melissa's credibility on her topic.

3 Elizabethan social historian Mike Bonk captures the excitement and fascination of this era on his current website, www.faires.com. He describes the Renaissance as "a period of intensity in all things: work, play, . . . the arts, world exploration, . . . , religion and superstition. Renaissance faires resurrect [these extremes], both as reenactment and as a way of life."

4 Some people live and die by their ability to re-create pre-seventeenth century Europe. They create elaborate costumes and have entire other personalities that they become on the weekends. Renaissance fairs are both exciting and educational, and anyone with curiosity and imagination can attend, observe, and even participate.

Paragraph 5 previews the main points Melissa intends to discuss.

5 It's easy for you to experience present-day Renaissance culture through three easy acts: imagine yourself as a Renaissance figure, affiliate with your local kingdom, and participate in a local Renaissance festival or event.

Here Melissa begins to apply the 4 S's to her first main point. She signposts ("To start") and states the point: becoming a part of the Renaissance world.

Melissa uses examples and testimony to support her point. Her sources (Boar and Smith) use narration, contrast, and statistics.

Melissa summarizes her first point by stressing the fun and educational value of becoming a Renaissance character.

6 To start on your journey into the Renaissance, imagine yourself becoming a part of the world of a Renaissance fair. This would mean becoming a person from the original world, letting that entire culture become part of who you are, and suspending normal belief about who you are in daily life. Renaissance fair enthusiast Mike Boar proclaims: "Monday through Friday, I'm Mike the Truck Driver. On the weekends, I'm the Barbarian King. Men fear me. Women can't get enough of me. Guess who I'd rather be?" And Mike isn't alone in his love of a personality switch for the weekend. According to Jules Smith, Sr., cofounder of International Renaissance Fairs Ltd., Renaissance fairs are the "new vaudeville," drawing a crowd of 193,000 people to the last fair he held in Maryland. That's a lot of people getting decked out in chain mail and corsets and going out for the weekend. Participants use traditional names and titles, wear period clothing, and even learn about a possible profession from that time period. Events are usually open to the public, and so even if you're not into wearing tights and riding horses, it's still fun to go and watch and learn about the diversity of the culture.

7 Learning how to do all of those character-altering activities is important, but the knowledge of all things Renaissance doesn't just come in a potion from

the apothecary. It is instead often achieved through the second aspect of Renaissance life: affiliating with your local kingdom. The Society for Creative Anachronism, Inc., an international organization dedicated to Renaissance culture, has divided the world into sixteen kingdoms, spanning the entire globe and allowing everyone in the world in on the fun. A map of these divisions can be found on its website, www.sca.org. Many of these sixteen kingdoms have their divisions within the United States. Virginia is located in the Kingdom of Atlantia, and each kingdom has at least one university in a central location. These universities are run by kingdom officials and offer classes in how to become more immersed in the culture; how to be a goldsmith, or lessons in jousting; or even a lecture on the political methods of King Arthur. You can learn how to fence or ride a horse, cook medieval delicacies, or shop for velvet gowns and leather boots. Each kingdom also allows any of its subjects to gain membership, come to the annual events and fairs, and immerse themselves fully in any events or activities that might help them understand Renaissance Europe.

8 While each kingdom provides the learning opportunities for and access to these festivals, the actual participation in them is the third, and most important, aspect of Renaissance fair culture. Without this participation, all the character changes and kingdom knowledge don't mean nearly as much. It is the practice of Renaissance life that makes it worthwhile, and the actual Renaissance fairs are the easiest and most fun way to do that. There are lots of different types of fair activities to participate in, from jousting festivals to chain mail competitions to cooking parties. You can take classes on spinning and weaving and chain mail or participate in the annual Saint Patty's Day Bloodbath ($5 for a day of swordsmanship and excitement). All aspects of Renaissance culture are available and represented, and all you have to do is go out and look for it. Particular festivals are held around present-day holidays, such as Halloween and feasting days, or events that were important in Renaissance culture. There is a very popular fair held in Pennsylvania every year at Halloween called Renaissance Fright Night that includes renditions of "Frankenstein" and poetry from Poe, goblins and gargoyles that come alive, and street peasants, roasted chestnuts, and fighting for the plenty. This is just one example. There are many websites, such as www.faires.com, that offer detailed information about specific fairs in your area. These festivals are the culmination of the work that people do in learning about the way things were in Renaissance Europe. It's a chance to show off your costumes, present your new persona, showcase your work, or just go and be a part of the festivities. The festivals are a time to enjoy the culture and community that is created and to relax and bask in all the entertainment that is offered through a Renaissance fair.

9 Transforming yourself into a Renaissance figure, affiliating with your local kingdom, and participating in a Renaissance fair are three main ways to experience Renaissance culture today. To get started on your journey, visit www.faires.com. Just make sure you spell it the Renaissance way: f-a-i-r-E-s. Here you will find all sorts of suggestions on integrating Renaissance culture into your life in fun and exciting ways. So take the hint from Mike Boar, the truck driver: lose the college student in you for the weekend, and see how much you like being a Barbarian King with a penchant for chain mail.

Reprinted with permission of the speaker.

A complementary transition links Melissa's first and second points. Notice Melissa's creativity in using the archaic phrase "potion from the apothecary."

Melissa signposts ("second") and states her next main point: affiliating with a local kingdom.

Melissa supports this point by providing examples of Renaissance activities.

Melissa summarizes this second point by reiterating the functions of Renaissance kingdoms.

Melissa signposts ("third") and states her final main point: participation in Renaissance fair culture.

Melissa provides examples of many fair activities and of particular fairs held annually.

Melissa summarizes the benefits of participation in Renaissance fairs.

Melissa clearly summarizes her three main points in the first sentence of her conclusion.

Melissa provides an easy-to-remember URL to help listeners extend their exploration of her topic.

Melissa's speech comes to a definite, satisfying close with this vivid, well-worded final image.

SUMMARY

- An informative speech requires you to research a subject of your choice, synthesize data from various sources, and pass it on to your listeners.

Goals of Informative Speaking

- Your goals as an informative speaker are to expand listeners' knowledge, assist their understanding, or help them apply the information you communicate.

Categories of Informative Speeches

- Classifying informative speeches by subject gives you an idea of the range of possible topics and the patterns of organization each subject typically uses. Informative speeches can be about people, objects, places, activities and events, processes, concepts, conditions, and issues.
- As you begin to prepare an informative speech, ask yourself three questions: (1) How much does the audience already know about this topic? (2) What does the audience need to know in order to understand this topic? (3) Can I present this information in the allotted time so that the audience will understand and remember it?

Guidelines for Informative Speaking

- To develop and deliver an effective informative speech: (1) Let your audience know that your purpose is to inform. (2) Be objective in your approach to the topic and the language you use. (3) Be specific. (4) Be clear. (5) Be accurate. (6) Limit the ideas and supporting material that you try to include. (7) Be relevant. (8) Use the pattern of organization best suited to achieving your specific purpose. (9) Use appropriate forms of support. (10) Use lively, effective speech delivery.

EXERCISES

1. **Practice Critique.** Goodrich's speech in Appendix B is an example of an informative speech delivered in an introductory public speaking class. Read the transcript or watch the video. Then, using the guidelines you have learned in this and previous chapters, compile a list of the speech's strengths and weaknesses. Select two weaknesses and suggest specific strategies Darla could use to improve her speech.

2. Write and bring to class five specific purpose statements for speeches on any topics you choose. Do not identify the general purpose (to inform or to persuade) in these statements; for example, "To _____ the audience on the effects of fragrance on personal health, worker productivity, and product sales." Two or three of these statements should be for informative speech topics; the remainder, for persuasive topics. Be prepared to exchange your paper with another classmate. Each person should write "inform" or "persuade" in the blank provided in each specific purpose statement. Return the papers and discuss the answers.

3. Suppose you are asked to speak to a group of incoming students on the topic "Using the Campus Library." Your objective is to familiarize new students with the physical layout of the library so that they can research efficiently. Outline the key ideas you would develop in your speech. What types of presentational aids would you use to reinforce your message?

4. Select an emotionally charged issue (political correctness, Internet filtering in public libraries, or legalization of drugs, for example). Brainstorm aspects of the issue that would be appropriate for an informative speech. State the specific purpose of the speech and briefly describe what you could discuss. In discussing

your topic, point out what makes the speech informative rather than persuasive.

5. Select an informative speech from *Vital Speeches of the Day*, some other published source, or the Internet. Analyze the speech to see if it adheres to the guidelines discussed in this chapter. If it does, show specifically how it fulfills the goals of each guideline. If it does not, list the guidelines violated, and give examples of where this occurs in the speech. Suggest how the speaker could revise the speech to meet the guidelines.

6. Using the speech you selected in Exercise 5, identify and write down the specific purpose of the speech. Does it meet the characteristics of a speech to inform? Why or why not? What method of organization did the speaker use? Do you think this is the best pattern to achieve the speech's specific purpose? Why or why not?

7. Analyze a lecture by one of your instructors to see if it adheres to the guidelines listed in this chapter. Which guidelines for informative speeches do you think also apply to class lectures? Which do not apply? If the instructor violated any guidelines you think apply to lecturing, how might the instructor remedy this?

The Strategy of Persuasion

16

After studying this chapter,
you should be able to

1. Define persuasion.

2. Describe the three types of
   influence.

3. Distinguish among three types
   of persuasive speeches.

4. Understand the stages of
   speaker credibility.

5. Apply the components of
   credibility to enhance your
   persuasiveness.

6. Focus your goals and connect
   with your listeners.

7. Organize and support
   your arguments to achieve
   maximum effect.

8. Apply four strategies to
   enhance your emotional
   appeals.

> The humblest individual
> exerts some influence,
> either for good or evil, upon
> others.
>
> —Henry Ward Beecher

Media specialist Tony Schwartz, producer of political commercials for presidential and other political candidates, combined *manipulation* and *participation* to create a new word: *partipulation*. He argues that voters are not simply manipulated by campaign and advertising strategists. Voters do, after all, have the option of rejecting the messages politicians present to them. So, Schwartz contends, "You have to participate in your own manipulation."[1]

Persuasion is similar to Schwartz's concept of partipulation. As a speaker, your goal should be to establish a common perspective and tap values your listeners share. Your goal should not be to manipulate or trick them. As a critical listener, you have a right and an ethical responsibility to choose whether you are persuaded. Charles Larson echoes this speaker–listener orientation:

> [T]he focus of persuasion is not on the source, the message, or the receiver, but on *all* of them equally. They *all cooperate* to make a persuasive process. The idea of *co-creation* means that what is inside the receiver is just as important as the source's intent or the content of messages. In one sense, *all* persuasion is *self-persuasion*—we are rarely persuaded unless we participate in the process.[2]

In this chapter, we examine how source, message, and receiver interact to co-create persuasion, and we introduce you to the *strategy* of persuasion. Why is persuasive speaking important? How does the persuasive process work? What are some principles and strategies you can use as you prepare your message? The answers to these questions provide a blueprint for your speech. In the next chapter, we introduce you to the *structure* of persuasion. You will use your blueprint as you build your persuasive speech. You will study how to organize and test the arguments of your speech. You will then discover how to integrate those arguments into a clear and convincing message.

The Importance of Persuasion

Delivering a persuasive message will challenge and benefit you in several ways. First, it will require you to select an issue you think is important and to communicate your concern to your audience. Voicing your beliefs will demand that you confront their logic and support; in other words, you must test your ideas for their validity. Second, that process, in turn, will require that you gather supporting materials and draw valid inferences from them as you develop your arguments. Approached seriously and researched energetically, a persuasive speech assignment can develop both your critical thinking and speech-making skills. Finally, you may also use it as an opportunity to improve your school or community. Change can occur when people speak and audiences act.

As a listener, you also benefit by participating in the persuasive process. A speaker can make you aware of problems and can show you how to help solve them. You hear other points of view and, consequently, may better understand why others have beliefs different from yours. A speech that challenges your beliefs often forces you to reevaluate your position. Participating as a listener also heightens your critical thinking and improves your ability to explain and defend your beliefs. Finally, as a listener, you have an opportunity to judge how others use persuasive speaking techniques, thus enabling you to improve your own persuasive speaking.

A Definition of Persuasion

Persuasion is the *process of influencing another person's values, beliefs, attitudes, or behaviors.* Persuasion does not necessarily require power. Power implies authority or control over another. For example, employers who want you to be on time will state that policy and then issue reprimands, withhold promotions, and even threaten to terminate your employment to ensure that you obey. They do not need to persuade you. Likewise, in this class, you probably speak on the days assigned because failing to do so would hurt your grade. In each instance, the power residing in some other person's position shapes your behavior, at least in part.

Persuasion, however, is more accurately equated with influence than with power. As a speaker, you try to influence the audience to adopt your position. You probably have little power over your listeners, and they have the freedom to reject your message. Suppose, for example, that your speech instructor wants your class to attend a lecture given on campus by author David Sedaris. You are not required to attend, and there is no penalty or reward. To influence you, however, your instructor emphasizes the importance of this opportunity by telling you about Sedaris's background and listing two of his best-known books: *Me Talk Pretty One Day* and *Dress Your Family in Corduroy and Denim*. Your instructor also mentions Sedaris's reputation as a lively, entertaining speaker and tells you that his sister is actress Amy Sedaris.

In this case, your instructor is using influence rather than power to persuade. The concept of persuasion as influence means that you can bring about change whether or not you are the more powerful party in a relationship. You can also see that compared to power, influence requires more effort, creativity, and sensitivity but in the long run is probably more effective. If persuasion is our attempt to influence others, let's look more closely at the types of influence we can achieve.

A persuasive speech provides you the opportunity to champion important causes, change audience beliefs and attitudes, and motivate their behaviors.

persuasion
The process of influencing another person's values, beliefs, attitudes, or behaviors.

Types of Influence

Our definition of *persuasion* suggests three types of influence. You can change, instill, or intensify your listeners' values, beliefs, attitudes, and behaviors. Your goal is to move your listeners closer to your position. It may help you to think of this process as a continuum:

Remember, when you speak to persuade, you are speaking to listeners who may oppose, be indifferent to, or support your position. If you've developed an audience profile as we recommended in Chapter 5, you will have a good idea of your target audience. The information you gather and the assumptions you make about your audience before your speech determine your strategy as you develop your remarks.

Many students preparing persuasive speeches make the mistake of thinking that they must change their audiences' opinions from "oppose" to "favor," or vice versa. Take the example of Chris, who argued in his persuasive speech that the National Collegiate Athletic Association should adopt a play-off system to determine each year's college football champion. After his speech, only one classmate who opposed a play-off system said that Chris had persuaded her to support the proposal. Chris thought he had failed to persuade. Further class discussion, however, proved him wrong. A few listeners said they had moved their position from strong opposition to mild opposition. In addition, several who already supported the play-off system said that Chris's arguments had strengthened their opinion. And several listeners who were neutral before the speech found that Chris persuaded them to agree with him. As you can see, even though Chris persuaded only one audience member to move from "oppose" to "favor," his speech was quite successful. Persuasion occurs any time you move a listener's opinion in the direction you advocate, even if that movement is slight.

Change

The most dramatic response you can request of your listeners is that they *change* a value, belief, attitude, or behavior. The response you seek is dramatic because you attempt to change opposition to support, or support to opposition. In terms of the continuum, you are trying to move listeners from one side of zero to the other. For example, if you discover that the majority of your listeners eat high-cholesterol foods, your persuasive speech could encourage them to alter their diets. You would be trying to change their behavior.

Instill

Second, you can attempt to *instill* a value, an attitude, a belief, or a behavior. You instill when you address a particular problem about which your listeners are unaware or undecided. If you persuade your audience that a problem exists, you have instilled a belief. A speaker trying to persuade an audience that intensive care unit psychosis is a serious health problem would first need to define that term for listeners. Then, by documenting cases of "psychotic activity occurring specifically in the intensive care unit among patients . . . which can cause them to fall out of bed, pull out breathing tubes, or . . . pull out central [arterial] lines," the speaker could instill a belief in the audience.[3]

Intensify

Finally, you may try to *intensify* values, beliefs, attitudes, or behaviors. In this case, you must know before your speech that audience members agree with your position or behave as you will advocate. Your goal is to strengthen your listeners' positions and actions—to move them even slightly in the direction you advocate on the continuum. For example, your audience may already believe that recycling is desirable. If your persuasive speech causes your listeners to recycle more frequently, you have intensified their behavior. Your persuasive speech may even encourage them to persuade family and friends to adopt similar behavior. When you change believers into advocates and advocates into activists, you have intensified their attitudes and behavior.

Types of Persuasive Speeches

Persuasive speeches are generally classified according to their objectives. An effective persuasive speech may change what people believe, what people do, or how people feel. Persuasive speeches, then, may be divided into speeches to convince, to actuate, or to inspire. Understanding these divisions can help you determine your primary objective as you work on your speech, but keep in mind that persuasive speeches often include two or more objectives. For example, if your purpose is to get your audience to boycott companies using sweatshop labor to produce their products, you must first convince them that your cause is right. We usually act or become inspired after we are convinced.

Speeches to Convince

In a **speech to convince**, your objective is to affect your listeners' beliefs or attitudes. Each of the following specific purpose statements expresses a belief the speaker wants the audience to accept:

> To convince the audience that "hate speech" is constitutionally protected
>
> To convince the audience that hydrogen fuel–celled cars are commercially feasible
>
> To convince the audience that there is a constitutional right to privacy
>
> To convince the audience that sealed adoption is preferable to open adoption

speech to convince
A persuasive speech designed to influence listeners' beliefs or attitudes.

SPEAKING WITH CONFIDENCE

Rather than trying to convince my classmates to tackle a world problem, I wanted to motivate them to begin making simple but important choices to improve their health. I had noticed that some of them (and their friends) had the habit of wearing unsupportive, ill-fitting shoes, such a flip flops. So, I decided to speak on the health benefits of wearing properly fitting shoes. One of my concerns, though, was being taken seriously by my listeners, so I made sure to use sound arguments and credible sources. I presented the medical issues that could result, using expert sources and an accompanying visual aid. After securing agreement on the problems, I then asked my audience to consider healthy options the next time they bought shoes. By keeping my goals focused, limited, and practical, I felt confident that I had made a constructive contribution to the immediate and long-term health of my audience.

Brittney Howell
Radford University

The speaker's purpose in each of these speeches is to establish belief, not to secure action.

Speeches to Actuate

speech to actuate
A persuasive speech designed to influence listeners' behaviors.

A **speech to actuate** may establish beliefs, but it always calls for the audience to act. The specific purpose statements listed here illustrate calls for action:

> To move, or actuate, the audience to donate nonperishable food to a local food bank

> To move the class to sponsor a Relay for Life team to benefit the American Cancer Society

> To move the audience to begin a low-impact aerobic workout program

Speeches to Inspire

speech to inspire
A persuasive speech designed to influence listeners' feelings.

A third type of persuasive speech is the **speech to inspire,** one that attempts to change how listeners feel. Examples include pep talks and motivational speeches as well as special occasion speeches such as commencement addresses and eulogies. Some specific purposes of speeches to inspire are these:

> To inspire the audience to honor the service of fallen firefighters

> To inspire the audience to appreciate those who made their education possible

> To inspire listeners to give their best efforts to all college courses they take

The purposes of inspiration are usually noble and uplifting. These speeches typically have neither the detailed supporting material nor the complex arguments characteristic of speeches to convince or actuate. Sometimes, speakers may ask their listeners to take a specific action to demonstrate their appreciation—for example, to donate to the National Fallen Firefighters Foundation. In this case, the speech to inspire transitions into a speech to actuate.

Thus far, we have seen the importance of audience involvement in the process of persuasion. We have provided a definition of *persuasion* and discussed the various goals that persuasive speakers can have. In the following section, we discuss six important strategies that apply to all persuasive speeches.

◗ Persuasive Speaking Strategies

As far back as ancient Greece, there is evidence of people giving advice on how to be an effective persuasive speaker. Aristotle, for example, devoted much space to the subject in his classic work *The Rhetoric*. He discussed three modes of persuasion: ethos, logos, and pathos.[4] These three modes remain an important foundation today for our understanding of persuasive speaking. What do these terms mean, and how can they help you prepare a persuasive speech?

Ethos, or speaker credibility, derives from the character and reputation of the speaker. **Logos,** or logical appeal, relies on the form and substance of an argument. **Pathos,** or emotional appeal, taps the values and feelings of the audience. Each variable—speaker, message, and audience—affects the finished product. No two people will give the same speech on the same topic to the same audience. Your strategy for each speech must be based on your unique situation and on your own creativity. Nevertheless, we can give you some strategies, or guidelines, to follow as you prepare your persuasive speech.

Establish Your Credibility

As a speaker, your first available source of persuasion is your own credibility, or ethos. **Credibility** is simply your reputation, and it helps determine how your listeners evaluate what you say. Research confirms that the higher your perceived credibility, the more likely the audience is to believe you.[5]

Speaker credibility is fluid, varying according to your listeners. You possess only the credibility your listeners grant you. If you pepper your speaking with humor, for example, some listeners may see you as lively and interesting, while others may think you frivolous. You probably have as many different images as you have audience members.

Stages of Credibility. Credibility also varies according to time. Your credibility before, during, and after your speech may change. These chronological divisions are sometimes referred to as *initial, derived,* and *terminal credibility.*[7]

EXPLORING ONLINE

Readings on Rhetoric
www.public.asu.edu/~macalla/logosethospathos.html

If you want to know more about how to incorporate ethos, logos, and pathos into your persuasive appeals, visit this student-friendly website. Dr. Michael Callaway of Mesa Community College defines, explains, and provides examples of these three concepts.

ethos
Speaker credibility.

logos
Logical appeal.

pathos
Emotional appeal.

One can stand as the greatest orator the world has known, possess the quickest mind, employ the cleverest psychology, and have mastered all the technical devices of argument, but if one is not credible, one might just as well preach to the pelicans.

—Gerry Spence[6]

credibility
The degree to which listeners believe a speaker.

Leaders in business, government, religion, education, and other areas need to know when and how to convince, actuate, and inspire their audiences.

initial credibility
A speaker's image or reputation before speaking to a particular audience.

derived credibility
The image listeners develop of a speaker as he or she speaks.

terminal credibility
The image listeners develop of a speaker by the end of a speech and for a period of time after it.

KEY POINTS

Guidelines for Enhancing Your Image of Competence

1. Know your subject.
2. Document your ideas.
3. Cite your sources.
4. Acknowledge personal involvement.

competence
Listeners' views of a speaker's qualifications to speak on a particular topic.

Initial credibility is your image or reputation prior to speaking. The more the audience knows about you, the firmer your image. Even if your listeners don't know you personally, you can still bring varying images to the speaking occasion. For example, if you are a spokesperson for an organization, your audience may make certain assumptions about you based on what they know about that organization. If a representative from EMILY's List, the Family Research Council, the National Rifle Association, or the Sierra Club were to speak to you, you would probably make certain assumptions about the individual based on what you know about that organization. Just as you do with strangers, you form impressions of your classmates based on what they say in class, how they dress, whether they arrive at class on time, their age, and any organization to which they belong. They have also formed impressions of you, of course. Such images constitute your initial credibility.

Derived credibility is the image the audience develops of you as you speak. The moment you enter your listeners' presence, you provide stimuli from which they can evaluate you. As you begin your speech, the number of stimuli multiplies quickly. If you begin your speech with an offensive joke, listeners' images of you will become more negative. When you appeal to your listeners' values and present reasoned arguments to advance your position, you enhance your image. Your information helps your audience judge your credibility. Listeners will also judge your nonverbal behaviors, such as gestures, posture, eye contact, and appearance. If you convey confidence, authority, and a genuine concern for your listeners, you will enhance your credibility.

Terminal credibility is the image the audience has of you after your speech. Even this credibility is subject to change. The listener may be caught up in the excitement and emotion of your speech and end up with an elevated opinion of you. As time passes, that evaluation may moderate. As you can see, the process of generating and maintaining credibility is ongoing. In this class, for example, your credibility at the conclusion of one speech will shape your initial credibility for your next speech.

Components of Credibility. Studies demonstrate that a highly credible speaker can more successfully persuade than a speaker having low credibility. Clearly, you need to pay careful attention to your credibility at each stage in order to deliver a successful persuasive speech. How do you enhance your image? Communication theorists agree that speakers who appear competent, trustworthy, and dynamic are viewed as credible.[8] If your audience believes that you possess these qualities, you can be effective in persuading them.

Convey Competence. In this class, you are among peers, and so your audience probably considers you a fellow student rather than an expert on your chosen topic. How can you get them to see you as knowledgeable and worthy of their trust? Four strategies will help you establish an image of **competence** on your subject.

1. *Know your subject.* To speak ethically, you must be well informed about your subject. The more you read and listen, the easier it is

to construct a message that is both credible and compelling. You should comprehend both the content and the context of your persuasive message. Persuading your classmates to begin recycling low-density plastics (LDPs) does you little good if your area has no processing plant for LDPs and thus recyclers will not accept them. A well-researched speech increases persuasion by contributing to your image as a well-informed individual. In a public speaking course such as this, the image-building you do is cumulative. Thorough, quality research enhances your credibility on the immediate topic and generates positive initial credibility for your next appearance before the same group.

2. *Document your ideas.* You document ideas by using clear, vivid, and credible supporting materials to illustrate them, as we discussed in Chapter 8. Unsupported ideas are mere assertions. Though your listeners may not expect you to be an expert on your topic, they need assurance that facts and experts corroborate what you say. Providing documentation supports your statements and increases your believability.

3. *Cite your sources.* You need to tell your listeners the sources of your information. Remember, your audience is not going to have the opportunity to read your bibliography. Citing sources enhances the credibility of your ideas by demonstrating that experts support your position. It also requires that your sources be unbiased and of good quality.

4. *Acknowledge any personal involvement or experience with your subject.* Listeners will probably assume that you have an edge in understanding color blindness if you let them know you are color-blind. If you have worked with terminally ill patients and are speaking on hospice care, mentioning your experience will similarly add authority to your ideas.

Convey Trustworthiness. A second criterion of speaker credibility is **trustworthiness**, and it should tell listeners two things about you—that you are honest and that you are objective in what you say. A speaker can demonstrate these attributes in two ways.

trustworthiness
Listeners' views of a speaker's honesty and objectivity.

1. *Establish common ground with your audience.* If listeners know that you understand their values, experiences, and aspirations, they will be more receptive to your arguments. You increase your persuasiveness when you identify with your listeners.

2. *Demonstrate your objectivity in approaching the topic.* The information and sources you include in your speech should demonstrate thorough, unbiased research. One student gave his speech on cigarette smoking, arguing that its harmful effects were greatly exaggerated. He relied on studies sponsored by the tobacco industry. Few in the audience were persuaded by his evidence. He undermined his image of trustworthiness because he limited his research to sources the audience considered biased.

dynamism
Listeners' views of a speaker's confidence, energy, and enthusiasm for communicating.

Convey Dynamism. A third element of credibility is **dynamism,** a quality closely associated with delivery. We enjoy listening to speakers who are energetic, exciting, spirited, and stimulating. But should speakers whose delivery is static, timid, and unexciting be considered less credible than their more exuberant counterparts? Perhaps not, and the ethical listener will focus more on the content than on the form of the message. Yet, studies continue to document that dynamism contributes to speaker credibility, and it would be wise for you to develop this attribute.

Dynamism contributes to persuasion because it conveys both confidence and concern. If you appear tentative or unsure of yourself, the audience may doubt your conviction. To the extent that you can strengthen your verbal, vocal, and physical delivery, you can enhance your image of confidence and, hence, your credibility.

Dynamism also demonstrates concern for the audience and a desire to communicate with them. If your delivery seems flippant, distracted, or detached from the audience, your listeners may assume that you are not concerned about the topic or about them. On the other hand, conveying enthusiasm for your topic and your listeners communicates a strong positive message.

Combining personal credibility with logic and emotion, Michael J. Fox advocates funding cutting-edge research to find a cure for Parkinson's disease.

As a speaker, present a well-researched and well-documented message and communicate it in an honest and unbiased manner. Your verbal, vocal, and physical delivery should show you to be a fluent, forceful, and friendly individual serious about the issue you address. If listeners perceive you to be competent, trustworthy, and dynamic, you will have high source credibility and, hence, be an effective persuader.

ETHICAL DECISIONS

Dynamism: Masking or Making Credibility

In this chapter, we note that a speaker's ability to influence an audience depends, in part, on his or her credibility. Credibility, in turn, is a function of an audience's perception of the speaker's competence, trustworthiness, and dynamism. Dynamic speakers convey confidence; they also communicate a sense of concern for their audiences, a desire to make a connection with their listeners.

Unfortunately, dynamism sometimes masks a speaker's questionable motives. Both Hitler and Mussolini, for example, were dynamic speakers. So were many other leaders throughout the ages who led their followers into battle for unjust causes. How can listeners separate a speaker's dynamism from his or her trustworthiness and competence? If a dynamic speaker seems to care about the audience, how do listeners determine whether the speaker's feelings are sincere? Moreover, what ethical responsibility do listeners have to evaluate the credibility of speakers whose delivery is timid and unexciting? Is it legitimate to tune out a speaker's message if he or she is not effective at making an emotional connection with the audience? In general, what guidelines should listeners follow when they evaluate a speaker's dynamism and credibility? Write your answers to these questions and be prepared to discuss them in class.

Focus Your Goals

A common mistake many beginning speakers make is to seek dramatic change in their listeners' values, beliefs, attitudes, and behaviors. The speaker who can accomplish this is rare—particularly if he or she seeks change on highly emotional and controversial issues such as abortion, gun control, capital punishment, religion, or politics. Keep in mind that the more firmly your audience is anchored to a position, the less likely you are to change their attitudes. It is unrealistic for you to expect dramatic change in a person's beliefs and values in a 5- to 10-minute speech. Instant conversions occur, but they are rare. Limiting your goals and arguing incrementally will help you focus your goals.

Limit Your Goals. Rather than try to convince your audience to support (or oppose) the death penalty, try to convince them of a limited goal, a smaller aspect of the topic; for example, argue that capital punishment deters crime (or does not). Once a listener accepts that belief, you or another speaker can build on it and focus on a successive objective: support for (or opposition to) the death penalty.

Which specific purpose statement in the following pairs is the more limited and reasonable goal?

> To persuade the audience that exposure to violent video games promotes aggression, *or*
> To persuade the audience that habitual exposure to violent video games promotes aggression in children

> To persuade the audience that actively involving students in classroom learning is desirable, *or*
> To persuade the audience that team learning is a cost-effective way to promote student learning

In both cases, the second statement is the more limited and potentially more persuasive. Remember the persuasive principle: *persuasion is more likely if your goals as a speaker are limited rather than global.*

Argue Incrementally. A second principle builds on the first one: *persuasion is more permanent if you achieve it incrementally.* To be effective and long-lasting, persuasion should occur incrementally, or one step at a time. This principle becomes more important if your audience is likely to hear counterarguments to your argument. In any speech, you speak for a fixed amount of time. The greater the number of points you must prove, the less time you have to support and explain each. Because you must move through several steps, your limited time may force you to abbreviate your support of some of these steps. When your listeners hear another speaker attack one of those steps later, they may lack sufficient evidence to counter those attacks; as a result, what you accomplished may be only temporary. Your goal should be to "inoculate" your listeners against possible counterarguments. The stronger your arguments, the greater the likelihood that you will bring about enduring change in your audience's opinions. If you know your audience has been exposed to counterarguments, you may need to address those arguments before introducing your own.

Connect with Your Listeners

You are probably more easily persuaded by people similar to you than by those who are different. We may reason that individuals having backgrounds like ours will view situations and problems as we would. Furthermore, we believe that people who share our beliefs will investigate an issue and arrive at a judgment in the same manner we would if we had the time and the opportunity. Thus, *persuasion is more likely if a speaker establishes common ground with the audience.*

One way to increase your persuasion, then, is to identify with your listeners. Sonja, a weekend news anchor for a local television station, was asked to speak to a college television production class on employment opportunities in television. Notice how Sonja used the strategy of identification in her introduction as she focused on experiences she shared with her listeners.

> Seven years ago a timid freshman girl sat in a college classroom much like this. Just like you, she was taking a TV production class. And like some of you, I suspect, she dreamed of being in front of a camera someday, sitting at an anchor desk, reporting the news to thousands of families who would let her come into their homes through the magic of television.
>
> There was little reason to predict that this girl would achieve her dreams. In many ways she was rather ordinary. She didn't come from a wealthy family. She didn't have any connections that would get her a job in broadcasting. She was a B student who worked part-time in the university food service to help pay for her education. But she had a goal and was determined to attain it. And then one day, it happened. An instructor announced that a local TV station had an opening for a student intern. The instructor said the internship would involve long hours, menial work, and no pay. Hardly the opportunity of a lifetime! Nevertheless, after class, she approached the instructor, uncertain of what she was getting into. With her instructor's help, she applied for and received the internship. It is because of that decision that I am now the weekend anchor of the city's largest television station.

The rest of Sonja's speech focused on the importance of student internships in learning about the reality of the broadcast media and making contacts for future references and employment. Her opening comments made Sonja a more believable speaker by bridging the gap between her and her listeners. Sonja's suggestions influenced her audience because she had established common ground with them.

Four principles of persuasion should guide how you establish common ground with your audience. Each of these principles requires you to analyze your audience carefully in order to understand your listeners.

Assess Listeners' Knowledge of Your Topic.   *Persuasion is more likely if the audience lacks information on the topic.* In the absence of information, a single fact can be compelling. The more information your listeners possess about an issue, the less likely you are to alter their perceptions.

Arturo applied this principle in a speech to persuade his audience that auto insurance companies should not be allowed to set rates based on drivers' credit ratings. Few of his listeners knew that the practice occurred. Yet, by citing just a handful of credible sources, Arturo proved that the practice increased beginning in the mid-1990s, had been adopted by 92 percent of insurers by 2001, and was "nearly universal" by March 2002. As a result, drivers with the worst credit ratings paid rates that were, in some cases, 40 percent higher than those with the best ratings.

New and surprising information such as this can have great persuasive impact. Of course, this principle also has significant ethical implications. Ethical speakers will not exploit their listeners' lack of knowledge to advance positions they know are not logically supported.

Assess How Important Your Audience Considers Your Topic

Ken, Andrea, and Brad gave their persuasive speeches on the same day. Ken's purpose was to persuade the audience to support the school's newly formed lacrosse team by attending the next home game. Andrea's topic concerned the increasing number of homeless adults and children in the city. She told the class about Project Hope, sponsored by the Student Government Association, and asked everyone to donate either a can of food or a dollar at designated collection centers in campus dining halls or in the Student Center. Finally, Brad advocated legalization of marijuana, citing the drug's medical and economic potential.

Which speaker do you think had the most difficult challenge? In answering this question, you must consider the audience. *Persuasion is related to how important the audience considers the topic.*

The perceived importance of a topic can increase the likelihood of persuasion. Audience members in the above example probably agreed with both Ken and Andrea, and both may have been successful persuaders. Listeners who viewed combating hunger as a more important goal than supporting the lacrosse team were probably more persuaded by Andrea and may have contributed to Project Hope.

Just as the importance of a topic can work for you as a persuasive speaker, it can also work against you and decrease the likelihood of persuasion. It is surely easier, for example, for someone to persuade you to change brands of toothpaste than to change your religion. The reason is simple: your religion is more important to you. Brad probably had a tougher time persuading his listeners than did either Ken or Andrea. Legalizing marijuana probably ran counter to some deeply held audience opinions, and the intensity of those beliefs and values may have made them more resistant to Brad's persuasive appeals. The importance of an issue will vary according to each audience member, and you need to take this into account as you prepare your persuasive appeal.

Motivate Your Listeners. A third principle of persuasion is that *persuasion is more likely if the audience is motivated in the direction of the message.* People change their values, beliefs, attitudes, and behaviors because they are motivated to do so. To be an effective persuader, you must discover what motivates your listeners. This requires an understanding of their needs and desires. How can you do this? You can enhance your persuasive appeal by following three steps. First, identify as many of the needs and desires of your listeners as possible. Second, review your list, and select those that your speech satisfies. Third, as you prepare your speech, explain how the action you advocate fulfills audience needs. If you discover that your speech does not fulfill the needs or desires of your listeners, then you have probably failed to connect with these listeners. They may receive your speech with interest, but such listeners will probably not act on your message. What you intended as a persuasive speech may in fact be received as informative.

Relate Your Message to Listeners' Values. Finally, *persuasion is more likely if the speaker's message is consistent with listeners' values, beliefs, attitudes, and behaviors*. We expect our actions to match our beliefs. In fact, we will call someone a hypocrite who professes one set of values but acts according to another. Your ability to persuade is thus enhanced if you request an action that is consistent with your audience's values.

Use this principle of consistency in constructing your persuasive appeal. For example, we have had students who persuaded their classroom audience to oppose the use of animals in nonmedical product testing. They first identified the beliefs that would cause a person to challenge such tests—for example, product testing harms animals and is unnecessary. Next they showed their audience that they share these beliefs. Once they accomplished that, the speakers then asked their listeners to act in accordance with their beliefs and boycott companies that continue to test cosmetics on animals.

Organize Your Arguments

In Chapter 4 you learned that most of us are inefficient listeners. A speech that is poorly organized has little chance of surviving in the minds of audience members. Using the organizational strategies presented in Chapters 9 and 10 can increase your listeners' retention of your message. This is especially important if you seek long-term changes in your audience's attitudes and behaviors.

In addition to what you've already learned about structuring your speech, we offer one more organizing principle: *persuasion is more likely if arguments are placed appropriately*. Once you have determined the key arguments in your speech, you must decide their order. To do that, you must know which of your arguments is the strongest. Assume for a moment that your persuasive speech argues that the public defender system must be reformed. Assume, too, that you are using a problem–solution organization (discussed in Chapter 9). Your first main point and the arguments supporting it could be:

1. The public defender system is stacked against the defendant.
   A. Public defenders' caseloads are too heavy.
   B. Public defenders have too little experience.
   C. Public defenders have inadequate investigative staffs.

EXPLORING ONLINE

Primer of Practical Persuasion

www.healthyinfluence.com/wordpress/steves-primer-of-practical-persuasion-3-0

For an excellent discussion of persuasion theories, visit this updated website authored by Dr. Steven Booth-Butterfield. Claiming to be the most popular persuasion website, the site presents an entire online textbook with links to 32 chapters grouped into seven content areas. You will enjoy the author's humor as you learn how to apply theory and research to various persuasive environments.

One of these three arguments will probably be stronger than the other two. You may have more evidence on one, you may have more recent evidence on it, or you may feel that one argument will be more compelling for your particular audience. Assume that you decide point B is the strongest. Where should you place it? Two theories of argument placement are the primacy and recency theories.

Primacy Theory. **Primacy theory** recommends that you put your strongest argument first in the body of your speech to establish a strong first impression. Because you are most likely to win over your listeners with your strongest argument, this theory suggests that you should win your listeners to your side as early as possible. Primacy theorists tell you to move your strongest argument to the position of point A.

primacy theory
The assumption that a speaker should place the strongest argument at the beginning of the body of a speech.

Recency Theory. **Recency theory**, on the other hand, maintains that you should present your strongest argument last, thus leaving your listeners with your best argument. Recency theorists would have you build up to your strongest argument by making it point C.

If your listeners oppose what you advocate, you may want to present your strongest argument first. Moving them toward your position early in the speech may make them more receptive to your other ideas. If your audience already shares your beliefs and attitudes and your goal is to motivate them to action, you may want to end with your most compelling argument. Both the primacy and recency theorists generally agree that the middle position is the weakest. If you have three or more arguments, therefore, do not place your strongest argument in a middle position. When you sandwich a strong argument between weaker ones, you reduce its impact.

recency theory
The assumption that a speaker should place the strongest argument at the end of the body of a speech.

Aristotle argued that logos relies on the form and substance of argument. Organizing and supporting your ideas, the subjects of this and the following section, will help you develop the logical appeal of your speech.

Support Your Ideas

Well-supported ideas benefit your speech in two ways. First, they provide an ethical underpinning for your position. Ethical speakers test their ideas for validity and share that support with their listeners. Second, well-supported ideas enhance your credibility. Using quality evidence, citing your sources, and employing valid reasoning increase your credibility as a speaker.[9]

Two sections of this book will help you construct a convincing case for your position. In Chapter 8, we discussed the types of supporting material and tests of evidence that you can use to prove your arguments. You can use examples, definitions, narration, comparison. contrast, statistics, and testimony to give your ideas credibility. In Chapter 17, we will introduce you to the elements of an argument, describe five types of argument you can use in your persuasive speaking, and define several categories of faulty reasoning you should avoid.

KEY POINTS

Persuasive Speaking Strategies

1. Establish your credibility.
2. Focus your goals.
3. Connect with your listeners.
4. Organize your arguments.
5. Support your ideas.
6. Enhance your emotional appeals.

Enhance Your Emotional Appeals

Pathos, Aristotle's third mode of persuasion, is the appeal to emotions. Among the emotions speakers can arouse are anger, envy, fear, hate, jealousy, joy, love, and pride. When speakers use these feelings to try to get you to believe something or to act in a particular way, they are using emotional appeals.

Because some of the feelings just listed seem negative, you may consider emotional appeals as unacceptable or inferior types of proof. Perhaps you have even heard someone say, "Don't be so emotional; use your head!" It is certainly possible to be emotional and illogical, but keep in mind that it is also possible to be both emotional and logical. Is it illogical, for example, to be angered by child abuse, to hate racism, or to fear chemical warfare? We don't think so. The strongest arguments combine reason with passion. Logos and pathos should not conflict but should complement each other.

Jessica began her persuasive speech by relating a personal narrative she remembered from her childhood.

> I was 4 years old; my sister was only 2. It was not long after we reached my grandma's house that the phone rang. I could hear ambulance and police sirens head toward the highway as tears were forming in my mom's eyes. There had been a car accident. My dad was rushed to the hospital; his little Fiesta car was totaled. He had been hit on the passenger side by a man driving a station wagon, and, fortunately, both my dad and the other driver survived. Because the other driver fell asleep at the wheel, my dad went to the hospital instead of coming home that night to his family.

Jessica quoted several sources with examples and statistics related to driver fatigue, including these powerful statistics:

> Drowsy driving is estimated to cause about 20 percent of [all vehicle] accidents, 1.2 million a year, more than drugs and alcohol combined. It accounts for an astonishing 5 percent of fatal crashes, and 30 percent of fatal crashes in rural areas.[10]

Did Jessica construct a logical argument? Yes. She presented examples and statistics to support her position. Did she construct an emotional argument? Again, yes. She tapped her listeners' need for safety and their compassion for those who have suffered because of drowsy drivers. Logos and pathos coalesced to form a compelling argument. You can use the guidelines in this chapter's "Theory Into Practice" feature to develop and enhance the pathos of your persuasive speech.

It is important to remember that these three modes of persuasion—ethos, logos, and pathos—all work to enhance your persuasive appeal. The best persuasive speeches combine all three. Effective persuaders are credible, present logically constructed and supported arguments, and tap their listeners' values.

THEORY INTO PRACTICE

TIP   Developing Emotional Appeals

Thoughtful emotional appeals can engage listeners in both the content and delivery of your message. Use the following four guidelines to connect with your audience and enhance the pathos of your speech.

Tap Audience Values

This guideline requires, first, that you carefully analyze your audience to identify their beliefs, values, and needs. Then, as you construct and deliver your speech, show that what you advocate is consistent with your listeners' values.

Duncan's specific purpose was to persuade his classmates to become members of Amnesty International. He had joined this organization because he felt that, as an individual, he could do little to help end torture and executions of prisoners of conscience throughout the world. As part of a concerted worldwide effort, however, he saw the opportunity to further social and political justice. Duncan surveyed his classmates and discovered that although many of them knew little about Amnesty International, most strongly supported freedom of expression and opposed governments' actions to suppress this right. Duncan used these shared values to establish common ground with his listeners and to frame what he would propose.

Use Vivid Examples

Vivid, emotionally toned examples illustrate and enliven your message. After presenting testimony of persecution coupled with statistical estimates of the extent of the problem, Duncan paused and then announced, "I want you not only to hear of the plight of these victims but also to see it." He pushed a remote control button and proceeded to show five slides of people brutalized by their own governments. He did not speak but simply showed each slide for 10 seconds. After the last slide, he spoke again:

> They say a picture is worth a thousand words. Well, these pictures speak volumes about human rights abuse. But these pictures should also speak to our consciences. Can we stand back, detached, and do nothing, knowing what fate befalls these individuals?

Duncan used dramatic visual examples to enhance the pathos of his speech.

Use Emotive Language

In Chapter 12, we discussed the power of words. Nowhere can words be more powerful than when they work to generate emotional appeals. Near the end of his speech, Duncan told his listeners, "In the last 4 minutes you've heard about the anguish, the pain, the suffering, and the persecution experienced by thousands of people, simply because they want to be free and follow their consciences." *Anguish, pain, suffering*, and *persecution* are all words Duncan carefully chose to evoke strong feelings among the audience.

Use Effective Delivery

As we discussed in Chapter 13, when a speaker's verbal and nonverbal messages conflict, we tend to trust the nonverbal message. For that reason, speakers who show little physical and vocal involvement with their speeches usually come across as uninterested or insincere. When you display emotion, you can sometimes generate audience emotion. Throughout his speech, Duncan made effective use of eye contact, gestures, pauses, and vocal emphasis to connect with his classmates. His speech had a powerful effect because his delivery demonstrated his concern for and commitment to his topic.

SUMMARY

The Importance of Persuasion

- As a speaker, persuasion challenges you to select topics important to your audience, evaluate possible supporting material, and construct valid and compelling arguments.
- As a listener, you should listen objectively, evaluate thoughtfully, and respond responsibly. Effective listening can enhance your ability to explain your beliefs and improve your own persuasive speaking.

A Definition of Persuasion

- Persuasion is the process of influencing (changing, instilling, or intensifying) another person's values, beliefs, attitudes, or behaviors.

Types of Persuasive Speeches

- A persuasive speech aimed at changing beliefs and attitudes, but not requesting any overt behavior of listeners, is a *speech to convince*. A *speech to actuate* seeks to change behaviors. A *speech to inspire* encourages positive changes in the way listeners feel about their beliefs or actions.

Persuasive Speaking Strategies

- Three modes of persuasion, discussed at least as early as the time of Aristotle, are *ethos* (ethical appeal), *logos* (logical appeal), and *pathos* (emotional appeal).
- The higher your perceived credibility, the more likely the audience is to believe you. A starting point for persuasion, then, is to establish your credibility. Some speakers have *initial credibility* with a particular audience, based on the listeners' prior knowledge of the speaker. All speakers have *derived credibility*, developed from the ideas they present in their speech and their speech delivery, and *terminal credibility* based on the audience's evaluation of the speaker and the message after the speech.
- *Competence, trustworthiness*, and *dynamism* are three components of a speaker's credibility.
- You are more likely to persuade if your goals are limited rather than global. In addition, your persuasiveness with an audience will be more enduring if you achieve it incrementally, or step by step.
- Persuasion is more likely if you establish common ground with the audience. You are more likely to persuade listeners who lack information on your subject, who are self-motivated in the direction of your message, and whose values, beliefs, attitudes, and behaviors are consistent with your message.
- Persuasion is more likely if the speaker's arguments are appropriately placed within the speech. *Primacy theory* asserts that you should place your strongest argument first in the body of your speech. *Recency theory* maintains that you should build up to your strongest argument, placing it last in the body of your speech. The lesson for public speakers is to avoid placing a strong argument between weaker ones.
- Provide solid support for your ideas. Well-supported ideas provide an ethical underpinning for your speech and enhance your ethos for the audience. Use a variety of quality supporting materials, cite your sources, and reason logically to increase your persuasiveness.
- Increase your persuasiveness by enhancing your message's emotional appeals. Tap audience values; use vivid, emotionally toned examples; use emotive language; and display emotion in the physical and vocal delivery of the speech.

EXERCISES

1. **Practice Critique.** Martin Luther King, Jr.'s "I Have a Dream" speech helped elevate a national debate on equal access to employment opportunities, public accommodations, home ownership, and voting rights. Some historians claim that Dr. King's powerfully persuasive speech spurred creation of a coalition to support this legislation. Access a transcript of Rev. King's speech by using one of the links included in Appendix B or by typing "I Have a Dream Speech" into an Internet search. As you read the transcript, note how he directed his arguments to several diverse audiences: black and white, rich and poor, powerful and powerless, nonviolent and militant. Identify appeals that are designed to convince, actuate, and inspire listeners. What values and beliefs did Dr. King tap to influence his listeners' attitudes and behaviors? How did he seek to establish common ground with such diverse audiences?

2. Select three print, broadcast, or Internet advertisements for the same kind of product (soft drinks, insurance, automobiles, and so on). Discuss the persuasive appeals of each ad. Which one do you think is the most effective? Why? Could any of these strategies of persuasion be incorporated in a speech? Provide some examples.

3. Select an editorial from your campus newspaper, a local or national paper, or *Editorials on File*. Identify the beliefs, attitudes, and values implicit in the editorial, as well as any behaviors the writer advocates.

4. Select a topic, and write a specific purpose statement that seeks dramatic change in the behavior or attitude of your audience. Divide the change you seek into several incremental steps. Discuss what you would need to prove to achieve each step. Could any of these steps be the basis for a speech by itself?

5. Listen to a speaker on C-SPAN, the *PBS NewsHour*, a news interview show, or some other broadcast. Keep a chronology of the speaker's initial, derived, and terminal credibility. What changes occurred in your impression of the speaker? What accounted for those changes? What might the speaker have done to improve his or her credibility?

6. Brainstorm a list of values you think the majority of your class holds. You might use the PERSIA (political, economic, religious, social, intellectual, and artistic) framework to get you thinking about a broad range of values. Refer to this list as you discuss how you could develop an audience-centered persuasive speech for an upcoming assignment.

7. Locate a speech that you feel includes examples of unethical emotional appeals. Many political campaign speeches are a good source of these examples. Explain why the emotional appeals are questionable.

The Structure of Persuasion

17

After studying this chapter, you should be able to

1. Describe and apply the steps to constructing an argument.

2. List and use the four steps of refuting an argument.

3. Compare and contrast five types of argument.

4. Construct and evaluate these types of argument.

5. Recognize and explain ten fallacies of argument.

6. Explain and apply the characteristics of propositions.

7. Identify three types of proposition.

8. Understand and use Monroe's motivated sequence.

Good argument, like good architecture, reveals its structural elements so that what is being said and how it is being supported lie open to the consideration of all.

—Perry Weddle

I n the previous chapter, we discussed the *strategy* of persuasion. You learned what persuasion is and strategies you can use to develop a convincing message. In this chapter, we discuss the *structure* of persuasion. Structuring sound arguments and detecting flawed reasoning are important skills for the public speaker.

Developing your own persuasive arguments and responding to others' persuasive appeals exercise all your critical thinking skills. Your research involves *information gathering* as you formulate questions and collect data to answer them. As you develop new lines of inquiry based on your research, you will use your *generating* skills. As you develop your arguments from various sources, you'll be *remembering*, *integrating*, and *organizing*. And throughout the process you'll be *analyzing* and *evaluating* your evidence, discarding weaker sources, and *focusing* your speech more sharply.

We will show you how to construct an argument and how to detect faulty arguments. In addition, you will study characteristics and types of persuasive propositions and special organizational patterns you can use in persuasive speeches.

● Making and Refuting Arguments

argument
The process of reasoning from evidence to prove a claim.

Aristotle's description of the effective persuasive speech sounds simple, doesn't it? An argument is more than an assertion, or claim. **Argument** is the process of reasoning from evidence to *prove* a claim. Before you can prove your case, however, you must understand the structure of arguments and how those arguments are organized in your speech. In the previous chapter, we referred to this type of persuasive appeal as logos. Let's see how all this works.

A speech has two parts. Necessarily, you state your case, and you prove it.

—Aristotle[1]

Steps of an Argument

Suppose you make the following statement: "I am more confident about public speaking now than I was at the beginning of this course." If someone asked you to justify your statement, you could respond in this way:

> I experience fewer symptoms of nervousness. I seem to worry less about facing an audience. The night before my speech, I sleep better than I used to. I establish eye contact with my audience now, rather than avoiding looking directly at them, as I did in my first speech. I no longer nervously shift my weight from foot to foot, and I have started gesturing.

Together, your statement and response constitute an argument. You have made a claim ("I am more confident about public speaking now") and then supported it with evidence—in this case, examples from personal observation. Aristotle would be pleased!

EXPLORING ONLINE

Constructing Arguments
http://owl.english.purdue.edu/owl/resource/659/02/

This section of the Purdue University Online Writing Lab website provides examples to help you understand logic and to practice constructing arguments. It also links to information on various types of logical fallacy.

At its simplest level, an argument includes three steps:

1. You make a claim.
2. You offer evidence.
3. You show how the evidence proves the claim.[2]

A *claim* is the conclusion of your argument. It is a statement you want your listeners to accept. Some examples of claims include:

The influence of race undermines the accuracy of eyewitness testimony.

The most important thing you can learn in college is how to learn.

Visual aids make ideas easier to remember.

The validity of any claim depends on the evidence behind it. **Evidence** is the supporting material you use to prove a point. As an advocate, you have an obligation to support your position with valid arguments. In other words, you must offer your listeners reasons to accept your conclusion.

Speakers may introduce a claim and then present supporting materials, or they may introduce evidence and show how that information leads to an inescapable claim. In her persuasive speech on the need to reform the organ donation system, Ali's first key idea was that an organ shortage existed. Notice how she gently introduced her claim and then presented statistical evidence and cited her sources. She let the evidence build to a more compelling claim—that "the demand for organs far outweighs the supply."

evidence
Supporting material a speaker uses to prove a point.

First, let us examine the extent of the organ shortage in the United States.

Every patient waiting for an organ transplant in the United States is registered with the United Network for Organ Sharing, or UNOS. The UNOS is a nonprofit organization established by Congress in 1984 that seeks to encourage organ donation. *U.S. News & World Report* of January 13, 2003, reports that every morning more than 83,000 people awaiting a new heart, liver, kidney, or other organ wake up to a brutal imbalance of supply and demand.

During the next 24 hours, while it is likely that 66 of them will receive a transplant, 17 will die. And by the way, another 115 new names will be added to the waiting lists. Day by day, the human toll and the organ deficit grow. For example, the *Tulsa World* of August 18, 2003, reports that one of the most common organ transplants is the kidney. Approximately 13,000 kidney transplants are done each year in the United States, but there are almost 50,000 patients waiting for kidneys. There are also approximately 5,000 liver transplants done in the U.S. every year, but the waiting list for these organs is still about 15,000.

Clearly the demand for organs is due to the low number of actual registered donors and a system unable to meet the exponentially growing demand for organ transplants in this country.[3]

Makes a claim.

Offers evidence.

Shows how the evidence proves the claim.

Refuting an Argument

In Chapter 9, we offered the "4 S" strategy for developing your key ideas in a speech. In a persuasive speech, you signpost your claim, state your claim, support your claim with quality evidence, and summarize, showing how your

refute
To dispute; to counter one argument with another.

refutational strategy
A pattern of disputing an argument by (1) stating the position you are refuting, (2) stating your position, (3) supporting your position, and (4) showing how your position undermines the opposing argument.

evidence proves your claim. But how do you refute another's argument? The question is relevant because topics you and your classmates select for your persuasive speeches will involve a spark of controversy. There is always another side, perhaps several sides, in addition to the one the speaker presents. You may even select a topic because you read or heard a statement with which you disagreed. Persuasive speakers and critical thinkers must know both how to prove arguments and how to refute them. For each argument you **refute**, you may want to use the following four-step **refutational strategy**:

1. State the position you are refuting.
2. State your position.
3. Support your position.
4. Show how your position undermines the opposing argument.

Seth selected his topic, the importance of language skills for career advancement, after hearing a comment by his roommate. He presented the following argument in his speech. The comments in the margin show how Seth used each of the four steps of refutation.

States position to be refuted.

Last week, my roommate stormed into the dorm room shaking a paper he just got back from his English composition teacher. He threw the paper on his bed and screamed, "I can't wait until I get out of college, away from teachers who are obsessed with grammar, and into the real world where people judge you on what you say, not how you say it!" Sound familiar? I bet many of us have felt the same way after getting back a paper with all those picky corrections marked in red ink. As my roommate says, "In the real world, you're not judged on your grammar."

States speaker's position.

Well, my roommate's wrong. Grammar is important in the business world just as it is here in the classroom. How we express our ideas *is* important to our success. At least that's the conclusion of Camille Wright Miller, and she ought to know. She's a Ph.D. and a consultant on workplace issues. In her January 13, 2002, *Roanoke Times* column, she told about a candidate who was interviewed for an important position in a company, one that would pay more than $100,000. After the interview, one of the owners said, "How many times did he say 'I seen'"? Those two words cost him the job. And this isn't an isolated example. Dr. Miller says, "Many . . . organizations recognize the power of language and the negative impact of grammatically flawed language on their customers and employees." Employers evaluate grammar "in determining an individual's intelligence, capabilities, and fitness to be a manager."

Supports speaker's position.

Shows how speaker's position undermines opposing argument.

Using incorrect language can keep us from landing a good job or getting promoted once we're hired. So, I'm going to tell my roommate that he probably should listen to what his English composition teacher says. And all of us should read those picky comments written in red on the papers we get back, too. Because there's some truth in the cliché "Good grammar never goes out of style."

The quality of your decisions—indeed, the quality of your life—depends on what you know and how you use that information.

◖ Types of Argument

Speakers can justify their claims by using any of five types of argument. You may offer proof by arguing from example, analogy, cause, deduction, or authority. The type of argument you select will depend on your topic, the available evidence, and your listeners. You may combine several types of argument in a single persuasive speech. Knowing how to construct and test arguments will also help as you listen to the speeches of others.

Argument by Example

Argument by example is an inductive form of proof. **Inductive argument** uses a few instances to assert a broader claim. For example, if you have struggled through calculus and analytic geometry, you may conclude that math is a difficult subject. We hear a few friends complain of electrical problems with a particular make of car and decide not to buy that model. A speaker relates several examples of corruption in city hall, and we conclude that political corruption is widespread. Those are all examples of inductive reasoning.

Kateri argued that a teacher shortage had forced school districts throughout the nation to lower their standards for substitute teachers. She used examples of eight states to suggest a larger trend:

> According to the March 19, 2000, *Denver Rocky Mountain News*, with thousands of openings and no substitutes "school districts are being forced to hire more substitute teachers with less experience and education." In Colorado, a teacher can obtain a one-year emergency substitute license without earning even a bachelor's degree or passing the state's teacher tests. According to the November 7, 2000, *Telegraph Herald*, "Illinois, South Dakota, Kansas, and Nebraska do not . . . require a teaching license." The previously cited *Press Enterprise* states that "in some districts of Maryland, Kentucky, and Idaho, only a high school diploma is required to substitute teach."[4]

How can you test whether an argument by example is sound? Argument by example is valid only if you can answer yes to each of the following four questions:

1. *Are the examples true?* In Chapter 8, we noted that hypothetical or imaginary examples can clarify a point, but they do not prove it. Only when verifiable examples are presented should you proceed to the next question.
2. *Are the examples relevant?* Suppose Susan presents the following evidence in her speech on homelessness: "According to police reports published in yesterday's *News Journal*, city police picked up three individuals who were found sleeping in the park this past weekend. So, you can see that even in our city homelessness is a serious problem." Do these examples really support the claim? Did these individuals not have homes? Had they passed out? Were they there for other reasons? Until you can answer these questions, you cannot assume that they were homeless. The examples must relate to the specific claim.
3. *Are the examples sufficient?* Susan must present enough examples to prove her assertion. In general, the greater the population for which you generalize, the more examples you need. Three examples of homelessness may be statistically significant in a small town, but that number is far below average for many large cities.

argument by example or inductive argument
Says that what is true of a few instances is true generally.

In the space of 176 years the Lower Mississippi has shortened itself 242 miles. That is an average of a trifle over one mile and a third per year. Therefore, any calm person, who is not blind or idiotic, can see that . . . just a million years ago next November, the Lower Mississippi River was upwards of 1,300,000 miles long.

—Mark Twain[5]

SPEAKING WITH CONFIDENCE

I began drafting a persuasive speech on business ethics, targeting my peers as the next generation of business leaders. It quickly became clear, however, that I failed to research my audience. Many of them intended to pursue professions other than business, so I decided to show why it's important for *all* students to take ethics courses. I supported my claims with evidence from expert and unbiased sources. I gave examples of recent business scandals to show some of the problems created by unethical behavior. I shared what I learned in my ethical leadership class and quoted from the textbook. I argued that a better understanding of ethics would give all of us guidelines to use when we faced unexpected and difficult decisions in the future. Near the end of my speech, I provided my audience with specific ethics courses for all the majors in our class, and asked them to look into these classes for fall registration. Knowing that I had supported my claims well, I was confident that I had persuaded my audience to consider taking these ethics courses.

Brian Davis
Virginia Tech University

4. *Are the examples representative?* Was the weekend Susan reported typical? How did it compare with other weekends, weekdays, or seasons? To prove her argument, Susan must present examples that are true, relevant, sufficient, and representative.

Argument by Analogy

argument by analogy
Says that what is true in one case is or will be true in another.

An analogy is a comparison. **Argument by analogy** links two objects or concepts and asserts that what is true of one will be true of the other. Argument by analogy is appropriate when the program you advocate or oppose has been tried elsewhere. Some states have no-fault insurance and the line-item veto; others do not. Some school systems allow corporal punishment, offer magnet programs, and require a passing grade for participation in extracurricular activities; others do not. A speech defending or disputing one of these programs could demonstrate success or failure elsewhere to establish its position.

Jon argued that pharmacists should not have the right to refuse to fill patients' prescriptions, even for moral or religious reasons. Notice how he used argument by analogy to support his position:

Trial lawyers know that cases— and arguments—cannot be won by eloquent language alone. The validity of any claim depends on the quality of the evidence supporting that claim.

The June 4, 2005, *Ledger Times* reminds us that in many ways pharmacists are like bus drivers and airline pilots. It would be outrageous for a pilot who disapproved of gambling to refuse transport to Las Vegas–bound passengers who wanted to visit casinos. Or for a bus driver, disturbed [by] tax dollars [that] went to a lavish new football stadium rather than a decrepit public school, to refuse to let sports fans off at the arena. Professional pharmacists hold a state-conferred monopoly on medications. In that respect, they are public servants. Their role calls for neutrality on the job—whether they prefer to or not.[6]

Do you find Jon's argument persuasive? The key to this pattern of argument is the similarity between the two entities. In testing the validity of your argument by analogy, you need to answer this question: "Are the two entities sufficiently similar to justify my conclusion that what is true of one will be true of the other?" If not, your reasoning is faulty. This question can best be answered by dividing it into two questions.

1. *Are the similarities between the two cases relevant?* For example, suppose you used argument by analogy to advocate eliminating Friday classes during summer school on your campus as State U has done. The facts that both schools have similar library facilities and the same mascot would be irrelevant. Equivalent summer enrollments, numbers of commuting students, and energy needs are highly relevant and can be forceful evidence as you build your case.

2. *Are any of the differences between the two cases relevant?* If so, how do those differences affect your claim? If you discover that your college has far fewer commuting students than State U does, this difference is relevant to your topic and will undermine the validity of your claim.

Argument by Cause

Argument by cause connects two elements or events and claims that one is produced by the other. Causal reasoning takes two forms—reasoning from effect to cause and from cause to effect. The difference between the two is their chronological order. An *effect-to-cause argument* begins at a point of time (when the effects are evident) and moves back in time (to when the cause occurred). When you feel ill and go to the doctor, the doctor will usually identify the symptoms (the effects) of the problem and then diagnose the cause. The doctor is reasoning from effect to cause. In contrast, *cause-to-effect argument* begins at a point of time (when the cause occurred) and moves forward (to when the effects occurred or will occur). Doctors reason from cause to effect when they tell their patients who smoke that this habit may result in emphysema or lung cancer.

In his persuasive speech "The Death of Reading," Nicholas used a book metaphor to organize and phrase his message. He previewed his key ideas: "Chapter 1: The Death of Reading; Chapter 2: The Autopsy; and Chapter 3: The Resurrection." Before presenting his solutions, Nicholas argued from effect to cause to explain why children today read less:

> **argument by cause**
> Says that one action or condition caused or will cause another.

> [Effect]

Reading leisurely, whether newspapers, magazines, or books, has decreased over 50 percent in today's families since 1975. The American Psychological Association on December 17, 2003, argued that reading is essential to childhood imaginative growth. Modern entertainment such as television and movies leaves little room for creative interpretations. "A lack of reading invites Big Brother, preventing our children from being able to create the world themselves. When reading, the children are in control of the reality, not the films."

> [Cause]

Now that we have looked at the symptoms, we must next crack open the spine of today's books and run an autopsy to discuss the inherent causes of the death of reading. To children the answer is simple: reading isn't fun anymore. The December 28, 2003, *St. Petersburg Times* tells us that many children believe that the only motivation that they have to read is to pass tests. In 2002 alone, over 85,000 third graders were not allowed into the fourth grade due to an inability to pass their FCAT reading scores, and over 43,000 were forced into summer reading to pass. This form of education is known as "extrinsic motivation." This means that America's schools rely on external rewards, such as grades and test scores. Extrinsic motivation does not teach our children to think independently and critically about situations. Reading, it seems, has fallen prey to this school of thought, because children are taught to read to get good test scores, not because reading is entertaining and intellectual.[7]

Rachel used a cause-to-effect argument in her speech on the lack of safety in nursing homes:

[Cause]   In 1965 the Fire Marshals Association of North America begged Congress to require sprinklers in all nursing homes. Forty years and 12 failed proposals later, Congress has yet to act. On December 16, 2005, *USA Today* reveals that there are 16,000 nursing homes that violate fire safety standards annually. Twenty-three thousand fires are reported every year. Four states—Massachusetts, Minnesota, Montana, and Hawaii—set no fire safety standards, only six states require fire sprinklers, and less than half require smoke alarms that alert authorities.

[Effect]   These statistics lead up to an average of at least one fatal fire every month, much like the one that occurred just before the holidays as reported by the Associated Press on December 13, 2005, where two were killed in a Michigan fire and dozens more injured. Fires in nursing homes are all too common, and with more than 1.6 million residents in need of assisted-living arrangements, the danger is real.[8]

When you argue by cause, test the soundness of your reasoning by asking and answering the following three questions:

1. *Does a causal relationship exist?* For an argument from cause to effect or effect to cause to be valid, a causal relationship must exist between the two elements. Just because one event precedes another does not mean that the first caused the second. One of our students argued that the scholastic decline of American education began with and was caused by the Supreme Court's decision outlawing mandatory school prayer. We doubt the connection.

2. *Could the presumed cause produce the effect?* During a period of rising inflation, one of our students gave a speech arguing that various price hikes had contributed to the inflation rate. She provided three examples: the cost of postage stamps had increased 87.5 percent, chewing gum 100 percent, and downtown parking meter fees 150 percent. While she was able to document the dramatic percentage increase in the prices of these products, her examples had more interest than impact. They did not convince her audience that these increases by themselves could significantly influence the inflation rate.

3. *Could the effect result from other causes?* A number of causes can converge to produce one effect. A student who argues that next year's increased tuition and fees are a result of the college president's fiscal mismanagement may have a point. But other factors may have made the tuition increase necessary: state revenue shortfalls, decreased

enrollment, cutbacks in federal aid, and so on. Speakers strengthen their arguments when they prove that the alleged cause contributed substantively to producing the effect and that without the cause, the effect would not have occurred or the problem would have been much less severe.

Argument by Deduction

Ben began his speech on time management with the following statement:

> All of us are taking courses that require us to be in class and to study outside class. In addition, many of us are members of social, academic, religious, or career-oriented clubs and organizations. Some of us work. All of us like to party! Crowded into our school and work schedules are our responsibilities to friends and family members. In short, we're busy!
>
> College is a hectic time in our lives. Sometimes it seems that we're trying to cram 34 hours of activity into a 24-hour day. In order to survive this schedule and beat the stress, college students need to develop effective time-management skills. You are no exception! If you listen to my speech today, you will learn how to set realistic goals, meet them, and still have time to socialize with friends and get a good night's sleep. Sound impossible? Just listen closely for the next 8 minutes.

Ben used two types of argument in his introduction. He opened by arguing from example, providing several instances to make his case that college life is busy. He then used deductive reasoning to make the speech relevant to each member of the audience. A **deductive argument** moves from a general category to a specific instance. In this sense, deductive arguments are the reverse of argument by example. To see why that's true, consider the structure of a deductive argument.

Deductive arguments consist of a pattern of three statements: a major premise, a minor premise, and a conclusion. This pattern of deductive argument is called a **syllogism**. The **major premise** is a claim about a general group of people, events, or conditions. Ben's major premise was this: "College students need to develop effective time-management skills." The **minor premise** places a person, event, or condition into a general class. Ben's minor premise could be phrased like this: "You are a college student." The **conclusion** argues that what is true of the general class is true of the specific instance or individual. Ben concluded that each college student in his audience needed to develop effective time-management skills.

Use the following steps to check the structure of your deductive argument:

1. State your major premise.
2. Say "because," and then state your minor premise.
3. Say "therefore," and then state your conclusion.

The resulting two sentences should flow together easily and make sense. Ben could have tested the clarity of his argument by saying the following:

He who will not reason is a bigot; he who cannot is a fool; and he who dares not is a slave.

—William Drummond

deductive argument
Says that what is true generally is or will be true in a specific instance.

syllogism
The pattern of a deductive argument, consisting of a major premise, a minor premise, and a conclusion.

major premise
A claim about a general group of people, events, or conditions.

minor premise
A statement placing a person, an event, or a condition into a general class.

conclusion
The deductive argument that what is true of the general class is true of the specific instance.

Participants in a political debate are judged on the quality of their arguments as well as their manner of presentation.

"College students need to develop effective time-management skills. *Because* you are a college student, *therefore* you need to develop effective time-management skills." Notice that if the two premises are true and relate to each other, the conclusion must also be true.

For deductive arguments to be valid, they must meet certain tests. Whether you are listening to others' arguments or evaluating arguments in your own speech, keep in mind three questions.

1. *Are the premises related?* "All men are created equal. Equal is an artificial sweetener. Therefore, all men are artificial sweeteners." This statement doesn't make much sense, does it? The first sentence uses the word *equal* to mean "equivalent." The second uses *Equal* as a product name for a sugar substitute. For an argument to be valid, the premises must relate to each other. In this case, they clearly do not.

Let's construct another example. Suppose John prepares a speech trying to persuade his classmates to apply for a new academic scholarship named after his father, James Burke. In his speech, John makes the following statement:

> Any student enrolled in State U who is a U.S. citizen can apply for the Burke Scholarship. That includes everyone in this class. Just think, next year you could have your entire tuition and fees paid, and you can spend your money for something you've been wanting but were unable to afford. Maybe even that new laptop computer.

Before John convinces his classmates to apply for the scholarship, he first tells them that they are eligible. His argument may be depicted as follows:

Major premise: Any State U student who is a U.S. citizen can apply for the Burke Scholarship.

Minor premise: Every student in this class is a State U student who is a citizen of the United States.

Conclusion: Therefore, every student in this class can apply for the Burke Scholarship.

The terms in the minor premise fall within the scope of the major premise. The two premises are related, and the conclusion seems logical.

2. *Is the major premise true?* Before John's classmates begin filling out a scholarship application form, they should ask the question, "Is the major premise of the argument true?" Suppose two prerequisites for application are full-time student status and good academic standing. The statement "any State U student who is a U.S. citizen can apply for the Burke Scholarship" is then false. Part-time and probationary

EXPLORING ONLINE

The Toulmin Model of Argument

www.unl.edu/speech/comm109/Toulmin

The Toulmin Project Home Page, created by Charles Soukup and Scott Titsworth of the University of Nebraska at Lincoln, offers a substantial introduction to Stephen Toulmin's popular model of argumentation. Designed specifically for students enrolled in communication classes, this website provides a thorough explanation of the model with examples and practice test questions.

students cannot apply. The conclusion of the argument ("every student in this class can apply for the Burke Scholarship") would therefore not necessarily be true. You must be able to prove your major premise before you draw a conclusion.

3. *Is the minor premise true?* A false minor premise is just as damaging to an argument as a false major premise. Let's suppose that John's major premise is true and that any State U student who is a U.S. citizen can apply for the Burke Scholarship. What if his class includes some foreign students? His minor premise ("every student in this class is a State U student who is a citizen of the United States") is then false. Those students are not eligible for the scholarship, and John's conclusion is false. Arguing a position entails ethical considerations. You must know your facts and reason logically from them.

Argument by Authority

Argument by authority differs from the four other forms of argument we have discussed. To see how it is different, consider the following example from Lynn's speech:

> I believe that every student should be allowed to vote for Outstanding Professor on Campus rather than having the award determined by a select committee of the faculty. And I'm not alone in my opinion. Last year's recipient of the award, Dr. Linda Carter, agrees. The President of the Faculty Senate spoke out in favor of this proposal at last week's forum, and the Student Government Association passed a resolution supporting it.

Argument by authority uses testimony from an expert source to prove a speaker's claim; its validity depends on the credibility the authority has for the audience. In this example, Lynn did not offer arguments based on example, analogy, cause, or deduction to explain the validity of her position. Instead, she asserted that two distinguished professors and the SGA agreed with her. She asked her audience to believe her position based on the credentials of the authority figures who endorsed her claim. Her rationale was that her sources had access to sufficient information and had the expertise to interpret it accurately; thus, we should trust their conclusions.

An argument based on authority is only as valid as the source's credibility. To test your argument, ask and answer two questions:

1. Is the source an expert?
2. Is the source unbiased?

Our discussion of these questions and other tests of evidence in Chapter 8 will help you select the best authority for your claim.

Testing the arguments you use and hear others use is crucial to effective, ethical speaking and listening. The "Theory Into Practice" feature summarizes these tests. When you analyze the arguments you use, you strengthen them and can save yourself the embarrassment of being caught

argument by authority
Uses testimony from an expert source to prove a speaker's claim.

THEORY INTO PRACTICE

TIP   Testing Your Arguments

Mario Cuomo, noted speaker and former governor of New York, encouraged leaders to persuade others "not so much with speeches that sound good, as with speeches that are good and sound."[9] As you select and develop the arguments for your speeches, ask and answer these questions that we discussed in this chapter. Remember to use these same guidelines when you listen to the speeches of others.

Argument by Example

- Are the examples true?
- Are the examples relevant?
- Are the examples sufficient?
- Are the examples representative?

Argument by Analogy

- Are the similarities between the two cases relevant?

- Are the differences between the two cases relevant?

Argument by Cause

- Does a causal relationship exist?
- Could the presumed cause produce the effect?
- Could the effect result from other causes?

Argument by Deduction

- Are the premises related?
- Is the major premise true?
- Is the minor premise true?

Argument by Authority

- Is the source an expert?
- Is the source unbiased?

---

fallacy
A flaw in the logic of an argument.

KEY POINTS

Fallacies of Argument

1. Hasty generalization
2. False analogy
3. Post hoc ergo propter hoc
4. Slippery slope
5. Red herring
6. Appeal to tradition
7. False dilemma
8. False authority
9. Bandwagon
10. Ad hominem

using illogical or invalid proof. However, it is just as important to check the validity of persuasive arguments you hear. By doing this, you avoid being duped into misguided thoughts and actions.

In spite of these tests, persuasive speakers sometimes incorporate certain errors of proof into their speeches. These errors are so widely used that they have been named and studied. In the following section, we examine some of these arguments that appear—but only appear—to say something authoritative. If you can identify these errors, you can avoid them.

◑ Fallacies of Argument

A **fallacy** is "any defect in reasoning which destroys its validity."[10] Fallacies can be dangerous and persuasive for the same reason: because they resemble valid reasoning, we often accept them as legitimate. They can produce bad decisions leading to harmful consequences.

Fallacies are flawed patterns of reasoning. Speakers who value civility respect the credibility of their ideas and the welfare of their listeners. As you construct your persuasive speech, make sure that the arguments you encounter in your research are valid. Then, use your research to develop sound arguments to support the ideas in your speech. As a listener, you have an ethical responsibility to evaluate critically the ideas other speakers present to you. Be alert for those arguments based on sound versus flawed reasoning. Consider the valid arguments and reject fallacious ones.

How can you tell the difference? We will discuss ten of the most common fallacies. As you read them, notice how many resemble the patterns of argument we have just discussed.

Hasty Generalization

People who jump to conclusions commit the fallacy of **hasty generalization,** a faulty form of argument by example. What distinguishes valid from fallacious inductive proof is the quantity and quality of examples. When speakers make claims based on insufficient or unrepresentative instances, their reasoning is usually flawed. For example, a speaker uses examples of three students convicted of plagiarism and concludes that cheating is widespread on campus. An advertisement shows a dentist recommending a particular brand of toothbrush, and the consumer assumes that it carries the endorsement of dentists in general. People who rely too much on first impressions, who do not read widely, or who spend little time researching are prime candidates for reasoning from hasty generalization. They often develop beliefs and opinions that later prove erroneous.

False Analogy

Speakers argue by analogy when they link two items and assert that what is true of one will be true of the other. If the two items are sufficiently similar, the speaker's claim may be valid. However, if the items differ in critical ways, the persuader may be guilty of using a **false analogy,** and the claim may be fallacious. You've probably heard someone respond to an argument by saying, "That's like comparing apples and oranges." That person just detected a faulty comparison. Read some of the arguments we've heard in students' speeches and see if you can detect some faulty reasoning:

> We license drivers; why shouldn't we license parents? You can't take to the road until you learn how to drive and pass a test. Aren't children more important than cars?
>
> Part of being an adult includes the right to make choices and accept the consequences of your actions. If it's legal to purchase tobacco, shouldn't it also be legal to buy marijuana?
>
> We prohibit cigarette advertising on television; why shouldn't we prohibit ads for beer?

What do you think of these arguments? Which comparisons are valid arguments by analogy? Which are fallacies? Your answers may differ from your friends and classmates; detecting fallacies is not always easy. You need to exercise your critical thinking skills as you read, listen to, and develop arguments by analogy.

hasty generalization
A fallacy that makes claims from insufficient or unrepresentative examples.

EXPLORING ONLINE

Fallacies of Reasoning
www.onegoodmove.org/fallacy/

For an explanation of the ten fallacies we discuss and for many more, visit Stephen's Guide to Logical Fallacies by Stephen Downes. Click on "Index" and begin your tour of definitions, examples, and explanations of more than 50 fallacies.

false analogy
A fallacy that occurs when an argument by analogy compares entities that have critical differences.

Post Hoc Ergo Propter Hoc

post hoc
A chronological fallacy that says that a prior event caused a subsequent event.

This fallacy uses the Latin title and literally means "after this, therefore because of this." A chronological fallacy, **post hoc** (as it is usually called) assumes that because one event preceded another, the first caused the second; it is an improper application of the argument by cause. Perhaps you have heard a friend comment, "I knew it would rain; I just washed my car!" Your friend is probably making a joke based on the post hoc fallacy. People exhibit post hoc reasoning when they expect something good to happen if they carry a lucky charm while gambling, wear a lucky shirt to a football game, or cross their fingers as a teacher returns an exam.

These defects in reasoning may seem obvious. Yet other examples of confusing coincidence with causation are more subtle and potentially more damaging. For instance, a person rejects medical treatment, relying instead on an unresearched cure because someone else tried it and subsequently got well. An incumbent mayor takes credit for every city improvement that occurred since she took office; her opponent blames her for everything bad that happened during this time. An event may have more than one cause. It is also preceded by occurrences having no effect on it whatsoever. As a result, determining the relationship between two events or conditions is often difficult. But you must examine that relationship if you are to avoid the post hoc fallacy.

EXPLORING ONLINE

Propaganda

www.propagandacritic.com

Why should we think about propaganda? You can find a discussion of that question on this excellent website constructed by Dr. Aaron Delwiche. Drawing from the work of the Institute for Propaganda Analysis, this communication professor discusses eight common techniques of propagandistic messages and offers numerous examples of faulty logic.

Slippery Slope

slippery slope
A fallacy of causation that says that one action inevitably sets a chain of events in motion.

Envision yourself at the top of a hill on a wintry day. You take one step, slip on a patch of ice, lose your footing, and begin sliding down the hill. You try to regain your balance, but you continue your slide, stopping only when you reach the bottom of the hill. This visual image depicts the slippery slope fallacy. **Slippery slope** asserts that one action inevitably sets in motion a chain of events or indicates a trend; it is an example of the faulty use of argument by cause. This defect in reasoning is exemplified in the following two arguments:

> If you amend the Constitution to prohibit flag burning, you open the door to other amendments to our Bill of Rights. Ultimately, you destroy the freedoms upon which our nation is based.

> If we begin to control the sale of guns by restricting the purchase of handguns, where will it end? Will shotguns be next? And then hunting rifles? Soon the right to bear arms will disappear from the Constitution, and sportsmen and sportswomen will be denied one of their basic freedoms.

These speakers' arguments imply that a single act will set in motion a series of events that no one will be able to stop, but that is not necessarily the case. Just because legislators support one constitutional amendment or one law doesn't always mean that they must support subsequent reforms. Usually, a slide down the slope is preventable. Each journey involves a series of decisions, and it is possible to retain or regain your footing.

Red Herring

The name of the **red herring** fallacy apparently originated with the English fox hunt. When the hunt was over, the hunt master would drag a red herring—a type of fish that is smoked and salted—across the path of the hounds. The pungent scent would divert the dogs from their pursuit of the fox, and they could then be rounded up. If you love to read murder mysteries, you may have trained yourself to be on guard for some incidental twist in the plot that seems to be there just to throw less attentive readers off track. Such devices have come to be called *red herrings*.

A red herring fallacy is another example of a faulty argument by deduction. An arguer makes a claim based on an irrelevant premise. How does the red herring fallacy work in a speech? Bruce Waller provides a vivid example and analysis of this defect in reasoning using the issue of gun control:

> If the debate is over whether handguns should be banned, it is relevant to consider how many people have been killed in handgun accidents. But suppose someone asserts, "Everybody talks about handgun accidents! But think of how many people are killed each year in auto accidents! Why don't we ban automobiles?" You must hold your breath and cover your nose and stay on the trail, for a red herring has just been dragged across the argument. The danger of auto accidents is certainly serious, and perhaps on another occasion we should discuss how to reduce that danger—but that has nothing to do with the question of banning handguns. Whether there are other unacceptable dangers in society is not the issue; the question is instead whether handguns pose an unacceptable risk. Perhaps they do, perhaps they do not, but no progress will be made on that issue if the arguers are distracted by irrelevant reasons.[11]

In essence, a speaker guilty of the red herring fallacy introduces an irrelevant issue to deflect attention from the subject under discussion. Both of the following speakers attempted to divert discussion from germane issues to irrelevant concerns:

> A politician answers charges that she accepted illegal campaign contributions by noting her service on the state's ethics advisory board.

> A student responds to a charge of plagiarism with the statement, "I was a Boy Scout throughout high school."

When you present a persuasive speech, you are an advocate for the position you present. As such, you have an ethical responsibility to defend your arguments. Answer criticisms of your argument with evidence and logic; don't deflect criticism by diverting your audience to another track.

Appeal to Tradition

This fallacy is grounded in a respect for traditional ways of doing things. On the surface, respect for tradition seems reasonable. But the fallacy commonly called **appeal to tradition** defends the status quo and opposes

red herring
A fallacy that introduces irrelevant issues to deflect attention from the subject under discussion.

appeal to tradition
A fallacy that opposes change by arguing that old ways are always superior to new ways.

change by arguing that old ways are superior to new ways; it is an improper use of an argument by authority. A speaker who argues against admitting men to her college because of the school's history as a women's school commits this fallacy unless she offers additional support for the claim. Its most common form of expression—"We've always done it that way"—is merely descriptive. It discourages discussion and reevaluation of our traditions.

As important as many traditions are to us, they should not be used to thwart needed change. The Constitution of the United States gave people many of the freedoms they enjoy. Yet it also precluded non-European Americans and women from full participation in society. The fight to secure the right to vote for all citizens challenged that tradition. Old ways are not always the best ways.

False Dilemma

When forced to choose between two alternatives, you face a dilemma. Dilemmas can be actual or false. In an actual dilemma, the alternatives you face are real; there is no room for compromise. Suppose you are asked to choose between going to a movie with friends and attending a review session for an upcoming test. If the review and theater hours coincide, your dilemma is real and you must forfeit either entertainment or study.

A **false dilemma** presents only two options when, in reality, there are more. For example, if there is a late showing of the movie, perhaps you can convince your friends to meet you at the theater after you attend the review. In this instance, the dilemma is false because you do not have to choose between studying and seeing the movie; you can do both. Woody Allen's quotation is an example of a false dilemma. Certainly, humans face alternatives other than utter hopelessness and total extinction.

The fallacy of false dilemma is sometimes called the *either–or fallacy*. The dilemma usually polarizes issues into two mutually exclusive categories, such as "Stand with America or stand for terrorism" and "When guns are outlawed, only outlaws will have guns!" Neither slogan allows for middle-ground positions.

Listeners should be especially attentive to all "either–or" and "if–then" statements they hear. These grammatical constructions lend themselves to the fallacy of false dilemma, as in the following examples:

> A person is either a Republican or a Democrat. Because I know Carolyn isn't a Republican, she must be a Democrat.

> The issue is very simple: Either you support the Constitution on which this nation was founded, or you're not a patriotic American.

> I don't support a cutback in defense spending. I don't want to see a weakening of America's strength.

Each of these examples presents the listener with only two choices. However, they disregard other legitimate options. Carolyn may be a Libertarian, a Socialist, an Independent, or a member of the Green Party or some other political party. We can exhibit patriotism and still question a nation's laws

---

More than at any time in history, mankind faces a crossroads. One path leads to despair and utter hopelessness, the other to total extinction. Let us pray we have the wisdom to choose correctly.

—Woody Allen

false dilemma
A fallacy that confronts listeners with two choices when, in reality, more options exist.

and policies. Eliminating unnecessary defense spending does not necessarily weaken the country. Using that money for other important projects—like major road and bridge repair—may make America stronger.

False Authority

The fallacy of **false authority** is an invalid form of argument by authority. This fallacy occurs when advocates support their ideas with the testimony of people who have apparent but not real expertise. Before deciding to accept someone's opinion or testimony, ask the question, "Is the person an objective expert on this topic?" Celebrity endorsements of commercial products frequently illustrate this fallacy. The famous sports personality who urges you to buy that 260-horsepower sedan with an all-aluminum, high-output, 3.5-liter, 24-valve, V6 engine may know only what she's reading from a script. Advertisers often use celebrities more for their popularity than their credibility.

It is important to exercise your critical thinking skills to avoid using the fallacy of false authority. If you cite information from a website without checking its authority and accuracy or if you quote from authors without knowing their credentials, you have used the fallacy of false authority, most likely unintentionally. The statement "I couldn't find any information about the author" is a recipe for irresponsibility. You can avoid the fallacy of false authority by using only information you know to be expert and credible.

false authority
A fallacy that uses testimony from sources who have no expertise on the topic in question.

Bandwagon

In the 1800s and early 1900s, political candidates held parades to meet the people. A band rode on a wagon leading the parade through town. As the wagon passed, local leaders would jump on the bandwagon to show their support. The number of people on board was considered a barometer of the candidate's popularity and political strength.

The **bandwagon** fallacy is also a faulty argument by authority. It assumes that popular opinion is an accurate measure of truth and wisdom. Frequently referred to as the "everybody's doing it" fallacy, bandwagon arguments commonly use phrases such as "everyone knows" or "most people agree." Door-to-door salespeople or intrusive phone solicitors who tell you that all your friends and neighbors are purchasing their products use the bandwagon appeal. They base their sales pitch on the product's popularity, not on its merits.

Speakers who defend the rightness of their positions by pointing to polls showing popular support similarly exploit the bandwagon fallacy. While agreement regarding a belief or action may be reassuring, it is no guarantee of accuracy or truth. "Truth is not always democratic."[12] History is cluttered with popularly held misconceptions. Remember, most people once believed that the world was flat and that the sun revolved around Earth. You should decide the validity of an argument by its form and substance, not merely by how many people agree on it.

bandwagon
A fallacy that determines truth, goodness, or wisdom by popular opinion.

Ad Hominem

ad hominem
A fallacy that urges listeners to reject an idea because of the allegedly poor character of the person voicing it; name-calling.

Ad hominem, literally meaning "to the man," arguments ask listeners to reject an idea because of the allegedly poor character of the person voicing it. Political speeches, especially those delivered at national conventions, are peppered with ad hominem arguments. These statements often evoke applause, cheers, and laughter, but they provide little insight into issues. When Rush Limbaugh refers to feminists as "feminazis," he is making an ad hominem attack rather than engaging in reasoned discourse. A club member commits this fallacy when he argues that Bryan's proposal for an alcohol-free party should not be taken seriously because Bryan has two DUI (driving under the influence) convictions.

In its most obvious form, this fallacy is name-calling. For some people, simply knowing that a speaker is liberal, conservative, feminist, or fundamentalist is sufficient to close their minds. They disregard the merits of an idea because of the person giving the message. An ethical listener has a responsibility to give all ideas a fair hearing.

> If you can't answer a man's argument, all is not lost; you can still call him vile names.
>
> —Elbert Hubbard

To speak ethically and with civility, you must know how to construct valid arguments and avoid defective ones such as those we have just discussed. Once you have mastered this ability, you can use your arguments to achieve the overall goal of your speech. In the remainder of this chapter, we will show you how to develop a persuasive proposition and how to organize your arguments effectively.

◗ Selecting Propositions for Persuasive Speeches

In Chapter 6, we explained that your first steps in constructing a speech are to select your topic, focus or narrow it, determine your general purpose, formulate your specific purpose, and construct a thesis statement. In persuasive speaking, you can add one additional step: state your proposition.

proposition
A declarative sentence expressing a judgment a speaker wants listeners to accept.

A **proposition** is a declarative sentence expressing a judgment you want the audience to accept. If you speak on the topic of improving education, you may narrow this broad subject and select as your specific purpose to persuade the audience that teacher salaries should be increased. Your basic position—"teacher salaries should be increased"—can be thought of as a proposition. Notice that this proposition *expresses a judgment* that *is debatable* and that *requires proof*. We will discuss these three characteristics of propositions in the next section.

Your thesis statement, in contrast, lists the reasons you offer to prove your proposition. In the preceding example, your thesis statement could be: higher teacher salaries would recruit better teachers, retain better teachers, and improve student learning. The following example illustrates the similarities and differences among the proposition, specific purpose, thesis statement, and key ideas of speech.

Proposition: The new campus classroom building should be named Richter Hall.

Specific Purpose: To persuade the audience that the new classroom building should be named for Louise Richter

Thesis Statement: The new classroom building should be named for Louise Richter, an outstanding teacher, advisor, and friend.

Key Ideas: I. The name of the new classroom building should honor an outstanding educator.

       II. Louise Richter deserves this recognition.

         A. She was an outstanding teacher.

         B. She was an outstanding advisor to student organizations.

         C. She was a cherished friend.

Notice that this proposition expresses a judgment, while the thesis statement includes the reasons the speaker will offer to prove the proposition.

Characteristics of Propositions

If you formulate a well-worded proposition early in preparing your persuasive speech, you will be sure of your persuasive goal and can keep it firmly in mind. Your proposition also helps you to focus your persuasive speech and test the relevance of supporting ideas as you develop them. Devising your proposition can be relatively easy. Propositions are marked by three characteristics.

Propositions Express a Judgment. A proposition for a persuasive speech states the position you will defend. Consequently, it should be worded as a declarative sentence expressing your position. If you advocate statehood for Puerto Rico, your proposition could be worded like this: "The United States should grant Puerto Rico statehood." This simple declarative sentence clearly states your position on the issue.

Sometimes, however, you may be interested in a topic but lack enough information to have developed a position on it. In this case, you may first want to phrase a question to guide your research. Once you answer the question, you can then develop your proposition.

Mark was a criminal justice student interested in the issue of the death penalty. He had read an article discussing the pros and cons of capital punishment for juveniles convicted of capital crimes, but he had not developed his own position on the issue. To guide his research, Mark worded the following question: Is the death penalty for juveniles cruel and unusual punishment? He researched the topic, reading articles by scholars and jurists on both sides of the issue. He made a list of arguments for and against capital punishment for juveniles. Although Mark supported capital punishment for adult offenders, his research convinced him to oppose it for juveniles. The proposition he subsequently decided to defend was "The death penalty for juveniles is cruel and unusual punishment." By phrasing his position statement, writing it out, and keeping it in front of him as he continued researching and assembling his arguments, Mark was able to keep his speech focused on arguments against capital punishment for juveniles.

KEY POINTS

Requirements of Propositions

1. Propositions express a judgment.
2. Propositions are debatable.
3. Propositions require proof.

The power of persuasion can mobilize students to debate issues, combining logic with passion.

Propositions Are Debatable. Propositions are appropriate for persuasive speeches only if they are debatable. In other words, the judgment must include some degree of controversy. The proposition "Earth revolves around the sun" is not a good proposition for a persuasive speech because you are unlikely to find any qualified authority today opposing that statement. We now accept it as fact. Once we accept a proposition as fact, it ceases to be an appropriate topic for persuasive speeches.

Propositions Require Proof. A proposition is an assertion, and assertions are statements that have not yet been proved. Your objective as a persuasive speaker is to offer compelling reasons for listeners to accept your proposition. As we discussed earlier in this chapter, you may support your proposition with arguments from example, analogy, cause, deduction, or authority.

Types of Propositions

Propositions for persuasive speeches are of three types: fact, value, and policy. The type of organization and support materials you will use depends on the type of proposition you defend.

Propositions of Fact. A **proposition of fact** focuses on belief. You ask the audience to affirm the truth or falsity of a statement. The following are examples of propositions of fact:

proposition of fact
An assertion about the truth or falsity of a statement.

> Access to math tutors increases students' grades in mathematics courses.
>
> An aspirin a day can reduce the risk of heart disease.
>
> Antimatter-powered space travel is technologically feasible.

In her speech on random drug testing, Jennifer defended this proposition: "Random drug testing on the job decreases workplace drug use." Her specific purpose and key ideas were as follows:

Specific Purpose: To convince the audience that random drug testing decreases workplace drug use

Key Ideas: I. Random drug testing deters casual drug use.
              II. Random drug testing helps decrease drug addiction.
                  A. It identifies users.
                  B. It encourages users to seek therapy.

proposition of value
An assertion about the relative worth of an idea or action.

Propositions of Value. A **proposition of value** requires a judgment on the worth of an idea or action. You ask the audience to determine the "goodness" or "badness" of something, as in this proposition: "Corporal punishment in schools is wrong." Propositions of value can also ask you to compare two items and determine which is better, as in Sir William Blackstone's statement, "It is better that ten guilty persons escape than one innocent suffer." Other propositions of value include the following:

Deterrence is a more important goal of criminal justice than rehabilitation.

Censorship is a greater evil than pornography.

Educational tracking of students by ability perpetuates social and racial inequality.

Suppose you decided to persuade your audience that free agency is bad for professional sports. You could develop your speech on this value proposition as follows:

Specific Purpose: To persuade the audience that free agency is hurting professional sports

Key Ideas: I. It destroys the competitive balance of teams.
               II. It undermines the financial solvency of teams.
               III. It creates bad role models for kids.

Propositions of Policy. A **proposition of policy** advocates a course of action. You ask the audience to endorse a policy or to commit themselves to some action. These statements usually include the word *should*. Here are some examples of policy propositions:

proposition of policy
A statement requesting support for a course of action.

Cell phones should be banned in college classrooms.

Nonviolent offenders should be excluded from "three strikes and you're out" sentencing.

Students should be able to repay student loans through community service.

Duane wanted to persuade his audience to support the student government association's proposal to change from a quarter to a semester academic calendar. Organizing his speech topically, he presented three benefits to a semester system.

Specific Purpose: To persuade the audience that this college should adopt a semester calendar

Key Ideas: I.   Semesters allow more time for research in theory courses.
               II. Semesters allow more time for skill development in performance courses.
               III. Semester credits are easier to transfer to other institutions.

Monroe's Motivated Sequence

In Chapters 9 and 10, we discussed how to organize the introduction, body, and conclusion of a speech. Those guidelines apply to the organization of persuasive and informative speeches. One type of persuasive speech, the speech to actuate, provides an interesting challenge to speakers. In the 1930s, Alan Monroe developed one of the most popular patterns for organizing the superstructure of a speech to actuate.[13] Called "the motivated sequence," this pattern is particularly appropriate when you discuss a well-known or easily established problem. Monroe drew from

Monroe's motivated sequence

A persuasive pattern composed of (1) getting the audience's attention, (2) establishing a need, (3) offering a proposal to satisfy the need, (4) inviting listeners to visualize the results, and (5) requesting action.

the conclusions of educator and philosopher John Dewey that persuasion is best accomplished if a speaker moves a listener sequentially through a series of steps.[14] **Monroe's motivated sequence** includes five steps, or stages: attention, need, satisfaction, visualization, and action.

Attention. Monroe argued that speakers must first command the *attention* of their listeners. Suppose your geographic area is experiencing a summer drought. You could begin your speech with a description of the landscape as you approached your campus a year ago, describing in detail the green grass, the verdant foliage, and the colorful, fragrant flowers. You then contrast the landscape of a year ago with its look now: bland, brown, and blossomless. With these contrasting visual images, you try to capture your audience's attention and interest.

Need. A speaker's second objective is to establish a *need*. This step is similar to the problem and need steps in the problem–solution and the need–plan patterns of organizing a speech. For example, your speech on the drought situation could illustrate how an inadequate water supply hurts not only the beauty of the landscape but also agricultural production, certain industrial processes, and, ultimately, the economy of the entire region.

Satisfaction. When you dramatize a problem, you create an urgency to redress it. In the *satisfaction* step of the motivated sequence, you propose a way to solve or at least minimize the problem. You may suggest voluntary or mandatory conservation as a short-term solution to the water shortage crisis. As a longer-range solution, you might ask your audience to consider the merits of planting grasses, shrubs, and other plants that require less water. You could advocate that the city adopt and enforce stricter regulations of water use by businesses or that it develop alternative water sources.

Visualization. Monroe argued that simply proposing a solution is seldom sufficient to bring about change. Through *visualization*, Monroe's fourth step, a speaker seeks to intensify an audience's desire to adopt and implement the proposed solution. You could direct the audience to look out the window at their campus and then ask if that is the scenery they want. More often, though, you create word pictures for the audience to visualize. Without adequate water, you could argue, crops will die, family farms will fail, industries will not relocate to the area, and the quality of life for everyone in the area will be depressed. In contrast, you could refer to the landscape of a year ago, the image you depicted as you began your speech. The future can be colored in green, red, yellow, and blue, representing growth and vitality.

Action. The final step of the motivated sequence is the *action* you request of your listeners. It is not enough to know that something must be done; the audience must know what you want them to do, and your request must be within their power to act. Do you want them to join you in voluntary conservation by watering their lawns in the evening when less water will evaporate or by washing their cars less frequently? Are you asking them to sign petitions pressuring the city council to adopt mandatory conservation measures when the water table sinks to a designated level? Conclude your speech with a strong appeal for specific, reasonable action.

Dolly decided that her final speech would be a speech to actuate; she wanted her classmates to decide to study a foreign language. She researched articles she found in the library and on the Internet. She interviewed a professor in the foreign languages department and borrowed some brochures published by the Modern Language Association. After taking extensive notes, she opened a new computer file and typed five phrases: Attention Step, Need Step, Satisfaction Step, Visualization Step, and Action Step. She then began to draft the framework for her speech. Using the motivated sequence helped Dolly move her listeners step by step to her final request for action:

Attention Step

In January 1997 Diane Crispell, executive editor of *American Demographics*, observed that "America is a linguistic paradox. Even as it boasts a richly diverse population speaking a host of languages, it encourages immigrants to forsake their mother tongues and doesn't encourage native English speakers to acquire foreign-language skills." Those who reject opportunities to connect with other cultures do so at their personal and professional peril. Studying a foreign language can give you a competitive edge. Learning a foreign language develops your communication skills, your analytical skills, and your employment opportunities.

Need Step

College students need a variety of competencies for personal, academic, and career success.
A. Communication skills are essential in each of these areas.
B. Problem-solving skills are necessary to function successfully in life.
C. An understanding of other cultures is increasingly important in a global society.

Satisfaction Step

Studying a foreign language can give you a competitive edge.
A. It improves your communication skills.
B. It develops your analytical skills.
C. It provides employment advantages.

Visualization Step

Wouldn't it be nice to take a friend to a romantic French movie and be able to understand the dialogue without having to read the translation? Or, when visiting another country, to be able to pick up a newspaper and to read the headlines? Or, when you land that dream job, to be able to negotiate an important business deal with that client from another country, in part because you spoke her language and understood the customs of her culture?

Action Step

Before the semester is over, I want you to take that step that will give you a competitive edge in your personal, academic, and professional life.
A. Enroll in a foreign language class while you are in college.
B. Visit the International Programs Office, and sign up for a study abroad program.
C. Buy some foreign language self-study learning tapes or CDs.
D. Begin learning a foreign language from a friend from another culture.

◖ Annotated Sample Speech

James Chang delivered the following persuasive speech and placed first at the 2003 Interstate Oratorical Association National Speech Contest. As you read his speech, notice how he used Monroe's motivated sequence to frame his problem–solution discussion of contributing to sustainable charity programs.

Sustainable Giving[15]

James Chang, Cypress College

Attention
In his introduction (paragraphs 1 and 2), James focuses his audience's *attention* on the pervasive problem of poverty. He appeals to his listeners' self-interest (values) by suggesting that they are, unintentionally, part of the problem.

1 Beatrice Biira, a 9-year-old girl in Uganda, lives in abject poverty. Living in a shanty home where the rain seeps through the roof every night, neither she nor any of her siblings has ever stepped foot in a school. Her story, sadly, is not unique. The World Bank in 2001 concluded that nearly three billion people live on less than two dollars a day. We hear this and we want to help, so we write checks to groups who claim that they will make a difference by donating food, clothing, and other short-term essentials, and we feel like we have helped make a difference in Beatrice's life, and, indeed, we probably have.

2 But what happens after the food runs out? Despite our best intentions, by donating to charities that offer short-term aid, we inadvertently perpetuate the cycle of poverty. Thus, I am advocating today that potential donors to charities should give to organizations that provide solutions that are sustainable in nature and that, furthermore, we change our very conception of the role of charities in fighting poverty. First, we will evaluate the problems caused by traditional conceptions of charitable giving, and then we will take a look at two examples of the solution—sustainable charity programs. Finally, we will see how we can personally take steps to implement these solutions.

Need
James discusses the problems of traditional charitable giving in paragraphs 3 and 4. He establishes a *need* for reform by demonstrating that traditional giving is not reducing poverty but is actually trapping millions in a cycle of poverty.

3 The American Association of Fundraising Counsel reports that Americans gave $212 billion to charity in 2001, and while that money was certainly donated with good intentions, much of it went to short-term causes that don't solve for poverty in the big picture. Certainly, charities that fight poverty see those horrors

on a daily basis. The UN Food and Agricultural Organization reports in their 2002 assessment of the State of Food Insecurity in the World that more than 840 million people in the world are malnourished and more than 150 million of them are under the age of 5. Six million children die every year as a result of hunger. The nonprofit almanac *In Brief* reported in July 2001 that there are more than 700,000 nonprofit charities registered in the United States. Many of these organizations are like the Children's Hunger Fund and Food for Life Global, which provide care packages of food to needy families. These programs certainly fulfill an immediate and important need in emergency situations like the aftermath of natural disasters or armed conflict.

4 Outside of these emergency situations, however, there is still massive poverty, and it is here where many of these programs fall short. The unfortunate result of this type of giving is that the families remain dependent on the charities as their very source of livelihood. Because no sustainable solution is ever given, recipients become trapped in a cycle of dependency. This problem is not caused by a lack of giving, for the Independent Sector Coalition reports that 89 percent of American households gave to charity in 2000. It is because of a lack of public awareness of the distinction between traditional charitable giving, as I have just described, and sustainable giving. Andrew Natsios, administrator of the United States Agency for International Development, puts this problem best in a speech delivered on May 31, 2001, when he said, referring to the term *sustainable development*, "it is just not a term that makes it easy for other people to understand what we do. If you explain that we do economic growth, . . . agriculture, . . . environmental program[s], . . . micro-enterprise programs, we perform all of these different functions, people intuitively know what we do."

5 In order to fight poverty successfully, then, we must learn what sustainable development means and its ramifications for solving the problems of poverty. There are some charities that already realize the importance of providing sustainable development measures. Unfortunately, these organizations do not receive the support that they need, still taking a back seat to traditional conceptions of giving. These organizations take different forms, but all share the common denominator of promoting self-reliance and sustainable, long-term solutions—powerful ends that they can only advance with your support.

6 The old adage goes, "Give a man a fish, and you feed him for a day; teach a man to fish, and you feed him for a lifetime." It was the belief of the founder in the simple premise that people should have the ability to feed themselves that was the foundation for the Heifer Project. Heifer International operates Animals to Families as sustainable gifts. The families raise the animals, benefiting from the products of those animals and selling them as a source of revenue. For example, beehives are given to many families for the sale of honey and beeswax. Of course, the Heifer Project also provides heifers—young female cows that provide up to four gallons of milk a day. The families benefit from the much-needed vitamins and protein in milk, and sell the surplus.

7 The effects of the Heifer Project on these families are very real indeed. Beatrice Biira was able to afford the $60 needed to go to school after the Heifer Project donated a goat to her family in 1994, as documented by *ABC News* in March 2001. Oliverio was a 15-year-old young man in Guatemala when the Heifer Project first helped him. Heifer International trained Oliverio to use rabbit droppings as manure on farms, and because rabbits have over 40 offspring a year, they

Satisfaction
In paragraphs 5 and 6, James seeks to *satisfy* the need for a change by explaining the merits of sustainable development.

Visualization
After introducing the solution to the problem, James asks his audience (in paragraphs 7 and 8) to *visualize* how sustainable giving can make a difference for those living in poverty. To intensify the desire to contribute, he describes specific success stories, using the examples of Beatrice, Oliverio, and Irma. James returns to that visualization in paragraph 10.

also provided much needed protein and food. Oliverio was then able to likewise train other members of his own village, selling the rabbits to them to raise enough money to pay for his and his sister's tuition. According to Heifer International's 2002 annual report, the Heifer Project has donated 28 different kinds of livestock, helping millions of families in 125 countries.

8 Programs like the Heifer Project are unique in providing permanent solutions. While other organizations continue to provide short-term aid and entrench dependency, sustainable programs make a long-term difference. Just as the Heifer Project donates animals to help its recipients, another organization, the Grameen Foundation, or the Grameen Bank, operates by issuing micro-credit loans that are interest- and collateral-free. The beneficiaries use the money to start businesses to become permanent sources of revenue. The foundation trains and supervises their recipients and organizes them into support groups. For example, Irma Hernandez, a woman from Honduras, joined with four other women in taking out a loan for $120 from the Adelante Foundation, a program supported by and modeled on Grameen. Her husband worked full-time as a farm laborer, but because work was not always available, the income was simply too low and too unstable to support the five children that they had. With the money that Irma borrowed, she was able to buy the necessary tools to start a clothes-making business that brought a steady second income to the family. Micro-credit loans are not a new concept—in fact, governments have used them effectively to spur development. *The Economist* of April 19, 2003, reports that the Thai government is now endowing each village in the country with a micro-credit fund worth about $23,000 each. Despite the success of sustainable programs where implemented, we as donors continue to choose the quick fix, contributing to organizations that provide short-term aid when in fact it is sustainable programs that are needed.

Action

In paragraph 9, James tells his listeners how they can *act* to implement the solution on an institutional and an individual level. He encourages his audience to contribute to two organizations, and he provides the URLs for their websites.

9 The most important question that should then remain is how you personally can help out. On an institutional level, the United States Agency for International Development, US-AID, is one of the leaders in fighting global poverty and should be encouraged to strengthen and increase its sustainable programs. Information about US-AID and the ability to contact the agency can be found on its website at usaid.org. On an individual level, the two private organizations I've talked about today provide detailed information about their ongoing operations as well as the opportunity to contribute on their websites. The Heifer Project, donating animals as sustainable gifts and having directly improved the lives of Beatrice and Oliverio, has a website at heifer.org. The Grameen Bank, issuing micro-credit loans and having directly helped Irma Hernandez and her family, has a website at gfusa.org. These are only two of a small but growing number of sustainable charities. Earlier, we learned that 89 percent of American households give regularly and that $212 billion was given in 2001. Clearly, we want to give, so the question is not whether or not we give, but to what we give.

10 Today, we've looked at the problems of poverty in the developing world and seen how the traditional conception of giving only traps recipients in a cycle of dependency and poverty. We then evaluated two examples of the solution—sustainable charities—and discussed action steps that we can all take. Sustainable charities empower people to help themselves. It is these organizations that give the needy people of the world not only a better today, but the opportunity for a better tomorrow—created by and for themselves.

SUMMARY

Making and Refuting Arguments

- Persuasion is the art of affecting other people's values, beliefs, attitudes, or behaviors. To be an effective persuader, you must know how to structure a valid argument, detect flaws in reasoning, and word propositions.
- The three steps of structuring an *argument* are to (1) make a claim you want the audience to accept, (2) supply evidence supporting that claim, and (3) explain how the evidence proves your claim.
- The act of countering one argument with another is called *refutation*. To refute an argument, follow this *refutational strategy*: (1) state the position you are refuting, (2) state your own position, (3) support your position with evidence, and (4) show how your position undermines the argument you oppose.

Types of Argument

- To give listeners a reason to accept a persuasive claim, speakers may use any of five types of argument: (1) *argument by example*, which uses specific instances to support a general claim; (2) *argument by analogy*, which links two concepts, conditions, or experiences and claims that what is true of one will be true of the other; (3) *argument by cause*, which links two concepts, conditions, or experiences and claims that one causes the other; (4) *deductive argument*, which employs a pattern called a *syllogism*, which consists of a major premise, a minor premise, and a conclusion; and (5) *argument by authority*, which uses testimony from an expert source to prove a speaker's claim.

Fallacies of Argument

- Fallacious arguments are dangerous because they may resemble sound reasoning.
- Ten fallacies of argument are common. (1) *The fallacy of hasty generalization* makes claims based on insufficient or unrepresentative examples. (2) *False analogy* compares entities that have critical differences. (3) *Post hoc ergo propter hoc* falsely confuses chronology with causation, arguing that because event A preceded event B, A caused B. (4) *The slippery slope* fallacy asserts that one event inevitably unleashes a series of events. (5) *Red herring* introduces irrelevant issues to deflect attention from the true question under discussion. (6) *Appeal to tradition* asserts that old ways of doing things are correct or best, simply because they are traditional. (7) *False dilemma* argues that we must choose between two alternatives, when in reality we may have a range of options. (8) *False authority* uses testimony from sources who have no real expertise on the topic in question. (9) The *bandwagon* fallacy argues that we should behave or think a particular way because most people do. (10) Finally, *ad hominem* urges listeners to reject an idea because of allegations about the character, politics, religion, or lifestyle of the person voicing the idea.

Selecting Propositions for Persuasive Speeches

- All persuasive speeches advocate *propositions*, position statements the speaker wants listeners to accept. A persuasive proposition must be stated as a declarative sentence that expresses a judgment, is debatable, and requires proof in order to be accepted. The three types of persuasive propositions are propositions of fact, value, and policy.

Monroe's Motivated Sequence

- A persuasive speech must move listeners through a series of steps. *Monroe's motivated sequence* is a formal, five-step pattern for moving listeners to belief or action: (1) get the attention of your listeners, (2) clarify the need, (3) show how to satisfy that need, (4) visualize the solution, and (5) request action.

EXERCISES

1. **Practice Critique.** Read the transcript of James Chang's speech, "Sustainable Giving," in this chapter. Before offering a solution, James discusses barriers of traditional charitable giving to combating long-term poverty. As you read his speech, make a list of the problems and causes he presents, and then analyze how he develops each. What is the claim? What material does James offer to support that claim? Does the evidence prove the point? Why or why not? Write a few suggestions for James to make his arguments stronger and more persuasive.

2. You have been asked to visit your former high school to speak to a group of college-bound students. The school's counselor has asked you to speak on the topic "College Years Are the Best Years of Your Life!" Construct three arguments that support this position. Give an example of how your speech could use each type of argument: example, analogy, cause, deduction, and authority.

3. Using argument by analogy, construct a short speech on one or more of the following topics. What similarities between the two entities make your analogy credible? What differences undermine the believability of each statement?

   a. Being in college is like being in a demolition derby.

   b. Life is like an athletic contest.

   c. Studying for an exam is like tying your shoe.

   d. Giving a speech to an audience of strangers is like going on a first date.

   e. A job interview is like an audition for a role in a film.

4. Determine whether each of the following statements is a proposition of fact, value, or policy.

   a. The university should build a new library.

   b. A new library would cost the university seven million dollars.

   c. It is more important to build a new library than to expand our athletic facilities.

   d. Access to math tutors increases students' grades in mathematics courses.

   e. The FDA should reduce required testing for experimental drugs to fight life-threatening illnesses.

   f. It is more important for a country to do good than to feel good.

5. Identify the major premise, minor premise, and conclusion in each of the following groups of statements:

   a. *Inquiring Minds* should be aired on the Trashy Cable Network.

   Inquiring Minds is a fluffy news show.

   All fluffy news shows should be aired on the Trashy Cable Network.

   b. A high grade point average is important to Charlotte.

   Today's college students value high grade point averages.

   Charlotte is a college student.

6. Find an editorial from a recent campus, local, or national newspaper. Identify the different types of argument used.

7. Locate examples of each fallacy discussed in this chapter. Examine advertisements in newspapers and in magazines and on radio, television, and the Internet. Read editorials, letters to the editor, and transcripts of speeches.

8. Apply the three criteria for well-worded propositions by writing specific propositions on the following topics:

   a. Hate crimes

   b. Lotteries

   c. Minimum legal drinking age

   d. Feminism

   e. Living wills

9. Write a proposition analysis think piece on the topic you have selected for a persuasive speech.

    a. Write the proposition you intend to support or oppose.

    b. Define key or ambiguous terms.

    c. Determine the important debatable issues.

    d. Suggest types of supporting material necessary to prove your points.

10. Write a proposition of fact, value, and policy for each of the following topic areas.

    a. Electric cars

    b. A foreign language requirement for all college students

    c. Competency tests for teachers

    d. Funding for cancer research

11. Consider the topic "This college should use only a pass–fail grading system." Prepare an argument for this topic using the "4 S" structure. Then refute your argument using the four-step refutational strategy.

12. Select a topic not discussed in this chapter, and describe how you might go about developing it using each step of Monroe's motivated sequence.

Speaking on Special Occasions

- **The Speech of Introduction**
- **The Speech of Presentation**
- **The Acceptance Speech**
- **The Speech of Tribute**

- **The Speech to Entertain**
- **The Impromptu Speech**
  Theory Into Practice: The Question–Answer Period

After studying this chapter, you should be able to

1. Understand and apply the five guidelines for a speech of introduction.

2. Understand and apply the four guidelines for a speech of presentation.

3. Understand and apply the four guidelines for an acceptance speech.

4. Understand and apply the five guidelines for a speech of tribute.

5. Understand and apply the five guidelines for a speech to entertain.

6. Understand and apply the four guidelines for an impromptu speech.

7. Understand and apply the four steps of answering a question from the audience.

If we use common words on a great occasion, they are the most striking, because they are felt at once to have a particular meaning, like old banners, or everyday clothes, hung up in a sacred place.

—George Eliot

EXPLORING ONLINE

Commencement Speeches

www.humanity.org/voices/
commencements/

This site includes transcripts of commencement speeches ranging from Theodor Geisel (Dr. Seuss) to Bill Gates and covering the years from 1936 to the present.

speech of introduction
A speech introducing a featured speaker to an audience.

KEY POINTS

Guidelines for the Speech of Introduction

1. Focus on the featured speaker.
2. Be brief.
3. Establish the speaker's credibility.
4. Create realistic expectations.
5. Set the tone for the speech.

On December 11, 2010, Cate Edwards stood beside her mother's casket in the Edenton Street Methodist Church in Raleigh and addressed more than eight hundred mourners who had assembled to celebrate the life of Elizabeth Edwards. Reflecting on her mother's courage and her six-year battle with breast cancer, Cate said: "I am who I am today, and I'll be whoever it is that I will become, in large part because she was my mom. . . ."[1]

Though we may not have the visibility of Cate Edwards, we can all count on being called on to deliver a speech on some special occasion: delivering a eulogy at the funeral or memorial service of a relative or friend, accepting an award from a civic group, or introducing a guest speaker at a club meeting.

To speak your best on any of these occasions, you must consider the customs and audience expectations in each case. In this chapter, we discuss seven special occasions or special circumstances for public speeches: the speech of introduction, the speech of presentation, the acceptance speech, the speech of tribute, the speech to entertain, the impromptu speech, and the question–answer period. You will learn guidelines for each of these types of speeches and read examples of many of them. This information can serve you well beyond the classroom and prepare you for any occasion when you are requested, invited, or expected to speak.

◖● The Speech of Introduction

One of the most common types of special-occasion speech is the **speech of introduction**. Some people use that phrase to indicate speeches by people introducing themselves to an audience. As we use the phrase in this chapter, however, we mean a speech introducing a featured speaker. The following guidelines will help you prepare such a speech of introduction.

- *Keep the focus on the person being introduced.* The audience has not gathered to hear you, so don't upstage the featured speaker. Keep your remarks short, simple, and sincere.
- *Be brief.* If you can, request and get a copy of the speaker's résumé. This will give you information to select from when preparing your introductory remarks. The key word in that last sentence is *select.* Your listeners will tune out quickly if your introduction is a lengthy chronology of jobs or events in a person's life. Highlight key information only.
- *Establish the speaker's credibility on the topic.* You do this by presenting the speaker's credentials. As you prepare, ask and answer questions such these: What qualifies the speaker to speak on the subject? What education and experiences make the speaker's insights worthy of our belief?
- *Create realistic expectations.* Genuine praise is commendable; just be careful not to oversell the speaker. Can you imagine walking

to the microphone after the following introduction? "Our speaker tonight is one of the great speakers in this country. I heard her last year, and she had us laughing until our sides hurt. Get ready for the best speech you've heard in your entire life!"

- *Establish a tone consistent with the speaker's presentation.* Would you give a humorous introduction for a speaker whose topic is "The Grieving Process: What to Do When a Loved One Dies"? Of course not. On the other hand, if the evening is designed for merriment, your introduction should help set that mood.

Communication professors should certainly know how to introduce a featured speaker. In the following example, Professor Don Ochs of the University of Iowa did an exemplary job of introducing his longtime colleague Professor Samuel L. Becker, the keynote speaker at a Central States Communication Association convention. You'll see that Ochs uses some communication jargon because he was speaking to a group of communication professionals. Notice, though, how Ochs's brief, cordial remarks focus on Becker, establishing his credibility and setting the tone for Becker's informative and inspirational speech:

Thirty years ago I walked out of an Iowa City store onto the main street and noticed Sam Becker walking about 20 feet ahead of me. His youngest daughter was alongside Sam but she was terribly upset about something, crying, and obviously hurt about something. Sam put his arm around his daughter and, in the space of two blocks, said something that comforted and fixed the problem. She was smiling when they parted company.

I share this snapshot of Sam with you because, for me, it captures Sam's approach to life, higher education, scholarship, and our profession.

Sam Becker has figuratively put his arm around difficulties and problems for his entire career. He's made all of us as teachers and scholars better persons and better professionals with his intellect, his vision, his energy, and his instinctive willingness to help.

As a rhetorician I would much prefer to introduce Sam with figures and tropes, with synecdoche, litotes, and hyperbole. But Sam is a social scientist, so I will be quantitative instead.

How much has Sam helped us? Sam has taught at four universities, written six books, been active in eight professional associations, authored 10 monographs, served on 12 editorial boards, worked on evaluation teams for 32 colleges and universities, served on 36 university committees, lectured at 50 colleges and universities, directed 55 PhDs, and authored 105 articles. Without doubt, he has helped and assisted and supported all of us. Our speaker today, Sam Becker.[2]

The Speech of Presentation

The **speech of presentation** confers an award, a prize, or some other form of special recognition on an individual or a group. Such speeches are typically made on special occasions: after banquets or parties, as parts of business meetings or sessions of a convention, or at awards ceremonies.

KEY POINTS

Guidelines for the Speech of Presentation

1. State the purpose of the award or recognition.
2. State the recipient's qualifications.
3. Adapt your speech's organization to audience knowledge.
4. Compliment finalists for the award.

speech of presentation
A speech conferring an award, a prize, or some other recognition on an individual or group.

ETHICAL DECISIONS

How (and Whether) to Polish a Bad Apple

King is president of the Porridge Players, an organization that stages musical comedies on his campus. This season, the Players have performed *South Pacific*, and the actress who played Nelly Forbush is Maria MacIntosh, an enormously talented singer, dancer, and actress with a horrible temper and an insufferably arrogant attitude. As president of the Players, King has been called on time after time to mediate disputes between this woman and other members of the cast and crew. By the time the season is over, he has little respect for her, despite her considerable talents.

At the end of each season, the faculty advisory board for the Players votes on awards for the best performers, director, technical people, and so forth. No one is very surprised when Maria is chosen to receive the award for best actress. King, however, is dismayed to learn that he has to present it, along with a short introductory speech. He wonders what to do. Should he simply praise Maria's performance and not mention the difficulties she caused, or is it his responsibility to make the faculty board aware of her flaws and negative impact on the company? What kind of information do you think King should include in his speech? Be prepared to discuss your answer with the class.

EXPLORING ONLINE

Sample Speeches

http://gos.sbc.edu

"Gifts of Speech" is an ongoing project from Sweet Briar College in Virginia. This site offers access to texts of speeches by influential women from around the world. You can search this collection alphabetically by particular speakers or chronologically by year. The site also lists the "Top 100 American Speeches of the 20th Century," with transcripts of the speeches by women.

When you give a speech of presentation, let the nature and importance of the award being presented as well as the occasion on which it is being presented shape your remarks. The following guidelines will help you plan this special-occasion speech.

First, as a presenter, you should *state the purpose of the award or recognition*. If the audience is unfamiliar with the award or the organization making the award, begin by briefly explaining the nature of the award or the rationale for presenting it. This is especially important if you represent the organization making the award. In contrast, an award having a long history probably needs little if any explanation.

A second guideline is to *focus your speech on the achievements for which the award is being made*; don't attempt a detailed biography of the recipient. Because you are merely highlighting the honoree's accomplishments, the speech of presentation will be brief, rarely more than 5 minutes long and frequently much shorter.

Third, *organize a speech of presentation primarily according to whether your listeners know the name of the recipient in advance*. If they do not know the honoree, capitalize on their curiosity. Begin by making general comments that could refer to several or many people; as the speech progresses, let your comments become more specific. Use gender-neutral descriptions ("this person" or "our honoree"), rather than using "he" or "she." In this way, you keep your audience guessing and allow them the pleasure of solving a puzzle. If the audience knows in advance the name of the person being recognized, begin the speech with specifics and end with more general statements that summarize the reasons for the presentation.

Finally, if a group of individuals has been nominated and you are announcing the winner with your speech of presentation, briefly *compliment the entire group of people who have been nominated for the award*.

We asked Josh McNair, a graduate teaching assistant, to create and present an award for the graduate student selected to follow him. Notice how he focuses on the reasons for the award and the honoree's qualifications. Josh also uses imagery and quotations appropriate to the occasion.

> Laurent A. Daloz, a twentieth-century educator, once observed, "In the end, good teaching lies in a willingness to attend and care for what happens in our students, ourselves, and the space between us." I couldn't agree more. Teaching is the dynamic process of filling the space between teacher and student through authentic and open communication.
>
> As part of a new tradition at Radford University, graduate students who have completed their teaching responsibilities are given the opportunity to recognize Graduate Teaching Fellows (GTFs), who will soon begin their teaching journey as communication instructors. The Great Teaching Future Award recognizes graduate students in the Department of Communication who have demonstrated academic excellence, teaching aptitude, and commitment to higher education. This year's honoree has shown all these qualities and now begins his journey to fill the space between himself and his students with knowledge, skills, and the desire for learning. It is both a privilege and pleasure to present the first Great Teaching Future Award to Mr. Zach Henning.
>
> This year's award recipient has demonstrated a unique commitment to teaching speech communication. This past year he independently sought out academic and applied opportunities for training as a college instructor. Last fall he successfully designed and delivered a public speaking teaching module in a graduate seminar in communication education. As an intern in Dr. George Grice's undergraduate persuasion class, Zach used multimedia and email to actively engage students in learning both in and out of the classroom. He completed his instructor training over the summer when, on a volunteer basis, he assisted Dr. Bill Kennan in teaching two sections of public speaking. Under Dr. Kennan's tutelage, Zach listened to and critiqued more than a hundred student speeches.
>
> Those of us who know Zach have witnessed his commitment to filling the space between himself and his students. First, Zach fills the space with knowledge of *what* to teach. The public speaking teaching module he developed includes clear teaching objectives that emphasize both the critical thinking and experiential components of constructing and delivering speeches. Second, Zach fills the space with skills on *how* to teach. In Dr. Grice's persuasion class, he successfully incorporated communication technology, traditional lecture, and small-group formats to motivate students. Finally, Zach fills the space with humor and his unique wit to foster in his students a desire for learning.
>
> As our teaching mentor, Dr. Grice, states in his teaching philosophy, "Understanding and applying knowledge comes from discovering relationships through communication, imagination, and invention." The Great Teaching Future Award follows this teaching philosophy and recognizes Graduate Teaching Fellows who have demonstrated excellence in attending to and caring for the space between themselves and their students. It is with great pleasure, then, that I present Zach Henning with this year's Great Teaching Future Award.[3]

◖ The Acceptance Speech

At some point in your life, you may be commended publicly for service you have given to a cause or an organization. You may be presented a farewell or retirement gift from your friends or coworkers. You may receive an award for winning a sporting event, an essay contest, or a speech contest. Although these are different occasions, they have at least one thing in

---

KEY POINTS

Guidelines for the Acceptance Speech

1. Thank those who bestowed the award.
2. Compliment the competition.
3. Thank those who helped you attain the award.
4. Accept the award graciously.

acceptance speech
A speech responding to a speech of presentation by acknowledging an award, a tribute, or recognition.

EXPLORING ONLINE

Sample Acceptance Speech

www.eliewieselfoundation.org

Visit this site for an excellent example of an acceptance speech that was both inspirational and persuasive. In the menu column, click on "Elie Wiesel" and then on "Nobel Prize Speech." On December 10, 1986, Elie Wiesel graciously accepted the Nobel Peace Prize. In this famous speech, he blended examples and evocative language to remind his audience of suffering and injustice and to call them to action, "the only remedy to indifference."

common—each requires a response. To accept a gift or an award without expressing appreciation is socially unacceptable. An **acceptance speech**, then, is a response to a speech of presentation. When a recipient acknowledges the award or tribute, he or she provides closure to the process. A gracious acceptance speech usually includes four steps.

First, *thank the person or organization bestowing the award*. You may wish to name the group sponsoring the award and the person who made the speech of presentation. In addition, you may want to commend what the award represents. Your respect for the award and its donor authenticates your statement of appreciation.

Second, if you are accepting a competitively selected award and especially if your competitors are in the audience, acknowledge their qualifications and compliment them. This step need not be lengthy; you can *compliment your peers* as a group rather than individually.

Third, *thank those who helped you achieve the honor*. Whether you are an accomplished pianist, vocalist, artist, athlete, or writer, you have usually had someone—parents, teachers, or coaches—who invested time, money, and expertise to help you achieve your best.

Finally, *accept your award graciously*. In response to Josh's speech of presentation, graduate student Zach Henning delivered the following acceptance speech. Notice how he incorporates all the guidelines we've discussed:

Thank you, Josh, for your kind words and for your support. It is with great honor that I accept this award. I realize that I have big shoes to fill and I will do my best to follow your example.

When I think about teaching, I'm reminded of what the great philosopher Aristotle said, "Teaching is the highest form of understanding." Through my internship and volunteer work with the communication department, I've learned more about who I am and how I can help others succeed. My understanding started with the feelings I experienced when I noticed thirty-four students looking up and paying attention to my words and thoughts. Their eagerness to learn inspired me to be the best instructor I can.

I know many qualified candidates who share my beliefs and feelings about teaching. Each could easily take my place with the experiences they bring to this department. I'm sure they would agree that teaching is more than a chore or an occupation. Instead, it's an art that is mastered through experience and guidance.

For that guidance, I turned to Dr. George Grice and Dr. William Kennan. They taught me about classroom logistics, lesson plans, and practical knowledge about the mechanics of teaching. More importantly, however, they taught me how to be passionate about what I am doing and how to positively influence the lives of students beyond the textbook and lecture material. For this I thank you both for your patience and generosity in offering me the opportunity to share in that passion.

I would also like to thank Dr. Gwen Brown, the director of our graduate program. Last year, new to the program and this university, I came to her wanting to know how I could become a graduate teaching fellow. Though there were no positions available at that time, Dr. Brown guided me to curricular and extracurricular opportunities that would heighten my interest in teaching. Her advice gave me the opportunity to reapply and accept this honor today.

And, most importantly, I would like to thank my students for their hard work and dedication. It is my goal not only to teach you about how to succeed in the classroom, but also to teach you about how to succeed in life. I am a firm believer in Dr. Martin Luther King, Jr.'s challenge that "the function of education is to teach one to think intensively and to think critically." I share this goal of education to teach both knowledge and character to prepare you for the challenges and opportunities you will encounter in your professional lives.

I hope that I never stop learning and understanding. There are always new challenges and new ways of thinking and teaching. I hope to continue to grow and change as I gain more experience and knowledge. Thank you for this first step to a lifetime of teaching and learning.[4]

The Speech of Tribute

A **speech of tribute**, or commemorative speech, honors a person, a group, or an event, and it can be one of the most moving forms of public address. A special form of this speech is the **eulogy**, a tribute to someone who has recently died. Vivid and memorable examples include Ronald Reagan's tribute to the crew of the Challenger after the shuttle explosion in 1986, Edward Kennedy's eulogy of his nephew John F. Kennedy, Jr., in 1999, and Abraham Lincoln's Gettysburg Address.

Peggy Noonan, presidential speechwriter, captures the power of eulogies:

They are the most moving kind of speech because they attempt to pluck meaning from the fog, and on short order, when the emotions are still ragged and raw and susceptible to leaps. It is a challenge to look at a life and organize our thoughts about it and try to explain to ourselves what it meant, and the most moving part is the element of implicit celebration. Most people aren't appreciated enough, and the bravest things we do in our lives are usually known only to ourselves. No one throws ticker tape on the man who chose to be faithful to his wife, on the lawyer who didn't take the drug money, or the daughter who held her tongue again and again. All this anonymous heroism. A eulogy gives us a chance to celebrate it.[6]

Five guidelines will help you write a eulogy or any other speech of tribute.

First, *establish noble themes*. As you begin developing a speech of tribute, ask, "Why is this person worthy of my respect and praise?" Answer this question by developing themes you want the audience to remember. Focus on the positive. A speech of tribute celebrates what is good about a person; it is not an occasion for a warts-and-all biography. You must be careful, however, not to exaggerate a person's accomplishments. To do so may undermine your speech by making it seem insincere or unbelievable.

Our student Stuart delivered a speech of tribute for one of his childhood heroes: Hall of Fame baseball player Ted Williams. He avoided the trap of organizing his speech as a biographical listing in an encyclopedia. Instead, he highlighted three lessons that all audience members, whether baseball fans or not, could learn from

KEY POINTS

Guidelines for the Speech of Tribute

1. Establish noble themes.
2. Provide vivid examples.
3. Express audience feelings.
4. Create a memorable image.
5. Be genuine

A great eulogy is both art and architecture—a bridge between the living and the dead, memory and eternity.
—Cyrus M. Copeland[5]

speech of tribute
A speech honoring a person, group, or event.

eulogy
A speech of tribute praising a person who has recently died.

Cate Edwards celebrated her mother's life, comforting and expressing the sentiments of those who loved and respected Elizabeth Edwards.

studying Williams's life. Stuart introduced these themes as he previewed his key ideas:

> He was given many eloquent nicknames by his teammates and the news media: The Splendid Splinter, The Kid, and Teddy Ballgame. All portray his amazing baseball talent, but all fail to capture the values that directed his life. Ted Williams taught us a lesson in *patriotism*, a lesson in *perseverance*, and a lesson in *charity*. And he did so not by lecturing or preaching, but by powerfully leading by example.

Second, *develop the themes of your speech with vivid examples*. Anecdotes, stories, and personal testimony are excellent ways of making your speech more vivid, humane, and memorable.

Third, *express the feelings of the audience assembled* or those whom you represent. The audience needs to be a part of the occasion for any speech of tribute. If you are honoring Mr. Crenshaw, a former teacher, you may speak for yourself and for all students who studied under him. The honoree should feel that the tribute expresses more than one person's view.

Your use of noble themes, vivid examples, and audience feelings should combine to *create a memorable image of the person being honored*. Your speech not only honors someone but also helps audience members focus on that person's importance to them.

Finally, *be genuine*. If you are asked to deliver a speech of tribute about someone you do not know, you may want to decline respectfully. The personal bond and interaction you develop in getting to know someone well is essential for a speech of tribute. Also, the person being honored may find the tribute more meaningful if it comes from a person he or she knows well.

◐ The Speech to Entertain

speech to entertain
A speech designed to make a point through the creative, organized use of humorous supporting materials.

The **speech to entertain** seeks to make a point through the creative, organized use of the speaker's humor. The distinguishing characteristic of this speech is the entertainment value of its supporting materials. It is usually delivered on an occasion when people are in a light mood: after a banquet, as part of an awards ceremony, and on other festive occasions.

A *speech to entertain* is different from *speaking to entertain*. In their opening monologues, Conan O'Brien and David Letterman are both speaking to entertain. Their purpose is to relax the audience, establish some interaction with them, and set the mood for the rest of the show. Their remarks are not organized around a central theme, something essential to a speech to entertain. If you combine the following five guidelines with what you already know about developing a public speech, you will discover that a speech to entertain is both challenging and fun to present.

The first requirement for a speech to entertain is that it *makes a point* or communicates a thesis. Frequently, the person delivering a speech to entertain is trying to make the audience aware of conditions, experiences, or habits that they take for granted. The following are examples of topics on which we have heard students present successful speeches to entertain:

KEY POINTS

Guidelines for the Speech to Entertain

1. Make a point.
2. Be creative.
3. Be organized.
4. Use appropriate humor.
5. Use spirited delivery.

The imprecision and incorrectness of language, especially that used in some advertisements

Many doctors' failure to speak language that their patients can understand and many patients' failure to ask their doctors the right questions

Our interest in or curiosity about tabloid news stories

The routine, expensive date versus creative, less expensive dating options

In some of these speeches, the speaker had stated the main point fairly bluntly by the end of the speech: Look carefully at the language used to sell you things; you owe it to your health to ask questions of your doctor; you do not have to spend a fortune to have an interesting time on a date. In other speeches, speakers simply implied their thesis.

Second, *a speech to entertain is creative*. To be creative, your speech to entertain must be your product and not simply a replay of an Ellen DeGeneres or a Jimmy Kimmel monologue. A replay is not creative, even if you do a great job of delivering the other person's lines. Moreover, if you copy other people's words and don't credit them, you are plagiarizing. Your speech to entertain should give your audience a glimpse of your unique view of the world.

Third, *a speech to entertain is organized*. It must have an introduction, a body, and a conclusion, just as informative and persuasive speeches do. The speech to entertain must convey a sense of moving toward some logical point and achieving closure after adequately developing that point. Failure to organize your materials will cause you to ramble, embarrassing both you and your audience. You will feel like the novice comic caught without a finish, a sure-fire joke that makes a good exit line. The audience will sense that you are struggling and will have trouble relaxing and enjoying your humor.

Fourth, *a speech to entertain uses appropriate humor*. The speech to entertain is difficult to do well for a simple reason: most people associate entertainment with lots of laughter and feel that if the audience is not laughing, they are not responding favorably to the speech. But consider the range of things that entertain you, from outrageous antics to quiet, pointed barbs. Your humor should be adapted to your topic, your audience, the occasion, and your personal style. The following four suggestions should guide your use of humor:

1. *Be relevant.* Good humor is relevant to your general purpose and makes the main ideas of your speech memorable. Michael's speech to entertain discussed the ways we label products and people. One of his points was that the product warnings printed on packaging tell us about various companies' views of their customers. His examples were relevant to that main idea and added humor to his speech by helping him show the absurdity of many product labels.

For example, the first thing I saw on the box my toaster came in was a warning. Warning—do not submerge in water, especially when the plug is connected to an electrical outlet. Now just at a practical level, I'm pretty sure that almost anyone should be able to figure out that the chances of getting your Pop-Tart to turn brown at the bottom of a Jacuzzi are pretty slim to begin with.[7]

2. *Be tasteful.* Audience analysis is vital for a speech to entertain. Taste is subjective. What delights some listeners may offend others. Do your best in analyzing your audience, but when in doubt, err on the side of caution. Remember, humor that is off-color is off-limits.

3. *Be tactful.* Avoid humor that generates laughter at the expense of others. There may be times when good-natured ribbing is appropriate, but humor intended to belittle or demean a person or group is unethical and unacceptable. For that reason, sexist and inappropriate ethnic humor is also off-limits.

4. *Be positive.* The tone for most occasions featuring speeches to entertain should be festive. People have come together to relax and enjoy each other's company. Dark, negative humor is usually inappropriate, as it casts a somber tone on the situation.

Finally, a speech to entertain benefits from spirited delivery. We have often heard good speeches to entertain and looked forward to reading transcripts of them later. We were usually disappointed. The personality, timing, and interaction with the audience that made the speech lively and unforgettable could not be captured on paper. We have also read manuscripts of speeches to entertain that promised to be dynamic when presented, only to see them diminished by a monotonous, colorless, and lifeless delivery.

◖ The Impromptu Speech

You are standing in the back of a crowded orientation session when, to your surprise, your supervisor introduces you and says, "Come up here and say a few words to these folks." Or you receive an award you didn't know you were being considered for. As people begin to applaud, you start walking to the front of the room. These are but two situations in which you would deliver an impromptu speech.

The **impromptu speech**, one with limited or no advance preparation, can be intimidating. You have not had time to think about the ideas you want to communicate. You begin speaking without knowing the exact words you will use. You have not practiced delivering your speech. Don't panic! By now you have a pretty good understanding of how to organize, support, and deliver a speech. You have practiced these skills in prepared speeches. All this practice will help you in your impromptu speech. With experience comes confidence. If you follow these four guidelines, you should be ready for almost any impromptu speech that comes along.

First, if you have a choice, *speak on a topic you know well.* The more you know about your topic, the better you will be able to select relevant ideas, organize them, and explain them as you speak. In addition, your confidence will show in your delivery.

Second, *make the most of the time you have.* Don't waste "walking time" from your seat to the front of the room worrying. Instead, ask

---

KEY POINTS

Guidelines for the Impromptu Speech

1. Speak on a topic you know well.
2. Make the most of the preparation time you have.
3. Focus on a single or a few key points.
4. Be brief.

impromptu speech
A speech delivered with little or no advance preparation.

By the end of this course, you should learn enough public speaking skills to comfortably and confidently offer your impromptu thoughts about a subject you know.

yourself, "What do I want the audience to remember when I sit down? What two or three points will help them remember this?"

Third, *focus on a single or a few key points*. If you have been asked to explain why you support building a new library instead of renovating the existing facility, think of the two or three most important reasons underlying your position. And remember to use the "4 S's" as you present those reasons to your audience.

Finally, *be brief*. One public speaking axiom is, "Stand up! Speak up! Shut up! Sit down!" Although this can be carried to an extreme, it is probably good advice for the impromptu speaker. An impromptu speech is not the occasion for a long, rambling discourse. Say what you need to say, and then be seated.

THEORY INTO PRACTICE

 **TIP   The Question–Answer Period**

Holding a question–answer period following your speech gives you the opportunity to interact directly with your audience. This usually results in a natural, lively delivery and makes for better speaker–listener rapport.

If questions are friendly, that is a high compliment: the audience is genuinely interested in you and your topic. If questions stem from audience confusion about your presentation, you have an opportunity to clarify. If someone asks you a combative and contentious question, you've just been given a second chance to win this person over to your point of view.

You will find the following guidelines helpful when you stand in front of an audience and ask, "Are there any questions?"

1. *Restate or clarify the question.* This is important for three reasons. First, repetition makes sure that the entire audience has heard the question. Second, repeating the question gives the questioner the opportunity to correct you if you misstate it, saving you the embarrassment of beginning to answer a different question. Third, if the question seems confusing to you or somehow misses the point, you can rephrase the question to make it clearer, more focused, and more relevant. Never answer a question you don't understand.

2. *Compliment the question whenever possible.* We have all heard speakers say, "I'm glad you asked that." Of course, you cannot repeat that same remark after each question. But you can say, "That's a good (or perceptive or interesting) question" or "I was hoping someone would ask that." This applies even to hostile questions. Sincerely complimenting a hostile questioner can defuse a tense situation and focus attention on issues rather than on personal antagonism.

3. *Answer the question.* Of course, the content and the form of your answers depend on the specific questions; nevertheless, the following suggestions may be helpful.

   • *Know your topic thoroughly.* Your success during the Q–A period will depend in large part on your research and preparation for your speech. You should always know more than you include in your speech. Most of the time, poor answers reflect poor preparation.
   • *Be as brief as possible.* Obviously, some questions require longer, more thoughtful answers than others. The question, "How much did you say it will cost to complete Phase II of the new library?" can be answered simply, "Two and a half million dollars." The question, "What will that $2.5 million provide?" will require a much longer answer.

(Continued)

- *Be methodical in giving lengthy answers.* When you need to give a detailed answer, use the organizational strategies that you've already learned and practiced: Signpost, state, and explain what you want the audience to remember.
- *If you don't know an answer, admit it.* Making up an answer is unethical. Fabricated answers can not only undermine your credibility, but the audience may also act on incorrect information you have provided. There is nothing wrong with saying, "I don't know" or "I don't know, but I'll check on it and let you know." If you give the second response, make sure you follow up promptly.
- *Be careful about what you say publicly.* Remember that in a public gathering there is no such thing as an off-the-record statement. If the press is present, what you say may indeed be reported. As a rule, never say anything that would embarrass you or slander others if it were to appear in the next morning's paper.

4. *Check the response with the questioner.* Did you answer the question to her or his satisfaction? Is there a follow-up question? Remember two drawbacks to this approach, however. If each person is allowed a question and a follow-up, you will be able to answer fewer people's questions. Second, if questioners are argumentative, asking them if you answered the question to their satisfaction gives them an opportunity to keep the floor and turn the Q–A period into a debate.

On a practical level, the question–answer period is one sure test of how well you know the topic of your speech. Handled effectively, a question–answer period gives you a final chance to clarify questions audience members might have, to reinforce your main points, and to cultivate the image you want to leave with your listeners.

❱ SUMMARY

The Speech of Introduction

- The *speech of introduction* presents a featured speaker to an audience. Be brief, focus your remarks on the featured speaker, establish that person's credibility, create positive but realistic audience expectations, and match the tone of the featured speech.

The Speech of Presentation

- The *speech of presentation* confers an award, prize, or special recognition on an individual or group. Such a speech should state the purpose of the award or recognition, particularly if it is new or unfamiliar to the audience. Reveal why the person deserves the award. If the audience does not know the name of the recipient in advance, create suspense, revealing the recipient's name only late in the speech. If the person being honored has been selected from nominees known to the audience, compliment those other individuals.

The Acceptance Speech

- The *acceptance speech* is an honoree's response to a speech of presentation. In accepting an award, thank the people bestowing it. You should also compliment your competitors if you know them. Then thank those who helped you attain the award, and accept the award graciously.

The Speech of Tribute

- The *speech of tribute*, or commemorative speech, honors an individual, a group, or a significant event. A *eulogy*, spoken to honor a person who has recently died, is one of the most familiar speeches of tribute. In delivering a speech of tribute, you should establish noble themes built on vivid examples from the subject's life. In addition you should express the collective feelings of the audience, create a memorable image of the subject, and be genuine.

The Speech to Entertain

- The *speech to entertain* seeks to make a point through the creative, organized use of the speaker's humor. Usually delivered on a light, festive occasion, your speech to entertain should make a point, be creative, be well organized, use appropriate humor, and be delivered in a spirited manner. The humor you use should be relevant to your point, tasteful, tactful, and positive.

The Impromptu Speech

- An *impromptu speech* is one delivered with little or no advance preparation. You speak impromptu whenever someone asks you a question or calls on you to speak with only a moment's notice. Speak on a subject you know well, use your limited preparation time constructively, cover only a few key points, and be brief.

The Question–Answer Period

- The *question–answer period* after your speech gives you the opportunity to interact with your audience. Restate or clarify what is asked, compliment the question or the questioner, answer the question, and check your response with the person who asked the question.

EXERCISES

1. **Practice Critique.** In 2008, family and friends of Timothy J. Russert gathered in the Kennedy Center to celebrate the life of this NBC newsman and favorite son of Buffalo, New York. Doris Kearns Goodwin delivered a moving eulogy about her friend. Read the transcript of her speech in Appendix B. Then, using the five guidelines discussed on pages 337–338, write a brief critique of the speech, noting places where the speaker did and did not follow each guideline.

2. Pair up with another member of the class. Discuss each other's speech topics and relevant personal background. Following the guidelines discussed in this chapter, prepare a speech introducing your partner on the day of his or her speech. Your partner will introduce you when you speak.

3. Pair up with someone and discuss what each of you does well. Create an award that one of you will receive. One of you will give a speech of presentation and the other a speech of acceptance.

4. Watch all or a portion of an awards ceremony (such as the Oscars or Grammys). Select the best and worst acceptance speeches; justify your choices.

5. Prepare and deliver a speech of tribute for someone you admire who is known to the class. This person may be a campus, local, national, or international figure.

6. Select a humorous magazine article or newspaper column. Discuss how you might edit, revise, and adapt the article for a speech to entertain, as well as how you would cite the source. Write a thesis statement, outline the key ideas, and develop entertaining examples to support those points.

7. Listen to or read a transcript of a question–answer period following a speech or at a press conference. Sources may include network broadcasts of presidential press conferences; C-SPAN broadcasts of interviews, National Press Club addresses, conference proceedings, news briefings, and call-in shows; and transcripts of presidential press conferences published in *Weekly Compilation of Presidential Documents* and *Public Papers of the Presidents of the United States*. Analyze the speaker's strategies and effectiveness in responding to audience questions.

Speaking in and as a Group

19

After studying this chapter, you should be able to

1 Recognize the importance of studying small group work as an adjunct to public speaking.

2 Identify four concepts that define a small group.

3 Compare and contrast different types of groups.

4 Explain the principles of group decision making.

5 Apply the seven-step process of group decision making.

6 Understand and incorporate the responsibilities of group members.

7 Understand and incorporate the responsibilities of group leaders.

8 Identify different formats for group presentations.

9 Apply the ten steps of preparing a group presentation.

Individual commitment to a group effort—that's what makes a team work, a company work, a society work, a civilization work.

—Vince Lombardi

Take out a sheet of paper and start listing all the small groups to which you belong. After a few minutes of brainstorming, you will probably be surprised at the length of your list. Groups are so prevalent in our society that it is estimated that there are more groups in America than there are people.[1] Unfortunately, small group communication seems not to be a skill most of us master easily. Estimates are that professionals lose 31 hours a month—nearly 4 workdays—in unproductive meetings.[2] The time you spend working in groups will be more valuable if you learn effective small group communication skills. This chapter will cover the relationship between small group communication and public speaking, the characteristics of a group, the types of groups, the principles of group decision making, the responsibilities of group leaders and members, and the most frequently used formats for group presentations.

◖ Small Group Communication and Public Speaking

Why study group work as an adjunct to public speaking? The answer is twofold: (1) Groups of people often make presentations, either internally or to the public; and (2) the quality of those presentations depends on how well group members have functioned together.

For most of your work in this class, you have operated alone. You selected, researched, and organized your speech topics. You have practiced and delivered these speeches standing alone in front of your classmates. Your individual work continues in a group. You must still present, support, and defend your ideas. The more you know about effective speech content, organization, and delivery, the better your individual speeches within the group will be.

As part of a group solving a problem and preparing a presentation, your work is more complex, however. On-the-spot interaction in a group elevates the importance of listening and critiquing. You will need to use all the critical thinking skills we discussed in Chapter 1. You'll also be challenged to provide feedback to other group members. Using the guidelines for critiquing that we discuss in Appendix A will help you do your part to create and maintain a constructive, supportive communication environment. Group processes will truly test your ability to work productively and congenially with other people.

EXPLORING ONLINE

Group Development

www.abacon.com/commstudies/ groups/devgroup.html

This Allyn & Bacon website presents several models that describe how groups develop. Click on "Small Group" at the bottom of the page for seven common questions about groups, and then access the answers.

◖ Small Groups Defined

small group
A collection of three or more people influencing and interacting with one another in pursuit of a common goal.

A **small group** is a collection of three or more individuals who interact with and influence one another in pursuit of a common goal. This definition includes four important concepts: individuals, interaction, influence, and goal.

The number of *individuals* in a group may vary. There must be at least three. Two people are not a group but rather an interpersonal unit, sometimes called a *dyad*. The addition of a third person adds a new dynamic, a new perspective. Paul Nelson describes the new relationship in the following way:

> Something happens to communication when it involves more than two people: It becomes much more complex. For example, imagine two people, A and B, having a conversation. There is only *one* possible conversation, A–B. Add one more person, C, however: Now there are *four* possible interactions, AB, A–C, B–C, and A–B–C. Add another person, D, and there are *eleven* possible interactions. And so on.[3]

Although we can all agree that three is the minimum number for a small group, we do not always agree on the maximum number. Even communication experts disagree, with some using seven as a workable maximum and others stretching the range to twenty. What characterizes a small group is not a specific number of participants, but the *type* of communication they undertake. A group that is too large cannot maintain meaningful interaction among members and may have to be divided into smaller working groups.

A second characteristic of a small group is *interaction*. A group cannot function if its participants fail to interact, and it functions ineffectively when a few members dominate. Generally, the larger the group, the fewer opportunities for any one member to participate and the greater the likelihood that a few members will dominate the flow of communication, making certain that meaningful interaction does not take place.

A third characteristic of small groups is *influence*. Group members interact in order to influence others. Groups function best when members express differences of opinions openly and try to persuade others with data and arguments.

Finally, a group has a purpose. As we noted in Chapter 1, a group is more than simply a collection of individuals who interact; it exists for a reason. Members interact and influence one another over a period of time in order to achieve a *goal*. The group process fails when members are unsure of their goal or when they fail to resolve conflicting perceptions of that goal.

> Never doubt that a small group of thoughtful, committed citizens can change the world. Indeed, it's the only thing that ever has.
>
> —Margaret Mead

Types of Groups

We can classify groups into two general types: socially oriented and task oriented. A **socially oriented group** is one that exists primarily because its members enjoy interacting with one another. Group members may not have a major task in mind but rather are concerned mainly with relationships, enjoying time spent with other members of the group. A **task-oriented group** is more formal. Members interact with a specific goal in mind. For example, you and a few classmates may form a study group to review for examinations and to be an audience for each other as you practice your speeches.

The objectives of socially and task-oriented groups often intermingle. Say you and your friends decide to go to a movie. Clearly, this is a social occasion, but you still must accomplish certain tasks: What movie does

socially oriented group
A small group that exists primarily because its members enjoy interacting with one another.

task-oriented group
A small group that exists primarily to accomplish some goal.

the group want to see? When is the best time for everyone to see it? Will you go together or just meet at the theater? At times you have probably been frustrated when your social group was unable to make some of these "easy" task decisions.

While socially oriented groups may have task objectives, the converse is also true. You form a study group to accomplish certain tasks, but as you get to know the others in the group, you discover that you enjoy their company. As social objectives emerge, the group meets more frequently and functions more effectively. If social purposes predominate, however, you may find that your group sacrifices studying for socializing. Even though most groups have both social and task objectives, one purpose usually takes precedence according to the situation. That purpose determines the structure of your group and the nature of the communication among its members.

In this chapter, we will focus on task-oriented groups, sometimes called *working groups*. These include study groups, problem-solving groups, and action groups. The objective of a **study group** is to learn about a topic. It gathers, processes, and evaluates information. When you and your classmates work together to prepare for an exam, you are a study group. A **problem-solving group** decides on courses of action. This type of group explores a problem, suggesting solutions to remedy it. The objective of an **action group** is, as its name implies, to act. It has the power to implement proposals. These categories may overlap. In fact, you may be a member of a group that studies a situation, devises a solution, *and* implements it.

Successful athletic teams recognize the importance of working together as a group of individuals to accomplish their goals. Business and professional organizations are increasingly using **work teams** to accomplish their objectives. Communication scholars Thomas Harris and John Sherblom argue, "Teams differ substantially from many small groups, because the teams themselves, rather than the leader, control the group process."[4] They rely on individual responsibility and shared leadership.

A type of action group that is increasingly common in the business world is the **self-directed work team**. Such work teams manage themselves, in addition to getting work done. Responsibilities and characteristics of self-directed work teams include

- sharing management and leadership roles;
- planning, controlling, and improving their own work;
- setting team goals, creating schedules, and reviewing group performance;
- identifying and securing necessary training;
- hiring and disciplining team members; and
- assuming responsibility for products and services produced.[5]

Work teams obviously require that traditional leadership responsibilities gradually shift to team members. Many teams rotate the role of team leader, with members occupying the position for a designated length of time.

study group
A task-oriented group devoted to researching and learning about a topic.

problem-solving group
A task-oriented group devoted to deciding on courses of action to correct a problem.

action group
A task-oriented group devoted to implementing proposals for action.

work team
A team or group of people who perform all activities needed to produce the product, service, or other goal specified by an outside leader, supervisor, or manager.

self-directed work team
A group of people who manage themselves by identifying, conducting, and monitoring all activities needed to produce a product or service.

As you go through this chapter, you will find that participating in task groups and delivering public speeches are similar in several ways. Both usually involve research, analysis of information and ideas, and the presentation of that information to others. Yet despite these similarities, there are notable differences between public speaking and group communication. The effective communicator will seek to master both sets of skills.

Group Discussion and Decision Making

One important reason we form groups is to make decisions. We may seek a friend's guidance because we believe that two heads are better than one. This philosophy is the foundation of group decision making. You may have heard the expression that in communication "the whole is greater than the sum of its parts." What this means is that if a group of five functions effectively, its product will be qualitatively or quantitatively superior to the total product of five people working individually. But a group is able to work most effectively only when members follow certain principles of group decision making.

Although a task-oriented group functions more effectively if members enjoy one another's company, social interactions should not take precedence over the group's basic objective: to accomplish the task.

Principles of Group Decision Making

Group Decision Making Is a Shared Responsibility. The presence of a group leader does not necessarily establish a leader–follower or even an active–passive association. In fact, the relationship among group members is usually better represented as a partnership. Group decision making requires the active participation of the group leader and group members performing mutually reinforcing responsibilities.

Group Decision Making Requires a Clear Understanding of Goals. Every group has a goal. Sometimes that goal is predetermined. Your instructor may, for example, divide your class into small groups, asking each group to generate a list of 25 topics suitable for a speech to inform. In your career, you may be part of a small group that must study specific job-related problems and propose workable solutions. In both instances, the group has a clear statement of its objective. In other situations, the goal of your group may be less clear. If that is the case, you will have to clarify, specify, or even determine your goals.

Group Decision Making Benefits from a Clear but Flexible Agenda. Every group needs a plan of action. Because a group's process affects its product, it is vital that members spend sufficient time generating an action plan. The leader can facilitate this process by suggesting procedures that

---

KEY POINTS

Principles of Group Decision Making

1. Group decision making is a shared responsibility.
2. Group decision making requires a clear understanding of goals.
3. Group decision making benefits from a clear but flexible agenda.
4. Group decision making is enhanced by open communication.
5. Group decision making requires adequate information.

the group may adopt, modify, or reject. The best plan, or agenda, however, is one not dictated by the leader, but rather one developed by all group members.

A group's agenda should be both specific and flexible. Group participants must know what is expected of them and how they will go about accomplishing the task at hand. Raising $1,000 for charity could be accomplished by dividing the membership into five teams, each having the responsibility for generating $200. These teams would need to communicate and coordinate to avoid unnecessary overlap as they decided on their fund-raising projects. Groups also need to be flexible as they pursue their goals. Unexpected obstacles may require revising the agenda. The group needs a backup plan, for example, if its car wash is canceled because of rain.

Group Decision Making Is Enhanced by Open Communication. If all members of a group think alike, there is no need for the group. One person can simply make the decision. Diversity encourages alternative perspectives. Both the group leader and individual members should protect and encourage the expression of minority views.

Groups should avoid **groupthink**, a term coined by Irving Janis. This occurs when group members come to care more about conforming and not making waves than they do about exercising the critical evaluation necessary to weed out bad ideas.[6] Groupthink reduces open communication and adversely affects the quality of decision making. To be effective, a group must encourage each member to exercise independent judgment.

Group Decision Making Requires Adequate Information. Access to information that is sufficient and relevant is extremely important. A group suffers if its information is based on the research of only one or two of its members. To avoid this problem, a group should follow a few simple steps. First, the leader should provide essential information to the group as a starting point. Second, each member should contribute critical knowledge to the group. Third, the group should divide the gathering of information in a way that is efficient and yet provides some overlap. Later in this chapter, we provide suggestions for gathering information.

Now that we understand the principles of group decision making, let's look at how the group makes decisions.

The Process of Group Decision Making

In his celebrated book *How We Think*, published in 1910, John Dewey argued that decision making should be a logical, orderly process.[7] His "Steps to Reflective Thinking" have provided one of the most useful, and we think one of the best, approaches to problem solving. We'll apply Dewey's steps to group decision making shortly, but first we need to clarify the group's discussion topic.

If you are a member of a problem-solving discussion group or a task-oriented group and you have not been assigned a topic, the group will need to select a topic and word it. A good discussion topic is current and

When all think alike, no one thinks very much.

—Walter Lippman

groupthink
Excessive agreement among group members who value conformity more than critical evaluation.

EXPLORING ONLINE

Groupthink

http://changingminds.org/explanations/theories/groupthink.htm

http://www.mindtools.com/pages/article/newLDR_82.htm

These websites discuss Irving Janis's concept of *groupthink*. You can learn eight symptoms of groupthink, as well as suggestions for improving group decision making.

KEY POINTS

The Steps to Problem Solving

1. Define the problem.
2. Analyze the problem.
3. Determine the criteria for the optimal solution.
4. Propose solutions.
5. Evaluate proposed solutions.
6. Select a solution.
7. Suggest strategies for implementing the solution.

controversial and has a body of data and opinion from which to construct and refute positions. Once you select a topic meeting these criteria, you must word the topic according to the following guidelines.

First, it should be worded as a question the group will seek to answer. "The campus parking problem" fails to meet this criterion and, consequently, does not direct participants in the discussion toward a goal.

Second, the question should be open rather than closed. Open wording might include "What can be done to alleviate the parking problem on campus?" or "How should this college solve the campus parking problem?" These questions are open because they do not direct the group to one particular solution. They invite a variety of solutions and can generate lively and productive discussion. The question "Should the campus build a multistory parking facility to solve the campus parking problem?" is an example of a closed question because it focuses attention on only one solution. This yes-or-no question limits discussion of alternative proposals. Because it forces individuals to choose sides, a closed question is probably more appropriate for a debate than for a discussion format.

After members have agreed on a topic question, the group should begin answering it in a logical, methodical manner. The following seven-step process, based on Dewey's model, will aid your group. It is important that you go through these steps chronologically and not jump ahead in your discussion. Solutions are best discussed and evaluated only after a problem is thoroughly defined and analyzed.

Define the Problem. Before you can solve a problem, you must first define it. By defining the key terms of the question, group members decide how they will focus the topic, enabling them to keep on track and to avoid extraneous discussion. Suppose your college asks you to be part of a student advisory committee to address the issue "What can be done to alleviate the parking problem on campus?" To answer the question, members must agree on what constitutes "the parking problem." Are there too few parking spaces? If there are sufficient spaces, are they not geographically located to serve the campus best? Is there congestion only during certain times of the day or week? Is the problem not the number of spaces but the condition of the parking lots? How your group defines the problem determines, to a large extent, how you will solve it.

Analyze the Problem. In analyzing a problem, a group looks at both its symptoms and causes. We gauge the severity of a problem by examining its *symptoms*. For example, the group needs to know the approximate number of students unable to find parking spaces and why that is detrimental. Students may be late for class because of parking congestion; accidents may occur as cars crowd into small spaces; students walking to dimly lit and distant parking spaces after an evening class may worry about physical attacks. These symptoms point to the magnitude of the problem. Certainly, some symptoms are more serious than others, and group members must identify those needing immediate action.

However, the group is still not ready to propose remedies. The group must now consider the *causes* of the problem. By examining how a difficulty developed, a group may find its solution. The parking problem may stem from a variety of causes, including increased enrollment, parking spaces converted to other uses, lack of funds to build new parking lots, too many classes scheduled at certain times, and inadequate use of distant parking lots.

Determine the Criteria for the Optimal Solution. Decision-making criteria are the standards we use to judge the merits of proposed solutions. It is wise to state these criteria before discussing solutions. Why select an action plan only to discover later that sufficient funding is unavailable? The group studying campus parking worked to avoid this pitfall. Some of the criteria they considered were as follows:

Criteria	Explanation
Economics	The proposal should be cost effective.
Aesthetics	The proposal should not spoil the beauty of the campus.
Legality	The proposal cannot force residents and businesses adjacent to campus to sell their land to the college.
Growth	The proposal should account for future increases in enrollment.
Security	The proposal should enhance the safety of students going to and from parking lots.

Propose Solutions. Only after completing the first three steps is the group ready to propose solutions. This is essentially a brainstorming step with emphasis on the quantity, not quality, of suggestions. At this stage, the group should not worry about evaluating any suggested solutions, no matter how far-fetched they may seem. This group's brainstorming list included the following:

Building a multistory parking lot in the center of campus
Constructing parking lots near the edge of campus
Lighting and patrolling lots in the evening
Initiating bus service between apartment complexes and campus
Encouraging students to carpool or to ride bicycles to campus

Evaluate Proposed Solutions. Now the group is ready to evaluate each proposed solution using the criteria listed in the third step. The group considers the advantages of the proposed solution and then assesses the disadvantages. The centrally located high-rise parking garage may use valuable land efficiently and limit the extent of late-night walking but may not be cost effective and may intrude on the beauty of the campus

Select a Solution. After evaluating each proposed solution, you and your fellow group members should have a good idea of those solutions to exclude from consideration and those to retain. You will then weigh the merits and deficiencies of each. Your final solution may be a combination of several of the proposed remedies. For example, the group working on the campus parking problem could issue a final report advocating a three-phase solution: short-range, middle-range, and long-range goals. A short-range approach may involve converting a little-used athletic practice field to a parking facility, creating more bicycle parking areas, and encouraging carpooling. A middle-range solution could involve creating a bus system between student apartments and the campus or trying to get the city transit system to incorporate new routes. The long-range proposal could involve building a well-lit multistory parking facility, not in the middle of campus but near the athletic complex, to be used during the week for general student parking and on weekends for athletic and entertainment events.

Suggest Strategies for Implementing the Solution. Once the small group has worked out a solution, members would normally submit their recommendations to another body for approval, action, and implementation. Sometimes, however, decision makers should not only select feasible and effective solutions but also show how they can be implemented. How would the small group incorporate suggestions for implementing its solution? Members may recommend coordinating their plan with the long-range master plan for the college. The group would probably also suggest a timetable detailing short- and long-range projects and might also identify possible funding sources.

In summary, the reflective thinking model enables a group to define a problem, analyze it, determine the criteria for a good solution, propose solutions, evaluate solutions, select a solution, and suggest ways to implement it. Decisions made by following this process are generally better, and group members are more satisfied with their work. This model can benefit groups in business, government, education, and other organizations, and it can improve your individual decision making.

The Responsibilities of Group Members

The ideal leader–member relationship is not an active–passive partnership. To enhance the quality of the group's product, all members must participate actively. Productive group members undertake five key responsibilities.

Inform the Group. Group members should enlarge the information base on which decisions are made and action is taken. A decision is only as good as the information that supports it. You enlarge the group's information base in two ways. First, you contribute what you already know about the issue being discussed. Hearsay is worth mentioning at this stage, as long as you acknowledge that it is something you have heard but cannot prove. Another member may be able to confirm or refute it, or it can be put on the agenda for further research.

Second, group members contribute to a group's understanding of a topic by gathering additional relevant information. You may hear ideas

> **KEY POINTS**
>
> **Responsibilities of Group Members**
>
> 1. Inform the group.
> 2. Advocate personal beliefs.
> 3. Question other participants.
> 4. Evaluate ideas and proposals.
> 5. Support and monitor other group members.

that you want to explore further. You may need to check out facts before the group can clarify the dimensions of a problem or adopt a particular plan of action. The research and thought you give to a topic before the next meeting will make that meeting more efficient and productive.

Advocate Personal Beliefs. Group members should provide information to help make decisions and should use that data to develop positions on the issues being discussed. Participants should be willing to state and defend their opinions. A good participant is open-minded, willing to offer ideas, and then willing to revise or retract them as additional facts and expert opinion surface. Your opinions may change as they are challenged throughout the discussion.

Question Other Participants. Effective participants not only give but also seek information and opinions. Knowing how and when to ask an appropriate question is an important skill. As one advertisement claims, "When you ask better questions, you tend to come up with better answers." Asking effective questions requires active listening, sensitivity to the feelings of others, and a desire to learn. Group members should seek clarification of ideas they do not understand and should encourage others to explain, defend, and extend their ideas.

Evaluate Ideas and Proposals. Too often we either accept what we hear at face value or remain silent even though we disagree with what is said. Yet, challenging facts, opinions, and proposals benefits the quality of discussion. It is the group's obligation to evoke a range of positions on the issue being discussed and then separate the good ideas from the bad. Each idea should be discussed thoroughly and analyzed critically. Thus, all group members are obligated to evaluate the contributions of others and to submit their own positions to rigorous testing. This is sometimes difficult to do. Yet participants should not be defensive about their ideas but should instead be open to constructive criticism.

Support and Monitor Other Group Members. A group is a collection of individuals having different personalities. Some may be less assertive than others and may have fragile egos. Reluctant to express their ideas because they fear criticism, they may cause the group to lose important information and to rush into a decision. They may even foster groupthink. In addition to providing support for reticent individuals, members should also take note of possible dysfunctional, self-oriented behaviors that impede the group's progress. Ronald Adler and Jeanne Elmhorst describe some of these roles and behaviors:

- *The blocker:* Prevents progress by constantly raising objections.
- *The attacker:* Aggressively questions the competence or motives of others.
- *The recognition seeker:* Repeatedly and unnecessarily calls attention to self by relating irrelevant experiences, boasting, and seeking sympathy.

ETHICAL DECISIONS

Leader and Member Responses When Groups Fail

An anonymous benefactor has contributed funds to sponsor a Career Day on Emily's campus. The president of the Student Government Association appoints Emily, a first-year student, to chair a committee charged with drafting a detailed proposal for Career Day activities. Despite Emily's efforts to encourage open discussion and to distribute the workload, two of the five committee members have contributed little. Kate, a junior, opposes most of the ideas offered by others, seldom volunteers any concrete suggestions of her own, and often wants to discuss issues unrelated to the committee's task. Gary, a senior, seldom attends meetings, and when Emily asks for his input, he usually shrugs and says, "Whatever you decide is fine with me." After three unproductive meetings with all five members present, Emily is concerned that the committee may not meet its deadline for the report. She decides to call a private meeting with the three productive members and draft the report. They finish it in a few hours and then present it to the full committee at the next meeting, allowing all the members to discuss and vote on it.

Is Emily's strategy an ethical one for a committee chair? When a group is not functioning effectively, should the leader do everything possible to ensure that all members participate in the decision-making process, or is it more important to ensure that the group takes action, even if it means giving more power to selected members? What responsibility do the members have to ensure equal participation?

- *The joker:* Engages in joking behavior in excess of tension-relieving needs, distracting others.
- *The withdrawer:* Refuses to take a stand on social or task issues; covers up feelings; does not respond to others' comments.[8]

The climate of the group should encourage openness and acceptance. It is the job of both the leader and the group members to create and reinforce this climate.

The Responsibilities of Group Leaders

Just as effective leadership depends on effective membership, so, too, does effective membership depend on effective leadership. Leaders have certain responsibilities that, if fulfilled, minimize negative roles and behaviors and help the group meet its goal.

Plan the Agenda.   A group leader has the primary responsibility for planning an agenda. This does not mean dictating the agenda; rather, the leader offers suggestions and solicits group input into the process.

Orient the Group.   How a meeting begins is extremely important in setting expectations that affect group climate and productivity. A leader may want to begin a meeting with some brief opening remarks to orient the group to its mission and the process it will follow. In analyzing business meetings, Roger Mosvick and Robert Nelson conclude, "The chairperson's orientation speech is the single most important act of the business meeting." They describe this speech as follows:

KEY POINTS

Responsibilities of Group Leaders

1. Plan the agenda.
2. Orient the group.
3. Establish an information base.
4. Involve all members in the discussion.
5. Encourage openness and critical evaluation.
6. Secure clarification of ideas and positions.
7. Keep the group on target.
8. Introduce new ideas and topics.
9. Summarize the discussion.
10. Manage conflict.

It is a systematically prepared, fully rehearsed, sit-down speech of not less than 3 minutes nor more than 5 minutes (most problems require at least 3 minutes of orientation; anything over 5 minutes sets up a pattern of dominance and control by the chairperson).[9]

For some groups that you lead, it will not always be appropriate or even desirable to begin a meeting with a structured speech. Still, leaders should try to accomplish several objectives early in the group's important first meeting. They should (1) stress the importance of the task, (2) secure agreement on the process the group will follow, (3) encourage interaction among members, and (4) set an expectation of high productivity.

Establish an Information Base. Leaders may wish to introduce background information to the group in an opening statement or to forward some relevant articles with background information to members before the first meeting. This sometimes makes the initial meeting more productive by establishing a starting point for discussion. Leaders should encourage input from all members, however, as the primary means of ensuring sufficient information for making decisions.

Involve All Members in the Discussion. A leader must make certain that participation among group members is balanced. A person who speaks too much is as much a problem as one who speaks too little. In either case, the potential base of information and opinion is narrowed. Leaders can encourage more thoughtful and balanced discussion by asking members to think about a particular issue, problem, or solution prior to the discussion and then asking each member to share ideas with the group before discussing each. This strategy often promotes a more thoughtful analysis of the topic and encourages each member to participate in the discussion. Remember our position that all members share the responsibility of group leadership. If someone is not contributing to the discussion, any member of the group can ask the silent person for an opinion.

> Freedom rings where
> opinions clash.
>
> —Adlai Stevenson

Encourage Openness and Critical Evaluation. After the group has shared information and ideas, the leader must guide the group in evaluating them. The leader may do this by directing probing questions to specific individuals or to the group as a whole. To achieve and maintain a climate of free and honest communication, the group leader must be sensitive to the nonverbal communication of participants, encouraging them to verbalize both their reluctance and their excitement about the ideas other members are expressing. At the same time, the sensitive leader will keep criticism focused on ideas rather than on personalities.

Secure Clarification of Ideas and Positions. Effective leaders are good at getting group members to make their positions and ideas clearer and more specific. They do this in two ways. First, the leader may encourage a member to continue talking by asking a series of probing follow-up questions ("So what would happen if . . . ?"). Even the use of prods ("Uh-huh." "Okay?") can force discussants to think through and verbalize their ideas and positions. Second, the leader may close a particular line of discussion by paraphrasing the ideas of a speaker ("So what you're saying is that . . ."). This strategy confirms the leader's understanding, repeats the idea for the benefit of other group members, and invites their reactions.

Keep the Group on Target. Effective leaders keep their sights on the group's task while realizing the importance of group social roles. There is nothing wrong with group members becoming friendly and socializing. This added dimension can strengthen your group. However, when social functions begin to impede work on the task, the group leader must "round up the strays" and redirect the entire group to its next goal.

Introduce New Ideas and Topics. We've already mentioned that it is important for leaders to prepare for the first group meeting. In addition, the leader should be the most willing researcher among the group. If discussion stalls because the group lacks focus or motivation, the leader must be willing and able to initiate new topics for research and talk. If a lapse in the group's progress signals that research and discussion have been exhausted, the leader must recognize this situation and be willing to move on to the next phase of group work.

Summarize the Discussion. A leader should provide the group periodic reviews of what has been decided and what remains to be decided. These summaries keep members focused on the group's task. Leaders may begin a group meeting with an *initial summary*, a brief synopsis of what the group decided previously. They may offer *internal summaries* during the discussion to keep the group on target. At the conclusion of the group task, leaders should provide a *final summary* that reviews what the group accomplished.

Manage Conflict. Conflict is both inevitable and essential in group discussion. When ideas collide, participants must rethink and defend their positions. This process engenders further exploration of facts and opinions and enhances the likelihood of a quality outcome. It is important that a group manage, not discourage, conflict.

While conflict of ideas contributes to group effectiveness, interpersonal antagonism may undermine it. When conflict becomes personal, it ceases to be productive, as it disrupts the group. Some members may stop expressing their opinions for fear of attack. If the climate becomes too uncomfortable, members may withdraw from the group. Thus, when conflict surfaces, it is essential that the group respond appropriately. At some point, it may become evident that conflict cannot be solved by the group or in the presence of group members. In this event, the leader may have to meet with the disruptive member and discuss the problem.

When a group is composed of members and a leader fulfilling the various roles we have just outlined, it should produce quality results. At times, the problem solving will benefit the group alone and no external report is needed. Often, however, the group will be requested or will want to present its findings to a larger group: coworkers, company stockholders, or just an interested public audience, for example. In such cases, the group must continue to work together to plan its presentation.

In a symposium, speakers offer their perspectives on a topic and then discuss those issues with other panelists, often answering questions from the audience.

The Group Presentation

Next, we discuss two popular formats for group presentations and provide a systematic checklist to help you develop a first-rate presentation.

Formats for the Presentation

There are several formats for a group presentation, two of which are the public discussion and the symposium.

The Public Discussion. In a **public discussion**, a group sits, often in a semi-circle, in front of the audience. Members are aware of an audience but usually address others in the group. The audience, in effect, eavesdrops on the group's conversation. If your public speaking class includes group presentations, your small group may be asked to use this format to present its report to the class.

The problem-solving classroom discussion usually requires extensive preparation. The group has researched the topic, planned the discussion, and possibly practiced the presentation. Members have a general idea of the content and organization of their own and other participants' remarks, although the presentation is not memorized or scripted. The presentation is intended to inform and persuade the audience on the issue being discussed. Sometimes a question–answer period follows.

The Symposium. A **symposium** is a series of speeches on a single topic presented to an audience. It differs from a public discussion in at least two ways. First, there is no interaction among the speakers during the presentation; however, a discussion period may follow. Each speaker has a designated amount of time to present her or his remarks. Second, speakers address members of the audience directly. Sometimes speakers are seated at a table; often they use a lectern. In most public symposiums, the speakers

public discussion
A small group exchange of ideas and opinions on a single topic in the presence of an audience.

EXPLORING ONLINE

Team Presentations
www-acad.sheridanc
.on.ca/~nowell/presentations/
grouppres.htm

Professor David Nowell of Sheridan College Institute of Technology and Advanced Learning in Canada has created this worthwhile website with links to information on building a team, the group presentation, and resources.

symposium
A series of public speeches on a single topic, possibly followed by group discussion or a question–answer period.

SPEAKING WITH CONFIDENCE

In my public speaking class I learned how to structure and present my ideas effectively. But team presentations offer an additional challenge. You need to care about other group members' opinions and input. Synergy just doesn't happen; it requires a lot of work. I've given team presentations in my English, communication, geology, and business classes. In my marketing class, for example, our group researched and presented a product analysis of the General Motors product line. Our presentation was more than just a collection of individual speeches. We met and planned our roles. Who would speak on what topics and in what order? Who was responsible for projecting visual aids? How would we dress to convey that we all took the presentation seriously? This required more preparation and practice than just rehearsing our individual parts. When each of us concluded our portion of the presentation, we previewed how it related to what the next person would talk about. A team presentation requires a smooth flow from person to person. Team presentations are a lot of work, but when they're done well, they can be exciting and rewarding.

Cynthia Opakunle
Radford University

have not met beforehand to discuss what they will say. If you are assigned to a group for a presentation in this class, you will likely want to meet several times, following some of the guidelines we discuss in the following section.

Preparing a Group Presentation

Although there is no one correct way to prepare for a group presentation, the following suggestions will help you work efficiently and produce an effective product. The symbol "•" denotes those steps requiring group interaction; the other steps can be done individually.

• Brainstorm about the Topic. Through brainstorming, you will discover what group members already know, and you will uncover numerous ideas for further research. In addition to providing content, brainstorming also serves a relationship function. By giving all members an opportunity to participate, brainstorming gives you a glimpse of your peers' personalities and their approaches to group interaction. You get to know them, and they get to know you. Maintaining an atmosphere of openness and respect during this first meeting gets the group off to a good start. Once you have generated a list of areas concerning your topic, you are ready for the second step.

Do Some Exploratory Research. The second phase of your group process is individual research. While there may be some merit in each person's selecting a different topic to research, research roles should not be too rigid. Rather than limiting yourself by topic, you may wish to divide your research by resource. One member may search the Internet, another the library's databases, while a third may interview a professor who is knowledgeable on the topic, and so forth. It is important that you not restrict your discovery to the list of topics you have generated. Exploratory research is also a form of brainstorming. As you look in indexes and read articles, you will uncover more topics. Each group member should try to find a few good sources that are diverse in scope.

KEY POINTS

Steps in Preparing a Group Presentation

•1. Brainstorm about the topic.

  2. Do some exploratory research.

•3. Discuss and divide the topic into areas of responsibility.

  4. Research your specific topic area.

  5. Draft an outline of your content area.

•6. Discuss how all the information interrelates.

•7. Finalize the group presentation format.

•8. Plan the introduction and conclusion of the presentation.

  9. Prepare and practice your speech.

•10. Rehearse and revise the presentation.

• Discuss and Divide the Topic into Areas of Responsibility. After exploratory research, your group should reconvene to discuss what each member found. Which expectations did your research confirm? Which were contradicted? What topics did you find that you had not anticipated? Your objective at this stage of the group process is to decide on the key areas you wish to investigate. Each person should probably be given primary responsibility for researching a particular area. That person becomes the content expert in that area. While this approach makes research more efficient, it has a drawback. If one person serves as a specialist, the group gambles that he or she will research thoroughly and report findings objectively. If either assumption is not valid, the quantity of information may be insufficient and its quality contaminated. An alternative approach is to assign more than one person to a specific area.

> The nice thing about teamwork is that you always have others on your side.
>
> —Margaret Carty

Research Your Specific Topic Area. Using the strategies discussed in Chapter 7, research your topic area. Your focus should be on the quality of the sources you discover, not on quantity. While your primary goal should be to gather information on your topic, you should also note information related to your colleagues' topics. Jot down sources that may help another group member. If you are researching a relevant Internet source that could benefit another group member, email her or him the URL. Group members who support each other in these and other ways make the process more efficient and, hence, more enjoyable. This usually results in a better product.

Draft an Outline of Your Content Area. After you have concluded your initial research but before you meet again with your group, construct an outline of the ideas and information you've found. This step is important because it forces you to make sense of all the information you have collected, and it will expedite the next step when you will share information with the group.

• Discuss How All the Information Interrelates. You are now ready to meet with your group. Members should summarize briefly what they have discovered through their research. After group members have shared their ideas, they should decide which ideas are most important and how these ideas are related. There should be a natural development of the topic that can be divided among group members.

• Finalize the Group Presentation Format. The speaking order should already be determined. There are, nevertheless, certain procedural details that the group must decide. Will the first speaker introduce all presenters or will each person introduce the next speaker? Where will the participants sit when they are not speaking: facing the audience or in the front row? The more details you decide beforehand, the fewer distractions you will have on the day you speak.

• Plan the Introduction and Conclusion of the Presentation. A presentation should appear to be that of a group and not that of four or five individuals. Consequently, you must work on introducing and concluding the group's comments, and you must incorporate smooth transitions from one speaker's topic to the next. An introduction should state the topic, define important terms, and establish the importance of the subject. A conclusion should summarize what has been presented and end with a strong final statement.

Prepare and Practice Your Speech. By this time, you know the requirements of an excellent speech and have had the opportunity to deliver a few. Most of our earlier suggestions also apply to your speech in your group's presentation. Some differences are worth noting, however. For example, as part of a group presentation, you will need to refer to your colleagues' comments and perhaps even use some of their supporting materials. The group presentation may also impose physical requirements you have not encountered as a classroom speaker, such as speaking to those seated around you in addition to making direct contact with the audience, or speaking from a seated position.

• **Rehearse and Revise the Presentation.** Independent practice of your portion of the presentation is important, but that is only one part

THEORY INTO PRACTICE

 Developing a Presentational Style

A team presentation is more than just a collection of individual speeches on the same topic. By coordinating your group's content and delivery, you will enhance your collective credibility and message impact. Consider the following guidelines to create a polished and proficient team presentation:

1. *Dress appropriately.* All presenters should be well groomed and dressed up, rather than dressed too casually.
2. *Introduce the presentation and team members.* Provide an agenda for your presentation. What will listeners learn and who will present each section? Will one person introduce all team members at the beginning, or will each person introduce the next presenter?
3. *Organize and deliver the team's ideas.* Throughout the presentation, use all those strategies you've learned in this class.
4. *Incorporate smooth transitions from one person to the next.* A seamless presentation requires planning and practice.
5. *Have one person design and produce all presentational aids.* This will ensure that their design and appearance are consistent.
6. *Have one person display all presentational aids except when he or she is speaking.* Assigning one person to handle and project all the aids will help make the presentation flow smoothly and consistently.
7. *Assign someone to keep time and provide other signals to the group.* Use subtle but clear time signals so that team members do not exceed their time limits. This person may also signal when presenters are speaking too softly or too rapidly.
8. *Conclude the main part of your presentation.* Often the person who introduced the presentation also concludes it.
9. *Conduct a question-and-answer session.* If you are allowed a Q–A period, decide who will manage it. Will one person or several answer questions from the audience? Who will recognize those who want to ask questions? Review the guidelines discussed in the TIP box in Chapter 18.
10. *And, of course, practice, practice, practice, both individually and as a group.*

of rehearsal. The group should practice its entire presentation. Group rehearsal will make participants more confident about their individual presentations and will give the group a feeling of cohesion.

Following the procedures we have described should result in a carefully planned, conscientiously researched, adequately supported, and well-delivered group presentation. More than that, however, your presentation should also demonstrate the spontaneity, goodwill, and camaraderie that will likely have developed if members of your group have functioned effectively and productively together.

● SUMMARY

Small Groups Defined

- A *small group* is a collection of three or more people influencing and interacting with one another in pursuit of a common goal.

Types of Groups

- Groups usually fulfill both *socially oriented* and *task-oriented* needs for their participants, though one of these types of needs will predominate depending on the situation. Task-oriented groups include the *study group*, which learns about a topic; the *problem-solving group*, which decides on courses of action; and the *action group*, which implements proposals. Businesses and professions rely increasingly on *work teams*, groups of people who perform all activities needed to produce some product, service, or other goal specified by an outside leader, supervisor, or manager. *Self-directed work teams* perform all the activities of work teams, but also set their own goals and monitor their own progress.

Group Discussion and Decision Making

- To ensure valid decisions, groups must abide by five principles: (1) group decision making is a shared responsibility and requires active participation of all members; (2) group members must share a specific, realistic goal; (3) groups make decisions best under a clear but flexible agenda; (4) groups make the best decisions when members are free to express opinions

openly; and (5) group decision making requires and benefits from the research and information shared by all participants.

- Problem-solving groups speed their progress and simplify their task by following a seven-step process: (1) define the problem, (2) analyze the symptoms and the causes of the problem, (3) determine the criteria that an optimal solution to the problem must satisfy, (4) propose various solutions to the problem, (5) evaluate each possible solution against the established criteria, (6) decide on the best solution, and (7) suggest ways of putting the solution into action. Following these steps in this order will streamline group problem-solving work.

- Responsibilities of group members include the following: (1) sharing information, (2) advocating personal beliefs, (3) questioning other participants, (4) evaluating data and opinions, and (5) supporting other participants in the group.

- Responsibilities of group leaders include the following: (1) planning the group's agenda, (2) orienting the group to the task at hand, (3) providing background information on the problem to be discussed, (4) involving all members in the group's discussion, (5) encouraging a climate of open and honest critical evaluation, (6) seeking clarification of members' ideas and positions, (7) keeping the group focused on its task, (8) introducing new ideas and topics for discussion, (9) summarizing the discussion at various points, and (10) managing interpersonal conflict.

The Group Presentation

- A group presentation may take the form of a *public discussion* before an audience. In this situation, participants speak to one another about aspects of the problem. Another format for a group presentation is the *symposium*, a series of formal individual speeches on different aspects of a problem.

- Group presentations benefit from a logical ten-step approach to developing them: (1) brainstorm the topic with colleagues in the group; (2) do some individual exploratory research; (3) discuss the topic with group members and divide areas of research responsibility by topic or source; (4) research your assigned area individually, noting sources in other group members' areas; (5) organize the data your research yields; (6) discuss with other group members how all the generated information interrelates; (7) determine the presentation format; (8) plan the introduction of group members and the material to be discussed; (9) prepare and practice speeches individually; and (10) rehearse and revise the entire group presentation.

EXERCISES

1. **Practice Critique.** Attend a meeting of a student, faculty, city, or some other decision-making group. Select a group with a limited number of members so that you can observe interactions among the members. Take notes during the meeting and then, using the lists of responsibilities of group members and group leaders on pages 353–357 as a guide, write a brief analysis of the group's interactions. Which responsibilities did the group perform well? Which responsibilities seemed to receive little attention? What could the group do to foster more effective interactions? If the group had a leader, what strengths and weaknesses did you observe in his or her communication behaviors?

2. Interview someone in a leadership position. The person may be a business executive, an officer in an organization, a school principal, a college president, or any other leader. Construct and ask a series of questions designed to discover his or her views on characteristics of effective and ineffective leaders. Record the answers and be prepared to discuss them in class.

3. Using the following topic areas, brainstorm and select a specific problem area. Word it in the form of a problem-solving discussion question.
   a. Addiction and substance abuse
   b. Education
   c. International relations
   d. Political campaigning
   e. Privacy issues

4. Choose four campus problems you think need to be addressed—for example, class registration. Word the topics as problem-solving questions. Analyze each topic, asking the following questions:
   a. How important is the problem?
   b. What information do you need to analyze and solve the problem?
   c. Where would you find this information?
   d. What barriers keep the problem from being solved now?
   e. Which steps in the problem-solving process do you think will generate the most conflict? Why?

   Based on your answers to these questions, select the best topic for a problem-solving discussion. Justify your choice.

5. Write a summary and evaluation of your participation in an assigned group discussion, using the five criteria for effective group participation. Write a critique of other members in your group using these same criteria.

6. Write a critique of your group leader using the ten criteria for effective leadership. If you served as leader, write a self-critique.

Giving and Receiving Criticism

After studying this
appendix, you should be
able to

1 Define criticism.

2 Identify the three elements
   of criticism.

3 Apply the model of
   criticism to explain how
   these elements function.

4 Discuss the value of giving
   and receiving criticism.

5 Incorporate the guidelines
   for critiquing speeches.

6 Use the guidelines for
   acting on criticism.

Appropriate feedback is crucial to your development as a public speaker. What you learn from your instructor and classmates about distractions caused by language, voice, or body will help you polish your speaking skills. You, in turn, want to be an incisive and sensitive critic when you write or speak about others' speeches.

Criticism is information given to others in a way that enables them to use it for self-improvement.[1]

This feedback includes both positive comments that reinforce what a speaker did well and negative comments that point to areas for improvement. If you say, "Your speech was well within the 7-minute time limit," you spotlight a positive aspect of the speech. If you write or say, "I liked your speech," you are also providing speech criticism. This last comment, however, doesn't really teach the speaker anything. There is nothing wrong with saying, "I enjoyed your speech," or "I didn't care for this speech as much as your last one." Just don't stop there. Explain why.

What is the shortest word in the English language that contains the letters a, b, c, d, e, and f? Answer: feedback. Don't forget that feedback is one of the essential elements of good communication.[2]

criticism
Feedback offered for the purpose of improving a speaker's speech.

A Model of Criticism

All criticism contains three parts: *judgments*, *reasons*, and *norms*.[3] Figure A.1 illustrates the relationships between these parts. The most familiar and superficial level of criticism consists of **judgments**. We make them frequently about many different subjects: "I loved the movie *Sweeney Todd*," "Dr. Venkat is an excellent teacher," or "I always enjoy your speeches."

judgments
A critic's opinions about the relative merits of a speech; the most common and superficial level of speech criticism.

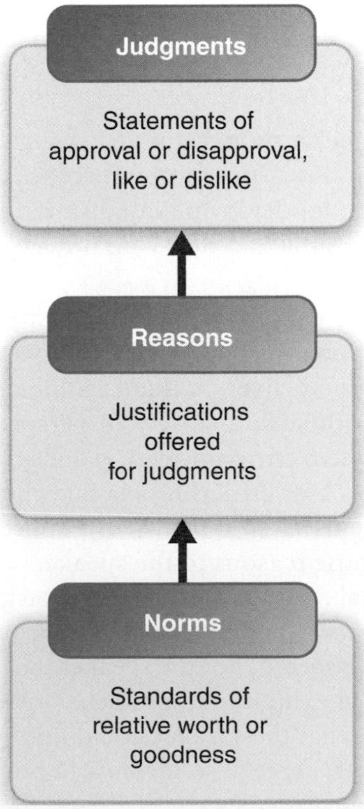

FIGURE A.1
A Model of Criticism

Judgments
Statements of approval or disapproval, like or dislike

Reasons
Justifications offered for judgments

Norms
Standards of relative worth or goodness

reasons
Statements that justify a critic's judgments.

norms
The values a critic believes necessary to make any speech good, effective, or desirable.

Underlying those judgments, whether we voice them or not, are **reasons**: "*Sweeney Todd* had a great cast and I really liked the music, but I thought the film was way too bloody," "Dr. Venkat is an excellent teacher because her lectures make a course I dreaded lively and interesting," or "I always enjoy your speeches because you choose such unusual topics." Statements such as these specify reasons for the critics' judgments.

The statements in the preceding paragraph are instructive and useful because they help others infer your **norms**—the values you believe make something good or effective or desirable. Such statements tell us that the critics dislike graphic violence in movies, appreciate liveliness in class lectures, and like unusual topics in public speeches. We may, of course, argue with the critics about whether these norms are valid. That's healthy and productive. As speech critics we must provide reasons for our judgments; only by doing so do we tell the speaker the basis of our reactions.

Here are some examples of helpful comments made by students about their classmates' speeches:

Karen, your concern for children certainly shows in this speech on rating day care centers. Your personal examples really helped make the speech interesting.

John, your speech on how to improve study habits was the best I heard. It was appropriate and beneficial to everyone in the class. Your language was simple and coherent. You explained just what we needed to know in the time you had.

Lettie, one problem I saw was your use of visual aids. Once you have finished with the visual aid, you should put it away rather than leave it where the audience can see it. That way, the audience will focus their attention on you rather than on the object.

One value of receiving well-written or thoughtful oral comments about your speeches is that repetition of a criticism will reinforce it. If one person tells you that you need to speak louder, you may dismiss the advice. If twelve people say that they had trouble hearing you, however, you are more likely to pay attention.

A second value of receiving criticism from many people, especially people from various cultures, is that different people value different aspects of a speech. Some may put a premium on delivery, others on speech content, and still others on organization. With such a variety of perspectives and values, it would be a shame if all their criticism were reduced to "Good job!" or "I liked it." To provide the best criticism you can, remember to specify the reasons for your judgments; ask yourself why a speech affects you and then try to communicate those reasons to the speaker.

We should also make a final note about the spirit in which you give speech criticism in this class. You should never make criticisms that are designed to belittle or hurt the speaker. Target the speech, not the speaker. Focus on specific behaviors rather than the person exhibiting those behaviors. You will probably never hear a speech so fine that the speaker could not make some improvement, and you will never hear a speech so inept or ill prepared that it does not have some redeeming value. *Listen evaluatively* and then *respond empathetically*, putting yourself in the speaker's place, and you should make truly helpful comments about your classmates' speeches.

Critiquing Speeches

To help you become a better critic, we offer ten suggestions you can use as you evaluate speeches. Remember, though, that to *critique* effectively you must first *listen* effectively. Use the eight guidelines we offer in Chapter 4 (see pages 63–68) to help you understand and remember more of what you hear.

One of our students, Susan, delivered an informative speech on three major tenets of the Amish faith. We asked some students to critique Susan's speech, and we have used their comments to illustrate our suggestions.

Begin with a Positive Statement

Do you remember being told, "If you can't say something nice, don't say anything at all"? Well, that's good advice to follow when you critique your classmates' speeches. Public speaking is a personal experience. You stand in front of an audience expressing *your* thoughts in *your* words with *your* voice and *your* body. When you affirm the positive, you establish a healthy climate for constructive criticism. Demonstrate to speakers that what they said or how they said it was worthy. Fortunately, you can always find something helpful to say if you think about it. Be positive—and sincere!

Two of our students began their critiques of Susan's speech with these opening statements:

> I found your speech on the Amish to be very interesting; their beliefs are fascinating. They seem very simple but very committed to their group—what a unique way of living.
>
> I have lived near the Amish in Pennsylvania. Your speech explained the reasons for their behavior. You clearly explained why they do what they do.

Notice that while both critics compliment the speaker, the second critic also demonstrates her involvement in the topic.

Target a Few Key Areas for Improvement

Imagine how you would react if you were told, "There are seventeen areas you need to work on for your next speech." You'd probably feel overwhelmed: *How can I possibly do all that in time for my next speech? Which of the seventeen suggestions should I focus on first?* Susan's critics focused on the most important strengths and weaknesses of her speech. In so doing, they provided her with manageable goals for her next speech. After accomplishing them, she could begin to improve other aspects of future speeches.

Organize Your Comments

A critique, just like a speech, is easier to follow if it is well organized. You can select from several options to frame your comments, and you should select the one that is most appropriate to you, the speaker, and the speech.

For example, you can organize your comments topically into the categories of speech *content*, *organization*, and *delivery*. A second option is chronological; you can discuss the speech's *introduction*, *body*, and *conclusion*. A third option is to divide your comments into speaking *strengths* and *weaknesses* (remember, give positive comments first). You could even combine these options. You could discuss the speaker's introduction, body, and conclusion and within each category discuss first the strengths and then the weaknesses.

Be Specific

Suppose, instead of this list of ten suggestions for offering criticism, we simply said, "When you critique your classmates' speeches, be as helpful as possible so that they can improve their speaking." Although that is good advice, it's not very helpful, is it? By being more specific, we hope to provide you with tools to improve your critiquing skills. Similarly, you will help speakers if you provide them with specific suggestions for improvement.

For speakers to become more proficient, they need to know *what* and *how* to improve. One student told Susan, "I liked the way you presented the speech as a whole." That statement provides a nice pat on the back, but it doesn't give Susan much direction. The qualifying phrase "as a whole" seems to suggest that the listener noticed small problems that were minimized by the generally positive effect of Susan's speech. What were those problems, and what could Susan have done to minimize them? Remember to provide reasons for your judgments. In the two statements below, the listeners' comments are specific.

> I was really impressed with the fact that you did not use your notecards while you delivered the introduction or the conclusion. That suggests that you were confident and well prepared.
>
> Susan, you used good transitional phrases or words to move from subtopic to subtopic within each main point. An example of this was when you said, "Not only do the Amish have simple ways of dressing, but they also provide very simple toys for their children."

Be Honest but Tactful

> Do not remove a fly from you friend's forehead with a hatchet.
>
> Chinese proverb

Providing suggestions for improvement tests your interpersonal skills. At times you may be reluctant to offer criticism because you think it may offend the speaker. If you are not honest, however, the speaker may not know that the topic was dull, the content superficial, and the delivery uninspiring. Still, you must respect the speaker's feelings. The statement "Your speech was dull, superficial, and uninspiring" may be honest, but it is hardly tactful. It may provoke resistance to your suggestions or damage the speaker's self-esteem.

One student thought Susan's speech content and organization were excellent but that her delivery was mechanical and lifeless. The student could have said, "Your delivery lacked excitement." Instead, she wrote, "The only problem I saw with your speech was a lack of enthusiasm. Maybe the speech was too rehearsed. It sounded kind of like a newscast. I think it needed some humor to break the monotony."

Personalize Your Comments

The more interest and involvement your critique conveys, the more likely the speaker is to believe in and act on your advice. You can personalize your comments in three ways. First, use the speaker's name occasionally, as in "Susan, your hand gestures would be more effective if you used them less. I found myself being distracted by them."

A second way of reducing a speaker's defensiveness and establishing speaker-critic rapport is by using I-statements in place of you-statements. Explain how the speech affected you. Instead of saying, "Your organization was weak," say, "I had trouble following your key ideas," and then give some examples of places where you got lost. The following is an example of what one of our students could have said and what she actually did say in her critique of Susan's speech:

> *She could have said:* "You lost my attention during the first part of your speech because you spoke so fast that I couldn't keep up with you."
> *Instead, she said:* "I had difficulty following your words at first because your rate seemed fast to me. After you settled down into the speech, though, I could listen with more attention."

A third way of personalizing your comments is by stating how you have benefited from hearing the speech. The following statement from a student critique let Susan know that her use of visual aids to illustrate Amish artifacts was interesting and helpful:

> Your speech . . . especially caught my attention when you showed the toys, the quilt, and the artwork. And putting the visual aids down after explaining them helped in keeping me interested in the next area.

Reinforce the Positive

Sometimes we want so much to help someone improve that we focus on what the speaker did wrong and forget to mention what the speaker did well. As you enumerate how speakers can improve, don't forget the things they did well and should continue doing. One student, impressed with Susan's language and vocal delivery, made the following comment:

> Susan, your delivery was excellent. You used your voice to emotionally color your message. I really felt as if I was living in the pictures that your descriptions created.

Problem-Solve the Negative

If you are serious about wanting to improve your speaking, you will want to recognize the weaknesses of your speech. Only then can you improve. As a critic, you have a responsibility to help others become better speakers. Don't be afraid to let them know what went wrong with a speech.

As a rule, though, do not criticize behaviors that the speaker cannot correct. On the day she spoke, Susan was suffering an allergic reaction. As a result of antihistamines she was taking, her throat was dry. Even if this had detracted significantly from her message, it would have been inappropriate for a student to comment, "I had trouble listening to what you said because your mouth seemed dry. Avoid that in your next speech." Such a request may be beyond the speaker's control. On the other hand, it would be useful to suggest that Susan take a drink of water immediately before speaking.

You will help speakers improve their speaking if you follow two steps in your criticism. First, point out a specific problem and, second, suggest ways to correct it.

One student was impressed with Susan's visual aids but offered her the following advice about one of them:

> You said that the Amish don't like to have their pictures taken, and yet you used a picture of an Amish man as a visual aid. Next time, if you'd explain how or where you got the picture, it wouldn't leave picky people like me wondering during the rest of your speech how you got that picture.

Provide the Speaker with a Plan of Action

When you give your comments, include a plan of action for the speaker. What should the speaker concentrate on when presenting the next speech? One student focused Susan's attention on her next speaking experience by suggesting the following action plan:

> Susan, your overall speech and style of presentation were very good. However, I detected two minor things that could be improved. First, except when you were moving toward or away from a visual aid, you remained in one place. I believe that taking a few steps when you begin a subtopic would emphasize your transitions and enhance your message. Second, take more time to demonstrate and talk about the boy's toy that you showed us. You said, "It has marbles and fun moving parts," but I didn't really get a chance to see how it operates. Your organization, your vocal emphasis and inflection, your eye contact, and your knowledge of the topic were all terrific. You're an effective speaker, and if you use these suggestions for your next speech, you will be even more effective.

End with a Positive Statement

Conclude your critique on a positive note. Remind speakers that both you and they benefited from this experience. One of the highest compliments you can give a speaker is that you learned something from the speech. Two of our students concluded their critiques of Susan's speech as follows:

> Great job, Susan! You were very specific and enthusiastic about your subject, and your visual aids reinforced what was already thorough.
>
> Susan, you did an outstanding job. Your speech was well organized and very informative. You showed some signs of nervousness, but more practice will alleviate most of them. Whenever and wherever you will be speaking next, I'd like to be there.

To see how one student applied these ten guidelines, read the "Theory Into Practice" feature.

KEY POINTS

Guidelines for Critiquing Speeches

1. Begin with a positive statement.
2. Target a few key areas for improvement.
3. Organize your comments.
4. Be specific.
5. Be honest but tactful.
6. Personalize your comments.
7. Reinforce the positive.
8. Problem-solve the negative.
9. Provide the speaker with a plan of action.
10. End with a positive statement.

Acting on Criticism

Most of us dislike receiving criticism, yet such feedback is important to our success as public speakers. If you want to communicate more effectively, you must seek feedback from your listeners. Ethical speakers respect their audiences. Consideration for the audience means, in part, trusting their opinions and advice. If you respect your listeners, you will value their questions and advice about your speech. The following suggestions will enable you to get the most out of this process.

Focus on *What* Your Critics Say, Not *How* They Say It

Listen to the content of the feedback, not the way it is presented. Too often, we become defensive when someone critiques us. Remember that offering criticism is not easy, and your critic may not have mastered the suggestions we've presented in the previous section. Avoid reacting emotionally to feedback, even if it is poorly worded and insensitive. Instead, focus on the content of the suggestions you receive.

Seek Clear and Specific Feedback

To improve your speaking, you must be aware of specific areas for improvement. Suppose a critic says, "Your organization could be improved." That may be an honest and valid statement, but it isn't very helpful. Ask the critic to be more specific. Is the problem with the introduction, body, or conclusion? What specific strategies could you use to improve your organization? It may take some good interpersonal communication to elicit the feedback you need to become a better public speaker.

Sometimes you may receive conflicting feedback. Don't dismiss criticisms simply because they seem contradictory. For example, one critic may comment that your eye contact was good, another that it was poor. Both may be right. Perhaps you spoke only to those in the center of the room; they may have liked your eye contact, while others felt excluded. Or a critic's reaction may have been based on cultural norms; some cultures value eye contact more than others. It's important to learn the reasons behind a critic's judgment before you can improve your public speaking.

Evaluate the Feedback You Receive

It's not enough just to receive and understand feedback. You must use your critical thinking skills to analyze and evaluate that feedback. Repetition is one standard of judgment. If only one classmate thought your attention-getting step was weak, don't be too concerned. However, if your instructor and the majority of your classmates thought it deficient, you should target that as an area for improvement.

THEORY INTO PRACTICE

Critiquing a Classmate

Melissa Janoske delivered her informative speech "Renaissance Fairs: The New Vaudeville" (see pages 276–277) in her public speaking class. We asked Donika Patel, a classmate of Melissa's, to write a critique of the speech. As you read Donika's critique, notice how she used the guidelines discussed in this appendix. Though most of the feedback you offer speakers may be less formal, more brief, or perhaps given orally rather than in writing, you should still use many of these critiquing strategies as you help others build their speaking competence and confidence.

Critique

Donika begins her critique by complimenting Melissa, establishing a supportive listener-speaker relationship.

Melissa, I'm always impressed with your choice of topics. They're both interesting and informative. You definitely understand that public speaking is an audience-centered activity, and you actively involved all of us with the Renaissance culture throughout the introduction, body, and conclusion of your speech.

Introduction of Speech

She organizes her comments chronologically.

Your introduction fulfilled the guidelines that we've studied in class. You captured my attention from the start with vivid narration. You painted a picture of a Renaissance scene and took us on a walk through the village. The use of the word *you*, combined with effective eye contact, helped me imagine that I was actually in the sword fight. For example, you described how I won the fight with my sword, pinning my opponent to the ground.

Donika offers specific examples to show how the speech engaged her.

After getting my attention, you introduced the topic of your speech, established the importance of people's interest in re-creating medieval England, and then previewed the key ideas you would discuss in the body of the speech. When you finished your introduction, I was ready to learn how I could participate in a Renaissance fair.

Body of Speech

The body of your speech was very well organized and easy to understand. Organizing your speech chronologically was appropriate because it told us step by step how we could get involved in a Renaissance fair. You used the 4 S's to present your three key ideas. You signposted and stated your key ideas, using action verbs to tell us each step of the process. Melissa, I was impressed with your transitions and how they incorporated the theme of Renaissance culture. I really liked the image of "a potion from the apothecary" as you moved from your first to your second key idea.

Notice how she reinforces what Melissa did well.

Not only was your speech well organized, it was also well supported. You supported your ideas with examples, statistics, and testimony. When quoting experts,

Develop a Plan of Action

After receiving feedback, summarize and record those comments. Then rank those areas needing improvement according to their importance. Rather than tackling every criticism, select a few to work on for your next you told us who they were, and you gave us the URLs of a couple of interesting websites. Though you had good information, I would like to have heard more. I was curious which university represents our kingdom in Virginia. I would also have enjoyed more descriptions of activities that women, as well as men, can participate in at Renaissance fairs. Maybe some pictures showing women and men in traditional costumes would make your speech content more vivid.

Melissa, in the introduction you had really enthusiastic vocal delivery and you used great hand gestures to describe the fight scene. You delivered that part of the speech without relying on your notes. I'd like to see that same delivery in the body of your speech. I noticed that you often glanced down at your notes, which sometimes disrupted the flow of the speech. Perhaps you had too many words in your notes. Limiting your notes to key ideas and supporting material, such as references, direct quotes, and statistics, might improve your eye contact. You also spoke a little quickly as you presented your key ideas. Try to include more and longer pauses to give the audience more time to understand each key point. Overall, I thought you had good poise and facial expressions that complemented what you were saying throughout your speech.

> Even when Donika discusses areas for improvement, she does so tactfully and offers some specific suggestions.

> Again, Donika helps Melissa problem-solve ways to relate to her listeners.

Conclusion of Speech

Your summary clearly reviewed the key points you discussed in the body of your speech. Remember that an important element of a conclusion is to activate audience response. What can we do next to get involved in Renaissance culture? Maybe you could give us the dates and locations of some upcoming fairs in our area, for example. I liked the way you used Mike the Truck Driver to connect your conclusion back to your introduction.

> Throughout her critique, Donika targets a few key areas for improvement.

Melissa, for your next speech, I suggest adding some more content in the body, working on the conclusion to activate audience response, and practicing your delivery a little more to help slow your pace and to improve your eye contact. With greater attention to these areas, your future speeches will be even better!

> Here, she offers a plan of action for Melissa's next speech.

As always, your topic was interesting, your speech was well organized, and your delivery was enthusiastic. Melissa, I learned a lot and look forward to hearing your next speech. Good job!

> Donika concludes her critique with a positive statement.

Donika K. Patel
Radford University

speech. Write a plan of action that states your goals and the strategies you will use to achieve them.

Remember that your goal as you move from one speech to the next is not consistency but consistent improvement. So, rather than defending what you said or did in your speech, listen carefully and act on those

KEY POINTS

Guidelines for Acting on Criticism

1. Focus on *what* your critics say, not *how* they say it.
2. Seek clear and specific feedback.
3. Evaluate the feedback you receive.
4. Develop a plan of action.

suggestions for improvement that you receive most frequently. If you have doubts about the validity of suggestions your classmates are making, discuss the matter with your instructor. You will make the most accelerated improvement if you graciously accept the compliments of your peers and your instructor and then work quickly to eliminate problems that they bring to your attention.

Speech criticism is further recognition of a commitment between speaker and listener. The ultimate aim of speech criticism is to make a particular speech more enjoyable or instructive for an audience. Speech criticism should amplify and clarify the terms of the contract that any individual speaker will enter with all her or his future audiences.

SUMMARY

A Model of Criticism

- *Criticism*—feedback offered for the purpose of improving a speaker's speech—consists of *judgments*, *reasons*, and *norms*.

Critiquing Speeches

- To be helpful, criticism must be balanced between positive and negative aspects of the speech, but it should begin and end with positive comments. Criticism should target a few key areas for improvement, be well organized, be specific, be honest but tactful, be personalized, and reinforce positive aspects of the

speech. In addition, criticism should problemsolve the negative and provide the speaker with a plan of action for future speeches.

Acting on Criticism

- As a speaker, focus on *what* your critics say rather than on *how* they say it. Seek clear, specific feedback. Evaluate that feedback and target a few areas for improvement. Develop a plan of action that sets goals for your target areas and states the strategies you will use to make those improvements.

EXERCISE

1. **Practice Critique.** Select a speech you've presented in this class. Using the guidelines discussed in this chapter, write a self-critique of your vocal and physical delivery, or other aspects your instructor identifies. Specifically, focus on your speaking rate, vocal variety, eye contact, gestures, and movement. Be sure to mention your strengths and areas for improvement. Finally, write a plan of action for your next speaking assignment.

Sample Speeches

The Problem with Food Aid[1]

Chiwoneso Beverley Tinago, William Carey University

Chiwoneso placed second at the 2009 Interstate Oratorical Association contest. Notice how she reveals her personal commitment and connection to the topic near the end of her persuasive speech.

1   Muna is an eight-year-old girl from Mulonda, Zambia. Every morning she walks to a food distribution point set up by the World Food Program at a nearby hospital. She holds tightly to her battered tin cup as she waits in line for hours to receive the mixture of corn and soy powder, but the stocks are running low and like every other day, she walks home empty-handed.

2   Muna's reality is that she is an AIDS orphan who struggles to stay alive, but she will not die from AIDS; more than likely she will die of hunger. This story is becoming all too common and was taken from the *New York Times* of January 17, 2009. The latest estimates from the UN Food and Agriculture Organization (FAO) show that another 40 million people were pushed into hunger in 2008 as a result of higher food prices. The FAO warned that the ongoing economic crisis could tip even more people into hunger and poverty.

3   Since the late 1960s, wealthy countries have been obligated by the Food Aid Convention to feed the hungry. However, a major part of the problem that the hungry face today is the nature of the food aid itself. This is not a new issue, but as the world's remaining arable farmland comes under increasing pressure from climate change and the development of biofuels, it is an issue that policy makers, humanitarian workers, and politicians need to resolve if widespread world hunger is ever to be alleviated.

4   Today, we will reveal the current problems inherent in the global food aid policy, then examine some of the causes before finally providing some workable and desperately needed solutions.

5   In August 2007, one of the biggest and well-known American charity organizations, CARE, announced that it was turning down $45 million a year in food from the United States government. According to the USAID [United States Agency for International Development] website updated daily, the U.S. provides nearly 60 percent of the world's food aid—that's nearly double the amount provided by European countries combined. Until this day, CARE claims that the way U.S. aid is structured causes, rather than reduces, hunger in the countries where it is received. Let's assess their claims by revealing the current problems in the food aid policy. These problems are threefold: ineffective use of aid money, monetization, and undercutting of local economies.

6   First. Transporting thousands of tons of food from the Unites States is a costly and timely process. The *Bloomberg News* of December 8, 2008, told the story of how a bag of corn stamped "US Aid from the American people" took more than 6 months to reach Ethiopian native Haylar Ayako. The corn had traveled more than 12,000 miles by rail, ship, and truck. Warehouse-stays punctuated each leg of the journey until the corn finally arrived in the village of Shala-Luka. But by that time Haylar had buried seven of his grandchildren. According to the *World Politics Review* of December 19, 2008, transporting the food drains needed funds from the actual provision of food aid. By the time all the costs are figured in, it's like every dollar worth of food ends up costing three dollars to get [the food] to the people who need it.

7 Second. Most of us view food aid as simply free food given to needy people. This is not entirely true. The *Seattle Times* of November 11, 2008, states that some food that is transported falls into the hands of aid agencies who in turn sell the grain to local communities and use the revenue to finance their development programs. This means that a large portion—even a majority—of food donated as project food aid is not used as food at all but is converted to cash. This is known as monetization. More than likely, food ends up going to those who can afford it instead of whose who desperately need it.

8 Third. The introduction of imported food in certain regions removes farmers' incentives to produce. According to the WTO [World Trade Organization] website updated daily, the grain that the agencies are selling is undercutting local farming since the aid grain is cheaper than the local grain. This puts local farmers out of business and deeper into poverty and, in the long run, becomes part of a process by which those countries lose the means to develop.

9 Now, the U.S. does not stand alone in the food aid problem. Countries like Canada and South Korea also sell food aid; however, more attention has been placed on the U.S. because it has a larger sphere of influence since it provides the most food aid. So with that in mind, having outlined the problem, let us move on and examine some of the causes. These problems are twofold: current U.S. legislation and lack of regulation.

10 First. According to the aforementioned *Seattle Times* article, U.S. legislation requires that 75 percent of all food aid shipments be sent aboard U.S.–flagged carriers. The U.S. also buys grain used for food aid from U.S. farms. But these are far from being family farms. A U.S. Government Accountability Office study released last year in April noted that just 18 U.S. companies were deemed eligible to bid for food aid contracts, with two of the country's largest agribusinesses, Cargill and Kalama Export Company, earning $28 million in food aid contracts in March and April 2008 alone.

11 Second. Another cause is lack of regulation. The Food Aid Convention is the main international agreement governing food aid. According to the WFP website updated daily, the convention has no mechanism for determining food aid effectiveness or for evaluating performance of individual donors. Moreover, it operates with little transparency, providing remarkably little public information on its deliberations. Thus, this lack of effectiveness and transparency allows for practices like monetization to take place.

12 By no means are we denying the positive accomplishments of food aid programs, but it is obvious that the current policy on food aid is both self-interested and politicized; thus, action needs to be taken on the international, governmental, and personal levels. First and most important, donor countries need to negotiate a new global food aid compact to replace the languishing Food Aid Convention. The new agreement would strengthen effectiveness and accountability by officially doing away with monetization of food aid and requiring that donors purchase food aid locally or closer to the needy region whenever possible. Programs like Purchase for Progress, which was formed by the World Food Program and the Bill and Melinda Gates Foundation in September 2008, now buy 70 percent of all their food aid in developing countries like Malawi and India. This allows countries to develop their own agriculture economies and allows food to move more quickly and cost-effectively to the people who need it most.

13 Second. Change is needed in the current U.S. food aid legislation. In January 2008, American growers, processors, and transporters fought off a proposal before

Congress that would speed deliveries of food aid by buying at least 25 percent more food closer to needy regions. This proposal must be reconsidered under the new Obama administration, and it is essential to point out that the proposal does not ask for more money, but rather, asks that the 2 billion dollars that is currently available for food aid be utilized wisely in order to feed the most people.

14 Finally, on a more personal level, if you donate money to any aid organizations, be more aware of how your money is being used. I recently started an initiative on campus called students turning hunger into hope, which encourages the other 44 organizations on campus to use the 2008–2009 school year as a food aid platform by supporting organizations that use cost-effective food aid programs. At the end of my speech, I will be handing out a card with a list of some of these organizations. Now if you are unable to donate money, then I encourage you to visit *www.thehungersite.com.* Click on the orange Give box on the main page, and the site sponsors led by Mercy Corps International will pay for cups of food to be given to children at numerous schools in developing countries at no cost to you. Last year the site fed over 72 million children.

15 Today, we have revealed the current problems inherent in the global food policy, then examined some of the causes before finally providing some solutions. The plight of the hungry is sometimes difficult to fathom. I have been a recipient of food aid after my country suffered a severe drought in the 90s, but unlike Muna, Haylar, and the other 25,000 people who die from hunger every day, the food arrived just in time. When President John F. Kennedy named the Food for Peace program in 1961, he said, "Food is strength, and food is freedom, and food is a helping to people around the world whose good will and friendship we want." That may be true, but it would be imprudent of us to forget that food is food. As governments and aid agencies worry about losing money if an overhaul of the global food aid policy is achieved, it is essential to remember now more than ever that losing once had a kinder, nobler name—giving.

Flash Mobs[2]

Jennell Chu, San Antonio College

Jennell Chu delivered the following classroom speech in the spring of 2011. Notice her simple structure and her use of examples that would be familiar to many of her listeners.

1 On June 3, 2003, over 100 people gathered in New York City's Macy's department store, on the ninth floor, around an expensive rug. When asked what they were doing, they would each respond that they all lived together on the outskirts of town and were buying a rug. Then they just left. Later that day about 200 people gathered in the lobby of the Grand Hyatt New York and clapped for 15 seconds. Then, once again, they just dispersed.

2 According to Kenneth Baldauf, who studied these and other such occasions for his ebook *Emerge with Computer Concepts*, these are part of a growing trend called flash mobs, which is what I will be talking about today.

3 According to Baldauf, a flash mob is a group of people who assemble suddenly in a public place, do something unusual, and then disperse in order to gain attention or to create confusion and sometimes amusement. Now I've actually participated in a few flash mobs myself and they have always been a lot of

fun without any ill intent behind them. And as flash mobs are a trend that you're seeing more and more today, it is good to know common types of flash mobs and why these occasions are becoming so common.

4   Now, first I will be speaking about the common types of flash mobs. Dance flash mobs are one of the most common types of flash mobs that you will see. And what happens in them is that a group of people get together and learn how to do choreography to set to music. And a lot of the times these are done as tributes to the artists themselves, such as the group Flash Amsterdam who does Michael Jackson tributes. So they would go out and do things to his classic songs such as "Beat It" and "Billie Jean" and so many others.

5   Now freeze flash mobs are another type of common flash mob. These began when the group Improv Everywhere started, filmed at the Grand Central Station in New York. You can read more about this at their website, www .improveverywhere.com underneath "Frozen Grand Central." What they did is a group of people just went to the station and then they just froze. It didn't matter if they were talking, whether they were taking a picture, or even one man I remember dropped his notes on the floor and was starting to pick them up. They just froze and did not move for a certain amount of time. Then, afterwards, by some certain signal, they just once again started going on with their daily lives. Now according to Baldauf the largest freeze flash mob ever done was in Paris, where over 3,000 people participated.

6   And another type of common flash mob that you've seen doesn't have a set method, such as dance and freeze flash mobs but it's more general, that you can come up with for yourself. These flash mobs are done in support or opposition to a certain idea. The World News Network picked up on a flash mob done by a group, United Way, in Washington Station. What this group did is they went into the station and then they just began undressing. And when they undressed, you could see across their T-shirts a slogan that said, "Live United." This was to show support of how all people in the world should live together in harmony, without any prejudice. So whether it's a dance flash mob, a freeze flash mob, or a flash mob to show your support or opposition against something, these are just some of the common types that you will see today.

7   Now the second thing I will be speaking about is why flash mobs are becoming so common in today's society. The Internet is a big reason why flash mobs are so common nowadays. Thanks to the Internet we have social networking sites such as Facebook, Twitter, MySpace, and so many others that it is just so easy for a large group of people to come together for one purpose. And of course there's also YouTube. With YouTube, if you search the words "flash mob," you can come up with thousands of videos that you just spend hours watching because it's very entertaining to watch. And once on to these videos, people watch them, think they're fun, then they eventually want to be part of one or they want to start their own. And that, of course, just helps spread the trend all over the world.

8   Cell phones are another big reason why flash mobs are so common. Nowadays cell phones are basically mini-computers. Everywhere you go, you have the Internet, so once again you have those social networking sites. Then you also have your instant access to your email, and there's also text messaging. So now it's just so easy to get the news spread out to everyone. And you can even make one up as soon as [you] get the idea because you can just send it out to everyone in your phone book, and they can send it out to more people and more people. And you can just have a huge group.

9 And, of course, flash mobs are themselves just becoming more mainstream these days. There are businesses around the world who are using flash mobs as a way of advertising. And then, of course, there are television shows which are becoming more used to the idea of flash mobs and are incorporating them in themselves. Erica Futterman even stated in the *Rolling Stone*'s February 9th edition that the popular show "Glee" used a flash mob in order for one of the show's characters to attempt to get a date on the Valentine's episode. So as you can see, the Internet, cell phones, and just by flash mobs becoming more mainstream is a reason why these occurrences are becoming so much more common in today's society.

10 So by now you should know some of the common types of flash mobs and why they are becoming so common. And, like I said, flash mobs can be anything from—they can be complex like a dance flash mob, where you have hundreds of people learning choreography. Or you can just get people to start a pillow fight in a random street. Or, if you're like me, you'll wind up downtown with a group of girls and start singing the "Sailor Moon" theme song. But any way you start, while each individual flash mob will appear and then quickly disappear, the trend of flash mobs themselves doesn't appear to be disappearing quite as quickly.

Steganography: Hidden Messages[3]

Julian Petrin Fray, San Antonio College

Julian found her informative speech topic during the flurry of Internet communication about national security following the tragedy of 9/11. She heightened listener interest in this novel topic by showing its ancient origins. Julian won first place in informative speaking at the Texas Community College Speech and Theater Association state tournament in the spring of 2002.

1 In the movie *Along Came a Spider*, students of influential Washington politicians attend an elite, private school. The classrooms in this school don't look like what you might see in an ordinary public school. Here, students are assigned their own computers, all of which are networked together. As the instructor proceeds through his lesson, the students are prompted to follow along on their own screens. The use of this kind of technology may suggest a wisdom beyond their years, but these students are still very much like other fourth graders. When the character Megan Rose wants to pass a note in class, she doesn't resort to the conventional folded-up piece of paper. Instead, she uses her computer to send an innocent-looking picture of a tiger to her friend, Dimitri. Dimitri then takes the picture and applies a simple program, thereby revealing a hidden message.

2 These students are using the very complex technology of steganography to accomplish a very simple goal. Steganography has existed throughout history, but just recently it has been given new attention. In fact, this old technique has been given new applications due to today's technology. This new use allows messages to pass, undetected, through many different media, including video, email, and digital photographs. This means that every image you view on your computer has the potential to contain a hidden message. This message can come in many different formats, including as a virus that can interfere with the files on your hard drive.

3 So today, we'll first discuss what steganography is and how it came into existence. Second, we will see exactly how steganography works. Finally, we'll look at its current uses and possible future applications.

4 First, then, what is steganography? As defined by Richard Lewis, of the System Administration, Networking, and Security Institute, steganography literally means "covered writing" and is the art of concealing the very existence of a message. The purpose of steganography is to hide a message within another form of communication in such a way that prevents an observer from learning that anything unusual is taking place.

5 Steganography has a long and rich history in warfare. One of the first recorded instances of its use is written in the *Histories* of Herodotus. In ancient Greece, messages were conveyed using wax tablets. In one story, Demeratus wanted to notify his hometown of Sparta that Xerxes was intending to invade the Peloponnesus. To ensure that the message would not be intercepted, he scraped the wax off of the tablets and wrote his message on the underlying wood. He recovered the tablets with wax so that they appeared to be blank. In this form, they could pass undetected back to Sparta. Once in Sparta, the wax was melted off, revealing the hidden message.

6 Another method of steganography is to use invisible inks. According to Declan McCullagh, in the February 2, 2001, edition of *Wired News*, these inks were used as recently as World War II. A covert message could be written between the lines of a seemingly innocuous letter. The most common inks used were milk, vinegar, fruit juices, and even urine. These liquids would darken when heated, thereby revealing the hidden messages. Later, with the use of other chemicals, the invisible ink became even harder to detect.

7 Just as Demeratus hid his message, we can now hide a message in an electronic format so that it's almost undetectable. The wax tablet has given way to the electronic file, but the goal remains the same: to obscure the message to all but the intended viewer. So, second, let's take a closer look at how steganography works.

8 In his article on steganography at the Johnson and Johnson Technology Consultants website, www.jjtc.com, last accessed on September 16, 2001, Neil F. Johnson, a professor at George Mason University, explains how these messages are embedded. In every computer file, there is a large amount of "empty" space, or space that is not integral to the file. These "low-order" bits can be changed slightly without alerting the human senses. Steganography takes advantage of this by embedding the digital message in these bits. You see, in a computer, an image is simply an array of numbers that represents light intensities at various points called pixels. Each pixel can contain up to three bytes of information, but most images do not require that amount of memory. So the steganographic program can simply utilize the "extra" bytes in those pixels. This creates a slight degradation in the quality of the photograph. Look at this picture of a chapel [showing Photograph 1]. Now, take a look at this picture [showing Photograph 2]. While they initially appear to be identical, you might notice the slight degradation in the second photograph. The reason for this is that Photograph 2 actually contains an aerial view of the Pentagon, encoded using steganography [showing Photograph 3]. The degradation, noted previously, is somewhat helpful in detecting a hidden message, but it's not a very effective tool. The degradation is so slight that most people won't even notice it, even when compared side by side with the original.

9 After hiding, then sending the message, the next step is to extract it. This is the easiest step because it's done by the computer. According to Dr. Johnson, using a steganalysis program, your computer can pull out the message and display it. Each day, many of us receive emails from various friends, family, and co-workers. Many of these contain jokes or images. These images are perfect

vessels for steganographic messages. Much like the U.S. postal workers were unwitting couriers of the anthrax virus, you too might just be propagating covert information without your knowledge.

10 Now that we understand how steganography works, let's look, finally, at some of its applications. One of the most unsettling aspects about this technology is its very nature: the sending and receiving of covert messages. Consider this example, given by Robert Vamosi, in the June 27, 2001, edition of the *ZDNet News:* You work for the National Security Agency monitoring terrorist activities. In the past week, you have recorded a large increase in the number of encrypted emails being sent. This may tip you off to a forthcoming event, or terrorist activity. At the very least, your suspicions will be aroused and cause you to take a closer look at those emails. Then consider that, instead of being able to monitor obviously encrypted emails, you had to monitor the subtle patterns of every single image on the Internet. This is the exact reason terrorists, including the infamous Osama bin Laden, use steganography to communicate. Because these embedded images can be posted to free websites, terrorists can convey their messages around the world without ever tipping off major security officials. Jack Kelley, in his June 6, 2001, article in *USA Today*, states that steganography has become so fundamental to the operations of these groups that bin Laden and other Muslim extremists are teaching it at their camps in Afghanistan and the Sudan.

11 On a more local level, steganography can be a very important tool for businesses. For example, let's say you work in New York City for a large software firm. You've just written a breakthrough program that has immense possibilities. The source code for this program needs to be sent to the parent company, located in California, but you're afraid that it may be intercepted. Prior to copyrighting the program, the only thing that keeps your program from being used by another developer is that they don't have access to your source code. Keeping this source code protected is very important and shouldn't be trusted to a simple encrypted email. So, you can embed the source code using steganography and send the email without worrying about its interception.

12 For the future, we can expect to see an increase in this type of communication. The technologies allowing messages to be hidden will increase in sophistication to reduce the amount of degradation, thereby making it even more difficult to detect these messages.

13 Today we have explored a new technology that can change the way we communicate. We have examined what steganography is and how it works. We have also explored current and future applications for this technology.

14 Current steganography is a new and exciting twist on an old form of communication. The uses I have shown you today are but a small portion of the possibilities for this technology. From terrorists to CEOs, this technology has a wide range of applications. So next time you open an email and see a picture of a family member or a familiar scene, you might think about what may be in the image that you're just not seeing.

How Old Is He Anyway? Aging the Whitetail Buck[4]

Darla Goodrich, San Antonio College

Whitetail deer are common in the Texas hill country. When they wander into suburban areas, however, deer can annoy as many residents as they charm. A hunter, Darla knew that her audience would include both hunters and animal welfare advocates. She delivered the following speech in an Internet class during the spring of 2005.

1 Imagine for a minute that you're sitting comfortably underneath a huge oak tree, smack dab in the middle of a hundred acres of prime whitetail country. It's nearly dawn and suddenly from out of the shadows trots an 8-point buck! You look him over and realize that he's immature, only about $2^1/_2$ years old. So you lower your scope, watch him a little longer, and then he's gone.

2 Can you really tell how old a buck is just by looking at him? Yes, you can, but until recently I couldn't and still feel bad that my first buck was so young. Had I only waited a couple more years, he could have grown into quite a trophy. And not only that, but even though the older bucks produce a healthier herd, you still need some younger ones around to reduce the breeding pressure on the older ones.

3 As you watch deer on the run around the city, or you watch them from your own backyard, have you ever wondered why one buck can look so different from another with the same point count? This evening I'm going to share some of the physical and behavioral characteristics of four different age groups of whitetail buck. I'm going to talk about yearlings, immature bucks, mature bucks, and post-mature bucks. So that whether you're a watcher or a hunter you too can age the whitetail buck on the hoof, and hopefully avoid the mistake that I made.

4 The first category that I want to discuss is yearling bucks. Now, these bucks are actually a year and a half old, born late in the spring of the previous year. Their antlers are thin with short tines and they can range anywhere from one to ten points. This buck has a cute, little baby face. And as you can see from this illustration, his neck is rather skinny, and it's quite obvious where it meets the shoulders and the chest. His legs are long and lanky compared to the rest of his body and if, from a distance, you cover his antlers with your thumb, he looks more like a doe than a buck. All of my illustrations come from a poster entitled "Field Guide for Buck Deer," published by Wildlife Enterprises in 2000.

5 In addition to looking like a youngster, this buck behaves like a youngster. Often heedless of his surroundings, he'll be the first buck out to the food plot in the early evening. You can tell fairly quickly that a yearling buck is just that. He's young and impertinent and very entertaining to watch.

6 The second category that I want to discuss is immature bucks. These bucks range in age from $2^1/_2$ to $3^1/_2$ years and generally have antlers with thicker main beams and longer tines. The face is still rather long and if you picture it as a triangle, you'll see that the distance from the top of the head to the bottom of the jaw is actually shorter than the distance down the nose or from the jaw to the nose. The neck is beginning to fill out, but it's still obvious where it meets the chest and shoulders, and the legs still look a little long in proportion to the body. And if you look at the distance from the ground to the bottom of the chest and the ground to the waist, it's clear that the waist is smaller than the chest.

7 Immature bucks are more cautious than yearlings and will typically follow them out to the food plot in the early evening. This age group is the most tempting to harvest because they can have impressive racks and are fairly easy to shoot because of their aggressive pursuit of the doe in heat.

8 Immature bucks still appear much like does without antlers at this stage and because of their relentless promiscuity, more of this age group are taken than any other.

9 By the way, you can find much of what I'm discussing, and a whole lot more, at www.whitetaildeer.com, which I accessed on March 14th, and it's periodically updated.

10 The third category that I want to talk about is mature bucks. These are the $4\frac{1}{2}$- to $6\frac{1}{2}$-year-olds. As you can see from this picture, the head creates an equilateral triangle and looks balanced. The neck is as thick as the shoulders and chest so there's no real distinction, and the legs are appearing a little shorter now in proportion to his body if you note the straight line from the bottom of the chest to the waist with just a slight amount of sag. Mature bucks are the trophy bucks. Until now most of their growing energy has been concentrated on skeletal development, but at maturity most of their energy is now concentrated on antler development.

11 Unfortunately, these bucks also undergo a major behavioral change as well. This age group is much more reclusive than their younger brothers and you'll be lucky to see them out at legal hunting time. Mature bucks are in their prime with full-size bodies, impressive antlers, and an evasive attitude.

12 The fourth and final category that I want to talk about is post-mature bucks. These are the $7\frac{1}{2}$-year-olds and older. As a buck continues to age he exhibits many of the characteristics of a "senior citizen." His face becomes rather stubby and his skin starts to sag and droop. His legs appear much shorter than his body because of the sagging midsection and swayed back. The antlers can still be quite impressive, but now they can begin to deteriorate because his teeth are getting old and worn, and so he's getting fewer nutrients.

13 Now this age group is the most challenging to hunt, having survived many hunting seasons already. And I was fortunate enough to see a buck at this stage. It was a few minutes past legal hunting time, and he was with a group of does that the younger bucks were herding out in front of them. He was an ugly old buck, and it looked like it really hurt his joints and his feet to walk.

14 Post-mature bucks look old, with pot bellies and sagging skin, and as whitetaildeer.com puts it, they are like "old grandfathers, but still the kind who truly enjoy interacting with their young grandchildren."

15 So now we've talked about some of the physical and behavioral characteristics of four different age groups of the whitetail buck. We've talked about the size and the shape of the head and the nose as it relates to a triangle. We've talked about how the neck and leg looks in proportion to the body, and how the chest and the back and the torso are shaped. We've also discussed some behavioral characteristics, ranging anywhere from heedless and impertinent, to wild-eyed and raring to go, to very cautious and solitary. So whether you want to be able to judge the ages of your bucks for effective herd management, or to grow trophy bucks, or for whatever reason you may have, the basic physical and behavioral characteristics of each age group can aid you in determining just how old that buck is and, in so doing, hopefully avoid the embarrassing mistake that I made with my first buck.

Speech of Tribute to Timothy J. Russert[5]

Doris Kearns Goodwin

Tim Russert, the longest serving moderator of NBC's *Meet the Press*, died on June 13, 2008. Five days later, an invited audience gathered for his memorial service at the Kennedy Center in Washington, D.C. Noted historian and author Doris Kearns Goodwin, one of ten speakers, shared her memories of Russert with 1,500 people in the concert hall and with those watching on television.

1 Hello. I'm Doris Kearns Goodwin, or as Tim would remind me, the Irish daughter of Michael Francis Aloysius Kearns. History at its best is about telling stories, stories about people who lived before, about events in the past that create the contours of the present. By studying the lives of others, we hope that we, the living, can learn from their struggles and their triumphs.

2 Today, as we who were lucky enough to have been Tim Russert's friends recount our stories about this remarkable man with the booming voice and the radiant smile, it becomes increasingly clear that while his professional achievements will long be remembered, the lasting legacy he leaves behind is the truly honorable life that he led. For it is in the elements of that life so exquisitely balanced between a profound commitment to work and an equally profound commitment to his family and his friends that we have the most to learn.

3 Now, to be sure, his professional success will long be remembered. Indeed, for future historians attempting to tell the political story of the last two decades, there will be no more valuable resource than the transcripts and the tapes of *Meet the Press*. We have lost the art of letter writing, the discipline of keeping a diary. But as Tim showed, we have not lost the capacity for talking, for sitting around a simple table and conversing in a civil and illuminating fashion about the most important issues of the day.

4 "Everyone has a purpose on Earth," Tim once said. His, he believed, was to understand public policies, interpret political events, and inform the public. And how magnificently he practiced that chosen vocation, providing us week after week with a consistently intelligent public discourse which is the heartbeat of democracy.

5 Moreover, years from now, historians will not only be able to read what our leading figures said but observe how they responded to Tim's penetrating questions. And these observations will provide the key to unlocking both character and temperament. Those who flinched with discomfort, who stubbornly resisted honest answers, they will not fare so well over time, while those who were willing to acknowledge errors, to laugh at themselves, to admit that, yes, those statements on the screen do seem contradictory, they will emerge in a far better light. Tim once said to me that he could never understand why a politician could not say, "You're right, I've changed my mind on that issue."

6 There is only one politician who could have consistently given Tim the answer he craved, but that would mean bringing Abraham Lincoln back as Tim's guest on *Meet the Press*. Just imagine it. On the screen, Tim would have put up several contradictory statements that Lincoln said about slavery in 1832, 1842, and 1852. This would not fluster Lincoln, however. For as history records, whenever he had to say that he had changed his position, he had a simple answer: "Yes, you're right. I have changed my position. I'd like to believe I'm smarter today than I was yesterday."

7 And yet while the core of Tim's work will live on for generations, it is the character of the man that tells the bigger story, the warmth, sensitivity, integrity, fairness and fundamental decency. His capacity to transmit his cheerful strength to others, reach out to people, pick up their emotions, put himself in their shoes, inspire their trust, the character of a gentle man who retained all his life his boyish sense of wonder, the character of a beloved figure whose death has produced an outpouring of emotion across our land. It has been said that, over time, friendship turns to love. You look back and you remember the experiences you shared, the joy at one another's achievements, the comfort provided in time of sorrow,

and you know these memories will last forever. Though you've heard each other's favorite stories, you take pleasure in hearing them again and again.

8 I cannot tell you how many times in the presence of others, Tim would spur me to tell a story I had long since told him, so that the people sitting with us could enjoy it. Tell me about Lincoln and the critic, he would prompt. And I would tell the story of the man who shouted at Lincoln, "You're two-faced, Mr. Lincoln." To which Lincoln responded, "If I had two faces, do you think I'd be wearing this face?"

9 And on and on it went. Tell me about FDR and the poker game. Tell me about LBJ and the Alamo. And Tim would sit there with this huge grin on his face, as if he were a proud parent, though, I, of course, was the older of the two. And so through these and a hundred other shared experiences, friendship turned to love.

10 A few weeks ago, in the aftermath of the sad news about Senator Kennedy's brain tumor, I told Tim of a conversation I had had with Rose Kennedy decades ago as she remarked on the shortened lives of her children, most notably, Jack and Bobby. She said she found solace in the thought that if they could come back, they would still choose the lives they'd been given to lead, for they'd been blessed with so much achievement and so much fulfillment.

11 Tim said he understood what she was saying, for he, too, had already been blessed with all that he could want, with work he adored and a family he loved, blessed beyond his wildest imagination. But if his length of years were denied to him, the hardest part, he said, would not be sharing with Maureen in the limitless future of their son, not seeing Luke get married and become a father of his own.

12 While Tim's shortened life means that the children of Luke will never meet their paternal grandfather on this Earth, they will surely come to know him. They'll know his heart and his soul through the memories of all who loved him, through the countless stories filled with love and laughter, stories that will be told and retold for generations.

13 I am honored to be one of those storytellers tonight. Thank you.

I Have a Dream

Martin Luther King, Jr.

Speaking from the steps of the Lincoln Memorial on August 28, 1963, Martin Luther King, Jr., delivered the keynote address of the March on Washington, D.C., for civil rights. Many scholars consider this the greatest American speech of the twentieth century. You can access a transcript, the audio, the video, and commentary of the Reverend King's address just by typing "I Have a Dream speech" into an Internet search. Our Google search generated more than 4 million hits in .15 seconds.

Three of our favorite sites can be accessed at the following links:

American Rhetoric provides free full text and audio and pay-for-play video of Dr. King's speech.

www.americanrhetoric.com/speeches/mlkihaveadream.htm

You can also find the full text of the speech—as well as other speeches and selected papers—at The Martin Luther King, Jr. Research and Education Institute, located at Stanford University. Click on "I Have a Dream" and "March on Washington" for excellent background information.

http://mlk-kpp01.stanford.edu/index.php

Coretta Scott King, King's widow, established The Martin Luther King, Jr. Center for Nonviolent Social Change as a "definitive source for accurate information on the life, legacy, and teachings of Dr. and Mrs. Martin Luther King, Jr." Click on "History & Resources" for a brief introduction to the center and links to Dr. King's speeches, sermons, quotations, and additional resources.

www.thekingcenter.org

Endnotes

Preface

1. Steve C. Beering, "The Liberally Educated Professional," *Vital Speeches of the Day* (April 15, 1990): 400.

Chapter 1

1. Nick Morgan, *Give Your Speech, Change the World* (Boston: Harvard Business School, 2005), 1.

2. Ernest L. Boyer, *College: The Undergraduate Experience in America* (New York: Harper, 1987), 73.

3. Cited in William E. Arnold and Lynne McClure, *Communication Training and Development*, 2nd ed. (Prospect Heights, IL: Waveland, 1996), 38.

4. "Job Outlook 2011," *Career Development and Job-Search Advice for New College Graduates* (Bethlehem, PA: National Association of Colleges and Employers, 2011), accessed June 30, 2011, www.naceweb.org/so12082010/college_skills/?menuID=91&referal=knowledgecenter.

5. Jerry L. Winsor, Dan B. Curtis, and Ronald D. Stephens, "National Preferences in Business and Communication Education: II." Speech Communication Association Convention, San Diego, CA, November 26, 1996.

6. Winsor, 11.

7. Thomas M. Scheidel, *Persuasive Speaking* (Glenview, IL: Scott, Foresman, 1967), 2.

8. C. K. Ogden and I. A. Richards, *The Meaning of Meaning*, 9th ed. (New York: Harcourt, Brace, 1953), 10–12. Chapter 1, "Thoughts, Words and Things" (pp. 1–23), explains in detail the relationships among symbols, referents, and interpreters.

9. HNN Staff, "So What Does Jihad Really Mean?" *History News Network,* accessed June 18, 2002, www.historynewsnetwork.org/articles/article.html?id=774.

10. "'Jihad' Dropped from Harvard Student's Speech," *CNN*.com, accessed June 18, 2002, wysiwyg://153/http://fyi.cnn.com/2002/f…dnews/05/31/harvard.jihad.ap/index.html.

11. Karlyn Kohrs Campbell, *The Rhetorical Act*, 2nd ed. (Belmont, CA: Wadsworth, 1996), 119.

12. National Center for Educational Statistics. *National Assessment of College Student Learning: Identifying College Graduates' Essential Skills in Writing, Speech and Listening, and Critical Thinking*. NCES 95-001 (Washington, DC: GPO, May 1995), 122.

13. Robert Ennis, "A Taxonomy of Critical Thinking Dispositions and Abilities," in *Teaching Thinking Skills: Theory and Practice*, ed. Joan Boykoff Baron and Robert Sternberg (New York: Freeman, 1987), 10.

14. June Stark, "Critical Thinking: Taking the Road Less Traveled," *Nursing 95* (November 1995): 55.

15. National Assessment of Educational Progress, *Reading, Writing and Thinking: Results from the 1979–80 National Assessment of Reading and Literature*. Report No. 11-L-01 (Washington, DC: GPO, October 1981), 5.

Chapter 2

1. Mark M. Monmonier, *Mapping It Out: Expository Cartography for the Humanities and Social Sciences* (Chicago: University of Chicago Press, 1993), 140. We are grateful to Professor Jeremy Crampton of George Mason University for directing us to this source.

2. Fabien A. P. Petitcolas, "Digital Watermarking and Steganography," *The Information Hiding Homepage*, last modified January 28, 2002, www.cl.cam.ac.uk/~fapp2/steganography. We are grateful to Jolinda Ramsey and her student Julian Petrin Fray for first introducing us to the field of steganography.

3. Donald K. Smith, *Man Speaking: A Rhetoric of Public Speech* (New York: Dodd, 1969), 228.

4. Kenneth Blanchard and Norman Vincent Peale, *The Power of Ethical Management* (New York: Fawcett-Ballantine, 1988), 9.

5. Mary Cunningham, "What Price 'Good Copy'?" *Newsweek* (November 29, 1982): 15.

6. James C. McCroskey, *An Introduction to Rhetorical Communication* (Upper Saddle River, NJ: Prentice, 1968), 237.

7. *Copyright and Fair Use in the Classroom, on the Internet, and the World Wide Web*, Information and Library Sciences, University of Maryland University College, accessed June 30, 2011, www.umuc.edu/library/copy.shtml.

8. U.S. Copyright Office, *Limitation on Exclusive Rights: Fair Use*, accessed June 30, 2011, www.copyright.gov/title17/92chap1.html#107.

9. Georgia Harper, "Using the Four Factor Fair Use Test," *Fair Use of Copyrighted Materials*, University of Texas, Austin, last modified August 10, 2001, www.utsystem.edu/ogc/intellectualproperty/copypol2.htm.

10. "Copyright Exceptions," Purdue University Copyright Office, accessed June 29, 2011, www.lib.purdue.edu/uco/CopyrightBasics/fair_use.html.

11. These guidelines have been shaped and reinforced by several excellent sources, including Harper, "Using the Four Factor Fair Use Test"; Georgia Harper, "Copyright Crash Course: Fair Use of Copyrighted Materials," University of Texas Libraries, accessed June 29, 2011, http://copyright.lib.utexas.edu/copypol2.html; "Copyright Exceptions," Purdue University Copyright Office; "Chapter 9, Fair Use," Stanford University Libraries, accessed April 26, 2011, http://fairuse.stanford.edu/Copyright_and_Fair_Use_Overview/chapter9/index.html.

12. Alexander Lindey, *Plagiarism and Originality* (New York: Harper, 1952), 2.

13. John L. Waltman, "Plagiarism: Preventing It in Formal Research Reports," *ABCA [American Business Communication Association] Bulletin*, June 1980, 37.

14. Michael T. O'Neill, "Plagiarism: Writing Responsibly," *ABCA Bulletin*, June 1980, 34, 36.

15. Erik Vance, "Genetically Modified Conservation," *Conservation Magazine*, July/September 2010. Reprinted as "Genetic Engineering for Good: A Researcher Modifies Crops to Feed the Hungry and Cut Pesticide Use," *Utne Reader*, January/February 2011, 23.

16. *Paraphrase: Write It in Your Own Words*, Purdue OWL (Online Writing Lab), Purdue U Writing Lab, accessed June 16, 2005, http://owl.english.purdue.edu/handouts/print/research/rphr.html.

17. Institute for Civility in Government. "Reclaiming Civility in the Public Square: 10 Rules That Work." September 21, 2008, www.instituteforcivility.org/what-we-do/reclaiming-civility-in-the-public-square-book.aspx.

18. Rod L. Troester and Cathy Sargent Mester, *Civility in Business and Professional Communication* (New York: Peter Lang, 2007), 10.

19. Quoted in Maureen Killoran, "Expanding Our Moral Imaginations," Sermon Presented at River Road Unitarian Universalist Congregation, Bethesda, MD, February 13, 2011, accessed August 17, 2011, www.rruuc.org/index.php? id=191&sermon=110213.

20. Rona Marech, "Thanks for the Civility: Mannerly Campaign Spread Nationwide." *Baltimoresun.com*, November 1, 2007, www.choosecivilitymc.org/published/dat/baltimore_sun.pdf.

21. Institute for Civility in Government.

Chapter 3

1. Virginia P. Richmond and James C. McCroskey, *Communication: Apprehension, Avoidance, and Effectiveness*, 5th ed. (Boston: Allyn & Bacon, 1998), 41.

2. David Wallechinsky, Irving Wallace, and Amy Wallace, *The Book of Lists* (New York: Morrow, 1977), 469–70.

3. John H. Greist, James W. Jefferson, and Isaac M. Marks, *Anxiety and Its Treatment* (New York: Warner, 1986), 33.

4. Richmond and McCroskey, 45.

5. James A. Belasco and Ralph C. Stayer, *Flight of the Buffalo* (New York: Warner, 1993), 327–28.

6. Belasco, 328.

7. Ralph B. Behnke, Chris R. Sawyer, and Paul E. King, "The Communication of Public Speaking Anxiety," *Communication Education* 36 (1987): 140.

8. Joe Ayres and Theodore S. Hopf, "Visualization: A Means of Reducing Speech Anxiety," *Communication Education* 34 (1985): 321.

9. Daryl J. Bem, *Belief, Attitudes, and Human Affairs* (Belmont, CA: Brooks/Cole, 1970), 57.

10. Jack Valenti, *Speak Up with Confidence* (New York: Morrow, 1982), 19.

Chapter 4

1. Bernard E. Farber, comp. *A Teacher's Treasury of Quotations* (Jefferson, NC: McFarland, 1985), 186.

2. Larry Barker, Renee Edwards, Connie Gaines, Karen Gladney, and Frances Holley, "An Investigation of Proportional Time Spent in Various Communication Activities by College Students," *Journal of Applied Communication Research* 8 (1980): 101–9.

3. Robert L. Montgomery, *Listening Made Easy* (New York: AMACOM, 1981), n.p.

4. William James, *The Principles of Psychology*, vol. 2 (Cambridge: Harvard University Press, 1981), 380. This is a reprint of the original 1890 Henry Holt edition.

5. Lyle V. Mayer, *Fundamentals of Voice and Diction*, 8th ed. (Dubuque, IA: Brown, 1988), 178. Laura Janusik, "Listening Facts," *International Listening Association*, accessed June 27, 2011, http://d1025403.site.myhosting.com/files.listen.org/Facts.htm.

Chapter 5

1. Mary Raymond Shipman Andrews, *The Perfect Tribute* (New York: Scribner's, 1906), 1–9.

2. Thomas M. Scheidel, *Persuasive Speaking* (Glenview, IL: Scott, Foresman, 1967), 97. For a fuller account, see Mark E. Neely, *The Last Best Hope of Earth: Abraham Lincoln and the Promise of America* (Cambridge: Harvard University Press, 1993), 154–55. Neely notes that Lincoln made these remarks to acknowledge a serenade celebrating recent Union victories at Gettysburg and Vicksburg.

3. Carl Sandburg, *Abraham Lincoln: The Prairie Years and the War Years* (New York: Harcourt, 1954), 443–44.

4. Newspaper reporters the next day began to reflect widely different public views of the president's surprisingly brief speech. *The Chicago Times* referred to "the silly, flat, and dish-watery utterances" of Lincoln; the *Harrisburg [Pennsylvania] Patriot and Union* simply reported, "We pass over the silly remarks of the President . . ." (Sandburg, 445). Other newspapers, however, made entirely positive evaluations of Lincoln's speech. *The Chicago Tribune*

predicted, "The dedicatory remarks of President Lincoln will live among the annals of man" (Sandburg, 445). The *Philadelphia Evening Bulletin* noted that thousands who would not wade through Everett's elaborate oration would read Lincoln's brief remarks, "and not many will do it without a moistening of the eye and a swelling of the heart" (Sandburg, 446). The *Providence Journal* reminded its readers of the adage that the hardest thing in the world is to make a good 5-minute speech and said, "We know not where to look for a more admirable speech than the brief one which the President made at the close of Mr. Everett's oration" (Sandburg, 446).

5. Robert Hughes, *Culture of Complaint: The Fraying of America* (New York: Oxford University Press, 1993), 14.

6. Jeffrey F. Milem, "Why Race Matters," *Academe*, September–October 2000, 28.

7. Terry Sanford, quoted in "Commencement Remarks: Learning to Care and Share," *Representative American Speeches 1988–1989*, ed. Owen Peterson (New York: Wilson, 1989), 154.

8. "Transcript for April 24th," *Meet the Press*, MSNBC, June 2, 2005, transcript www.msnbc.com/id/7619740/. O'Neill attributes the quotation to Karen Armstrong, *The Spiral Staircase: My Climb Out of Darkness* (New York: Anchor-Random House, 2004), 298. Armstrong's actual words: "I tremble for our world, where, in the smallest ways, we find it impossible, as Marshall Hodgson enjoined, to find room for the other in our minds." Armstrong is quoting from Marshall G. S. Hodgson, *The Venture of Islam: Conscience and History in a World Civilization*, 2 vols. (Chicago and London, 1974), I: 379.

9. Abraham H. Maslow, *Motivation and Personality*, 2nd ed. (New York: Random, 1970), 35–47.

10. Maslow, 38.

11. Maslow, 41.

12. Lawrence R. Frey, Carl H. Botan, and Gary L. Kreps, *Investigating Communication: An Introduction to Research Methods*, 2nd ed. (Boston: Allyn & Bacon, 2000). In constructing our suggestions regarding audience questionnaires, we drew from advice in this excellent text.

13. Ari Posner, "The Culture of Plagiarism," *New Republic*, April 18, 1988, 19.

Chapter 6

1. Ralph Fletcher, *What a Writer Needs* (Portsmouth, NH: Heinemann, 1993), 101.

2. Leonard J. Rosen and Laurence Behrens, *The Allyn & Bacon Handbook*, 4th ed. (Boston: Allyn & Bacon, 2000), 68.

Chapter 7

1. Patricia Senn Breivik, *Student Learning in the Information Age* (Phoenix, AZ: Oryx Press, 1998), 2.

2. Brevik.

3. Wayne C. Booth, Gregory G. Colomb, and Joseph M. Williams, *The Craft of Research* (Chicago: University of Chicago Press, 1995), 35.

4. Jenny Sinclair, "The Information Challenge," *The Age*, February 6, 2002, http://theage.com.au.

5. Robert C. Jeffrey and Owen Peterson, *Speech: A Text with Adapted Readings*, 2nd ed. (New York: Harper and Row, 1983), 169.

6. "How Academic Librarians Can Influence Students' Web-based Information Choices," *OCLC [Online College Learning Center] White Paper on the Information Habits of College Students*, June 2002, accessed August 7, 2002, www2.oclc.org/oclc/pdf/printondemand/informationhabits .pdf.

7. Frederick J. Friend, "Google Scholar: Potentially Good for Users of Academic Information," *The Journal of Electronic Publishing*, 9, no. 1 (2006). doi:10.3998/3336451.0009.105.

8. "Google Scholar," Lehigh University, Library & Technology Services, last modified April 14, 2005, www .lehigh.edu/helpdesk/docs/google/.

9. Michael K. Bergman, "White Paper: The Deep Web: Surfacing Hidden Value," *The Journal of Electronic Publishing*, 7, no. 1 (August 2001) accessed August 19, 2011, http://hdl.handle.net/2027/spo.3336451.0007.104.

10. Stephen Dingman, email to the authors, September 2, 2005.

11. Bergman, 1.

12. Alison J. Head and Michael Eisenberg. "How Today's College Students Use Wikipedia for Course-related Research," *First Monday* 15, no. 3 (Mach 2010), accessed July 25, 2011, www.uic.edu/htbin/cgiwrap/bin/ojs/index .php/fm/article/view/2830/2476.

13. We adapted this checklist from Serena Fenton and Grace Reposa, "Evaluating the Goods," *Technology & Learning* (September 1998): 28–32; "Module IX: Evaluating Information Sources," McConnell Library, Radford University, accessed September 2, 2002, http://lib.runet .edu/highlanderguide/evaluation/intro.html; Esther Grassian, "Thinking Critically about Web 2.0 and Beyond," UCLA College Library, last modified November 4, 2006, www .sscnet.ucla.edu/library/modules/Judge/CLThinkWeb20 .pdf; and Keith Stanger, "Criteria for Evaluating Internet Resources," University Library, Eastern Michigan University, accessed August 30, 2002, http://online.emich .edu/~lib_stanger/ineteval.htm.

14. "Wikipedia FAQ/Schools," Wikipedia, last modified June 10, 2011, http://en.wikipedia.org/wiki/ Wikipedia:FAQ/Schools.

15. "Preface," *Ulrich's Periodicals Directory 2009*, serials dir. Laurie Kaplan (New Providence, NJ: ProQuest, 2008), vii.

16. Chris Dodge, "Knowledge for Sale," *Utne* (July-August 2005): 73.

17. Alden Todd, *Finding Facts Fast*, 2nd ed. (Berkeley: Ten Speed, 1979), 14.

Chapter 8

1. Ross Petras and Kathryn Petras, *The 365 Stupidest Things Ever Said* (New York: Workman, 1999), n.p.

2. Kyle Zrenchik, "9/11 Rescue Workers: The Forsaken Heroes," *Winning Orations, 2007* (Mankato, MN: Interstate Oratorical Association, 2007), 42. Coached by Ray Quiel.

3. *Encarta World English Dictionary* (New York: St. Martin's, 1999), 1600.

4. *Urban Dictionary*, s.v. "krumping," accessed May 12, 2011, www.urban dictionary.com/define.php?term =krumping.

5. Kimberly Paine, "Red Light Running," *Winning Orations, 2001* (Mankato, MN: Interstate Oratorical Association, 2001), 41. Coached by Susan Miskelly.

6. Ben Bradley, "The New College Disease," *Winning Orations, 2000* (Mankato, MN: Interstate Oratorical Association, 2000), 132. Coached by Terry West.

7. Paul Starbuck, "Exercise Anorexia: The Deadly Regimen," *Winning Orations, 2007* (Mankato, MN: Interstate Oratorical Association, 2007), 5. Coached by Ana Petero.

8. Zrenchik, 42.

9. C. Everett Koop, address, National Press Club, Washington, DC, September 8, 1998.

10. Tony Martinet, "Ribbons: Function or Fashion," *Winning Orations, 2004* (Mankato, MN: Interstate Oratorical Association, 2004), 79. Coached by Christina Ellis.

11. Tasha Carlson, "License to Save," *Winning Orations, 2009* (Mankato, MN: Interstate Oratorical Association, 2009), 34. Coached by Kristofer Kracht.

Chapter 9

1. Robert Half, "Memomania," *American Way* (November 1, 1987): 21.

2. Robert L. Montgomery, *Listening Made Easy* (New York: AMACOM, 1981), 65–78.

3. Matthew Whitley, "Involuntary Commitment Laws," *Video User's Guide for the Allyn & Bacon/AFA Student Speeches Video I* (Boston: Allyn, 1997), 43–45.

4. B. Scott Titsworth, "Students' Notetaking: The Effects of Teacher Immediacy and Clarity," *Communication Education* (October 2004): 317.

5. Glenn Leggett, C. David Mead, Melinda Kramer, and Richard S. Beal, *Prentice Hall Handbook for Writers,* 11th ed. (Upper Saddle River, NJ: Prentice Hall, 1991), 417–18. We have drawn on examples these authors use in their excellent section on connecting language.

6. Robert DiYanni and Pat C. Hoy, *The Scribner Handbook for Writers*, 3rd ed. (New York: Longman, 2001), 196.

7. DiYanni, 197.

Chapter 10

1. Jake Gruber, "Heart Disease in Women," *Winning Orations, 2001* (Mankato, MN: Interstate Oratorical Association, 2001), 16. Coached by Judy Santacaterina.

2. David Slater, "Sharing Life," *Winning Orations, 1998* (Mankato, MN: Interstate Oratorical Association, 1998), 63.

3. Hillary Rodham Clinton, "Remarks on the Working Women's Forum," Speech, Working Women's Forum, Chennai, India, July 20, 2011, accessed September 29, 2011, www.state.gov/secretary/rm/2011/07/168835.htm.

4. Brian Bauman, Untitled Speech, *Winning Orations, 2001* (Mankato, MN: Interstate Oratorical Association, 2001), 74. Coached by Al Golden.

5. Gruber, 16.

6. Jayme Meyer, Untitled Speech (University of Texas at Austin, 2001–2002).

7. Paul Starbuck, "Exercise Anorexia: The Deadly Regimen," *Winning Orations, 2007* (Mankato, MN: Interstate Oratorical Association, 2007), 5. Coached by Ana Petero.

8. Kimberly Paine, "Red Light Running," *Winning Orations, 2001* (Mankato, MN: Interstate Oratorical Association, 2001), 41. Coached by Susan Miskelly.

9. Paine, 42.

10. Viqar Mohammad, "Ovarian Cancer," *Winning Orations, 2007* (Mankato, MN: Interstate Oratorical Association, 2007), 17. Coached by Judy Santacaterina.

11. Mohammad, 19.

Chapter 11

1. E. D. Hirsch, Jr., *Cultural Literacy: What Every American Needs to Know* (New York: Vintage-Random, 1988), 34.

2. Jeff Kirvin, "I Don't Really Have to Use Roman Numerals, Do I?" *Writing on Your Palm*, accessed August 2, 2005, www.writingonyourpalm.net/column030310.htm.

3. Many people who teach creative writing prefer visual brainstorming, or "branching," to the traditional linear outlines such as the ones we illustrate. For interesting discussions of how outlining by visual brainstorming draws on both sides of the brain, see Henriette Anne Klauser, *Writing on Both Sides of the Brain: Breakthrough Techniques for People Who Write* (San Francisco: HarperSanFrancisco, 1987), 47–55, and Gabriele Lusser Rico, *Writing the Natural Way: Using Right-Brain Techniques to Release Your Expressive Powers* (New York: Tarcher/Putnam, 2000).

4. "Getting Started: Outlining," *Guide to Writing Research Papers*, Capital Community College Foundation, accessed August 2, 2005, http://webster.comnet.edu/grammar/composition/brainstorm_outline.htm.

5. This example is based on John M. Kennedy, "How the Blind Draw," *Scientific American* (January 1997): 76+.

Chapter 12

1. Gerald Parshall, "A 'Glorious Mongrel,'" *U.S. News & World Report*, September 25, 1995, 48.

2. Richard Lederer, *Anguished English: An Anthology of Accidental Assaults upon Our Language* (Charleston, SC: Wyrick, 1987), 8.

3. Gloria Cooper, ed., *Red Tape Holds up New Bridge, and More Flubs from the Nation's Press* (New York: Perigee, 1987), n.p.

4. This discussion of language is based on Roman Jakobson, "Closing Statement: Linguistics and Poetics," in *Style in Language*, ed. Thomas A. Sebeok (Cambridge: MIT Press, 1964), 350–74.

5. Charles L. Barber, *The Story of Speech and Language* (New York: Crowell, 1965), 9–10.

6. Jeffrey McQuain, *Power Language: Getting the Most out of Your Words* (New York: Houghton, 1996), 3–4.

7. This discussion of two ways of responding to language is based on Louise M. Rosenblatt, *The Reader, the Text, the Poem: The Transactional Theory of the Literary Work* (Carbondale: Southern Illinois University Press, 1978), particularly Chapter 3, "Efferent and Aesthetic Reading."

8. Miriam Ringo, *Nobody Said It Better!* (Chicago: Rand, 1980), 201.

9. Cherie Spurling, "Batter Up—Batter Down," *Winning Orations, 1992* (Mankato, MN: Interstate Oratorical Association, 1992), 12. Coached by Janet Hunn.

10. Raymond Gozzi, "Metaphors around the TV Remote Control," *ETC: A Review of General Semantics* (Winter 1998): 441.

11. Gozzi, 438.

12. Elyse Sommer and Dorrie Weiss, eds., *Metaphors Dictionary* (Detroit: Gale, 1995), xi.

13. Phillip J. Wininger, "The Unwanted Neighbor," *Winning Orations, 2001* (Mankato, MN: Interstate Oratorical Association, 2001), 36, 38. Coached by Judy Woodring.

14. Elie Wiesel, "The Shame of Hunger," *Representative American Speeches: 1990–1991*, ed., Owen Peterson (New York: Wilson, 1991), 70–74.

15. Travis Kirchhefer, "The Deprived," *Winning Orations, 2000* (Mankato, MN: Interstate Oratorical Association, 2000), 151. Coached by Ron Krikac.

16. Mario Cuomo, Keynote Address, Democratic National Convention, *Vital Speeches of the Day* (August 15, 1984): 647.

17. Sarah Meinen, "The Forgotten Four-Letter Word," *Winning Orations, 1999* (Mankato, MN: Interstate Oratorical Association, 1999), 26–29. Coached by Dan Smith.

18. William Safire, "On Language: Marking Bush's Inaugural," *New York Times Magazine*, February 5, 1989, 12.

19. Our guidelines have been shaped and reinforced by suggestions in these two excellent publications: *Publication Manual of the American Psychological Association*, 6th ed. (Washington, DC: American Psychological Association, 2010), 70–77, and Rosalie Maggio, *Talking about People: A Guide to Fair and Accurate Language* (Phoenix, AZ: Oryx, 1997).

20. Rosalie Maggio, *The Bias-Free Word Finder: A Dictionary of Nondiscriminatory Language* (Boston: Beacon, 1991), 7.

21. Maggio, *Talking about People*, 1.

22. Richard Price, interview with Terry Gross, *Fresh Air*, National Public Radio, WHYY, Philadelphia, May 9, 1995.

23. Lewis, M. Paul, ed., *Ethnologue: Languages of the World*, 16th ed. (Dallas, TX.: SIL International, 2009), online version accessed August 10, 2011, www.ethnologue.com/.

24. Quoted in George Plimpton, ed., *The Writer's Chapbook: A Compendium of Fact, Opinion, Wit, and Advice from the 20th Century's Preeminent Writers* (New York: Viking, 1989), 176.

Chapter 13

1. Elinor Donahue, "Writing Your Own Speeches," *Fund Raising Management*, accessed July 7, 1999, http://web4.infotrac.galegroup.com/itw/i...5!xrn_49_0_A18711219?sw_aep=viva_radford.

2. Mario Cuomo, "Introduction," in *More than Words: The Speeches of Mario Cuomo* (New York: St. Martin's, 1993), xiv–xv.

3. Achim Nowak, *Power Speaking: The Art of the Exceptional Public Speaker* (New York: Allworth, 2004), 11.

4. Barack Obama, "Remarks by the President at a Memorial Service for the Victims of the Shooting in Tucson, Arizona," Speech Delivered in Tuscon, Arizona, January 12, 2011, www.whitehouse.gov/the-press-office/2011/01/12/remarks-president-barack-obama-memorial-service-victims-shooting-tucson.

5. Deborah Blum, "Face It! Facial Expressions Are Crucial to Emotional Health," *Psychology Today*, September 19, 1998, 32. Blum uses Paul Ekman's estimate of 5,000 facial expressions. Ray Birdwhistell posited the number 250,000 in his *Kinesics and Context: Essays on Body Motion Communication* (Philadelphia: University of Pennsylvania Press, 1970), 8.

6. Donna Frick-Horbury and Robert E. Guttentag, "The Effects of Restricting Hand Gesture Production on Lexical Retrieval and Free Recall," *American Journal of Psychology* (Spring 1998): 45–46.

7. "Gestures May Trigger Ability to Recall Words," *Roanoke Times*, June 10, 2005, A12. See also Sharon Begley, "Living Hand to Mouth," *Newsweek*, November 2, 1999, 69.

Chapter 14

1. We adapted this chapter opening from four images described in an effective Nikon advertisement we saw for the first time in *American Photo*, March/April 1991, 19.

2. Kit Long, *Visual Aids and Learning*, August 12, 1997, University of Portsmouth, accessed September 21, 2002, www.mech.port.ac.uk/av/ALALearn.htm.

3. Michael Antonoff, "Meetings Take off with Graphics," *Personal Computing*, July 1990, 62.

4. Achim Nowak, *Power Speaking: The Art of the Exceptional Public Speaker* (New York: Allworth, 2004), 192.

5. Freddy Silva, *Secrets in the Fields: The Science and Mysticism of Crop Circles* (Charlottesville, VA: Hampton Roads, 2002).

6. Elizabeth Downs and Judi Repman, "Picture Perfect!" *Library Journal*, September/October, 2001, 39.

7. Chris Gurrie and Brandy Fair, "(Re)Discovering PowerPoint: Retooling the PowerPoint Pedagogy for 2009 and Beyond," National Communication Association Convention, Chicago, November 12, 2009, 1.

8. Dave Paradi, "Ten Secrets for Using PowerPoint Effectively," accessed April 27, 2009, www.thinkoutsidetheslide.com/articles.ten_secrets_for_using powerpoint.htm.

9. Guy Kawasaki, "How to Change the World: A Practical Blog for Impractical People," December 30, 2005, http://blog.guykawasaki.com/2005/12/the_102030_rule.html#axzz1F4K0TMii.

10. Nick Morgan, *Give Your Speech, Change the World* (Boston: Harvard Business School, 2005), 139.

11. These guidelines were part of a handout, "When Not to Use PowerPoint," distributed by Prof. Barbara Strain and Prof. Karen Wilking during a workshop at San Antonio College, Spring 2008. Used by permission.

12. Michael Talman, *Understanding Presentation Graphics* (San Francisco: SYBEX, 1992), 270.

13. Edward R. Tufte, *Visual Explanations: Images and Quantities, Evidence and Narrative* (Cheshire, CT: Graphics Press, 1997), 74.

14. We adapted this list of guidelines from multiple sources including Ann Luck, *Visual Aid Checklist for Interactive Video Presentation* (1997). Used by permission of the author. Also from Joyce Kupsch and Pat R. Graves, *Create High Impact Business Presentations* (Lincolnwood, IL: NTC Learning Works—NTC/Contemporary, 1998), 89–90, 95–96, 107–09.

15. Edward R. Tufte, *The Visual Display of Quantitative Information* (Cheshire, CT: Graphics Press, 1983), 121. See also Tufte's richly illustrated later works: *Envisioning Information* (Cheshire, CT: Graphics Press, 1990) and *Visual Explanations*.

Chapter 15

1. Internet World Stats, "Internet Usage and Population Statistics for North America," last modified June 26, 2011, www.internetworldstats.com/stats14.htm.

2. Pew Internet & American Life Report, "Internet Evolution," accessed July 2, 2005, www.pewinternet.org/PPF/r/148/report_display.asp.

3. Melissa Janoske, "Renaissance Fairs: The New Vaudeville," Speech Delivered at Radford University, Radford, Virginia, Spring 2002. Used with permission.

Chapter 16

1. "The 30-Second President," narr. Bill Moyers, *A Walk through the 20th Century with Bill Moyers*, PBS, 1984.

2. Charles U. Larson, *Persuasion: Reception and Responsibility*, 9th ed. (Belmont, CA: Wadsworth, 2001), 10.

3. Neel Bhatt, Untitled Speech, *Winning Orations*, 2004 (Mankato, MN: Interstate Oratorical Association, 2004), 21. Coached by David Moscovitz.

4. *The Rhetoric of Aristotle*, trans. Lane Cooper (New York: Appleton, 1960), 8.

5. James Benjamin, *Principles, Elements, and Types of Persuasion* (Fort Worth, TX: Harcourt, 1997), 122, 124.

6. Gerry Spence, *How to Argue and Win Every Time* (New York: St. Martin's Griffin, 1995), 47.

7. James C. McCroskey, *An Introduction to Rhetorical Communication*, 7th ed. (Boston: Allyn, 1997), 87–88.

8. McCroskey, 89. McCroskey credits D. K. Berlo and J. B. Lemmert with labeling these three dimensions of credibility in "A Factor Analytical Study of the Dimensions of Source Credibility," a paper they presented at the 1961 convention of the Speech Association of America, New York.

9. Benjamin, 129. See also Robert H. Gass and John S. Seiter, *Persuasion, Social Influence, and Compliance Gaining* (Boston: Allyn, 1999), 89.

10. Jessica J. Jones, "Are You Guilty?" *Winning Orations*, 2004 (Mankato, MN: Interstate Oratorical Association, 2004), 93. Coached by Barbara F. Sims.

Chapter 17

1. Aristotle, *The Rhetoric of Aristotle*, trans. Lane Cooper (New York: Appleton, 1932), 220.

2. For a more elaborate discussion of the structure of an argument, see Stephen Toulmin, *The Uses of Argument* (New York: Cambridge University Press, 1974).

3. Ali Heidarpour, "Organ Donation Reform," *Winning Orations, 2004* (Mankato, MN: Interstate Oratorical Association, 2004), 69. Coached by Stacy Schrank and Thomas Bartl.

4. Kateri Mintie, "Failing Our Students: America's Misuse of Substitute Teachers," *Winning Orations, 2001* (Mankato, MN: Interstate Oratorical Association, 2001), 31. Coached by Alexis Hopkins.

5. Mark Twain, *Life on the Mississippi* (New York: Harper, 1917), 156.

6. Jon Meinen, Untitled Speech, *Winning Orations, 2006* (Mankato, MN: Interstate Oratorical Association, 2006), 17. Coached by Dan Smith.

7. Nicholas Barton, "The Death of Reading," *Winning Orations, 2004* (Mankato, MN: Interstate Oratorical Association, 2004), 32. Coached by Craig Brown and Robert F. Imbody, III.

8. Rachel Resnick, "The Nursing Home Catastrophe," *Winning Orations, 2006* (Mankato, MN: Interstate Oratorical Association, 2006), 1. Coached by Josh Miller.

9. Mario Cuomo, Keynote Address, Democratic National Convention, *Vital Speeches of the Day* (August 15, 1984): 647.

10. John M. Ericson and James J. Murphy with Raymond Bud Zeuschner, *The Debater's Guide*, rev. ed. (Carbondale, IL: Southern Illinois University Press, 1987), 139.

11. Bruce N. Waller, *Critical Thinking: Consider the Verdict* (Upper Saddle River, NJ: Prentice, 1988), 30.

12. W. Ward Fearnside and William B. Holther, *Fallacy—The Counterfeit of Argument* (Upper Saddle River, NJ: Prentice, 1959), 92.

13. Raymie E. McKerrow, Bruce E. Gronbeck, Douglas Ehninger, and Alan H. Monroe, *Principles and Types of Speech Communication*, 14th ed. (New York: Addison-Longman, 2000), 153–61. See also: Alan H. Monroe, Principles and Types of Speech (Chicago: Scott, 1935).

14. See our discussion of Dewey's Steps to Reflective Thinking in Chapter 19.

15. James Chang, "Sustainable Giving," *Winning Orations*, 2003 (Mankato, MN: Interstate Oratorical Association, 2003), 3–4. Coached by Liana Koeppel.

Chapter 18

1. Shushannah Walshe, "Cate Edwards' Quiet Courage Delivering Eulogy," *The Daily Beast*, December 14, 2010, www.thedailybeast.com/blogs-and-stories/2010-12-14/cate-edwards-quiet-courage.

2. Don Ochs, "Introduction of Samuel L. Becker, Central States Communication Association Convention, April 12, 1991," *The CSCA News*, Spring 1991, 2.

3. Josh McNair, Speech of Presentation, Radford University, Virginia, Summer 2002. Reprinted with permission of the author.

4. Zachary Henning, Acceptance Speech, Radford University, Virginia, Summer 2002. Reprinted with permission of the author.

5. Cyrus M. Copeland, ed., *Farewell, Godspeed: The Greatest Eulogies of Our Time* (New York: Random-Harmony, 2003), xv.

6. Peggy Noonan, *What I Saw at the Revolution* (New York: Random, 1990), 253.

7. Michael McDonough, Untitled Speech, *1990 Championship Debates and Speeches* (Annandale, VA: Speech Communication Association, 1990), 86.

Chapter 19

1. Bobby R. Patton and Timothy M. Downs, *Decision-Making Group Interaction*, 4th ed. (Boston: Allyn, 2003), 1.

2. "The State of Meetings Today," *EffectiveMeetings.com*, accessed August 25, 2011, http://www.effectivemeetings.com/meetingbasics/meetstate.asp.

3. Paul E. Nelson, "Small-Group Communication," in Lilian O. Feinberg, *Applied Business Communication* (Sherman Oaks, CA: Alfred, 1982), 27.

4. Thomas E. Harris and John C. Sherblom, *Small Group and Team Communication*, 3rd ed. (Boston: Allyn, 2005), 156.

5. Richard S. Wellins, William C. Byham, and Jeanne M. Wilson, *Empowered Teams: Creating Self-Directed Work Groups That Improve Quality, Productivity, and Participation* (San Francisco: Jossey-Bass, 1991), 4–5.

6. Irving L. Janis, *Groupthink: Psychological Studies of Policy Decisions and Fiascoes*, 2nd ed. (Boston: Houghton, 1982), 9.

7. John Dewey, *How We Think* (Boston: Heath, 1910).

8. Ronald B. Adler and Jeanne Marquardt Elmhorst, *Communicating at Work: Principles and Practices for Business and the Professions*, 6th ed. (Boston: McGraw, 1999), 241. These authors and other scholars base their discussion of these group roles on Kenneth D. Benne and Paul Sheats, "Functional Roles of Group Members," *Journal of Social Issues* 4 (1948): 41–49.

9. Roger K. Mosvick and Robert B. Nelson, *We've Got to Start Meeting Like This!* rev. ed. (Indianapolis, IN: Park Avenue-JIST Works, 1996), 147.

Appendix A

1. This definition is adapted from Hendrie Weisinger and Norman M. Lobsenz, *Nobody's Perfect: How to Give Criticism and Get Results* (New York: Warner, 1981), 9–10.

2. ThinkExist.com Quotations, "feedbackquotes," *ThinkExist.com Quotations Online*, last modified September 6, 2011, http://thinkexist.com/search/searchquotation.asp?search=feedback.

3. This model of criticism is adapted from Beverly Whitaker Long, "Evaluating Performed Literature," *Studies in Interpretation*, vol. 2, eds. Esther M. Doyle and Virginia Hastings Floyd (Amsterdam: Rodopi, 1977), 267–81. See also her earlier article: Beverly Whitaker, "Critical Reasons and Literature in Performance," *The Speech Teacher* 18 (November 1969): 191–93. Long attributes this three-part model of criticism to Arnold Isenberg, "Critical Communication," *The Philosophical Review*, July 1949, 330–44.

Appendix B

1. Chiwoneso Beverley Tinago, "The Problem with Food Aid," *Winning Orations, 2009* (Mankato, MN: Interstate Oratorical Association, 2009), 38–39. Coached by Jennifer Talbert.

2. Jennell Chu, "Flash Mobs," Speech Delivered at San Antonio College, San Antonio, Texas, Spring 2011. Used with permission.

3. Julian Petrin Fray, "Steganography: Hidden Messages," Speech Delivered at the Texas Community College Speech and Theater Association State Tournament, Spring 2002. Coached by Jolinda Ramsey. Used with permission.

4. Darla Goodrich, "How Old Is He Anyway? Aging the Whitetail Buck," Speech Delivered at San Antonio College, San Antonio, Texas, Spring 2005. Used with permission.

5. Doris Kearns Goodwin, Speech of Tribute to Timothy J. Russert, June 18, 2008, Kennedy Center, Washington, DC, MSNBC, June 20, 2008, www.huffingtonpost.com/2008/06/18/doris-kearns-goodwin-at-t_n_107943.html.

Glossary

Consult the pages on which these terms are defined and discussed for a fuller, contextual understanding of the term's use and the definition's origins.

acceptance speech   A speech responding to a speech of presentation by acknowledging an award, a tribute, or recognition. (p. 336)

action group   A task-oriented group devoted to implementing proposals for action. (p. 348)

actual example   A true instance or illustration. (p. 131)

ad hominem   A fallacy that urges listeners to reject an idea because of the allegedly poor character of the person voicing it; name-calling. (p. 318)

alliteration   The repetition of beginning sounds in words that are adjacent, or near one another. (p. 214)

antithesis   The use of parallel construction to *contrast* ideas. (p. 214)

appeal to tradition   A fallacy that opposes change by arguing that old ways are always superior to new ways. (p. 315)

appearance   A speaker's physical features, including dress and grooming. (p. 233)

argument   The process of reasoning from evidence to prove a claim. (p. 302)

argument by analogy   Says that what is true in one case is or will be true in another. (p. 306)

argument by authority   Uses testimony from an expert source to prove a speaker's claim. (p. 311)

argument by cause   Says that one action or condition caused or will cause another. (p. 307)

argument by example or inductive argument   Says that what is true of a few instances is true generally. (p. 305)

articulation   The mechanical process of forming the sounds necessary to communicate in a particular language. (p. 232)

attitude   A statement expressing an individual's approval or disapproval, like or dislike. (p. 78)

audience disposition   Listeners' feelings of like, dislike, or neutrality toward a speaker, the speaker's topic, or the occasion for a speech. (p. 82)

audience-generated topics   Speech subjects geared to the interests and needs of a speaker's listeners. (p. 94)

audience profile   A descriptive sketch of listeners' characteristics, values, beliefs, attitudes, and/or actions. (p. 84)

audience segmentation   The strategy of dividing an audience into various subgroups based on their demographic and psychographic profiles. (p. 74)

audience targeting   The strategy of directing a speech primarily toward one or more portions of the entire audience. (p. 74)

audio aid   A cassette tape, compact disc, or record used to clarify or prove a point by letting listeners hear an example. (p. 251)

bandwagon   A fallacy that determines truth, goodness, or wisdom by popular opinion. (p. 317)

bar graph   A diagram used to show quantitative comparisons among variables. (p. 246)

behavior   An individual's observable action. (p. 79)

belief   A statement that people accept as true. (p. 78)

brainstorming   Noncritical free association to generate as many ideas as possible in a short time. (p. 92)

captive audience   A group of people who are compelled or feel compelled to assemble to listen to a speaker. (p. 83)

causal division   Organization of a speech from cause to effect, or from effect to cause. (p. 152)

causal transition   Establishes a cause-effect relationship between two ideas. (p. 162)

channel   The way a message is sent. (p. 12)

chart   A graphic used to condense a large amount of information, to list the steps in a process, or to introduce new terms. (p. 247)

chronological division   Organization of a speech according to a time sequence. (p. 150)

chronological transition Shows how one idea precedes or follows another in time. (p. 162)

circular conclusion A conclusion that repeats or refers to material used in the attention-getting step of the introduction. (p. 178)

civility Communication behaviors that reflect respect for others and foster harmonious and productive relationships. (p. 33)

cliché A once-colorful figure of speech that has lost impact from overuse. (p. 210)

cognitive restructuring A strategy for reducing communication anxiety by replacing negative thoughts and statements with positive ones. (p. 43)

communication The process of sharing meaning by sending and receiving symbolic cues. (p. 5)

communication apprehension The fear or anxiety associated with real or anticipated communication with another person or persons. (p. 38)

comparison The process of associating two items by pointing out their similarities. (p. 135)

competence Listeners' views of a speaker's qualifications to speak on a particular topic. (p. 288)

complementary transition Adds one idea to another. (p. 162)

complete sentence outline An outline in which all numbers and letters introduce complete sentences. (p. 187)

conclusion The deductive argument that what is true of the general class is true of the specific instance. (p. 309)

connotation The emotional association(s) that a word or phrase may evoke in individual listeners. (p. 207)

contrast The process of distinguishing two items by pointing out their differences. (p. 136)

contrasting transition Shows how two ideas differ. (p. 162)

coordinate ideas Ideas that have equal value in a speech. (p. 185)

credibility The believability or dependability of speakers and their sources. (pp. 129, 287)

critical thinking The logical, reflective examination of information and ideas to determine what to believe or do. (p. 14)

criticism Feedback offered for the purpose of improving a speaker's speech. (p. 365)

database A huge collection of information arranged for quick retrieval by computer using key words stipulated by a researcher. (p. 113)

decoding The process of attaching meanings to symbols received. (p. 11)

deductive argument Says that what is true generally is or will be true in a specific instance. (p. 309)

deep Web Huge databases of Internet information posted by public, government, corporate, and private agencies and available only by specific queries. (p. 111)

definition An explanation of the meaning of a word, phrase, or concept. (p. 132)

definition by etymology Explanation of the origin of the word being defined. (p. 133)

definition by example Providing an instance or illustration of the word being defined. (p. 133)

definition by operation Explanation of how the object or concept being defined works, what it does, or what it was designed to do. (p. 134)

definition by synonym Substitution of a word having similar meaning for the word being defined. (p. 132)

delivery The way a speaker presents a speech, through voice qualities, bodily actions, and language. (p. 224)

demographics Characteristics of the audience, such as age, gender, ethnicity, education, religion, economic status, and group membership. (p. 74)

denotation The literal meaning or dictionary definition of a word or phrase. (p. 206)

derived credibility The image listeners develop of a speaker as he or she speaks. (p. 288)

diagram A graphic, usually designed on a computer or drawn on poster board, showing the parts of an object or organization or the steps in a process. (p. 246)

direct question A question that asks for an overt response from listeners. (p. 168)

dynamism Listeners' views of a speaker's confidence, energy, and enthusiasm for communicating. (p. 290)

encoding The process of selecting symbols to carry a message. (p. 10)

environment The occasion, social context, and physical setting for communication. (p. 12)

ethics Standards used to discriminate between right and wrong, good and bad, in thought and action. (p. 20)

ethos Speaker credibility. (p. 287)

eulogy A speech of tribute praising a person who has recently died. (p. 337)

evidence Supporting material a speaker uses to prove a point. (p. 303)

example A sample or illustration of a category of people, places, objects, actions, experiences, or conditions. (p. 130)

eye contact Gaze behavior in which a speaker looks at listeners' eyes. (p. 236)

facial expression   The tension and movement of various parts of a speaker's face. (p. 235)

factual distractions   Listening disturbances caused by attempts to recall minute details of what is being communicated. (p. 63)

fair use provision   Section of U.S. copyright law allowing limited noncommercial use of copyrighted materials for teaching, criticism, scholarship, research, or commentary. (p. 28)

fallacy   A flaw in the logic of an argument. (p. 312)

false analogy   A fallacy that occurs when an argument by analogy compares entities that have critical differences. (p. 313)

false authority   A fallacy that uses testimony from sources who have no expertise on the topic in question. (p. 317)

false dilemma   A fallacy that confronts listeners with two choices when, in reality, more options exist. (p. 316)

feedback   Verbal and nonverbal responses between communicators about the clarity or acceptability of messages. (p. 11)

figurative comparison   Associations between two items that do not share actual similarities. (p. 136)

figurative contrast   Distinctions between two items that do not have actual differences. (p. 136)

film and video   Moving projections used to enhance a speaker's point. (p. 248)

formal outline   A complete sentence outline written in sufficient detail that a person other than the speaker could understand it. (p. 192)

general purpose   The broad goal of a speech, such as to inform, to persuade, or to entertain. (p. 102)

gestures   Movements of a speaker's hands, arms, and head while delivering a speech. (p. 237)

group communication   Three or more people interacting and hoping to influence one another to pursue a common goal. (p. 8)

groupthink   Excessive agreement among group members who value conformity more than critical evaluation. (p. 350)

handout   Any graphic visual aid distributed to individual audience members. (p. 249)

hasty generalization   A fallacy that makes claims from insufficient or unrepresentative examples. (p. 313)

hearing   The continuous, natural, and passive process of receiving aural stimuli. (p. 59)

hypothetical example   An imaginary or fictitious instance or illustration. (p. 132)

impromptu speaking   Speaking without advance preparation. (p. 225)

impromptu speech   A speech delivered with little or no advance preparation. (p. 340)

inductive argument   Says that what is true of a few instances is true generally. (p. 305)

inflection   Patterns of change in a person's pitch while speaking. (p. 232)

initial credibility   A speaker's image or reputation before speaking to a particular audience. (p. 288)

intentional plagiarism   The deliberate, unattributed use of another's ideas, words, or pattern of organization. (p. 30)

interpersonal communication   Communication between individuals in pairs; also called *dyadic communication.* (p. 8)

interpreter   Any person using symbols to send or receive messages. (p. 5)

intrapersonal communication   Cognition or thought; communicating with oneself. (p. 7)

jargon   The special language used by people in a particular activity, business, or group. (p. 209)

judgments   A critic's opinions about the relative merits of a speech; the most common and superficial level of speech criticism. (p. 365)

key word or phrase outline   An outline in which all numbers and letters introduce words or groups of words. (p. 187)

line graph   A diagram used to depict changes among variables over time. (p. 246)

listener   The receiver, or decoder, of the message. (p. 11)

listening   The intermittent, learned, and active process of giving attention to aural stimuli. (p. 59)

literal comparison   Associations between two items that share actual similarities. (p. 135)

literal contrast   Distinctions between two items that share actual differences. (p. 136)

logos   Logical appeal. (p. 287)

major premise   A claim about a general group of people, events, or conditions. (p. 309)

map   A graphic representation of a real or imaginary geographic area. (p. 247)

Maslow's hierarchy   A model of five basic human needs—physiological, safety, belongingness, esteem, and self-actualization—in an ordered arrangement. (p. 80)

mass communication   One person or group communicating to a large audience through some print or electronic medium. (p. 9)

message   Ideas communicated verbally and nonverbally. (p. 10)

metaphor   An implied comparison of two things without the use of *as* or *like*. (p. 213)

minor premise   A statement placing a person, an event, or a condition into a general class. (p. 309)

mnemonic division   Organization of a speech according to a special memory device, such as alliteration, rhyme, or initial letters that spell a word. (p. 153)

Monroe's motivated sequence   A persuasive pattern composed of (1) getting the audience's attention, (2) establishing a need, (3) offering a proposal to satisfy the need, (4) inviting listeners to visualize the results, and (5) requesting action. (p. 322)

movement   A speaker's motion from place to place during speech delivery. (p. 236)

narration   The process of describing an action or series of occurrences; storytelling. (p. 134)

need–plan division   A variation of problem–solution organization that (1) establishes a need or deficiency, (2) offers a proposal to meet the need, (3) shows how the plan satisfies the need, and (4) suggests a plan for implementing the proposal. (p. 155)

noise   Anything that distracts from effective communication. (p. 13)

nonsexist language   Language that treats both genders fairly and avoids stereotyping either one. (p. 216)

norms   The values a critic believes necessary to make any speech good, effective, or desirable. (p. 366)

object   An actual item or three–dimensional model of an item used during the delivery of a speech. (p. 244)

occasion-generated topics   Speech subjects derived from particular circumstances, seasons, holidays, or life events. (p. 95)

organizing question   A question that, when answered, indicates the ideas and information necessary to develop your topic. (p. 148)

parallelism   The expression of ideas using similar grammatical structures. (p. 214)

paraplage   Plagiarism consisting of half original writing and half quotation from an unattributed source. (p. 30)

pathos   Emotional appeal. (p. 287)

pause   An intentional or unintentional period of silence in a speaker's vocal delivery. (p. 230)

personal narrative   A story told from the viewpoint of a participant in the action and using the pronouns *I* or *we*. (p. 134)

personification   A figure of speech that attributes human qualities to a concept or inanimate object. (p. 213)

persuasion   The process of influencing another person's values, beliefs, attitudes, or behaviors. (p. 283)

physical distractions   Listening disturbances that originate in the physical environment and are perceived by the listener's senses. (p. 62)

physical noise   Distractions originating in the physical environment. (p. 13)

physiological distractions   Listening disturbances that originate in a listener's illness, fatigue, or unusual bodily stress. (p. 62)

physiological noise   Distractions originating in the bodies of communicators. (p. 13)

picture   A photograph, painting, drawing, or print used to make a point more vivid or convincing. (p. 244)

pie, or circle, graph   A diagram used to show the relative proportions of a whole. (p. 246)

pitch   The highness or lowness of a speaker's voice. (p. 231)

plagiarism   The unattributed use of another's ideas, words, or pattern of organization. (p. 29)

post hoc   A chronological fallacy that says that a prior event caused a subsequent event. (p. 314)

posture   The position or bearing of a speaker's body while delivering a speech. (p. 234)

PowerPoint   A software program that enables speakers to supplement their presentations with text, graphics, images, audio, and video. (p. 251)

preview   A statement that orients the audience by revealing how the speaker has organized the body of a speech. (p. 175)

primacy theory   The assumption that a speaker should place the strongest argument at the beginning of the body of a speech. (p. 295)

problem–solution division   A rigid organizational pattern that establishes a compelling problem and offers one or more convincing solutions. (p. 154)

problem-solving group   A task-oriented group devoted to deciding on courses of action to correct a problem. (p. 348)

pro–con division   Organization of a speech according to arguments for and against some policy, position, or action. (p. 152)

projection   A manner of presenting visual aids by casting their images onto a screen or other background. (p. 251)

pronunciation   How the sounds of a word are to be said and which parts are to be stressed. (p. 233)

proposition   A declarative sentence expressing a judgment a speaker wants listeners to accept. (p. 318)

proposition of fact   An assertion about the truth or falsity of a statement. (p. 320)

proposition of policy   A statement requesting support for a course of action. (p. 321)

proposition of value   An assertion about the relative worth of an idea or action. (p. 320)

psychographics   Characteristics of the audience, such as values, beliefs, attitudes, and behaviors. (p. 77)

psychological distractions   Listening disturbances that originate in the listener's attitudes, preoccupations, or worries. (p. 63)

psychological noise   Distractions originating in the thoughts of communicators. (p. 13)

public communication   One person communicating face to face with an audience. (p. 9)

public discussion   A small group exchange of ideas and opinions on a single topic in the presence of an audience. (p. 358)

rate   The speed at which a speech is delivered. (p. 229)

reasons   Statements that justify a critic's judgments. (p. 366)

recency theory   The assumption that a speaker should place the strongest argument at the end of the body of a speech. (p. 295)

red herring   A fallacy that introduces irrelevant issues to deflect attention from the subject under discussion. (p. 315)

referent   The object or idea each interpreter attaches to a symbol. (p. 5)

refutational strategy   A pattern of disputing an argument by (1) stating the position you are refuting, (2) stating your position, (3) supporting your position, and (4) showing how your position undermines the opposing argument. (p. 304)

refute   To dispute; to counter one argument with another. (p. 304)

repetition   Restating words, phrases, or sentences for emphasis. (p. 214)

research   The process of gathering evidence and arguments to understand, develop, and explain a speech topic. (p. 108)

research-generated topics   Speech subjects discovered by investigating a variety of sources. (p. 98)

rhetorical question   A question designed to stimulate thought without demanding an overt response. (p. 168)

search engine   A tool for locating information on the Internet by matching items in a search string with pages that the engine indexes. (p. 110)

self-directed work team   A group of people who manage themselves by identifying, conducting, and monitoring all activities needed to produce a product or service. (p. 348)

self-generated topics   Speech subjects based on the speaker's interests, experiences, and knowledge. (p. 93)

semantic distractions   Listening disturbances caused by confusion over the meanings of words. (p. 63)

sexist language   Language that excludes one gender, creates special categories for one gender, or assigns roles based solely on gender. (p. 216)

signpost   Numbers (*one*) or words (*initially, second,* or *finally*) that signal the listener of the speaker's place in the speech. (p. 157)

simile   A comparison of two things using the words *as* or *like*. (p. 213)

slippery slope   A fallacy of causation that says that one action inevitably sets a chain of events in motion. (p. 314)

small group   A collection of three or more people influencing and interacting with one another in pursuit of a common goal. (p. 346)

socially oriented group   A small group that exists primarily because its members enjoy interacting with one another. (p. 347)

spatial division   Organization of a speech according to the geography or physical structure of the subject. (p. 151)

speaker   The sender, encoder, or source of the message. (p. 10)

speaking extemporaneously   Delivering a speech from notes or from a memorized outline. (p. 226)

speaking from manuscript   Delivering a speech from a text written word for word and practiced in advance. (p. 226)

speaking from memory   Delivering a speech that is recalled word for word from a written text. (p. 226)

speaking outline   A brief outline for the speaker's use alone and containing source citations and delivery prompts. (p. 196)

specific purpose   A statement of the general purpose of the speech, the speaker's intended audience, and the limited goal or outcome. (p. 103)

speech of introduction   A speech introducing a featured speaker to an audience. (p. 332)

speech of presentation   A speech conferring an award, a prize, or some other recognition on an individual or group. (p. 333)

speech of tribute   A speech honoring a person, group, or event. (p. 337)

speech to actuate   A persuasive speech designed to influence audience behaviors. (p. 102, 286)

speech to convince   A persuasive speech designed to influence audience beliefs and attitudes rather than behaviors. (pp. 102, 285)

speech to entertain   A speech designed to make a point through the creative, organized use of humorous supporting materials. (pp. 102, 338)

speech to inform   A speech designed to convey new or useful information in a balanced, objective way. (pp. 101, 262)

speech to inspire   A persuasive speech designed to influence listeners' feelings. (p. 286)

speech to persuade   A speech designed to influence listeners' beliefs or actions. (p. 102)

statistics   Data collected in the form of numbers. (p. 137)

study group   A task-oriented group devoted to researching and learning about a topic. (p. 348)

subordinate ideas   Ideas that support more general or more important points in a speech. (p. 185)

summary   A statement or statements reviewing the major ideas of a speech. (p. 177)

syllogism   The pattern of a deductive argument, consisting of a major premise, a minor premise, and a conclusion. (p. 309)

symbol   Anything to which people attach meaning. (p. 5)

symposium   A series of public speeches on a single topic, possibly followed by group discussion or a question–answer period. (p. 358)

task-oriented group   A small group that exists primarily to accomplish some goal. (p. 347)

terminal credibility   The image listeners develop of a speaker by the end of a speech and for a period of time after it. (p. 288)

testimony   Quotations or paraphrases of an authoritative source to clarify or prove a point. (p. 138)

thesis statement   A one-sentence synopsis of a speaker's message. (p. 103)

third-person narrative   A story told from the viewpoint of a witness and using the pronouns *he*, *she*, or *they*. (p. 135)

tone   The relation established by language and grammar between speakers and their listeners. (p. 217)

topical division   Organization of a speech according to aspects, or subtopics, of the subject. (p. 150)

transition   A statement that connects parts of the speech and indicates the nature of their connection. (p. 161)

trustworthiness   Listeners' views of a speaker's honesty and objectivity. (p. 289)

unintentional plagiarism   The careless or unconscious unattributed use of another's ideas, words, or pattern of organization. (p. 30)

URL (uniform resource locator)   The standard notation for each Internet website's unique address, often beginning with "http://," "https://," or "www." (p. 110)

value   Judgment of what is right or wrong, desirable or undesirable, usually expressed as words or phrases. (p. 77)

visual brainstorming   Informal written outline achieved by free associating around a key word or idea. (p. 98)

visualization   A strategy for reducing communication anxiety by picturing yourself delivering a successful speech. (p. 44)

vocalized pause   Sounds or words such as *ah*, *like*, *okay*, *um*, *so*, and *you know* inserted to fill the silence between a speaker's words or thoughts. (p. 230)

volume   The relative loudness or softness of a speaker's voice. (p. 230)

voluntary audience   A group of people who have assembled of their own free will to listen to a speaker. (p. 83)

working outline   An informal, initial outline recording a speaker's process of narrowing, focusing, and balancing a topic. (p. 189)

work team   A team or group of people who perform all activities needed to produce the product, service, or other goal specified by an outside leader, supervisor, or manager. (p. 348)

Name Index

Subject Index

Note: Page numbers followed by *t* indicate tables; those followed by *f* indicate figures. Boldface page numbers indicate marginal glossary entries.

Photo Credits

p. 2, Marty Heitner/The Image Works; p. 4, Kevin Lamarque/Reuters/Corbis Wire/Corbis; p. 6, Danny Shanahan/Conde Nast Publications/www.cartoonbank.com; p. 8, IT Stock/ Polka Dot/Thinkstock; p. 13, Danita Delimont/Alamy; p. 18, Anthony Harvey/AP Images for VH1; p. 21, ©1992 by P. S. Mueller, used by permission; p. 23, Eric Feferberg/AFP/ GETTY Images/Newscom; p. 27, Bob Daemmrich/The Image Works; p. 36, Cleve Bryant/ PhotoEdit; p. 39, Image Source/Alamy; p. 42, Mariely Sanchez-Moronta, Marymount; p. 43, Jeff Greenberg/PhotoEdit; p. 52, Mary Kate Denny/PhotoEdit; p. 56, Richard Levine/Alamy; p. 59, © United Features Syndicate, Inc. Reprinted by permission; p. 61, Bob Daemmrich/PhotoEdit; p. 64, Jodie Moody; p. 66, John Warburton-Lee Photography/ Alamy; p. 68, Mark Richards/PhotoEdit; p. 70, Jeff Greenberg/PhotoEdit; p. 73, Bob Daemmrich/The Image Works; p. 76, Bob Daemmrich/The Image Works; p. 77, Krystal Grave; p. 82, 1982 Thaves. Reprinted with permission; p. 87, Kayte Deioma/PhotoEdit; p. 90, s70/ZUMA Press/Newscom; p. 93, Du Jian/Xinhua/Landov; p. 96, Wally Herbert/ Robert Harding World Imagery; p. 98, AISPIX/Shutterstock; p. 99, Bryan McClure; p. 101, Bob Daemmrich/The Image Works; p. 107, Beyond Fotomedia GmbH/Alamy; p. 110, Stockbyte/Getty Images; p. 113, Tetra Images/Alamy; p. 118, Elizabeth Crews/The Image Works; p. 121, Matthew Williams; p. 126, Directphoto.org/Alamy; p. 129, Tetra Images/Alamy; p. 136, Sean Sprague/The Image Works; p. 139, Jovan Coker; p. 143, Ed Fisher/Conde Nast Publications/cartoonbank.com; p. 146, James Woodson/Digital Vision/ Thinkstock; p. 149, Wendy Connett/Robert Harding Picture Library Ltd/Alamy; p. 151, s70/ZUMA Press/Newscom; p. 156, (top) Bob Daemmrich/Alamy, (bottom) Corey Town; p. 160, Neale Cousland/Shutterstock; p. 166, Realistic Reflections/Alamy; p. 171, Spencer Grant/Art Directors & TRIP/Alamy; p. 173, Amanda Gipson; p. 174, Ashley Cooper/ Global Warming Images/Alamy; p. 178, Bill Bachmann/Alamy; p. 182, Purestock/Alamy; p. 185, Michael Newman/PhotoEdit; p. 186, Alana Kwast; p. 197, AP Photo/Scott Heppell; p. 198, Photograph courtesy of Gateshead Council; p. 202, Photoshot/Newscom; p. 205, Cleve Bryant /PhotoEdit; p. 206, Suzanne L. Hamilton; p. 210, AP Photo/The Waterloo/ Cedar Falls Courier, Dan Nierling; p. 216, Jeff Greenberg/Alamy; p. 222, Martin Poole/ Riser/Getty Images; p. 227, Hill Street Studios/Blend Images/PhotoLibrary; p. 231, Brandy Baker/Detroit News/PSG/Newscom; p. 237, (top) Michael Gino, (bottom) Jack Hollingsworth/Corbis Premium RF/Alamy; p. 240, Davis Barber/PhotoEdit; p. 243, Lauren Fishman; p. 245, (left and right) Digital Vision/Getty Images; p. 253, Image Source/Alamy; p. 260, Luc Novovitch/Alamy; p. 264, Alexander Sandvoss/Alamy; p. 269, A. Ramey/ PhotoEdit; p. 272, Patty Pak; p. 273, Kristoffer Tripplaar/Alamy; p. 274, Jeff Greenberg/ Alamy; p. 280, Craig Golding/Ed Stock/iStockphoto; p. 283, Richard Wareham Fotografie/ Alamy; p. 286, Brittney Howell; p. 288, Marty Heitner/The Image Works; p. 290, AP Photo/Charles Krupa; p. 300, Kennell Krista/SIPA/Newscom; p. 306, (top) Brian Davis, (bottom) Heide Benser/Comet/Corbis; p. 310, Chris Sweda/EPA/Landov; p. 320, AP Photo/ San Francisco Examiner, Dave Kennedy; p. 330, Jason Szenes/EFE/Newscom; p. 337, Robert Willett/MCT/Newscom; p. 340, Bob Daemmrich/PhotoEdit; p. 344, GoGo Images Corporation/Alamy; p. 349, Yuri Arcurs/Shutterstock; p. 358, Jeff Greenberg/Alamy; p. 359, Cynthia Opakunle; cover, Diana Ong/SuperStock.